PHILOSOPHICAL FOUNDATIONS OF FIDUCIARY LAW

Philosophical Foundations of Fiduciary Law

EDITED BY ANDREW S GOLD AND PAUL B MILLER

OXFORD
UNIVERSITY PRESS

OXFORD
UNIVERSITY PRESS

Great Clarendon Street, Oxford, OX2 6DP,
United Kingdom

Oxford University Press is a department of the University of Oxford.
It furthers the University's objective of excellence in research, scholarship,
and education by publishing worldwide. Oxford is a registered trade mark of
Oxford University Press in the UK and in certain other countries

First Edition published in 2014

Impression: 1

Published in the United States of America by Oxford University Press
198 Madison Avenue, New York, NY 10016, United States of America

British Library Cataloguing in Publication Data
Data available

Library of Congress Control Number: 2014934941

ISBN 978–0–19–870172–9

Printed and bound by
CPI Group (UK) Ltd, Croydon, CR0 4YY

In loving memory of my parents, Arthur and Estella Gold—A.S.G.

For Stella, Serena, and Kieran Miller, with love—P.B.M.

Table of Contents

List of Abbreviations

AktG	Aktiengesetz
art	article
BGB	Bürgerliches Gesetzbuch
BGH	Bundesgerichtshof
BGHZ	Entscheidungen des Bundesgerichtshof in Zivilsachen
BVerfG	Bundesverfassungsgericht
CC	civil code
C Com	Code de commerce
CCQ	Quebec civil code
CEO	chief executive officer
CJ	Chief Justice
CPR	*Critique of Practical Reason*
ERISA	Employee Retirement and Income Security Act
ICJ	International Court of Justice
J	Justice
JJ	Justices
LJ	Lord Justice
LLC	Limited Liability Company
MitbestG	Mitbestimmungsgesetz
MoM	*Metaphysics of Morals*
NJT	normal justification thesis
s	section
UCITS	Undertakings for the Collective Investment of Transferable Securities

List of Contributors

Richard R W Brooks is the Charles Keller Beekman Professor of Law at Columbia Law School.

Evan J Criddle is Professor of Law at William & Mary Law School.

Hanoch Dagan is the Stewart and Judy Colton Chair in Legal Theory and Innovation and former Dean of the Tel-Aviv University Faculty of Law.

Deborah A DeMott is the David F Cavers Professor of Law at Duke Law School.

Avihay Dorfman is Senior Lecturer in Law at the Tel-Aviv University Faculty of Law.

The Hon Justice James Edelman is a Justice of the Supreme Court of Western Australia, Conjoint Professor at the University of New South Wales and Adjunct Professor at the University of Western Australia and University of Queensland, and former Professor of the Law of Obligations at the University of Oxford Faculty of Law.

Evan Fox-Decent is Associate Professor of Law at the McGill University Faculty of Law.

Tamar Frankel is Professor of Law and Michaels Faculty Research Scholar at the Boston University School of Law.

Martin Gelter is Associate Professor of Law at Fordham Law School.

Joshua Getzler is Professor of Law and Legal History at the University of Oxford Faculty of Law.

Andrew S Gold is Professor of Law at the DePaul University College of Law.

Michele Graziadei is Professor of Law at the University of Turin Faculty of Law.

Sharon Hannes is Professor of Law and Director of the Cegla Center for Interdisciplinary Research at the Tel-Aviv University Faculty of Law.

Geneviève Helleringer is Associate Professor in the Department of Public and Private Policy at ESSEC Business School, and Fellow at the Institute of European and Comparative Law, Oxford University.

Ethan J Leib is Professor of Law at Fordham Law School.

Daniel Markovits is the Guido Calabresi Professor of Law at Yale Law School.

Paul B Miller is Assistant Professor of Law at the McGill University Faculty of Law.

J E Penner is Professor of Law at the National University of Singapore Faculty of Law.

David L Ponet is a Parliamentary Specialist at UNICEF.

Irit Samet is a Senior Lecturer in the Dickson Poon School of Law at King's College London.

Michael Serota is a Criminal Code Reform Attorney in the United States.

Robert H Sitkoff is the John L Gray Professor of Law at Harvard Law School.

Henry E Smith is the Fessenden Professor of Law and Director of the Project on the Foundations of Private Law at Harvard Law School.

Lionel D Smith is James McGill Professor of Law and Director of the Paul-André Crépeau Centre for Private and Comparative Law at the McGill University Faculty of Law. He is also Professor of Private Law at the Dickson Poon School of Law, King's College London.

Introduction

Andrew S Gold and Paul B Miller

Whether it is viewed from the perspective of relationships, rights and duties, or wrongs and remedies, fiduciary law is a distinctive body of law. Fiduciary law governs relationships marked by asymmetries of power. Fiduciaries enjoy power over beneficiaries. And fiduciary law expresses an expectation that fiduciaries act in their beneficiaries' interests. It does so through a range of important legal duties. There is little doubt that fiduciary relationships generate at least one distinctive legal duty, the duty of loyalty. And fiduciary relationships ordinarily attract other legal duties, including duties of care, candor, confidence, and good faith. Compliance with these duties, particularly the duty of loyalty, is unusually demanding. The remedial response to the wrongful violation of fiduciary duties is also notoriously harsh. Disloyal fiduciaries are liable to be stripped of wrongful gains through a constructive trust or disgorgement order. Careless fiduciaries are liable to be ordered to make good losses suffered by beneficiaries on terms more favorable than those that govern the availability of compensatory damages at common law.

Fiduciary law is also a critically important body of law. Fiduciary duties ensure the integrity of a remarkable variety of relationships, institutions, and organizations. They apply to relationships of great personal significance, including those between parents and children. They structure a wide variety of commercial relationships, including those between partners, joint venturers, agent and principal, and director and corporation. Fiduciary duties are essential to the regulation of relationships between professional service providers and their clients, including relationships between lawyer and client, doctor and patient, and investment manager and client. Fiduciary principles govern the administration of money and property for others, as is evident in the central place reserved for fiduciary duties in the law of trusts, estates, and fund management. Fiduciary duties are also central to the governance of private institutions, ranging from universities, hospitals, and museums to churches and unions. Fiduciary duties, perhaps uniquely in private law, challenge traditional ways of marking the boundaries between private and public law, inasmuch as they figure prominently in public governance. Indeed, there is even a storied tradition of thinking of the authority of the state in fiduciary terms.

Notwithstanding its importance, fiduciary law has been woefully under-analyzed by legal theorists. Private law theorists have lavished attention on property, contract, tort, and unjust enrichment. They have examined philosophical questions concerning the forms of, and justification for, private ownership; the nature of contracts and contractual obligation; the bases of restitutionary liability for unjust enrichment; and the character of, and basis of responsibility for, tortious wrongdoing. However, fiduciary law has attracted comparatively little attention.

Given that fiduciary law offers so much undiscovered terrain, this volume has a distinctive aim. Like the other volumes in the *Philosophical Foundations* series, the present volume includes contributions by leading legal theorists whose work represents the state-of-the-art in a branch of specialized jurisprudence. However, it does more than present the best contemporary work of legal theory in a field. The book contributes to the very definition of the field. We believe that the essays collected here will set the agenda for philosophical study of fiduciary law for generations to come.

Our contributors have identified a wide range of deep and challenging theoretical questions about fiduciary law. Amongst these are questions relating to the nature of fiduciary relationships; the scope of fiduciary obligation; the nature of fiduciary loyalty (eg, whether it is the object of duty or virtue); the content of fiduciary duties; the nature and limits of fiduciary principles of public and private governance; and the relationship between fiduciary and non-fiduciary principles of private ordering. Of course, our contributors have done more than identify challenging questions. They have also ventured original and important answers. The answers offered are enlightening and will repay close scrutiny. However, whether or not one ultimately agrees with the answers given, the questions themselves are profound. We hope and expect that the manner in which these questions are framed and addressed will foster interest in this new and important topic of theoretical inquiry.

The chapters collected here, like the field about which they are written, defy easy categorization. Many chapters address several distinct philosophical questions and there are many cross-cutting themes amongst them. Nevertheless, in organizing this book and these introductory remarks, we have grouped the chapters according to their predominant focus. First is a set of chapters that addresses the nature and formation of fiduciary relationships. Second is a collection of chapters that focuses on the basis, scope, and content of fiduciary duties. The third set of chapters offers new constructive and critical insights about fiduciary law from the perspective of economic theory. The fourth grouping of chapters examines the operation of fiduciary principles across systems of private law and within particular private law fields. The final set of chapters investigates fiduciary principles in the context of public and international law.

I. Fiduciary Relationships

Fiduciary relationships are important to fiduciary law. They are the footing on which fiduciary duties are imposed, interpreted, and enforced. Nevertheless, fiduciary relationships raise difficult philosophical questions. Are fiduciary relationships a coherent category of legal relationship, distinctive relative to other categories of private law relationship? What role does status, or conventional characterization of relationships, serve in fiduciary law? How do consent and prescription factor in the formation of fiduciary relationships and in adjustment of the terms governing them? Are fiduciary relationships unitary or are there a number of irreducible kinds of fiduciary relationship? What purposes do fiduciary relationships serve; ie, what do they allow individuals, and society more generally, to accomplish? What values do fiduciary relationships implicate? Several chapters in this volume address these and other theoretical questions concerning fiduciary relationships.

Most relationships considered to be fiduciary are treated as such as a matter of status or convention. To say that a relationship enjoys fiduciary status is simply to say that it is habitually treated as fiduciary, such that a given relationship will be presumed to be fiduciary if it falls within a category of relationship that has fiduciary status. Relationships between partners, trustees and beneficiaries, agents and principals, directors and corporations, lawyers and clients, parents and children, the state and aboriginal peoples, amongst others, have recognized fiduciary status, at least in some jurisdictions. Many think that fiduciary law's reliance on status is unusual and that status in itself determines the application of fiduciary liability rules to fiduciary relationships.

In his contribution, Justice James Edelman encourages reconsideration of these views about the role of status in fiduciary law. In other work, Edelman has argued that fiduciary obligations arise on the basis of voluntary undertakings by fiduciaries. A puzzle generated by this view is that it seems not to account for the role of status, or relationship characterization more generally, in fiduciary liability. "Why" asks Edelman "do courts emphasise the duties that arise in relationships of particular status?" His chapter provides an answer. Courts refer to status as an evidentiary factor in placing a proper, objective construction on an undertaking made by the fiduciary. More specifically, status figures in construction of the content and scope of duties undertaken by the fiduciary. Status does not, as is commonly believed, determine the incidence of fiduciary duties. Instead, it influences the shape of consensually undertaken duties.

Edelman views undertakings and status in fiduciary law as conceptually continuous with undertakings and status elsewhere in the law of obligations. Status, he tells us, plays an important role in the implication of terms in contract law and in the law of common callings. Its role in fiduciary law, while equally important, is not distinctive. Here, as elsewhere, status informs judicial determination whether "reasonable expectations of particular duties" are associated with a particular consensual undertaking. An implication is that we should place less weight on the *fiduciary* character of an undertaking. The fiduciary "label" signifies only that courts are to consider whether, in all the circumstances, a purported fiduciary has undertaken to act exclusively in the interests of the beneficiary.

Edelman's consent-based theory of fiduciary obligation is simple and elegant. However, parsimony sometimes risks obscuring the object of theorization. In his contribution, Joshua Getzler suggests that this risk is realized here. He explains that "[t]he observation that fiduciary duties commonly arise from consent... [is]... entirely valid. But it risks distortion to work these observations into simple formulae that claim to encompass the entire field." Consent is important to the ascription and limitation of fiduciary duties. But its role is far more complicated, and in places uncertain, than the consent-based theory would have us believe.

The consent-based theory bypasses analysis of the nature of fiduciary relationships and duties in favor of analysis of the formation of fiduciary relationships and of the ascription of fiduciary duties. Getzler expresses doubts about this move. He notes that in many cases, consent factors in the *limitation* rather than *ascription* of fiduciary duties. Even where it underlies ascription, consent is often implicated in the formation of contractual *and* fiduciary relationships that are interrelated in complicated ways not captured by the consent-based theory. Getzler frames these complexities in light of three types of terms: mandatory terms, default terms, and structuring terms. Where mandatory terms apply, one may be consensually involved in an activity or relationship but the terms governing that activity or relationship are mandated. Where default terms apply, one again may be consensually involved in an activity or relationship and one may, but needn't, consensually alter (via *ex ante* or *ex post* consent) the terms governing it. Where structuring terms apply, one may be consensually involved in an activity or relationship, and unless one clearly stipulates otherwise, one will find that one's conduct will be governed by terms derived from relevant customs or practices. Consent is complicated in fiduciary law, Getzler reveals, precisely because fiduciary relationships are variably governed by each of these three different kinds of terms. Indeed, some relationships are governed by unique combinations of kinds of terms. This alone makes it difficult to generalize about the consensual basis of fiduciary relationships and duties.

Getzler illustrates these complexities by flagging a number of questions on which the law is presently unclear. For example, what significance does consent have in the attribution and/or limitation of fiduciary duties to a relationship that was consensually formed on a non-fiduciary basis, but which has since become fiduciary? In what circumstances can one limit fiduciary duties by invoking the consensual basis of a relationship? For example, can one look to the consensual basis of the relationship as a reason for exiting it unilaterally to pursue an opportunity that would be foreclosed if the relationship were continued? These issues should give the theoretician pause: "Each. . . has been the subject of significant litigation, reflecting doubt over how ascription and limitation operate. Stating that fiduciary duties are based on consent does not yield a magic bullet that solves such problems, nor even a superior language for analyzing the issues."

Whereas Edelman and Getzler focus on the ascription of fiduciary duties through fiduciary relationships, Paul Miller's contribution is focused on the nature of the fiduciary relationship. Miller begins by noting a puzzling feature of fiduciary law and scholarship. Judicial opinion and practice make the fiduciary relationship conceptually central to fiduciary liability. But dominant scholarly opinion suggests that it is meaningless to talk of fiduciary relationships as such. This disjuncture raises the question whether the fiduciary relationship is a distinctive and definable kind of legal relationship.

Miller argues that the fiduciary relationship is distinctive and definable. He provides a conceptual theory of the fiduciary relationship—the fiduciary powers theory—that articulates and explains the formal properties of the relationship. According to Miller, all fiduciary relationships are distinguished by the fiduciary's possession of discretionary power over significant practical interests of the beneficiary. Fiduciary power is not, Miller argues, mere factual power, nor is it simply a legal power in the general, Hohfeldian, sense. Fiduciary power is rather a peculiar kind of legal power. It is a form of authority in the nature of particular legal capacities (eg, the capacity to contract, or to own, alienate, or manage property) derived from the legal personality of a person (ordinarily, the beneficiary or a third-party benefactor). Fiduciary power is thus representative or substitutive in nature. In his chapter, Miller elaborates on the notion of fiduciary power and other properties of fiduciary relationships. He then argues that the theory can explain the presumptive fiduciary nature of several categories of relationship that have recognized fiduciary status and that it can help resolve debates over the fiduciary character of other kinds of relationship.

Hanoch Dagan and Sharon Hannes agree that fiduciary relationships involve the fiduciary's possession of power in the sense described by Miller. But they express reservations about the unitary ambitions of Miller's theory. They suggest that fiduciary law, like contract, offers a number of distinct forms of relationship. They also argue that Miller's juridical account of the justification for fiduciary duties does not press as far, or as wide, as it ought to in picking out those aspects of fiduciary relationships that warrant the imposition of fiduciary duties. According to Dagan and Hannes, the values engaged by fiduciary relationships are multiple and variable.

Dagan and Hannes approach their subject through the framework of private law pluralism, which "embraces the vast heterogeneity of private law and celebrates the multiple forms characterizing its landscape." Given that they favor contextual analysis, it should be unsurprising that Dagan and Hannes focus on a particular subset of fiduciary relationships; namely, those implicated in finance. According to Dagan and Hannes, *financial* fiduciary relationships have unique qualities and engage a distinctive set of values. They argue that "the law of financial fiduciaries is a private law institution aimed at enhancing people's autonomy by allowing them to safely delegate to others. . . authority over a significant aspect of their welfarist interests." While accepting "the important autonomy-enhancing role of financial fiduciaries. . . as the telos of that institution" they argue that the fact that power is enjoyed by financial fiduciaries over *welfarist* interests supports normative economic analysis of the incentive effects of fiduciary liability rules.

Dagan and Hannes argue that their approach offers important interpretive advantages. Clarification of differences in the character of specific welfarist interests implicated by financial fiduciary relationships aids in our understanding of differences in standards of conduct applicable to financial fiduciaries (ie, it can explain why the exclusive interests standard of loyalty prevails in trust law but not corporate law). Equally, their account avoids the "hazard of apology" associated with conceptualist theories by providing a basis for critical evaluation of controversial points of fiduciary doctrine (eg, the practice of tolerating forms of compensation of fiduciaries that generate conflicts of interest). In these and other ways, a pluralist approach promises a capacious framework within which to analyse fiduciary relationships and duties in the varied contexts in which they arise.

II. Fiduciary Duties

The duty of loyalty is one of the most prominent features of fiduciary law. Loyalty is often considered essential to fiduciary relationships, and in fiduciary settings it has distinctive features. These features also raise interesting philosophical questions. What is fiduciary loyalty, and how does fiduciary loyalty relate to loyalty more generally? What is the relationship between fiduciary loyalty and moral character, values, and principles? Is fiduciary loyalty a virtue? Is fiduciary loyalty truly the object of a duty, or is it better understood in different terms? Several chapters in this volume address these and other questions about fiduciary duties.

Irit Samet notes that fiduciary law might have conceived of loyalty in a thin or thick sense. But she suggests that it has adopted a thick sense of loyalty. Loyalty, like justice, calls on the fiduciary to suppress greed, but it does more: the loyal fiduciary will have the feeling that the well-being of the object of his or her loyalty takes precedence over the fiduciary's own good. The loyal fiduciary will possess the proper emotion; namely, devotion to his or her principal. From this perspective, loyalty may be seen as a virtue. As Samet indicates, understanding loyalty as a virtue could raise difficulties under certain interpretations of Kant's moral theory. Moral worth, on this reading of Kant, only attaches to actions done from the right motive, and motivations of loyalty—as opposed to motivations based on respect for moral law—would not qualify because they are rooted in emotion. Arguably, then, the highly personal attachment that loyalty calls for poses challenges under a Kantian approach. But Samet contends that this concern is misplaced; the thick loyalty that is required of fiduciaries actually complements a Kantian understanding of virtue.

Samet suggests that emotions can play an important motivational role within a Kantian account of practical reasoning. On her account, one might adopt a policy of acting consistently with one's moral duties, and one might cultivate morally oriented emotions—such as sympathy or kindness—in an effort to increase the likelihood of one's adherence to this policy. Actions that are motivated by emotion may then be rooted in reasoned respect for the moral law, even where respect for the moral law does not play a direct motivational role. Loyalty, in Samet's view, can then be a rational strategy for adoption by morally worthy agents who recognize their own weaknesses. On this basis, she concludes, fiduciary loyalty can be understood as a Kantian virtue.

Lionel Smith also takes a Kantian perspective, but he focuses on different aspects of Kant's philosophy. Smith is interested in determining whether fiduciary loyalty can qualify as a legal or juridical duty as Kant understood these concepts. On this approach, in order to have a juridical duty it must be possible to comply with the purported duty for any end or objective that the duty bearer may have. As Smith explains: "[I]t must be possible to say objectively whether the duty was performed, without knowing why it was performed. If I pay my taxes only because I don't want to go to jail, I have complied with the duty, and this shows that the duty can qualify as a legal one." In addition, the duty must be narrowly defined, so that one can decide clearly whether or not the duty has been fulfilled. And this raises interesting questions about the status of fiduciary loyalty.

On Smith's view, the fiduciary duty of loyalty prescribes how the fiduciary's judgment is to be exercised. The fiduciary must exercise judgment in what the fiduciary *perceives* to be the best interests of the beneficiary. Accordingly, fiduciary loyalty is a subjective requirement. One might worry that if loyalty is a subjective requirement it will fail to meet the Kantian mandate that legal duties must be narrowly defined. Yet Smith finds that the resulting duty is sufficiently narrow to qualify as a duty under a Kantian approach, despite this subjective aspect. Drawing an analogy to criminal law *mens rea* elements, he explains that a subjective aspect need not preclude a duty from being a legal duty. That said, on Smith's account, fiduciary loyalty is not truly a duty. Instead, it is a juridical constraint on fiduciaries. The requirement of loyalty operates analogously to certain rules in contract law that may make a contract voidable, such as the rules that address some types of mistake. A failure to meet this type of condition is a failure to meet the requirements of a rule, but not a failure to meet the requirements of a duty. Fiduciary loyalty operates in a similar fashion: A valid exercise of a fiduciary power must be done properly; that is, it must be done loyally.

James Penner argues that fiduciary loyalty is neither a value nor a virtue. While friendship, for example, has intrinsic value, Penner claims that loyalty in itself does not. Penner challenges the idea that we should seek out opportunities to be loyal, for its own sake. And, he suggests, a person who is generally loyalty-minded has a vicious rather than a virtuous disposition in respect of this trait. On the other hand, Penner raises the possibility that fiduciary loyalty could be a negative virtue. Here, Penner draws on Joseph Raz's account of the rule of law as a negative virtue. On Raz's account, there are certain wrongs we can only commit once we have a legal system, and the rule of law is a virtue of a legal system to the extent it limits the commission of such wrongs. But the rule of law on this view is not something that is valuable in its own right; the rule of law, accordingly, is a negative virtue. If it is a negative virtue, loyalty would likewise involve the absence of a certain type of disvalue or vice. In this case, disloyalty or betrayal. Penner claims that certain relationships, such as friendships, provide unique opportunities for wrongdoing of this kind. While loyalty may not be intrinsically valuable in Penner's view, it does limit betrayals, as loyal parties will be incapable of, or at least averse to, committing these wrongs.

In addition, Penner rejects the idea that fiduciary loyalty is a duty. He sees fiduciary loyalty instead in terms of liability. A fiduciary has no duty to avoid conflicts of interest and being in a conflict is not in itself a wrong. Even so, when a fiduciary acts in conflict of interest and acquires a gain as a consequence, the fiduciary will have a duty to account for that gain to the fiduciary's principal. As Penner understands this duty, then, it is an example of a primary, remedial duty (and in this sense analogous to the primary, remedial duties found in the law of unjust enrichment). Penner's account is also relevant to the relationship between fiduciary liability and other spheres of private law. It is sometimes thought that independent, non-fiduciary wrongs (eg, a breach of contract) can qualify as fiduciary wrongs, at least where disloyalty is also involved in the underlying conduct. On Penner's view, however, wrongs are not *fiduciary* wrongs simply because they happen to manifest disloyalty. As he suggests, with fiduciary liability, the issue is that the wrong party has taken part in a transaction, not that the transaction is itself a wrong. Penner's arguments thus have significant implications for the proper extension of fiduciary remedies in areas of overlap with other private law fields.

Andrew Gold accepts the premise that fiduciary loyalty implicates a duty, and he takes this premise as a starting point. Gold, however, considers a distinct question: does the conception of loyalty in fiduciary law have any core minimum content? Many fiduciary theorists think it does. Some theorists suggest that the core minimum content of fiduciary loyalty is an anti-conflicts rule. Others suggest that the core minimum content is a requirement that the fiduciary act in what he or she perceives is the best interest of the beneficiary. Gold contends that fiduciary loyalty takes many forms, potentially including (or excluding) either of these conceptions. Fiduciary law adopts different conceptions of loyalty for different types of fiduciary relationships, and it adopts different conceptions in different jurisdictions.

In Gold's view, the different conceptions of fiduciary loyalty are not readily reducible into each other. Moreover, each of the leading accounts faces significant counterexamples. For instance, in some settings, a loyal fiduciary need not try to act in the best interests of the beneficiary; in other settings a loyal fiduciary is free to act with a conflict of interest, and would not face liability for doing so. It may be that each type of fiduciary loyalty is an expression of a single overarching loyalty concept—but even so, the common features will at best provide a very thin account of loyalty's essential content. Gold concludes, however, that the varied aspects of fiduciary loyalty may in turn provide insights into the nature of fiduciary law. On this account, the reasons why the concept of loyalty varies are themselves worthy of study.

III. Economic Theory

Classically, economic accounts see fiduciary law as a response to a principal–agent problem. On this view, agency is understood broadly as involving one party undertaking imperfectly observable discretionary actions that affect the interests of the principal. For a variety of reasons, these relationships implicate agency costs, and these are not readily addressed by the parties' efforts to set precise contractual terms *ex ante*. Contractarian law and economics suggests that fiduciary law responds to agency costs by supplying duties that fill gaps in contracts involving the hiring of an agent. The content of these duties is derived from a hypothetical bargain: the law provides terms that the parties would have selected in a world of zero transaction costs.

Robert Sitkoff's chapter adopts many of the premises of the standard, contractarian account. He sees fiduciary law as a response to a principal–agent problem, with the task being to minimize agency costs while still retaining the benefits of agency. Sitkoff, however, shows how a re-imagined economic approach can solve various problems that beset earlier economic analyses of fiduciary law. In doing so, he shows the breadth of phenomena that an economic theory can explain. Sitkoff contends that both per se and ad hoc fiduciary relationships involve agency problems, and he suggests that in each case the law imposes fiduciary obligations to address these problems. Yet fiduciary duties, such as duties of loyalty and care, have distinctive features. The law makes use of broad standards in these settings, thus enabling courts to provide context-specific terms to complete the parties' contract and minimize error costs. The law also adopts a panoply of subsidiary rules, such as the duty of impartiality and the principal and income rules in trust law. Subsidiary rules simplify enforcement of fiduciary obligations, reducing decision costs. The result is a structure that offers the decision cost advantages of rules while offering the error cost advantages of standards.

Sitkoff also emphasizes the context specific features of fiduciary law. Different fiduciary relationships raise different principal–agent problems, and the law reflects these differences. The variations in fiduciary law are adaptations to address the particular concerns each relationship and type of fact pattern raises. In addition, Sitkoff addresses one of the more fundamental challenges for contractual accounts of fiduciary law: mandatory rules. While much of fiduciary law comprises default rules that parties may change by appropriate contractual provisions, certain fiduciary obligations are immutable. Sitkoff argues that there are two functional bases for these mandatory rules. First, they serve a protective and cautionary function: A prophylactic rule may be justified in cases where the principal is commonly an unsophisticated party or not fully informed. Second, they serve an external categorization function: by delineating specific obligations that correspond to specific legal relationships, information costs are reduced.

Lastly, Sitkoff offers a functional account of both the compensatory and disgorgement remedies in fiduciary law. Both remedies, in his view, serve a deterrent purpose. The disgorgement remedy, however, serves as a penalty default to encourage disclosure by parties with superior information.

Daniel Markovits argues that the contractarian account fails to capture the actual requirements of fiduciary loyalty. In part, this is because fiduciary law does not allow for the practice of "efficient breach" in the way that contract law does. Strictly speaking, Markovits does not see efficient breach to be an actual breach of an agreement (he understands the parties to have contemplated the "breach" at formation). But with that caveat, efficient breaches are a common outcome of contractual relationships, and they are facilitated by the standard expectation damages remedy. In fiduciary law, unlike contract law, disgorgement remedies are a common feature. This divergence marks a major difference between contractual and fiduciary practices.

At a more fundamental level, Markovits suggests that contract sharing differs from fiduciary sharing. Contracting parties must go as far as their contract requires, but may otherwise act in a self-interested fashion towards each other. There is a duty of good faith, but it is good faith with respect to whatever agreement was reached by the parties *ex ante*. As Markovits indicates, contract sharing is sharing *ex ante*. In contrast, fiduciary sharing is sharing *ex post*. Contractual parties are not only less other-regarding than fiduciaries, but, in Markovits's view, they are differently other-regarding. Fiduciary sharing is different from that contemplated by contractual good faith; fiduciary sharing requires the fiduciary to take the initiative on her beneficiary's behalf. In turn, this contrast between *ex ante* and *ex post* sharing has profound implications for fiduciary law.

Richard Brooks provides an efficiency-based account of fiduciary relationships, but one with a very different focus from the standard economic account. Brooks does not take issue with the idea that contractarianism can help us understand fiduciary law. His contention is that the contractual account misses other important phenomena. Brooks is interested in understanding fiduciary law as it relates to knowledge, and a concern with knowledge brings different features to our attention. While many accounts of fiduciary law focus particularly on duties of care and loyalty, Brooks is interested in accounting for duties of confidence, candor, and disclosure, along with a fiduciary's obligation to be informed.

In Brooks's view, the standard contractual understanding of fiduciary law errs in its emphasis on the fiduciary's knowledge and expertise. Much of a fiduciary's knowledge is acquired during the course of a fiduciary relationship, rather than prior to its existence. In addition, contractual accounts generally take for granted that a court or the parties can fill in contractual gaps *ex post*, even if the parties could not readily determine appropriate terms *ex ante*. If, however, there are verifiability problems *ex post*, the court (and the parties) may not be able to fill in the appropriate terms after the fact. There may be a problem of "non-contractibility." As Brooks explains, the fiduciary duties that govern information can help to address these challenges.

Tamar Frankel focuses on the practical effects of legal theories on fiduciary law. Frankel suggests that fiduciary law can be re-characterized in various ways, with the consequence that fiduciary duties are watered down. Among other concerns, she argues that viewing fiduciary relationships as essentially contractual in nature renders irrelevant the power relationship between the parties. She further suggests that this perspective erodes the expressive impact of the law on the conscience of the fiduciary. Frankel contends that rules in fiduciary law are perceived differently when framed in terms of contract. In particular, she suggests that contractarianism will decrease the likelihood that prohibitions that limit fiduciaries' freedom will be observed in practice.

Frankel also challenges the usage of terms and concepts from other disciplines in the fiduciary setting. In her view, agency costs terminology leads to confusion, as the word "agency" has distinct meanings in economic and legal contexts. More broadly, Frankel raises concerns about agency relationships themselves, even when understood in the narrow, legal sense of agency. In certain cases, a fiduciary relationship that historically falls into one fiduciary category may subsequently fall into another fiduciary category. For example, Frankel argues that fiduciary duties may be watered down when a trust relationship is transformed into an agency relationship. Both trust and agency relationships are fiduciary, but the responsibilities of the fiduciary actor will vary depending on our categorization of the relationship.

Henry Smith approaches fiduciary law from a different angle; he considers the ways in which fiduciary law functions as a part of the law of equity. Equity, on Smith's account, serves as a means to counter opportunism. Fiduciary law is a setting in which there is a substantial risk of opportunistic conduct, given the amount of discretion fiduciaries have in carrying out their responsibilities. And the classic contexts that implicate fiduciary loyalty—self-dealing and conflicting interest transactions—correspond to a particularly high risk of opportunism. As Smith notes, a common equitable response to risks of opportunism is to make use of proxies and presumptions. Fiduciary law adopts this approach as well. Fiduciary law, however, often employs more categorical rules than we typically see in equity. The presumptions adopted in fiduciary law may be harder to overcome. Furthermore, the remedies for fiduciary breaches are often stringent. The challenge, then, is one of balancing the risks. If equity is seen from an anti-opportunism perspective, the question is "whether the proxies for opportunism and the effect of the presumptions based on them are unpredictable enough to keep the opportunists guessing but without destabilizing the law."

A frequent concern with equity is that it may serve as a largely unbounded means for courts to police the fairness of deals *ex post*. Yet there are also ways to cabin the scope of fiduciary law. Fiduciary law makes use of commonsense morality, and it draws on community and industry custom. Smith argues that these features constrain the fact-based analyses in fiduciary law, at least to some extent. Likewise, the largely *in personam* effect of fiduciary duties limits the information costs imposed by fiduciary law. Situating fiduciary law within a system of equity can thus provide an explanation for a variety of different fiduciary doctrines. Smith's chapter shows how these different features fit together, in the process accounting for the characteristic mix of formalism and contextualism in fiduciary law.

IV. Fiduciary Principles in Context: Private Law

A variety of contextual factors have influenced the development, interpretation, and application of fiduciary principles in private law. Some of these factors are rooted in differences amongst systems of private law; others are based on differences in the character of the relationships that attract fiduciary constraints. Fiduciary principles in civil and common law jurisdictions have common origins and reflect shared concerns. But the development of fiduciary law has taken different paths in different jurisdictions, reflecting the influence of underlying social, economic, and legal histories as well as differences in legal tradition and culture. Fiduciary principles also have common features across the relationships in which they figure, but again, categories of fiduciary relationships are clearly not identical.

Contextual factors raise a host of theoretical questions about fiduciary principles in private law. For example, what differences are there in the form given to fiduciary principles in civilian and common law systems? What do these differences suggest about the values engaged, and functions served, by fiduciary law? What, if anything, is distinctive in the nature of fiduciary relationships, content of fiduciary duties, or menu of fiduciary remedies in particular fields, such as trust law or agency law? Several chapters in this volume address these and other questions concerning the contexts in which fiduciary principles arise in private law.

Michele Graziadei's contribution provides a comparative assessment of fiduciary principles in civil and common law systems. Many scholars study fiduciary principles exclusively within the context of the Anglo-American common law tradition. As a result, one might think that fiduciary law is an exceptional product of that tradition; an outgrowth, more particularly, of the law of equity. Graziadei shows that this is a mistake. Fiduciary principles are prominent in modern civilian legal systems: "[t]he belief that fiduciary law is an unimportant minor field in civil law countries is based on false assumptions." Nor is it the case that fiduciary principles arose independently in civil and common law jurisdictions; in both systems they have a common origin in Roman law. Graziadei explains that "the label 'fiduciary relationship' in continental Europe is usually not employed to refer to the same set of facts and problems designated by that expression in common law jurisdictions." Nevertheless, the "province of fiduciary law in civilian countries is quite large and rich," and though "highly fragmented," it is marked by similar legal norms designed to prevent or redress abuse of power and conflicts of interest.

Beyond explaining points of convergence and divergence between civil and common law, Graziadei shows that comparative legal history holds important lessons for contemporary legal theory. We continue to grapple with problems generated by conflicts of value in the economies in which fiduciary relationships arise. Centuries ago, fiduciary relationships were premised on an "economy of honour" which promoted self-sacrifice as an element of virtue. These values are still reflected in certain non-commercial fiduciary relationships. But the "economy of honour" has been eclipsed by the "economy of commerce," which legitimates self-interested behavior and promotes maximization of utility. These values are, Graziadei suggests, reflected in many commercial fiduciary relationships. The dominance of the value of utility in commercial fiduciary law should not be surprising. But more surprising, and potentially worrisome, Graziadei explains, is the promotion of this value at the expense of non-mercantile values in non-commercial fiduciary relationships. Attention to historical and jurisdictional context is valuable in its own right but it is also useful, Graziadei shows, in suggesting the need for greater sensitivity to the various social and economic contexts in which fiduciary relationships arise.

The contribution of Martin Gelter and Geneviève Helleringer also provides a comparative analysis of fiduciary duties in civil and common law jurisdictions. Gelter and Helleringer focus on differences in the conceptualization of fiduciary relationships and duties in corporate law, and on the implications of those differences. In the United States, the canonical view is that the corporate fiduciary relationship is between directors and corporations, with the interests of corporations being equated with the interests of shareholders. The content of the corporate law duty of loyalty reflects this view of the fiduciary relationship, insofar as loyalty is understood as a matter of fidelity to the interests of shareholders. In certain European civil law jurisdictions, corporate fiduciary relationships and duties are understood differently. Directors still have an obligation to act in the best interests of the corporation, but the corporation's interests are understood as encompassing those of a broad range of stakeholders.

These different ways of casting corporate fiduciary law reflect fundamentally different views about the constitution of corporations and the values that should be promoted by corporate law. The prevalence of "stakeholderism" in Europe has raised interesting theoretical and practical challenges. One set of challenges lies in construing the fiduciary mandate of the constituency director. Constituency directors are appointed to represent the interests of a constituency group (eg, employees or creditors). Formally, their fiduciary duty is identical to that of other directors; they are to act in the best interests of the corporation. But how much, if any, latitude do constituency directors have to privilege the interests of their constituents?

On the whole, the law suggests that constituency directors are not permitted to favor constituents; fiduciary duties are *uniform* and are owed to the *corporation*. Gelter and Helleringer argue that this is paradoxical given differences in underlying bases of representation, given the inherent ambiguity of corporate interests, and given that fiduciary duties are framed negatively in terms of conduct to be avoided rather than positively in terms of interests to be served. They argue that, in interpreting corporate fiduciary duties, greater attention should be paid to the basis of authority under which a director acts. If directors are authorized to act for the corporation as a whole, their fiduciary relationship is with the corporation alone and their duty should be understood as owed to the enterprise. However, if a director is authorized to act for a constituency, their fiduciary relationship with the corporation and duty to it ought to be understood as mediated through their representation of that constituency.

Deborah DeMott's contribution focuses on fiduciary principles in the context of agency law. She explores the fiduciary character of agency relationships, highlighting aspects of these relationships that differ from other kinds of fiduciary relationships often misleadingly framed in terms of agency. DeMott also attends to an under-analyzed topic in agency law that is of general interest to legal theorists; namely, the normative horizon within which legal interpretation should take place. DeMott here offers an extended reply to Kent Greenawalt's reflections on her work on the interpretation of instructions in agency.

DeMott points out that a distinctive feature of the agency fiduciary relationship is the principal's responsibility for, and control over, the actions of the agent. Unlike other fiduciary relationships in which the beneficiary is passive in law (and, often, in fact), the principal has a "right or power to control the agent." The principal exercises control mainly by issuing instructions. Respect for the control rights of the principal requires clarification of the proper approach to interpreting these instructions. DeMott suggests that the proper normative horizon is one informed by the fiduciary character of agency itself: "[t]he fiduciary benchmark requires the agent to interpret instructions reasonably in light of the principal's wishes... [it] does not permit the agent to exploit gaps or arguable ambiguities in the principal's instructions to further the agent's self interest or that of a third party, without the principal's consent."

Recognition of the foundational importance of control within the agency fiduciary relationship has important implications for agency theory and for our understanding of the functional advantages and disadvantages of agency. It suggests that Hohfeldian accounts of agency that emphasize the power of the agent to bind the principal are flawed given their failure to account for the principal's control of the agent in the exercise of agency powers. DeMott points out that the control rights enjoyed by the principal also impact the functionality of agency relationships. The expectation that the principal will control the agent, and the principal's right to do so at any juncture, means that agency is a poor choice of relationship for those who wish to bind themselves prospectively or who wish to delegate discretion to a fiduciary more fulsomely.

Avihay Dorfman's contribution examines fiduciary principles in the context of trust law. As was true of DeMott, so too Dorfman believes that the particular fiduciary relationship with which he is concerned is structurally distinctive. He also believes that it raises distinctive normative issues. Like Dagan and Hannes, Dorfman favors contextual over unitary analysis of fiduciary relationships and duties. In addition, he endorses value pluralism with the caveat that, while "context matters... it *supervenes on* the formal structure of the trust... [and thus] it is both necessary and desirable to understand this form before accounting for context." Dorfman, like Miller, therefore focuses on identifying and exploring *formal* properties of fiduciary relationships. But he is skeptical of the breadth of the conceptual analysis offered by Miller. He argues that "by moving from the most abstract generalization of the fiduciary relationship *directly* to concrete doctrine... the unitarist approach *necessarily* obscures distinctions that may exist amongst fiduciary relationships that arise in different forms."

Dorfman argues that trust law fiduciary relationships are distinctive partly as a result of the function they serve; they "respond to a... difficulty introduced by beneficiaries who lack personality." Beneficiaries like children and incapacitated adults, being incapable of owning property and enjoying associated benefits of ownership, suffer the "excesses of ownership" (inasmuch as personality is a precondition of fee simple ownership). The trust responds to this problem in a distinctive way: "[i]t provides access [to ownership] through the familiar division of ownership labor between trustee and beneficiary: The former is vested with title over a particular asset, whereas the latter holds... the entitlement to the *ownership of another* over this asset." Dorfman maintains that the trust should therefore be understood as a "derivative" form of ownership.

The position of the trustee is characterized by more than her possession of legal title to the trust corpus; according to Dorfman, it is also characterized by "transubstantiation," whereby "the trustee can assert the power to author acts and decisions with respect to the trust property in the name of the beneficiary." Through the person of the trustee a beneficiary can avail herself of the exercise of powers rooted in legal personality notwithstanding that she may lack such personality herself. This has ramifications for our understanding of the hallmark fiduciary duty of loyalty. According to Dorfman, the duty of loyalty ought not to be understood as *responsive* to formal properties of the trust. It is "partly *constitutive* of what it is to be a trustee." The duty of loyalty is the doctrinal basis for attributing gains associated with trust administration to the beneficiary and in functioning as such it simply requires that "the trustee assume the distinctive ownership personality of the beneficiary."

V. Fiduciary Principles in Context: Public Law

Public fiduciary theory has a long history and prominent political theorists—including John Locke and Hugo Grotius—have offered important fiduciary accounts of the state. In recent years, there has been a resurgence of public fiduciary theory. Fiduciary principles have been applied to administrative law, election law, and the practice of judging. In addition, fiduciary principles have recently been offered as a source of citizens' political obligations. Given these developments, public fiduciary theory now raises a variety of significant questions. Who qualifies as a public fiduciary—the state, a branch of the state, or one or more of its organs or officeholders? Who is the proper beneficiary of public fiduciaries? Is it the general public or particular constituents? To the extent public fiduciary principles may be drawn from private fiduciary analogues, which private law relationships should serve as models? And finally, how far does public fiduciary theory reach? For example, does it apply to international law? Many of these questions are assessed by the chapters in this Part.

Evan Fox-Decent suggests that fiduciary principles can help explain legitimate authority—not only for private parties, but also for the state. He takes Joseph Raz's account of authority as a starting point. Under this account, authorities are legitimate only if the authority's directives enable its subjects to better conform to reason. One of the central components of this account is the Normal Justification Thesis that a subject of authority would better comply with reasons that apply to him if he intends to be guided by the authority's directives than otherwise. Raz's account has recently been critiqued on several grounds including that it allegedly fails to show why the purported authority has standing to complain about or punish disobedience. Fox-Decent seeks to build on elements of Raz's account while avoiding these critiques.

Fox-Decent's fiduciary account of authority incorporates the Normal Justification Thesis. And he begins his analysis with the parent–child relationship. In this setting, he argues, parental powers are linked to parental duties. Parents have powers to issue and enforce directives to their children in part because of their fiduciary duties to help their children better comport with reason. Parents' fiduciary duties, in turn, arise given their custody of a legally incapable child and a prohibition on unilateralism. The child's duty to obey is implicit in parental authority, since parental authority "consists in a moral power to impose duties on the child only to the extent that those duties serve her."

Fox-Decent suggests that the fiduciary relationship between the state and its citizens is similar, and that these similarities reflect constitutive features of all fiduciary relationships. According to Fox-Decent, all fiduciaries hold administrative power over another person or her interests. And the beneficiary "must be incapable of guiding or exercising it on account of her circumstances (contextual incapacity), or on account of the nature of the alleged fiduciary's power (juridical incapacity)." Fiduciary duties are triggered in these circumstances, and they must be understood in terms of the reasons for which fiduciary powers are held. The fiduciary, he argues, has service reasons that warrant her fiduciary powers. In respect of the state–citizen relationship, Fox-Decent contends that citizens are juridically incapable of exercising public powers. The state is authorized "to establish legal order in a manner consistent with its overarching fiduciary duty, and on behalf of every subject, since every subject has an interest in security against unilateralism." In exercising its fiduciary powers, however, the state must be accountable to legal standards. And this has an important implication: "With accountability in place, subjects can properly be held to a moral duty to obey because they have legal assurance that the state is not entitled to subject them to domination."

Ethan Leib, David Ponet, and Michael Serota focus on a key challenge for public fiduciary theory: the mapping of public fiduciary relationships. As they suggest, private fiduciary theory has long struggled with identifying which parties are fiduciaries and which are their beneficiaries. Corporate law provides a well-known example—courts and commentators often diverge on the question whether directors owe their fiduciary obligations to shareholders, the corporation, or a range of stakeholders. Public fiduciary theory faces a similar set of puzzles.

When determining who is a public fiduciary, some theorists identify the federal state as the fiduciary, but others point to a body such as a legislature or an individual state or municipal government. Yet other theorists see officeholders themselves as fiduciaries. Alternatively, each of these state actors might be fiduciaries. Public fiduciary theory needs to have answers to these questions if it is to provide useful accounts of public fiduciary responsibilities. Furthermore, when determining who is a beneficiary, another set of problems arises. It may not be clear, for example, whether a member of Congress is a fiduciary for the people of her district, her state, her nation, present generations, or future generations. In addition, a public officeholder's oath of office may have a significant effect on this analysis.

Leib, Ponet, and Serota work through a variety of possible permutations of public fiduciary relationships and in doing so demonstrate just how complex the mapping concern is. As they indicate, correctly mapping fiduciary relationships is vital to the application of fiduciary principles to public law problems. They also suggest that a study of the private law can help political theorists in this endeavor, as long-standing debates in private law fields bear similarities to the puzzles faced by public fiduciary theory. A good example is the shareholder–stakeholder debate in corporate law. The shareholder primacy approach might suggest, by analogy, that in the public fiduciary setting a public official should owe her fiduciary obligations to the local constituency that elected her to office. A stakeholder view, in contrast, might suggest that this public official would have a duty both to represent this constituency, and also to represent a broader public whose interests need protection.

Evan Criddle considers public fiduciary theory from a different perspective—international law. Criddle argues that a state's responsibility to protect the people of other states, like its primary responsibility to its own people, can be understood in fiduciary terms. He traces the history of this fiduciary principle back to Francisco de Vitoria. In the sixteenth century, Vitoria sought to justify Spanish rule over indigenous peoples in the Americas based on the objective of protecting the natural rights of Spanish citizens who might travel there. Vitoria also based his argument on the objective of protecting the natural rights of indigenous peoples. This account ultimately proved highly influential for international institutions. As examples, Criddle points to various trusteeship relations between Western governments and first nations. He also indicates that fiduciary theory underpins the modern law of military occupation.

This is not to say that fiduciary principles have always been applied to desirable effect. There are many instances in which they have been abused as a cover for self-seeking behavior by states. Nevertheless, Criddle contends that assuming they are taken seriously and acted on in good faith, fiduciary principles provide noteworthy benefits. Amongst other things, fiduciary principles may serve as a basis for intervention to protect human rights. Criddle argues that, under a fiduciary conception of international law, the international community has an affirmative legal obligation to intervene to protect beneficiaries from human rights abuses. As he notes, the international community's recognition of sovereign states may be understood as a recognition of preexisting sovereign status. Or, this recognition may be understood as a necessary condition for such status. In either case, Criddle argues, the international community's responsibility is more than a moral ideal—it is a legally binding obligation, grounded in the responsibilities of the international community itself. Just as, in private law, courts have a responsibility to arbitrate when fiduciaries fail to meet obligations to their beneficiaries, so too the international community must intercede when fiduciary states fall short in the execution of their fiduciary mandate.

The chapters collected in this volume cover and chart a wide expanse of challenging philosophical terrain. In many cases, the questions addressed by our authors are novel. Invariably, their answers are original and challenging. There is some agreement amongst some of the chapters on some points (eg the tenability or lack thereof of contractarian economic analyses of fiduciary duties). But fortunately, for those of us who hope that the present volume will foster lively debate, the chapters also reveal diversity of opinion in answers given to several foundational philosophical questions about fiduciary law. There is difference of opinion, for example, on the question whether the fiduciary relationship has any defining qualities, whether these qualities are essential and uniform or contingent and particularistic, and what these qualities are. Opinion is also split on the moral and juridical expression given to the value of loyalty in fiduciary law; some of our authors think loyalty is a virtue, others that it is the object of a legal duty, while other authors deny both claims. There are also a variety of views on the content of standards of loyalty and the justification for these standards. Some argue that these standards are fixed and justified on moral or juridical grounds that apply universally across various kinds of fiduciary relationship. Others argue that these standards are variable and are justified either by moral values implicated by particular fiduciary relationships or by economic efficiency considerations that are manifested differently in different circumstances. Public fiduciary theorists are more univocal but not entirely so. Some of our contributors believe that public law is animated by a general fiduciary idea of state authority and assume that discrete public fiduciary relationships are instantiations of this idea. Others argue that there are important differences in the constitution of different public fiduciary relationships and suggest that these differences impact the application of fiduciary principles to public offices. This is but a sampling of the diversity of opinion amongst our contributors on answers to some important questions of fiduciary theory. An incurious person might be surprised and disappointed to find such disagreement on foundational philosophical questions concerning an important body of law. But we hope that the reader will find cause for celebration in the variety of views on offer and the rigor with which the arguments supporting them are put. At the very least, disagreement on answers to philosophical questions should be seen as an invitation to further philosophical inquiry.

PART I

FIDUCIARY RELATIONSHIPS

1

The Role of Status in the Law of Obligations

Common Callings, Implied Terms, and Lessons for Fiduciary Duties

*The Hon Justice James Edelman**

> Even in the case of a solicitor–client relationship, long accepted as a status based fiduciary relationship, the duty is not derived from status. As in all such cases, the duty is derived from what the solicitor undertakes, or is deemed to have undertaken, to do in the particular circumstances.[1]
>
> In some [exceptional] cases, it is simply not reasonable for a client to claim that it expected a law firm to owe it exclusive loyalty and to refrain from acting against it in unrelated matters. . . [The Court will consider various factors] when determining whether there was a reasonable expectation that the law firm would not act against the client in unrelated matters.[2]

The focus of this book is the law of fiduciaries. This chapter addresses an important and difficult question at the heart of the fiduciary law. But the question is not confined to fiduciary law. It has repercussions throughout the law of obligations. The question is the role played by the status or office of a person in determining the obligation owed. One possible answer to this question forms part of a larger perspective which can reduce the tesserarian nature of fiduciary litigation.

The New South Wales Court of Appeal makes an important point in the quotation at the start of this chapter. This point is that a fiduciary's duty is not derived from status. A similar point is made in the second quotation above taken from a recent decision of the Supreme Court of Canada.[3] But if fiduciary duties are not derived from status then this gives rise to a conundrum. Why do courts commonly speak of fiduciary *relationships*? Why do courts emphasize the duties that arise in relationships of a particular status? The answer which I will tentatively suggest is that status may play an important part of the background material by informing the duties which are undertaken by particular persons. In other words, where a duty arises because of a manifest, or objective, undertaking the status or office held by a person is an important circumstance in determining the scope of the duties which the officeholder may reasonably be held to have undertaken.

This chapter makes one assumption which is justified only briefly here. The assumption is that the existence of an undertaking, objectively manifested, is a precondition

* My thanks to Daniella Spencer-Laitt for research assistance.

[1] *Beach Petroleum v Kennedy* (1999) 48 NSWLR 1, 188 (Spigelman CJ, and Sheller and Stein JJA). The only quibble which one might have with this quotation is that an objective undertaking does not involve a "deeming" or any fiction. It is not a proxy for subjective thoughts.

[2] *Canadian National Railway Co v McKercher LLP* [2013] SCC 39 [37] (McLachlin CJ for the Court).

[3] *Canadian National Railway Co v McKercher LLP* [2013] SCC 39.

in equity for a fiduciary obligation to arise. I have made a more substantial argument concerning this precondition elsewhere.[4] There are many authorities which emphasize the need for such an undertaking.

Not every undertaking, nor even every undertaking said to be made by a person in a fiduciary relationship,[5] is a *fiduciary* undertaking. The dominant position in authority is that before an undertaking can become a *fiduciary undertaking* the undertaking must include a pledge to act, or behave, in a particular *manner*. Sometimes this pledged manner of performance of the undertaking is described as a requirement that performance will be in the other party's best interests. Sometimes it is expressed as a requirement that the undertaking be performed "loyally" to that other party. On other occasions it is expressed as a requirement that the duty be performed for the "proper purposes" for which it was conferred. All of these formulations can be problematic. But the important point is that however the manner of acting or behaving is expressed, the manner of performance of an undertaking is not a freestanding duty.[6] An "obligation" to be "loyal" invites the question: loyal to what end? Loyalty can be infinitely variable as Horace illustrated, and Owen satirized: *dulce et decorum est pro patria mori.* In law as in life, loyalty cannot be understood without knowing the performance in relation to which loyalty is required. For fiduciary duties, the performance is the obligation undertaken. The manner in which the duty is performed is part of the undertaking but it is generally said to be that manner of performance that attracts the epithet *fiduciary*.

There is a conundrum which arises from a focus upon construction of an undertaking to determine the content of a fiduciary duty. The conundrum is why we speak of fiduciary *relationships*. If (i) the content of the fiduciary duty is determined by the content of the objective undertaking and (ii) the distinctiveness, or fiduciary nature, of the undertaking is determined by a particular undertaken manner of the exercise of the undertaken duty, then why should it matter whether the undertaking is made as part of a particular relationship or not? In other words, what is the relevance of *status* or *relationships* in determining the content of objectively undertaken duties?

The answer to the conundrum is that the role of a fiduciary relationship depends upon an understanding of the role of *status* in the law concerning voluntary undertakings. The essential point in this chapter is to float the thesis that status performs the same role in relation to fiduciary duties that it performs generally in the law of obligations.

This chapter is divided into three parts. First, I explain the nature of a fiduciary duty: how it arises and how the content of the duty is determined. This part is in the nature of a summary of more detailed arguments which I, and others,[7] have made elsewhere.

Second, I turn to the role of status in the law of obligations generally. Two examples are given: the role of status in relation to implied terms and the role of status in relation

[4] J Edelman, "When Do Fiduciary Duties Arise?," 126 *LQR* 302 (2010).

[5] P Finn, *Fiduciary Obligations* (1977) 2; *Bristol and West Building Society v Mothew* [1998] Ch 1, 18 (Millett LJ); *Arklow Investments Limited v MacLean* [2000] 2 NZLR 1 (PC); *Chirnside v Fay* [2006] NZSC 68; [2007] 1 NZLR 433 [15] (Elias CJ).

[6] *Pilmer v The Duke Group (in Liq)* (2001) 207 CLR 165, [70]–[71] (McHugh, Gummow, Hayne, and Callinan JJ).

[7] Finn (n 5).

to the law of common callings. In each case, it is strongly arguable that status operates as part of the context by which reasonable expectations are formed.

Third, I return to fiduciary duties and explain how an understanding of the operation of status in the law of obligations can help us understand its role in determining the content of a fiduciary undertaking.

There is one significant topic excluded from discussion in this chapter. This chapter is concerned only with fiduciary duties as they arise in equity. It does not deal with duties which a statute might describe as "fiduciary" or the interrelationship between fiduciary duties in equity and those under statute. Parliament can create new duties which in equity would not be considered "fiduciary," and can attach the same remedial consequences upon those duties. Parliament might even attach the label "fiduciary" to duties which had never previously been regarded as fiduciary. Or it can redefine and shape fiduciary duties and their remedial consequences. For instance, in *United States v Mitchell*,[8] Marshall J, for the majority, spoke of the fiduciary duty "established by the Act [Indian General Allotment Act 1887] and of the subsequent statutory and administrative developments which clarified and fleshed out that duty." One of the most significant examples of interaction between statutory and equitable duties is found in company law. A company, and its directors, are the creation of statute. The powers of the directors derive from statute. In many jurisdictions those powers have not been codified, so the construction of the statute will take place as set against the historical background of fiduciary duties in equity.

I. The Nature of a Fiduciary Duty

The word "fiduciary" derives from the Latin *fiducia* meaning trust or confidence.[9] The origins of a fiduciary duty depend upon the extent of the link between concepts that are thought to be necessary and the point at which it might be thought that one concept ceases being developed and a new concept is born. Some association might, nevertheless, be drawn between the modern conception of a fiduciary duty and the Roman law concept of *fiducia*. In Roman law, *fiducia* was a pactum. It was an "appendage to a conveyance."[10] Its primary use was a direction to the holder of property concerning that person's obligations in relation to the property. The Roman concept of *fiducia cum amico*,[11] which still exists in Civilian jurisdictions,[12] requires a person who receives assets of another to deal with them in good faith.

There are two important preliminary points which must be understood in order to comprehend the operation of fiduciary duties.

First, a fiduciary duty requires an undertaking. I have made this point elsewhere[13] but the notion most famously derives from the academic[14] and judicial[15] work of Paul

[8] 445 US 535 (100 S Ct 1349, 63 L Ed 2d 607 (1980)).

[9] J Morwood (ed), *Pocket Oxford Latin Dictionary* (2001) 56; *Oxford English Dictionary* (2nd edn, 1989) definition 3: "Of the nature of, proceeding from, or implying trust or reliance."

[10] W Buckland, *A Textbook of Roman Law* (3rd edn, 1966) 431.

[11] Gaius 2.60.

[12] G Gretton, "Trusts without Equity," 49 *ICLQ* 499 (2000) at 501.

[13] Edelman (n 4).

[14] P Finn "The Fiduciary Principle," in T Youdan (ed), *Equity, Fiduciaries and Trust* (1992).

[15] *Grimaldi v Chameleon Mining NL (No 2)* [2012] FCAFC 6; (2012) 200 FCR 296 [177].

Finn. The core proposition of this section is that the fiduciary undertaking is always manifested by the conduct of the fiduciary. In this sense the fiduciary undertaking is voluntary: it is not imposed by law independently of the fiduciary's manifest intentions. But it is not concerned with the subjective knowledge or subjective intentions of the fiduciary. The undertaking is construed from manifest words, conduct, and circumstances.

One particularly relevant circumstance is the office held by a person. A person might be appointed as a trustee, or as a solicitor. In some cases, the person's undertaking upon appointment might provide clearly that he or she can perform duties in a manner which involves putting himself or herself in a position of conflict or that he or she might be permitted to use the position to make profit in a particular way, possibly at the expense of the principal. Equity does not prohibit such agreement, whether in a contractual context or in a trust deed or other settlement or undertaking. Indeed, in commercial trusts it is almost universal today for trustees to profit, via remuneration, from their positions. In other cases there might be no such expressed undertaking. If not, the history and nature of the office of trustee or solicitor will carry with it reasonable expectations of particular duties. A reasonable expectation is the converse of the manifestation of an undertaking viewed from the perspective of the right-holder.

The importance of the fiduciary undertaking is also not confined to fiduciary duties in equity. For instance, in the United Kingdom it has an important statutory role in the Charities Act 2006 (UK) which has, at the heart of its definition of charity in s 1(1), the concept of an "institution." Section 78(5) defines an institution as including "a trust or undertaking." The Charities Act 1960 also referred to undertakings in s 46(1).

The second preliminary point is that a subdivision within undertakings, involving a class of undertaking as "fiduciary," is a modern conception. As Sealy and Finn observed decades ago, the term "fiduciary" only became common in the law reports of the mid-nineteenth century.[16] But although the concept of a "fiduciary" undertaking is a recent one, the concept of an undertaking itself is extremely old. The undertaking, initially genuine and later also fictional, was central to the plea of *assumpsit* (he undertook). Prior to the emergence of a distinct law of contract, an undertaking did not require consideration from the plaintiff for a successful action based upon mis-performance of an undertaken responsibility.[17]

Today, an undertaking which is supported by consideration will usually be legally binding as a contract. Historically, however, consideration was not necessary for an undertaking to be a binding *assumpsit*. And even today a unilateral undertaking can be binding without consideration in various situations such as where the undertaking is in the form of a deed, or if it involves a letter of credit, or if it involves an undertaking to hold rights on trust.

The characterization of an undertaking as "fiduciary" might be seen as a general example of another situation in which courts will treat undertaken obligations as binding even if they are unilateral. But it may, nevertheless, be doubted whether there is any

[16] L Sealy "Fiduciary Relationships," [1962] CLJ 69; and [1962] CLJ 119; Finn (n 5) 1.

[17] D Ibbetson, *A Historical Introduction to the Law of Obligations* (1999) 133 and *Powtuary v Walton* (1598) Ro Abr 1.10, *Action sur Case*, P5.

utility in a quest to identify a precise boundary between those undertakings which are fiduciary and those undertakings which are not. Making consequences depend upon whether a misleading label is attached to the undertaking is almost certain to cause confusion in the law. Nearly 40 years ago in the first page and core proposition of his great work on fiduciaries, Finn observed that the "rules are everything. The description 'fiduciary,' nothing."[18] The label "fiduciary" is also misleading due to its etymology in "trust" and "confidence." It is well known that "fiduciary duties" can arise despite the absence of any relationship of trust or confidence. Even when a fiduciary duty is owed by a trustee, the duty does not arise because of the *fiducia* or "trust" which is sometimes said to inhere in that relationship. There need be no relationship of trust or confidence between a trustee and a beneficiary; the beneficiary might not know of the trust and the beneficiary might not even be born.[19]

Nevertheless, on the state of the current law, it is often necessary to decide whether the label "fiduciary" should be attached to a particular undertaking in order to determine whether various consequences should arise. On one view, the undertaking is "fiduciary" if it incorporates a pledge that the duty will be performed in a particular way. Sometimes this particular manner of performance is described as being in the "best interests" of the principal. In the United States, Scott made this point more than 60 years ago, saying that the fiduciary undertaking could be contractual or gratuitous, but the key point was that the nature of the undertaking involved acting in the interests of another person.[20] In Australia, in the leading Australian formulation of the fiduciary duty, Mason J explained that the "critical" feature of fiduciary relationships was that the fiduciary "undertakes or agrees to act for or on behalf of or in the interests of another person in the exercise of a power or discretion which will affect the interests of that other person in a legal or practical sense."[21] This statement has been quoted with approval in Australia on many occasions.[22]

The same is true in Canada. Putting aside the reference to statute, in *Galambos v Perez*[23] the Supreme Court of Canada said of fiduciary duties in equity that "[i]t is fundamental to all ad hoc fiduciary duties that there be an undertaking by the fiduciary, which may be either express or implied, that the fiduciary will act in the best interests of the other party. . . In cases of per se fiduciary relationships this undertaking will be found in the nature of the category of relationship in issue." This final, and important, sentence is considered in greater detail in Section III of this chapter. Again, in the Supreme Court of Canada in *Hodgkinson v Simms*,[24] La Forest, L' Heureux-Dubé, and Gonthier JJ explained, quoting from Finn, that "the 'end point' in each situation is to ascertain whether the one has the right to expect that the other will act in the former's interests (or, in some instances, in their joint interest) to the exclusion of his own

[18] Finn (n 5) 1.

[19] *Swain v Law Society* [1982] 1 WLR 17, 48 (Fox LJ); J D Heydon and M J Leeming (eds), *Jacobs' Law of Trusts in Australia* (7th edn, 2006) 4 [107].

[20] A Scott "The Fiduciary Principle," 37 *Calif Law Rev* 539, 544 (1949).

[21] *Hospital Products Ltd v United States Surgical Corporation* [1984] HCA 64; (1984) 156 CLR 41, 96–7.

[22] In the High Court, for example, *Pilmer v Duke Group (In liq)* (2001) 207 CLR 165, [70]–[71] (McHugh, Gummow, Hayne, and Callinan JJ); *John Alexander Tennis Club v White City Tennis Club* (2010) 241 CLR 1, [87] (French CJ, Gummow, Hayne, Heydon, and Kiefel JJ).

[23] [2009] 3 SCR 247, 249. [24] [1994] 3 SCR 377.

several interests." Most recently, the Supreme Court of Canada held that even in a per se fiduciary relationship such as that of lawyer–client there can be examples where a law firm might not owe exclusive loyalty to its client. Whether or not this proposition applies in other jurisdictions especially in the context of different statutes and regulations, the essential basis for the conclusion of the Supreme Court was whether there is a reasonable expectation by the client of such loyalty from the law firm.

Although it is not necessary for the purposes of this chapter to quibble with the widely accepted formulation that a fiduciary duty requires that the undertaking be performed in the best interests of the principal, it suffices to say that there may be some difficulties with the expression of that proposition in those terms. There are three difficulties with this common "best interests" formulation.

First, a trustee might undertake to hold assets on trust subject to a general power to distribute the assets to anyone in the world (including himself or herself). No decision has yet held a general power to be invalid. The existence of this power, if valid, must mean that there is no requirement for the trustee to act in the best interests of the beneficiaries since a duty to act in a particular manner, with a power not to do so, permits a trustee to act in a manner which is not in the best interests of beneficiaries.

Second, consider an example. Suppose a trustee holds a trust fund on a discretionary trust for three objects with an absolute discretion as to the amount, if any, which will be distributed to each. The trustee carefully considers the circumstances of the beneficiaries and distributes all of the trust funds to person B. Unbeknownst to the trustee, person B has a chronic gambling habit and the distribution is soon gambled and lost. On the assumption that the distribution was not in the best interests of any of the objects, still less in the best interests of all of them, could it be said that the trustee is liable for failing to distribute the trust fund in the best interests of the objects of the trust? The answer is "no." As the joint judgment in the High Court of Australia of McHugh, Gummow, Hayne, and Callinan JJ explained in *Pilmer v Duke Group*,[25] "there is not imposed upon fiduciaries a quasi-tortious duty to act solely in the best interests of their principals." As the House of Lords and High Court of Australia have both emphasized, the description of the manner of exercise of fiduciary powers[26]

> clearly cannot be done by enumeration, since the variety of situations facing directors of different types of company in different situations cannot be anticipated. No more, in their Lordships' view, can this be done by the use of a phrase—such as "bona fide in the interest of the company as a whole," or "for some corporate purpose." Such phrases, if they do anything more than restate the general principle applicable to fiduciary powers, at best serve, negatively, to exclude from the area of validity cases where the directors are acting sectionally, or partially i.e. improperly favouring one section of the shareholders against another.

A third difficulty with the broad "best interests" or "loyalty" formulation of fiduciary undertakings is that it can require a fiduciary duty to be "filleted" into fiduciary and

[25] *Pilmer v The Duke Group (in Liq)* [2001] HCA 31; (2001) 207 CLR 165 [74].

[26] *Howard Smith Ltd v Ampol Ltd* [1974] AC 821, 835; *Whitehouse v Carlton Hotel Pty Ltd* [1987] HCA 11; (1987) 162 CLR 285 (Mason, Deane, and Dawson JJ).

non-fiduciary components such as an undertaken duty of care.[27] It can create a distinction between fiduciary powers of care and (non-)fiduciary duties of care.[28] It can require that fiduciary duties are all proscriptive.[29] Each of these points is controversial; different countries, and different courts, have reached different conclusions on them.

For these reasons there are problems with the current requirement of "best interests" or "loyalty" as an essential component in that which makes an undertaking a *fiduciary undertaking*. But the most fundamental point is the centrality of a manifest undertaking coupled with a reasonable expectation of loyalty. The circumstances which support such an expectation include any office assumed by the fiduciary, the words and conduct spoken or expressed by the fiduciary in the assumption of any office or making of any undertaking. This underscores the importance of the point made by Fletcher Moulton LJ almost a century ago: "There is no class of case in which one ought more carefully to bear in mind the facts of the case."[30] Or, as the matter was put in the Supreme Court of Canada,[31] and also in *Grimaldi v Chameleon Mining NL (No 2)*[32] by the Full Court of the Federal Court in Australia:

> A person will be in a fiduciary relationship with another when and insofar as that person has undertaken to perform such a function for, or has assumed such a responsibility to, another as would thereby reasonably entitle that other to expect that he or she will act in that other's interest to the exclusion of his or her own or a third party's interest.

II. The Evolution of Status in the Law of Obligations: Two Examples

This section considers the role of status in two areas of the law of obligations. The point made is that in areas where an obligation is based upon an objectively manifested undertaking, as it is in these examples, relationship status or officeholding is one relevant factor in construing that undertaking.

A. Example 1: Common callings

The first example where status or office is sometimes thought to dictate the nature of obligations owed is in relation to "common callings." Holdsworth argued that the origin of liability upon a common calling was the notion that persons holding a particular status were regulated by law. Hence "persons like innkeepers or common carriers, and perhaps persons like smiths or surgeons, were considered to be bound by their calling to show a certain degree of skill in their respective callings."[33] The basis for the action,

[27] See J D Heydon, "Are the *Duties* of Company Directors to Exercise Care and Skill Fiduciary?," in S Degeling and J Edelman (eds), *Equity in Commercial Law* (2005). See also *United States v White Mountain Apache Tribe* 537 US 465; 249 F 3d 1364 (2003).

[28] Heydon (n 27). [29] See *Futter v Revenue & Customs* [2013] UKSC 26.

[30] *Re Coomber* [1911] 1 Ch 723 at 728–9.

[31] *Canadian National Railway Co v McKercher LLP* [2013] SCC 39 [37].

[32] [2012] FCAFC 6; (2012) 200 FCR 296 [177].

[33] W S Holdsworth, *A History of English Law*, vol 3 (3rd edn, 1923) 385.

Holdsworth asserted, was "at bottom public policy. It was for the interest of the community—then as now—that persons who professed a particular calling should show an adequate amount of care, skill and honesty in following their calling."[34]

Holdsworth's version of the history of the common callings is controversial. The late A W B Simpson argued that no particular categories of common calling ever existed. The adjective "common" applied to hangmen, prostitutes, informers, serjeants, laborers, attorneys, innkeepers, carriers, and many others: it "means no more than available to or for the public."[35]

In any event, the "status" conception of the liability of a common calling gradually receded. In a later consideration of the evolution of special assumpsit, Holdsworth explained that by the seventeenth century the centrality of the undertaking had meant that the adoption of "these forms of assumpsit in these cases tended to promote and emphasise a transition from status to contract."[36] A general consensus emerged that it was not the particular status of an individual which gave rise to the duties of a common calling but the nature of the undertaking made by the individual.

In Sir Percy Winfield's famous history of negligence in torts,[37] he traced the different conceptions of the basis for rules concerning the common callings including that which was floated by Coke after the *Ipswich Tailor's Case*;[38] namely, that the liability based upon a common calling, such as that of a common carrier, was based upon a general undertaking of safe delivery. By the time of Blackstone this undertaking conception had become central. Blackstone explained that this class of contracts "arises upon this supposition that everyone who undertakes any office, employment, trust, or duty contracts with those who employ or entrust him, to perform it with integrity, diligence and skill."[39]

The modern conception is now firmly rooted in the notion of an undertaking. In the leading Australian case of *James v Commonwealth*,[40] Dixon J rejected the argument that the Commonwealth had induced common carriers to breach their duty to carry Mr James's fruit, finding that the carriers had not undertaken or assumed a common duty:[41]

> The holding out or profession of the character of common carrier may be expressed, or it may be, and usually is, implied by a course of business or other conduct. It is in every case a question of fact whether the character of a common carrier has been assumed. In considering that question an important matter is whether the carrier holds himself out as ready without discrimination to carry the goods of all persons who may choose to employ him or send him goods to be carried. If, instead of inviting all persons without discrimination to use his ships or vehicles, he reserves the right of choosing among them, independently of the suitability of their goods for his means of transportation

[34] Holdsworth (n 33) 385–6.

[35] A W B Simpson, *A History of the Common Law of Contract: The Rise of the Action of Assumpsit* (1987) 230.

[36] Holdsworth (n 33) 448.

[37] P Winfield, "The History of Negligence in Torts," 42 *LQR* 184, 188–90 (1926).

[38] 11 Coke Rep 53a, 53b; 77 ER 1218, 1219.

[39] J Chitty (ed), *Blackstone's Commentaries of the Laws of England* (1826) Book III, ch 9, p 164.

[40] [1939] HCA 9; 62 CLR 339.

[41] [1939] HCA 9; 62 CLR 339 at 367–9.

and without regard to the room or space he has available, then he is not a common carrier.

Although the common calling arises as a matter of an undertaking, one particular aspect of the *common* calling should however be emphasized. That aspect is that the undertaking is to the public *at large*. As Dixon J explained, a person is not required to make an undertaking to the public generally to perform a service, but if he or she does so then that duty can be breached if it is not performed in relation to an individual. For this reason, the duties arising from the common callings are sometimes described as "public" duties and the possibility arose of proceeding for breach upon a criminal indictment.[42] So "if an inn-keeper... hangs out a sign and opens his house for travellers, it is an implied engagement to entertain all persons who travel that way and upon this universal *assumpsit* an action on the case will lie against him for damages."[43] Similarly, a standard common law count in the case of a common carrier for the refusal to carry goods was as follows:[44]

> That the defendant was a common carrier of goods for hire... and the plaintiff at a reasonable and proper time... tendered to him... at his place of business for the receipt of goods to be carried by him as such carrier to receive the same and carry them [for delivery] for hire to the defendant; and the plaintiff was then ready and willing and offered to pay to the defendant his reasonable hire... and the defendant then had sufficient time, means and convenience to receive and carry and deliver the said goods as aforesaid, and could and ought to have done so; yet the defendant did not nor would receive and carry the said goods for the plaintiff.

Common callings still exist. But an undertaking to the public to perform a service without discrimination is not common. Hence, the onus of proving that there has been no reservation of a right to discriminate is on the person who alleges that some particular carrier is a common carrier.[45] The question has become one of construction of an undertaking.

Although the question is one of construction of the undertaking, the status or office held remains relevant. There are some instances where status leads to a reasonable expectation that the undertaking is one to act in a common calling. Barristers and taxi drivers are examples. Further, if a common calling is found, the status of the obligor might affect the nature of the particular rights and duties found to be undertaken. An example is the common law lien which is imposed upon the recipient of a service provided by common calling. The "common law lien" was differentiated by Lord Kenyon from liens which the common law recognized by usage or agreement. When the common calling obligations were thought to be based upon considerations of public policy the lien was rationalized as a corresponding benefit to the obligor. It was said that the common law lien arose "where a party was obliged by law to receive goods... in

[42] See discussion in *Stapley v Towing Masters Pty Ltd (trading as Dynamic Towing)* [2009] NSWCA 382 [92]; *Pozzi v Shipton* (1838) 1 Per & Dav 4, 12 per Patteson J (arguendo, although the passage does not appear in the report at [1838] Eng R 205; 8 Ad & E 1106; 112 ER 1106); *Belfast Ropework Co v Bushell* at 212 per Bailhache J.

[43] Chitty (n 39), Book III, ch 9, p 165.

[44] E Bullen and S M Leake, *Precedents of Pleadings* (3rd edn, 1868) 277.

[45] *Stapley v Towing Masters Pty Ltd (trading as Dynamic Towing)* [2009] NSWCA 382 [98] (Campbell JA).

which case as the law imposed the [burden] it also gave him a power of retaining for his indemnity."[46] But, as the basis of the common calling moved to a model concerned with undertakings, the basis for the common law lien became rooted in the *expectation* that the status of a person as a common obligor in that industry would generally carry a right to a lien. By the time of the Bills of Lading Act 1855, it became recognized that the "receipt of the cargo by the indorsee of the bill of lading is evidence of an agreement to be bound by its terms, whatever they may be."[47] As the House of Lords later explained, "[t]he inferred contract is not a fiction. It is a contract which the court concludes has come into existence because that is the proper finding of fact to make on the evidence in the case."[48] The common law lien for freight or for general average arose as part of the contractual undertaking "unless the bill of lading contained words waiving or negativing the lien (as by stamping the bill of lading "freight prepaid")."[49]

B. Example 2: Implied terms

Another area in which it has been thought that a duty is imposed upon a person due to status or office held is where the term is implied by custom or usage in an industry in which a person holds an office or status. But, properly understood, the role of status or offices in these cases is developing towards being merely a factor in determining what a reasonable person would expect.

It is not clear upon what basis the obligation arising from custom or usage was originally imposed. The concept of a "general custom" was described by reference to the operation of the common law itself: where "a new case has to be decided, where analogy will not help as an authority or a guide, the lawyer must have recourse to what is called his discretion or common-sense, which is, in fact, customary reason."[50] On this broad view of custom, all duties arising from custom would properly be seen as imposed as a matter of law rather than arising from construction of an undertaking.

But, there was a more limited use of custom as a basis for importing obligations. In *Hutton v Warren*[51] Parke B spoke of the obligation from custom or usage being imported into a lease "by implication." The basis for the imposition of an obligation arising from custom was therefore implication of that obligation as a term of an undertaking. In the United States Supreme Court, in *Barnard v Kellogg*,[52] Davis J said:

> The proper office of a custom or usage in trade is to ascertain and explain the meaning and intention of the parties to a contract, whether written or in parol, which could not be done without the aid of this extrinsic evidence. It does not go beyond this, and is used as a mode of interpretation on the theory that the parties knew of its existence,

[46] *Naylor v Mangles* (1794) 1 Esp 109, 109; 170 ER 295, 296.

[47] *Allen v Coltart* (1883) 11 QBD 782, 785, Cave J citing *Young v Moeller* (1855) 5 E&B 755.

[48] *Borealis Ab v Stargas Limited and Others and Bergesen DY A/S* [2001] UKHL 17; [2001] 2 All ER 193 [20] (Lord Hobhouse).

[49] *Borealis Ab v Stargas Limited and Others and Bergesen DY A/S* [2001] UKHL 17; [2001] 2 All ER 193 [20] (Lord Hobhouse).

[50] J H Browne, *The Law of Usages and Customs* (1875) 79.

[51] *Hutton v Warren* (1837) 1 M&W 466, 475;150 ER 517, 521.

[52] 77 US 383 (1869) [5].

> and contracted with reference to it. . . But if it be inconsistent with the contract, or expressly or by necessary implication contradicts it, it cannot be received in evidence to affect it.

The role of status, or office, was as a background fact about an industry in which there was broad acceptance of particular conduct and from which one might deduce the terms of an agreement. In *Browne on Usage and Custom* this more limited conception of duties that can arise by custom was explained in the following way:[53]

> Seeing that custom is only to be inferred from a large number of individual acts, it is evident that the only proof of the existence of a usage must be by the multiplication or aggregation of a great number of particular instances; but these instances must not be miscellaneous in character, but must have a principle of unity running through their variety, and that unity must shew a certain course of business and an established understanding respecting it.

One of the most famous examples of undertakings implied by custom was the law merchant. The law merchant custom varied. Sometimes it was local. Sometimes it was general. Sometimes law merchant custom was accepted without evidence. Sometimes evidence was required. In *Edie v East India Co*,[54] Wilmot J said that "[t]here may indeed be some questions depending upon customs amongst merchants, where if there is a doubt about custom it may be fit and proper to take the opinions of merchants thereupon; yet that is only where the law remains doubtful, and even then the custom must be proved by facts not by opinion only."

An example of an obligation, and corresponding right, which arose as a consequence of status was the lien at common law which arose as a matter of custom or usage in particular relationships involving a particular status. The source of this right was an implied undertaking. In *Brandao v Barnett*,[55] Lord Campbell explained that these liens arose as "part of the law merchant" because "when a general usage has been judicially ascertained and established it becomes a part of the law-merchant, which courts of justice are bound to know and recognize." In Australia, Stephen J explained that "it is by such a process that the general liens of solicitors, stockbrokers, factors and insurance brokers have been established."[56]

In the leading case in Australia, *Con-Stan Industries of Australia Pty Ltd v Norwich Winterthur Insurance (Australia) Ltd*,[57] the High Court of Australia made the same point, describing the evolution of the concept of custom:

> A person may be bound by a custom notwithstanding the fact that he had no knowledge of it. Historically the courts approached this question in a rather different way. It was said that, as a general rule, a person who was ignorant of the existence of a custom or usage was not bound by it. To this rule there was a qualification that a person would be presumed to know of the usage if it was of such notoriety that all persons dealing in that sphere could easily ascertain the nature and content of the

[53] Browne (n 50) 79. [54] 2 Burr 1228.
[55] (1846) 12 Cl & F 787, 805; 8 ER 1622, 1629. See also Lord Lyndhurst 810, 1631.
[56] *Majeau Carrying Co Pty Ltd v Coastal Rutile Ltd* [1973] HCA 22; (1973) 129 CLR 48.
[57] [1986] HCA 14; (1986) 160 CLR 226, 237–8.

> custom. It would then be reasonable to impute that knowledge to a person, notwithstanding his ignorance of it.[58] In this way, the issue of notoriety. . . came to be co-extensive with the question of imputed knowledge. The achievement of sufficient notoriety was both a necessary and sufficient condition for knowledge of a custom to be attributed to a person who was in fact unaware of it. The result is that in modern times nothing turns on the presence or absence of actual knowledge of the custom; that matter will stand or fall with the resolution of the issue of the degree of notoriety which the custom has achieved. The respondent's contention that industry practices unknown to the assured are incapable of forming the basis of an implied term of the contract cannot be sustained.

The same is true in Canada.[59]

However, the acceptance that a term is *implied* into an undertaking is not the same as saying that the term arises as a matter of *construction* of the undertaking. In *Liverpool City Council v Irwin*,[60] Lord Wilberforce spoke of three different classes of implication of term. One class involved implication of terms by custom which was said to be founded upon "what both parties know and would, if asked, unhesitatingly agree to be part of the bargain." The second is where courts add a term to a contract without which the contract will not work. The third (which Lord Wilberforce doubted) was Lord Denning MR's view that terms could be implied if they were reasonable. The fourth was where the parties had not stated all the terms of the contract and the court needed to search for the terms by implication to complete the undertaking. On Lord Wilberforce's view, it is only the fourth of these categories which is expressly concerned with construction of a contract or undertaking.

But if the other three classes of implication of terms are not really concerned with a question of construction, then why do they arise? The view of Lord Denning MR, in the Court of Appeal in *Liverpool* was that the implication had nothing to do with the intention of the parties. Quoting from an extra-judicial speech of Lord Wright to the Holdsworth Club, Lord Denning argued that "[t]he truth is that the Court decides this question in accordance with what seems to be just and reasonable in its eyes. . . The Court is, in this sense, making a contract for the parties—though it is almost blasphemy to say so."[61] A non-religious lawyer might quibble with Lord Denning's use of the word "almost." The same view was expressed more recently by Kirby J in *Roxborough v Rothmans of Pall Mall Australia Ltd.*[62] His Honour said that "the time may be coming where the fiction is dispensed with completely and the courts acknowledge candidly that, in defined circumstances, the law to which they give effect permits, according to a desired policy, the imposition upon parties of terms and conditions for which they have omitted to provide expressly." The ultimate purpose of this chapter has been to reject this view.

[58] *Halsbury's Laws of England* (4th edn, 1973–87) vol 12, paras 467–8; *Jones v Canavan* (1972) 2 NSWLR 236, 243.

[59] See, eg, *Georgia Construction Co v Pacific Great Eastern Railway* [1929] SCR 630; *Gainers Ltd and Local 319 United Packing House Workers of America* (1964) 47 WWR 544, 552 (Riley J).

[60] [1977] 1 AC 239, 253.

[61] *Liverpool v Irwin*, unreported Court of Appeal decision, 22 July 1975, p 9.

[62] *Roxborough v Rothmans of Pall Mall Australia Ltd* [2001] HCA 68; (2001) 208 CLR 516, 575 [159].

The reason why this "policy" approach to implied terms is incorrect was explained by the Privy Council in *AG of Belize v Belize Telecom Ltd.*[63] In that case, Lord Hoffmann, giving the advice of the Privy Council, considered the leading Privy Council decision in *BP Refinery (Westernport) Pty Ltd v Shire of Hastings*,[64] on appeal from the Supreme Court of Victoria. In that case the Privy Council set out five criteria which must be "satisfied" for the implication of a term.[65] Those criteria were:

(i) must be reasonable and equitable;
(ii) must be necessary to give business efficacy to the contract so that no term will be implied if the contract is effective without it;
(iii) must be so obvious that "it goes without saying";
(iv) must be capable of clear expression; and
(v) must not contradict any express terms of the contract.

Lord Hoffmann rejected the suggestion that the *BP Refinery* indicia must all be satisfied. Instead, his Lordship explained that the factors were merely indicia to be used in the assessment of the meaning which words bear to the reasonable addressee. This approach assimilates the process of implication of terms with the exercise of construction and interpretation. In relation to implication, Lord Hoffmann's approach asks whether such a provision would spell out in express words what the instrument, read against the relevant background, would reasonably be understood to mean.[66] Lord Hoffmann's approach has been approved in New Zealand,[67] and in England.[68]

Lord Hoffmann's approach is also supported by the fact that courts often divide on the issue of whether they are involved in an exercise of "implying" a term or "construing" the terms of the contract by "the drawing out of what is implied by the language of the contract itself."[69] In Australia, the High Court of Australia has, on a number of occasions, divided in approach concerning whether the exercise in which it was engaged was one of interpretation or construction, or one of implication. For instance, in *Butt v Long*,[70] two judges in the High Court considered the issue to be one of interpretation[71] whilst the Chief Justice considered the issue to be one of implication.[72] In *Lewis Construction (Engineering) Pty Ltd v Southern Electric Authority of Queensland*,[73]

[63] *AG of Belize v Belize Telecom Ltd* [2009] UKPC 10; [2009] 1 WLR 1988 [21]–[27] referred to without disapproval in *The Bell Group Ltd (in liq) v Westpac Banking Corporation [No 3]* [2012] WASCA 157 [342] (Lee AJA).

[64] *BP Refinery (Westernport) Pty Ltd v Shire of Hastings* (1977) 180 CLR 266, 283 (Lord Simon and Lord Keith).

[65] *BP Refinery (Westernport) Pty Ltd v Shire of Hastings* (1977) 180 CLR 266, 283 (Lord Simon and Lord Keith).

[66] *AG of Belize v Belize Telecom Ltd* [2009] UKPC 10; [2009] 1 WLR 1988 [21].

[67] *Dysart Timbers Ltd v Nielsen* [2009] NZSC 43; [2009] 3 NZLR 160 [25] (Tipping and Wilson JJ) [62] (McGrath J).

[68] *Mediterranean Salvage & Towage Ltd v Seamar Trading and Commerce Inc ("The Reborn")* [2009] EWCA Civ 531.

[69] *Brambles Holdings Ltd v Bathurst City Council* [2001] NSWCA 61; (2001) 53 NSWLR 153, 165 [30] (Heydon JA); *Boreland v Docker* [2007] NSWCA 94 [110]–[111] (Beazley JA; Mason P and Ipp JA agreeing).

[70] *Butt v Long* [1953] HCA 76; (1953) 88 CLR 476.

[71] *Butt v Long* [1953] HCA 76; (1953) 88 CLR 476, 489–90 (Webb J), 490–1 (Fullagar J).

[72] *Butt v Long* [1953] HCA 76; (1953) 88 CLR 476, 487–9 (Dixon CJ).

[73] *Lewis Construction (Engineering) Pty Ltd v Southern Electric Authority of Queensland* (1976) 50 ALJR 769.

three judges[74] considered the exercise as one of interpretation whilst two judges considered it as a question of implication.[75]

Nevertheless, the step of conflating implication and construction has not yet been taken in Australia. In *Codelfa Construction Pty Ltd v State Rail Authority of NSW*,[76] the five requirements were described by Mason J (with whom Stephen and Wilson JJ agreed) as necessary conditions. Mason J (Stephen and Wilson JJ agreeing) also said that "[w]hen we say that the implication of a term raises an issue as to the meaning and effect of the contract we do not intend by that statement to convey that the court is embarking upon an orthodox exercise in the interpretation of the language of a contract, that is, assigning a meaning to a particular provision."[77]

There are signs that the approach in Australia might change. In relation to *in*formal contracts it has been said that the five *BP Refinery* criteria are replaced with a single question: is it "necessary for the reasonable or effective operation of a contract of that nature in the circumstances of the case."[78] However, that expression of the test for implication was subject to a proviso: "a term may be implied in a contract by established mercantile usage or professional practice or by a past course of dealing between the parties."[79] The state of the law is therefore that different approaches may apply to identification of the terms of an undertaking by (i) express formal contract or deed; (ii) informal contract; or (iii) custom or usage. But the common feature is that each is found to be part of an undertaking based upon manifestations of the intention of the relevant party or parties.

III. Status and Fiduciary Undertakings

With this background on the role of status in informing the objective construction of an undertaking, we move to the meaning of the "fiduciary *relationship*." A question posed at the start of this chapter is: if the duty of a fiduciary is determined by the content of a manifest undertaking, then what is the relevance of the fiduciary *relationship*?

The answer to that question must be that the relationship will often provide crucial context for the construction of an undertaking. For instance, in a case where the fiduciary duties are undertaken as part of a contract, the relationship will not be "superimposed" upon those duties. Instead, it will inform their content. Often the relationship is the reason why undertaken duties are fiduciary. That is, the relationship is the reason why a duty will be required to be performed in a manner which shows regard to the interests of the principal.

[74] *Lewis Construction (Engineering) Pty Ltd v Southern Electric Authority of Queensland* (1976) 50 ALJR 769, 770–1 (Barwick CJ, dissenting), 773–5 (Gibbs J), 778 (Mason J).

[75] *Lewis Construction (Engineering) Pty Ltd v Southern Electric Authority of Queensland* (1976) 50 ALJR 769, 777 (Stephen and Murphy JJ).

[76] *Codelfa Construction Pty Ltd v State Rail Authority of NSW* [1982] HCA 24; (1982) 149 CLR 337, 345.

[77] *Codelfa Construction Pty Ltd v State Rail Authority of NSW* [1982] HCA 24; (1982) 149 CLR 337, 347. See also *Secured Income Real Estate (Australia) Ltd v St Martins Investments Pty Ltd* [1979] HCA 51; (1979) 144 CLR 596, 605–6 (Mason J).

[78] *Hawkins v Clayton* (1988) 164 CLR 539, 573 (Deane J); *Breen v Williams* (1996) 186 CLR 71, 90–1 (Dawson and Toohey JJ), 123–4 (Gummow J).

[79] *Hawkins v Clayton* (1988) 164 CLR 539, 573 (Deane J); *Breen v Williams* (1996) 186 CLR 71, 91 (Dawson and Toohey JJ).

This notion was expressed in *Hodgkinson v Simms*[80] in the majority joint judgment of La Forest, L'Heureux-Dubé, and Gonthier JJ. Speaking of the relationship of agency, and the status of a person as an agent, their Honours said that:

> . . . the legal incidents of many contractual agreements are such as to give rise to a fiduciary duty. The paradigm example of this class of contract is the agency agreement, in which the allocation of rights and responsibilities in the contract itself gives rise to fiduciary expectations.[81] In other contractual relationships, however, the facts surrounding the relationship will give rise to a fiduciary inference where the legal incidents surrounding the relationship might not lead to such a conclusion. . . However, as Professor Finn puts it, the "end point" in each situation is to ascertain whether "the one has the right to expect that the other will act in the former's interests (or, in some instances, in their joint interest) to the exclusion of his own several interests."[82]

One of the most famous passages in fiduciary law might be easily explained in this way. Various judgments in the High Court of Australia, the Privy Council,[83] the House of Lords,[84] and the Supreme Court of Canada,[85] have all endorsed and emphasized the importance of a crucial passage from Mason J in the High Court of Australia:[86]

> ...the existence of a basic contractual relationship has in many situations provided a foundation for the erection of a fiduciary relationship. In these situations it is the contractual foundation which is all important because it is the contract that regulates the basic rights and liabilities of the parties. The fiduciary relationship, if it is to exist at all, must accommodate itself to the terms of the contract so that it is consistent with, and conforms to, them. The fiduciary relationship cannot be superimposed upon the contract in such a way as to alter the operation which the contract was intended to have according to its true construction.

The point being made by Mason J is that the fiduciary "relationship" is a matter which informs the terms which arise under the contract. The relationship thus "accommodates" itself to the contract and is not "superimposed" upon the contract. Where, in light of the surrounding circumstances, a particular "fiduciary" duty is not expressed or implied in the contract then it cannot be imposed on the parties.[87]

This explanation can clarify why status is not essential to the existence of a fiduciary duty. The classic English exposition of the fiduciary concept has been one of "status." The

[80] [1994] 3 SCR 377.

[81] *Johnson v Birkett* (1910) 21 OLR 319; *McLeod v Sweezey* [1944] SCR 111; P D Finn, "Contract and the Fiduciary Principle," 12 *UNSWLJ* 76 (1989).

[82] Finn (n 81) 88.

[83] *Kelly v Cooper* [1993] AC 205, 215.

[84] *Hilton v Barker Booth & Eastwood* [2005] UKHL 8; [2005] 1 WLR 567 [30].

[85] *Strother v 3464920 Canada Inc* [2007] 2 SCR 177; 2007 SCC 24 [141] (McLachlin CJ, Bastarache, LeBel, and Abella JJ agreeing).

[86] *Hospital Products Ltd v United States Surgical Corp* (1984) 156 CLR 41, 97.

[87] *ASIC v Citigroup Global Markets Australia Pty Ltd (No 4)*, (2007) 160 FCR 35, 77 [281] (Jacobson J); *Henderson v Merrett Syndicates Ltd* [1994] UKHL 5; [1995] 2 AC 145, 206 (Lord Browne-Wilkinson); *Canberra Residential Developments Pty Ltd v Brendas* [2010] FCAFC 125; (2010) 188 FCR 140 [36]; *Noranda Australia Ltd v Lachland Resources NL* (1988) 14 NSWLR 1 [17] (Bryson J). Cf the more tentative expression in *John Alexander Tennis Club v White City Tennis Club* [2010] HCA 19; (2010) 241 CLR 1 [87], French CJ, Gummow, Hayne, Heydon, and Kiefel JJ that "it will be very difficult to superimpose the suggested fiduciary obligation upon that limited contract."

exemplar of a fiduciary has been thought to be a trustee.[88] Company directors have been considered to be an obvious extension given the power they have to deal with company property.[89] This is an error. Early in the development of fiduciary law it was clear that the notion of a fiduciary had extended so far beyond this analogy that this "status" conception of a fiduciary could no longer have any real explanatory power. Fiduciary duties are now recognized between parties despite the absence of any proprietary connection: lawyer to client,[90] doctor to patient,[91] partner to partner,[92] bailee to bailor,[93] stockbroker to client,[94] joint venturer to joint venturer,[95] parent to child,[96] the State to its Aboriginal people.[97] And they are recognized between persons who cannot be categorized as falling within any status category at all: in Canada this residuary category was described as ad hoc fiduciary relationships. As early as 1885, Field J said that "the fiduciary relation, as it is called, does not depend upon any particular circumstances. It exists in almost every shape."[98]

Conclusions

Writing in sixteenth-century Elizabethan England, Shakespeare observed the importance of "degree, priority and place, Insisture, course, proportion, season, form, Office, and custom, in all line of order." But "Take but degree away, untune that string, And, hark! what discord follows; each things meets In mere oppugnancy. . ."[99] In various areas of the law of obligations, including obligations arising from common callings and obligations arising from custom or usage, it was also thought that the obligation was imposed on a person due to that person's status or office.

That view is no longer held. Instead, status or office serves as a basis from which an implication can be drawn in an undertaking by the obligor. That implication is based upon the manifestations by, or objective conduct of, the obligor. The office or status held by the obligor will shape the understanding that a reasonable person will have of their conduct.

The same should be true of the role of status in relation to duties undertaken by fiduciaries. A dominant view of the law concerning fiduciary duties is that an undertaking will become a *fiduciary undertaking* when the undertaking involves an obligation to act or behave, and also to do so in a particular *manner*. The undertaking, and the manner in which the undertaking must be performed, may be influenced by the status or office of the person giving the undertaking. But, in every case, the ultimate question should be one of construction or implication.

This view is not universally held in relation to fiduciary duties, nor in relation to common callings nor terms implied by custom. There are still views that these terms

[88] P Birks, "The Content of Fiduciary Obligation" *TLI* 34 (2002).

[89] *Regal (Hastings) Ltd v Gulliver* [1967] 2 AC 134.

[90] *Maguire v Makaronis* (1997) 188 CLR 449.

[91] *Norberg v Wynrib* [1992] 2 SCR 226; *Breen v Williams* (1996) 186 CLR 71 (Gaudron, McHugh, and Gummow JJ; contra Brennan CJ, Dawson and Toohey JJ).

[92] *Helmore v Smith* (1886) 35 Ch D 436 at 444.

[93] *Hallett's Estate; Knatchbull v Hallett* (1879) 13 Ch D 696 at 709.

[94] *Daly v Sydney Stock Exchange Ltd* (1986) 160 CLR 371.

[95] *United Dominions Corporation Ltd v Brian Pty Ltd* (1985) 157 CLR 1; *Chirnside v Fay* [2006] NZSC 58; [2007] PNLR 6.

[96] *M(K) v M(H)* [1992] 3 SCR 6; *Plowright v Lambert* (1885) 52 LT 646 at 652; *Clay v Clay* (2001) 202 CLR 410.

[97] *Guerin v R* [1984] 2 SCR 335.

[98] *Plowright v Lambert* (1885) 52 LT 646 at 652.

[99] *Troilus & Cressida*, I, iii.

are implied as a matter of policy, or judicial assessment of reasonableness, independently of the manifest intentions of the parties.

There is a grave danger which can arise unless we are vigilant with an understanding of status as only a factor in the process of construction or implication of terms of an undertaking. The danger arises because the same status can describe many different types of relationship. The "archetypal" fiduciary,[100] the trustee, can be used as an example.

Historically, the nomenclature of trust was almost exclusively used to describe circumstances of declared trusts, that is trusts which were either expressly or impliedly declared. In *Cook v Fountain*,[101] the Lord Chancellor, Lord Nottingham, giving the opinion of himself and two Chief Justices, said of declarations of trust:

> [E]xpress trusts are declared either by word or writing; and these declarations appear either by direct and manifest proof, or violent and necessary presumption. These last are commonly called presumptive trusts; and that is, when the Court, upon consideration of all circumstances presumes there was a declaration, either by word or writing, though the plain and direct proof thereof be not extant.

In this period, "almost all the lands in England were conveyed to Uses" to evade "the hardships of the feudal tenures... [and] to secure estates from forfeitures for high treason."[102] Hence, it was unsurprising that there was a common recognition that particular duties would attach to this common undertaking of trustee. When lands were placed into the management of another person, there was a common, perhaps near-universal, expectation arising from the acceptance of the office. In *Ex parte Lacey*[103] Lord Eldon said that a "trustee, who is entrusted to sell and manage for others, undertakes in the same moment, in which he becomes a trustee, not to manage for the benefit and advantage, of himself."

The same is not true today. The office of trustee assumes many different forms and the nature of the trust can vary dramatically. There will be many express trusts where Lord Eldon's implication can be easily made. But this is far from universal. It is well recognized that some trustees do not owe fiduciary duties at all.[104] Other trustees, who might usually owe fiduciary duties, will not do so if the express or implied terms of the trust instrument deny those duties.[105] In every case, courts must be vigilant not to impose particular duties without examining carefully the terms of the undertaking. Although the status or office of a person as a trustee is an important and relevant matter in construing the scope of the undertaking and the duties which arise from it, it is only part of the inquiry concerning construction of the undertaking.

The same is true of a person in a position such as a financial adviser. In one recent Australian case it was suggested that financial advisers are one of the "well recognized

[100] *Maguire v Makaronis* [1997] HCA 23; (1997) 188 CLR 449, 473 quoting *Hospital Products Ltd v United States Surgical Corporation* [1984] HCA 64; (1984) 156 CLR 41 at 68 (Gibbs CJ).

[101] (1676) 3 Swan 585, 591; (1676) 36 ER 984, 987,

[102] W Cruise *An Essay on Uses* (1795) 30; see also T Plucknett and J Barton, *St German's Doctor and Student* (1523; edn 1974) ch 22, p 222, "Howe uses of lande began and by what law and the cause why so moche lande is put in use;" W Swadling, "Explaining Resulting Trusts," 124 *LQR* 72, 80 (2008).

[103] (1802) 6 Vesey Junior 625, 626–7, 31 ER 1228, 1228–9.

[104] *Giumelli v Giumelli* [1999] HCA 10; (1999) 196 CLR 101, 112 [5] (Gleeson CJ, McHugh, Gummow, and Callinan JJ).

[105] *Sargeant v National Westminster Bank* (1990) 61 P&CR 518; *Hayim v Citibank NA* [1987] AC 730; *Citibank NA v QVT Financial LP* [2007] EWCA 11, 1 All ER (Comm) 475; *Elovalis v Elovalis* [2008] WASCA 141 [67] (Buss JA); *Re Beatty* [1990] 1 WLR 1503, 1506 (Hoffmann J); *Edge v Pensions Ombudsman* [2000] Ch 602, 621, 627–30 (Chadwick LJ for the Court of Appeal).

categories" of fiduciary agent.[106] But it was also emphasized that this was because the financial adviser had "voluntarily assumed the well established obligations such a person owes to its clients.. . . That relationship attracted the above fiduciary obligations that, in the absence of contractual or other modifications, for over two centuries have overlaid contractual dealings between fiduciary agents in well recognised categories, such as financial advisers, stockbrokers, real estate agents and, of course, solicitors, and their clients." The same point was made in *Commonwealth Bank of Australia v Smith*[107] where Davies, Sheppard, and Gummow JJ said that where a bank gives a customer advice upon financial affairs, "it may have created in the customer the expectation that nevertheless it will advise in the customer's interests as to the wisdom of a proposed investment." As Jagot J recently explained, a financial advisory firm will owe fiduciary duties when the firm moves beyond being a "mere salesman."[108]

It may be that this understanding of the role of fiduciary relationships, and fiduciary duties, will ultimately prove the point made more than four decades ago by Finn that the label "fiduciary" is the unnecessary expression of a conclusion. Indeed, there are already areas where the law functions, and has long functioned, without the necessity of hanging consequences upon the label. An example is the duties of employees. Employees may owe fiduciary duties to their employers which are similar to the duty of good faith and fidelity. The employment relationship was recognized as one of the categories of relationship where fiduciary duties are owed in *Hospital Products Ltd v United States Surgical Corporation*.[109] But the same fiduciary analysis, with the same consequences, is employed in many cases by implication of terms without the need for the fiduciary epithet. Hence, in *Pearce v Foster*[110] the English Court of Appeal held that an employee had breached an implied contractual duty because he "had deliberately placed himself in that position which rendered his interest conflicting with his duty."[111] The duty was implied because "the relation of master and servant implies necessarily that the servant shall be in a position to perform his duty duly and faithfully."[112] Again, in *Malik v Bank of Credit and Commerce International SA*[113] the House of Lords accepted as properly made a concession that contracts of employment contained implied terms that "the bank would not, without reasonable and proper cause, conduct itself in a manner likely to destroy or seriously damage the relationship of confidence and trust between employer and employee."[114] Lord Steyn observed that this implied term in law was probably just part of the very long established implied term in law "to serve his employer loyally and not to act contrary to his employer's interests."[115]

[106] *Wingecarribee Shire Council v Lehman Bros Australia Ltd (in liq)* [2012] FCA 1028 [733] (Rares J).

[107] [1991] FCA 375; (1991) 42 FCR 390, 391.

[108] *Bathurst Regional Council v Local Government Financial Services Pty Ltd (No 5)* [2012] FCA 1200 [2324].

[109] [1984] HCA 64; (1984) 156 CLR 41, 68 (Gibbs CJ), 96 (Mason J), 141 (Dawson J).

[110] (1886) 17 QBD 536. See also *Sterling Engineering Co Ltd v Patchett* [1955] AC 534.

[111] (1886) 17 QBD 536 at 541–2 (Lindley LJ).

[112] (1886) 17 QBD 536 at 539 (Lord Esher MR). See also at 543 "their position is highly fiduciary" (Lopes LJ).

[113] [1998] AC 20.

[114] [1998] AC 20 at 34–5 (Lord Nicholls). See also at 45 (Lord Steyn).

[115] [1998] AC 20 at 46 (Lord Steyn).

2

Ascribing and Limiting Fiduciary Obligations

Understanding the Operation of Consent

*Joshua Getzler**

Introduction

The ideal underpinning fiduciary law is utopian—to ensure that fiduciaries serve with undivided loyalty the interests of those who reasonably repose trust in them. The reality is a little grimier, for trust and reliance provide the opportunity for fraud and exploitation: it is difficult to defraud someone who does not trust, and law will often be a frail and partial shield when trust is ruptured.[1] Yet like love, the ideal of fiduciary obligation in relationships of trust and dependency seems to survive its long catalogue of betrayals, and courts continue to evoke the protections of fiduciary law, even if they cannot quite agree on how that law should operate.

Reacting, perhaps, against the utopian and moralistic language of classical fiduciary law, jurists today have looked for a new basis to explain these puzzling duties that mandate trust and altruism. Two fresh answers have been given attempting to clarify the terrain. The first answer is that fiduciary duties are properly proscriptive only, and must be disentangled from prescriptive duties setting standards of positive performance;[2] the fiduciary obligations are reframed as "parastic" duties that exist only to fence and protect duties of performance that take their source from outside fiduciary law proper.[3] The second answer proposes that these fiduciary duties are themselves based on consent, and so fall to be interpreted as objective undertakings ultimately sourced in the will of the parties. Hence the law is not legislating good conduct, but carrying out the parties' own will to engage with each other on fiduciary terms of self-denial.[4]

* My initial arguments were presented to the Chancery Bar Association at Lincoln's Inn, the Supreme Court of Western Australia, and the Western Australian Bar Association. For fruitful discussion I thank John Armour, Matthew Conaglen, James Edelman, Matthew Howard, Nicholas Le Poidevin, Nicholas Morris, Edward Rock, David Vines, Christopher Zelestis, and the participants in the Duty of Care in Finance Study Group at Oxford and the Fiduciary Law Workshop at De Paul University. I am particularly grateful to James Goudkamp, Dyson Heydon, Clare McKay, and Paul Miller for detailed comments. I remain accountable for all errors.

[1] Robert Axelrod, *The Evolution of Cooperation* (1984, rev edn 2006); Diego Gambetta (ed), *Trust: Making and Breaking Cooperative Relationships* (1988). A telling case-study of the dialectic of trust and fraud is given in Tamar Frankel, *The Ponzi Scheme Puzzle: A History and Analysis of Con Artists and Victims* (2012).

[2] *Girardet v Crease & Co* (1987) 11 BCLR (2d) 361, 362; *Breen v Williams* (1996) 186 CLR 71, 113 (HCA); *Bristol & West Building Society v Mothew* [1998] Ch 1, 16–18; *Pilmer v The Duke Group Limited (in liq)* (2001) 207 CLR 165, 198 (HCA); *Friend v Brooker* (2009) 255 ALR 601 at [84] (HCA).

[3] Peter Birks, "The Content of Fiduciary Obligation," 34 *Israel L Rev* 3 (2000); Matthew Conaglen, *Fiduciary Loyalty: Protecting the Due Performance of Non-fiduciary Duties* (2010) 7–11 and ff.

[4] *Hospital Products Ltd v United States Surgical Corporation* (1984) 156 CLR 41, 96–7 (HCA) per Mason J; *Vivendi SA Centenary Holdings III Ltd v Richards* [2013] EWHC 3006 (Ch); James Edelman, "When do

The observations that fiduciary duties commonly arise from consent, and regularly operate to prohibit certain behavior, are each entirely valid. But it risks distortion to work these observations into simple formulae that claim to encompass the entire field, sufficiently explaining the genesis of fiduciary obligations, their content, and the proper remedies for breach. The problem here is reproduced in much contemporary theorizing which seeks to position the law around a constrained core of abstract principles, on the model of parsimonious modeling in microeconomics or moral philosophy. We see this drive in operation in other areas of law such as contract, tort, or property, where the theorist announces that beneath the doctrinal detail cultivated over time by courts and legislatures, one can say truly that "*X* is based on *Y*," where *X* is some synchronous construct of a body of law and *Y* is some favored monistic moral principle (be it autonomous will; sanctity of bargain; Kantian promise-keeping; the harm principle; collective welfare maximization; variant forms of corrective justice, or whatever). Moreover it is often the case that a normative argument—"*X should* be based on *Y*"—is lurking in what purports to be a resolutive positive description. For convenience we may label this approach the "base/superstructure" model, where some important principle at the base holds up the superstructure of detailed law. "Base/superstructure" modeling is a perfectly valid exercise, yet other methods of analysis may capture the nature of practical legal reasoning more authentically. Legal rights and duties are commonly generated in a dialectic of oscillating claims: "If fact *A* pertains, then *prima facie* or in a general case duty *B* arises, unless *B* is countered by a defence or counter-claim *C*; but *C* may in turn be adapted or nullified by factor *D, et cetera.*" The technique of the law here involves an initial ascription of duty in certain conventional core cases; the ascribed duty may then be limited or rendered defeasible, in whole or part, by adducing fresh factors justifying or excusing departures from the initial position.

The technique of ascription and limitation, drawing originally on the casuistic model of common law pleading as a method of moral judgment, was cultivated in linguistic philosophy in Herbert Hart's earliest work in the late 1940s,[5] and in the contemporaneous work of Hart's colleague and collaborator John L Austin.[6] It was then imported back into legal discourse and applied in the 1960s to property law by Tony Honoré,[7] and to tort law by Richard Epstein in the 1970s;[8] it makes a late appearance in Hugh Collins's contract jurisprudence of the 1980s.[9] This chapter makes a tentative start in

Fiduciary Duties Arise?," 126 *LQR* 302 (2010), and "The Importance of the Fiduciary Undertaking," 7 *J Equity* 128 (2013).

[5] H L A (Herbert) Hart, "The Ascription of Responsibility and Rights," 49 *Proceedings of the Aristotelian Society* (ns) 171 (1948), reprinted in Anthony Flew (ed), *Logic and Language* (1951) 145. The ascription model was later disowned by Hart, but still attracts defenders as well as detractors, eg J R Lucas, "The Ascription of Actions" (MS *c*1975), at <http://users.ox.ac.uk/~jrlucas/ascript.html#r-1>.

[6] J L Austin, "A Plea for Excuses," 57 *Proceedings of the Aristotelian Society* (ns) 1 (1956–7), reprinted in J O Urmson and G J Warnock (eds), *Philosophical Papers* (1961) 175.

[7] A M (Tony) Honoré, "Rights of Exclusion and Immunities against Divesting," 34 *Tulane L Rev* 453 (1960).

[8] Richard Epstein, "Defenses and Subsequent Pleas in a System of Strict Liability," 3 *J of Leg Stud* 165 (1974); "Pleading and Presumptions," 40 *U Chi L Rev* 556 (1973). For a detailed treatment of defeasibility in tort, distinguishing denials of the elements of liability from (*inter alia*) excuses, justifications, and incapacities, see James Goudkamp, *Tort Law Defences* (2013).

[9] Hugh Collins, *The Law of Contract* (1986).

applying the techniques of ascription and defeasibility to fiduciary law, to see if it can add a fresh dimension to our understanding. But first we must map the field, to discover what duties are being ascribed and what is then made defeasible. We will discover that consent plays a role in both ascription and limitation of fiduciary obligations, but that the operation of consent is far from simple and does not explain everything.

I. The Province and Operation of Fiduciary Duties

A. What are fiduciary duties?—Denial, best interests, office

To rephrase the present subheading: what do these duties require of the fiduciary? At the core lies a suite of duties designed to nullify any temptation to sacrifice the interests of the beneficiary.[10] In other words, fiduciary duties are applied when it is important to prevent a person from being distracted from or corrupted in his or her role as an obligee and power-holder by conflicting interest or obligation. The policy of nullification or prophylaxis is so crucial that even where no harm to beneficiary interests is demonstrated and even where good faith is shown, the full gamut of remedies may be applied to ensure that there is no taint affecting the fiduciary's conduct. In this sense the core rules are comparable to public law controls of decision-makers such as the stringent rules concerning bias, improper purpose, and avoidance of irrelevant decisional criteria.[11]

The chief nullifying duties comprise (i) the duty not to profit from a fiduciary position;[12] and (ii) the duty not to have conflicting interests or duties that prevent or might inhibit single-minded service to a beneficiary.[13] These correlate with various powers in the beneficiary, namely to elect to avoid any inconsistent transactions whether executed or executory provided there are no bars to rescission; alternatively to affirm any profit-making transaction made from within the scope of the fiduciary duty as if made on the beneficiary's behalf and so take any gains; and finally to disaffirm any harmful transaction and seek an account to compensate loss or restore the position as if no breach had occurred.[14]

Is the ban on conflicting interests and duties one prohibition or two? Self-interest will often accompany conflicted duties, as where a fiduciary receives remunerations from multiple employments. In law the line between conflicted duties and conflict of interest blurs and it is self-interest or profit which is the most litigated as the more

[10] *Harris v Digital Pulse* (2003) 56 NSWLR 298 (NSWCA) at [404]–[420] and [470] per Heydon JA. Nullification of temptation is often described as "prophylaxis;" Lionel Smith explores this concept in "Deterrence, Prophylaxis and Punishment in Fiduciary Obligations," 7 *J Equity* 87 (2013).

[11] Matthew Conaglen, "Public–Private Intersection: Comparing Fiduciary Conflict Doctrine and Bias," *Public L* 58 (2008). The key modern case remains *Attorney-General for Hong Kong v Reid* [1994] 1 AC 324 (PC). There is a historical backdrop of fiduciary doctrine being used more broadly to discipline public officials using tests developed for trusts powers: see, eg, *R v Windham* (1776) 1 Cowp 377, 98 Eng Rep 1139 (*The Wadham College case*); *Charitable Corporation v Sutton* (1746) 2 Atk 400; 26 Eng Rep 642.

[12] *Keech v Sandford* (1726) Sel Cas Ch 61; 25 Eng Rep 223; *Boardman v Phipps* [1967] 2 AC 46.

[13] *Commonwealth Bank of Australia v Smith* [1991] FCA 375; 102 ALR 453 per Davies, Sheppard, and Gummow JJ; *Kelly v Cooper* [1993] AC 205 (PC); *Bristol and West Building Society v* Mothew [1998] Ch 1 at 18–19 per Millett LJ.

[14] Joshua Getzler, "'As If:' Accountability and Counterfactual Trust," 91 *BU L Rev* 931 (2011); Charles Mitchell, "Equitable Compensation for Breach of Fiduciary Duty," 66 *Current Legal Problems* 307 (2013).

salient infraction. Historically the law tended to see the conflicted fiduciary as participating as a principal in the inconsistent second employment. But later it came to be recognized that there can be a conflict of duties apart from or in the absence of any interest, as where one undertakes conflicting gratuitous relationships. In the absence of profit-taking, fiduciary law is gentler in disciplining agents with multiple employments, looking for evidence that adequate service was degraded by the existence of the conflict. Where there has been some consent to multiple employments, the law may still apply sanctions to discipline a fiduciary who intentionally favors one of the parties he serves.[15] No such evidence of harm or intentionality need be adduced when accountability for wrongful gain is the prime issue.[16]

More controversial are claims that there are affirmative fiduciary duties requiring positive conduct from the fiduciary. The foundational positive duty is stipulated as a duty to seek the "best interests" of beneficiaries, which would seem to correlate with a right to have one's interests served. The over-arching "best interests" duty can be broken down into component parts, for example to offer due care and prudent management; to exercise powers and wield discretions with a proper purpose, and with advertence only to due decisional considerations; to act in good faith. Most of these tend to be process duties with a subjective element, stating the goal that the fiduciary ought to be pursuing, rather than the goal that must be achieved. Duties of positive performance have attracted at least some degree of recognition in most common law jurisdictions.[17] Moreover it is a commonplace of United States fiduciary law that positive duties form part of the fiduciary suite.[18] However influential decisions of appellate courts in England, Australia, and elsewhere have now asserted that there are properly no positive *fiduciary* duties; such duties must find their source in contract or tort, or elsewhere in equity doctrine.[19]

There is yet another theory, one which sees fiduciary duties as forming an office or a status. The idea comes from the classical Roman concept of an *officium*, a standard set of primary duties pertaining to a person with recognized responsibilities. The nature of that office will then accent and shape all the relevant duties of the officeholder, both

[15] *Hilton v Barker Booth & Eastwood* [2005] 1 WLR 567 (HL).

[16] It has been suggested that some element of dishonesty may be required to trigger full accountability for wrongful profits (*Swindle v Harrison* [1997] 4 All ER 705 (CA)), but this position has not commanded support: Conaglen (n 3) 90–4.

[17] See, eg, *Cowan v Scargill* (1985) Ch 270, 286–7; *Item Software (UK) Ltd v Fassihi* [2004] EWCA Civ 1244; [2005] 2 BLHC 91 at [40]–[44]; *Gwembe Valley Development Company Ltd v Koshy* [2003] EWCA Civ 1048; [2004] 1 BCLC 131.

[18] See, eg, *In Re El Paso Corporation Shareholder Litigation*, 41 A 3d 432 (Del Ch, 29 Feb 2012) per Chancellor Strine; *In re Answers Corp Shareholder Litigation (No 1)*, WL 1253072 and *(No 2)* 2014 Del Ch LEXIS 17 (Del Ch, 11 Apr 2012 & 3 Feb 2014) per Vice Chancellor Noble; *In re Trados Inc Shareholder Litigation* 73 A 3d 17 (Del Ch, 21 May 2013) per Vice Chancellor Laster; Skadden Arps, *Delaware Corporate Litigation: 2012 In Review* (11 Jan 2013) at: <http://www.skadden.com/sites/default/files/publications/Del.%20Corporate%20Litigation_2012%20In%20Review.pdf>.

[19] The leading cases are *Bristol Building Society v Mothew* [1998] Ch 1 (CA); *Breen v Williams* (1996) 186 CLR 71 (HCA); implications are explored in Conaglen (n 3), 32–58, 201–3. The prescriptive theory as stated in *Breen* was debated, and perhaps evaded, in recent litigation in Western Australia: see *Bell Group (in liq) v Westpac Banking Corporation* (2008) 39 WAR 1 per Owen J; [2012] WASCA 157; J Dyson Heydon, "The Duty to Act in Good Faith in the Best Interests of the Company, in the Light of the *Bell Group* Case" (Paper at the Annual Corporate Law Conference, Supreme Court of New South Wales, 27 Aug 2013).

positive and negative. This means that duties owed by a fiduciary to a beneficiary may have a depth or intensity that would not be owed by a shopkeeper or a plumber on whom a customer relies for goods and services. The bridge from the Ciceronian concept of *officium* to modern fiduciary law runs through civilian and canon law concepts, entering into common law in the context of executorship.[20] This older theory has not quite been abandoned in the common law world, as courts regularly find that certain statuses presumptively give rise to fiduciary duties that will color, intensify, and constrain all dealings, simply by virtue of the position or personality of the actors, as with trustees, partners, agents, directors, financial and other advisers, responsible professionals such as doctors, and intimate roles such as those of spouses, parents, religious leaders, and other mentors.[21]

So we have three distinct theories of the core nature of fiduciary duties: to avoid conflict and so nullify corrupting temptations to misperformance; to promote the best interests of beneficiaries; to execute an office and thereby uphold status relationships.

B. When are fiduciary duties imposed?—Discretion, monitoring, and vulnerability

The courts have tended to impose fiduciary duties where one party has a continuing authority or power over another, which is hard to monitor and control, and which exposes the entrusting party to a special vulnerability.[22] In many cases vulnerability has been evoked as the main reason for enforcement, but it must be tempered by the other components of liability. One is vulnerable to the performance of one's car mechanic, but you can easily monitor by showing the mechanic's work to another garage; not so with a trustee of funds or an investment broker.[23] Historically it was important to show that a person had continuous control of another's assets or affairs and was accountable for what happened to those assets before a fiduciary duty could be recognized; fiduciary duties governed relationships, not merely transactions.[24] Custodial trusts involving ownership powers were an obvious case, but fiduciary law could also apply where a person exercised any considerable power over the affairs of another, whether arising from contractual authority or some other mandate, including a unilateral seizing of control over the affairs of another, as with a trustee *de son tort*. In all such cases fiduciary law

[20] See especially A M (Tony) Honoré, "On Fitting Trusts into Civil Law Jurisdictions," 27 *Oxford Legal Studies Research Paper* (2008), <http://ssrn.com/abstract=1270179>; *Honoré's South African Law of Trusts* (1st edn, 1966; 5th edn, 2002); "Trust," in Reinhard Zimmermann and Daniel Visser (eds), *Southern Cross: Civil Law and Common Law in South Africa* (1996) 849; Michele Graziadei, "The Development of *Fiducia* in Italian and French Law from the 14th Century to the End of the Ançien Régime," in Richard Helmholz and Reinhard Zimmermann (eds), *Itinera Fiduciae: Trust and Treuhand in Historical Perspective* (1998) 327; Maurizio Lupoi, "Trust and Confidence," 125 *LQR* 253 (2009).

[21] See, eg, Jeffrey Hackney, "More than a Trace of the Old Philosophy," in Peter Birks (ed), *The Classification of Obligations* (1997) 123; Paul B Miller in this volume; and for classical common law authority, *Birtchnell v Equity Trustees, Executors and Agency Co Ltd* (1929) 42 CLR 384 (HCA) per Dixon J.

[22] Tamar Frankel, "Fiduciary Duties as Default Rules," 74 *Or L Rev* 1209 (1995); "Fiduciary Law," 71 *Cal L Rev* 795 (1983); *Fiduciary Law* (2010); Robert Flannigan, "The Core Nature of Fiduciary Accountability," *NZ L Rev* 375 (2009).

[23] Cf Robert Flannigan, "Fiduciary Mechanics," 14 *Can J Lab & Emp L* 25 (2008).

[24] Joshua Getzler, "Rumford Market and the Genesis of Fiduciary Obligations," in Andrew Burrows and Alan Rodger (eds), *Mapping the Law: Essays in Memory of Peter Birks* (2006) 577.

gave the vulnerable party confidence in the dedicated behavior of the fiduciary *without* having to monitor, which is a pretty good description of what it means to trust someone.[25] At the same time the fiduciary duty to account embraced a duty to provide information to the beneficiary as to how the trust had been carried out; a fiduciary had a duty to self-monitor on behalf of the beneficiary, and the court had a supervisory jurisdiction to make sure the accounting was kept up.[26]

Another way to reframe the vulnerability test would be to ask if there is anything special about the position of the obligor or the nature of obligations owed that would be undermined in the presence of a conflicted or ungoverned discretion in the hands of the obligee. We have seen the argument that fiduciary duties are proscriptive protections that assist in the due performance of affirmative non-fiduciary duties. But this model does not explain which non-fiduciary duties deserve fiduciary protection, and why banning conflicts makes for better performance in any case.

One way forward is to give greater scrutiny to the mischief that the proscriptive duties address. Lionel Smith has proposed that the mischief is biased or swayed motive.[27] But this raises another question: when is motive significant in adapting obligations? Another way to reframe the proscriptive theory is to distinguish between *contending* interests and duties, where there is rivalry for resources of an agent such as attention, effort, time, and skill, and *conflicting* interests and duties, where commitment to one party is destructive of the interests of the other. In the former case competition for resources might be seen as a zero-sum game best controlled by the allocative or distributive rules of contract and tort. But where an agent is found to be subject to conflicting interests and duties, then attention to the interests of self or some other party is more actively harmful to the beneficiary. Here, the rivalrous interests are not just in competition; they cannot coexist. This is where fiduciary law plays its special proscriptive role. In practice, distinguishing destructive from innocent conflicts may be difficult. Courts have long observed that where intense reliance and trust are reposed, a serious shortfall in performance may indicate a deeper and more destructive disloyalty where the entrusted person has simply thrown over their duty.[28]

We can find all three elements of discretionary power, difficulty of monitoring, and special vulnerability in Lord Chancellor Eldon's classic exposition in *Ex parte Lacey* in 1802. The case involved a trustee who bid to buy for himself the trust property he was selling at an open auction, thus falling into a breach of fiduciary duty:

> The rule I take to be this; not, that a trustee cannot buy from his Cestuy que trust, but, that he shall not buy from himself.... A trustee, who is entrusted to sell and manage for others, undertakes in the same moment, in which he becomes a trustee, not to manage for the benefit and advantage, of himself. It does not preclude a new contract with those, who have entrusted him. It does not preclude him from bargaining, that he will

[25] Tamar Frankel, *Trust and Honesty: America's Business Culture at a Crossroad* (2005).

[26] Getzler (n 14); the leading modern case is now *Schmidt v Rosewood Trust Ltd* [2003] 2 AC 709 (PC).

[27] Lionel Smith, "The Motive, Not the Deed," in Joshua Getzler (ed), *Rationalizing Property, Equity and Trusts: Essays in Honour of Edward Burn* (2003) 53; and Lionel Smith in this volume.

[28] Joshua Getzler, "Duty of Care," in Peter Birks and Arianna Pretto (eds), *Breach of Trust* (2002) 41; Leon Fioris, "Precluding Prescriptive Duties in Fiduciary Relationships: The Problems with the Proscriptive Delimitation," 40 *Austl Bus L Rev* 166 (2012).

> no longer act as a trustee. The Cestuys que trust may by a new contract dismiss him from that character: but even then that transaction, by which they dismiss him, must according to the rules of this Court be watched with infinite and the most guarded jealousy; and for this reason; that the Law supposes him to have acquired all the knowledge a trustee may acquire; which may be very useful to him; but the communication of which to the Cestuy que trust the Court can never be sure he has made, when entering into the new contract, by which he is discharged. I disavow. . . that the trustee must make advantage. I say, whether he makes advantage, or not, if the connection does not satisfactorily appear to have been dissolved, it is in the choice of the Cestuy que trusts, whether they will take back the property, or not if the trustee has made no advantage. It is founded upon this; that though you may see in a particular case, that he has not made advantage, it is utterly impossible to examine upon satisfactory evidence in the power of the Court, by which I mean, in the power of the parties, in ninety-nine cases out of an hundred, whether he has made advantage, or not. Suppose, a trustee buys any estate; and by the knowledge acquired in that character discovers a valuable coal-mine under it; and locking that up in his own breast enters into a contract with the Cestuy que trust: if he chooses to deny it, how can the Court try that against that denial? The probability is, that a trustee, who has once conceived such a purpose, will never disclose it; and the Cestuy que trust will be effectually defrauded.[29]

The importance of self-monitoring and disclosure identified in older fiduciary law is not accepted as foundational by every jurist. John Langbein has argued that, with the heightened powers of monitoring available in a modern age of paper and electronic trails and professional audit, the classical proscriptions of fiduciary law could be relaxed and replaced with a generalized duty to seek beneficiaries' best interests, without blanket prohibitions inhibiting agents' efforts.[30] The exposure of fiduciary breach at the heart of the corporate and financial economy since Professor Langbein wrote has not helped validate his argument.

C. How are fiduciary obligations imposed?—Expectations, status, consent

We have now identified some plausible legal policies for applying fiduciary duties—but what is the precise *causa*, the juristic trigger for imposition? And how may the *causa* inform our understanding of the fiduciary institution itself?

Paul Finn opened his leading study of this area of law with the claim that a person "is not subject to fiduciary obligations because he is a fiduciary; it is because he is subject to them that he is a fiduciary."[31] This may be taken as a critique of status-based theories of fiduciary obligation, where mandatory terms are applied to certain settled classes

[29] *Ex parte Lacey* (1802) 6 Ves Jun 625, 626–7; 31 Eng Rep 1228, 1228–9 (LC). See also *York Buildings Co v MacKenzie* (1795) 8 Bro 42; 3 Eng Rep 432.

[30] John H Langbein, "Questioning the Trust-Law Duty of Loyalty: Sole Interest or Best Interest?," 114 *Yale LJ* 929 (2005).

[31] Paul Finn, *Fiduciary Obligations* (1977), 2, cited *inter alia* by Millett LJ in *Bristol and West Building Society v Mothew* [1998] Ch 1, 18; and by the Privy Council in *Arklow Investments Ltd & Wingate v Maclean* [2000] 1 WLR 594; [1999] UKPC 51.

of relationship.[32] Also often cited is Justice Finn's claim that one can enforce fiduciary duties when one has a justifiable or legitimate expectation of such protection.[33] Finn's anti-conceptual approach influenced Anglo-Commonwealth courts for over a generation, perhaps because his open-textured tests allow for discretion in determining when fiduciary obligations arise.

In a shift in juristic thought over the past two decades, it has become popular to describe fiduciary duties as neither status nor expectation based, but rather as founded directly on consent or voluntary undertakings. In the language of American economic analysis, the law erects fiduciary duties as default law in cases where it is difficult to specify a complete contract due to the continuing nature and intrinsic discretion of the parties' dealings. Both custodial trusts[34] and corporate fiduciary duties[35] can therefore be reduced to branches of contract law. Opponents have countered that contractarian analysis does not capture unique features of fiduciary law, including its blend of default and mandatory terms, its extensive remedial structure, and its overriding emphasis on accountability.[36]

Consent theory has been expressed rather differently in the Anglo-Commonwealth legal tradition. It begins with the idea that consent can modify the operation of extant fiduciary relationships, not that consent is the origin of those relationships. In other words consent tends to be seen as an aspect of defeasibility, not of ascription.

This distinction can be seen in Mason J's minority opinion in the Australian case of *Hospital Products v USSC*. In that case a distributor cynically exploited the trust bestowed upon him by an overseas manufacturer in order to flood the local market with his own copied manufactures. Could fiduciary duties be applied to support disgorgement remedies on top of contractual damages for loss? The majority found that the contractual, mutually self-seeking nature of the relationship necessarily excluded a finding of fiduciary duties. Mason J countered this finding as follows:

> That contractual and fiduciary relationships may co-exist between the same parties has never been doubted. Indeed, the existence of a basic contractual relationship has in many situations provided a foundation for the erection of a fiduciary relationship. In these situations it is the contractual foundation which is all important because it is the contract that regulates the basic rights and liabilities of the parties. The fiduciary relationship, if it is to exist at all, must accommodate itself to the terms of the contract

[32] See *Birtchnell v Equity Trustees, Executors and Agency Co Ltd* (1929) 42 CLR 384 (HCA) per Dixon J, and discussion herein, following n 19.

[33] Paul Finn, "The Fiduciary Principle," in Timothy Youdan (ed), *Equity, Fiduciaries and Trust* (1992) 1, 26; a similar approach is stated in Deborah A DeMott, "Breach of Fiduciary Duty: On Justifiable Expectations of Loyalty and their Consequences," 48 *Ariz L Rev* 925 (2006).

[34] John H Langbein, "The Contractarian Basis of the Law of Trusts," 105 *Yale LJ* 625 (1995); Robert H Sitkoff, "An Agency Costs Theory of Trust Law," 89 *Cornell L Rev* 621 (2004).

[35] Frank Easterbrook and Daniel Fischel, "Contract and Fiduciary Duty," 36 *J of L and Econ* 425 (1993); Robert H Sitkoff, "The Economic Structure of Fiduciary Law," 91 *BU L Rev* 1039 (2011).

[36] Deborah DeMott, "Beyond Metaphor: An Analysis of Fiduciary Obligation," 37 *Duke LJ* 879 (1988); Scott Fitzgibbon, "Fiduciary Relationships Are Not Contracts," 82 *Marq L Rev* 303 (1999); Tamar Frankel, *Fiduciary Law* (2011); M W Lau, *The Economic Structure of Trusts* (2011) 21–58; Getzler (n 14).

> so that it is consistent with, and conforms to, them. The fiduciary relationship cannot be superimposed upon the contract in such a way as to alter the operation which the contract was intended to have according to its true construction.[37]

Mason J's argument has been adopted many times, in many common law jurisdictions, and has been deeply influential.[38] A number of observations may be taken from his judgment. The contract founding the close commercial relationship in that case was seen by Mason J as separate from the fiduciary relationship; the two categories "co-exist" such that the fiduciary duties are erected on the foundation of the contract so as to "conform" to it. The nature of the contractual relationship can help determine the scope and intensity, as well as the existence, of fiduciary duties. But this does not mean that the contract and the ensuing fiduciary duties are identical or have an identical juristic source.[39]

Next we must recall that the issue at stake in *Hospital Products* was primarily remedial. Fiduciary duties were asserted in order to justify an account of profits via a constructive trust as a more penetrating profit-stripping remedy, with added insolvency-shielding effects. Arguably the better analysis was not to find a fiduciary duty in the distributor relationship itself, but rather to identify a cynical or intentionally exploitative breach of the distributorship contract as the mischief that warranted a profit-stripping remedy.[40] In effect, Mason J was proposing to apply an attenuated fiduciary duty to the contract in order to intensify the duties of due performance and curb the contractor's power of efficient breach. In other words, the ascribed contract was made partially defeasible by the overlay of fiduciary law, not the other way round. Today we might solve the problem more directly by implying good faith duties of performance as the avenue to provide a profit-stripping remedy, or expand the range of remedies available for breach of contract generally.

The final point about *Hospital Products* concerns the authority of Mason's judgment. Gibbs CJ's majority judgment reached a more conservative conclusion and refused to characterize a distributor relationship as fiduciary, but offered a rich set of tests for measuring the existence and scope of fiduciary duties, much of it based on older status models. Mason J did not carry the court, but his contractarian mode of expression clearly appealed to the future more than Gibbs CJ's traditional approach.[41]

[37] *Hospital Products Ltd v United States Surgical Corporation* (1984) 156 CLR 41, 97 (HCA).

[38] Eg *Kelly v Cooper* [1993] AC 205 (PC), and over 100 other cases citing the judgment, eg *Benedetti v Sawiris* [2009] EWHC 1330 (Ch) at [502] per Patten J; *Rossetti Marketing Ltd v Diamond Sofa Company Ltd* [2012] EWCA Civ 1021 at [21] per Lord Neuberger MR.

[39] *In re Coomber* (1911) 1 Ch 723, at 728–9; *Hospital Products Ltd v United States Surgical Corporation* (1984) 156 CLR 41 at [27]–[39] (HCA) per Gibbs CJ; Mark Leeming, "The Scope of Fiduciary Obligations: How Contract Informs, But Does Not Determine, the Scope of Fiduciary Obligations," 3 *J Equity* 181 (2009).

[40] Peter Birks, "Restitutionary Damages for Breach of Contract: Snepp and the Fusion of Law and Equity," *Lloyds Maritime and Commercial LQ* 421 (1987).

[41] *Hospital Products* at [30]–[40] per Gibbs CJ. The minority status of Mason J's judgment is affirmed by the High Court of Australia in *John Alexander's Clubs Pty Limited v White City Tennis Club Limited* (2010) 241 CLR 1 at [86] (HCA).

D. Restatements of the consent theory

A restatement of consent theory was offered by Millett LJ in the leading case of *Bristol Building Society v Mothew*:

> A fiduciary is someone who has undertaken to act for and on behalf of another in a particular matter in circumstances which give rise to a relationship of trust and confidence.[42]

It is not entirely clear from this how the undertaking leads to fiduciary liability. The duties could be consciously or subjectively assented to one by one; or supplied by law as objective default terms subject to defeasance; or imposed by law as mandatory terms or duties responding to a voluntary act.

In a further restatement of the undertaking theory recently offered by James Edelman, the default interpretation is propounded rather than the subjective consent or mandatory terms interpretations.[43] Justice Edelman also discards Mason J's model of contract and fiduciary law "conforming" or interacting, arguing instead that fiduciary duties are *identical* to the agreement bringing the parties into their relationship. The fiduciary duties are, on his view, "based simply upon a construction of the undertaking itself to determine the expressed or implied duties undertaken by the parties." This also goes a step beyond Lord Millett's more tentative formulation in *Mothew*, by seeing the undertaking itself as the operative *causa*, albeit the terms are to be determined using the objective test of construction as in contract.[44] The theory draws from a tendency in recent English law to characterize all duties arising in contract, both primary and secondary, as rooted in the intentions of the parties, rather than legally imposed duties where the law reacts to the factum of voluntary conduct.[45] It is also important to note that on the remedies side, Edelman has argued that profit-stripping remedies should be used more extensively to uphold obligations, bringing the remedial armory of fiduciary law into contract itself[46]—and thus supplying an alternative answer to the cynical breach problem evoked in *Hospital Products*. This suggestion has not as yet been embraced by the courts.[47] Fiduciary relationships may have become more like contracts, but contracts have not become more like fiduciary relationships. Nonetheless

[42] *Bristol Building Society v Mothew* [1998] Ch 1 at 18 per Millett LJ.

[43] Edelman, "When Do Fiduciary Duties Arise?" and "The Importance of the Fiduciary Undertaking" (n 4), further articulated in James Edelman's chapter in this volume. See also Anthony Duggan, "Contracts, Fiduciaries and the Primacy of the Deal," in Elise Bant and Matthew Harding (eds), *Exploring Private Law* (2010) 275; Colin Feasby, "Fiduciary Obligations and Exculpatory Clauses," 36 *Alta L Rev* 923 (1998).

[44] See also *Twinsectra Ltd v Yardley* [2002] 2 AC 164, 185 [71] per Lord Millett, and *Byrnes v Kendle* (2011) 243 CLR 253 (HCA) where settlement of trusts was also held to be voluntaristic but based on an objective test.

[45] *Investors Compensation Scheme v West Bromwich Building Society* [1998] 1 WLR 896 (HL) per Lord Hoffmann; see also Lord Hoffmann, "'The Achilleas,'" 14 *Edin L Rev* 47 (2010). Lord Hoffmann has also tilted English law towards a search for the parties' contractually expressed intentions through ready use of extrinsic evidence, converting the objective test into a quest for the parties' own conceptions of their expressed meanings: see *Chartbrook Ltd v Persimmon Homes Ltd* [2009] 1 AC 1101, criticized by J Dyson Heydon, "Implications of Chartbrook Ltd v Persimmon Homes Ltd for the Law of Trusts" (Paper at the STEP Annual Trusts Symposium, Adelaide, 18 Feb 2011).

[46] James Edelman, *Gain-Based Damages* (2002); "Fiduciaries and Profit Disgorgement for Breach of Contract," 6 *J of Equity* 115 (2012).

[47] *Devenish Nutrition Ltd v Sanofi-Aventis SA (France)*[2009] Ch 390 (CA).

Justice Edelman's undertaking thesis, shorn of the parallel remedial arguments, has been cited with approval by a number of courts.[48] We therefore need to understand where this newly popular theory of fiduciary undertakings based on objective consent may take us.

II. Fiduciary Obligation and Objective Consent—General Implications

A. Objectivism merges consent with *ex lege* duties

Some jurists have seen objectification of the legal interpretation of conduct as the essence of a mature legal system,[49] whether we speak of unilateral voluntary conduct that impacts on third parties or consensual conduct that involves a common enterprise. For the sake of exposition we may divide the types of objectification of consent into three further ideal types—mandatory terms, default terms, and structuring terms.

To give examples within the first category: a person who voluntarily elects to drive a car will find that the law requires that due care be taken as a mandatory requirement of the voluntary conduct, whether duties of care are willed or not; likewise a person who elects to have a child will find many legal duties follow entirely outside his or her will. At the broadest level, a person who voluntarily enters a jurisdiction is taken to be subject to the laws of that jurisdiction whether known and consented to by the entrant or not. In such cases, the will or consent of a person is not determinative of the ensuing duties; rather the general law applies rules regulating certain types of voluntarily initiated conduct.

The second category typically applies to cases of interactive consensual conduct. Here objectivism may involve an evidential method used to fix default packages of assumed or accepted duties, which can in turn be varied by further evidence of consent. For example, many of the terms of sale of goods as listed in controlling legislation may be varied by the parties at will.

The third mode of objective construction, labelled here as "structuring" interpretation, merges the first two *ex lege* and putative consent theories. A court may assume as a heuristic of private law that parties will *expect* to incorporate as implied or imputed terms those regular duties ascribed by general law or practice or the custom of a trade. A general or particular practice thereby structures the terms of all legal relationships within that practice. This means that, even on the basis that all the duties arising from voluntary undertakings are to be seen as based upon and legitimated by the parties' intentions, one will still have to turn to the general law or to contextual practice to find out what was objectively "intended" or undertaken. Indeed, not only *ex lege* fiduciary, contract, and tort rules, but statutory regulations become part of the "voluntary" deal

[48] See, eg, *John Alexander's Clubs Pty Limited v White City Tennis Club Limited* (2010) 241 CLR 1, [44] (HCA); *Red Hill Iron Ltd v API Management Pty Ltd* [2012] WASC 323, [372]; *F&C Alternative Investments (Holdings) Ltd v Barthelemy* [2012] Ch 613, [225]; *Vivendi SA Centenary Holdings III Ltd v Richards* [2013] EWHC 3006, [137] (Ch).

[49] See, eg, H L A Hart, "Diamonds and Strings: Holmes on the Common Law," in *Essays in Jurisprudence and Philosophy* (1983) 278; Peter Cane, "Mens Rea in Tort," 20 *OJLS* 533 (2000).

unless somehow excluded. This point was key in the great United States Supreme Court case of *Ogden v Saunders*, interpreting the Contract Clause in 1827.[50] It also operates in areas adjacent to fiduciary law, such as resulting and constructive trusts and estoppels, where the court finds dispositive intentions by reference to standards of reasonable expectations and just conduct. Some have thought that the older "quasi-contractual" theory of unjust enrichment used such a mode of implication.[51]

The courts do not necessarily distinguish these models of consensual obligation when describing fiduciary duties as undertakings. But as with the muddle over implied contract in the law of unjust enrichment, the new "quasi-contractual" or objective undertaking theory of fiduciaries needs to be refined to determine more precisely the role of consent in fixing duties. The key questions can be investigated through the lens of ascription and defeasibility—how, in practice, and in particular pockets of the law, the parties can design and vary the usual package of fiduciary rights and duties. The rest of this chapter pursues this inquiry.

B. Powers of variation and irreducible cores

Many assumed duties fall into the first category of mandatory, non-defeasible requirements. Simply because one enters into a legal set of duties by a voluntary act does not necessarily entail a power to pick and choose elements from that usual package of rights and duties. The law may see the package of duties as unseverable; by choosing to enter the field, you must assume the legally mandated suite of duties. This requirement may be based on policy reasons. For example those affected by the conduct of the obligee may not be privy to negotiation of the level of obligation. The reckless driver who put a sign on his car warning pedestrians to keep out of his way would remain liable to pedestrians harmed by dangerous driving even if they saw the sign; the law will not accept his disclaimer, for the driver cannot force others to accept that he will not care about their fate. In other cases parties in more obviously consensual relationships may be unable to bargain effectively to define and fix an acceptable level of performance and so protect their interests. For example patients contracting to have an operation done may find it hard to assess the skills of a doctor. Standardization reflects the fact that the mandatory package ordained by law is usually optimal for most players who wish to (or have to) enter the game, or in a variation, leaving it open for parties who need non-standard terms to negotiate to the desired equilibrium.

In other cases an attempt to carve out exemptions from the normal duty package will be seen as inimical to or repugnant to the foundational undertaking; a "derogation from grant," if you like. Thus exemption clauses that undermine the primary obligations fail because they purport to create an asymmetric exchange undermining the consideration of the contract. Moreover, derogation is suspect because it often seems to be pursued by stealth. Further, the law may not permit renegotiation of the baseline

[50] 25 US 213 (1827); and see Joseph Story, *Commentaries on the Constitution of the United States* (1833), vol 3, ch 34: Prohibitions on the States—Impairing Contracts §§ 1368–94.

[51] Peter Birks and Grant McLeod, "The Implied Theory of Quasi-Contract," 6 *OJLS* 46 (1986); cf Samuel J Stoljar, *The Law of Quasi-Contract* (2nd edn, 1989), viewing the term "quasi-contractual" as adjectival rather than substantive or causal in the application of *ex lege* duties to surrender unjust enrichments.

even in a non-oppressive case because of the risk of destabilizing the position for all others who benefit from enforcement of the standard duties.

Questions such as these are especially relevant where trust property is the subject of the fiduciary undertaking. Here we find a mixture of mandatory and default rules, where a good deal of the normal package of duties can be sliced away by agreement. Yet the courts have found that not all terms may be discarded lest there be no trust institution left. In such cases we find an "irreducible core"[52] of fiduciary duties relating to the title, a minimum that must be preserved if a trust is to exist, especially in order to justify the strong asset partitioning effect of the trust.[53] Millett LJ used such language in *Armitage v Nurse* when he hemmed in trust exemption clauses with the notion of an irreducible core of loyalty obligations, while at the same time permitting liability for even gross negligence to be excluded.[54]

A contrary approach would be to reject the notion of an irreducible core and claim that the rights and duties undertaken by the trustee can be set at any level that the privy parties wish, quite independently of the question of third-party effects. On this view, a trustee can negotiate any terms with a settlor (or settlor-beneficiary), provided no oppression is used in the bargaining process. Trust law thus becomes default law all the way down, with no significant core. But is there really no logical minimum of trust duties, not even loyalty? The courts have experimented with such ideas, and have found that the most attenuated duties can be stipulated within a trust provided that some restraint on the trustee treating the property as the trustee's own is left in place. This explains why it was decided in *Citibank v MBIA* that a trust agreement could license conflicted duties and cut down any general requirement to consider the best interests of beneficiaries.[55] The facts of *Citibank* were that a structured finance agreement allowed a trustee to ignore the claims of beneficiaries whose debt entitlements were wrapped in a trust, where a clause adopted by agreement of all the parties allowed the trustee to direct payments to favor outside non-beneficiary financiers. The power to prefer outsiders was held to be valid, although it cut the beneficiaries' trust rights to vanishing point, because it was prospectively consented to by those privy to the trust. There was still a trust institution in place, since the trustees could not self-deal or appropriate the assets for themselves, and hence asset partitioning still operated in case of wrongful assignment by, or insolvency of the trustees. The result of the case has been seen as

[52] See David Hayton, "The Irreducible Core Content of Trusteeship," in A J Oakley (ed), *Trends in Contemporary Trust Law* (1996) 47.

[53] Sitkoff (n 35) develops an interesting economic explanation of mandatory terms in fiduciary law in terms of third-party interests and duties. There is currently an intense debate in the Commonwealth as to how strong the third-party asset partition effects have to be to uphold trust and non-trust fiduciary duties: see *Attorney-General for Hong Kong v Reid* [1994] 1 AC 324 (PC); *Ultraframe (UK) Ltd v Fielding & Ors* [2005] EWHC 1638(4) (Ch); *Sinclair Investments (UK) Ltd v Versailles Trade Finance Ltd* [2012] Ch 453 (CA); *Grimaldi v Chameleon Mining NL (No 2)* (2012) 200 FCR 296; 287 ALR 22; *FHR European Ventures LLP v Ramsey Makarious* [2013] 3 WLR 466 (CA). Discussion of this important problem will have to be deferred to another occasion.

[54] [1998] Ch 241 (CA); and see *Spread Trustees Co Ltd v Hutcheson* [2012] 2 AC 194 (PC); James Penner, "Exemptions," in Peter Birks and Arianna Pretto (eds), *Breach of Trust* (2002) 241.

[55] *Citibank NA v (1) MBIA Assurance SA (2) QVT Financial LP (3) Fixed-Link Finance BV* [2006] EWHC 3215 (Ch); [2007] EWCA Civ 11.

extreme.[56] We will explore next how consent operates in more nuanced forms in other areas where parties purport to vary their fiduciary duties.

III. The Operation of Consent on Fiduciary Obligations—Seven Practical Issues

A. Duties *de novo* rest on objective consent

Where the parties stand in no prior relationship, the ascription of fiduciary duties *de novo* is governed by objective consent. But this blank rule can yield disparate results. Where the court perceives an equilibrium of expectation in the community or the sector that the type of relationship normally demands fiduciary regulation, then objectivism will imply fiduciary duties even where the parties do not advert to or wish for such duties.[57]

However, objectivism can cut the other way to prevent ascription. Before a legal relationship is constituted, it is possible for the parties to narrow the scope of any fiduciary duties or eliminate them entirely by normal contractual negotiation. This is true even in cases of sensitive relationships that would normally attract presumptive fiduciary protection. The more demanding requirements of informed consent do not apply since the parties are not yet in fiduciary relations; they are free to exclude fiduciary duties as they would any implied terms. This rule obviously impacts very heavily on trustee, managerial, and advisory services, especially where financial services are purveyed to inexpert purchasers; and with parties regularly excluding fiduciary controls from financial instruments, legislatures have responded by shoring up protection of purchasers using open-textured regulatory duties.[58]

Objective consent to the exclusion of fiduciary duties can also take effect impliedly, without formal discussion, where the general standards of a market permit conflicted interests and duties within a particular type of managerial or agency relationship. For example, in *Kelly v Cooper*[59] the Privy Council held that custom or a general course of

[56] Alexander Trukhtanov, "The Irreducible Core of Trust Obligations," 123 *LQR* 342 (2007); and for a more general argument that such reductions of trust duties go too far, see Adam Hofri-Winogradow, "The Stripping of the Trust: From Evolutionary Scripts to Distributive Results," 75 *Ohio St LJ* (forthcoming 2014). The Law Commission of England and Wales investigated control of exemption clauses in 2003 but finally decided to leave the statutory rule licensing extensive exemptions in place: *Trustee Exemption Clauses* (Law Com No 301, Cmd 6874, 2006). The problem is again under the scrutiny of the Law Commission due to concern at poor standards in finance: *Fiduciary Duties of Investment Intermediaries* (Law Com CP No 215, 2013) 65–99.

[57] *McKenzie v McDonald* [1927] VLR 134 per Dixon J, and developed in *Daly v Sydney Stock Exchange Ltd* (1986) 160 CLR 371 (HCA); *Hospital Products Ltd v United States Surgical Corporation* (1984) 156 CLR 41 (HCA) at [27]–[39] per Gibbs CJ; *Wingecarribee Shire Council v Lehman Brothers Australia Ltd (in Liq)* [2012] FCA 1028; *Bathurst Regional Council v Local Government Financial Services Pty Ltd (No 5)* [2012] FCA 1200; John Glover, "Reflections on Identification of Fiduciaries," in Peter Birks (ed), *Privacy and Loyalty* (1997) 270; Laura Hoyano, "The Flight to the Fiduciary Haven," in Birks (ed), *Privacy and Loyalty*, 169.

[58] See, eg, *Financial Conduct Authority Handbook* (2013), particularly the "Conduct of Business Sourcebook" (<http://fshandbook.info/FS/html/FCA/COBS>), applying a "best interests" standard to control sale of financial products. The policy debate in this area of regulation continues: see Law Commission, *Fiduciary Duties of Investment Intermediaries* (n 56); Parliamentary Joint Committee on Corporations and Financial Services, *Inquiry into Financial Products and Services in Australia* (2009).

[59] [1993] AC 205, 214–15 (PC).

dealing in the community can limit the scope of the loyalty obligation so as to allow simultaneous representation of contending clients. A client retaining an agent to sell real estate could be taken to understand from the practices of the market that the agent would be representing other clients trying to sell like properties to the same limited group of buyers; and similar rules have been applied to dealers and brokers.[60] *Kelly v Cooper* was taken to legalize the device used especially in City finance, law, and accountancy, where a professional firm erects an information and personnel wall so that rival clients can each deal with an independent fiduciary within the same organization, with such fiduciaries also insulated from contact with the trading parts of the firm. Or there can even be consent to overt minglings of duty and interest where this can be seen to be beneficial to all, as where clients of a bank agree to information sharing through a syndicate. Constructive knowledge of, and consent to, these practices is attributed to clients, where the very existence of the practice is taken to give due notice.[61]

Courts have pushed the principle of implied objective consent very far in some instances. In an important English pension trust case, the customary practices of pension management were held to license by implication decision-making by a trustee board where the representatives of one faction of beneficiaries took decisions at the expense of another pensioner class, which lacked representation but whose interests were directly affected by the trustees' self-interested surplus allocation decisions.[62]

The parameters of objective consent in *de novo* relationships were raised squarely by the Federal Court of Australia in *ASIC v Citigroup*.[63] The court had to determine which levels of disclosure and awareness of the terms of an instrument were necessary in order to eliminate fiduciary duties in a financial managerial relationship where fiduciary duties might normally have been expected to arise. In that case a corporation bargaining at arm's length agreed to a non-fiduciary retainer with an investment bank for the purposes of launching a hostile takeover of a third entity. The retainer, if effective, would have shrunk the scope of fiduciary relations to nil. The retainer document explained that Citigroup as a "wide bank" had to maintain its freedom to serve multiple clients with interests that might come into tension, but it promised to respect clients' confidential information even though fiduciary duties were excluded. After the client agreed to the retainer, a Citigroup executive inadvertently sent a strong signal to the Sydney capital markets that a deal was likely. On this basis, one of Citigroup's proprietary traders on the other side of an internal information wall was induced to take a speculative stake for the bank in the takeover target. The trader was then summoned to a casual meeting by a Citigroup executive on the adviser side of the bank, and told to stop buying the target shares. This was done in order to extricate the bank from a position competing with its advisory client as its acquisitions drove up the target

[60] *Parker v Parker* [2003] EWHC 1846 (Ch) at [248] per Lewison J; *In Plus Group v Pyke* [2002] EWCA Civ 370 at [79]–[90] per Sedley LJ.

[61] *Prince Jefri Bolkiah v KPMG* [1999] 2 AC 222; Law Commission of England and Wales, *Fiduciary Duties and Regulatory Rules* (Law Com No 236, 1995).

[62] *Edge v Pensions Ombudsman* [2000] Ch 602 (CA); cf Jonathan Hilliard, "The Flexibility of Fiduciary Doctrine in Trust Law: How Far Does it Stretch in Practice?," 23 *Trust Law International* 119 (2009).

[63] *ASIC v Citigroup Global Markets Australia Pty Limited* (2007) 241 ALR 705; analyzed in Joshua Getzler, "*ASIC v Citigroup*: Bankers' Conflict of Interest and the Contractual Exclusion of Fiduciary Duties," 2 *J of Equity* 62 (2007).

share price. However, the trader thought he was being tipped that the deal was off, and promptly divested the bank of all the target shares. The sudden divestment itself generated a strong market signal that Citigroup was seeking to avoid a conflict of interest, thereby revealing the likelihood of a takeover, and exciting further public trading inimical to the client's project. As it turned out the takeover succeeded, at a greatly inflated cost. ASIC, the regulator, then brought a regulatory action against Citigroup for breach of statutory duties that tracked fiduciary duty at general law. Jacobson J held that the exclusion of fiduciary duties was contractually binding and covered the terrain of conflict of interest as well as conflict of duty. In the result no breaches of fiduciary duty were found because there were no fiduciary duties, even though the consenting client may not have adverted to the kind of misfeasance that Citigroup ended up committing. The case was difficult because there was a prior relationship of non-discretionary banking and brokerage services offered by the defendant bank to the client before their relationship was upgraded to a full advisory relationship. The client's *pro forma* consent to a non-fiduciary retainer without full explanation of the risks of hostile proprietary trading by the retained bank and release of sensitive information was held to be valid, despite the existence of a close relationship prior to the new retainer. The case must be regarded as finely balanced. An oddity of it is the failure of ASIC to rely on the High Court decision in *United Dominions Corporation v Brian*, where Mason, Brennan, and Deane JJ held that that "[a] fiduciary relationship can arise and fiduciary duties can exist between parties who have not reached, and who may never reach, agreement upon the consensual terms which are to govern the arrangement between them."[64] By contrast, the recent High Court decision of *John Alexander's Clubs* allowed a succession of collateral contracts to exclude by implication any nascent fiduciary relations between the parties,[65] though lower-court judges and commentators have not found the ratio of *John Alexander's Clubs* easy to frame or follow.[66] The law is unclear.

B. Renegotiated or suspended duties rest on informed consent

Ex post renegotiation of fiduciary duties must be given enhanced procedural protection due to the power of the fiduciary to conceal necessary information and abuse his or her power within the relationship.[67] The fiduciary duty is in a sense double-entrenched—not only must the fiduciary show good faith and loyalty in performance of the obligations arising from the relationship, but any attempt to vary the fiduciary protections is itself subjected to fiduciary standards of accountability, disclosure, and good faith. The courts have put these requirements in a variety of forms. In the case of *Maguire v Makaronis* it was stated that for an existing fiduciary –

[64] *United Dominions Corporation Ltd v Brian Pty Ltd* (1985) 157 CLR 1 at 11–12 (HCA).

[65] *John Alexander's Clubs Pty Limited v White City Tennis Club Limited* (2010) 241 CLR 1 (HCA).

[66] *Thomas v SMP International (No 4)* [2010] NSWSC 984 at [70] per Pembroke J; *Red Hill Iron Ltd v API Management Pty Ltd* [2012] WASC 323 at [358]–[382] per Beech J; Robert Flannigan, "Collateral Contracting Implicitly May Vary Fiduciary Accountability," 126 *LQR* 496 (2010); cf "The Joint Venture Fable," 50 *Am J of Legal Hist* 200 (2010).

[67] Cf *Erlanger v New Sombrero Phosphate Co* (1878) 3 App Cas 1218. Note also Lord Eldon's policy of disclosure in *Ex parte Lacey* (n 29).

> to escape the stigma of an adverse finding of breach of fiduciary duty, with consequent remedies, it was for them to show, by way of defence, informed consent by the [beneficiary]. . . to. . . a divided loyalty. [F]ully informed consent is a question of fact in all the circumstances of each case. . . The circumstances of the case may include. . . the importance of obtaining independent and skilled advice from a third party.[68]

Such statements give little clarity or guidance. In the conflict of interest and profit cases there have been widely varying treatments of what "informed" consent requires; some cases have suggested that disclosure of an opportunity which is then renounced by or for a beneficiary suggests consent to the fiduciary taking the opportunity for him or herself;[69] other decisions have required comprehension by the beneficiary of the legal and factual situation and advertent consent to the fiduciary taking any benefit.[70] Another source of uncertainty is the juristic effect of informed consent—does it eliminate the pre-existing duties,[71] or set up a defence without extinguishing the duties?[72] It is a point of central doctrinal and practical importance, yet the authorities are divided.

Some of the most interesting discussions of these points have come from cases involving conflicts of duty and duty.[73] In a much cited formulation, Richardson J in the New Zealand Court of Appeal stated:

> A solicitor's loyalty to his client must be undivided. He cannot properly discharge his duties to one whose interests are in opposition to those of another client. If there is a conflict in his responsibilities to one or both he must ensure that he fully discloses the material facts to both clients and obtains their informed consent to his so acting. . . And there will be some circumstances in which it is impossible, notwithstanding such disclosure, for any solicitor to act fairly and adequately for both.[74]

[68] (1997) 188 CLR 449 at 466 (HCA) (footnotes omitted). In *Maguire* authority supporting the necessity of informed consent in order to shield from breach of fiduciary duties was found in *Birtchnell v Equity Trustees, Executors and Agency Co Ltd* (1929) 42 CLR 384 at 398 (HCA), where Isaacs J was concerned with placing the onus of proof of consent on the fiduciary; Dixon J by contrast looks for "knowledge and information" of a partnership opportunity to be given to the partnership before acting. The other authorities cited in *Maguire* concerned issues of consent to breach in areas of trust law quite distant from fiduciary disloyalty: 1. whether a beneficiary having sufficient freedom of will to consent to a wrongful appointment need understand that he is concurring in a breach of trust in order to be estopped from suing (answer: no) (*In re Pauling's Settlement Trusts* [1962] 1 WLR 86 at 108 (Ch) per Wilberforce J); *Spellson v George* (1992) 26 NSWLR 666 at 669–70, 673–5, 680 per Hope JA; 2. whether knowledge of a wrongful payment by itself can be tantamount to acquiescence or consent (answer: no): *Life Association of Scotland v Siddal* (1861) 3 De G F & J 58 at 73; 45 Eng Rep 800 at 806. Cases involving solicitors drafting wills are clear that the testator must fully understand both legal and practical consequences of all terms.

[69] *Queensland Mines Ltd v Hudson* (1978) 18 ALR 1.

[70] *Boardman v* Phipps [1967] 2 AC 46, 109 per Lord Hodson; *Murad v Al-Saraj* [2005] EWCA Civ 959; and note especially *Bogg v Raper* (1998) 1 ITELR 267; [1998] EWCA Civ 661 per Millett LJ (a solicitor with an interest in the will could still draft provisions benefiting himself, but not "if the draftsman inserted the provision without calling the settlor's attention to it and knowing that the settlor did not realise its effect").

[71] "Under the general law, full disclosure and informed consent simply prevent a breach of duty from arising:" *Eastland Technology Australia Pty Ltd v Whisson* [2005] WASCA 144 at [73] per McLure JA.

[72] *In re Pauling's Settlement Trusts* [1962] 1 WLR 86; [1961] 3 All ER 713 per Wilberforce J.

[73] See further Matthew Conaglen, "Fiduciary Regulation of Conflicts between Duties," 125 *LQR* 111 (2009); "Remedial Ramifications of Conflicts between a Fiduciary's Duties," 126 *LQR* 72 (2010); Conaglen (n 3) 142–76.

[74] *Farrington v Rowe McBride & Partners* [1985] 1 NZLR 83 at 90 (NZCA), approved in *Clark Boyce v Mouat* [1994] 1 AC 428 (PC); *Maguire v Makaronis* (1997) 188 CLR 449 at 465 (HCA); *Beach Petroleum NL v Abbott Tout Russell Kennedy & Ors* [1999] NSWCA 408 at [203].

In 1991 the Federal Court of Australia put it thus:

> Not only must the fiduciary avoid, without informed consent, placing himself in a position of conflict between duty and personal interest, but he must eschew conflicting engagements. The reason is that by reason of the multiple engagements, the fiduciary may be unable to discharge adequately the one without conflicting with his obligation in the other. Thus. . . where an adviser in a sale is also the undisclosed adviser of the purchaser, an actual conflict of duties arises.[75]

Millett LJ cited this decision in *Mothew* as a basis of his own restatement:

> The fiduciary must take care not to find himself in a position where there is an *actual* conflict of duty so that he cannot fulfil his obligations to one principal without failing in his obligations to the other.[76] If he does, he may have no alternative but to cease to act for at least one and preferably both. The fact that he cannot fulfil his obligations to one principal without being in breach of his obligations to the other will not absolve him from liability.[77]

The parties may yet wish to proceed with a *potential* conflict of duties in play. Solicitors can usefully serve both sides of a transaction; and bankers may wish to serve many parties competing in the same market. Likewise factors, agents, financial advisers, and professional service providers generally may find it convenient to take retainers simultaneously or serially from persons with potentially conflicting duties. The gains of shared information and saved costs outweigh the potential losses, even if a core prohibition of fiduciary law is thereby discarded. A glance at the case law reveals that this is not just a modern issue but has been a constant bugbear. Lord Eldon acknowledged grudgingly in the 1802 case of *Lacey* that the practice of solicitors acting for buyer and seller in the same transaction was very common, though he decried it—as indeed have modern courts on occasion.[78] This neurosis in fiduciary law thus lies very deep, with condemnation of conflicted loyalty being accompanied by a toleration of conflict in practice and a ready set of tools to allow defeasibility of duty.

Perhaps the best discussion of this was provided in *Hilton v Barker Booth & Eastwood*,[79] a House of Lords decision of 2005. *Hilton* was argued as a contractual case, but Lord Walker in his leading judgment seemed to assume that the contractual duties erected by a solicitor's retainer tracked fiduciary obligation.[80] The contractual

[75] *Commonwealth Bank of Australia v Smith* [1991] FCA 375; 102 ALR 453 at [81], citing Finn (n 31) 253–4.

[76] Citing *Moody v Cox and Hatt* [1917] 2 Ch 71; *Commonwealth Bank of Australia v Smith* (1991) 102 ALR 453.

[77] *Bristol Building Society v Mothew* [1998] Ch 1 at 19. To like effect, *Prince Jefri Bolkiah v KPMG* [1999] 2 AC 222, 233–7 per Lord Millett.

[78] *Ex parte Lacey* (1802) 6 Ves Jun 625, 631, 31 Eng Rep 1228, 1231: "there is no case, in which it is useful upon general principles, that the same Solicitor should be employed on all sides: in many cases it is a great saving of expense certainly: but, where property is to be brought to sale, to pay creditors &c. great mischief is occasioned by it;" *Commonwealth Bank of Australia v Smith* [1991] FCA 375; 102 ALR 453 at [84]: "We pause to say that various courts in a number of jurisdictions have decried the practice of the one solicitor acting for both vendor and purchaser;. . . It is an undesirable practice and it ought not to be permitted." To similar effect: *Hilton v Barker Booth & Eastwood* [2005] 1 WLR 567 (HL).

[79] [2005] 1 WLR 567 (HL).

[80] For detail see Joshua Getzler, "Inconsistent Fiduciary Duties and Implied Consent," 122 *LQR* 1 (2006).

framework meant that it was possible to identify a positive primary duty to act in the client's best interests, including a duty to disclose information that would help the client as well as a duty to keep confidential any sensitive information about the client.

The problem in *Hilton* arose from the nature of the prohibition on double retainers. In the leading case of *Moody v Cox and Hatt*,[81] the English Court of Appeal held that a fiduciary who undertakes conflicting duties to more than one person by that act alone breaches fiduciary duty, and further that the duty owed to one client cannot justify breach of a duty owed to another client. The fiduciary must abide by the primary duties of all protected relationships; and if this is impossible the fiduciary must then pay compensation for any breach. We can call this the theory of "double breach"—one breach in entering into a potential conflict that can inhibit service; a second breach when the conflict is actualized.[82] In England, New South Wales, and other common law jurisdictions, solicitors' rules guard against such breaches by refusing a solicitor liberty to engage in conflicting duties, even if a waiver is procured;[83] but this is a regulatory pressure, not law (and it must always be judged if duties truly conflict, or if a lawyer is performing non-discretionary or ministerial duties for both sides of a deal with no scope for conflict, as in a simple conveyance). In *Hilton* a solicitor acted for both sides of a land deal, but concealed from the seller (1) that he knew that the buyer was an unreliable fraudster with a criminal record, having defended the buyer in an earlier criminal prosecution, and (2) that the solicitor was secretly interested in the transaction, having lent the deposit money to the buyer. The breach of the prohibition on conflict of interest went to undermine the solicitor's veracity only and did not give rise to liability. More serious was the double-duties conflict; the defendant solicitor could not do his duty and disclose data to the plaintiff client without breaching a parallel duty of confidence to his other client. The Court of Appeal found that since both clients had authorized the lawyer to work on both sides, they each impliedly agreed to shrink the best interests duty and waive their right to disclosure of the others' confidential or sensitive information. Lord Walker attacked this model on two grounds: one was that taking on a severely conflicted retainer in the first place breached the *Moody and Cox* ban on actual inhibition of service; and secondly that no implied consent to the shrinkage of duty could be allowed without full disclosure of the kind of risks that were being faced. The lawyer owed Hilton disclosure of the risk of dealing with the other client when taking on the fiduciary retainer. But this would have breached the duty to the other side, as well as probably scotching the deal. This suggests that the *Kelly v Cooper*

[81] [1917] 2 Ch 71.

[82] This distinction is unpacked in Conaglen (n 3) 142–76; also "Fiduciary Regulation of Conflict between Duties" and "Remedial Ramifications of Conflicts between a Fiduciary's Duties" (n 73). In *Mothew*, Millett LJ further suggested that where there is a valid consent to a double retainer involving some risk of conflict, then consciously acting to take the part of one side against the other is a breach of duty since balanced service as agreed to by the parties is inhibited.

[83] Eg, NSW Revised Professional Conduct and Practice Rules 1995, Rule 9.3: "If a practitioner, who is acting for more than one party to any proceedings or transaction, determines that the practitioner cannot continue to act for all of the parties without acting in a manner contrary to the interests of one or more of them, the practitioner must thereupon cease to act for all parties." Cf Solicitors' Code of Conduct 2007 (England and Wales), Rule 3.02(1)(2).

theory of implied consent to conflict, derived from the praxis of the parties judged in their market context, does *not* apply to each and every fiduciary situation. Lord Walker also disposed of the Court of Appeal's finding that the breach (namely the failure to eschew the double retainer) had not caused the relevant loss using but-for causal reasoning (since Hilton would in all likelihood have gone ahead with a different lawyer who would not have known of the risks from the purchaser and could not have warned Hilton to avoid the transaction). The relevant breach related to the second duty, to disclose data in order to advance Hilton's best interests, and here the failure to warn Hilton of the rogue's record, even though such a warning would have betrayed a confidentiality duty and best interest duty owed to a rogue, was a cause of the vendor's loss-making transaction. The Court of Appeal had toyed with a theory of "internal Chinese Walls"[84] namely that a solicitor need only warn of data arising from the actual transaction of the parties, not knowledge gleaned from other transactions, but in the end preferred a theory of implied consent to shrinkage of duty. This was the very theory shot down by Lord Walker in the Lords appeal, on the basis that you cannot consent to dangers that are not explained to you. It is one of the strongest cases we have setting out how informed consent should work to control the scope of fiduciary obligations. But the equally strong case of *Kelly v Cooper* pushes the other way. The law is unclear.

The next areas are particularly troublesome cases of exemptions from, and transitions in and out of, fiduciary relationships:

C. Moving from an existing non-fiduciary relationship to a fiduciary relationship

Where parties have commenced certain business or intimate relations but not yet crystallized the final form of their relationship, what happens where the parties then gradually deepen their relationship? Can one party benefit from entry into the initial relationship and then, even after commitments are made and valuable assets and information transferred or exchanged, seek maximal profits or withdraw to pursue the project alone, without reference to the interests of the other party? Can fiduciary controls accrete to the relationship as the parties take increasing powers over each other's interests? The dominant party will typically claim that there has been valid consent to the succeeding relationship being non-fiduciary. The vulnerable party will claim a legitimate expectation that fiduciary protections would apply as the relationship deepens, requiring consent to profit-taking or exit by one of the parties. Must a person in a prior relationship seek informed consent, or merely formal consent, in order to modify or exclude fiduciary obligations, where a later relationship on a new basis emerges?[85] The law is unclear.

[84] Derived from Chadwick J's judgment on mortgage solicitors' duties in *Bristol & West Building Society v Baden, Narnes and Grove* [2000] Lloyd's Rep PN 241 at 263.

[85] This issue was also raised in *ASIC v Citigroup Global Markets Australia Pty Ltd* (2007) 241 ALR 705. In a context of joint venture: *Cobbe v Yeoman's Row Management Ltd* [2008] UKHL 55; [2008] 1 WLR 1752; Joshua Getzler, "Quantum Meruit, Estoppel, and the Primacy of Contract," 125 *LQR* 196 (2009). See further Ben Mcfarlane, "The Problem of Pre-Contractual Reliance: Three Ways to a Third Way" (NYU Working Paper, 15 October 2006). Available at SSRN: <http://ssrn.com/abstract=1348134>.

D. Application of fiduciary duties to new circumstances within a relationship

Take a case where formal *ex ante* consent to a limited set of fiduciary duties is given at the time when the relationship is constituted, without the parties considering the extent of the consent. For example a principal agrees that an agent shall be allowed to pursue multiple employments to the advantage of all concerned. The agent then pursues self-interested profits directly at the expense of the principal, in a manner not foreseen by the latter. Can the agent rely on a formal consent that on its face relieves him of all fiduciary duty? Partners agree to form a partnership, or directors to give executive services to a company, or agents to assist a family trust in its investments, with implicit fiduciary duties across the scope of the business. If a new line of business emerges, who is to decide whether it falls within the scope of the fiduciary protections or not?[86] The law is unclear.

E. Moving down from a fiduciary relationship to no relationship

What if the parties have terminated a close relationship with fiduciary qualities, but one side continues to exploit opportunities, information, or other benefits emanating from that past relationship? When can a fiduciary work with former clients' rivals or pursue their own interests in competition with a former client? The termination of fiduciary relationships raises a risk of posterior abuse. Must the fiduciary seek informed consent to post-relationship conflicts, or does the termination of the fiduciary relationship presumptively end all duties?[87] The law is unclear.

F. No sensitive fiduciary service is at stake

Fiduciary protection may not be required where a professional serving two sides of a transaction exercises no ministerial discretion, but is offering only a mechanistic service, as where a solicitor serving both sides of a deal is asked simply to explain the terms of a conveyance and execute the paperwork. Because no fiduciary protection would normally apply to that part of the work, the functionary, who has not here been asked to serve in a fiduciary capacity, can go forward without worrying about conflict of duties.[88] But discerning which parts of the relationship are fiduciary and which not is difficult. The law is unclear.

[86] An issue identified by Robert Austin in his influential article "Fiduciary Accountability for Business Opportunities," in Paul Finn (ed), *Equity and Commercial Relationships* (1987) 141, cited in *Western Areas Exploration Pty Ltd v Streeter [No 3]* [2009] WASC 213 at [51]. The same issue was enlivened in the classic case of *Boardman v Phipps* [1967] 2 AC 46, and further explored in *Hilton v Barker Booth & Eastwood* [2005] 1 WLR 567 (HL) and *Rossetti Marketing Ltd v Diamond Sofa Company Ltd* [2012] EWCA Civ 1021 (CA).

[87] *Strother v 3464920 Canada Inc* [2007] SCC 24.

[88] *Clark Boyce v Mouat* [1994] 1 AC 428 (PC); *Pilmer v The Duke Group Limited (in liq)* (2001) 207 CLR 165 (HCA); cf John Glover, "Conflicts of Interest, Conflicts of Duty and the Information Professional," 23 *Adel L Rev* 215 (2002).

G. Subject separation

If one fiduciary relationship is limited in scope such that it covers a different area of activity than another fiduciary relationship, then the fiduciary can legitimately serve two masters.[89] And in tandem, if a fiduciary relationship has a subject matter of limited scope then the fiduciary agent may be allowed to take profit outside that subject. These principles can be seen in *London and Mashonaland Exploration Co Ltd v New Mashonaland Exploration Co Ltd*,[90] which assumes that the scope of a director's duty is limited by his contract of engagement and the business of the company. In the normal case undivided loyalty is not expected and a director is free to serve as director of a rival company; the potential conflict is acceptable, provided he does not use confidential information and avoids actual conflict. This doctrine may reflect a time when companies were hemmed in by clearly stipulated corporate purposes; the contrast lay with partnerships where the partners enjoyed a general attornment or wide ostensible authority for the partnership; there fiduciary doctrine was more jealous of rival service to another entity.[91] In a significant statement in the 2009 case of *Western Areas Exploration Pty Ltd v Streeter [No 3]*, Heenan J summarized and then contained the *Mashonaland* doctrine:

> It does not extend beyond the proposition that merely being a director of one company, which is in competition with another company of which the person is also a director, does not constitute any breach of fiduciary duty at least insofar as no misuse is being made of confidential information or of assets or connections of the other company. This approach is itself based on the assumption that a director in such a dual position might occasionally be faced with a situation where there is a direct conflict of interest between some decision or activity of one of the companies in which he may otherwise be expected to participate and the interests of the other but that in such circumstances the director will recognise the conflict and abstain from participating in the action or in the activity.[92]

This is a highly sensitive area. Companies, partnerships, and looser joint ventures raise special problems since actors with multiple roles may mix self-interest with multiple duties to intersecting entities. Examples are varied and legion. Thus promoters of a company owing one set of obligations to subscribers may, if they become directors, owe a different and conflicting obligation to the company itself. A subgroup of partners or directors may break free to pursue a business opportunity that might have belonged to the parent partnership or company; in such a case, apart from the problem of illegal profit to the individual, the breakaways may owe inconsistent fiduciary duties to the new partnerships or companies. Another case is where the trustee of a shareholding

89 *Lagunas Nitrate Company v Lagunas Syndicate* [1899] 2 Ch 392; cf *Erlanger v New Sombrero Phosphate Co* (1878) 3 App Cas 1218, and in the different context of conflict of interest and wrongful profits, *New Zealand Netherlands Society "Oranje" Inc v Kuys* [1973] 1 WLR 1126 (PC); *Aas v Benham* [1891] 2 Ch 244, interpreted in *Birtchnell v Equity Trustees, Executors and Agency Co Ltd* (1929) 42 CLR 384 (HCA) per Dixon J; *Boardman v Phipps* [1967] AC 46, at 108 per Lord Hodson, at 117 per Lord Guest; *O'Donnell v Shanahan* [2009] EWCA Civ 751 per Rimer LJ; *Links Golf Tasmania Pty Ltd v Sattler* [2012] FCA 634.

90 [1891] WN 165; approved *Bell v Lever Brothers Ltd* [1932] AC 161, 195 per Lord Blanesburgh.

91 See *Birtchnell* (n 21) per Isaacs J, Dixon J.

92 [2009] WASC 213 at [77]–[78], reversed for different reasons on appeal: [2011] WASCA 17.

takes a seat on a company board in order to protect the interests of the trust. The interests of the company may diverge from the interest of the trust, even if the trust controls a majority or sole shareholding.[93] Again, the requirement of informed *ex post* consent seems well established.[94] But deciding the scope of an extant fiduciary relationship is never an easy question. The law is unclear.

Each of these seven areas concerning variation or limitation of the suite of fiduciary duties has been the subject of significant litigation, reflecting doubt over how ascription and limitation operate. Stating that fiduciary duties are based on consent does not yield a magic bullet that solves such problems, nor even a superior language for analyzing the issues. The key question is how to set standards of disclosure and consent when changing the intensity and scope of fiduciary duties, where such duties would normally be applied due to the sensitivity of the relationship. One important conclusion is that the rules of defeasibility based on consent must be crafted independently of the *causae* of ascription.

Conclusion

Consensual exclusion and reshaping of fiduciary duties is so common that some commentators have argued that the present default position should be reversed—no loyalty duties unless the parties expressly prescribe for them.[95] The better analysis is that fiduciary law here can serve as what law and economics scholars have described as a "penalty default rule."[96] This is a rule set at an equilibrium that perhaps the majority of market actors would not have chosen; the penalty of sticking to the default rule encourages release of information and revealing of preferences by self-aware and rational actors who will renegotiate terms and tailor the level of protection to their needs. In fiduciary law the default rule sets a very high, perhaps too high, protection against conflict of interests and duties; the parties are free to adapt these rules where this brings countervailing advantages. The law can then leave in place a highly protective default position for less sophisticated actors who cannot easily bargain or do not know which equilibrium to bargain for. Thus fiduciary law emerges as a well-designed union of penalty default and standard efficient default rules. Moral hazard and temptation to abuse fiduciary power to redraw relationships in favor of the fiduciary is reduced when the law applies stringent disclosure rules to ensure that any departures from the default rule are well understood and consent is well informed. The cost of forcing many or most parties to bargain around the default rules is justified because the payoff to individuals and society of honest and faithful service is very high.[97] The fiduciary disclosure and consent rules ensure that the balance of risk and protection is set to the level

[93] Tony Molloy, "Trustees of Controlling Shareholdings Who Take Directorships or Senior Executive Posts in the Company," 16 *Tr & Trustees* 741 (2010).

[94] *Erlanger v New Sombrero Phosphate Co* (1877–8) LR 3 App Cas 1218 (HL); *Boardman v Phipps* [1967] 2 AC 46 (HL); [1964] 1 WLR 993 (Ch) per Wilberforce J.

[95] Langbein (n 30).

[96] Cf Ian Ayres and Robert Gertner, "Filling Gaps in Incomplete Contracts: An Economic Theory of Default Rules," 99 *Yale LJ* 87 (1989).

[97] Conaglen (n 3) 219–21, drawing from Michael Whincop, "Of Fault and Default: Contractarianism as a Theory of Anglo-Australian Corporate Law," 21 *Melb UL Rev* 187 (1997).

the parties actually accept with full information and awareness; absent such consent and the default position should be very demanding of the fiduciary. In other words, a fiduciary standard is applied to attempts to vary the fiduciary standard, a precautionary double entrenchment that still permits variation if the parties truly wish it. There may be a good case for setting efficient rather than penalty default rules in normal contracting, where the majority of parties do not win much value from having to release information and dicker over the precise setting of contractual standards. Objective consent there suffices to shift the goalposts.[98] But in long-term discretionary fiduciary relationships, where value is easily destroyed or appropriated by opportunistic agents, it is important that the law help the parties set workable incentives, which means that parties should be encouraged in the first instance to bond to give up self-interest and divided loyalties as a condition of service, with consensual variation of reduced protection being harder to attain than in finite term or non-discretionary contracts; in those latter cases the potential for abuse is lessened and market discipline can be most effective. It would disrupt this finely balanced system between fiduciary and non-fiduciary dealings if the courts would allow informed consent to turn into a merely formal process; and as we have seen, there are plenty of precedents to help the judges hold the line, and prevent too easy a limitation of the initially ascribed obligations. For it is in the area of limitation or defeasibility of duty that much of the important work of setting standards now occurs. Not "who is a fiduciary," or "what is a fiduciary duty," but "how are fiduciary duties changed" is now the compelling question.

[98] Eric Posner, "There are No Penalty Default Rules in Contract Law," 33 *Fla St UL Rev* 563 (2006).

3

The Fiduciary Relationship

*Paul B Miller**

Introduction

The conceptual structure of private law is, to a considerable extent, formal in nature. Principles of private liability are mediated by relatively stable forms of action, interaction, and organization. The formal character of private law is reflected in the fact that the application of liability rules is often preconditioned on judicial determination that the interaction of the plaintiff and defendant fell within a form (or kind) of action, interaction, or organization to which certain mandatory or default rules apply. Thus, for example, a simple claim for breach of contract turns on the existence of a primary obligation of contractual performance, which is in turn rooted in a particular form of legal relationship—ie, a contractual relationship.[1] The claim for breach of contract will fail unless the claimant can establish that the underlying relationship was actually contractual—ie, that it possessed the formal properties (validity conditions) of a contract. Similarly, a claim of trespass to real property turns on establishment of ownership or a lesser interest in the real property (eg, a leasehold interest) that generates a right of exclusive possession. Here, too, we have a liability rule the application of which is conditioned on the form of the relationship between litigants (owner and non-owner; leaseholder and non-leaseholder). Modifications of, or deviations from, a rule may also be formally determined (eg, the nature of the relationship between landlord and leaseholder informs rules governing the rightfulness of the former's presence on leased property).

Many of the forms of action, interaction, and organization in private law are well understood or at least widely analyzed. However, that is not true of fiduciary law. There is considerable uncertainty over the basis, nature, and scope of fiduciary duties as well as their justification. These uncertainties necessarily raise questions about the structure of fiduciary law.

Is fiduciary liability, like some other bases of equitable intervention, largely discretionary?[2] Or is it, at least in part, structured formally? Addressing this question requires

* I am grateful to participants in the 2013 Fiduciary Law Workshop at Notre Dame Law School for their input. I am also appreciative of questions and comments provided by participants at the Philosophical Foundations of Fiduciary Law Workshop held at the DePaul College of Law. For detailed comments, I am particularly grateful to Christopher Bruner, Evan Fox-Decent, Andrew Gold, and Julian Velasco.

[1] The fact that there may be several variants on a given form, such as a contract, does not detract from the formal character of liability. It is instead a reflection of the mutability and complexity of legal forms as constructions of reason. On varieties of contract, see Hanoch Dagan and Michael Heller, *Freedom of Contracts*, forthcoming.

[2] As Laycock suggests in his essay on the influence of equity on the common law. See Douglas Laycock, "The Triumph of Equity," 56 *Law & Contemp Probs* 53 (1993). See also Peter Birks, "Equity in the Modern Law: An Exercise in Taxonomy," 26 *UW Austl L Rev* 1 (1996).

that one consider shared experience as reflected in doctrine and the practices of lawyers and judges. To what extent, if at all, are we concerned with the *general* nature of the relationship between litigants when determining whether fiduciary liability rules apply? Supposing we are concerned with the general nature of their relationship, do we treat it as distinctive? I shall presently argue that we are (as a matter of practice), and should be (as an analytical matter), very much concerned with the fiduciary relationship and its distinctive, formal, properties.

Let us begin at a pre-critical level, with our habits of thought and speech. As lawyers and legal scholars we are, I think it is fair to say, in the habit of referring to people as fiduciaries, and offices and relationships as having a fiduciary character, with the implication that they are instances of a general kind or category.[3] So, for example, we say with confidence that lawyers, directors, agents, and trustees are fiduciaries, and perhaps with some diffidence that parents, doctors, and public officials are (or should be) so considered. Similarly, we say of offices that they, too, have a fiduciary character (and, by extension, we treat occupation of an office as a reason for considering a person or relationship to be fiduciary). Finally, we speak of persons and offices as being implicated in fiduciary relationships. Hence, we say that lawyers have a fiduciary relationship with their clients, that corporate directors stand in a fiduciary relationship to the corporation they serve, and so on. On a critical level, the implication of kind-status is reflected positively in efforts to identify common characteristics of fiduciaries.[4] It is reflected negatively in our opinions, beliefs, and decisions (authoritative or otherwise) that certain people are not and could not be fiduciaries.

These practices may simply reflect a shared intuition that there are salient resemblances between particulars; resemblances for which a collection of loosely related terms (fiduciary, fiduciary office, fiduciary relationship) provide suitable shorthand.[5] But given that these are technical legal terms, and our practices are the practices of lawyers, it seems more likely that they reflect conceptual and practical exigencies generated by customary usage. And in law, the usage implies more than ease of reference. To refer to a person, office, or relationship as fiduciary is to suggest certain significant legal consequences. A fiduciary is subject to a range of distinctive and demanding legal obligations.[6]

Given customary usage, the suggestion that the fiduciary relationship is an indefinable construct may seem surprising. Nevertheless, this is conventional wisdom amongst leading fiduciary law scholars. In Section I of this chapter, I introduce and challenge this view by contrasting it with judicial practice and opinion. In Section II, I offer a theory of the fiduciary relationship—*the fiduciary powers theory of the fiduciary relationship (hereinafter: fiduciary powers theory)*—centered on a definition of the relationship. The viability of a definition is partly a function of its capacity to encompass

[3] Hereinafter, I shall speak of "kinds" and "forms" interchangeably as shorthand for general kinds or categories of roles, offices and relationships.

[4] See generally Tamar Frankel, *Fiduciary Law* (2001) 4–6; and Laura Hoyano, "The Flight to the Fiduciary Haven," in Peter Birks (ed), *Privacy and Loyalty* (Oxford: Clarendon Press, 1997) 169.

[5] As suggested by John Glover, "The Identification of Fiduciaries," in Peter Birks (ed), *Privacy and Loyalty* (Oxford: Clarendon Press, 1997) 269.

[6] See generally Peter Birks, "The Content of the Fiduciary Obligation," 34 *Israel L Rev* 3 (2000).

phenomena commonly understood as denoted by the defined term. Accordingly, in Section III I show how the fiduciary powers theory explains the kind-status of a set of relationships widely considered fiduciary. The utility of a definition lies in its capacity for differentiation of phenomena and is best revealed where differentiation is hard due to confounding similarities. Thus, in Section IV I show how the fiduciary powers theory enables principled resolution of disagreements over the fiduciary character of other relationships. In the final section, I offer some brief conclusions.

I. Conflicting Views on Fiduciary Relationships

Current thinking about fiduciary law features two prominent views on fiduciary relationships. The dominant academic view is that the fiduciary relationship is indefinable.[7] The dominant judicial view is that the existence of such a relationship is a precondition of fiduciary liability. These views conflict. Judges treat the fiduciary relationship as conceptually central to fiduciary liability; leading academics deny the coherence of the concept. This conflict is paradoxical. Judges condition liability on the existence of a relationship that falls within a general kind or category that many academics insist is illusory or incoherent. The paradox is troubling in itself but also because it generates certain complexities for our understanding of fiduciary duties. Case law predominantly suggests that fiduciary duties are responsive to something in the nature of the fiduciary relationship, and thus that fiduciary liability is formally structured. But leading academic opinion seems to imply otherwise.

A. The fiduciary relationship is indefinable

The notion that the fiduciary relationship is indefinable is venerable. It has also proved remarkably durable.[8] Len Sealy was an early proponent of this view. In an article on fiduciary relationships, Sealy averted to the "problem of defining a fiduciary situation."[9] He concluded that the problem is irresolvable: "The word 'fiduciary'. . . is *not* definitive

[7] I attribute this position primarily to academics because definitional reasoning is itself largely an academic preoccupation. It is rare to find direct judicial pronouncements on point. But see Wilson J, dissenting in *Frame v Smith* [1987] 2 SCR 99 (SCC) 135, who noted that: "there is no definition of the concept "fiduciary" apart from the contexts in which it has been held to arise." Likewise, Brennan CJ in *Breen v Williams* (1996) 186 CLR 71 (HCA) 92 noted that "the law has not, as yet, been able to formulate any precise or comprehensive definition of the circumstances in which a person is constituted a fiduciary in his or her relations with another." Fletcher Moulton LJ's famous warning in *Coomber v Coomber* [1911] 1 Ch 723 about "unthinking resort to verbal formulae" in fiduciary law has been interpreted by some as a condemnation of definitional reasoning. But I think that the best interpretation of the dictum in *Coomber* is that given to it by Millett LJ in *Bristol & West Building Society v Mothew* [1998] Ch 1. Millett LJ takes the dictum to mean that greater care is required in definition of terms. Thus he began his analysis of a claim of fiduciary breach involving negligence by stating that it is "necessary to begin by defining one's terms." More specifically, it is necessary that we think about fiduciary law in terms of concepts that are distinctive to it (though Millett LJ was concerned with identifying what is distinctive about fiduciary obligations, not fiduciary relationships).

[8] This is true, notwithstanding some significant attempts to define the fiduciary relationship or to clarify its basic nature. See especially Ernest J Weinrib, "The Fiduciary Obligation," 25 *U Toronto LJ* 1 (1975); J C Shepherd, "Towards a Unified Concept of Fiduciary Relationships," 97 *LQR* 51 (1981); and D Gordon Smith, "The Critical Resource Theory of Fiduciary Duty," 55 *Vand L Rev* 1399 (2002).

[9] L S Sealy, "Fiduciary Relationships," *Cambridge LJ* 69, at 69 (1962).

of a single class of relationships to which a fixed set of rules and principles apply... the mere statement that John is in a fiduciary relationship towards me means no more than that in some respects his position is trustee-like."[10]

An influential endorsement of this view was subsequently offered by Paul Finn in his classic treatise, *Fiduciary Obligations*.[11] Finn's book was ventured on the basis of his immediate and unequivocal rejection of the notion that the fiduciary relationship is a distinctive and coherent kind of legal relationship. On the very first page of his book, Finn proclaimed:

> [I]t is meaningless to talk of fiduciary relationships as such. Once one looks to the rules and principles which actually have been evolved, it quickly becomes apparent that it is pointless to describe a person... as being a fiduciary... The rules are everything. The description "fiduciary," nothing.[12]

The views of Sealy and Finn have proven widely influential and are shared by leading contemporary scholars. For instance, Deborah DeMott argues that fiduciary law has "developed through a jurisprudence of analogy rather than principle" and insists that "the law of fiduciary obligation is situation-specific."[13] The situation-specificity of the law is such as to render definitional reasoning futile. DeMott argues that "the characteristics of even the standard or conventional fiduciary relationships... are too variable to enable one to distill a single essence or property that unifies all in any analytically satisfactory way."[14]

Similarly, Matthew Conaglen argues that fiduciary duties can and ought to be analysed independently of fiduciary relationships.[15] He, too, recognizes that there are categories of relationship in which "fiduciary duties are indubitably owed" but thinks there is little to be gained in analysing them as a kind or type.[16] Indeed, he claims that efforts to define the fiduciary relationship rest on "vain hope."[17]

Finally, James Edelman claims that it is possible to analyse the ascription of fiduciary duties independently of an inquiry into the nature of fiduciary relationships.[18] He argues that "we can only understand when fiduciary duties arise if we conceive of them as obligations based upon manifestations of a voluntary undertaking to another."[19] Edelman considers it unnecessary to characterize the nature of the undertaking, claiming that fiduciary duties are not "necessarily referable to a relationship or status."[20]

[10] Sealy, "Fiduciary Relationships," at 73 (original emphasis).

[11] P D Finn, *Fiduciary Obligations* (1977).

[12] Finn, *Fiduciary Obligations*. Interestingly, in his later writings Finn recanted, expressing worry over indiscriminate use of the word "fiduciary:" "our present uncertainty is thought to be exacerbated by the lack of a workable and unexceptionable definition of a fiduciary... Definition, however imperfect, has its place." P D Finn, "The Fiduciary Principle in Equity," T G Youdan (ed), *Equity, Fiduciaries and Trusts* (1989) 26.

[13] Deborah A DeMott, "Beyond Metaphor: An Analysis of Fiduciary Obligation," 37 *Duke LJ* 879, 879 (1988).

[14] Deborah A. DeMott, "Breach of Fiduciary Duty: On Justifiable Expectations of Loyalty and their Consequences," 48 *Ariz L Rev* 925, 934–5 (2006).

[15] Matthew Conaglen, "The Nature and Function of Fiduciary Loyalty," 121 *LQR* 452 (2005).

[16] Conaglen (n 15) at 454.

[17] Matthew Conaglen, *Fiduciary Loyalty: Protecting the Due Performance of Non-Fiduciary Duties* (2010) 9.

[18] James Edelman, "When do Fiduciary Duties Arise?," 126 *LQR* 302 (2010).

[19] Edelman (n 18) at 302.

[20] Edelman (n 18) at 302.

B. The fiduciary relationship grounds fiduciary liability

The view that the fiduciary relationship is indefinable conflicts with prevailing judicial opinion, according to which fiduciary liability is premised on breach of one or more duties occasioned by the formation of a fiduciary relationship. Contra Edelman, fiduciary duties *have* historically been "necessarily referable to a relationship." They arise where a fiduciary relationship arises and they govern the conduct of fiduciaries within the ambit of this relationship, however far it happens to extend.

The conventional wisdom of judges implies the analytical priority of relationship over duty in the structure of fiduciary liability. This priority is reflected in what judges say about fiduciary liability as well as what they do in adjudicating liability.

Let us start with what matters most—the practices whereby litigants argue, and judges adjudicate, fiduciary liability claims. Here, relationship characterization figures centrally. Plaintiffs do not simply assert a duty and plead facts showing breach. Instead, they first claim that their relationship with the defendant was fiduciary. More particularly, they claim that it was fiduciary as a matter of status or fact.[21] Courts adjudicate claims accordingly. They determine whether the relationship was, in fact, fiduciary as a matter of status or fact. Once that determination is made, recognition of fiduciary duties, and analysis of allegations of breach, follows.

Appreciation of the role of relationship characterization in fiduciary liability requires brief explanation of dominant methods of identifying fiduciary relationships.[22] In the usual case, a plaintiff will argue that she and the defendant are in a relationship of fiduciary *status*. The relationships that most think of as fiduciary are so recognized as a matter of status (eg, agent and principal, trustee and *cestui*, director and corporation). Confronted with a claim of this sort, the court will determine whether the relationship is of a type that has settled fiduciary status. If so, it is almost invariably treated as fiduciary and the defendant will be deemed to have been subject to fiduciary duties.

In the rare case that a plaintiff is unable to prove a relationship of settled fiduciary status, she may argue either for a *de novo* extension of status or a one-off judgment that the relationship is fiduciary. Sometimes litigants manage to convince the courts that an extension of status is in order. However, the bar is very high given the precedential implications. It is thus more typically argued that the relationship is fiduciary by virtue of its actual (rather than presumed) characteristics. Here, facts rather than status drive the analysis. A relationship is identified as fiduciary by virtue of its possession of characteristics of recognized fiduciary relationships (ie, those that have settled fiduciary status). There is considerable difference of opinion amongst judges on the characteristics of fiduciary relationships.[23] However, commonly cited characteristics include discretion, power, inequality, vulnerability, trust, and confidence.

I have elsewhere criticized these methods of identifying fiduciary relationships.[24] However, their defensibility is immaterial here. The important point for present purposes is that the kind-status of a relationship (whether in its own right or by virtue of its status) determines whether fiduciary duties apply to it. Fiduciary liability is formally

[21] See Smith (n 8).

[22] I discuss these methods in greater detail in Paul B Miller, "A Theory of Fiduciary Liability," 56 *McGill LJ* 235 (2011). See also Smith (n 8) and Glover (n 5).

[23] Hoyano (n 4). [24] Miller (n 22).

structured even if we don't understand well the formal properties of the kind of relationship on which fiduciary duties are based.

Given that relationship characterization is central to the formulation and adjudication of liability claims, it should be unsurprising that judges frequently say as much. Consider *Guerin v Canada*, in which Dickson CJ had to decide whether the incidence of fiduciary duties is controlled wholly (and merely) by status or rather follows from something in the nature of the fiduciary relationship. He found the latter to be the case:

> [I]t is sometimes said that the nature of fiduciary relationships is both established and exhausted by the standard categories of agent, trustee, partner, director, and the like. I do not agree. *It is the nature of the relationship, not the specific category of actor involved that gives rise to the fiduciary duty.*[25]

Also instructive are comments on methods of identifying fiduciary relationships. For example, in *Lac Minerals Ltd v International Corona Resources Ltd*, La Forest J said of the status-based approach that:

> The focus is on the identification of *relationships which, because of their inherent purpose or presumed factual or legal incidents, the courts will impose a fiduciary obligation* on one party to act or refrain from acting in a certain way.[26]

Of the fact-based approach, he said:

> The imposition of fiduciary obligations is not limited to those relationships in which a presumption of such an obligation arises. Rather, *a fiduciary obligation can arise as a matter of fact out of the specific circumstances of a relationship.*[27]

Similar statements are found in other leading cases. For instance, in *Hospital Products Ltd v United States Surgical Corporation*, Dawson J made it clear that fiduciary duties arise from, and are responsive to, properties of the fiduciary relationship:

> There is. . . the notion underlying all cases of fiduciary obligation that *inherent in the nature of the relationship itself is a position of disadvantage or vulnerability* on the part of one of the parties. . . *From that springs the requirement* that a person under a fiduciary obligation shall not put himself in a position where his interest and duty conflict.[28]

In the United States, courts have also emphasized that fiduciary duties arise by virtue of fiduciary relationships. For example, in *United States v Chestman*, the US Court of Appeals for the Second Circuit said:

> A fiduciary relationship involves discretionary authority and dependency. . . the beneficiary of the relation may entrust the fiduciary with custody over property of one sort or another. *Because the fiduciary obtains access to this property to serve the ends of the fiduciary relationship, he becomes duty-bound* not to appropriate the property for his own use.[29]

[25] [1984] 2 SCR 335 (SCC) 341 (emphasis supplied).
[26] [1989] 2 SCR 574 (SCC) 646 (emphasis supplied).
[27] [1989] 2 SCR 574 (SCC) at 648 (emphasis supplied).
[28] (1984) 156 CLR 41 (HCA) 142 (emphasis supplied).
[29] 947 F 2d 551, 569 (2d Cir 1991) (emphasis supplied). See also the Restatement (Third) of Trusts § 2 cmt. b: "Despite the differences in the legal circumstances and responsibilities of various fiduciaries, one

Of course, courts are evidently not of one mind on the nature of the fiduciary relationship or the link between it and fiduciary duties. However, they are predominantly of the view that fiduciary relationships ground fiduciary duties and thus fiduciary liability.

II. Resolving the Conflict: The Fiduciary Powers Theory of the Fiduciary Relationship

We have established that there are two important, but conflicting, views on fiduciary relationships. Leading academics hold that the fiduciary relationship is indefinable; judges treat it as a lynchpin of liability. Scholarly opinion reflects real uncertainty about the nature of the fiduciary relationship. However, in the conflict between it and the judicial opinion, the latter must prevail. Lawyers and judges reason and act as though the fiduciary relationship is a distinctive form or kind of legal relationship. We cannot but take these practices seriously. Indeed, I suggest that they supply the basis for definitional reasoning. In previous work I have offered a working definition of the fiduciary relationship as part of a broader fiduciary powers-based theory of fiduciary liability.[30] I shall now develop the definition more fully, explain its implications, and argue for its viability and utility.

A. A definition of the fiduciary relationship

I suggest that the fiduciary relationship is a distinctive and coherent kind of legal relationship that may be defined as follows:

> A fiduciary relationship is one in which one party (the fiduciary) exercises discretionary power over the significant practical interests of another (the beneficiary).[31]

The above definition identifies formal properties of the fiduciary relationship. These properties establish the content and parameters of the relationship as a general kind of legal relationship; some are definitive properties, others are structural properties. The definitive properties are kind-defining terms and thus drive the taxonomical function of the kind or category of relationship picked out by the definition. Kind-defining terms make it possible to use the definition to sort, categorize, and differentiate particulars. The structural properties identify implications of kind-status for the parties to a relationship falling within it.

We may first consider the definitive properties of the fiduciary relationship under the fiduciary powers theory. The most significant of these is, unsurprisingly, the exercise of *power* by the fiduciary relative to the beneficiary. It is commonly suggested that fiduciaries possess power over others.[32] However, power is conceptually ambiguous.

characteristic is common to all: a person in a fiduciary relationship to another is under a duty to act for the benefit of the other as to matters within the scope of the relationship."

[30] Miller (n 22) at 261–5. [31] Miller (n 22) at 262.

[32] *United States v Chestman* (n 29); *Hospital Products Ltd v United States Surgical Corporation* (n 28); *Norberg v Wynrib* [1992] 2 SCR 226 (SCC); and *Galambos v Perez* 2009 SCC 48 (SCC). See also Shepherd (n 8); Smith (n 8); Evan Criddle, "Fiduciary Administration: Rethinking Popular Representation in Agency Rulemaking," 88 *Texas L Rev* 441 (2010); and Evan Fox-Decent, *Sovereignty's Promise: The State as Fiduciary* (2012). While many courts analyze the relationship in terms of power, some conceive of it in terms of trust and confidence. See the judgment of Millett LJ in *Mothew* (n 7), at 18: "A fiduciary is someone who has

Power may mean control, authority, strength, or influence, amongst other things. And many of these concepts are, in turn, ambiguous. Even Hohfeld's well-known definition of a legal power won't do.[33] Hohfeld conceives of legal powers in general as capacities (devised or sanctioned by law) to alter the legal position or relationship of another.[34] Whether or not this is an adequate account of the juridical character of legal powers in general, it does not fully encompass fiduciary powers or express well their juridical character. Some fiduciaries in some cases wield powers over the material rather than legal interests of beneficiaries (eg, physicians and parents) and in exercising those powers influence the material but not legal position of the beneficiary. The *possession* of such a power alters the terms on which the fiduciary and beneficiary and/or benefactor of the power relate (inasmuch as possession of these powers entails authorization) but the *exercise* of the power needn't alter the legal character of these or other relationships, much less the legal position of the parties to them. Fiduciaries in these relationships wield a kind of legal power not captured by Hohfeld's definition. Similarly, some people wield powers that are clearly legal powers in Hohfeld's sense but are not powers that could reasonably be considered fiduciary. The simplest example may be the exercise of powers inherent in options arising under contract (eg, an option to purchase land at an agreed price within a fixed term). The exercise of an option influences the legal position or relationship of another (at the very least, the counter-party who gave the option and is liable to its exercise) but the power to act on an option is not (or is at least not inherently[35]) other-regarding; instead, it may be and ordinarily is exercised self-interestedly. To say simply that a fiduciary relationship is one in which one person possesses power—or even legal power of some sort—relative to another is therefore inadequate. The concept of *fiduciary* power must be disambiguated from other varieties of power.

I suggest that fiduciary power is distinguishable from other varieties of power by virtue of the fact that it is a form of *authority* ordinarily derived from the *legal personality* of another (natural or artificial) person.[36] The fiduciary, by virtue of the power vested

undertaken to act for or on behalf of another in a particular matter in circumstances which give rise to a relationship of trust and confidence." In my view, the stipulation of an undertaking as one to "act for or on behalf of another" implies a relationship of power of the sort described in Section II.A. This view is resonant with Mason J's statement in *Hospital Products* at 96–7, that "[t]he critical feature of [fiduciary] relationships is that the fiduciary undertakes or agrees to *act for or on behalf of* or in the interests of another person *in the exercise of a power or discretion* which will affect the interests of that other person in a legal or practical sense" (emphasis supplied).

[33] Compare Lionel Smith, "Can We Be Obliged to Be Selfless?" in this volume.

[34] See Wesley N. Hohfeld, "Some Fundamental Legal Conceptions as Applied in Judicial Reasoning," 23 *Yale LJ* 16, 55 (1913): "a power is one's affirmative 'control' over a given legal relation as against another."

[35] I recognize that an option may be held under a fiduciary mandate in which case its exercise is other-regarding in the sense that the fiduciary is obligated to act in the interests of the beneficiary. But this is a function of the fact that exercise of the option (a kind of legal power) is subject to the exercise of fiduciary power (a different kind of legal power). There is nothing in the juridical character of the option *itself* that makes *it* a kind of power that attracts fiduciary duties.

[36] I therefore follow Hobbes in conceiving of fiduciary authority as inherently representational and rooted in the concept of personality as such; persons acting on those capacities that are inherent in their legal personality and held relative to their person or property needn't *claim* authority as such for the rightfulness of their action is entailed by the connection between the capacities and their personality. Persons may be said to *act* with authority when they exercise these powers or capacities but in speaking of authority as such we are ordinarily concerned with their conferral—ie, with the *authorization* upon which legal representation depends. Authority as a form of representation signifies that the exercise of conferred (ie, acquired) powers

in her, stands in substitution for the beneficiary or a benefactor in exercising a legal capacity that is ordinarily derived from the beneficiary or benefactor's legal personality.[37] Personal legal capacity consists in the ability to act in legally effective ways as well as the susceptibility to being held responsible for so acting. It is through the exercise of legal capacities that one acts as a legal person as such.[38]

Given that fiduciary power consists in the substitutive exercise of legal capacity, it follows that varieties of fiduciary power reflect varieties of legal capacity. Fiduciary power may thus entail the capacity to: enter into legally binding relationships for another, including contractual relationships; acquire, invest, use, administer, or alienate property owned by or held for another; to authorize the use of another's name, likeness, or confidential information; to license or permit access to, contact with, or use of, another's physical person or property; to make decisions relating to the health and personal welfare of another; to hold and claim benefit entitlements; to institute legal proceedings to enforce or seek vindication of legal rights for another; and to be held responsible for or answer claims of civil, criminal, or regulatory liability of another.[39]

Fiduciary power as a form of authority implies the freedom to engage in conduct, and more specifically to make decisions, not otherwise open to its bearer.[40] This follows

is rightful. The person wielding fiduciary authority invariably does so as a representative; it is for that reason that Hobbes speaks of those acting with authority on behalf of another as "personating" the other. Acting with authority in this sense is an extension, through representation, of the personality of another (or of oneself as donor of powers given over to another). See Thomas Hobbes, *Leviathan*, ed R Tuck (1996) 112: "the Right of doing any Action, is called AUTHORITY and sometimes *warrant*. So that by Authority, is alwayes understood a Right of doing any act; and *done by Authority*, done by Commission, or Licence from him whose right it is." Hobbes's account of authority is distinctive in its capacity to encompass private and public forms of fiduciary power. On the significance of the concept to our understanding of the state, and its exercise of public powers, as fiduciary see Fox-Decent (n 32), at 5–13. See also David Runciman, *Pluralism and the Personality of the State* (1997) 6–33.

[37] I repeat with the caveat that the power is "ordinarily" derivative in recognition of the fact that in a limited set of circumstances a fiduciary may declare that a capacity of her own will be henceforth held by her on a fiduciary basis for the benefit of a beneficiary. The transformation of personal powers to fiduciary powers by declaration may be part and parcel of a benefaction (as is true of self-declaratory trusts) but it may also arise in the context of incorporation or partnership (as where a director or partner transfers personal property to a corporation or partnership). In such cases the representative character of fiduciary power reflects *not* its derivation as such but the fact that, by virtue of an underlying benefaction or transaction, the power has been devoted to an object and as such no longer belongs within the residuum of powers and capacities through which the donor may pursue ends of his choice. The fiduciary who declares herself to be a fiduciary in respect of the disposition of certain powers (and, normally, associated property) stands in substitution for her beneficiary in the sense that her now-fiduciary powers have been dedicated to the ends of her chosen beneficiary. She exercises them for, or on behalf of, her beneficiary rather than on her own behalf. On the substitutive or representational character of fiduciary power, see the judgment of Mason J in *Hospital Products* (n 28), at 97: "The expressions 'for,' 'on behalf of' and 'in the interests of' signify that the fiduciary acts in a 'representative' character."

[38] Exercise of legal capacity is ordinarily, but not inherently, volitional; sometimes a person will be taken to have acted in a legally effective way notwithstanding that he did not specifically intend to so act (let alone to bring about associated legal consequences).

[39] This list is illustrative, not exhaustive.

[40] This should be uncontroversial in respect of most fiduciaries; however, it is true even where it seems nonsensical. One might think that a fiduciary who has declared that certain of her personal powers will be held on a fiduciary basis is not, in subsequently exercising those powers in a fiduciary capacity, doing anything other than what she may have freely done in exercising the powers in a personal capacity. But this thought is mistaken. It fails to account for the normative implications of the benefaction or transaction through which the powers were devoted to the beneficiary. Whether the transformation in the character of the power is accomplished by way of gift or through contract, the powers must, from the moment at which fiduciary mandate has been formalized, be taken as powers belonging rightfully to the beneficiary (the *cestui*, the partnership, or the

from the fact that capacities associated with legal personality are themselves personal in nature. The individual possessed of personality is the presumptive bearer of the legal capacity to act in her own name and to be recognized and held accountable for so acting. Thus the capacity to enter into a contract is presumptively held by individuals in their own right rather than by agents (agency requires showing of authority). Likewise, the capacity to decide whether to consent to treatment presumptively lies in the patient who will be subject to it (substitute decision-making likewise requiring proof of authority). The authorization through which the fiduciary is invested with fiduciary powers has a transformative effect. It alters the normative basis upon which fiduciaries, beneficiaries, and benefactors interact for it enables (literally, authorizes) the fiduciary to act in ways she would otherwise be legally disabled and/or prohibited from acting.

In some cases, the substitutive exercise of legal capacity might simply entail an extension of legal personality through which the capacity is given effect by another. For example, one person might cede a capacity to another but dictate how it is to be exercised. In such cases, the legal and practical effect of the substitution is limited. The person exercising the capacity simply effectuates the will of the person from whom it was derived. The law does facilitate substitutive exercise of capacity in this rather thin sense. Nevertheless, these powers are normally not considered fiduciary. As prominent authorities attest, powers are ordinarily considered fiduciary only if they are *discretionary*.[41] Discretion entails freedom of choice in the exercise of the power.[42] This in turn means that beneficiaries and benefactors are not merely subject to the conduct of fiduciaries; they are subject as well to their will. Fiduciaries decide, as well as act, for others.

The requirement of discretion is important but should not be overstated. The fiduciary has freedom of choice and action but it is not unlimited. Indeed, it is also an essential characteristic of fiduciary power that it is *specified*. Specification is ordinarily found in the express terms of a grant of authority but may also be supplied by law. Fiduciary power may be specified in any number of ways. It may be subject to triggering conditions (ie, powers may arise at a certain date or upon the occurrence of a certain event). It will usually be subject to conditions that define its scope (ie, specific matters or mandates are reserved for the judgment of the fiduciary) or constrain its exercise (eg, considerations are mandated or prioritized).

Fiduciary power is also inherently *relational*. Private fiduciaries are not sovereigns; they do not enjoy authority at large relative to a populace with diffuse and markedly divergent interests. Rather, their authority is held relative to particular beneficiaries and benefactors with clearly defined personal or common interests. Fiduciaries *exercise*

corporation, as the case may be). The fiduciary cannot rightfully exercise those powers *as a fiduciary* unless she has been properly constituted a fiduciary (ie, unless her acts have effectively authorized her to carry on in the exercise of the transferred powers in her new, fiduciary, capacity).

[41] See *United States v Chestman* (n 29), at 569: "A fiduciary relationship involves discretionary authority and dependency;" *Galambos v Perez* (n 32), at para 70: "The particular relationships on which fiduciary law focuses are those in which one party is given a discretionary power to affect the legal or vital practical interests of another;" and Weinrib (n 8) at 5: "if [the fiduciary has] no discretion to advise or negotiate and if their instructions are narrow and precise there is nothing on which the fiduciary obligation can bite." See also authorities cited in Miller (n 22) at 261–3 and Smith (n 8) at 1397.

[42] On the relationship between discretion in contractual performance and the execution of fiduciary mandates, see D Gordon Smith and Jordan Lee, "Fiduciary Discretion," 78 *Ohio State LJ* (forthcoming).

power in the world at large and thus relative to third parties but they *hold* it relative to a specific individual or group. The relational character of fiduciary power is a function of its derivation and implied purpose. Fiduciary power is derived from the legal personality of another and/or is expressly devoted to the ends of another; in any case, it founds a *relationship* in which one acts for the purpose of advancing the ends of another.

The relational character of fiduciary power provides a natural segue to another definitive property of the fiduciary relationship; namely, that practical interests of the beneficiary serve as the ground of fiduciary power. *Practical interests* include matters of personality, welfare, or right pertaining to persons or their causes. Matters of personality include determination of the interests of incapable persons. Matters of welfare include decisions pertinent to the physical, mental, and material well-being of persons or to the advancement of their causes. Matters of right include decisions relating to the exercise, enforcement, performance, discharge, or alienation of legal rights, obligations, powers, and liabilities of persons. *Practical* interests are, as a matter of conceptual necessity, such that they can be implicated by an individual acting personally on one or more of her legal capacities. The requirement of *significance* follows. Significance is not a function of the value or importance of an interest. It is, rather, a matter of the objective subsistence of an interest, such that the law can recognize it as such. An interest is not significant in this sense if a casual observer cannot see how it is or might be affected by the exercise of a legal capacity.

Structural formal properties of the fiduciary relationship are, by their nature, not immediately apparent in the above definition of the relationship. However, they, too, reflect the nature of fiduciary power and thus form an important part of the fiduciary powers theory of the fiduciary relationship. There are three related structural properties of the fiduciary relationship. The first is *inequality*. The fiduciary is, simply by virtue of the establishment of a fiduciary relationship, in a dominant position relative to the beneficiary. Wherever one person enjoys discretionary power over the practical interests of another, their relationship will be unequal in respect of the possession and exercise of fiduciary power itself. It must be emphasized that this inequality, being structural, is a matter independent of any circumstantial inequality that might exist between the parties. The beneficiary is always subordinate in respect of the possession and exercise of fiduciary power itself, notwithstanding that in other respects he may be ascendant.

The second and third structural properties of the fiduciary relationship are *dependence* and *vulnerability*. These properties are each, in turn, reflections of the structural inequality generated by the formation of a fiduciary relationship. Fiduciary power entails influence, including the risk of adverse influence. The fiduciary is to exercise power to achieve certain ends for the beneficiary. The beneficiary is thus invariably dependent upon the fiduciary as power is exercised so as to affect her practical interests. Vulnerability is a corollary of dependence, so understood. Fiduciaries are expected to exercise power to salutatory effect, but beneficiaries' interests might instead be set back. The degree of vulnerability faced by the beneficiary might be controlled in various ways (eg, by incentive, monitoring, and enforcement mechanisms). However, it cannot be eliminated. The susceptibility of the beneficiary to the influence of the fiduciary in the exercise of fiduciary power entails some risk of adverse influence.

B. Some doctrinal implications

The fiduciary powers theory of the fiduciary relationship has implications for key doctrinal issues. I can mention only a few presently and so will briefly comment on implications relating to the identification of fiduciary relationships, the incidence of fiduciary duties, and the scope of fiduciary duties.

The most important implications of the fiduciary powers theory arise simply by virtue of its clarification of the formal properties of the fiduciary relationship. At a general level, the fiduciary powers theory contributes to broader efforts to map the conceptual landscape of private law.[43] It does so by clarifying the nature of the fiduciary relationship such that it may be distinguished from other kinds of private law relationship, and by clarifying the incidence and function of fiduciary duties relative to other kinds of private law duty. More significant, though, is the primary sorting function served by the definition of the fiduciary relationship in the fiduciary powers theory. Existing methods of identifying fiduciary relationships do not perform this function well because they sort by approximation.[44] By contrast, a definition of the kind offered here permits sorting directly by reference to properties of the kind or category on which the whole enterprise of sorting is premised. Faced with a particular relationship, one can simply determine whether it possesses properties constitutive of the kind or category of relationship and so falls within or outside it.

Another important issue is that of determining the incidence of fiduciary duties. When do fiduciary duties arise? This is, as Edelman notes, a matter of some uncertainty.[45] The dominant judicial view supplies a pat answer: When a fiduciary relationship is established. This answer is important but has been unsatisfying given confusion over the nature of the fiduciary relationship. If it is unclear what makes a relationship fiduciary, it must be unclear when and how a fiduciary relationship may be established and, by extension, when fiduciary duties will arise. The fiduciary powers theory offers clarity. Fiduciary duties arise where one person receives or undertakes discretionary power over the significant practical interests of another. The nature of the relationship determines the means by which it may be formed; these methods of relationship formation amount to modes of authorization.

There are three principal modes of authorization: mutual consent, unilateral undertaking, and legal decree. In most cases, given the nature of the power conveyed, the relationship is established by mutual consent. Consent is often signified by contract. But it may be demonstrated otherwise (eg, by written consent, oral agreement, or by implication). However evidenced, mutual consent founds a fiduciary relationship by signaling that transferor and transferee intend the underlying transfer of power. Where the transfer of power is part of a benefaction it is impressed with the donative intent of the benefaction itself. More rarely, a fiduciary relationship may be established through unilateral undertaking by the fiduciary (eg, voluntary assumption of fiduciary power) or by decree (eg, through legislation or by court order). Usually, recourse to these modes of authorization is made necessary by the incapacity of the beneficiary

[43] Peter Birks, *English Private Law* (2004) and Andrew Burrows and Lord Rodger of Earlsferry (eds), *Mapping the Law: Essays in Memory of Peter Birks* (2006).
[44] See Miller (n 22) at 247–52. [45] See Edelman (n 18).

or benefactor to consent or by the impracticality of authorization being provided on a case-by-case basis.[46]

A final issue is that of determining the scope of fiduciary duties.[47] This issue has proven particularly pressing in commercial fiduciary relationships. In such relationships, the fiduciary will often have a pecuniary interest in an area of business in which her beneficiary has, or might come to have, a like interest. It is virtually impossible to rule out potential conflicts. This has become apparent in cases involving alleged appropriation of business opportunities.[48] A disappointed beneficiary has an incentive to over-state the scope of fiduciary duty to reach profits realized on an opportunity by a fiduciary. Courts have recognized the importance of delineating the scope of fiduciary duties, but have struggled to find a principled basis for, and method of, delineation.

The fiduciary powers theory fills that gap. Under this theory, the fiduciary relationship grounds fiduciary duties and determines their sphere of operation. It suggests that fiduciary duties ensure that fiduciary powers are exercised in a manner consistent with the beneficiary's exclusive claim relative to them. Fiduciary duties have no juridical purpose independent of the relationship that gives rise to them. It follows that, to define the scope of fiduciary duties, one must define the scope of the fiduciary relationship. This is necessarily a fact-based exercise in construction of the terms of particular fiduciary mandates. However, attention to the formal character of the fiduciary relationship allows one to focus the construction.

To ascertain the scope of a fiduciary relationship, and by extension the sphere of operation of fiduciary duties, it is necessary that one clarify the relative positioning of fiduciary and beneficiary under the mandate in question. One must identify particular capacities held by the fiduciary and the practical interest(s) of the beneficiary directly implicated by their exercise. One must also determine whether particular purposes have been specified (or may be implied) in the grant of power. In this way, the scope of fiduciary duties may be ascertained by determining *what* the fiduciary is expected to accomplish for the beneficiary through the exercise of *which* powers. Fiduciary duties constrain the conduct of the fiduciary within the ambit of the relationship so ascertained, but not beyond it.

III. Testing the Fiduciary Powers Theory: Core Cases

The fiduciary powers theory of the fiduciary relationship suggests that identification of fiduciary relationships should proceed by way of definitional reasoning. A critical test of any definition of the fiduciary relationship lies in its ability to encompass relationships of unquestioned fiduciary status. Status is an imperfect proxy for definitional

[46] Though in the case of personal powers that are declared fiduciary, unilateral undertaking is the only appropriate mode of authorization; the beneficiary has no standing to consent or object to the authorization as such.

[47] Lionel Smith, "The Motive, Not the Deed," in J Getzler (ed), *Rationalizing Property, Equity and Trusts* (2003) 53.

[48] See, eg, *Peso Silver Mines Ltd (NPL) v Cropper* [1966] SCR 673 (SCC); *Industrial Development Consultants v Cooley* [1972] 1 WLR 443; *Canadian Aero Service Ltd v O'Malley* [1974] SCR 592 (SCC); and *Bhullar v Bhullar* [2003] EWCA Civ 424.

reasoning, but we should have little reason for confidence in a definition of a concept if it does not comport with common usage of the concept. In fiduciary law, we have greatest apparent confidence in the fiduciary nature of a few core categories of relationship. In this section, I will show how the fiduciary powers theory of the fiduciary relationship explains the presumptive fiduciary status of trustees, agents, and corporate directors.

A. Trustees as fiduciaries

The trustee is widely considered to be the prototypical fiduciary.[49] When asked what makes the trustee a fiduciary, some hearken to the Latinate *fiducia* and its signification of social practices of trust reposed and undertaken in respect of property.[50] It is unclear whether this is as insightful as is supposed (mostly because it is unclear what it means to repose and undertake trust in general), but even supposing that trusteeship reflects a social economy of trust it is also the case that a trustee is one in whom legal power is reposed.

The notion that the trustee is a fiduciary by virtue of his possession of legal powers over trust property is not new.[51] Nevertheless, the basis for the fiduciary characterization of these powers has rarely been explained. I suggest that ordinary powers of trusteeship (administrative and dispositive) are fiduciary powers in the sense explained in Section II.A. The trustee of a private donative trust acts as a trustee through the authority he enjoys as such. This authority is in the nature of legal capacity to act in legally effective ways relative to the trust corpus. The powers of the trustee are sometimes (perhaps misleadingly) said to be those entailed by legal ownership of trust property. Precise delineation of these powers is a matter best left to treatise writers. But even

[49] By "trustee" I here mean the trustee of an ordinary express trust with a primarily donative purpose. I shall not presently explore complexities associated with public trusts, commercial trusts, and remedial trusts.

[50] Birks (n 6).

[51] Many authorities make reference to these powers when defining the nature of the trust or the office of trusteeship. Several statutes likewise refer to offices of trusteeship in terms of administrative and investment powers in relation to trust property. See, for example, *Halsbury's Laws of England*, vol 25 at 5: "A trust, in the modern and confined sense of the word, is a confidence reposed in a person with respect to property, of which he has possession or over which he can exercise a power, to the intent that he may hold the property or exercise the power for the benefit of some other person or object;" and the reasons of Lord Eldon in *Brown v Higgs* (1801) 8 Ves Jun 561, 570, 574: "[T]here are not only a mere trust and a mere power, but there is also known to the Court a power which the party to whom it is given is intrusted and required to execute; and with regard to that species of power, the Court considers it as partaking so much of the nature and qualities of a trust, that if the person, who has that duty imposed on him does not discharge it, the Court will to a certain extent discharge the duty in his room and place." See also *Restatement (Second) of Trusts*, vol 1, ch 7.3—"Powers of the Trustee;" Trustee Act, 1925, 15 Geo 5 Ch 19 (describing general and particular powers of trustees); Trustee Act, RSO 1990, c T23 (likewise, characterizing trusteeship in terms of possession of powers); J E Penner, *The Law of Trusts* (6th edn, 2008) 21, explaining that, by virtue of the division of legal and equitable title, "the trustee has all of the legal rights and powers associated with the property" and explaining the nature of the trust and relationships between its constituents in terms of powers and constraints thereon; and Graham Virgo, *The Principles of Equity and Trusts* (2012) 381, explaining that: "once appointed, trustees have a wide variety of powers" and explaining the nature of trusteeship in terms of possession of powers subject to fiduciary and other constraints. While some have endeavored to distinguish trusts and powers of trusteeship, courts have considered the concept of power to be so essential to the nature of the trust as to make any such distinction artificial. See *McPhail v Doulton* [1971] AC 242 (HL) 448G per Lord Wilberforce, "It is striking how narrow and in a sense artificial is the distinction. . . between trusts, or as the particular type of trust is called, trust powers and powers. . . A layman and, I suspect, a logician would find it hard to understand what the difference is."

cursory analysis reveals that trustees exercise legal capacities ordinarily associated with legal ownership. These capacities include powers of appointment, distribution, maintenance, and advancement.[52] They also include powers of delegation and of satisfying debts and settling claims.[53] Needless to say, only one with powers of ownership—held personally or on trust—is permitted to make decisions about the investment or maintenance of property, to license access to or use of the property, and so on.

The powers wielded by trustees are derivative, discretionary, relational, and specified within the meaning of the fiduciary powers theory. As is true of most fiduciaries, most trustees enjoy their powers *derivatively*. Apart from trustees acting under self-declaratory trusts, they obtain their powers through authorization by another. In some cases (eg, where trust property is that of a person who died intestate), trustees obtain their authority by decree (eg, under a Trustees Act). However, in most cases it is received from a settlor via a trust deed. An ordinary express trust for a donative purpose effectuates a benefaction of property and power for the benefit of another. The power and property are both derived from the settlor, who in settling the trust gives effect to her intent to do more than merely pass title by gift.

The powers of a trustee are specified. Indeed, *specificity* is a condition of validity for express trusts, as reflected in the "three certainties" requirements.[54] Amongst other things, for a purported declaration of trust to be effective in creating a trust, the powers devolved upon the trustee must be certain in their own terms as well as in respect of their objects (purposes or beneficiaries) and the property to which they relate. Beyond these *de minimis* requirements, the powers of trustees are ordinarily further specified in the trust deed.

The *discretionary* nature of trustees' powers is reflected in the traditional distinction between bare versus fixed and discretionary trusts. Under bare trusts, the trustee has no discretion in the administration of the trust. He serves as mere nominee, taking title but acting at the direction of the settlor-beneficiary. Bare trustees have passive responsibilities of maintenance but no positive fiduciary mandate requiring exercise of independent judgment. It is for this reason that bare trustees are not fiduciaries.[55] The trustee of a fixed trust, in contrast to that of a discretionary trust, does not have discretion in determining the interests of beneficiaries in trust property. But trustees of both fixed and discretionary trusts have discretion in administering the trust (eg, in making investment and maintenance decisions). It is thus unsurprising that no one doubts the fiduciary character of trusteeship of fixed and discretionary trusts.

[52] See Virgo (n 51) at 459–78. [53] Virgo (n 51) at 454–7 and 458.

[54] *Knight v Knight* (1840) 3 Beav 148.

[55] See *Ironside v Smith*, 1998 ABCA 366 (per Fruman J: "An individual may hold property on behalf of another as bare trustee without taking on all the onerous trappings of a fiduciary. A bare trustee has no further duty to perform except to convey the property to the beneficiary on demand and, so long as he holds it, to exercise reasonable care over the property, by maintaining or investing it") and *Financial Management Inc. v Associated Financial Planners Ltd* (2006) 367 WAC 70 (per McFayden, Picard, and O'Brien JJ: "while a trustee may owe fiduciary duties to its beneficiary, a bare trustee does not"). See also Penner (n 51), at 435–6, saying, of bare trusts, "Recall that for fiduciary obligations to arise, there must be some scope for discretion or leeway in the fiduciary's performance of her duties. No such discretion or leeway arises in the case of nomineeship, because in such cases the trustee is only to follow the beneficiary's instructions exactly. If the nominee breaches the trust in some way, he will certainly be liable for breach of trust, but as we know, not all breaches of trust are breaches of fiduciary obligation."

The powers of trustees are also *relational*. However the trust is effectuated, the trustee receives her authority through an intentional transfer of property and power. Powers are settled on trust along with property because this is essential to the settlor achieving her purpose for the transfer—ie, making a *mediated*, and in most cases *conditional*, benefaction. As is true generally, authorization has important relational effects. Whereas in most fiduciary relationships, it alters the legal basis on which fiduciary and beneficiary interact, with trusts things are rather more complicated. Here, the authorization transforms the terms on which settlor, fiduciary, and *cestui* relate, and it does so in different ways depending on the nature of the trust.

In self-declaratory trusts, the declaration entails transformation in the character of powers held with respect to the property settled on trust; these powers are, by virtue of the declaration, henceforth to be held by the settlor-trustee for the benefit of the *cestui*, bringing the parties into a new legal relationship with respect to the property and its administration. The settlor-trustee, in settling the trust, renders fiduciary powers that would otherwise be personal in the course of making a conditional transfer of property; the *cestui* receives, in consequence, new rights relative to the settlor-trustee in respect of both the exercise of powers and the disposition of associated property.

In ordinary express trusts, a valid declaration of trust effectuates a transfer of power from settlor to trustee; the trustee enjoys power over property formerly held by the settlor as legal owner. But given that a private donative trust is, first and foremost, a benefaction, the most significant relational effect is that which obtains between trustee and *cestui*. An ordinary express trust is a means by which to make a mediated benefaction that might otherwise have been unmediated. In establishing a trust rather than making a gift, the settlor interposes the trustee between herself and her intended beneficiaries. An implication of the interpolation of the trustee is that the beneficial interest of *cestui* in the trust is made subject to the authority of the trustee. Depending on the terms of the trust, it may be for the trustee to determine whether, when, how, and how far the beneficial interest of the *cestui* is to be served in the maintenance, investment, disposition, and distribution of trust property.

It is sometimes said that one of the defining features of the trust is that trustees receive rights or powers relative to property subject to duties to exercise those rights or powers in the interests of the *cestui*.[56] We are now in a position to better appreciate the truth of statements like this. Trustees are fiduciaries, and so subject to fiduciary duties, simply by virtue of the nature of the powers under which they act as trustees.

[56] F W Maitland, *Equity* (1936) 44: "I should define a trust in some such way as the following,—when a person has rights which he is bound to exercise on behalf of another or for the accomplishment of some particular purpose, he is said to have those rights in trust for that other or for that purpose and he is called a trustee;" *Underhill on Trusts* (2010) 1: "A trust is an equitable obligation, either expressly undertaken, or constructively imposed by the court, under which the obligor (who is called a trustee) is bound to deal with certain property over which he has control (and which is called trust property), for the benefit of certain persons (who are called the beneficiaries or *cestuis que trust*);" and Lionel Smith, "Trust and Patrimony," 38 *Rev Gen Droit* 379, 381 (2008): "the trust beneficiaries hold rights *in* the rights that the trustee holds as trust property" (original emphasis).

B. Agents as fiduciaries

The presumptively fiduciary character of agency is a matter of general consensus as well. Like trustees, agents enjoy power relative to their beneficiaries.[57] These powers are also evidently fiduciary.

Agency powers are powers in the sense described in Section II.A; namely, they are legal capacities derived from the legal personality of another person. In the context of agency, that person is the principal. An agent in the technical legal sense is one with authority to make legally binding arrangements for her principal.[58] This authority takes the form of specific legal capacities that are presumptively personal capacities of the principal. Consider the most typical kind of agency power—the power to enter into, and act under, a legally valid contract on behalf of the principal. The power to contract depends on a legal capacity inherent in the legal personality of one with actual capacity to act on it (an adult of sound mind). Conferral of this power on an agent brings about a substitution. The agent stands in for the principal in exercising powers to make, perform, breach, or renounce contracts that will be binding just as if these powers had been exercised personally. Consider another kind of agency power—the power of a lawyer to make binding representations on behalf of her client in filing, answering, amending, and defending claims, in drafting and filing legal documents, in making submissions to regulators, or in negotiating transactions.[59] The agency powers exercised by lawyers are also legal capacities derived from the legal personality of the person on whose behalf they are exercised (ie, the client). People may, and sometimes against strenuous advice do, exercise these capacities personally. But they typically cede them to a lawyer. In doing so, they authorize the lawyer to act in their stead. In accepting a retainer and undertaking powers associated with it, the lawyer acts as a fiduciary of her client.

Agency powers are also derivative, discretionary, relational, and specified within the meaning of the fiduciary powers theory of the fiduciary relationship. Their *derivative* character should be plain. The agent does not enjoy her powers innately. No one has the power, at large, to make legally binding arrangements for another. Instead, agency powers are derived from the legal personality of the principal. The agent cannot act as such (ie, as an agent) without authorization because her power is derived wholly from the authorization provided by the principal.[60]

[57] Restatement (Third) of Agency, §1.01, Comment c: "As defined by the common law, the concept of agency posits a consensual relationship in which one person... acts as a representative of or otherwise acts on behalf of another with power to affect the legal rights and duties of the other person... The common-law definition requires that an agent hold power;" *Mecham on Agency* s 26 (2nd edn, 1914): "'An agent' is a person who has authority, express or implied, to act on behalf of another person (the 'principal'), and to bind that other person by his acts or defaults;" Warren A Seavey, "The Rationale of Agency," 29 *Yale LJ* 859, 861 (1920): "a principal is bound where the agent acts in the exercise of power" (but insisting upon a sharp distinction between power and authority); Deborah A DeMott, "Disloyal Agents," 58 *Ala L Rev* 1049, 1050–1 (2007), explaining that the language "on behalf of" in standard definitions of agency means "that an agent acts with power to affect the principal's legal relations."

[58] I follow DeMott (n 57) in distinguishing the legal conception of agency from colloquial and other (eg, economic) conceptions.

[59] See generally Deborah A DeMott, "The Lawyer as Agent," 67 *Fordham L Rev* 301 (1998).

[60] See Restatement (Third) of Agency, §1.01, Comment c: "An agent who has actual authority holds power as a result of a voluntary conferral by the principal and is privileged, in relation to the principal, to exercise that power."

The *specificity* of agency powers is amply evidenced in practice. Contracts, retainers, and the like specify agency powers in a variety of ways. The power(s) themselves will ordinarily be described (eg, a power to enter into a contract of a particular sort). The object of the power will usually also be specified (eg, a power to renegotiate a contract of employment). A temporal term will typically be placed on the agent's powers. Finally, the exercise of agency powers is characteristically conditioned by instructions from the principal.[61]

Unlike trustees, agents act subject to the instruction of their beneficiaries. However, virtually all agents have *discretion* in the exercise of powers notwithstanding the presence of instructions.[62] This may be so even where instructions are quite detailed, insofar as they are subject to interpretation by the agent. Consider the purchasing agent who acts under instructions to obtain a particular good for a specified maximum price, but is otherwise free to negotiate purchase terms. The agent's discretion is limited by *ex ante* instruction and may be further limited by *ex post* consultation, but very rarely is it eliminated. This is unsurprising, for usually it would be pointless to hire an agent without affording her some discretion. If the principal intends not to avail himself of her judgment, he would do as well to exercise the powers personally.

Finally, agency powers are relational. An agent has the authority to act for and on behalf of the principal in dealing with third parties. The authorization of an agent transforms the basis on which these parties interact. The principal will be held accountable for actions of the agent in the exercise of the specific powers vested in the agent as if the actions were her own. The agent, otherwise incapable of binding the principal, obtains that ability. Possession and exercise of agency powers also alters the basis on which agent and principal interact with third parties. Provided notice is given of the agency relationship, contracts or other transactions entered into by an agent for a principal with a third party will be binding on the principal rather than the agent. The direct, personal, and bilateral character of most ordinary legal arrangements is thereby altered by agency.

C. Directors as fiduciaries

Corporate directors are quintessential fiduciaries.[63] And they, too, are commonly said to be fiduciaries insofar as they occupy a position of power.[64] Indeed, the fiduciary

[61] See DeMott (n 57) at 1051: "A defining characteristic of relationships that are ones of agency under the common law is the principal's power to give interim instructions to the agent although principal and agent have previously agreed the principal will not give such instructions, and although, in giving them, the principal breaches a contract with the agent. This power is a crucial aspect of the principal's position of control over the agent, itself necessitated by the agent's power to subject the principal to liability to third parties."

[62] The personal character of fiduciary liability and its dependence on there being an element of discretion in the exercise of a power conferred is reflected, even if only indirectly, in the rule prohibiting delegation by agents where the agent's powers are discretionary. *Summers v Commercial Union Assurance Co* (1881), 6 SCR 19 (SCC).

[63] Justice J Walsh, "The Fiduciary Foundation of Corporate Law," 27 *J Corp L* 333 (2002) and Leo Strine et al, "Loyalty's Core Demand: The Defining Role of Good Faith in Corporation Law," 98 *Geo LJ* 629 (2010).

[64] See Strine (n 63) at 633: "Delaware law has traditionally subjected. . . the use of authority under the statutory corporate law to the important condition that fiduciary power be exercised for proper corporate reasons and not to advance a personal agenda of any kind;" and Margaret Blair and Lynn Stout, "A Team Production Theory of Corporate Law," 85 *Va L Rev* 247, 291 (1999): "Like trustees, directors, once elected, become the ultimate decision-making authority within the firm, constrained primarily by their fiduciary duties."

administration of corporations was famously long ago analogized with that of trusts on the basis that directors, like trustees, wield power over property for the benefit of others.[65]

As we can now appreciate, the relevant basis of analogy lies in the nature of the power and not its object. The director of a corporation can only act as such through the exercise of certain powers over the corporation. Directors' powers, being residuary in nature under most statutes of incorporation, are so broad that they are implicated in virtually everything that directors do to effectuate the productive and other functions of the corporation. They are implicated in the hiring of employees, the acquisition and extension of credit, supplies, and property, the delegation of power to, and supervision of, officers, decision-making on ordinary and extraordinary matters of business, and the retention of, and issuance of instructions to, outside fiduciaries.

Directors have unusually broad powers. Nevertheless, they are fiduciary in the sense described in Section II.A. Directors' powers are in the nature of authority derived from the legal capacity of another person or group of persons. For corporations incorporated under a general statute of incorporation, the powers are ordinarily bestowed on directors by its express terms. These powers are, in turn, entailments of legislative concession of legal personality to the corporation. Corporations receive legal personality from the state but can only act on that personality—ie exercise particular legal capacities—through directors and their delegates.

The powers of directors are derivative, discretionary, relational, and specified. The *derivative* nature of their powers follows from the recognition that no one enjoys the power to represent an organization innately; they must be authorized to so act through legislative enactment or by the express will of its members. The derivative character of directors' powers is perhaps seen most clearly in their susceptibility to annulment or reclamation. The state ordinarily reserves the right to dissolve corporations and/or to remove and replace directors under general statutes of incorporation. Shareholders are also ordinarily given the power to displace directors by voting them out in elections or by asserting the authority to act in their stead under a shareholder agreement.

The *specificity* of directors' powers may be less evident, given that they are residual and granted in very broad terms.[66] However, though broad, directors' powers are limited. The director may exercise only those powers that the corporation or its members enjoy as such, for genuine corporate purposes, and only for the term of her office.[67] Further, whether or not directors' powers are *actually* specified, they are *susceptible* to specification in constating documents either *ex ante* or through *ex post* amendment by resolution of members of the corporation.

The *discretionary* nature of directors' powers is well known. Directors are elected by, and answerable to, shareholders. However, it is settled law that directors are not bound

[65] Adolf Berle, "Corporate Powers as Powers in Trust," 44 *Harv L Rev* 1049 (1931); Merrick Dodd, "For Whom Are Corporate Managers Trustees?," 45 *Harv L Rev* 1145 (1932); and Adolf Berle, "For Whom Corporate Managers Are Trustees," 45 *Harv L Rev* 1365 (1932).

[66] Specificity is more evident in contractarian and special act corporations, in that directors of these corporations have only those powers specifically conferred.

[67] Berle, "Corporate Powers" (n 65); *Re Smith and Fawcett Ltd* [1942] Ch 304; and *Teck Corp Ltd v Millar* (1972) 33 DLR (3d) 288 (BCSC).

to abide by the express will of shareholders on matters within their authority.[68] Rather, they are free to exercise discretion in the best interests of the corporation. The scope for discretion enjoyed by directors is in some jurisdictions underscored by the business judgment rule. Formulations of the rule vary, but in general it provides that powers of judicial review may not be exercised so as to erode the discretion afforded to directors in the exercise of their powers.

Directors' powers are also *relational*. Consider first an old variant on the corporate form—the contractarian (or memorandum) corporation, wherein directors act for shareholders in aggregate on the basis of *their* authorization. Shareholders' appointment of a director transforms the basis on which she interacts with them. The director exercises power relationally in that she must be taken to be acting on behalf of shareholders, jointly and severally, by virtue of their membership of the corporation. Personified corporations complicate the analysis, but only slightly. Here, the fact that directors' powers are bestowed by the state over a statutorily created entity gives directorship the appearance of a public office. However, appearances deceive. For all of their similarities to public offices, corporate offices are private, and powers associated with them are wielded relationally in respect of constituents of the organization itself. Personification means only that directors derive their powers from, and wield them directly in relation to, the organization rather than its members. These powers alter the terms on which directors and the organization (including shareholders, in and through identification of their interests with those of the personified entity) interact, for it is only through fiduciary administration that the organization is able to act as person.

IV. Testing the Fiduciary Powers Theory: Hard Cases

A basic test of the functionality of a definition is whether it permits identification of exemplars that one believes *ex ante* should fall within an adequately stipulated definition. Our core cases, above, provided such a test for the definition of the fiduciary relationship stipulated by the fiduciary powers theory. But of course a basic test is not necessarily the best test. In the real world, identification of particulars as being of a defined kind or category is not always simple. A more demanding test is that of identification through differentiation in hard cases (ie, cases requiring one to sort out potentially confounding similarities or differences).[69]

[68] *Automatic Self-Cleansing Filter Syndicate Co Ltd v Cuninghame* [1906] 2 Ch 34 (CA); and *Scott v Scott* [1943] 1 All ER 582 (Ch D).

[69] Cases that are hard in this sense have proven difficult to resolve because confounding similarities strain working criteria of kind-status upon which differentiation is based. The cases have proven hard to resolve through shared experience over time. Of course, cases could be hard in another sense; there might be relationships that are fiduciary as a matter of custom and consensus but seem difficult to explain in light of the fiduciary powers theory. Consider relationships in which the fiduciary wields power over the interests of multiple beneficiaries. In such cases, the existence of a group of beneficiaries complicates the idea that the fiduciary derives power from a process of authorization that involves transfer of capacity. The transfer of capacity is readily identified in cases in which there is one fiduciary, one beneficiary (and, perhaps, one benefactor). It is less readily identified otherwise. Consider as well the relationship between parents and children. In many, if not most, common law jurisdictions, the parent–child relationship is considered fiduciary as a matter of status. Parents wield discretionary power over their children. However, children lack capacity. Thus, though the law might insist (or imply) that the parent be understood as having derived power from the legal personality of the child, the parent's power cannot be understood as taking the form of

As it happens, there are several hard cases of relationship characterization in fiduciary law. Courts and commentators have disagreed, sometimes vehemently, about whether a particular sort of person, office, or relationship should be considered fiduciary. The fiduciary powers theory promises principled resolution of these debates. I here consider three hard cases. The first is whether advisers should, in general, be considered fiduciaries by virtue of the properties of advisory relationships in general. The second is whether confidants should, again in general, be considered fiduciaries. The third and last involves public officials. Here, the question is whether there is something in the nature of a public office or of state authority that would suggest that public officials are fiduciaries.

A. Advisers as fiduciaries

It is sometimes thought that all manner of advisers—lawyers, doctors, bankers, tax and investment advisers, and others—are fiduciaries of their clients simply by virtue of their advisory function.[70] This characterization seems supportable on the basis of some loose comparisons. Like trustees, certain advisers have access to the property of others. Many are expected to exercise discretion in advising their clients. Advisory relationships are frequently characterized by trust, confidence, inequality, and vulnerability.[71] Why, then, should we not say that advisers in general are fiduciaries of their clients?

One might think we should not say this because it is not true.[72] Loose comparisons provide insufficient support for general characterization, particularly where the characterization is so important. The question of the fiduciary character of advisory relationships arose in *Hodgkinson v Simms*, a case in which the Canadian Supreme Court had to decide whether a financial adviser was a fiduciary in the provision of tax and investment advice.[73] The Court was divided on several issues but was unanimous in holding that an advisory relationship is not inherently fiduciary. Justice La Forest, writing for the majority, explained that for an advisory relationship to be fiduciary "there must be something more than a simple undertaking by one party to provide information and execute orders for the other."[74] The dissenting justices agreed. Justice McLachlin cautioned that: "a false indicator of a fiduciary obligation is the "category" into which the relationship falls. Professional relationships like doctor–patient and lawyer–client often possess fiduciary aspects. But equally, many of the tasks undertaken pursuant to these relationships may not be trust-like or attract a fiduciary obligation."[75]

a capacity of the child because the child's personality does not entail (realized) capacities. I believe that the fiduciary powers theory can account for these cases, however neither is a hard case in the sense used here. They test the limits of the explanatory potential of the theory but they have no bearing on its capacity to resolve controversies over the fiduciary character of certain relationships. I am grateful to Evan Fox-Decent for raising this issue.

[70] J C Shepherd, *The Law of Fiduciaries* (1984) 28: "any person can, by offering to give advice in a particular manner to another, create in himself fiduciary obligations stemming from the confidential nature of the relationship created, which obligations limit the adviser's dealings with the advisee."

[71] Kenneth M Lodge and Thomas J Cunningham, "The Banker as Inadvertent Fiduciary: Beware a Borrower's Special Trust and Confidence," 98 *Comm LJ* 277 (1993).

[72] Jill E Fisch, "Fiduciary Duties and the Analyst Scandals," 58 *Ala L Rev* 1083 (2007).

[73] [1994] 3 SCR 377 (SCC). [74] [1994] 3 SCR 377 (SCC) at 409–10.

[75] [1994] 3 SCR 377 (SCC) at 464.

The fiduciary powers theory provides necessary conceptual support for this view. It suggests that advisers are not fiduciaries as such. That is to say, advisers are not fiduciaries by virtue of giving advice.[76] Instead, they are fiduciaries only where they exercise discretionary power over the practical interests of their clients. In such cases, provision of advice is incidental to the exercise of discretionary power.

This is consistent with cases that have investigated the circumstances in which advisory relationships are, or may become, fiduciary. For example, in *Hodgkinson*, Justice McLachlin said that "the cases suggest that the distinguishing characteristic between advice *simpliciter* and advice giving rise to a fiduciary duty is *the ceding by one party of effective power to the other*. It is this mutual conferring and acceptance of power to the knowledge of both parties that creates the special and onerous trust obligation."[77] To much the same effect is a distinction drawn in US law between investment advisers and brokers. Investment advisers are assumed to be fiduciaries insofar as they are presumed to enjoy discretionary power in making investment decisions for clients; brokers are not assumed to be fiduciaries as it is presumed that they lack such power. Jill Fisch explains: "as a general matter, brokers do not owe broad fiduciary obligations to their customers. . . [but] special circumstances *such as investor allocation of discretionary authority* to the broker may lead to the imposition of fiduciary principles."[78] Similarly, Arthur Laby observes that "[m]any courts adhere to a general rule that brokers are not subject to fiduciary duties unless they have investment discretion over an account."[79]

The fiduciary powers theory may assist in the resolution of debate over the fiduciary character of particular kinds of advisory relationships. Fiduciary characterization of doctor–patient relationships has, for example, proven to be highly controversial.[80] The fiduciary powers theory provides a basis upon which to differentiate amongst doctor–patient relationships. Where services to be performed are such that the doctor must seek authorization to act on the patient (eg, to perform an invasive procedure) and this will necessarily require her to exercise independent judgment, the doctor is a fiduciary. However, where the doctor's role is limited to providing information to enable the *patient* to exercise independent judgment or where the doctor provides information to a third party she exercises no power per se and is not a fiduciary.

B. Confidants as fiduciaries

It is also commonly suggested that confidants are or should be considered fiduciaries. Sometimes this is a matter of semantic slippage,[81] "confidence" being understood as

[76] Save for the rare circumstance in which the advisee is so epistemically dependent on the adviser that he is incapable of exercising independent judgment in determining how to act in reliance on the advice. In cases characterized by total reliance the adviser enjoys *effective* discretionary power over the advisee; though there is no formal cession of capacity the advisee's exercise of it is effectively determined by the advice given.

[77] [1994] 3 SCR 377 (SCC) at 466 (emphasis supplied).

[78] Fisch (n 72) at 1094–5.

[79] Arthur Laby, "Fiduciary Obligations of Broker-Dealers," 55 *Vill L Rev* 701, 704–5 (2010). See also Donald C Langevoort, "Brokers as Fiduciaries," 71 *U Pitt L Rev* 439 (2010).

[80] *Norberg v Wynrib* (n 32); *Breen v Williams* (n 7); Peter Bartlett, "Doctors as Fiduciaries: Equitable Regulation of the Doctor-Patient Relationship," 5 *Mod LR* 193 (1997).

[81] See generally Dennis Klinck, "Things of Confidence: Loyalty, Secrecy and Fiduciary Obligation," 54 *Sask L Rev* 73 (1990).

synonymous with "trust" or "reliance."[82] To place confidence in another in this sense is to trust another with some interest one cares about and/or to rely upon them to have a certain attitude to, or inclination to act in a certain way toward, you. For present purposes, I am interested in the distinct suggestion that relationships of confidence are fiduciary, where "confidence" consists in the disclosure and knowing receipt of confidential information. A number of courts and commentators have suggested that confidants in this sense are fiduciaries.[83] And here, too, the characterization seems supportable on the basis of loose comparisons. A confidant, like a trustee, has access to a "resource" (information) that "belongs" to someone else. Furthermore, relationships of confidence, like many fiduciary relationships, involve trust or engender dependence. Nevertheless, others have insisted that confidants are *not* fiduciaries.[84]

The fiduciary powers theory may assist in the resolution of this controversy as well. As was true of advisers, it suggests that confidants are not fiduciaries as such; ie, by virtue of their knowing receipt of information disclosed in confidence. Rather, confidants are fiduciaries wherever they happen to wield discretionary power relative to the practical interests of a person who might also have made a disclosure of confidential information. Invariably, where the exercise of power entails disclosure and use of confidential information, fiduciary regulation of power will constrain the handling of the information. But these consequences are incidental.

It should be recognized that fiduciaries are often in receipt of confidential information.[85] Indeed, disclosure of such information is effectively necessary for proper discharge of some fiduciary mandates. Nevertheless, as a conceptual matter, the disclosure and receipt of confidential information does nothing to alter the basis for considering a relationship to be fiduciary. One is a fiduciary by virtue of one's possession of fiduciary power, regardless of whether the mandate under which one receives such power, or

[82] Klinck (n 81) at 77–9, citing by way of illustration, *Billage v Southee* (1852) 9 Hare 534, 540 (68 ER 623) (Ch), in which Sir George Turner said: "No part of the jurisdiction of the Court is more useful than that which it exercises in watching and controlling transactions between persons standing in a relation of confidence to each other. . . The jurisdiction is founded on the principle of correcting abuses of confidence and I shall have no hesitation in saying that it ought to be applied, whatever may be the nature of the confidence reposed or the relation of the parties between whom it has subsisted I take the principle to be one of universal application, and the cases in which the jurisdiction has been exercised—thus of trustee and cestui que trust—guardian and ward—attorney and client—surgeon and patient—to be merely instances of the application of the principle."

[83] See *Lac Minerals* (n 26) per Wilson J (according to whom a fiduciary relationship was established between two companies negotiating toward a joint venture on the basis of disclosure of confidential information relating to the venture by one party to the other); Finn (n 11) at 36 "[disclosure of] confidential information. . . will attract fiduciary law's protection in Commonwealth jurisdictions provided the circumstances are such as to give rise to a duty of confidence;" R A Brait, "The Unauthorized Use of Confidential Information," 18 *Can Bus LJ* 323, 336 (1991); Robert Flannigan, "The Fiduciary Obligation," 9 *Oxford J Legal Stud* 285, 286 (1989); and Daniel Bayliss, "Breach of Confidence as a Breach of Fiduciary Obligations: A Theory," 9 *Auck U L Rev* 702 (2000).

[84] See *Lac Minerals* (n 26) per Sopinka J (dissenting) at 600: "the fact that confidential information is obtained and misused cannot of itself create a fiduciary obligation;" R G Hammond, "Is Breach of Confidence Properly Analyzed in Fiduciary Terms?," 25 *McGill LJ* 244 (1979); and Tamar Frankel, "Fiduciary Law," 71 *Cal L Rev* 795, 825 (1983): explaining that "[t]rust and confidence alone are not grounds for imposing fiduciary duties on the confidant," citing *Vai v Bank of America* (1961) 56 Cal 2d 329, 337–8.

[85] See Klinck (n 81) at 80: "Fiduciaries often are given, or are placed in a position that gives them access to, information."

circumstances in which one exercises it, also happen to involve disclosure of confidential information.

C. Public officials as fiduciaries

Thus far, we have been considering the fiduciary relationship as a distinctive kind of private law relationship. This is appropriate enough, for fiduciary duties are first and foremost a manifestation of private right. They govern the administration of certain private institutions and relationships in civil society. Nevertheless, one might wonder whether, and if so under what circumstances, public officials might be fiduciaries.

There is a large and growing body of work in public law theory that argues that public officials are fiduciaries.[86] The argument has been developed in different ways. For example, Evan Criddle claims that the administrative state is inherently fiduciary and that principles of administrative law may be usefully reinterpreted in this light.[87] Teddy Rave argues that politicians should be considered fiduciaries and thus be prohibited from gerrymandering.[88] Sung Hui Kim argues that the fiduciary nature of political representation entails limits on Congressional insider trading.[89] Ethan Leib contends that judges are fiduciaries and that this has important implications for our understanding of principles of adjudication, judicial ethics, and the place of the judiciary in democratic government.[90] Evan Fox-Decent provides a richly developed argument that all manner of public officials are fiduciaries in his book, *Sovereignty's Promise*.[91] Fox-Decent argues that public officials are fiduciaries insofar as the execution of official functions rests on an assertion of sovereign power that can only be understood as legitimate if conditioned in fiduciary terms.[92]

Claims that public officials are fiduciaries have met with some skepticism. As Fox-Decent explains, "[m]any common law courts have shown considerable reluctance to characterize as fiduciary the relationship between front-line decision-makers and the individuals subject to them."[93] For instance, in *Harris v Canada*, Dawson J held that a federal Minister could not be a fiduciary lest he face conflicting and irreconcilable duties to multiple beneficiaries.[94] More recently, in *Alberta v Elder Advocates of Alberta Society*, McLachlin CJ stated that: "the special characteristics of governmental responsibilities and functions mean that governments will owe fiduciary duties only in limited

[86] Though prominent private law scholars have also argued that public officials are fiduciaries. See Paul Finn, "The Forgotten 'Trust': The People and the State," in M Cope (ed), *Equity: Issues and Trends* (1995) and Frankel (n 4).

[87] Evan J Criddle, "Fiduciary Foundations of Administrative Law," 54 *UCLA L Rev* 117 (2006).

[88] D Theodore Rave, "Politicians as Fiduciaries," 126 *Harv L Rev* 671 (2013).

[89] Sung H Kim, "The Last Temptation of Congress: Legislator Insider Trading and the Fiduciary Norm against Corruption," 98 *Cornell L Rev* 845 (2013).

[90] Ethan J Leib, David L Ponet, and Michael Serota, "A Fiduciary Theory of Judging," 101 *Cal L Rev* 699 (2013).

[91] Fox-Decent (n 32).

[92] Relying on Wilson J's analysis of fiduciary relationships in *Frame v Smith*, Fox-Decent argues more specifically that public officials are fiduciaries to the extent that they: (a) wield power; (b) relative to practical interests of other persons; (c) in circumstances in which those other persons are vulnerable in the sense of being incapable of exercising or controlling the power; (d) and thus in circumstances characterized by presumed trust; (n 32) at 89–112.

[93] Fox-Decent (n 32) at 152.

[94] 2001 FCR 1408 (FCTD).

and special circumstances"[95] and further that "no fiduciary duty is owed to the public as a whole."[96] The Chief Justice reiterated concerns voiced by Dawson J in *Harris*, reasoning that imposing a duty of loyalty on the state would be "inherently at odds with its duty to act in the best interests of society as a whole, and its obligation to spread limited resources among competing groups with equally valid claims to its assistance."[97]

The decisions in *Harris* and *Elder Advocates* reflect a perceived problem of translation from private to public law; namely, how to reconcile public officials' duty to be responsive to the diverse (and often conflicting) interests of all citizens with a duty of loyalty giving rise to a private right of action by individual citizens demanding special consideration of *their* interests. This problem, though real, misses the mark. It is rarely argued that the fiduciary constitution of public office is such that it generates private law duties, breach of which may give rise to a private right of action. Public law theorists instead argue that recognition that public officials are fiduciaries offers valuable interpretive and normative perspectives on established principles of public law (eg, constraints on administrative discretion) or positions of public policy (eg, limiting gerrymandering). To the extent that private law rights and duties are discussed at all, it is to suggest that public law principles are animated by cognate concerns (eg, the concern over self-interested abuse of power).

As was true of our hard cases in private law, uncertainty over the appropriateness of characterizing public officials as fiduciaries is hard to resolve without clarity on the nature of the fiduciary relationship itself.[98] Under the fiduciary powers theory, it is important to distinguish two ways in which public officials may be thought to be fiduciaries. First, a public official might be said to be a fiduciary of an individual or defined group in just the way that ordinary private fiduciaries are, with the implication that private law duties enforceable by private right of action apply to the official. Second, one might say that a public official is a *sui generis* fiduciary of the public given the nature of the relationship between the state and its people. This kind of claim does not necessarily imply that public officials are subject to private law duties. Rather, it may instead be that the fiduciary character of public office informs existing principles of public law (enforceable, if at all, in the usual ways). An advantage of the fiduciary powers theory is that it permits us to make this distinction and to evaluate each claim about the fiduciary character of public office in its own right.

[95] [2011] 2 SCR 261 (SCC) at para 37. [96] [2011] 2 SCR 261 (SCC) at para 50.

[97] [2011] 2 SCR 261 (SCC) at para 44. The perceived inconsistency between public mandates and the duty of loyalty may be attributable in part to an overly narrow view of judges about the content of the duty of loyalty. See Andrew Gold, "The Loyalties of Fiduciary Law," in this volume. See also Andrew Gold, "Reflections on the State as Fiduciary," 63 *U Toronto LJ* 655 (2013).

[98] Many who claim that public officials are fiduciaries say very little about fiduciary relationships in general. However, Fox-Decent offers a particularly detailed account of the nature of the fiduciary relationship. We agree that the fiduciary relationship involves exercise of discretionary power by one person relative to another. However, there are important differences in our accounts. We both understand fiduciary power as a form of authority, but Fox-Decent has not argued that fiduciary power is rooted in the concept of legal personality. At times, he appears to suggest that fiduciary authority may be in the form of factual or legal power. I also believe that some of the characteristics Fox-Decent ascribes to fiduciary power are inessential (eg, its allegedly administrative and institutional nature). Furthermore, Fox-Decent suggests that trust and vulnerability are amongst the definitive properties of the fiduciary relationship, and that they are pertinent to the legal justification for fiduciary duties, both propositions that I resist.

The court in *Elder Advocates* was surely right to deny that the state is in general a fiduciary of the public in the ordinary sense; ie, in a relationship giving rise to private law duties enforceable by way of a private right of action. That does not mean that public officials are not *sui generis* fiduciaries of the public. But for the moment, let us consider when public officials might be fiduciaries in the ordinary sense. *Elder Advocates* clearly contemplates that there will be such cases. McLachlin CJ said that: "generally speaking, a strong correspondence with one of the traditional categories of fiduciary relationship. . . is a precondition to finding an implied fiduciary duty on the government."[99] She also explained that an aggrieved beneficiary must establish "a specific *private law* interest to which the person has a pre-existing distinct and complete legal entitlement."[100] Finally, and most intriguingly, she held that the power wielded by the state relative to the beneficiary must of a direct nature:

> [T]he degree of control exerted by the government over the interest in question must be equivalent or analogous to *direct administration of that interest* before a fiduciary relationship can be said to arise. The type of legal control over an interest that arises from the ordinary exercise of statutory powers does not suffice. Otherwise, fiduciary obligations would arise in most day to day government functions making general action for the public good difficult or almost impossible.[101]

These conditions are consistent with the fiduciary powers theory of the fiduciary relationship. A public official may be a fiduciary of an individual or defined group only where the official enjoys discretionary power directly in relation to the practical interests of that individual or group. In these cases, the official must have undertaken powers identical in kind to those held by private fiduciaries. These powers, again, are in the nature of legal capacities ordinarily derived from the legal personality of a *particular individual* beneficiary or benefactor (or *group* of same). Fiduciary powers in this sense are not capacities associated with the *sui generis* legal personality of the state (ie, its legislative, administrative, police, or judicial powers). Rather, they are powers of legal personality *simpliciter* (eg, capacities to make, vary, or enforce contracts, to manage, alienate, or invest property, and so on). Ordinarily, these powers are conferred on private persons acting as fiduciaries. However, in certain instances, the state might assume them. For instance, the state might undertake powers on trust to administer lands for aboriginal bands;[102] it might act as executor or trustee of last resort, administering property of those who die intestate or fail to make a valid appointment of an executor or trustee; it might undertake powers to invest pension funds for veterans;[103] or it might undertake powers of guardianship over children abandoned by or removed from their families.[104]

This suggests that there is nothing distinctively *public* about certain mandates undertaken by public officials. A public official just might undertake powers relative to specific individuals or groups that have an inherently fiduciary character. The state in these cases acts as trustee, agent, executor, or guardian. Where it does so, it may exercise

[99] [2011] 2 SCR 261 (SCC) at para 47. [100] [2011] 2 SCR 261 (SCC) at para 51.
[101] [2011] 2 SCR 261 (SCC) at para 53. [102] *Guerin v The Queen* (n 25).
[103] *Authorson v Canada (Attorney General)* (2002) 58 OR (3d) 417; rev'd (on other grounds) 2003 SCC 39.
[104] *KLB v British Columbia* [2003] 2 SCR 403 (SCC).

certain prerogative powers of the state (eg, in asserting jurisdiction over neglected or abused children), but the *fiduciary* powers are indistinguishable from those wielded by private fiduciaries. Being held for, and wielded relative to, a defined individual or group, the state owes ordinary private law duties to act in the interests of the individual or group in the exercise of its fiduciary powers.

Let us now turn to the claim that public offices are *inherently* fiduciary. We have established that fiduciary power is a kind of authority in the form of legal capacities derived from the *legal personality* of an ordinary person. As just noted, the state can and does from time to time undertake power in this sense. Might we say that public officials in general are fiduciaries to the extent that exercise of official functions invariably entails exercise of capacities inherent in the legal personality of the *state*? While this line of argument seems promising, it presents one obvious problem. The personality of the state is *sui generis*. The personality of the state parallels that of private persons to the extent that (a) it consists of certain legal capacities and (b) some of these capacities are the very capacities that individuals have. However, the parallels are limited. The state is, in addition to powers of ordinary personality, possessed of powers of a fundamentally different character. These are *powers of statehood* that permit the state to function as such; ie, as an organization capable of making, giving, and enforcing law. The basic categories of powers of statehood bespeak the distinctiveness of the personality of the state. They include legislative powers (ie, the power to make laws of general application), administrative powers (eg, the power to administer the state through bureaucracy and to administer revenue-generating and benefit-conferring programs), enforcement powers (ie, the power to ensure compliance with laws through policing and prosecution), and judicial powers (eg, the power to adjudicate civil, criminal, and other legal matters). If public offices are inherently fiduciary, it cannot be because powers of statehood are identical to powers of ordinary personality. This being so, it is necessary to consider the extent to which powers of statehood and ordinary personality share common properties.

Proper exploration of these commonalities will be intricate; it calls for more nuanced analysis of the concepts of ordinary and state personality than I am able to provide here. Nevertheless, a plausible line of argument might emphasize that both kinds of power are ultimately rooted in parallel forms of legal personality that reflect individuals' capacity for self-determination. Powers of ordinary personality are the means by which individuals are self-determining in law; ie, by which they may fix and pursue their own ends and are recognized as responsible as such. Powers of statehood relate to the capacity of individuals to demand establishment of a rightful condition through the person of the state. To the extent that the personality and authority of the state must be understood as derived ultimately from our moral capacity for self-determination, powers of statehood may well be of a kind with powers of ordinary personality. Both forms of power are essentially representative in character. They are held on the footing that they are to be exercised for and on behalf of another and in their interests alone.

Conclusion

Fiduciary liability is premised on the nature of the relationship between the fiduciary and beneficiary. However, leading scholars have suggested that it is meaningless to talk of *fiduciary relationships* as such; the fiduciary relationship is not a distinctive and coherent general kind of legal relationship. An implication is that fiduciary principles can, and must, be understood in abstraction from analysis of general characteristics of the relationships in which they arise.

I have here argued that this view is wrong. The fiduciary relationship is a distinctive and coherent general kind of legal relationship. It is definable. Furthermore, it is important that it be defined, given the central role played by the construct in the conceptual structure of fiduciary law.

Beyond arguing that the fiduciary relationship is definable, and that it should be defined, I have here offered my own definition and associated theory of the fiduciary relationship. The fiduciary powers theory suggests that the essential characteristic of all fiduciary relationships is possession by the fiduciary of discretionary power over the practical interests of the beneficiary. Fiduciary power takes the form of legal capacities derived from the legal personality of persons (ordinarily, the personality of a person other than the fiduciary—a beneficiary, or a third-party benefactor). I have shown that the fiduciary powers theory can explain the presumptive fiduciary character of relationships of recognized fiduciary status, and that it promises to advance debates over the fiduciary character of other relationships. However, perhaps the most important demonstration of the value of the fiduciary powers theory—its capacity to support a unified theory of fiduciary law—must await further analysis of the significance of fiduciary relationships in fiduciary law.

4

Managing Our Money

The Law of Financial Fiduciaries as a Private Law Institution

*Hanoch Dagan and Sharon Hannes**

Introduction

Courts and commentators invoke fiduciary duties in rather divergent contexts, that is, with respect to a diverse range of relationships, from the most intimate (parents and children) to the most commercial (directors and corporations), with numerous other categories in between (think lawyers, physicians, agents, trustees, guardians, etc).[1] This chapter focuses on one type of fiduciary: those who manage our money.[2] The typical example of a financial fiduciary is the professional trustee, but some financial fiduciaries are neither professional nor trustees.[3] Financial fiduciaries are responsible for people's savings, pensions, and bequeathable fortunes. Their relationships with the beneficiaries of these enormous amounts of money—it is estimated that as much as $14 trillion are managed by the trustees of the US pension funds system alone[4]—warrant special attention even if our conclusions turn out to be inapplicable to the other (also important, to be sure) types of fiduciary relationships.

Like other fiduciaries, financial fiduciaries are bound by a duty of loyalty, which is oftentimes (justifiably) treated as a (if not the) defining characteristic of fiduciary law overall.[5] If they are found in breach of this duty, they are required to disgorge their profits, a remedy that is also viewed as characterizing this area of law.[6] But while both the core

* Our thanks to Rick Brooks, Deborah DeMott, Avihay Dorfman, Andrew Gold, Matthew Harding, Ron Harris, Adam Hofri-Winogradow, Shelly Kreiczer-Levy, Roy Kreitner, Shay Lavie, Amir Licht, Yoram Margalioth, Daniel Markovits, Paul Miller, Ariel Porat, Irit Samet, Rob Sitkoff, and Stewart Sterk for helpful comments, to Osher Ben-Ami, Dana Goldstein, and Guy Goldstein for their research assistance, and to the Cegla Center for Interdisciplinary Research of the Law for financial support.

1 See, eg, Paul B Miller, "Justifying Fiduciary Duties," 58 *McGill LJ* 969, 971 (2013).

2 As the text implies, we narrowly circumscribe the ambit of our inquiry around money managers and invoke corporate fiduciaries only for purposes of comparison.

3 Examples of financial fiduciaries who are not trustees are executors, conservators, receivers, and trustees in bankruptcy (who are not trustees despite their title). *Restatement (Third) of Trust* § 5 (1992).

4 See Federal Reserve Statistical Release, Flow of Funds Accounts of the United States 113 (6 Dec. 2012), available at <http://www.federalreserve.gov/releases/z1/Current/z1.pdf>. We acknowledge that a subset of these pension account holders make some of their own investment decisions. But on the other hand, while the funds managed by pension trustees are probably the largest component of all funds held by trustees, there are other funds managed by financial fiduciaries, the composition and amounts of which are much less transparent. In any event, we note by comparison that the value of all corporate shares held directly by US households stands at about $9 trillion, and the market value of US households' real estate is estimated at $17 trillion against which there are $9.5 trillion in mortgages.

5 See, eg, Ernest J Weinrib, "The Fiduciary Obligation," 25 *U Toronto LJ* 1, 16 (1975).

6 See, eg, Hanoch Dagan, *The Law and Ethics of Restitution* (2004) 237.

content of the fiduciary relationship and its potential remedial implications are undisputed, the normative underpinnings of this body of law as well as many specific doctrinal issues, including the precise contents of the duty of loyalty, are far from being settled. (Another controversy, which we set aside here for reasons that will be clarified shortly, is whether we should think of fiduciary law as property-like, contract-like, or *sui generis*.)

We contend that the law of financial fiduciaries is a private law institution aimed at enhancing people's autonomy by allowing them to safely delegate to others (typically specialists) authority over a significant aspect of their welfarist interests.[7] In this chapter, we hope to explain why we find this conception of the relationship normatively attractive, to show how it accommodates the most convincing insights of other approaches to the field, and to explore the ways in which our account both elucidates important aspects of doctrine and offers some critical bite, namely: it reaffirms certain disputed rules and suggests the reform of others.

Section I sketches briefly the conceptual and normative framework of our inquiry: the construction of private law as a diverse set of institutions designed to empower people's ability to be the authors of their lives. Section II extracts some building blocks for our theory from the existing literature on fiduciary law: private law formalists helpfully insist that we understand fiduciary law as part of private law and that we focus accordingly on the parties' relationships and their rights and duties; lawyer economists, in turn, helpfully remind us that the main good people seek in having other people manage their money is utilitarian in nature; and moralists helpfully highlight both the material and expressive roles of the duty of loyalty in cultivating the intricate relationship such a delegation of authority entails.

Armed with these insights, we proceed, in Section III, to develop our own theory: we articulate and defend an animating principle of the law of financial fiduciaries, consider its prescriptions, and discuss its doctrinal implications. We argue that enabling the safe delegation of management of our money is autonomy enhancing because it allows people to enlist others for this increasingly complex task and focus their time and attention on their intrinsically valuable projects. We further explain how the *telos* of enabling the reliable delegation of money management entails a delicate balance between material effects (emphasized by lawyer economists) and expressive ones (highlighted by moralists). Financial fiduciaries law must be attuned to the complicated incentive structure generated by the peculiar mission of managing other people's money, which implies a discretionary authority that is particularly susceptible to both carelessness and abuse. But in addition to tailoring optimal incentives, the law of financial fiduciaries should also aim at ingraining a moral vocabulary epitomized by the loyalty injunction, for the cultural perception of financial fiduciaries as the quintessential figures of the ethical subject as economic subject[8] has a significant, if instrumental, role in the functioning of this private law institution.

[7] To be sure, unlike private law purists, we do not claim that concerns that are external to the pertinent parties are never legitimate considerations for private law. See Hanoch Dagan, *Reconstructing American Legal Realism & Rethinking Private Law Theory* (2013) ch 5. Considering whether the macroeconomic or distributive consequences of financial fiduciaries law pass the threshold of legitimacy in this respect is beyond the scope of this chapter. Cf Joshua Getzler, "'As If:' Accountability and Counterfactual Trust," 91 *BUL Rev* 973, 975–6 (2012).

[8] See Ritu Birla, *Stages of Capital: Law, Culture, and Market Governance in Late Colonial India* (2009) 71.

Translating these prescriptions into legal technology can explain and justify the traditional structure of loyalty doctrine in fiduciary law, composed as it is of the strict sole interest rule and a long list of exceptions and exemptions. More critically, our analysis demonstrates that in order to properly shape financial fiduciaries' investment policies, and thus the content of their duty of care, lawmakers should reexamine the traditional fiduciary fee structure and, we further insist, fiduciary pay should be treated as an exception to the duty of loyalty and be carefully scrutinized and periodically reassessed. Finally, under our account, although rules of financial fiduciaries law should not be mandatory, they should be shaped as sticky defaults that are tilted towards serving relatively weak and unsophisticated beneficiaries (or settlors).

I. Structural Pluralism in Private Law[9]

Private law theorists typically strive to formulate broad and unified normative theories of property, contracts, torts, and restitution. These structurally monist accounts suggest that there is one regulative principle—one value or one particular balance of values—that underlies (or should underlie) the various doctrines in these complex legal fields. Structural pluralism challenges this dominant paradigm; it embraces the vast heterogeneity of private law and celebrates the multiple forms characterizing its landscape. Multiplicity, under this approach, is neither a symptom of disorder nor a source of confusion. Quite the contrary: what looks like a random mess from a monist viewpoint, which struggles to pigeonhole the entire terrain of a heterogeneous field (property, contracts, and the like) into one regulative principle, is a rich mosaic from the perspective of structural pluralism. And this mosaic is indispensable for people's autonomy.

To see why, consider the conception of autonomy as self-authorship, under which people should, to some degree, be the authors of their own lives, choosing among worthwhile life plans with the ability to pursue those choices. As Joseph Raz explains, autonomy requires not only appropriate mental abilities and independence, but also "an adequate range of options." Whereas a wide spectrum of sets of social forms is available in societies pursuing the ideal of autonomy, autonomy "cannot be obtained within societies which support social forms which do not leave enough room for individual choice." For autonomy to be meaningful (other things being equal), there must be "more valuable options than can be chosen, and they must be significantly different," so that choices entail "tradeoffs, which require relinquishing one good for the sake of another." Thus, because autonomy underscores "the value of a large number of greatly differing pursuits among which individuals are free to choose," valuing autonomy inevitably "leads to the endorsement of moral pluralism."[10]

Given the variety of acceptable human goods from which autonomous people should be able to choose, the state must recognize a sufficiently diverse set of robust frameworks through which people can organize their lives. And because many of these goods

[9] This section draws on Hanoch Dagan, "Pluralism and Perfectionism in Private Law," 112 *Colum L Rev* 1409 (2012). For an application in property law and a preliminary one in contracts, see Hanoch Dagan, *Property: Values and Institutions* (2011); Hanoch Dagan, "Autonomy, Pluralism, and Contract Law Theory," 76 *Law & Contemp Probs* 19 (2013) [hereinafter Dagan, "Contract Theory"].

[10] Joseph Raz, *The Morality of Freedom* (1986) 372, 381, 395, 398–9.

cannot be realistically actualized without the active support of viable legal institutions, private law should ensure a wide range of such facilitative institutions.[11] Hence, private law should incorporate more than one set of principles and, consequently, more than one set of coherent doctrines; it should include, for each major category of human activity or interaction, sufficiently diverse types of institutions, each governed by a distinct regulative principle (namely, a different value or different balance of values); the boundaries between these institutions must be open to enable people to freely choose their goals, principles, forms of life, and associations.

Proactively facilitating the multiplicity of private law through such structural pluralism curbs law's power without undermining its normativity. The combination of the seemingly mundane ability of the law's carriers to recruit the state's monopolized power to enforce their judgments and the institutional and discursive features that tend to downplay law's coercive power mandates wariness of assigning much power to lawmakers who, as human beings, can make mistakes and, at times, even prefer their self-interest to the public good. A commitment to structural pluralism follows this injunction, because it opens up alternatives for choice rather than channeling everyone to the one possibility privileged by law. A pluralist private law regime thus allows individuals to navigate their course so as to bypass certain legal prescriptions, avoiding their implications and, hence, the power of those who have issued them.

Structural pluralism's acute attention to the power of law does not lead it to neglect law's normativity.[12] Quite the contrary: a structurally pluralist private law is profoundly normative. Each one of its categories encompasses a set of precise rules and informative standards that are shaped by a distinct regulative principle. Although many of these rules and standards function—as they should in an autonomy-based private law regime—as defaults, the frameworks of social interaction and cooperation that private law facilitates are necessarily limited in number and their contents relatively standardized. These features enable private law not only to consolidate people's expectations regarding the core types of human relationships, but also to express the law's normative ideals for these types of social interaction.

Structural pluralism advocates a major shift in private law theory, which informs this chapter: that rather than searching for unifying normative accounts of property, contracts, torts, restitution, and, for that matter, fiduciary law in their entirety, we should redirect our efforts towards reviving the inquiry of the specific private law institutions. Accordingly, the main task of private law theory is to distil the distinct human ideals embodied in the various private law institutions and elucidate how each of those institutions contributes to human flourishing. To be sure, with many private law institutions, the law often falls short of the human ideals their regulative principle purports to represent. But rather than challenging structural pluralism, these discrepancies highlight its practical significance as a source of critique and reform that can force private

[11] Indeed, while structural pluralism is animated by private law's commitment to one value—personal autonomy—this value requires law to not only tolerate, but rather actively facilitate, the institutional infrastructure necessary for the pursuit of a variety of values. See text accompanying n 74.

[12] This accommodation of law's power and normativity is one manifestation of structural pluralism's reliance on the legal realist conception of law. See Dagan (n 7) at chs 1, 8, 9.

law institutions to live up to their implicit promises and push lawmakers to craft innovative private law institutions.

II. New Lessons from the Received Wisdoms

Our understanding of fiduciary law fits squarely within the structural pluralist conception of private law. For us, the law of financial fiduciaries is a private law institution aimed at expanding people's autonomy by allowing them to safely delegate to others (typically specialists) authority over a significant part of their welfarist interests. As with other private law institutions, fleshing out the regulative principle of fiduciary law can enhance our understanding of this important body of law while pointing to ways to reform it. But before we outline this understanding and investigate its doctrinal implications, it is worthwhile visiting three perspectives on fiduciary law. Although we do not endorse any of these accounts, each provides useful building blocks for our own theory.

A. Formalism

Paul Miller has developed a sophisticated account of the "juridical justification" of fiduciary duties and fiduciary remedies. Miller's theory does not look at fiduciary law as an "object of justification." Rather, it "treats the juridical character of [fiduciary law] as a source. . . of justification," seeking to "reveal" the "internal principle of organization" embedded in this "juridical concept or form" of liability.[13] As such, Miller claims, his formal account "implies nothing beyond the normative coherence of [a given basis] of private liability,"[14] yet it does, he insists, "enjoy analytical priority over philosophical justification."[15]

Miller argues that "fiduciary duties are distinctive and supported by reasons derived from formal properties of the fiduciary relationship."[16] He defines a fiduciary relationship as "one in which one party (the fiduciary) exercises discretionary power over the significant practical interests of another (the beneficiary)."[17] More specifically, fiduciary power, which is "the constitutive characteristic of the fiduciary relationship," is "a form of authority derived from capacities constitutive of the *legal personality*" of another person (typically the beneficiary). This authority applies to a variety of "objects of decision-making ordinarily within the exclusive legal capacity of the person granting authority to the fiduciary," ranging from "aspects of personality of corporate or natural persons who lack legal capacity" to matters of rights or welfare of corporate and natural persons. In all these matters, "[p]ower is vested in fiduciaries to enable them to act for or on behalf of beneficiaries or to otherwise serve their interests," rendering "rightful conduct that would otherwise be wrongful." This fiduciary authority has three important qualities: it is "*discretionary* in nature," allowing "latitude for judgment by the person invested with authority in determining its exercise"; it is "*relational*" to "a specific

[13] Paul B Miller, "Justifying Fiduciary Remedies," 63 *U Toronto LJ* 570, 582 (2013).
[14] Miller (n 1) at 1008. [15] Miller (n 13) at 584. [16] Miller (n 1) at 1023.
[17] Paul B Miller, "A Theory of Fiduciary Liability," 56 *McGill LJ* 235, 262 (2011).

individual or group" and "*derivative*" of the legal capacities of others; and it is "*specific*," as opposed to "plenary."[18]

These "formal properties of the fiduciary relationship" explain Miller's understanding of fiduciary power as "a capacity integral to the legal personality of another;" they also underlie, for him, both the content and function of the duty of loyalty. Fiduciary power legitimates "a limited form of legal substitution" by enabling the fiduciary to exercise "legal capacities of the beneficiary or those of a benefactor." This means that "the fiduciary relationship has an asymmetrical formal structure," with the fiduciary occupying the "dominant position," thereby setting up dependence and vulnerability to misuse (or careless exercise) of authority as inherent features of the relationship. Furthermore, "[t]he purpose for which fiduciary power is held" is also "implicit in [this] substitutive nature." Fiduciary power "enables one person to act purposively on behalf of another." More importantly (at least for us), "[t]he ability to confer fiduciary power... enhances [one's] ability to effectively pursue her purposes, for it enables her to draw upon a fiduciary's means (e.g., skills, knowledge, experience, professional licensure) in the exercise of her capacities."[19]

The substitutive nature of the fiduciary relationship justifies, Miller contends, both the fiduciary obligation and the typical consequence of its breach. Being "an extension of the legal personality of the person from whose capacity it is derived," fiduciary power should be treated as a means "derived from or devoted to the beneficiary" and, thus, "belonging rightfully" and "exclusively" to the beneficiary and "held for advancement of [her] ends alone."[20] The duty of loyalty "secures this status" of fiduciary power "by proscribing its appropriation by the fiduciary,"[21] thereby ensuring that the beneficiary's claim over fiduciary power is "exclusive."[22] In other words, because this claim derives from the beneficiary's personality, fiduciary disloyalty "entails exploitation in the sense of a person being treated as a mere means." This is, Miller asserts, the rationale for the harsh disgorgement remedy typifying fiduciary law. A fiduciary who "receives unauthorized profit from the exercise of fiduciary power" is treating that power as "a means of her own." This violation of the beneficiary's exclusive entitlement "necessarily extends to gains associated" with the fiduciary's exercise of this power, because these gains "belong" to the beneficiary "as an incident of its exclusive claim over the powers constitutive of [her] personality." Thus, disgorgement simply vindicates the beneficiary's right by restoring to her "gains to which she was entitled by virtue of [that] right and [its] juridical justification."[23]

Miller argues that the explanatory force of his theory is boosted by its ability to account for hard cases in which full disgorgement is currently available although "the wrong done is merely technical." For example, Miller accepts the applicability of the conflicts rule even where a fiduciary acts "in, and because of, a genuine belief that in so doing she is [serving] the best interests of the beneficiary." Although the fiduciary's "salutary motivation" may be "morally and practically significant," it properly bears no legal significance since the no-conflicts rule is not concerned with "potentially adverse outcomes," but is rather grounded on the beneficiary's exclusive ownership of "the

[18] Miller (n 1) at 1013.
[19] Miller (n 1) at 1019.
[20] Miller (n 1) at 1020.
[21] Miller (n 1) at 1021.
[22] Miller (n 13) at 611.
[23] Miller (n 13) at 617.

power acted upon through judgment." Similarly, Miller endorses the strict application of disgorgement where "the fiduciary profits from a conflict but causes no harm to, or [even] achieves a good outcome for, the beneficiary," because "outcomes are immaterial to the beneficiary's *legal entitlement* to [these] profits," which is "rooted in his exclusive claim over fiduciary power as a means." In the same vein, Miller argues that his theory nicely explains why the conflict of interest rule focuses on personal interests that "arise during the execution of the mandate" and not on the fiduciary's "interests in compensation," which "are determined before the mandate is undertaken on the understanding that the interests of the beneficiary will govern its execution." Although he realizes that remuneration arrangements may be structured in a way that generates a conflict, Miller seems content with the conventional view under which they are not covered by the conflicts rule.[24]

Miller mentions (almost in passing) the autonomy-enhancing function of the fiduciary relationship, but his juridical analysis does not rely on this *telos*. Rather, the engine of his account is the claim that the beneficiary *necessarily* holds a "sole and despotic dominion"[25]—to use Blackstone's conception of property, which Miller repeatedly invokes as analogy[26]—over fiduciary power. And the reason for the alleged necessity of the beneficiary's exclusivity lies, in his view, in the nature of that power as an extension of the beneficiary's personality.

Miller's claim seems to rest on the presupposition that whereas in certain categories of fiduciary law the fiduciary's authority relates to welfarist interests of the beneficiary, in others it implicates "matters of rights" and "aspects of personality." Should, indeed, all of these very different interests have been necessarily lumped together, a "leveling up" of the beneficiary's claim to the fiduciary power might have been required to prevent the use of the beneficiary's person as a means to the fiduciary's ends. Exclusivity could have then been safely regarded as conceptually necessary. But there is in fact no need—certainly not an a priori one—to assume that the delegation of all these interests is governed by a sole regulative principle.[27] Rather, the substantive differences among the types of interests at hand could justify divergent treatment; fiduciary law could encompass, as structural pluralism prescribes, a number of distinct private law institutions.[28] And once we limit our focus to welfarist interests, there is no longer a conceptual necessity to perceive the beneficiary's entitlement to the fiduciary power as exclusive.[29] Certainly, this conclusion does not suggest that beneficiaries are *not* exclusively entitled to the fiduciary's power or that the specific rules Miller discusses are *necessarily* wrong. But the failure of the attempt to derive the content of the duty of loyalty and the implications of disloyalty from the duty's juridical form means that these propositions should not be taken as a given. Moreover, caution is also called for regarding Miller's celebration of his theory's successful accounting for rules that seem

24 Miller (n 13) at 606.
25 William Blackstone, *Commentaries on the Laws of England* (1765–9; 1979 edn) vol 2, *2.
26 Miller (n 1) at 998, 1006; Miller (n 13) at 611.
27 This critique applies also to Avihay Dorfman in this volume.
28 Cf Tamar Frankel, *Fiduciary Law* (2011) 8–10.
29 This critique echoes the conceptual critique of Blackstone's understanding of property. See generally Dagan (n 9) Part I.

substantively questionable, because—like other legal theories that take accepted adjudicative law as their source of justification—his theory of fiduciary law is susceptible to the "professional hazard" of apology.[30]

These faults notwithstanding, Miller's account offers two important lessons. First, although the notion that form (or juridical justification) enjoys analytical priority over substance (or normative justification)—or even that form can be analyzed while bracketing substance—is misguided, the idea that fiduciary law, typified by the structural features Miller highlights, should be analyzed within the framework of private law (rather than as a means to promote the aggregate welfare or society's overall morality) is valuable. Second, although Miller's theory improperly sets aside the *telos* of fiduciary law, it helpfully mentions the good that fiduciary law as a private law institution can advance when alluding to its autonomy-enhancing potential.

As we argue in Section III, the key to understanding the law of financial fiduciaries and guiding its proper interpretation and future development is to figure out its precise role in an autonomy-based private law and to study the ways in which it can best perform this function. In engaging in this task—and so as to avoid the "juridical trap" of over-abstraction—we need to direct some attention to the specific type of beneficiary interests on which this chapter focuses. Although our account begins with autonomy as private law's ultimate value and, thus, also the animating value of fiduciary law, we take seriously structural pluralism's dictate to shape private law institutions along the lines of the goods they offer. Insofar as welfarist types of fiduciary relationships are concerned, this means that our autonomy-based perspective is necessarily interested in—and should potentially incorporate—the economic analysis of fiduciary law.

B. Efficiency

Conventional economic analysis conceptualizes private law as a complex set of incentives for inducing potential transactors to maximize aggregate social welfare, conventionally interpreted in terms of preference satisfaction.[31] But the leading economic account of fiduciary law focuses on the micro interaction fiduciary law anticipates, rather than on its aggregate consequences, and is thus helpful for our analysis.

Frank Easterbrook and Daniel Fischel advance a contractarian view of the fiduciary relationship, which leaves no room for anything else: "Fiduciary duties are not special duties; they have no moral footing; they are the same sort of obligations... as other contractual undertakings."[32] When one person seeks the help of another to achieve a certain goal, the parties can write an explicit contract—if the task is simple enough and efforts sufficiently observable and verifiable. However, "when the task is complex, when efforts will span a substantial time, when the principal cannot measure (or evaluate) the agent's effort, when an assessment of the outcome is not a good substitute for measuring effort... a detailed contract would be silly."[33] In this world

[30] Cf Robin West, *Normative Jurisprudence: An Introduction* (2011) 26–7.
[31] See, eg, Robert Cooter and Thomas Ulen, *Law & Economics* (6th edn, 2011) 307.
[32] Frank H Easterbrook and Daniel R Fischel, "Contract and Fiduciary Duty," 36 *JL & Econ* 425, 427 (1993). See also, eg, Richard A. Posner, *Economic Analysis of Law* (3rd edn, 1986) 100–1.
[33] Easterbrook and Fischel (n 32) at 426.

of incomplete contracts,[34] where an agent's efforts and achievements are exceedingly hard to monitor, fiduciary duties replace explicit contracting. The easily observable and verifiable no-conflict rule of the duty of loyalty ensures that the agent remains committed to achieving the objectives of the contract,[35] and the duty of care ensures that she performs her role well. Most importantly, "because this process is contractual—because both the principal and agent enter this [undertaking] for gain—the details should be those that maximize that gain, which the contracting parties can divide."[36] Legal decision-makers should follow what the parties themselves would do in a world of complete contracts, by filling fiduciary duties with content that maximizes their welfare. Any effort to hold fiduciaries to a higher standard would be doomed, since "a beneficiary who does not value the new service or higher degree of loyalty at more than the cost of providing it is worse off, the opposite of the court's objective."[37] One important implication of this analysis is its strong endorsement of mutability, which explains why lawyer economists typically view the fiduciary duties as a simple garden-variety default that the parties should be able to override at will.[38]

This approach to shaping the contents of fiduciary duties explains their substantial variation across different types of fiduciary relationships. Consider the duty of care. In corporate law, the duty is quite lax. Managers make their business decisions with virtually no prospect of review for reasonableness thanks to the business judgment rule, which shields them from liability for any but the most egregious behavior.[39] In trust law, by contrast, the duty of care is quite stringent. A trustee is held to a relatively strict standard of prudence.[40] Economic analysis, by drawing on the welfare-maximization hypothetical-contracting standard, provides a rationale for this divergence. Since corporate managers are required to take on risky ventures, they must be shielded from judges' and juries' hindsight bias when their decisions turn out badly. Since shareholders want their managers to engage in such ventures, they would agree to protect them from this bias.[41] In contrast, trustees typically can diversify their trusts, so as to protect the beneficiaries, at low cost.[42] The difference in the content of these duties of care, therefore, derives from the divergent interests of the beneficiaries.

Finally, by focusing on the incentive structure typifying fiduciary relationships, the economic analysis provides a powerful justification for disgorgement as a remedy for disloyalty. As Robert Cooter and Bradley Freedman note, breaches of the duty of loyalty

[34] See generally Oliver Hart and John Moore, "Incomplete Contracts and Renegotiation," 56 *Econometrica* 755 (1988); Oliver Hart and John Moore, "Foundations of Incomplete Contracts," 66 *Rev Econ Stud* 115 (1999).

[35] See Robert Cooter and Bradley J Freedman, "The Fiduciary Relationship: Its Economic Character and Legal Consequences," 66 *NYU L Rev* 1045, 1074 (1991).

[36] Easterbrook and Fischel (n 32) at 426.

[37] Easterbrook and Fischel (n 32) at 431.

[38] See John Langbein, "The Contractarian Basis of the Law of Trusts," 105 *Yale LJ* 625, 629 (1995). See also, eg, Easterbrook and Fischel (n 32) at 429; Henry Hansmann and Ugo Mattei, "The Functions of Trust Law: A Comparative Legal and Economic Analysis," 73 *NYU L Rev* 434, 447 (1998).

[39] See Bernard Black et al, "Outside Director Liability," 58 *Stan L Rev* 1055, 1064–74 (2006).

[40] See text accompanying nn 116–20.

[41] See Hal R Arkes and Cindy A Schipani, "Medical Malpractice v the Business Judgment Rule: Differences in Hindsight Bias," 73 *Or L Rev* 587, 613–17 (1994); Jeffrey J Rachlinski, "A Positive Psychological Theory of Judging in Hindsight," 65 *U Chi L Rev* 571, 574, 619–23 (1998).

[42] We refine this statement in Section III.B.3.

may be hard to detect, because of two structural features of the fiduciary relationship.[43] First, the beneficiary's interests are subject to the fiduciary's discretion; the fiduciary is charged with controlling and managing an asset so as to serve the beneficiary's best interests and must use her own expertise and judgment to do so. Second, the management of the asset in question involves inherent risk and uncertainty, and therefore, a bad outcome cannot easily be tied to breach of the duty of loyalty. Under these conditions, the economics of enforcement suggest that "the optimal sanction for breach of the duty of loyalty must exceed the fiduciary's profit."[44] Fiduciary law usually achieves this through the remedy of disgorgement of profits, fortifying it with burden-shifting rules and strict presumptions.[45]

This understanding of disgorgement implies that its availability is related to the problem of deterrence. This could explain why in some fiduciary settings—particularly the corporate kind (especially in the United States)—disgorgement is less prevalent. In these contexts, underdeterrence may be beneficial in order "to spur the fiduciary to discover and exploit opportunities,"[46] due to the market devices that provide the fiduciary "with incentive compensation to align her interest with that of the [beneficiary]."[47] To be sure, in many (most?) fiduciary contexts, setting up the most efficient remedial response is quite an intricate task. But even in these contexts, focusing on the parties' incentives helps account for the broad prevalence of disgorgement as a species of "penalty default" rule, which induces fiduciaries to express contracting, namely: to negotiate with their beneficiaries to secure their specific consent to transactions that would ostensibly violate the duty of loyalty.[48]

Economic analyses that take private law to be merely a form of aggregate-welfare-increasing regulation prompt familiar debates as to the desirability of conceptualizing the public good in terms of aggregate preference satisfaction and—more relevant for our purposes—the legitimacy of using private law for such purposes.[49] Rehashing this controversy is not necessary here.[50] The account summarized here presents welfare maximization as an *instrumental* good, being the typical goal of the people who use financial fiduciaries law.[51] Framed this way, a welfarist analysis provides important data for any autonomy-based account of financial fiduciaries law properly attuned to the welfarist goods this institution can help people secure. What ultimately matters, in this view, is the way law offers people choices—safely delegating the authority over an important aspect of their welfarist interests—that would otherwise be practically unavailable.

[43] See Cooter and Freedman (n 35) at 1046–7.

[44] Easterbrook and Fischel (n 32) at 426. See generally Steven Shavell, *Foundations of Economic Analysis of Law* (2004) 351–4.

[45] See Cooter and Freedman (n 35) at 1053–5.

[46] See Easterbrook and Fischel (n 32) at 436.

[47] Roberta Romano, "Comment on Easterbrook and Fischel, 'Contract and Fiduciary Duty,'" 36 *JL & Econ* 447, 449–50 (1993).

[48] See Easterbrook and Fischel (n 32) at 445; Getzler (n 7) at 989. See generally Ian Ayres and Robert Gertner, "Filling Gaps in Incomplete Contracts: An Economic Theory of Default Rules," 99 *Yale LJ* 87 (1989).

[49] See, eg, Ernest J Weinrib, *The Idea of Private Law* (1995).

[50] For a review, see Dagan (n 7) at ch 5.

[51] We do not deny the possibility of an inverse reading, in which the parties' choices acquire their significance only for epistemological reasons, as a means to secure the maximization of aggregate utility.

And yet this canonical economic analysis, which insists that there is nothing special ("there is no subject"[52]) to a fiduciary relationship, is disappointing. To begin with, the notion that identifying a fiduciary relationship as a species of contract straightforwardly prescribes the content of fiduciary duties is misguided. Properly understood, contract law is not a simple, unified body of doctrine, but rather a quite diverse body of contract types.[53] Contract law actively empowers people to form collaborative voluntary arrangements—both discrete and impersonal as well as long term and relational—by providing a broad menu of divergent background regimes for risky undertakings in the various relevant spheres of contracting (home, intimacy, work, and commerce). An autonomy-based contract theory should, therefore, be attentive to the structural pluralist prescription that people be provided with a sufficiently diverse set of frameworks to organize their various endeavors and interpersonal relationships.[54] Hence, even were we to classify fiduciary law as a form of contract, we would still have to think about the distinct features of this contract type and their doctrinal implications.

The main insight of the economic analysis lies in clarifying the inherent challenge of expanding people's autonomy by allowing them to delegate the authority over a significant share of their estate—namely, the systemic reasons that render this authority particularly susceptible to abuse. It further prescribes that in figuring out how to contend with this challenge, we need to keep in mind both the welfarist goals of all the parties involved and the divergent consequences likely to arise in the different legal regimes given the distinct incentives they generate to the parties. This line of analysis elucidates the significance of the duty of loyalty as well as the disgorgement remedy. Indeed, unlike its formalist counterpart, the economic analysis accounts for this typical remedy for fiduciary disloyalty without stipulating the content of the beneficiary's entitlement and, thus, provides useful tools for refining its details.[55]

Yet by dismissing the unique quality of fiduciary law as a private law institution—by arguing, for example, that "some persons [simply] start calling some contractual relations 'Fiduciary,'" whenever "transaction costs reach a particularly high level"[56]—lawyer economists obscure, and may undermine, important aspects of this body of law. To see why, recall that under structural pluralism, private law institutions have two chief roles: stabilizing the expectations of people who invoke them and expressing our social ideals with respect to the institutions. Discarding the normative core of fiduciary law disables these functions, which is particularly detrimental in light of their subtle interaction. As Melanie Leslie argues, stripping fiduciary duties of their moral content might "dilute the stigma" of opportunistic behavior.[57] This unfortunate expressive

[52] Easterbrook and Fischel (n 32) at 438.

[53] See Roy Kreitner, "Multiplicity in Contract Remedies," in Nili Cohen and Ewan McKendrick (eds), *Comparative Remedies for Breach of Contracts* (2005) 19, 19–20; Roy Kreitner, "On the New Pluralism in 'Contract Theory,'" 45 *Suffolk U L Rev* 915, 915, 923–4 (2012).

[54] See Dagan, "Contract Theory" (n 9); Hanoch Dagan and Michael A Heller, "Freedom of Contracts" (unpublished manuscript).

[55] See also Joshua Getzler, "Rumford Market and the Genesis of Fiduciary Obligations," in Andrew Burrows and Alan Rodger (eds), *Mapping the Law: Essays in Memory of Peter Birks* (2006) 577, 586.

[56] Easterbrook and Fischel (n 32) at 438.

[57] Melanie B Leslie, "Trusting Trustees: Fiduciary Duties and the Limits of Default Rules," 94 *Geo LJ* 67, 90 (2005).

consequence, she maintains, may, in turn, have implications on the material front as well, given the typical weakness of other means of guarding against financial fiduciaries abuse (such as exit, monitoring, or market discipline).[58] Chipping away at the normative force of the duty of loyalty not only can damage the functioning of the law of financial fiduciaries but may also impair its ability to optimally promote autonomy. Thus, our autonomy-based theory of financial fiduciaries law must also look to virtue-based accounts of this institution for some insights.

C. Virtue

Peter Birks has suggested that to capture the distinctive feature of trust fiduciary law we should organize the "primary obligations recognized by the law" according to the "degree of altruism" they entail. In general, law is quite cautious in its demands, requiring only that we "take other people into consideration, and to that extent curb our pursuit of our own interests, where reasonable care would prevent reasonably foreseeable harm." Only in "special circumstances"—think of the duty of rescue type of cases—does law go beyond the first, negative "degree of legally obligatory altruism" and "requires us to take positive action to improve another's position." Finally, the "third and highest degree of legally obligatory altruism" is that of the trustee, who "must not only take care of the interests of another but must do so disinterestedly,"[59] namely: "uninfluenced by any competing interest of [her] own."[60] Indeed, for Birks, "the core fiduciary obligation—the core trust obligation—is the compound obligation to take active care and to do so disinterestedly." This "very rare obligation in the third degree of altruism is found in the express trustee." In line with our cautious approach regarding the multiplicity of fiduciary institutions, however, Birks adds that although the word "fiduciary" may be used to refer to "persons in trustee-like positions," we should be careful in so doing because this degree of altruism "does not attach to every fiduciary."[61]

Birks's "positive duty" approach is "incomplete,"[62] Lionel Smith claims, and he refines it in two ways. First, Smith insists on understanding the fiduciary relationship as "premised on a voluntary undertaking to assume an office to which the law attaches fiduciary obligations, or. . . to put another's interests ahead of one's own." This ensures that fiduciary law's prophylactic rules are not "inconsistent with the internal rationality of private law," namely, that it properly focuses on "the relationship between plaintiff and defendant, and their conduct that gave rise to the litigation," rather than on attempting to "influence the conduct of others in the future." Furthermore—and here is Smith's second refinement—the duty of loyalty is qualitatively different from other duties. The duty of loyalty is "distinct in character, and not just in the particularly high standard" it prescribes, and therefore the attempt to understand it "in terms of results will always fail." The duty of loyalty "is a kind of adjectival obligation," which focuses

[58] See Melanie B Leslie, "In Defense of the No Further Inquiry Rule: A Response to Professor John Lengbein," 47 *Wm & Mary L Rev* 541, 555–63 (2005).
[59] See also Leonard I Rotman, *Fiduciary Law* (2005) 244.
[60] See also *Meinard v Salmon* 164 NE 545, 546–8 (NY 1928) (per Cardozo CJ).
[61] Peter Birks, "The Content of the Fiduciary Obligation," 34 *Isr L Rev* 3, 17–20, 37–8 (2000).
[62] This may derive from Birks's reference to legal altruism, which means that his account is not moralistic.

on the "*manner* of doing what one does." A fiduciary must exercise fiduciary powers "in what *he perceives to be* the best interests of the beneficiary." Thus, "the real heart" of the duty of loyalty is "in the justiciability of motive"; it is "a duty to act (or not) with the right motive."[63]

Under this construction, fiduciary law's prophylactic rules are intended not to prevent "any particular result" but to protect "against disloyalty, which is not motivated by harm as such, but rather by motive." Smith acknowledges that these duties (the no-conflict rule and the no-profits rule) "are not judged by motives but by events in the world"; however, he insists that they "are triggered by situations in which it may be especially difficult to know with what motive the fiduciary acted, because the fiduciary is subject to conflicting motivational pressures." In such circumstances, "to leave your beneficiary wondering whether you had been disloyal, or to force him to prove disloyalty" would be "inconsistent" with an "undertaking to be loyal."[64]

Standing on its own, this moralist account of fiduciary law is questionable. It is unclear why beneficiaries are owed the highest degree of altruism (à la Birks), or why law should be particularly concerned with motives in the context of fiduciary relationships (à la Smith). After all, as Annette Baier contends, whereas in the context of moral relationships, fidelity is virtuous, it is immoral in the context of immoral relationships, where "trust-busting" can actually be the "morally proper goal."[65] And while many fiduciary relationships are moral, neither Birks nor Smith explains why they are subject to higher moral standards than other categories of interpersonal relationships. Furthermore, whereas with some other private law institutions, such as marital property and certain types of relational contracts, trust is a constitutive, intrinsically valuable component of the relationship,[66] there are no parallel intrinsic communal goods in our relationship with our money managers. The latter relationship is purely instrumental for us, which means that people care about their fortunes and not about the virtues of their managers. A law that respects, as it must, the reasons why people typically resort to this private law institution should respect their approach to the relationship created.[67] It should therefore come as no surprise that "a breach of fiduciary duty may be committed without the fiduciary necessarily acting immorally."[68]

But as with the efficiency analysis, we read these moralist accounts not as stand-alone theories but as valuable input for our autonomy-based account. The starting point of this reading is Smith's refinements, which construct the fiduciary relationship as a form of voluntary obligation[69]—a private law institution—that is dependent upon intense

[63] Lionel Smith, "The Motive, Not the Deed," in Joshua Getzler (ed), *Rationalizing Equity, Property and Trusts* (2003) 53, 61–2, 65, 69–70, 73. Smith revised his view, to some extent, in his chapter in this volume.

[64] Smith (n 63) at 73–6.

[65] Annette Baier, "Trust and Antitrust," 96 *Ethics* 231, 232 (1986).

[66] See respectively Dagan (n 9) ch 9; Ian Macneil, "The New Social Contract: An Inquiry into Modern Contractual Relations," in David Campbell (ed), *The Relational Theory of Contract* (2001) 127, 136.

[67] Thus, although we agree with Matthew Harding that "a main purpose of fiduciary law ought to be to enable people to form, maintain and develop relationships characterized by a cycle of trust and trustworthiness," we insist that in the context of financial fiduciaries, the parties' attitudes are of purely instrumental value, so that facilitating such relationships in "terms of detachment" by "mimic[king] the normative world of trust" is *not* "a matter of regret." Matthew Harding, "Trust and Fiduciary Law," 33 *Oxford J Legal Stud* 81, 96–7, 100–2 (2013).

[68] Matthew Conaglen, *Fiduciary Loyalty: Protecting the Due Performance of Non-Fiduciary Duties* (2010) 108.

[69] See also James Edelman, "When Do Fiduciary Duties Arise," 126 *Law Q Rev* 302 (2010).

emphasis on the fiduciary's other-regarding dispositions. However, in order to understand why "the theme of morality" ("Loyalty, fidelity, faith, and honor") should form the "basic vocabulary" of this private law institution,[70] we need to recall some of the insights gleaned from the economic analysis regarding the perverse incentives inherent to the fiduciary relationship and appreciate, with Leslie, fidelity's *instrumental* role in contending with these incentives.[71]

Irit Samet's justification for stringent disgorgement for disloyalty reinforces this point. She argues that the fiduciary's discretionary authority is vulnerable to abuse because fiduciaries—facing the temptation of profit in instances of potential conflict of interest—are "especially prone to self-deception and the biased judgment it yields." This is a significant risk because "[t]he all too human tendency to give charitable interpretation to our own actions and motivations endangers any social institution that is based on trust and integrity." Self-deception "enables virtuous people to justify their dishonest actions to themselves" by "turn[ing] off the inner voice of conscience so that immorality can go through undetected by the conscious self" and "subverting the process of evidence and weighing, thus. . . (mis)leading one to view illegitimate actions as permitted (or even prescribed)." The solution to this problem is "to eliminate the process of deliberation." That is to say, fiduciaries must be "prevent[ed]. . . from asking *themselves* whether a transaction that serves their interest is also good for their principals," which is exactly what the law does when it sets a bright-line no conflict rule.[72]

III. Financial Fiduciaries in the Service of Autonomy

A. The regulative principle of financial fiduciaries law

Our main claim regarding the law of financial fiduciaries emerges from this survey of the formalist, economic, and moralist accounts of fiduciary law. Like formalists, we believe that financial fiduciary law should be analyzed as a private law institution and, furthermore, accept the important autonomy-enhancing role of financial fiduciaries vis-à-vis the beneficiaries and/or benefactors as the *telos* of that institution.[73] For this reason we also endorse the economic account mandate that financial fiduciaries law must be attuned to the good for which people invoke it, which is welfarist in nature: people want to be able to rely on the time and expertise of others to manage

[70] Tamar Frankel, "Towards Universal Fiduciary Principles" (2013) § 5 (unpublished manuscript).

[71] This role may have its historical roots in an era when the fiduciary relationship was governed solely by ethical norms. See David J Seipp, "Trust and Fiduciary Duty in the Early Common Law," 91 *BU L Rev* 1011, 1016 (2011).

[72] Irit Samet, "Guarding the Fiduciary's Conscience—A Justification of a Stringent Profit-stripping Rule," 28 *Oxford J Legal Stud* 763, 765, 773–5, 781 (2008). See also Margaret M Blair and Lynn A Stout, "Trust, Trustworthiness, and the Behavioral Foundations of Corporate Law," 149 *U Pa L Rev* 1735, 1785, 1787 (2001).

[73] We bracket the difficult issue of possible tensions between the autonomy of beneficiaries and that of benefactors. One notorious aspect of this difficulty, which arises especially in the context of family trusts, is that of the "dead hand" dilemma: "Individual freedom to dispose of [property] cannot simultaneously be allowed and fully maintained. If the donor of a property interest tries to restrict the donee's freedom to dispose of that interest, the legal system, in deciding whether to enforce or void that restriction, must resolve whose freedom it will protect, that of the donor or that of the donee." Gregory S Alexander, "The Dead Hand and the Law of Trusts in the Nineteenth Century," 37 *Stan L Rev* 1189, 1189 (1985).

significant aspects of their welfarist interests. Finally, the moral vocabulary of financial fiduciaries law is also important given the significant, albeit instrumental, role of trust and fidelity in this private law institution.

To appreciate these lessons, we need to return to our starting point, namely, that the role of private law is to enhance people's autonomy by facilitating forms of interpersonal interactions that are conducive to human flourishing. People, of course, need not resort to any of these private law institutions. They are simply a repertoire of frameworks for voluntary arrangements available to people in pursuing their projects and ends of choice. The law of financial fiduciaries exemplifies a main tenet of structural pluralism, that law is a major instrument for facilitating many of these forms of interaction. These forms of interaction face endemic difficulties, such as information costs (symmetric and asymmetric), cognitive biases, and heightened risks of opportunistic behavior, alongside more cultural obstacles, that make it hard to imagine forms of interaction that are not (yet) widely recognized and named. The task of recognizing and naming is, especially in modern times, often performed by the law. Indeed, private law's autonomy-enhancing function is rarely exhausted by way of a hands-off policy and receptive approach to freedom of contract. Rather, law must actively empower its institutional arrangements, including through reliable guarantees against opportunistic behavior.[74]

Financial fiduciaries law is one—particularly challenging—type of these arrangements.[75] It complies with the Razian injunction of autonomy-enhancing because it adds an option, and a valuable one at that: the reliable delegation of authority over a significant aspect of one's welfarist interests. Delegating this authority bolsters autonomy because it enables us to enlist the superior skills, knowledge, and experience (and thus, arguably, judgment), or the professional licensure of others for a task that is, for most of us, crucial, either because it impacts our own financial future (as with savings and pensions) or because it affects our ability to secure the well-being of our loved ones or advance a cause we care about after we die (as with many trusts). Enabling such a delegation is autonomy enhancing also because the alternative seems daunting given the resources—in time and expertise—that the proper management of our money requires. The ability to *safely* delegate this task to others removes these burdens so that we can focus on intrinsically valuable projects.

To properly perform this twofold autonomy-enhancing role, financial fiduciaries law must be responsive to the goal for which it is invoked, namely: managing the beneficiary's estate (or a significant portion thereof). It must be suited to the particular incentive structure created by its inherent circumstances, where the discretionary authority is particularly susceptible to both carelessness and (even more prominently) abuse. Fiduciary law's openly prophylactic treatment of disloyalty should therefore not be

[74] See generally Dagan and Heller (n 54) at pt III.A.

[75] Cf J E Penner, "An Untheory of the Law of Trusts, or Some Notes Towards Understanding the Structure of Trust Law Doctrine," 63 *Cur Legal Probs* 653, 665 (2010). Like us, Penner characterizes trust law as a facilitative legal device, but he claims that moral principles have no role to play in arguing about law's core principles (at 665–7). Our treatment of the various doctrines we address herein demonstrates, *pace* Penner, the role normative arguments can, and should, play in the ongoing interpretation, elaboration, and development of such facilitative institutions.

understood (as private law formalists often argue) as an illegitimate use of private law to promote collectivist purposes.[76] Rather, the ambitious facilitation of this vulnerable type of interpersonal relationship implies that the core task of fiduciary law is to structure the *ex ante* entitlements of the parties *inter se* in a way that deters abuse.[77]

Although the economic analysis offers the sharpest account of the significance of deterrence to the integrity and viability of the law of financial fiduciaries, it has, surprisingly, neglected one of the most important means for securing that deterrence. By discarding fiduciary law's normativity, the economic analysis fails to appreciate law's role in preserving, sustaining, and reinforcing social norms crucial for the functioning of this type of fiduciary relationship.[78] Law is more than a set of incentives that serve as the basis for predicting some external reaction to deviation from or compliance with its dictates. As H L A Hart argued, legal norms are also taken as bases for claims, demands, and criticism, as standards and guides for conduct and judgment.[79] Structural pluralism takes seriously the normativity of private law; in fact, in addition to stabilizing expectations, this expressive role of law is, as noted, the reason for the significance structural pluralism accords to the internal coherence of our private law institutions.[80] Accordingly, structural pluralism prescribes that alongside its pursuit of optimal incentives for the proper management of other people's money, the law of financial fiduciaries should continue to inculcate the traditional cultural perception of trustees and similar financial fiduciaries as "the quintessential figure(s) of the ethical subject *as* economic subject."[81]

Performing both these roles is the main challenge of financial fiduciaries law.[82] An autonomy-based conception of this private law institution cannot understate the importance of its incentives, as formalists and moralists tend to, given the predominantly welfarist purpose for which it is invoked. Respecting fiduciary law's modus operandi—the particular way in which it enhances people's autonomy—responsible decision-makers must consider the effects of the rules they prescribe on the intended beneficiaries. But because these effects are mediated by fiduciaries' self-understanding of their role, which is, in turn, affected by the normative content the law expresses, our

[76] See, eg, Ernest J Weinrib, "Restitutionary Damages as Corrective Justice," 1 *Theoretical Inquiries L* 1, 33–4 (1999).

[77] See Dagan (n 6) at 236. See generally Dagan (n 7) at ch 5.

[78] This neglect of law's expressive function and its attendant role in reinforcing desirable social norms is not inherent to the economic analysis of law. See Robert Cooter, "Expressive Law and Economics," 27 *J Legal Stud* 585 (1998). Nonetheless, it may be no mere coincidence that the accounts of the law and economics luminaries discussed in Section II.B fail to take this function into consideration: sidestepping the significance of factors that are difficult to measure may be the economist's professional hazard.

[79] See H L A Hart, *The Concept of Law* (1961) 79–88.

[80] See text accompanying n 12.

[81] Birla (n 8) at 71. We do not deny the limits of law's prescriptive effects and the possibility that in certain cases legal intervention might actually backfire by crowding out internal motivations. The literature on these dynamics of the interaction between law and culture is divided. See Yuval Feldman and Tom R Tyler, "Mandated Justice: The Potential Promise and Possible Pitfalls of Mandating Procedural Justice in the Workplace," *Reg & Gov't* 46 (2012). We do not purport to resolve this matter here, but see no reason to suspect a moral backlash that would undermine the instrumentally beneficial role of the expressive function of financial fiduciaries law.

[82] Another important challenge of our doctrine is to examine whether there are uses, within the broad range of uses trust law currently facilitates, that undermine, rather than enhance, autonomy. A possible candidate for such critical inquiry is the spendthrift trust. See, eg, Gregory S Alexander and Hanoch Dagan, *Properties of Property* (2012) 306–7.

doctrine must also be sensitive to the potential counterproductive effects of incentives that could dilute the normativity of financial fiduciaries law, thereby undermining its material functioning.[83] There is probably no precise formula for optimally balancing these effects. This articulation of the regulative principle of the law governing financial fiduciaries thus requires a critical examination of its main doctrinal features, with an eye to the need to accommodate material incentives and expressive effects as well as to the possible legal techniques that may be available at any given doctrinal junction.[84] The remainder of this chapter will be devoted to this task.

B. Reassurance and critique

1. Sole or best interest?

We begin with the most significant doctrinal detail of trust law: the standard of trustees' loyalty. The traditional standard of loyalty is strict. It prescribes that "[t]he trustee is under a duty to administer the trust *solely* in the interest of the beneficiaries,"[85] so that any transaction that implicates the trustee's personal interests will be struck down, even if she can prove that it was in the best interest of the beneficiary. This "sole interest" standard and its attendant "no further inquiry" rule are not absolute, however. The sole interest standard gives way, as John Langbein demonstrated, to a long list of exclusions and categoric exceptions. A transaction or set of transactions that are tainted by the benefit they bestow upon the trustee but are in the best interest of the beneficiary are deemed acceptable where the trustee obtains the settlor's authorization, the beneficiary's informed consent, or the court's prior approval. Likewise, courts and legislatures have exempted classes of transactions that implicate the trustee's self-interest, granting special prerogatives to institutional trustees in the financial-services industry, such as the authority to deposit trust funds in a financial institution affiliated with the trustee's intrafamilial transactions.[86]

Taking a welfarist perspective, Langbein argues that the traditional sole interest rule should be replaced with a "best interest" rule, although he would still require the trustee to prove the fairness of a given transaction. This reform, he argues, would conform to a parallel shift in corporate law; it would also make trust law more transparent, given the existing array of exclusions and exceptions that are aimed at incentivizing transactions best promoting beneficiaries' interests; finally, such a reform would properly protect good faith non-professional trustees, who are the main victims of the traditional rule.[87] We share many of Langbein's premises. Like him, we reject the purported moralist foundation of trust law and the attempt to provide conceptual grounding for the sole interest standard. Furthermore, our autonomy-based theory of the law of financial fiduciaries is committed to the law being shaped to maximize beneficiaries' welfare. And yet we cannot support his proposed reform.

[83] Cf Lynn Stout, *Cultivating Conscience* (2011)106–8, 249–52.

[84] Cf Penner (n 75) at 668, 670.

[85] *Restatement (Second) of Trusts* (1959) § 170(1).

[86] John H Langbein, "Questioning the Trust Law Duty of Loyalty: Sole Interest or Best Interest?," 114 *Yale LJ* 929, 931–2, 963–5, 968–79 (2005).

[87] Langbein (n 86) at 980–2, 989, 987, 984–5.

There are three reasons to suggest that the lessons Langbein draws from corporate law lack the force he attributes to them. The first reason aligns with our general emphasis on the diversity of fiduciary forms. Although corporate law considers officers, directors, and controlling shareholders to be fiduciaries, Langbein's analogy ignores important distinctions between them and fiduciaries subject to trust law. As others demonstrated, these differences are significant and may justify the relative harshness of trust law either due to the availability of alternative means for securing loyalty in the corporate context (notably, the prospect of shareholder exit and shareholders' ability to replace the managerial team) or due to the relative complexity of the task of corporate directors.[88] Delving into the implications of these differences is beyond the scope of this chapter,[89] but suffice it to say that they justify a cautious attitude to this analogy.[90] This is reinforced by the fact that developments in corporate law, especially those involving conflicts between shareholders and managers, might not be triggered by the innocuous pursuit of maximizing shareholders' welfare but, rather, by a race to the bottom between states competing over incorporation fees and prestige and driven by managers armed with corporate money.[91]

Finally, and maybe most tellingly, the analogy to corporate law may work *against* Langbein's normative prescription, because the leading trend over the last decade or so has been a shift away from "best interest" and towards "sole interest."[92] This has occurred in important (perhaps the most important) areas of conflict-of-interest transactions in the corporate setting: the managerial loan, executive compensation, and the "freeze-out" merger. In the early years of the twenty-first century, it became evident that managers were abusing the opportunity to borrow from their corporations. A substantial portion of American corporations granted hefty loans to top executives;[93] the full extent of the benefits built into these loans was partially hidden from the public eye.[94] Concluding that instances of abuse were too frequent, Congress enacted the 2002 Sarbanes–Oxley Act, prohibiting public corporations, almost without exception, from giving loans to their executives even if in the best

[88] See, eg, respectively, Robert H Sitkoff, "The Economic Structure of Fiduciary Law," 91 *BU L Rev* 1039, 1045 (2011); Leslie (n 57) at 99–100. Moreover, the decisions of corporate directors regarding shareholders' money implicate many other individuals, a complexity that is absent in our case.

[89] It is unclear that either the prospect of exit or the ability to replace the managerial team significantly protects shareholders. An exit exercised in the wake of managerial abuse is exit at an inferior price, and thus does not offer much protection. Takeovers are also imperfect since they require a complex collective action and considerable costs, and are often hampered by anti-takeover devices used by the incumbent managers. See Sharon Hannes, "The Market for Takeover Defenses," 101 *Nw U L Rev* 125 (2007).

[90] Another complication stems from the fact that shareholders are not the sole beneficiaries of the corporation. See Andrew S Gold, "Dynamic Fiduciary Duty," 34 *Cardozo L Rev* 491 (2012).

[91] This is admittedly a controversial claim. Compare, eg, Lucian Arye Bebchuk, "Federalism and the Corporation: The Desirable Limits on State Competition in Corporate Law," 105 *Harv L Rev* 1435, 1441 (1992) with Marcel Kahan and Ehud Kamar, "The Myth of State Competition in Corporate Law," 55 *Stan L Rev* 679 (2002).

[92] Langbein focuses on much earlier developments in corporate law. But in order for his argument to hold, corporate law must not have reversed its preference.

[93] See, eg, Paul Hodgson, *My Big Fat Corporate Loan* (2002) 1.

[94] See Lucian A Bebchuk and Robert J Jackson, Jr, "Executive Pensions," 30 J Corp L 823, 824 n 2 (2005). Moreover, executive loans were often forgiven by companies, in whole or in part—yet another boon for managers. See Kathleen M Kahle and Kuldeep Shastri, "Executive Loans," 39 *J Fin & Quant Analysis* 791, 798 (2004).

interests of the shareholders[95] (and even if preapproved by the latter[96]). Similar developments—which, taken together, could be an indication of a "glorious resurgence" of the "sole interest rule" in corporate law—include the emerging legislative requirement that executive compensation be approved by the shareholders[97] and the recent shift in the Delaware courts' treatment of the freeze-out merger,[98] moving from the "entirely fair to the minority" standard[99] (a typically lenient best interest rule) to a sole-interest-like requirement of preapproval by a majority of the minority shareholders.[100]

Although the fact that these developments are taking the path that trust law has long preferred is not indicative of definitive reform, it does suggest a need for some caution before jettisoning the traditional trust law doctrine. This is supported by the regulative principle underlying, in our view, the law of financial fiduciaries, which vindicates the seemingly awkward normative structure of a sweeping rule with numerous exceptions.

A financial fiduciaries law aimed at serving the welfare interests of beneficiaries should favorably carve out, as trust law did, exceptions to the sole interest rule to cover categories of cases in which optimizing beneficiaries' interests requires allowing fiduciaries some incidental benefits. Therefore, unlike moralist accounts of this doctrine, our theory is not shaken by the proliferation of such exceptions. In fact, because we share Langbein's critique of the treatment of good-faith nonprofessional trustees, we are unwilling to join Miller in endorsing this aspect of traditional law[101] and instead commend the emerging jurisprudence that sets new exceptions covering these (relatively rare) cases.[102] But whereas Langbein's strictly economic perspective implies that once the "bark" of the sole interest rule has become much "worse than its bite,"[103] its baseline prescription should be reversed, we applaud the doctrinal structure that supplements a sole interest baseline with as many exceptions as a sound welfarist account prescribes. Our account suggests that this combination constructs a legal edifice that is well suited to the main doctrinal challenges of the regulative principle of financial fiduciaries law.

The unique development of the duty of loyalty in trust law subtly, if unintentionally, utilizes the gap between law's material effects and its expressive function in order to accommodate the law's expressive and material goals. Because financial fiduciaries law typically targets sophisticated professionals who have access to ample legal advice,

[95] As is the case with loans to cover managers' relocation costs or for them to buy shares in the corporation so as to align their incentives with those of the shareholders.

[96] Section 402 of the Sarbanes–Oxley Act, which added s 13(k) to the Exchange Act of 1934 (48 Stat 894). Sarbanes–Oxley Act § 402(a), Pub L No 107–204, 2002 USCCAN (116 Stat) at 745, 787 (codified at 15 USC § 78m(k) (Supp 2006)).

[97] See text accompanying nn 165–70.

[98] The freeze-out merger—a device used by controlling shareholders to buy out the corporation's public shareholders and go private—is perhaps the most extreme example of a conflict-of-interest transaction.

[99] Robert C Clark, *Corporate Law* (1986) 518–30.

[100] See *In re Pure Resources, Inc*, Shareholder Litigation 808 A 2d 421 (Del Ch 2002); Guhan Subramanian, "Fixing Freezeouts," 115 *Yale LJ* 2, 59 (2005). True, Delaware still leaves the door open for controlling shareholders to conduct freeze-out mergers without the minority shareholders' prior approval. But its court discourages this practice. See, eg, *In re Emerging Communications, Inc*, Shareholders Litigation No 16415, 2004 Del Ch LEXIS 79 (Del Ch 3 May 2004). Moreover, modern codes of corporate law grant minority shareholders veto rights with regard to crucial self-dealing transactions, including freeze-outs. Related Party Transactions and Minority Shareholder Rights 30–6 (OECD 2012), available at <http://www.oecd.org/daf/ca/50089215. pdf>.

[101] See text accompanying n 24.

[102] Leslie (n 58) at 570, 574, 579.

[103] Langbein (n 86) at 933.

most doctrinal details are likely to be translated into incentives and to generate corresponding behavioral outcomes. But doctrinal details rarely produce broad cultural consequences and, thus, rarely impact broader social norms. Rather, what may affect people's preferences and social norms are "more fundamental legal concepts and institutions."[104] Accordingly, in sticking to the conception of the trustee as a person who is morally obligated to serve the beneficiary alone, trust law reinforces this socially popular perception, which is instrumental in facilitating the safe delegation of welfarist interests to trustees.

The existing structure and language of the duty of loyalty in trust law may seem puzzling for Langbein because he fails to consider the instrumental value of the social expectations created by the virtuous image of fiduciaries and trust law's contribution to this image. By contrast, our analysis appreciates the expressive effect of law and how broad social norms, alongside the corresponding moral commitments and reputational concerns they may consolidate, can have desirable behavioral effects. We therefore caution against discarding the existing doctrinal design, which neatly serves financial fiduciary law that must both entrench this social norm and allow conflicted transactions when they typically serve the interests of beneficiaries.

There is another benefit to the unique structure of trust law—another challenge it contends with—which might also be at risk under Langbein's proposed reform. Conceptualizing deviations from the sole interest rule as exceptions could serve as a reminder of the need to scrutinize the justifiability of these exceptions. The ongoing inquiry into these exceptions that could thus be facilitated is particularly worthwhile given the strong prospect of abuse—the source of the persistent threat to the functioning of financial fiduciaries law as an autonomy-enhancing private law institution.

Consider the debate over a 2003 amendment to the Uniform Trust Code that allows a trustee to purchase investment services from a company to which she is connected.[105] This new rule permits investments by institutional trustees in mutual funds run by companies related to them and sanctions the entailed fees and commissions they can thus capture. Langbein argues that the new rule makes good sense, because a settlor who chooses a trustee for her investment expertise will often wish to benefit from the investment vehicles (mutual funds) created by that trustee, rather than use investment services from a third party.[106] Leslie disagrees, contending that even without this rule, settlors could have captured this purported benefit by preapproving such investment strategies, whereas the new rule might encourage trustees to invest in inferior vehicles in order to reap extra fees, thus requiring the weak party to the transaction—the settlor or beneficiary—to pursue protection where they think it necessary.[107]

We do not claim that it is easy to determine the desirability of this new rule. Quite the contrary: a careful comparison of the benefits and costs of this innovative exception is required. More specifically, once enough data have accumulated on this rule, empirical inquiries should examine the relative performance of mutual funds with a trustee as a sponsor vis-à-vis independent mutual funds as well as the portfolio returns of beneficiaries whose trustees invest in related funds (taking into account the returns net of all

[104] Dagan (n 9) at 133.
[105] Unif. Trust Code § 802(f) (amended 2003).
[106] Langbein (n 86) at 976–8.
[107] Leslie (n 58) at 570, 574, 579.

fees and commissions) in comparison to the returns of other beneficiaries. Fashioning the trustee's permission to make self-interested investments exceptions makes them salient for investigation, whereas reversing the baseline may obscure the subject's analytical significance.[108]

2. *Investment policy*

We now turn to the second important duty borne by fiduciaries—the duty of care—and focus on the investment strategy that the fiduciary should adopt on behalf of the beneficiary. Whereas the duty of loyalty may well be fiduciary law's most distinctive feature, it is the duty of care and, more specifically, the investment policy it prescribes that are paramount in the context of the autonomy-enhancing promise of enabling people to safely delegate the authority to manage their financial resources.

The literature on investment policy is mostly economic. But its starting point—in line with our approach—is that efficiency in our context means an investment policy tailored to the preferences of the particular beneficiary.[109] On this background, we attempt to contribute to the debate over the lessons to be drawn from the 2008 financial crisis regarding the regulation of trustee investment policy. In order to set the stage for this discussion, we begin with some conventional wisdom that shows that the prudence of investment policies that satisfy the duty of care varies for different types of fiduciaries. As supported by our structural pluralist approach, rather than looking for a unifying principle, an account of fiduciaries' duties of care must analyze the diverging tasks performed by different fiduciaries.[110]

Individuals tend to diversify their passive investments.[111] The commonsensical idea of refraining from putting all of one's eggs into one basket dovetails with modern portfolio theory, which teaches that diversification allows investors to avoid idiosyncratic risks of individual investments.[112] For quite some time, corporate managers acted as though their companies' wealth was their own and diversified "their" portfolios. This led to the creation of enormous conglomerates, which controlled multiple subsidiaries in different sectors of the economy. Such internal diversification turns out to be a particularly pernicious strategy, however: The resulting corporate structures are too complex to manage, rendering their central administration an overhead consumer that adds no significant managerial value. They are also extremely opaque and therefore very hard for analysts to read and for markets to discipline. Moreover, they facilitate a harmful process of cross-subsidization, whereby a weaker arm of the conglomerate is

[108] We acknowledge that a system based on a rule with exceptions that often kick in might put an extra burden on unsophisticated parties. This observation may imply that financial fiduciaries law should prescribe disclosure as a prerequisite to the application of at least some of these exceptions (as it does, for example, regarding the double commission earned when the trustee uses investment vehicles that she herself manages, Leslie (n 58) at 576–7)). It also underlies the significance of stickiness we discuss in Section III.B.3.

[109] See Max H Schanzenbach and Robert H Sitkoff, "The Prudent Investor Rule: A Theoretical and Empirical Reassessment" (2013) 17 (unpublished manuscript).

[110] These differences also affect the pertinent standard of care. See text accompanying nn 39–41.

[111] When a person manages her own business, she is unable to diversify her wealth. But given passive investments and liquid markets, diversification can be achieved at a relatively low cost.

[112] See Harry M Markowitz, "Portfolio Selection," 7 *J Fin* 77 (1952).

subsidized by its healthy subsidiaries, thus distorting the incentives of division managers[113] and insulating their tenure from downturns in specific sectors of the economy.[114] The ensuing losses suffered by these conglomerates resulted in a broad process of "deconglomeration" throughout the 1980s.[115] Once the markets came to appreciate the downside of internal corporate diversification, it became common wisdom that corporate managers should stick to a single area of expertise and allow investors to take care of diversification.

In sharp contrast to the optimal investment strategy of corporate fiduciaries, money-manager trustees should generally diversify the assets in the trust's portfolio as a prudent investor would normally do with her own portfolio. To be sure, the current rigorous prescription of diversification is relatively new. The traditional common law rule set an exhaustive list of permissible investments, which included (extremely) safe investments and emphatically excluded risky securities.[116] The standard then gradually shifted in both the UK and US toward the so-called (old) "prudent man" standard, which abolished the fixed list of investments and directed the trustee to instead adhere to the practices of prudent marketplace investors.[117] The courts, however, continued to be partial to safer investments.[118] And since the conventional form of trustee compensation does not give the trustee a cut of the trust's profits, the threat of liability, however slight, led trustees to be highly conservative in their investment strategies. Scholars began to argue that the law should be modified so as to encourage trustees to make riskier investments for their beneficiaries, as prescribed by modern portfolio theory.[119] The law finally changed, moving towards the modern "prudent investor" standard.[120] Under this new standard, trustees were granted the discretion to invest in any asset they saw fit. And while they were still required to take into account the settlor's and beneficiary's penchant for risk, riskiness was to be evaluated vis-à-vis the portfolio as a whole, not specific investments. The rationale for the rule is that the riskiness of any particular investment may be uncorrelated with the riskiness of other investments so that the inclusion of a risky investment in a portfolio may increase returns without adding a significant amount of risk. This modification to the law—even though only a default

[113] Such cross-subsidization alleviates the pressure on underperforming division managers and penalizes successful ones.

[114] See David S Scharfstein and Jermey C Stein, "The Dark Side of Internal Capital Markets: Divisional Rent-Seeking and Inefficient Investment," 55 *J Fin* 2537 (2000); Owen Lamont, "Cash Flow and Investment Evidence from Internal Capital Markets," 52 *J Fin* 83 (1997).

[115] See Sanjai Bhagat et al, "Hostile Takeovers in the 1980s: The Return to Corporate Specialization," in *Brookings Papers on Economic Activity: Microeconomics* (1990) 1; Steven N Kaplan and Michael S Weisbach, "The Success of Acquisitions: Evidence from Divestitures," 47 *J Fin* 107 (1992).

[116] See Joshua Getzler, "Fiduciary Investment in the Shadow of Financial Crisis: Was Lord Eldon Right?," 3 *J Equity* 1, 13–16 (2009).

[117] *Restatement (Second) of Trusts* (1959) § 227; *Harvard College v Armory*, 26 Mass (9 Pick) 446, 461 (1830); *In re Speight; Speight v Gaunt* [1883] 22 Ch D 727 (CA); [1883] 9 App Cas 1; 48 JP 84; 53 LJ Ch 419; 50 LT 330 (HL).

[118] See Bevis Longstreth, *Modern Investment Management and the Prudent Man Rule* (1986) 5.

[119] See, eg, John H Langbein and Richard S Posner, "Market Funds and Trust Investment Law," 3 *Am B Found Res J* 1 (1976).

[120] Unif Prudent Investor Act § 2 cmt (1994); *Restatement (Third) of Trusts* (1992) § 227; Pensions Act 1995 § 34(1); Trustee Act 2000 § 3(1).

rule—changed the way institutional trustees handle their trusts. The proportion of the average trust portfolio devoted to stock rose by as much as 4.5 percent.[121]

In the wake of the 2008 crisis, some scholars suggested that these most recent changes did not serve beneficiaries well and should be reevaluated. Joshua Getzler argues that a reversal should be considered—not merely back to the prudent man standard, but to the "court list" rule that prohibits altogether certain investments, such as corporate stock.[122] Stewart Sterk offers a less restrictive suggestion—to enact a pair of safe harbors: one that protects trustees from liability for excessive risk if they invest less than 60 percent of the trust's portfolio in equity, and another that precludes liability for *insufficient* risk if trustees invest at least 40 percent of the portfolio in equity. Moreover, in order to prevent a trustee from investing in specific, overpriced assets (since occasional market bubbles are presumably inevitable), Sterk would require a trustee engaged in active investment practices to explain to the court, in the event of failure, why he made each specific investment. Sterk claims that once trustees were permitted to invest in all possible ventures without fear of liability, they began to consider extremely risky investments with high returns. Then, when they achieved high returns, they were able to attract more clients by advertising these returns but downplaying the levels of risk they entailed. During market downturns, Sterk further argues, competing money managers are unlikely to advertise their returns at all, and therefore a highly risky investment strategy generates minimal risk for trustees. Sterk believes that the introduction of his safe harbors would help to reduce these excessive risk levels.[123]

Max Schanzenbach and Robert Sitkoff reject Sterk's proposal as well as any other alternative to the modern prudent investor standard. They argue, first, that there is no evidence that alternative investment strategies would have served beneficiaries better during the recent crisis. Second, they offer their own empirical study showing that the institutional trustees, who substantially increased their trusts' investment in shares after the adoption of the modern prudent investor standard, were those whose beneficiaries were well suited to bearing the additional risk. Finally, Schanzenbach and Sitkoff claim that a safe harbor that shields trustees from liability if they follow certain guidelines would cause too many trustees to follow these guidelines, because—being compensated by a percentage of the corpus—"they have little incentive to increase returns."[124]

Both sides of this debate make valid points. It is true, as Schanzenbach and Sitkoff note, that the old regime did not encourage enough risk-taking and that "formerly disfavored assets" may actually be "an important part of a diversification strategy" insofar as they are "not perfectly correlated with other asset classes."[125] By the same token, although given the heterogeneity of beneficiaries' preferences we are hesitant to endorse the idea of *general* thresholds of investment in equity (even if crafted as safe harbors),[126] Sterk may be right that the new, more fluid, standard drives trustees

[121] Max M Schanzenbach and Robert H Sitkoff, "Did Reform of Prudent Trust Investment Laws Change Trust Portfolio Allocation?," 50 *JL & Econ* 681, 707 (2007).

[122] Getzler (n 116) at 26–7.

[123] Stewart E Sterk, "Rethinking Trust Law Reform: How Prudent Is Modern Prudent Investor Doctrine?," 95 *Cornell L Rev* 851, 882, 887–8, 891, 896 (2010).

[124] Schanzenbach and Sitkoff (n 109) at 2, 7, 13, 26–40.

[125] Schanzenbach and Sitkoff (n 109) at 10.

[126] If investments of a specific kind are overseen by a regulator, such as a pension regulator, it would seem reasonable for her to set thresholds that are circumstance dependent and subject to periodic revision.

towards excessive risk-taking, especially in times of market bubbles and overpriced equity. To be sure, some of Sterk's concerns may (and should) be ameliorated through rules that prevent trustees from attracting clients by advertising inflated returns that stem from extreme risks: trustees who publicize their past returns should be required to provide information for a long period of time along with data on the riskiness of their investments. But it is not clear that these measures can sufficiently overcome the concern with excessive risk-taking.

These valid and conflicting concerns can be attributed to the detrimental impact of the traditional way trustees (and trust advisers) are compensated, which is typically computed as a set annual percentage of the value of the trust's assets.[127] The prudent man standard might have worked well had it paired the relatively mild threat of liability for speculative investing with some type of performance-based remuneration allowing the trustee to enjoy more of an upside from fruitful investments.[128] Similarly, the threat of excessive risk-taking could be alleviated were trustees to share in the risk by way of a suitable fee formula (or share the investments themselves). Moreover, the prevailing percentage-of-the-assets fee structure, in which financial fiduciaries can gain or lose mostly from getting a larger or smaller market share, exacerbates a herding problem. A money manager currently loses almost nothing by performing badly if her peers do not perform much better. And since the upside of outsmarting the market is likewise limited, she will often opt to mimic her peers' investment strategies. This herding tendency is particularly harmful during market bubbles, when overpriced investment opportunities become readily available, because herding exacerbates bubbles. Since this may have been a background factor in the recent financial crisis (especially the subprime crash),[129] it may be high time for a change to the traditional fee structure for financial fiduciaries.[130]

A thorough discussion of what fee structure could produce optimal incentives for money managers' investment policy is unnecessary for our purposes, but two conclusions seem appropriate. First, we assert that an analysis of financial fiduciaries' investment policy must reexamine their compensation structure. (Hence our treatment of the relationship between fiduciary compensation and the duty of loyalty in our last section.) Second, although we find overly aggressive the suggestion that financial fiduciaries' fees follow hedge-fund managers' fees, a generous (usually 20 percent) cut of the profits,[131] we believe that a balanced scheme can be reached. For instance, the fee structure could be along the lines of restricted stock grants to corporate managers, so

[127] See Robert C Illig, "The Promise of Hedge Fund Governance: How Incentive Compensation Can Enhance Institutional Investor Monitoring," 60 *Ala L Rev* 41, 68 (2008).

[128] The trustee's upside under the percentage-of-the-corpus-based compensation structure is mild. Thus, if the annual return earned is 5 percent and the percentage-of-the-corpus is 1 percent, the trustee enjoys an upside of only 0.05 percent of the assets she manages.

[129] See generally Adam J Levitin and Susan M Wachte, "Explaining the Housing Bubble," 100 *Geo LJ* 1177 (2012).

[130] Untraditional fee structures may be found even today in the incentive schemes of investment advisers. In a directed trust it is possible to outsource the investment function to an investment adviser who directs the trustee how to invest the assets of the trust. In such cases it is common to find success fees and untraditional fee arrangements for the adviser. Interestingly, it is unclear to what extent the investment adviser is subject to the requirements of trust law. See Jesse Dukeminier and Robert H Sitkoff, *Wills, Trusts and Estates* (9th edn, 2013) 654.

[131] Illig (n 127) at 102.

that the fiduciary would share the fate of her beneficiary for better or worse.[132] Such a fee structure would be symmetric in that managers would enjoy part of the fruits of success, but their exposure to the downside could prevent them from taking excessive risks.

3. *Opt-outs*

We began our doctrinal survey with the duty of loyalty because it is the signature feature of fiduciary law. Adding to this our earlier discussion of the disgorgement remedy for disloyalty[133] and the duty of care just covered, we have canvassed much of the doctrinal fabric of the law of financial fiduciaries. Our next inquiry relates to the status of this doctrine: Is it, as its canonical economic analysis suggests, "naturally" open to contrary agreement by the parties,[134] just like any other default, or should it instead be deemed immutable, as the moralist account of the duty of loyalty may suggest? We believe that it should be neither. Rather than comprising "mere" defaults or fully mandatory rules, we conceptualize financial fiduciaries law as a set of "sticky" default rules[135] wrapped in two standards—the duty of loyalty and the duty of care—which can be similarly derogated, but not completely set aside.

Our starting point is structural pluralism's emphasis on private law's autonomy-enhancing role, which implies a wide scope of freedom of contract. For pluralists, private law institutions offer unifying normative ideals for core categories of interpersonal relationships. People should be able to choose from these institutions in line with their own conceptions of the good and the means necessary for its realization given their particular needs and circumstances. This fundamental commitment to self-authorship—accompanied by a degree of caution regarding legal regimes that put too much power in the hands of lawmakers—requires that, in general, people should be able to choose not only from among the various private law institutions, but also within each of them. Immutability is troublesome from this perspective, because it does not accommodate heterogeneity, let alone idiosyncrasy, nor does it sufficiently accommodate the possibility of mistaken rules. Thus, where no third-party negative externalities are at stake, private law should not force its rules; rather, people should be able to consensually modify the rules of the pertinent institution if they so choose. Of course, at times the law might legitimately regulate and even strictly scrutinize such opt-outs in order to guarantee that they reflect people's informed choices. Nonetheless, to the extent possible, private law should attempt to overcome problems of information asymmetry and cognitive biases by prescribing sticky defaults rather than by curtailing choice through mandatory rules.[136]

[132] See Kevin J Murphy, "Executive Compensation: Where We Are, and How We Got There," in George Constantinides et al (eds), *Handbook of the Economics of Finance* (forthcoming 2014), available at <http://ssrn.com/abstract=2041679> (manuscript at 10).

[133] See text accompanying nn 43–8.

[134] See Sitkoff (n 88) at 1045. See also text accompanying n 38.

[135] On sticky defaults, see Ian Ayres, "Regulating Opt Out: An Economic Theory of Altering Rules," 121 *Yale LJ* 2032, 2084–8 (2012).

[136] See Dagan (n 9) at 1436.

It is hard to see why any specific rule of financial fiduciaries law should not be subject to these conclusions.[137] After all, significant welfare interests of the beneficiaries are on the line, and it is unlikely that government officials will inevitably do better than the parties at analyzing the situation and choosing the optimal solution. And while it is true that private parties suffer from cognitive-behavioral biases, limited willpower, and many other imperfections that may well justify stickiness, public officials are not necessarily immune from these either or, for that matter, other similar biases.[138] Even the expressive function of the duty of loyalty does not justify immutability, as opposed to stickiness. To be sure, we do not deny that immutability may send a clear message that, arguably, supports a particular social norm, and there may be cases where there is no other viable way to express such a message (the legal regime governing insider trading in securities law may be a case in point). But we do dispute that all default rules, irrespective of their structure and degree of stickiness, carry no normative content or signal indifference regarding the law's expressive message. While the rhetoric of gap-filling and optionality may dilute this expressive function,[139] the law can structure its doctrine so as to preserve, even inculcate, the social norms it deems of value, without sacrificing people's ability to opt out of its rules.[140]

Financial fiduciaries law can, and to some extent already does, address both the behavioral and expressive concerns while avoiding immutability. One important way to do this is by offering loyalty and care as defaults. As we argue, while embracing the traditional sole interest rule, such a default rule—like the reasonableness counterpart insofar as the duty of care is concerned—serves an important expressive function, especially in an environment that increasingly requires the carving-out of exceptions and exemptions. These traditional defaults are also justified on behavioral grounds that seem particularly pertinent to weak and unsophisticated parties. Even if most beneficiaries prefer a different default, opting out of the sole interest rule yields lower expected costs for them than the expected costs entailed by a more subtle default for unsophisticated beneficiaries (and settlors). Therefore, even if it were to turn out that most fiduciary relationships choose to opt out of a sole interest default rule, financial fiduciaries law should not replace its demanding defaults with simple majoritarian rules.[141]

A second, no less important legal device that can help law attain the delicate balance between opting out and expressiveness, while properly addressing these behavioral

[137] The rule governing delegation of investment decisions, which we do not discuss in detail, can exemplify this. Prior to the Uniform Prudent Investor Act of 1994, the default was that investment decisions should not be delegated by the trustee, but if the trustee does decide to delegate, then she is liable for any negligent act by the investment adviser. Given the enhanced duty to diversify and thus the greater need to delegate investment decisions, section 9 of the Uniform Prudent Investor Act changed the default, and the trustee is currently liable only for negligent selection of the investment adviser. Schanzenbach and Sitkoff (n 109) at 14, hail this change, whereas Sterk (n 123) at 898, prefers the old default. We would opt for a middle-ground default rule that imposes liability on the trustee if the delegation was to an entity or person who was (1) professionally unfit for the stint or (2) lacked the financial resources or insurance that could meet potential liability. The trustee could opt out of this standard after alerting the settlor or receiving permission from the beneficiary.

[138] See Christine Jolls et al, "A Behavioral Approach to Law and Economics," 50 *Stan L Rev* 1471, 1543 (1998).

[139] See Leslie (n 57) at 69–70, 91, 116.

[140] See Dagan (n 9) at 1436. But cf Leslie (n 57) at 89.

[141] Cf Lucian Bebchuk, "The Debate on Contractual Freedom in Corporate Law," 89 *Colum L Rev* 1395 (1989). Contra Langbein (n 38) at 660; Langbein (n 86) at 987–90.

concerns, is "impeding altering rules."[142] We join Leslie in insisting that although parties should be (and, in fact, are) able to "authorize particular acts that would otherwise be a breach of the duty [of loyalty]," this should be allowed by way of "limited, specific initial waivers," and they should not be able (and, in fact, are unable) to "agree to dispense with the duty entirely."[143] Sweeping exculpatory clauses run counter to the regulatory principle of financial fiduciaries law—to its distinct autonomy-enhancing function, which is the rationale for resorting to it—and a fully informed settler would be unlikely to agree to them. With Leslie we believe that a similar approach should apply regarding the duty of care for professional financial fiduciaries,[144] or at least that the law should resort to a "thought-requiring altering rule"[145] by requiring fiduciaries who offer a broad exculpatory clause for a discount to offer two different prices for the two types of services.[146]

Other impeding altering rules could further enable opting-out without diluting law's normative force or risking suboptimal opt-outs, especially by less sophisticated parties who may otherwise be misled by fiduciary law's expressive function. Leslie supports, as do we, requiring financial fiduciaries who offer "suspicious" waivers (eg, investing in their own investment vehicles and thus earning double commissions) to at least notify their beneficiaries about their conflicting interest.[147] Financial fiduciaries law could similarly use a "reversibility altering rule" to contend with the concern that if circumstances change and pro-fiduciary norms become outdated, it tends to be difficult for beneficiaries to adjust them.[148] This rule could take the form of a sunset provision, requiring beneficiaries to periodically confirm that they are still interested in these provisions.[149] Alternatively, the legislature or courts could be authorized to create new, future-oriented defaults if they identify a market-wide change in circumstances that calls into question all choices made by parties to fiduciary relationships at earlier dates.[150] Such unique altering rules would override all prior opt-outs from anti-fiduciary rules, while allowing parties to reaffirm their wish to deviate from the default by choosing to opt-out once again.

[142] Ayres (n 136) at 2086. [143] Leslie (n 57) at 112–13.

[144] Leslie (n 57) at 95–110. But cf Adam S Hofri-Winogradow, "The Stripping of the Fund: From Evolutionary Scripts to Distributive Results" (unpublished manuscript) (arguing, based on a UK empirical study of settlors' attitudes towards exculpatory clauses, that "most settlors are unlikely to be sufficiently aware of the implications" of such clauses).

[145] Ayres (n 136) at 2069–71.

[146] Leslie (n 57) at 102.

[147] See Leslie (n 57) at 116. This obligation seems to be entailed by the duty of candour.

[148] See Ayres (n 136) at 2083–4. Ayres does not address sunset provisions of the type we recommend here. His example of a reversibility altering rule—of cooling-off periods—has the effect of allowing the reconsideration of decisions that were initially mistaken and is especially effective against aggressive marketing techniques. Sunset provisions are important for allowing people to correct their decisions following changed circumstances that demonstrate that they either were initially mistaken or no longer properly serve the intended interests.

[149] For examples of sunset provisions, see Hong Kong law on prolonged interested party transactions, Related Party Transactions and Minority Shareholder Rights (n 99) at 35, and similar legislation in Israel, Companies Law 5759–1999, 44 LSI 119 § 275(a1), § 121(c) (1999). Beneficiary-reconfirmation requirement could, however, cause holdout problems in certain circumstances.

[150] See Sharon Hannes, "Corporate Stagnation: Discussion and Reform Proposal," 30 *J Corp L* 51, 61–73 (2004).

These and other possible measures would all be intended to ensure that an opt-out is deemed valid if and only if (1) it is sufficiently detailed and refers to circumstances the beneficiary (or testator) can reasonably assess *ex ante* (this requirement implies that no wholesale list of all possible exemptions should be validated) and (2) it is carried out in a way that conforms with an altering rule tailored to address the problem this category of exemption could raise for weak and unsophisticated beneficiaries (or testators).[151] Focusing on these latter actors is the most important prescription of an autonomy-based analysis of the law of financial fiduciaries (given that there is no simple way of splitting up the universe of beneficiaries into distinct categories).

4. *Fiduciaries' compensation*

Our last doctrinal question concerns fiduciary compensation. Although historically, the paradigmatic financial fiduciary was a trusted family or community member who performed the task of trusteeship gratuitously, nowadays it is a professional profit-making firm.[152] This is not necessarily a detrimental development and understandable given the increasingly complicated tasks involved. What we do find worrisome is fiduciary law's standard disinterest in the fiduciary's pay, which is perceived as exogenous to the duty of loyalty[153] despite the truism that this compensation comes at the beneficiary's expense.

Two explanations have been offered for this approach. Miller suggests that because the duty of loyalty focuses on the fiduciary's execution of the beneficiary's mandate, it cannot conceptually cover compensation arrangements, which are determined before the fiduciary takes office.[154] Leslie provides practical support for the same comforting conclusion: that "allowing settlors to compensate professional trustees generate[s] obvious benefits for the trust, with no offsetting risk."[155] We find neither of these arguments convincing. Perhaps the currently prevalent compensation arrangements are indeed innocent, but this is a contingent conclusion; and it is misguided and potentially damaging to view fiduciary pay as lying outside the ambit of the duty of loyalty. This may well be the most significant doctrinal implication of our account.

If there is one area in fiduciary law that can benefit from the corporate experience it is fiduciary pay, given the overwhelming contribution of modern schemes of executive compensation to two financial mega-crises over the last decade or so. The corporate context demonstrates that fiduciary compensation cannot be regarded as temporally extrinsic to the fiduciary relationship, because compensation is often adjusted during their term. In the last four decades, these adjustments resulted in an enormous upsurge in corporate executive pay,[156] a shift which is partly attributed to managers' ability to

[151] Corporate law also took a similar position. Thus, when Delaware allowed companies to exempt directors from monetary liability for breaches of duty of care, it maintained a full liability default, although as expected, most companies immediately opted out and exempted their directors. See Henry N Butler, "*Smith v Van Gorkom*, Jurisdictional Competition, and the Role of Random Mutations in the Evolution of Corporate Law," 45 *Washburn LJ* 267 (2006). This minoritarian standard may have been justified in order to protect shareholders who prefer to preserve liability but would have found it hard to opt out from a reverse no-liability standard.

[152] See Leslie (n 57) at 86.

[153] See text accompanying n 24.

[154] Miller (n 13) at 606; see also text accompanying n 24.

[155] Leslie (n 58) at 568.

[156] See Murphy (n 132) at 14; Lucian A Bebchuk and Yaniv Grinstein, "The Growth of Executive Pay," 21 *Oxford Rev Econ Pol'y* 283, 285 tbl 1 (2005).

influence their own compensation.[157] This "managerial power hypothesis"—which may be relevant also in fiduciary settings in which compensation is determined while the relationship is ongoing—is cogent and convincing. Yet traditional corporate law also contributed to this unjustified trend because, in line with the conventional divorce of fiduciary pay from the fiduciary relationship, it did not view pay practices as conflict-of-interest transactions and, therefore, did not set the appropriate safeguards.[158]

This cautionary note is bolstered by the fact that, *pace* Leslie, compensation formulas could generate conflicts of interest resulting in severe and hard to predict effects. The corporate setting thus offers a further, disturbing lesson: pay formulas designed to enhance the fiduciary's incentives and to align her interests with those of the beneficiary may, ironically, exacerbate the agency problem and aggravate the prospect of abuse by the fiduciary. Indeed, the sharp rise in corporate executive compensation can be attributed to the corresponding dramatic increase in stock-option grants to executives.[159] Moreover, empirical research has shown that equity-based compensation has perverse negative effects, which intensify as salary is dwarfed by options and, more generally, by incentive pay.[160] Equity-based compensation, it turns out, is a major catalyst for all forms of corporate misrepresentation, from mere abuse of accounting discretion by whitewashing or sugarcoating harmful disclosures, to paltering and outright fraud. Simply put, once managers' pay is dependent on share prices, it is hard to detach their incentives to improve the firm from their incentives to artificially misrepresent the firm's performance.[161] Thus, even after Congress made it much harder for managers to engage in manipulative practices following the 2001–2 accounting scandals,[162] deleterious incentive-based pay practices persisted. Because stock options and annual bonuses yield attractive profits in good scenarios versus mild penalties in bad scenarios, this feature of executive compensation is widely claimed to have led to the excessive risk levels that culminated in the recent financial crisis.[163]

Ultimately, Congress had to switch course and incorporate a "say-on-pay" mechanism into the Dodd–Frank Act.[164] And while the outcome of the shareholders' vote is currently only precatory in the US[165]—but might soon become binding overseas[166]—more

[157] Lucian Bebchuk and Jesse Fried, *Pay without Performance: The Unfulfilled Promise of Executive Compensation* (2004) 80.

[158] See Clark (n 98) at 192.

[159] See Bebchuk and Grinstein (n 158) at 290 tbl 4; Kevin J Murphy, "Explaining Executive Compensation: Managerial Power Versus the Perceived Cost of Stock Options," 69 *U Chi L Rev* 847, 848 (2002).

[160] For a literature review, see Sharon Hannes and Avi Tabbach, "Executive Stock Options: The Effects of Manipulation on Risk Taking," 38 *J Corp L* 533 (2013).

[161] See, eg, John C Coffee, Jr, "What Caused Enron? A Capsule Social and Economic History of the 1990s," 89 *Cornell L Rev* 269 (2004).

[162] See Sarbanes–Oxley Act of 2002, HR 3763, 107th Cong (2002); Sharon Hannes, "Compensating for Executive Compensation: The Case for Gatekeeper Incentive Pay," 98 *Cal L Rev* 385 (2010).

[163] See, eg, Sanjai Bhagat and Roberta Romano, "Reforming Executive Compensation: Focusing and Committing to the Long-Term," 26 *Yale J on Reg* 359 (2009); Lucian A Bebchuk and Holger Spamann, "Regulating Bankers' Pay," 98 *Geo LJ* 247 (2010).

[164] Dodd–Frank Wall Street Reform and Consumer Protection Act § 951 (codified as section 14A of the Securities Exchange Act of 1934, 15 USC § 78a).

[165] Shareholders litigation aimed against corporate directors that approved compensation packages against the shareholders vote have consistently failed. See, eg, *Raul v Rynd* No 11-560-LPS, 2012 US Dist LEXIS 25256, at 28–32 (D Del 14 March 2013).

[166] A government-sponsored bill in the UK aims to contend with this shift. Dep't for Bus Innovation & Skills, Enterprise & Regulatory Reform Bill: Directors' Pay, <http://discuss.bis.gov.uk/enterprise-bill/files/2012/11/12-1255-enterprise-regulatory-reform-bill-directors-pay.pdf>.

than half of the firms respond to an adverse shareholder vote by engaging with investors and making changes to their compensation plans.[167] This new requirement for shareholder approval of compensation properly mirrors the traditional trust-law structure of a sole interest rule paired with an exception for conflict-of-interest transactions that are approved by the beneficiaries (here, the shareholders). Compensation arrangements should not be regarded as intrinsically beyond the scope of the duty of loyalty. Delaware's Chancery Court recently affirmed this important understanding when it decided (in departure from earlier decisions) to carefully scrutinize the directors' stock-option plan, even though the plan had been generally approved by the company's stockholders.[168]

These changes have been triggered by the macro consequences of the fiascos that generated the recent financial crisis. But behind these consequences stand real people whose trust has been betrayed and fortunes depleted. Corporate law had to experience crisis in order to appreciate that the compensation of corporate managers should be subject to careful scrutiny and approval processes. Because fiduciary pay is no different, a credible theory of financial fiduciaries cannot ignore these lessons. Compensation of financial fiduciaries may well be unavoidable nowadays and thus warrants an exemption from the sole interest rule. But it is wrong and, as we have seen, potentially devastating to treat it as exogenous to the fiduciary relationship. Construing fiduciary pay as an exception to the rule implies that those crafting or sanctioning remuneration schemes must keep the beneficiaries' interests in mind. It also preserves the presumption that this kind of transaction should be carefully scrutinized and periodically reexamined.

This conclusion is, by and large, forward-looking: The typical compensation schemes for financial trustees are presently not afflicted with the most severe problems that plagued its corporate counterparts. But because, as noted, more sophisticated pay structures may be in the making, certain safeguards are required. Thus, the current fee structure for pension plan trustees, based on a fixed annual percentage of the assets they oversee,[169] does not incentivize short-termism or intense risk-taking. Quite the contrary: Under such a scheme, not only does the money manager not reap immediate profit from short-term gains or excessively risky investments, but she can also expect to be rewarded for long-term successes. For once performance can be assessed, more money is likely to be channeled to the best money managers, and consequently, the fees generated as a percentage of the assets they manage will increase. But given the significant distortions (noted above) this conventional fee structure yields for financial fiduciaries' investment strategies,[170] the formula may eventually change. If and when this happens, it will be important to keep in mind the conflict of interest that more sophisticated pay structures tend to produce. Here lies the importance of monitoring fiduciary pay as an exception to the sole interest rule and of periodically reexamining

[167] See Yonca Ertimur et al, *Shareholder Vote and Proxy Advisors: Evidence from Say on Pay* (2013), available at <http://papers.ssrn.com/sol3/papers.cfm?abstract_id=2019239>. Many other firms avoid such an outcome at the outset by adapting to shareholders anticipated wishes.

[168] *Seinfeld v Slager* Civ No 6462-VCG, 2012 WL 2501105 at *32 (Del Ch 29 June 2012). Cf *In re 3COM Corp Shareholders Litigation* No CA 16721, 1999 WL 1009210, at *1 (Del Ch 25 Oct 1999).

[169] See text accompanying nn 127–32. [170] See text accompanying nn 127–32.

its impact for the sake of the economy and of the beneficiaries whose pensions, savings, and bequests are at stake.

Finally, even today, with the traditional compensation formulas for money-managers still in place, their pay should be conceptualized as an exception to the sole interest rule and closely scrutinized, because fiduciary pay is often not an arm's length transaction. *Jones v Harris*,[171] dealing with the review standard for compensation of a mutual fund adviser (the fund's de facto money manager) who is by law "deemed to have a fiduciary duty with respect to the receipt of compensation,"[172] is illustrative. Whereas Judge Easterbrook refused to examine the "reasonableness" of the adviser's fee,[173] Judge Posner's dissent—highlighting the adviser's influence on its own pay-setting mechanism, expressing concern that "the advisor's charging its captive funds more than twice what it charges independent funds," and advocating more careful scrutiny of the size of the adviser's fee package—is clearly preferable.[174] Furthermore, because fiduciary pay should be governed by norms similar to those governing other deviations from the sole interest rule, his approach should apply to all instances of fiduciary pay that are not set by a market mechanism or other reassuring device.

Concluding Remarks

Financial fiduciaries law is an important case study on the contribution of private law to our personal autonomy. In a complicated world, with increasingly complex challenges to our ability to manage our finances and secure our welfare, law offers the option of delegating the authority to do so to others. For this option to be viable and enable us to focus on our intrinsically valuable projects, financial fiduciaries law must appreciate the significant risks of abuse and carelessness inherent to the delegation of such discretionary authority, while keeping in mind beneficiaries' welfarist purposes. The law should accordingly tailor its rules to provide fiduciaries with optimal incentives while inculcating the social norms associating these rules with the virtues of trust and loyalty.

This chapter celebrates the structure of traditional financial fiduciaries law, which tackles this challenging mission by entrenching a strict sole interest rule alongside many exceptions and exemptions that serve beneficiaries' best interests. Yet it also offers some direction for reform that could further the law's ability to pursue this task. The law should allow opt-outs but also design a range of sticky defaults that respond to the needs of weak and unsophisticated beneficiaries. The law should also realize the significance of revisiting the fee structure for fiduciaries, as well as reexamine its investment policy prescriptions. Finally and significantly, it should renounce its traditional treatment of fiduciary pay so that it is no longer considered exogenous to the duty of loyalty.

[171] *Jones v Harris Assoc LP* 527 F 3d 627 (No 07-1624) (7th Cir 19 May 2008), reh'g denied, 537 F 3d 728 (7th Cir 8 Aug 2008).
[172] Investment Company Act of 1940 § 36(b), 15 USC § 80a-35(b).
[173] *Jones* 537 F 3d at 733.
[174] *Jones* (n 173) at 731–2.

PART II

FIDUCIARY DUTIES

5

Fiduciary Loyalty as Kantian Virtue

*Irit Samet**

Introduction

The concept of loyalty carries heavy baggage. It calls to mind deep feelings for family, homeland, and friends. Its opposite, disloyalty, is associated with vengeance and humiliation. Loyalty is thus hardly the kind of concept you would expect to find at the heart of an eminent private law doctrine. Yet, many cases and scholarly works on fiduciaries cite with approval the statement of Millett LJ in *Bristol & West* that "the distinguishing obligation of a fiduciary is the obligation of loyalty."[1] And so it came about that a concept first invoked more than 200 years ago, at a time when explicit appeals to inter-personal morality were common in courts of equity, is still fundamental to the modern legal regulation of economic relationships. Some academics, like Peter Birks, find the concept of loyalty to be "less than useful [as it] fails to hit the nail on the head."[2] Most, however, treat the duty of loyalty as the centerpiece of their theory of fiduciary doctrine.

Consensus on the significance of the concept of loyalty to fiduciary law has not put an end to the controversy concerning the precise *nature* of the fiduciary's duty to be loyal to her principal. Indeed, there is disagreement whether the duty of loyalty has any *independent* content at all. Some, like Matthew Conaglen, argue that fiduciary duties fulfil a purely prophylactic role of ensuring that other, non-fiduciary duties (like the duty of care) are complied with.[3] I will not presently engage the debate over the content of the duty of loyalty. Instead, I accept, without further argument, Lionel Smith's opposite view that the duty of loyalty has the following highly specific content: when deciding how to act in matters that concern the principal, fiduciaries should not employ any considerations other than the advancement of their principal's interest(s). Since the fiduciary is placed in a distinctive position of authority, in which she has to make decisions about the resources (and sometimes even the body) of other people, in conditions where there is a serious gap in her favor in terms of information (always) and power (very often), we can expect the law to regulate her decision-making process via the duty of loyalty so construed.

* I am very grateful to Hanoch Dagan, Andrew Gold, Ori Herstein, Nick McBride, Paul Miller, Prince Saprai, Lionel Smith, Sandy Steel, and the participants of the conference on Philosophical Foundations of Fiduciary Duty for their helpful comments. The usual caveat applies.

1 *Bristol and West Building Society v Mothew* [1998] Ch 1 CA.

2 Peter Birks, "The Content of Fiduciary Obligation," 34 *Israel Law Journal* 3, 12 (2000).

3 "[T]he concept of 'loyalty'... operates so as to increase the likelihood of the fiduciary's faithful adherence to duty... by protecting the fiduciary from influences that are likely to interfere with proper performance of the fiduciary's *non*-fiduciary duties." Matthew Conaglen, *Fiduciary Loyalty: Protecting the Due performance of Non-fiduciary Duties* (2010) 61.

The duty of loyalty, on this interpretation, instructs fiduciaries to take the principal's good as the sole end of their actions. The duty is further grounded in the no-conflict rules, which forbid the fiduciary from taking any (unauthorized) actions that may, even accidently, serve her own interests. These strict rules are in place because, in situations of conflict, the risk that something other than the principal's best interest will influence the fiduciary is high. The working of the human mind is such that it is extremely difficult, if not impossible, to exercise judgment in a proper manner (ie, as required by the duty of loyalty) where the personal interests of the decision-makers are involved.[4] The prohibition on conflicts when making a decision about other people's affairs is not unique to fiduciaries: as Lionel Smith points out, parallel rules are scattered all over administrative law.[5]

Yet, only in fiduciary law is the requirement to discount extraneous considerations put in terms of "loyalty." In this chapter, I want to ask why equity resorts to this freighted concept. Is "loyalty" merely a romantic name or does it reflect a substantive aspect of the fiduciary doctrine? Does equity take "loyalty" to mean something narrow and distinctive or does it tap on the full-bodied sense of the word? In this chapter I argue that the latter is the case. By importing the loaded concept of loyalty from ethics and sociology, equity endeavors to encapsulate a subtle and complex aspect of the fiduciary relationship. Fiduciary loyalty does not just encompass the thin sense of loyalty associated with the proscriptive rules. It also incorporates a much thicker sense of loyalty. To show this, I proceed in Section I to unpack the concept of loyalty and then offer a preliminary account of how equity regards it as a virtue to be cultivated in fiduciaries. Section II then considers a possible objection to this view. In Section III I endeavor to refute this concern.

I. Loyalty, Thick and Thin

Loyalty, like love and jealousy, can take different shapes, and stretch over a wide range of emotional states, according to the type of relationship in which it is anchored. Expectations of loyalty vary so greatly from one type of relationship to another that we may come to wonder whether there is indeed much point in talking about it as one unified concept. Is there a common thread running through the loyalties of a wife to her ailing husband, the *mafioso* to his *famiglia*, the soldier to his country, and the consumer to a brand of deodorant? In his monograph on the subject, George Fletcher offers a scale of loyalties that spans from a mere expectation not to be betrayed, to an all-encompassing anticipation of union between the loyal and the subject of her loyalty.[6] Nevertheless, he finds that all loyalties exhibit one common trait: they make it

[4] Even the fiduciary herself cannot tell for sure whether illegitimate considerations were involved in the decision; see more on this in Irit Samet, "Guarding the Fiduciary's Conscience—A Justification of a Stringent Profit-stripping Rule," 28 *Oxford Journal of Legal Studies* 763 (2008).

[5] Lionel Smith "Fiduciary Obligations: Ensuring the Loyal Exercise of Judgement," a lecture given at King's College, London, in March 2013.

[6] George P Fletcher, *Loyalty: An Essay on the Morality of Relationships* (1993) 41–77. In my view, Fletcher's methodology is more fruitful than Simon Keller's, who sets out looking for a conceptual definition that captures all instances of loyalty. When, expectedly, he cannot find such definition he concludes that "loyalty is a fairly thin concept. [It] does not tell you. . . much. . . about how [the loyal] is disposed to think and behave". In that way Keller is missing out on many of the nuances and insights that are embedded in the thick concept of loyalty (Simon Keller, *The Limits of Loyalty* (2007) 21).

more difficult to break away from the relationship. The great benefits of loyalty's propensity to raise the "exit price" were demonstrated by Albert Hirschman in his ground-breaking study of loyalty in economic relationships. The loyal employee or consumer does not opt for the competitor in times of trouble; instead, she speaks out about things she is unhappy with, and thus gives the organization a valuable chance to fix what needs fixing without losing stakeholders in the process. The trademark of loyalty, says Hirschman, is "reluctance to exit in spite of disagreement."[7] In personal relationships, like friendship and marriage, disinclination to quit helps sustain the bond through inevitable strain.

On Fletcher's scale, the loyalty of fiduciaries rests near the minimal end. But if the core of loyalty is persistence in the face of difficulties, it seems hard to see why we would want to use it as an organizing concept in fiduciary law. After all, the fiduciary is generally free to leave her post.[8] Yet, if we go deeper into what underlies the disinclination to exit, we find a willingness to set aside self-interest. The employee who sticks with a company in difficulties, the wife who works hard to make a marriage work, the famous actress who chooses to pay "rich tax" rather than emigrate to Russia—what drives them to stay put is a commitment to the *relationship*.[9] This attitude of selflessness is also what lies at the heart of the fiduciary duty. The requirement to put other people's interest in front of your own interests is basic to the fiduciary duty no matter how it is conceptualized.

This sense of selfless devotion has, however, a dark side to it. Josiah Royce, for example, demands of the loyal that he be able to say: "I am the servant of [the object of my loyalty], its reasonable, its willing, its devoted instrument, and being such I have neither eyes to see nor tongue to speak save as this cause shall command."[10] These allusions to servitude and blindness are alarming. Loyalty, it is implied, can be heedlessly directed to unworthy objects, and even where the objects are worthy it can easily blind us to the needs and rights of people outside the relationship. I will comment first on the risk of unworthy objects, and then discuss the bias problem.

Loyalty can be found in the most appalling contexts and motivate gruesome actions.[11] This should make us wonder whether the idea of loyalty as a virtue has any plausibility. One easy way forward is to link loyalty and justice. David Ladd's definition of loyalty, for instance, suggests just that: "at the very least, loyalty requires the complete subordination of one's own private interests in favour of giving what is due."[12] If we describe loyalty by reference to "what is due" we restrict the range of its objects to worthwhile ones. But this,

[7] Albert O Hirschman, *Exit, Voice, and Loyalty: Responses to Decline in Firms, Organizations, and States* (1970) 98.

[8] *Hunter Kane Limited Watkins* [2002] EWHC 186 (Ch). That does not mean, of course, that fiduciaries can escape their duties (eg, not to exploit company's opportunities) simply by resigning (see for instance, *Canadian Aero Services v O'Malley* [1974] 1 SCR 592 (SCC)).

[9] Things are more complicated than this of course. Loyalty tends to attach to relationships which form part of our identity. In close relationship of that type, the distinction between actions that serve "me," actions that serve "you," and those that serve "us" is not always well defined. Nevertheless, even in the most intimate relationship, selfless actions are the mark of loyalty.

[10] Josiah Royce, *The Philosophy of Loyalty* (1908) 106. See also David Ladd: "at the very least, loyalty requires the complete subordination of one's own private interests in favour of giving what is due, and perhaps also the exclusion of other legitimate interests" (R E Ewin, "Loyalty and Virtues," 42 *Philosophical Quarterly* 403, at 405 (1992)).

[11] Here is an extreme example: "we teach our SS men that there are many things that can be forgiven on this earth, no matter how evil they be, but one thing never: disloyalty to the Fuhrer;" Heinrich Himmler, *Die Schutzstaffel* (1938), cited in Eric Felten, *Loyalty: The Vexing Virtue* (2011) 11.

[12] Ewin (n 10) at 405.

unfortunately, does not work. The "loyal Nazi" makes perfect sense, and the "disloyal Nazi" (say the party member who betrays the party's principles for a bribe) lacks exactly that kind of admirable trait that we try to capture with the notion of loyalty.[13]

Like sincerity, integrity, and (arguably) courage, loyalty is the kind of virtue which does not guarantee the moral quality of actions that are informed by it. You could, however, argue that the character of *agents* who lack these dispositions is diminished for that reason. The loyal Nazi will probably not strike you as virtuous, but a person who is indifferent or disloyal where loyalty is expected is repulsive. We tend to feel that there is something *morally* wrong with such behavior, and this provides a good indication of a conceptual connection between loyalty and virtue.[14] Conversely, when loyalty is attached to a morally worthy object we feel that it reflects very well on the agents who display it. So much so, that for some writers loyalty is the bedrock of virtues, an encapsulation of the crucial move from self-interest to selflessness.[15] The problem of unworthy objects is, however, only peripheral to fiduciary loyalty. In the large majority of cases, the loyal fiduciary's decision to pursue the principal's best interest will coincide with the demands of justice.[16] But this raises a different problem: where the requirements of justice and fiduciary loyalty coincide, what does loyalty add to justice? In other words, in what way will the conduct of the loyal *and* just person be different, indeed superior, to the action of the merely just? This is a more general way of asking the question with which I started this chapter; namely, what does loyalty in the thick sense add to the mixture of legal duties that define what the fiduciary should and should not do?

To understand the relationship between justice and loyalty, we must get a better understanding of virtue. For the ancient philosophers, virtue was a stable *disposition*, nurtured by the virtuous because she *knows* that people with virtuous dispositions tend to do the right thing. But, as Aristotle shows, even as the cultivation of virtue is driven by reason, emotions play a crucial role in the moral psychology of the virtuous. For the virtuous is expected not only to subject her emotions to reason but also to train her emotions to work in tandem with what virtue requires.[17] Aristotle's view of the interaction between reason and emotion in virtue occupies a middle ground between two antagonistic alternative

[13] Ewin (n 10) at 415; Keller (n 6) 22.

[14] Ewin (n 10) at 407; compare with Keller (n 6) 159, who argues that only people who quench natural feelings of loyalty that arise in them are morally reproachable.

[15] Ewin (n 10) 418: in order to overcome the problem of unworthy objects, Ewin suggests that loyalty is not exactly a virtue but "the raw material for [virtues]." Fletcher also has in store a highly ambitious plan for loyalty: in his view, it can function as an alternative basis for moral theory, which would replace the faulty objectivist ethics of Kant and Bentham (Fletcher (n 6) especially 164–8). Keller, in contrast, thinks that loyalty has no intrinsic value, that is, a value which is independent of the relationship within which it is embedded like friendship and parenthood (Keller (n 6) 146). Consequently, he argues that a tendency to form bonds of loyalty is not in and of itself a virtue (155). The question whether loyalty in general is a virtue is beyond the scope of the present chapter. But the kind of loyalty that is professed by honest fiduciaries is, I will argue, highly valuable (see Dagan and Hanesin this volume). The question that will keep us busy here is whether the loyal fiduciary displays a *moral* virtue.

[16] You could, of course, think of a case where this is not so. For example, where the fiduciary's wife needs an expensive medicine, and the only way to pay for it is through exploiting an opportunity that comes to the fiduciary as a result of his position. Another unfortunate example is the duty of the trustee to engage in unethical practices like "gazumping," if that will enhance the profits from selling the land held on trust (*Buttle v Saunders* [1950] 2 All ER 193). I will ignore these problematic cases here.

[17] Aristotle, *The Ethics of Aristotle: the Nicomachean ethics* (rev edn, 1976) 1102a13–1103a3, 1104b4–9. For an excellent detailed account of Aristotle's view of the role of emotion in virtue see Nancy Sherman, *Making a Necessity of Virtue: Aristotle and Kant on Virtue* (1997) ch 2.

accounts. According to the stoics, emotion has no significant place in the acquisition or expression of virtue. The virtuous, they thought, is a person who managed to free himself from the passions and the blurring effect which they have on judgment.[18]

At the other extreme, we find David Hume, for whom virtue is all about emotion: virtue, he says, is a disposition that begets that sentiment which is proper in the situation (eg, compassion, sympathy, or disgust).[19] But neither the Humean nor the stoic accounts are of much help when it comes to the analysis of the fiduciary duty. For one thing, with the stoic concept it is hard to make out the just fiduciary from the loyal one. If subjecting one's emotions to reason is all there is to virtue, then different virtues can only be distinguished according to the particular emotions that were suppressed to achieve them (eg, "fear" for courage, or "erotic love" for temperance). But in the fiduciary context, justice and loyalty suppress the same inclination, namely, "greed." The more fundamental problem with the stoic account is, however, its excessive sterility. When it comes to virtues like loyalty and confidence, the stoic account is thoroughly unsatisfactory. What loyalty adds to action in accordance with "what is due" is exactly an attachment which translates into a *feeling* that the well-being of the object of one's loyalty takes precedence over one's own good.[20] The virtuous fiduciary does not merely suppress greed; he also harbors the *proper emotion*, namely, devotion to her principal. The Humean account of virtue, as you would expect, runs into trouble from the opposite direction. For unlike loyalty to one's mother or school friend, which are more susceptible to analysis on a purely emotional basis, the loyalty of fiduciaries is based on a mature objective perception of the intricate power relations between fiduciaries and principals. The Humean account cannot but fail to capture the interdependence of emotion and reason in virtuous fiduciary loyalty, and is thus found wanting.

If we go back to the Aristotelian view of virtue, we find a picture of the virtuous as a composed person in whom the relationship between the emotional and rational side are typically of cooperation and agreement, rather than conflict and discord.[21] Thus, when we say that a fiduciary displays the virtue of loyalty, we suggest that his *emotions* reflect the *understanding* that his fiduciary status requires selfless action. The potential of loyalty to rearrange the order of priority within the conative part of the psyche is exactly what equity is tapping on in urging fiduciaries to be loyal. Thus, the fiduciary position is one in which "[l]oyalty is obligatory. . . [so that if] you are able to make choices that will reinforce your feelings of loyalty. . . you are morally required to do so."[22] There is no guarantee, of course, that feelings of loyalty coupled

[18] Eg, Seneca in the *De Matrimonio* says that "the wise man loves his wife by judgement not by passion" (cited in Martha Craven Nussbaum, *Upheavals of Thought: The Intelligence of Emotions* (2001) 235 n 118).

[19] David Hume, *A Treatise of Human Nature* (2nd edn, 1978) 498.

[20] For a similar emphasis on emotion as a necessary component of loyalty see Ewin (n 10): "loyalty is the emotional setting for the virtues and vices," at 418; Felten (n 11): "Loyalty, by contrast [to obligation], is an emotional response; it wells up inside us and carries us along", at 44; and the discussion in Keller (n 6) 15–17 and the conclusion that "an emotional attachment is found whenever we look closely at our own displays of loyalty" (17).

[21] Some would say too composed. Aristotle was very optimistic about the ability of the virtuous to train his emotions and achieve a genuine peace of mind, rather than mere control. Kant was more sceptical in this point, see herein text around n 66, and Sherman (n 17) 136–7.

[22] Keller (n 6) 144 and ch 6.

with understanding of one's duty will effectively suppress greed, but loyalty is a pretty good antidote to temptation.

The thick sense of loyalty can thus play an important role in guiding the behavior of fiduciaries: the association of fiduciary duty with loyalty conveys a strong message to the fiduciary that if he wishes to do his job well, he should develop and nurture the virtue of loyalty in the context of his relationship with the principal. True, the adoption of dispositions cannot be enforced. As Birks remarked in this context, "what the law requires when it requires altruism is at most action in the interest of others, outcomes, not motives."[23] But the function of law is not limited to the issuance of enforceable directives. The law can influence social norms in many ways. As expressive theories of law remind us, the value of legal norms cannot be measured solely on the basis of the consequences of its enforcement; a significant part of its value lies in the "statement" it makes. It is therefore easy to come by a law that "announces or signals a change in social norms [and is yet] *unaccompanied by much by way of enforcement activity.*"[24] The real importance of such laws is the long-run effect of the message they send out about the impropriety of certain behavior and the change they inculcate in social norms and the social meaning of action.

Thus, by presenting loyalty as an organizing theme for the legal duties of fiduciaries, equity communicates that compliance with this duty is more probable if fiduciaries develop a sense of loyalty to their principals. By drawing on the common understanding of loyalty equity sends a powerful message about the disposition appropriate to fiduciaries. And though it cannot be enforced, this recommendation is still highly significant since "the expression of social value. . . [is] possibly, the most important function of the courts."[25]

In what follows I identify and try to resolve a serious challenge for this interpretation of the term loyalty in the context of fiduciary relationship. As I work my way towards dispelling the difficulty, I wish to come up with a richer and more nuanced understanding of loyalty as the right disposition for fiduciaries.

II. Loyalty and the Fiduciary Relationship as a Moral Project

The interpretation of fiduciary loyalty as a recommendation to adopt a loyal disposition raises an interesting problem. The puzzle is premised on the observation that the most convincing justifications for fiduciary duties suggest that they embody moral duties which can be legitimately enforced by the state. Although disputed, this idea has now been accepted in numerous cases. [26] Some serious writers in the field undertook to find the

[23] Birks (n 2) 17.

[24] Cass Sunstein, "On the Expressive Function of Law," 144 *University of Pennsylvania Law Review* 2021, 2032 (1996); for a full presentation of the expressivist theory of law see Elizabeth S Anderson and Richard H Pildes, "Expressive Theories of Law: A General Restatement," 148 *University of Pennsylvania Law Review* 1503 (2000). Obvious examples are laws that forbid littering, or unenforced sodomy laws.

[25] Robert Cooter, "Expressive Law and Economics," 27 *The Journal of Legal Studies* 585, 585–6 (1998).

[26] See for instance *Parker v McKenna* (1874–5) LR 10 Ch App 96 CA, where Lord Cairns LC expressed the view that the no-conflict principle is a "rule founded upon the highest and truest principles of morality" (118); see similarly McCardie J in *Armstrong v Jackson*, the "rule is not one merely of law but of obvious morality" ([1917] 2 KB 822, 824).

precise principle of morality that informs the fiduciary duty and came up with interesting suggestions as to the "moral mischief" which it is out to prevent or correct.[27] I therefore endorse this understanding of the purpose of fiduciary duties without further comment.

Many chapters in this volume focus on the moral transgression which underlies breach of fiduciary duty. But the potential for mischief is only one side of the story. In fact, the fiduciary relationship can be an arena for morally commendable other-regarding action. In managing other people's money the fiduciary makes it easier for them to attend to their life projects;[28] in advising people who are inexpert the fiduciary allows them to make informed choices about their body and property; when she manages property for the unfit and under-aged the fiduciary enables them to be less dependent on family members who may have their own agenda. Whether it is a profession or a one-off favor to a friend, the principal–fiduciary relationship can provide people with ample opportunity to do good. A fiduciary who does her job conscientiously, as many fiduciaries doubtless do, will engages in benevolent activity which can raise a major contribution to her *Bildung* as a righteous person. This rather neglected perspective of the honest fiduciary, for whom the relationship with the principal is an occasion for morally worthy activity, will be the focus of my discussion here.

It is, as I said, beyond my present scope to show that fiduciary duties embody moral duties. But assuming that, it is pretty obvious that many of the most successful accounts explain the fiduciary duty as an embodiment of the Kantian duty of respect for autonomy. Matthew Harding, for example, defends the no-conflict rule as an incident of the duty to respect the humanity in every person.[29] In taking advantage of an opportunity that came to you as a result of your fiduciary role, without asking for the principal's permission, you would be using him as a mere means to your own ends.[30] And conversely, a fiduciary who is working for the principal's best interests shows respect for his humanity. In the same spirit, Arthur Laby has argued that the fiduciary is obligated to "adopt the principal's objectives, goal or ends."[31]

This direct application of Kant's account of imperfect duties is problematic.[32] But an improved analysis was suggested by Lionel Smith: when one person has the power to

[27] Sources for the contrary view can be found in Matthew Harding, "Manifesting Trust," 29 *Oxford Journal of Legal Studies* 245 n 26 (2009) and Arthur B Laby, "The Fiduciary Obligation as the Adoption of Ends," 56 *Buffalo Law Review* 99 n 1 (2008). For systematic refutation of the such contractual and other reductivist justifications of fiduciary duties see Paul B Miller, "Justifying Fiduciary Duties," 58 *McGill LJ* 12–30 (2013). Note, though, that even if fiduciary duties indeed embody moral obligations, it does not mean that there are no other justifications working in tandem with the moral one. It may well be the case that the law ought to respond to and be formulated in light of these other justifications as well.

[28] See Dagan and Hannes in this volume.

[29] Which is Kant's second formula of the categorical imperative, see Immanuel Kant, *Groundwork of the Metaphysics of Morals*, trans Mary J Gregor, introd Christine M Korsgaard (1998) 4: 428.

[30] Harding (n 27) 93–4. Harding offers this argument from respect as a justification for the "no-conflict" rule. But if we accept the Lionel Smith definition of the duty of loyalty the argument applies to fiduciary duties in general. Herding's justification of the fiduciary doctrine is Razian: state enforcement is legitimate in this case as compliance is necessary for the flourishing of a valuable social practice, viz., the formation of trust-based relationships (s IV); see also P D Finn, *Fiduciary Obligations* (1977) at 26. Others, like Tamar Frankel and Robert Flannigan argue that the moral wrong which Fiduciary duties set to uproot is abuse of trust (Robert Flaningan, "The Fiduciary Obligation," 9 *Oxford Journal of Legal Studies* 285, at 297 (1989); Tamar Frankel, *Fiduciary Law* (2011) at 78). Trust abuse arguments have some challenges to answer, and I will not pursue this line of argument here (see Miller (n 27) 32–6).

[31] Laby (n 27) 129 and s II.

[32] See Lionel Smith in this volume.

make decisions on behalf of another she has acquired part of that person's autonomy. If the fiduciary were to use these controls as pecuniary assets, she would be using another person as a means to an end.[33] And again, the reverse is also true: when the fiduciary forgoes an opportunity to advance his own interests and focuses instead on the sole interest of the principal, she acknowledges his irreducible humanity. The fiduciary position should therefore give you plenty of opportunity to engage in morally valuable activity. In a similar vein, Paul Miller proposes a "juridical" explanation that is very hospitable to Smith's autonomy-based account.[34] Following a careful reading of the case law he concludes that fiduciary power, "being an extension of the legal personality of the person from whose capacity it is derived, is... properly understood as a means... belonging rightfully to the beneficiary."[35]

We can see then that Kant's formula of respect for humanity, where moral duties are analyzed as originating from a conceptual truth about our fellow human beings, provides a most appropriate framework for identifying the moral foundations of the fiduciary duties. Kant's great achievement in showing how impersonal laws of morality can motivate agents to great acts of sacrifice makes his theory particularly attractive for those who seek to explain a duty to selfless pursuit of the interest of others in circumstances where fear of punishment is under-deterring (see text around n 46 herein). Another attractive feature of Kant's theory is the way in which the *source* of the moral duty is practical reason which calls for a universal application of the duty regardless of time and personal aptitude.

But now a problem arises: if we adopt a Kantian framework for understanding fiduciary duties, the suggestion that loyalty in the thick sense should inform the fiduciary's attitude to her principal seems to deprive the fiduciary of the opportunity to act in a morally praiseworthy way. The fiduciary who takes up the law's recommendation to act from a disposition of loyalty, in other words, will not be able to realize the ethical potential of the fiduciary position, as her actions will be worthless from a moral point of view. Here is why: to be sure, once the fiduciary acts in the way required of him by the moral law (that is, avoid conflicts of interests), he is clean of any wrongdoing. But moral *worth*, Kant argued, only attaches to actions that are done from the right *motive*.[36] And if we follow a widely accepted picture of Kant's moral theory, fiduciaries who act out of a sense of loyalty do not display the right motive, and their actions are therefore devoid of any moral value. Loyalty, it is argued, can never be a moral virtue and actions that are done out of loyalty (in the sense I developed here) cannot have any moral merit, for the following two reasons:

1. Dispositions and emotions cannot stand at the basis of a moral action because they are involuntary and unreliable. Seeing emotions as deserving of moral praise or blame would contradict one of Kant's most important aims,

[33] Lionel Smith: "Fiduciary Obligations: Ensuring the Loyal Exercise of Judgment," a lecture given at King's College in March 2013.

[34] Miller (n 27) 65.

[35] Miller (n 27) 62, and later on, "the duty of loyalty secures the beneficiary's legitimate expectation that fiduciary power, as one of her means, will be used only to achieve her ends... The wrongful nature of fiduciary disloyalty is that the fiduciary has treated fiduciary power as means at his disposal" (64–5).

[36] For a detailed analysis of the Kantian view of the "independence thesis" see Mark Timmons, "Motive and Rightness in Kant's Ethical System," in Mark Timmons (ed), *Kant's Metaphysics of Morals: Interpretative Essays* (2002).

namely, to liberate moral worth from the vagaries of fortune and human fickleness.

2. Loyalty is particularistic. When you ask the loyal "why did you act in that way?," the reason he gives would run along the lines of "I did this for X because he is my Y (e.g. partner/schoolmate/principal etc)." This answer is at odds with the formula for *moral* reason, which says "I did this because X is a human and I therefore owe him respect and must not use him as a means to my ends."

This interpretation of Kant's moral theory as holding that only the rather peculiar emotion of "respect for moral law" can motivate a morally worthy action, is very common. Here, for example, is how Bernard Williams presents it:

> if one is going to suggest that those things that a man does as the expression of certain emotions, can contribute to our view of him as a moral agent; if, further, one is going to say (as I have perhaps not yet said explicitly, but am very happy to) that one's conception of an admirable human being implies that he should be disposed to certain kinds of emotional response, and not to others; one has to try to answer the very powerful claim of Kant that this is impossible.[37]

Indeed, this familiar interpretation of Kant has a firm textual basis in the *Groundwork*. In this text, Kant defines virtue as a disposition to do one's duty out of respect for the moral law (4: 435). Other positive natural inclinations such as sympathy and kindness, he says, "deserve praise and encouragement, but not esteem" (4: 398). As Kant clarifies in the introduction, the reason why inclinations and other emotions (excepting "respect for the moral law") cannot be the basis of moral law is that they fail to accomplish two crucial tasks: (a) produce a *rule* that would tell us what moral duty requires, and (b) instill a *reliable* motivation to act as moral duty instructs (4: 390). As a result, if we are to have a proper concept of moral duty, we must identify an a priori law that is independent of sentimentality and attachment to a group or an individual. Kant's ingenuity lies in the way he shows that reason is both the ground of our moral duties towards others (as a supreme expression of humanity that is worthy of deep respect) as well as what determines the content of these duties.[38]

In this early *Groundwork* picture, everything that makes Kant's theory attractive for interpreters of fiduciary duties is already in place: the universal applicability and the transparency to the agent, as well as the motivating sense of duty; but loyalty to your principal (in the thick sense) does not fit in. For loyalty seems to exemplify everything that is wrong with emotions as a basis for moral merit. As Marcia Baron puts it: "What kind of reason is 'Because it is mine'?. . . loyalty seems at best silly."[39] And if "silly" is as good as loyalty ever gets, then in many other cases it is just a synonym for prejudice. When the basis of moral law is universal humanity it is hard to see how the highly personal attachment which is loyalty can be morally commendable. Even David

[37] Bernard Williams, "Morality and the Emotions," in *Problems of the Self* (1973) at 226.

[38] This is the crucial point where Kant departs from Aristotle, for whom practical reasoning is a basic component of ethical practice but not the source of autonomy humanity and the duties that attach to them (Sherman (n 17) 137–8). This leads, of course, to the differences between their respective concepts of virtue, as we shall see.

[39] Marcia Baron, *The Moral Status of Loyalty* (1984) 6; see also Ewin (n 10) 412.

Hume, for whom virtue *is* the tendency to display the proper emotion, considered loyalty worse than "bigotry and superstition."[40] And from the opposite direction, George Fletcher who is a great admirer of loyalty, believes that it can serve as the cornerstone of a non-Kantian ethics precisely because of the friction between loyalty and what he calls "impartial morality."[41]

Whether you think of loyalty as a moral myopia, or as the ultimate answer to the modern malaise of alienation, it is interesting to see how the tension between objectivity and partiality, which is embedded in the concept, is present in discussions of fiduciary duties. Thus, we find Arthur Laby saying that "the fiduciary's role identification with the principal requires him to re-orient his moral view-point away from pursuing the overall best state of affairs to furthering agent-oriented objectives. Just like spouses, parents and friends prefer the interests of those closest to them."[42] For the honest fiduciary this is bad news. While heading the advice of equity to foster a sense of loyalty to the principal may raise the chances that a morally *right* action is produced, once motivated by a sense of loyalty, her actions will have no moral *merit*, as they would be premised on a subjective principle that is morally irrelevant; for if the best description of your reason for action is "I do this for X because I am loyal to her," your action—even if it is selfless, even if it achieved fabulous results—is not a product of proper moral reasoning, and you do not deserve any moral tribute for it. This is a sad predicament for the fiduciary who (justly) conceives of his role as a morally valuable project.

In what follows, I will argue that this is an illusory problem. In truth, the thick loyalty that is expected of a fiduciary lends itself very well to analysis as a Kantian virtue and complements, rather than contradicts, those features of Kant's theory that make it so appealing to interpreters of the fiduciary doctrine. The argument that actions out of loyalty are, by definition, devoid of moral worth is also a misreading of Kant's own position. For unlike the stern line attributed to him by Fletcher and Williams, Kant has a complex, psychologically-sensitive approach to the place of emotions in moral virtue. The insights that made him famous, and his theory so appealing, need not (and did not) lead him to a stiff denial of the place of emotions and personal attachment in virtue. In what follows, I will therefore use Kant's own writing to show how loyalty in the thick sense complements an understanding of the fiduciary duty as an instantiation of the Kantian duty to respect the humanity of each and every person. In Section III I consider how the concerns that led the Court of Equity to develop the fiduciary doctrine echo Kant's writings on the subject of human weakness; I will also examine how Kant's view on the role which emotions can play in assisting us to cope with weakness can inform the interpretation of fiduciary loyalty as a virtue.

As you would expect, Kant's notion of virtue is miles apart from Hume's "virtue is all about emotions" account; it is also very different from the stoic "no-role-for-emotion" explanation. And it is not Aristotelian either. In Kant's view, Aristotle was wrong in identifying virtue with habit, ie, "a uniformity in action that has become a *necessity* through frequent repetition."[43] Virtue, he says,

[40] Hume (n 19) 562. [41] Fletcher (n 6) 13–16. [42] Laby (n 27) 134.
[43] Kant (n 29) 6: 407.

> is not to be defined and valued merely as an *aptitude* and a long standing *habit* of morally good actions acquired by practice. For unless this aptitudes results from considered, firm, and continually purified principles,. . . it is neither armed for all situations nor adequately secured against the changes that new temptations could bring about.[44]

In this passage, Kant identifies two difficulties with Aristotle's "virtue as good habits" position: one is that, once the habit sets in, the agent is no longer reflective and/or critical about the way it is exercised (eg, in asking "is this president, now that he has broken his promises, still worthy of my allegiance?"); a second, closely related, problem is that old habits may not be enough to motivate the right action in situations that are sufficiently different from the situations experienced thus far (eg, "this time I will not come around with a cake because the new neighbours are a gay couple"). Both problems are acutely relevant to fiduciaries. For as we have seen, the (juridical) duty of loyalty applies *only* in situations of discretion.[45] The whole point of the fiduciary relationship is to allow an expert to exercise discretion in novel situations that cannot be defined with any precision in the agreement that gave rise to the relationship.[46] As the fiduciary sets to work, the incoming stream of new opportunities for the principal requires constant diligence on his part. Loyalty that takes root in old routines may well be insufficient to ensure that illicit considerations do not slip into the fiduciary's decision-making process as she faces novel situations. Kant's solution to the shortages of habit as the basis of virtue, as we shall presently see, is to ground the virtue in an ever reflective and critical *reason*. Yet this grounding in reason does not entail the banishment of emotions from the arena of moral virtue.

The big stumbling block on the way to incorporating positive emotions and dispositions into Kant's picture of a morally worthy action is that they do not seem to be the product of free choice.[47] That we are responsible only for what we freely choose is a (if not "the") most basic principle of Kant's ethics.[48] Thus, in the *Groundwork*, sentiments (that we cannot fully control) and innate inclinations are sharply distinguished from practical reasoning that is free from external constraints, and are consequently left out of the definition of moral virtue. Nevertheless, the resources for developing a more complex link between emotions and moral worth can already be found in the *Critique of Practical Reason* (*CPR*). In contrast with the picture we find in the *Groundwork*, the *CPR* conceives of the relationship between emotions and reason as a dynamic affair: rather than a bundle of a fixed set of natural inclinations and erratic assortment of emotions, we find a a fairly harmonious emotive part of the psyche that can interact with, and be influenced by, reason: the morally good person, Kant says, will have a cheerful heart upon fulfilling her duty.[49] The text of the *Religion* is even more explicit

[44] Kant (n 29) 6: 383–4; and 6: 409 *remark*: "if the practice of virtue were to become a habit the subject would suffer a loss of that *freedom* in adopting his maxims which distinguishes an action done from duty."

[45] See Lionel Smith in this volume.

[46] Robert D Cooter and Bradley J Freedman, "The Fiduciary Relationship: Its Economic Character and Legal Consequences," 66 *New York University Law Review* 1045, at 1046 (1991).

[47] Paul Guyer, *Kant and the Experience of Freedom: Essays on Aesthetics and Morality* (1993) 344–5; Barbara Herman, *The Practice of Moral Judgment* (1993) ch 1.

[48] "Only. . . what does not serve my inclination. . . or at least excludes it from the calculation in making a choice, can be the object of respect, and thus a command;" Kant (n 29) 4: 400.

[49] Guyer (n 47) 344–5.

on this blissful effect: "the joyful heart in the *prosecution* of its duty. . . is a sign of the genuineness of virtuous disposition."[50]

Yet, this semi-automatic impact of reasoned choice over the emotions, whereby the genuine embrace of moral duty leads to joyful spirits, assigns a fairly minimal role to sentiment in the development and exercise of virtue. In the *Metaphysics of Morals* (henceforward *MoM*) Kant's view of the relationship between reason and emotions matures, and he now comes to appreciate the huge potential of emotions to assist us in the progress towards virtue. The *MoM* prescribes an *obligation* to work on our emotions and train them to support and complement reason. It is our duty, Kant says, "to cultivate [our] natural power (powers of spirit, mind and body) as means to all sorts of possible ends."[51] In the complex matrix of the *MoM*, with its distinction between *juridical* and *ethical* duties on the one hand, and perfect and imperfect duties on the other hand, the duty to engage in such emotional coaching comes under the rubric of *ethical* duties.[52] The cultivation of beneficial dispositions and positive emotions is something we owe both to ourselves and to others.[53] These two aspects of duty are closely linked, and, as we shall see, both are highly relevant for fiduciary loyalty.

Training the emotions to become means to morally worthy ends is not easy. The road to self-perfection is long and torturous. "Virtue is the concept of strength" Kant tells us.[54] And this moral strength, which he emphasizes repeatedly in the *MoM*, is required not only for neutralizing the destructive potential of the emotive part (as the stoics thought); we also need to devote large quantities of this will power to the incessant effort to "cultivate the compassionate natural (aesthetic) feeling in us, and make use of them as so many means to sympathy based on moral principles and the feelings appropriate to them."[55] Emotions and personal attachment can help us to make the morally right choices in several ways: first, emotions are a mode of attention. Compassion, for instance, can send us right in the direction of the suffering refugee, and help us to ignore various smoke screens cast by their and our governments.[56] Kant embraces this auxiliary function of the emotions in a famous passage from the *MoM* in which he advocates regular visits to debtors' prisons and sick beds.[57]

Emotions are also an important instrument of communicating our moral interest to other people.[58] In paying a tribute to the role of emotions in moral psychology and actions Kant corrects the bad impression of his commendation of cold-hearted actions in the *Groundwork*.[59] But the really important question for us is whether emotions can have a *motivational* role in Kant's scheme. For Aristotle acting out of emotions of pity, compassion etc. in a situation which calls for it, is precisely the right *moral* response. This can obviously not be the case for Kant. But can a positive emotion be a necessary

[50] Immanuel Kant, "Religion within the Limits of Reason Alone," in Allen W Wood (ed), *Religion and Rational Theology* (1996) 6: 23–4 n; and "what is not done with pleasure but merely as compulsory service has no inner worth, for one who attends to his duty in this way. . . is not loved by him;" Kant (n 29) 6: 484; Guyer (n 47) 367.

[51] Kant (n 29), 6: 444.

[52] As only perfect duties to others can be coerced form the outside Kant (n 29) 6: 38.

[53] The concept of a duty to oneself was criticized as incoherent as well as foreign to the Kantian system in its entirety. These arguments can however be countered, see Robert B Louden, *Kant's Human Being: Essays on his Theory of Human Nature* (2011) 17.

[54] Kant (n 29) 6: 392.

[55] Kant (n 29) 6: 457.

[56] Sherman (n 17) 145–6.

[57] Kant (n 29), 6: 457.

[58] Sherman (n 17) 147–9.

[59] 4: 398.

part of what motivated morally good action? If the answer is positive, as I think it is, the loyal fiduciary can be an epitome of a morally good agent.

III. Shoring up the Decent Fiduciary

One of the central tenets of Kant's moral theory, and the one for which it is so helpful as explanation of fiduciary duties, is that the morally worthy action is anchored in respect for the humanity in each of us. The basic "maxim" (ie, guiding principle) of your actions must be "treat humanity. . . never simply as a means but always at the same time as an end."[60] It is this universal law that stands at the basis of moral actions, not some subjective, accidental *attachment* to this or that individual. Kant never retreated from his position in regards to the huge significance of acting out of respect for humanity, or the risk of allowing our subjective feelings and/or innate inclinations to guide us in questions of morality. In one of his late texts—*Religion within the Boundary of Reason Alone*—he describes the middle stage of immorality as a state of an "impure heart," ie, a heart which "has not, as it should have, adopted the [moral] law alone as its all-sufficient incentive: instead, it usually (perhaps, every time) stands in need of other incentives beyond this, in determining the will to do what duty demands."[61] Can agents who act out of loyalty display anything but "impure heart"?

If Kant's position with regard to the moral superiority of actions that are independent of erratic emotions, involuntary inclinations and self-serving ends is to be reconciled with his attractive account of virtue in the *MoM*, we must rethink his idea that all morally worthy actions are motivated solely by a sense of (moral) duty (ie, by "respect for the moral law"). In her response to the "virtue ethics" criticism of Kant's moral theory, Onora O'Neill explains that we must understand Kant's notion of a "maxim [as referring to] the *underlying intention* by which the agent orchestrates his numerous more specific intentions. . ."[62] Kant's requirement that morally worthy actions be based on reasoned rules of behavior therefore means that, out of respect for moral law, you must always intend to do what duty requires of you. "Respect for the moral law" is understood as a second-order motivation that inspires the agent's conduct as a *whole*, rather than as the motivation behind every *specific* action.[63] And thus, the requirement that only "respect for moral law," and not any other emotion, be the motivation behind your actions does not refer to concrete actions, but only to the fundamental *policy* decisions on how to orient your activity in the world. Motivated by the will to abide by the moral law for its own sake, you should adopt the following strategy: I will work on myself to develop *all* those mental powers that could help me implement my policy, namely, to always act according to my moral duty. The cultivation of morally oriented emotions like sympathy and kindness will naturally be part of this strategy. Concrete actions that are motivated by sympathy, kindness, and the like can thus be attributed

[60] Kant (n 29) 4: 428. [61] Kant (n 50) I, ii (6: 29–30).

[62] Onora O'Neill, "Kant after Virtue," 26 *Inquiry* 387, at 393 (1983).

[63] Guyer (n 47) 380; Lara Denis, "Kant's Conception of Virtue," in Paul Guyer (ed), *The Cambridge Companion to Kant and Modern Philosophy* (2006) 513; Sherman (n 17) 33.

to a fundamental emotion of "respect for the moral law," even if it did not play a direct role in motivating the agent in this case.

All this can be directly applied to the emotion of loyalty in the context of fiduciary actions. A fiduciary who recognizes the depth of her commitment to the principal, and who, as a result, nurtures a sense of loyalty to him, is a perfect example of this inner process of self-perfection. This fiduciary will be better positioned to resist temptation to act self-interestedly.[64] The virtuous fiduciary's *recognition* that the moral law orders fiduciaries to pursue only the interests of their principals is fortified with an earnest *feeling* of responsibility for *her* principal. This will make it easier for her to identify situations in which her private interest may be influencing her decisions; it will help her avoid self-deception, and boost morally righteous *motivation* via emotional aversion to exploitation of the principal.

Some writers try to come up with a "virtue reading of Kant's ethics" in which the underlying principle is: "[you must] strive for a way of life in which all of one's acts are a manifestation of a character which is in harmony with moral law." But even if taking Kant to be a virtue ethicist is too far-fetched, it is obvious that the way he includes emotion in the motivational structure of the virtuous person results in a highly plausible picture of the relationship between moral virtue and human psychology. Importantly, this account of the place of emotions in moral virtue supports and complements his famous pessimism about the attainability of complete purity of heart.[65]

The incorporation of emotion into the basic structure of virtue is a compromise driven by a realistic appreciation of the unholy nature of human beings.[66] The fact that humans do not possess a "holy will" was crucial for Kant. As finite creatures, endowed with reason, but not a holy will, our natural inclinations always tempt us to do other than the moral law instructs. This vulnerability to temptation is the starting point of Kant's duty-based system.[67] A tight connection between virtue and temptation is already drawn in the *Critique*: "Virtue," Kant tells us there, is "a disposition conformed with law *from respect* for the law, and thus consciousness of a continuing propensity to transgression."[68] As a result, human virtue can only be an approximation of the perfect good will.[69] Nurturing the right moral sentiments is a sensible strategy for morally worthy agents who recognize their innate weakness.[70] The recruitment of emotion and inclination to help reason in motivating us to do good is indeed a concession to our

[64] The fear of being caught, punished, and shamed is a rather weak incentive for compliance with fiduciary duty. This is because the relationship inherently makes it very difficult to detect fiduciaries' wrongdoing see n 47 in Irit Samet, "What Conscience Can Do for Equity," 3 *Jurisprudence* 13 (2012). The big chance that breach of fiduciary duty will go undetected is one of the main reasons for the unusual strictness with which it is enforced. Whether this harsh treatment does indeed incentivize compliance is an open question, but either way, fortification of the fiduciary's inner resistance to wrongdoing is crucial: Samet, 775.

[65] Examples of this pessimism are numerous, see for example *Virtue* s 11, 6: 436; or Kant (n 50) 6: 32, where he declares blatantly that "the human being is by nature evil."

[66] Here is the colorful way in which he puts it in one place: "every human virtue in circulation is small change; only a child takes it for real gold. Nevertheless it is better circulating pocket pieces than nothing at all. In the end they can be converted into genuine gold coin. . ." (Immanuel Kant, *Anthropology from a Pragmatic Point of View* (1978) 39).

[67] Kant (n 29) 4: 414.

[68] Immanuel Kant, *Critique of Practical Reason*, ed Mary J Gregor (1997) 5: 128.

[69] Louden (n 53) 7. [70] Louden (n 53) 7.

unholy will, but it is one we must make if we wish to restrain self-love and promote an attitude of respect for the moral law. Virtue for Kant, as Lara Dennis explains, should be understood in less ambitious terms as "the form in which a rational being with a non-holy will expresses her supreme commitment to morality."[71]

Perhaps nowhere in the law do we find a more explicit acknowledgment of this battle against temptation than in fiduciary law. In one of the earliest cases in which an independent fiduciary doctrine starts to emerge—*Whichcote v Lawrence* (1798)—the danger of succumbing to the lure of easy profit at other people's expense is clearly recognized: "where a trustee has a prospect of advantage to himself, it is a great temptation to him to be negligent."[72] Things did not look better a hundred years later, when the Court of Appeal explained the unusual strictness of the fiduciary duty as a necessary means to remove "the temptation to embark on what must always be a doubtful transaction."[73] More recently in *Harris v Digital*, Haydon JA vividly explained that fiduciary rules "tend to prevent the disease of temptation in the fiduciary."[74] Reference to "disease" suggests a kind of moral pathology that threatens not only the principal, but also the fiduciary who wishes to do his job well but gives in to forces that are beyond his control. As Kant reminds us, even fiduciaries who are committed to compliance with their moral duties do not possess a perfect, holy, will; their position of power will necessarily tempt them to pursue self-interest.

Since the fiduciary status entails temptation and inner struggle, the fiduciary who wishes to be dutiful must adopt a long-term strategy to handle temptation. One important component of that strategy can, and should, be an attempt to harness one's emotions to the cause of compliance with one's duties. And here loyalty in the thick sense comes in. A fiduciary who is sincerely concerned about the corrosive effects of the temptation to act in self-interest will work to develop a sense of loyalty to his principal. If the fiduciary who knows what is right finds it easier to act conscientiously due to his feelings of loyalty, his selfless action is no less praiseworthy for that reason. For his feelings of loyalty were cultivated in an expression of free will, out of respect for the moral law, and this respect is therefore the ultimate motive of his actions vis-à-vis the principal; he therefore gets full points in the moral game. The presence of loyalty to one's principal(s) is thus a genuine virtue, and actions that are informed by it exhibit great moral merit.

Conclusion

In this chapter, I have argued that the term "loyalty," as it is used in the context of fiduciary duties, has two senses: one, technical, in which loyalty stands for the requirement that fiduciaries act only in the best interests of their principals. In this thin sense of loyalty, the duty to be loyal embodies a "juridical" moral duty, ie, a duty to act in a certain way which can be legitimately enforced by the state. The other "thick" sense of loyalty implies a specific emotional and intellectual orientation towards one's principals.

[71] Denis (n 63) 513. [72] *Whichcote v Lawrence* (1798) 34 Eng Rep CC, at [751].
[73] *De Bussche v Alt* (1878) 8 Ch D 286, at 316.
[74] *Harris v Digital Pulse Pty Ltd* (2003) 56 NSWLR 298.

It is an attitude in which selfless action comes easily, and exploitation of weakness is unthinkable. By invoking this rich concept of loyalty the courts of equity advise fiduciaries that the serious commitment they took upon themselves calls for the adoption of an unusual disposition. A detached and purely instrumental approach to her relationship with the principal may get the fiduciary to abide by her legal duties. But this unique position of great power over other people, combined with an information gap that renders detection of abuse quite unlikely, generates a temptation for wrongdoing that can be very hard to overcome. And this is true even for an honest, well-intentioned fiduciary.

Cultivating a sense of loyalty to the principal is therefore well advised even for the most conscientious fiduciary. In this chapter I wanted to show that the recommendation to adopt a stance of fully-fledged loyalty can be incorporated into a Kantian analysis of the fiduciary duty. The fiduciary position is a space of selflessness—an arena where morally commendable actions are naturally called for. It would have been a great drawback for the interpretation of loyalty suggested here if it meant that the fiduciary who adopts it thereby gives up all the moral *Bildung* potential of the fiduciary relationship. But, as we saw, such narrow reading of the Kantian framework, according to which loyalty, like any emotion, cannot be the motivating power behind a morally praiseworthy action, is unwarranted. Kant himself encourages his readers to make a strategic decision to cultivate these emotions which may help them to perform their duty. The conscious decision to enlist the emotive part to assist in the battle against weakness of will, is itself motivated by respect for the moral law, and it is this ultimate motivation that grants the concrete action (out of emotion) its moral value.

The loyal fiduciary is a perfect example of an agent who is acting in accordance with this recommendation: given the great difficulty of resisting the temptation to exploit her position to make private profit, she engages in emotional self-coaching which aims to nurture a sense of loyalty to her principal—a sentiment that will make it emotionally difficult for her to betray his trust. Her concrete actions out of loyalty are thus informed by a policy which was adopted out of deep respect for the moral law together with an acute awareness of our shortfalls as human beings. And it is this combination of commitment to the moral law and humbleness which makes the loyal fiduciary a morally virtuous agent.

6

Can We Be Obliged to Be Selfless?

*Lionel D Smith**

Introduction

This chapter seeks to examine a question in relation to fiduciary obligations. It is generally agreed that this part of the law is concerned with obligations that relate in some way to loyalty. The question I wish to explore is whether there is a *legal* obligation of loyalty; and if so, what does it require?

To show why I am interested in this question, let me refer to the recent analyses of two authors. One is Matthew Conaglen. On the first page of his monograph, he states that "[t]he concept of loyalty is now well established as the core—indeed the defining—concept of fiduciary doctrine."[1] At the end of the work, he states his conclusion in this way: ". . . the fiduciary concept of loyalty, as it is used in Anglo-Australian legal doctrine, is best understood as the summation of the various doctrines that are applied peculiarly to fiduciaries, rather than as a legal duty that is directly enforceable in its own right."[2] In other words, while fiduciaries are peculiarly subjected to the no-conflict rules and the no-profit rule, there is no legal duty of loyalty as such.

The other analysis is that of Arthur Laby. He has a positive definition of the duty of loyalty, as a duty that "entails a commitment by the fiduciary to adopt the principal's objectives, goals or ends as the fiduciary's own and to promote those ends."[3] On the face of it, this appears to be a much stronger idea of the duty of loyalty than that of Conaglen. And yet, Laby appears to be led to a very similar conclusion to that of Conaglen. Adopting a Kantian analysis, Laby argues that the duty as he defines it is an imperfect duty, because it does not prescribe particular actions or omissions, and for this reason it cannot be a legal duty.[4]

George Fletcher's book *Loyalty* is not about fiduciary obligations, but is more concerned with the constitutional dimensions of loyalty.[5] Interesting for this discussion are

* I am grateful to Matthew Conaglen, Stephen Galoob, Andrew Gold, Arthur Laby and Irit Samet for helpful comments and to Dennis Klimchuk for his comments and for discussion, over a long period of time, of many of the points addressed in this chapter.

[1] M Conaglen, *Fiduciary Loyalty: Protecting the Due Performance of Non-Fiduciary Duties* (2010) at 1, with a long list (in n 5) of case citations.

[2] Conaglen (n 1) at 269. In deploying a concept of "Anglo-Australian legal doctrine," Conaglen implies that in his view, English and Australian law are in agreement on this point, while other common law jurisdictions are not necessarily so. See at 24–6, where he argues in this sense with respect to a related but different point, namely which duties are properly called fiduciary duties.

[3] A B Laby, "The Fiduciary Obligation as the Adoption of Ends," 56 *Buffalo L Rev* 99, at 129 (2008).

[4] This is how I read Laby (n 3) at 140–3. His lengthy n 190 at 143 argues, in a way not wholly dissimilar to Conaglen, that the law uses other duties to enforce indirectly the duty of loyalty. Differently from Conaglen, Laby relies on the duty of care.

[5] G P Fletcher, *Loyalty: An Essay on the Morality of Relationships* (1993).

two of his chapter titles. Chapter 3 is entitled "Minimal Loyalty: 'Thou Shalt Not Betray Me.'" This seems to capture Conaglen's understanding of how the law implements loyalty, by prohibiting unauthorized conflicts and profits. Chapter 4 is entitled "Maximum Loyalty: 'Thou Shalt Be One with Me.'" This seems to capture Laby's strong conception of the duty of loyalty, even though Laby is apparently led to the conclusion that this duty cannot be implemented as a legal duty. Neither Conaglen nor Laby is saying that there is no legal duty of loyalty, in the sense that the law does not require loyalty. They are both supporters of the legal implementation of loyalty, but they conclude that the law does not, or cannot, directly enforce loyalty.

In my view, there are important truths in the arguments of both of these commentators, but also serious weaknesses. I will argue that there is a *legal* requirement of loyalty, which is found in the positive law of fiduciary obligations and which is consistent with the requirements of the law's philosophical foundations. But, perhaps similarly to Conaglen and Laby, I will suggest that the legal requirement of loyalty is not properly called a duty.

I. The Sphere of Legality

In this section, I will articulate the criteria which help us to decide whether a duty can be a legal duty. Like Laby, I will use a Kantian framework. For Kant, the sphere of legality ("the concept of Right"[6] as opposed to that of virtue), has, at a high level of generality, three features. First, it is concerned "only with the external and indeed practical relation of one person to another, insofar as their actions, as deeds, can have (direct or indirect) influence on each other."[7] Second, it does not address the relation of one person's choice to the *mere* wishes or needs of another, only the relationship between one person's choice and another person's choice. Choosing to fulfil another's needs may be morally worthy, but it is not the province of legal relationships, which are concerned with and arise from external manifestations of our autonomy. Third, juridical relationships are not concerned with "the end each has in mind;"[8] the question whether one has fulfilled one's legal duties stands apart from the reasons for which one has conducted oneself. All three elements include aspects of externality, a crucial feature for Kant in distinguishing the field of legal duties from the field of morality.[9]

More concretely, Kant's understanding of the sphere of legality leads to particular elements that must inhere in a duty in order for it to qualify as a legal duty. A duty can only be a duty of right—that is, a legal or juridical duty—if it "does not include the incentive of duty in the law and so admits an incentive other than the idea of duty itself."[10] In other words, it must be possible to comply with the duty for any end or objective that one may have.[11] This relates especially to the first and third elements set

[6] I Kant, *The Metaphysics of Morals*, trans M Gregor (1996), at 6: 230. [7] Kant (n 6).

[8] Kant (n 6).

[9] For analysis of the three elements and their interrelationship, see E Weinrib, *The Idea of Private Law* (1995) at 94–100.

[10] Kant (n 6) at 6: 230. See also at 6: 383: "What essentially distinguishes a duty of virtue from a duty of right is that external constraint to the latter kind of duty is morally possible, whereas the former is based only on free self-constraint."

[11] Conversely, a duty of virtue is a duty to adopt a particular end, such as improving the well-being of others, and thus it is *only* possible to fulfill a duty of virtue by adopting the relevant end.

out above: in the case of a duty of right, it must be possible to say objectively whether the duty was performed, without knowing why it was performed. If I pay my taxes only because I don't want to go to jail, I have complied with the duty, and this shows that the duty can qualify as a legal one.

There is also a distinction in Kant's analysis, somewhat less rigorously articulated, between duties that are wide (*weit*) and those that are narrow (*eng*). This distinction relates to how precisely the duty specifies what action it requires or forbids. A wide duty leaves latitude for choice among a range of ways in which it may be performed. For Kant, duties of right must be narrowly defined, so that it is possible to decide clearly whether or not they have been fulfilled.[12] Duties of virtue, by contrast, may be wide duties (although they may also be narrow). Kant also describes wide duties as imperfect (*unvollkommen*).[13]

II. Formulations of the Duty of Loyalty

Everyone agrees that fiduciary obligations are, in some way, about being loyal. In this section we will consider different understandings of how that requirement of loyalty is translated into the law.

A. A duty to act in the best interests of the beneficiary

In discussions of fiduciary obligations, whether in cases or in commentary, there are constant references to a duty to act in the interests, or the best interests, of the beneficiary. One formulation of the duty of loyalty, therefore, is simply as a duty to act in the best interests of the beneficiary. The Supreme Court of Canada has described the duty in this way.[14] This sounds plausible but taken literally, it leads immediately to grave difficulties. It is entirely open-ended. Any fiduciary could always do something more in the interests of his beneficiary; not only would that be asking too much, but in any event we could never know that the duty had been fulfilled.[15] In Kantian terms, the duty is a very wide one, like the duty of beneficence, and for this reason it could only be a duty of virtue and not a duty of right.

[12] Kant (n 6) at 6: 390, 6: 411. See also Kant's footnote to 6: 433, the importance of which is discussed in the Introduction by Roger J. Sullivan (at xix). In E Weinrib, "The Case for a Duty to Rescue," 90 *Yale LJ* 247 (1980), Weinrib argues that the common law should recognize a duty of easy rescue in emergencies, noting that if the duty is properly formulated, it can be narrow in Kant's sense.

[13] Kant (n 6) at 6: 390. This is arguably confusing as there is a separate sense of "imperfect obligation" which aims to capture the idea of a duty in relation to which no one holds a legal right of enforcement. Laby (n 3) at 140–1, traces the origin of this idea to Grotius and Pufendorf, and he treats this sense of "imperfect" as synonymous with Kant's idea of a wide duty. But it seems that a duty may be imperfect in this Grotian sense, but be perfectly clearly defined (and so "narrow" in Kant's distinction between wide and narrow duties). An example would be the duty to pay a debt, after the time limitation for legal enforcement had passed. Kant mentions (at 6: 383) duties in respect of which there is no right of coercion, and disqualifies them as duties of right.

[14] *BCE Inc v 1976 Debentureholders* 2008 SCC 69; [2008] 3 SCR 560, at [37]: "The fiduciary duty of the directors to the corporation. . . is a duty to act in the best interests of the corporation."

[15] This defect could not be cured by reformulating the duty as a duty to act *in what the fiduciary perceives* to be the best interests of the beneficiary. We will see, however, that this addition is an important part of the correct formulation of the requirement of loyalty.

But quite apart from Kant, the indeterminacy of such a duty is such that any lawyer would agree that this cannot be its correct formulation. Indeed, although the Supreme Court of Canada has articulated the duty of loyalty in this way, it rejected this formulation when a claim was made that was based upon this formulation. In *KLB v British Columbia*,[16] the plaintiffs suffered abuse as children in foster homes. The defendant Crown was *in loco parentis* to the children, and under Canadian law this meant that the Crown was in a fiduciary relationship with the children. One of the claims was that the Crown had breached its fiduciary duty "to act in the best interests of foster children." The Crown argued for a narrower duty, and the Court agreed with the Crown, holding that "a simple injunction to act in the best interests of the child, however laudable, does not provide a workable basis for assigning legal liability," and that the parental fiduciary duty "does not include a broad and unspecified duty to act in the child's best interests." Rather, the duty of loyalty is a duty "not to put one's own or others' interests ahead of the child's in a manner that abuses the child's trust."[17]

The difficulties in formulating the duty in this way have led to unpredictable results. In *McInerney v MacDonald*,[18] the Supreme Court of Canada held that a physician stands in a fiduciary relationship to his patient, with the result that the patient is entitled to all of the information in the doctor's records that was used in administering treatment.[19] The result was not directly based on a duty to act in the patient's best interests, but rather on the theory that the patient had a right to the information, because it was acquired for the benefit of the patient.[20] Subsequently, in *Breen v Williams*, a patient seeking information from a physician in Australia sought to establish that she had a right of access to the physician's records (as opposed merely to a right to the information, or some of the information, therein).[21] The High Court of Australia was not wholly opposed to the idea that the relationship might be fiduciary.[22] But the Court rejected the argument that there was a fiduciary obligation that entailed a right of access to records.[23]

The judgment of Gaudron and McHugh JJ did so in a way that has had significant, and perhaps unforeseen, consequences. Those judges wanted particularly to reject an argument that a patient's right of access to records grows out of the doctor's duty to

[16] *KLB v British Columbia* [2003] 2 SCR 403; 230 DLR (4th) 513.
[17] *KLB v British Columbia* (n 16) at [46], [47], [49].
[18] *McInerney v MacDonald* [1992] 2 SCR 138; 93 DLR (4th) 415.
[19] The physical records, however, typically belong to the doctor.
[20] *McInerney* (n 18) at 150, 424.
[21] *Breen v Williams* (1995) 186 CLR 71, HCA.
[22] Gummow J stated (at 134) that the relationship is fiduciary. See also Dawson and Toohey JJ (at 92–3) and Gaudron and McHugh JJ (at 107–8), accepting that some aspects of the relationship might be fiduciary in nature.
[23] Some of the judges of the High Court of Australia were rather scathing about the Supreme Court of Canada's decision; see Gaudron and McHugh JJ (at 111–12) and especially Dawson and Toohey JJ (at 95). This judgment itself, however, is not without flaws. It states (at 93) that a fiduciary obligation is "inappropriate" because the relationship is governed by contract and tort, which "leaves no need, or even room, for the imposition of fiduciary obligations." But this does not follow at all, as all three bodies of law are applicable in many situations. The judges note this (at 93–4), which undermines their own argument, and in so doing they make a cardinal jurisprudential error: "it is conceivable that a doctor may place himself in a position with potential for a conflict of interest—if, for example, the doctor has a financial interest in a hospital or a pathology laboratory—so as to give rise to fiduciary obligations. But that is not this case." It is not the breach of an obligation that creates the obligation. If there is no fiduciary obligation, the doctor is allowed to be in a conflict of interest.

act in the best interests of the patient. In doing so, they distinguished Australian from Canadian law by saying, with sparse authority, that "Canadian cases also reveal a tendency to view fiduciary obligations as both proscriptive and prescriptive. However, Australian courts only recognise proscriptive fiduciary duties."[24] In my view, this is a mischaracterization of both Canadian and Australian law. As far as Canadian law, the judges seemed to believe that the right to information recognized in *McInerney* was based on the "best interests" duty, understood as a prescriptive duty. Not only is the "best interests" duty not an open-ended duty to act, as we have seen, but moreover the right to information is not founded on it; it is founded on the fact that the doctor acquires the information for the patient's benefit, and must so hold it. For Australian law, this judgment has led to a far-reaching dogma, unfamiliar in the rest of the common law world, that fiduciary duties are only ever proscriptive: they forbid things, but do not require action. This has led to commentators arguing that the "best interests" duty is not a fiduciary duty, since it can be understood as a prescriptive duty, even though it seems to lie at the core of fiduciary law.[25] Similarly, this "proscriptive only" approach has led to the argument that fiduciaries' duties of disclosure are not fiduciary duties.[26] Presumably it must also mean that a fiduciary's positive duty to hand over an unauthorized profit is not a fiduciary duty, even though it arises from the no-profit rule which is clearly part of fiduciary law.

B. A duty to adopt the principal's objectives, goals, or ends

This is Laby's formulation, as we have seen. It is not entirely clear whether Laby thinks that the duty as he formulates it can be a legal duty. He shows that within Kant's framework, which Laby seems to adopt, it cannot be such a duty, because it is an imperfect duty, in the sense of being a wide and not a narrow duty; it prescribes no particular action.[27] He argues that this helps us to see "why fiduciary law has bedeviled courts and commentators for years."[28] But he goes on to claim that "courts have adopted an imperfect duty as a legal standard,"[29] even though, according to Kant, this is not merely a bad idea but is not actually possible.

There is another problem with Laby's formulation of the duty of loyalty. As we have seen, one implication of Kant's understanding of duties of right is that it must be possible to perform them with any end or purpose in mind. A duty to adopt the ends of another person could, however, only be complied with by someone because they had adopted the ends of the other person.[30] In Kant's analysis, a duty to set an end as one's

[24] *Breen v Williams* (n 21) at 113.

[25] It is said to be "foundational" in G Thomas, "The Duty of Trustees to Act in the 'Best Interests' of Their Beneficiaries," 2 *J of Equity* 177 (2008), and this must surely represent the dominant view. The Western Australian Court of Appeal recently held, contrary to the "proscriptive only" approach, that the "best interests" duty of corporate directors is a fiduciary duty: *Westpac Banking Corporation v The Bell Group Ltd (in liq) (No 3)* [2012] WASCA 157. For an overview of the Australian debate, see R T Langford, "Solving the Fiduciary Puzzle: The Bona Fide and Proper Purpose Duties of Company Directors," 41 *Australian Business L Rev* 127 (2013), arguing that the "best interests" duty can be a fiduciary duty despite *Breen v Williams*.

[26] V J Vann, "Solicitors and the Duty to Disclose," 2 *Univ of New England LJ* (2005) 67.

[27] For another sense of "imperfect duty," see n 13.

[28] Laby (n 3) at 142.

[29] Laby (n 3) at 142.

[30] It might be asked whether A could not adopt the ends of B simply because A, a professional fiduciary, wishes to earn fees. But this is a misunderstanding of the idea of adopting another's ends. One person,

end can only be a duty of virtue and not a duty of right. The two problems are related, of course, because both are tied to the external aspect of duties of right.

So Laby's formulation of the duty of loyalty cannot be a legal duty, at least within Kant's understanding of the nature of legal duties.

C. No free-standing duty of loyalty

As we have seen, this is Conaglen's approach. He argues that although the courts speak about a duty of loyalty, there is no free-standing duty of loyalty. The law aims to bring about loyalty only through the no-conflict rules and the no-profit rule.

How does Conaglen reach this conclusion? The methodology he adopts is to ask which duties are peculiar to fiduciaries; only these are properly called "fiduciary duties" and can be understood to be part of the law's implementation of what Conaglen calls "fiduciary loyalty."[31] So, for example, the duty of care, skill, and diligence which is presumptively owed by all fiduciaries is not a fiduciary duty, because it is a duty owed also by non-fiduciaries.[32] Conaglen ultimately concludes that the only duties left standing, after this exercise in elimination, are the no-conflict rules and the no-profit rule, which he therefore calls "peculiarly fiduciary duties."[33]

How can he conclude that the "best interests" duty, which many consider to be at the heart of fiduciary law, is not a fiduciary duty? How can he say that "while some fiduciaries owe a duty to act in the best interests of their principals, that is not itself a fiduciary duty"?[34] Conaglen adopts the approach mentioned above, that fiduciary duties are purely proscriptive.[35] To the extent that the "best interests" duty requires positive action, therefore, he says that it likely describes conduct that is required by the duty of care, skill, and diligence, which is prescriptive in part, and which on Conaglen's analysis is not a peculiarly fiduciary duty. To the extent that it requires conduct in good faith, it describes conduct that is required by the duty to act in good faith, which again is not a peculiarly fiduciary duty for Conaglen, because non-fiduciaries may owe a duty of good faith. And to the extent that it requires fiduciary powers to be used for proper purposes, the same result follows, because Conaglen notes that the exercise of powers

A, cannot adopt the ends of another person, B, for A's own purposes or ends. If A adopts B's ends, then A makes B's ends into A's ends; B's ends become A's ends. Conversely, if A is acting for some other end, such as getting paid for his work as a professional fiduciary, then it is not true that A has adopted B's ends. It could however be true that A is acting *as though* he had adopted B's ends. However, a legal duty to so act would still encounter the difficulty that it would be too wide and unspecific.

[31] Conaglen (n 1) ch 3.

[32] Unlike the general duty of care in negligence, however, the duty of care, skill, and diligence owed by a fiduciary cannot be fulfilled by complete inaction. In this sense, there are important differences between duties that are often similarly referred to in short as "duties of care."

[33] It is not, however, clear that these *rules*, as they are traditionally called, are *duties* in the normal sense that one commits an unlawful act by infringing them. I will return to this point herein.

[34] Conaglen (n 1) at 57. This implies that some fiduciaries do not owe such a duty, and on the same page Conaglen suggests that trustees and solicitors do not owe such a duty. This seems puzzling, but if, in addressing this question, Conaglen has in mind the open-ended formulation that was considered and rejected in Section II.A, then it is probably true that no one owes such a duty, for the reasons there discussed.

[35] Conaglen (n 1) at 59. His list of authorities begins with *Breen v Williams*, and apart from one *dictum* in a judgment of the English Court of Appeal (later reversed on a different point, and itself citing only *Breen*), consists entirely of Australian cases.

may be constrained by an objective "proper purposes" doctrine, even where the powers are held by non-fiduciaries. Ultimately, he suggests that the "best interests" duty is a kind of composite of these three duties, and since none of them is peculiarly fiduciary, then neither is this one.[36]

Conaglen is, in general, careful and thorough in his analysis. This part of the argument is, however, unsatisfying. In less than three pages, he reaches the conclusion that the requirement that a fiduciary act (in some sense) in the best interests of his principal is not part of fiduciary law, contrary to basic thinking all over the common law world (with the possible exception of Australia).[37] In reaching this conclusion, Conaglen does not even stay true to his own methodology. Even if he were correct that the "best interests" duty is an amalgam of three other duties, none of which he considers to be fiduciary, it would not follow that the "best interests" duty is not a fiduciary duty. This is because Conaglen's methodology is based on identifying duties that are only owed by fiduciaries. He does not point to any non-fiduciary who owes a duty to act in the best interests of someone else.

More fundamentally, the analysis is unsatisfying in treating the duty as a kind of amalgam, without a careful attempt to unpack the case law to give it a more precise content; although, to be fair, the present chapter is exactly concerned with the difficulty of that enterprise. Conaglen rightly notes that the duty of care, skill, and diligence is objective, while the "best interests" duty is purely subjective: it is a duty to act (in some sense) in *what the fiduciary subjectively believes* to be the best interests of the beneficiary.[38] This itself is enough to tell us that it stands apart not only from the duty of care, skill, and diligence, but also from the objective rules about proper purposes. It is clear, moreover, that when a person is under a duty of good faith, he is not under a duty that requires him to act in another's best interests. So the "best interests" duty actually has little in common with the three duties that, according to Conaglen, compose it. At least, it does not follow that it must lack any characteristic (such as being a peculiarly fiduciary duty) that they individually lack. None of the ingredients of gunpowder is explosive on its own.

Overall, Conaglen is led to the view that the law has a very minimal understanding of loyalty. For him, loyalty is nothing more than properly performing one's (non-fiduciary) duties.[39] The "peculiarly fiduciary duties" exist only to make that result more likely.[40] But of course, everyone is obliged to perform their duties, whether or not

[36] Conaglen (n 1) at 55–6.

[37] My hedging insertion of "(in some sense)" is justified because, in this part of my chapter, I am testing different formulations of this duty. The possible exception of Australia is due to the dominance of the "proscriptive only" dogma which has led many commentators there to think that the "best interests" duty is not a fiduciary duty.

[38] Conaglen (n 1) at 55. [39] Conaglen (n 1) at 202.

[40] It follows that Conaglen's understanding of the rule against conflicts of interest is that it forbids action if there is a conflict between the fiduciary's self-interest and *any* duty that that the fiduciary owes. This leads to an extraordinarily wide understanding of the idea of conflict. If a corporate officer is offered a bribe to hand over corporate secrets, he is in a conflict of interest on Conaglen's view, regardless of whether the offer is seriously entertained. Indeed, if he feels tempted by self-interest to take a day off work, without being so entitled, he is in a conflict, even if he later rejects the temptation. But what action is forbidden, in these situations, by the rule against conflicts? It can only be actions that are already forbidden by the applicable non-fiduciary duties. The better understanding of the rule against conflicts of interest is that it forbids *the exercise of judgment that is to be exercised in a fiduciary capacity*, when the fiduciary's exercise of judgment

they are a fiduciary. So fiduciary law ends up being about particular, deterrent sanctions that are applied to some people, in order to make it more likely that they will do what they are anyway obliged to do.[41] As far as the result, fiduciary loyalty is the same as non-fiduciary loyalty.

D. A requirement to exercise judgment in what the fiduciary perceives to be the best interests of the beneficiary

This is my formulation of the duty of loyalty. It is part of a larger account which aims to explain the domain of fiduciary obligations as composed of the duty of loyalty, the no-conflict rules, and the no-profit rule. In my account, each is an element of a unified whole.

1. Summary of the larger argument

The argument can be very briefly summarized as follows. The diagnostic feature of fiduciary relationships is that the fiduciary owes to the beneficiary a duty to exercise judgment in what the fiduciary perceives to be the best interests of the beneficiary. The duty is owed in any situation where one person holds authority to make discretionary decisions that will affect another person's legal situation and where, on a proper interpretation of the grant of the authority, the authority was granted to permit the grantee to manage the affairs of the other person. The second part of this description distinguishes situations where a person merely has power *over* another person from fiduciary situations, where a person holds power *on behalf of* another person. The duty of loyalty also arises in true advisory situations, where one person undertakes to advise another person to help that other person make their own decisions. In both situations—the holding of legal powers, and the advisory context—one person holds some control over another person, but holds that control on behalf of and for the benefit of the other person.

This duty of loyalty is not a prescriptive duty inasmuch as it does not prescribe any particular course of action. It does, however, prescribe how judgment is to be exercised, but in an entirely subjective way. It requires the fiduciary to exercise judgment in *what the fiduciary perceives* to be the best interests of the beneficiary. This means that it may require different decisions from different fiduciaries who are in what is otherwise the same situation. This does not mean that fiduciaries are not subjected to objective legal controls. First, the duty of care, skill, and diligence is tied to an objective standard of reasonableness.[42] Second, the no-conflict and no-profit rules are not tied to any subjective element. But the importance of the subjective nature of the duty of loyalty is that the duty evaluates, not whether the fiduciary has done their job well, but whether they

is liable to be affected by considerations of self-interest. This understanding, which gives the rule an independent scope of operation, is discussed further in Section II.D.1.

[41] For a full argument that deterrence accounts of fiduciary law are not adequate, see L Smith, "Deterrence, Prophylaxis and Punishment in Fiduciary Obligations," 7 *J of Equity* 87 (2013).

[42] D W M Waters, M Gillen, and L Smith, *Waters' Law of Trusts in Canada* (4th edn, 2012) at 908–9.

have done it loyally, that is, with an eye solely on what they perceive to be the best interests of the beneficiary.[43]

This formulation helps us to understand all of the rules about delegation that apply to fiduciaries. The general law (amended by statute in some contexts) is that fiduciaries can only delegate ministerial functions; in other words, those that do not involve the exercise of judgment.

This formulation also explains the review of fiduciary decision-making that can apply outside of any invocation of the rules about conflicts of interest. If a fiduciary exercises her judgment otherwise than in what she perceives to be the best interests of the beneficiary, she will find that the exercise of judgment can be reviewed and set aside. The most recent example is the decision of the UK Supreme Court in *Pitt v Holt*.[44] Unusually, the appeal was heard by a panel of seven judges, underlining its importance. They unanimously upheld the decision of the Court of Appeal, to the effect that a decision made by a fiduciary is "voidable if, and only if, it can be shown to have been done in breach of fiduciary duty."[45] Since the case had nothing to do with the no-conflict or no-profit rules, the implication is that the "breach of fiduciary duty" that was discussed was indeed a free-standing norm of fiduciary law.[46]

My account also provides a clear role and scope for the no-conflict rules. A conflict of self-interest and duty arises when a fiduciary exercises judgment, and the exercise of his judgment has the potential to be affected by his own self-interest. His self-interest conflicts with his duty of loyalty in a way that it cannot conflict with non-fiduciary duties, because the duty of loyalty is exactly about exercising judgment in the beneficiary's (not the fiduciary's) best interests. A conflict of duty and duty arises when a fiduciary exercises judgment, and the exercise of his judgment has the potential to be affected by a duty of loyalty that he owes to a third person. Again, it is because both duties of loyalty require decisions to be made while taking account of the best interests of two different persons that the conflict arises.

The conflict rules only apply (in their full private law form) to fiduciaries, because only fiduciaries owe duties of loyalty that require the exercise of judgment in what the fiduciary believes to be the best interests of another. But this helps us to see why we have analogous concerns in other situations: a person should disqualify himself from a scholarship committee if his relative is a candidate, and a politician should not participate in policy decisions where his financial self-interest is implicated. All of the situations where we are concerned about conflicts are situations where people are required to exercise judgment in an other-regarding, and not a selfish, way.

The duty of loyalty is subjective, and so (unlike in the case of non-fiduciary duties), whether or not it is complied with depends upon internal decision-making processes of

[43] See *Bristol & West Building Society v Mothew* [1998] Ch 1, CA at 18: "A servant who loyally does his incompetent best for his master is not unfaithful and is not guilty of a breach of fiduciary duty."

[44] *Pitt v Holt* [2013] UKSC 26. This is only the most recent affirmation of a long-standing principle. See L Smith, "The Motive, Not the Deed," in J Getzler (ed), *Rationalizing Property, Equity and Trusts: Essays in Honour of Edward Burn* (2003) 53, at 68–73, discussing examples from trust law and corporate law.

[45] *Pitt v Holt* [2011] EWCA Civ 197; [2011] 2 All ER 450, CA, at [127], quoted by the Supreme Court, ibid, at [70] and upheld in the paragraphs following.

[46] Contrary to the view espoused by Conaglen, that the no-conflict and no-profit rules exhaust the norms of fiduciary law: see text at n 2 herein.

the fiduciary. Moreover, even a decision-maker in good faith can never be certain that in a conflict situation, he or she has successfully excluded competing considerations. The law is aware of this, which is why, in general, it requires fiduciaries to refrain from exercising their duty-bound judgment in conflict situations.[47] Good faith is irrelevant, because it does not solve the problem of the impossibility of excluding extraneous influences on judgment.[48] As a result, when a fiduciary power is exercised in breach of the no-conflict rules, it is voidable, just like an exercise in breach of the duty of loyalty.[49] This underlines the connection between the no-conflict rules and the duty of loyalty.

The no-profit rule has a different foundation. To repeat, fiduciary relationships are characterized by the duty of loyalty, that is owed in any situation where one person holds authority to make discretionary decisions that will affect another person's situation and where, on a proper interpretation of the grant of this authority, it was granted to permit the grantee to manage the affairs of the other person. The no-conflict rules, as we have seen, exist to protect the loyal exercise of judgment. The no-profit rule exists because the fiduciary acts *on behalf of* the beneficiary (and therefore not on his own behalf). The relationship is one in which the fiduciary manages the affairs of the beneficiary, within a defined sphere. It is not possible, within the logic of such a relationship, for the fiduciary lawfully to extract wealth from the sphere of fiduciary management (except as authorized). On the contrary, everything in that sphere is attributed to the beneficiary.

Just as the costs of fiduciary management are attributed to the beneficiary (the fiduciary is entitled to reimbursement for expenses), so are the profits. Any benefit or advantage acquired by the fiduciary in the exercise of his or her duty-bound management is attributed, as a matter of primary right, to the beneficiary by the no-profit rule.[50] This applies even to a benefit whose acquisition was unauthorized, if the beneficiary so chooses. When I say "as a matter of primary right," I mean that this rule is not a sanction for wrongdoing. It does not depend on proof of the breach of any duty. This is why, like the no-conflict rule, it can apply to people who are in perfectly good faith.

Although information does not belong to anyone in a strict legal sense, the same principle of attribution that applies to profits is capable of explaining the obligations of fiduciaries in relation to information. Trustees must tell beneficiaries of the existence of the trust; trustees and other property-handling fiduciaries must keep and render accounts; and fiduciaries have been found liable for losses caused by failure to disclose conflicts of self-interest and duty, conflicts of duty and duty, and other breaches of duties of disclosure.[51] Again, because the fiduciary manages a sphere of activity on

[47] Compare I Samet, "Guarding the Fiduciary's Conscience—A Justification of a Stringent Profit-stripping Rule," 28 *OJLS* 763 (2008).

[48] This part of the argument owes a great deal to the work of Dr Remus Valsan and to his doctoral thesis, "Understanding Fiduciary Duties: Conflict of Interest and proper Exercise of Judgment in Private Law" (2012).

[49] Conaglen (n 1) at 76–9. As he notes (at 77), avoidance may be denied if the interests of third parties in good faith would be adversely affected. Like many authors, Conaglen uses the terminology of "rescission;" my use of "voidable" and "avoidance" is intended to refer to exactly the same recourse.

[50] Again, the fiduciary may retain any benefits that are authorized. My argument here is similar to that of P Miller, "Justifying Fiduciary Remedies," 63 *UTLJ* 570 (2013). My argument, however—possibly differently from that of Miller—does not rely on disloyalty, or any other wrongdoing, to explain the beneficiary's entitlement.

[51] I expand on this in the text at n 71.

behalf of and for the benefit of the beneficiary, the beneficiary is entitled to receive all relevant information concerning that sphere of activity.

2. *Is this duty too wide to be a legal duty?*

As we have seen, on Kant's approach, a duty cannot be a legal duty unless it specifies sufficiently narrowly the conduct that it requires. The duty of loyalty, as I have formulated it, does not prescribe any particular course of action. At the same time, in my view it does not suffer from the defect of being too wide. It is not like the formulation that says that the fiduciary must act in the interests of the beneficiary, but fails to say what action is required.[52] Nor does my formulation of the duty say that the fiduciary must *act* in what she perceives to be the best interests of the beneficiary; that would also be an open-ended duty, seeming to require action but not saying what action is required. As I formulate it, the duty only says that *when* a fiduciary exercises judgment to which the duty applies, he or she must do so in a particular way. In that sense, the duty is narrow; it does not require an undefined range of actions, and it only applies in situations where the fiduciary exercises his duty-bound judgment. When it applies it states quite clearly (and narrowly) how that judgment must be exercised: in what the fiduciary perceives to be the best interests of the beneficiary.

It falls to other duties to tell the fiduciary exactly what to do. The terms of a trust may require certain actions, as may the terms of an agent's or officer's contract. It is also true that it falls to other duties to stipulate whether there is some minimum frequency with which the fiduciary must turn his mind to the exercise of the powers that he holds in a fiduciary capacity. If this minimum frequency is not explicitly set out in the terms of a trust or contract, it will usually be stipulated by the duty of care, skill, and diligence, which is an objective duty tied to a standard of reasonableness.

Is my duty of loyalty too wide because it is subjective? It is subjective in the sense that it requires the fiduciary to exercise judgment in what *he or she believes to be* the best interests of the beneficiary. This is tied to the fact that the judgment belongs to the fiduciary. No one, not even a judge acting in that capacity, can say that the judgment was wrongly exercised merely because that person would have exercised it differently. But this subjective element does not, in itself, make the duty too wide. Here we can take note of aspects of the criminal law. Most "true" crimes have a subjective *mens rea* element; typically, they require a subjective intention to bring about some result. Murder requires a subjective intention to kill.[53] But this subjective intention is understood to be, itself, a matter of fact.

So too, in relation to the exercise of judgment by fiduciaries, the question of what factors they took into consideration is a matter of fact and evidence. If the court concludes that they took the wrong factors into consideration, it will conclude that there

[52] Section II.A herein.

[53] When Kant refers to suicide, he says that killing oneself is murdering oneself if it be *willkürlich*: Kant (n 6) at 6: 422. Gregor translates this as "wilfully," and other translations are "voluntarily" or "arbitrarily," in the technical sense "imposed by will alone." This implies that Kant understood both murder and suicide to require a subjective intention, and this did not prevent him from seeing them as forbidden by narrow, perfect duties (a duty of right in the case of murder, and a (narrow) duty of virtue in the case of suicide).

has been a breach of duty and that the judgment was not properly exercised. A striking example from the cases is that of a trustee who takes into consideration that a trust beneficiary has married against the trustee's wishes.[54]

3. *Is this a duty to adopt an end?*

As we have seen, for Kant a duty to adopt an end can only be a duty of virtue, and not a duty of right. Conversely, it must be possible to fulfill a duty of right for any end at all. In my view, the duty of loyalty as I have formulated it is not a duty to adopt an end, and therefore it can be a duty of right. A trustee could exercise her powers, say in choosing investments, in what she honestly thought were the best interests of the beneficiaries, while doing so *only because* she wanted to get paid her agreed compensation; or, because she was afraid of being found liable for breach of trust; or for any other motivation. In so acting, she would be acting loyally.

In an earlier text, I described the duty of loyalty in this way: "The fiduciary obligation is a duty to act (or not to act) with a particular motive: you must act (or not) in what you perceive to be the best interests of the beneficiary."[55] I would now change the formulation of what is demanded by the duty of loyalty: it is not a duty to act, or not to act, but rather a duty to exercise judgment in an other-regarding way. It is by so confining it that one can produce a defensible account of the no-conflict rules, including their scope and their relationship to the duty of loyalty. It is in relation to the exercise of duty-bound, other-regarding judgment that conflicts are forbidden.[56]

4. *Is it really a duty?*

There is, however, a problem about this formulation of the duty of loyalty. Normally, as I have said, it governs the exercise of fiduciary powers. If a power is exercised in violation of the duty, any resulting legal transaction is voidable. This would typically apply to a contract, although it might also be an issue of shares by a corporation, or the execution of a unilateral deed by a trustee, for example to exercise a dispositive discretion. As we have seen, the same consequence follows if such a transaction is entered into in breach of one of the no-conflict rules.[57]

[54] *Klug v Klug* [1918] 2 Ch 67; *Fox v Fox* (1996) 28 OR (3d) 496, CA. These are cases of the exercise (or non-exercise) of dispositive discretions, in which the requirements of loyalty are slightly different; I will return to this in Section II.D.4.

[55] Smith (n 44) at 73.

[56] Moreover, I no longer think it is necessary, or perhaps even desirable, to formulate the duty in terms of motive. It is true that many of the decisions on the review of fiduciary powers speak in these terms. What they are seeking to capture is the justiciability of the fiduciary's subjective decision-making process, as opposed to its objective result. But to phrase the matter in terms of a requirement as to motive arguably comes very close to suggesting that there is a requirement of adopting an end. For a careful philosophical analysis of the relationship between and among reasons, judgment, beliefs, intentions, and motives, see J Broome, "Motivation," 75 *Theoria* 79 (2009).

[57] There are many cases in which the beneficiary is not concerned to avoid any contract, but to capture a gain acquired by the fiduciary. A recent example is *FHR European Ventures LLP v Mankarious* [2013] EWCA Civ 17. Although the judgments refer to conflicts of interest, the only rule needed to deal with such cases is the no-profit rule.

Let us assume that the fiduciary has made a contract, and it is voidable because he did not believe that the contract was in the best interests of the beneficiary. The question is whether it is necessary, or helpful, or correct, to see the underlying problem that makes the contract voidable as a breach of duty, in the strict sense. A duty in the strict Hohfeldian sense corresponds to a claim-right held by the person to whom the duty is owed.[58] There are, however, many important juridical relationships that are not duties in this strict sense. Some of them are, imprecisely, called duties. For example, the "duty to mitigate" is not a duty.[59]

If we turn to rules that affect the validity of legal transactions, we can observe that in order to convey an estate in land at common law, you have to use a deed. We do not say that you have a duty to use a deed. If you don't use a deed, you don't convey the estate. A more relevant analogy is to other factors that, like breach of the "duty" of loyalty, make contracts voidable (not void): if a contract is made under certain kinds of mistake, or certain kinds of pressure, it will be voidable. We do not say that a person has a duty not to be mistaken or pressured. Contracts depend on volition, and the volition is vitiated by mistake and pressure. Hence, we might say with Hart that there has been a failure to fulfil the requirements, not of a duty, but of a *rule*; in particular, a rule that confers powers on individuals.[60]

In the same way, one might say instead that in order to make a valid exercise of a fiduciary power, it has to be done in the right way: the fiduciary must exercise judgment in what she perceives to be the best interests of the beneficiary; if she does not, the legal act is voidable, because the power was not exercised according to the rules that govern its exercise.[61] This does not show that there is a *duty*, in the strict sense, to exercise judgment according to those rules. If the requirement of loyalty is seen as a rule, or as part of what a power-conferring rule requires, it is still a juridical and not a moral construct. But it is not a duty in the Hohfeldian sense, namely that there is someone who holds a corresponding claim-right that the fiduciary must act, or not act, in a particular way.

If what I have been calling the "duty of loyalty" is really a required mode of exercise of fiduciary powers, then the position would end up being not that different from that

[58] W N Hohfeld, *Fundamental Legal Conceptions as Applied in Judicial Reasoning*, 3rd printing with new foreword by A L Corbin (1964) at 36–8.

[59] *Southcott Estates Inc v Toronto Catholic District School Board* 2012 SCC 51; [2012] 2 SCR 675 at [72]: "A plaintiff is not contractually obliged to mitigate, and in this sense the term 'duty to mitigate' is misleading."

[60] H L A Hart, *The Concept of Law* (3rd edn, 2012) at 26–42. Of course the same facts may reveal both a breach of a duty and a failure to comply with a power-conferring rule. If I make a gift of property to A because I was threatened with violence by A, I can avoid the gift and get my property back. A has clearly breached a duty; for my part, I can rely on that if I choose, perhaps seeking damages for mental distress in addition to restitution. But the independence of the failure to comply with a power-conferring rule is revealed if I make a gift of property to A because I was threatened with violence by B, A being totally innocent. I can avoid the gift and recover my property against A, who has breached no duty, because my volition was vitiated. I could also claim damages against B, who was not a party to the gift.

[61] The fact that the legal act is voidable, not void, is significant. The law does not judge it to be wholly without effect. The beneficiary may choose to let it stand, as can a person who makes a contract under a mistake or unlawful pressure; and stand it will. In the fiduciary context, this is why we cannot understand the "duty" of loyalty simply as an objective limit on the fiduciary's power. If a trustee has a fiduciary power to give property to any or all of A, B, and C, a disposition to D will be void (in equity at least) as outside the power. If she gives all the property to A and B because she does not like who C has married, the disposition is voidable (see n 54). This is *not* because she did not have the power to do so; she clearly did; it is because she exercised the power improperly. See P Watts, "Authority and Mismotivation," 121 *LQR* 4 (2005).

described by Conaglen and Laby, albeit according to a line of reasoning that is quite different from both. Loyalty would impose a juridical constraint on fiduciaries, but not one that amounted to a duty, in the strictest sense of that word.

Let me explore some implications of that approach. It may seem strange to argue that the duty of loyalty that lies at the heart of fiduciary law is not a duty at all. But on the other hand, as we have seen, one of the core features of the fiduciary relationship is that the fiduciary *always* holds discretionary powers for the benefit of the beneficiary. It is in the nature of such powers that they are *not* duties; they neither forbid nor require action.[62] The requirement of loyalty entails that in exercising judgment in relation to these powers, the fiduciary must act in what she perceives to be the best interests of the beneficiary. That is a juridical requirement, and as we have seen it has the potential to make legal acts voidable; but it cannot be constructed in such a way as to change the fundamentally discretionary character of the fiduciary's powers. It cannot turn them into duties in the strict sense. Seeing it as a required mode of exercise avoids this.

Moreover, this way of seeing the "duty" of loyalty helps us to better understand how it applies to dispositive powers. An example is the case in which property is held in trust for A, but the trustee holds a power of appointment over the trust property in favor of B. This power has an object, B, whose interests are potentially *opposed* to the interests of the trust beneficiary, A.[63] In general, the "duty" of loyalty is owed by a trustee to the beneficiary, and requires the trustee to act in what she perceives to be the best interests of the beneficiary. For example, in using an administrative power (such as a power to insure trust property) the trustee must so act. But in relation to a dispositive power, the position is different. The trustee has express authority to favor the interests of B, a non-beneficiary, over the interests of A, the beneficiary to whom the basic "duty" of loyalty is owed; indeed, the trustee could give all of the trust property to B, thus eliminating A's interest. And yet, the trustee is not *required* to favor B, and indeed has the power to give B nothing at all. If the law required the trustee to be guided only by the best interests of A, then presumably the trustee could never, or very rarely, use the dispositive power in favor of B. On the other hand, if the trustee had a duty to exercise the power in what he perceived to be the best interests of B, presumably he would effectively be required, at least in almost every case, to exercise the power in favor of B. How does the law deal with this problem? It says that in exercising a dispositive power, the fiduciary is not required to be guided by the best interests of one or more beneficiaries, nor those of objects of the power. Instead, he is required to do what he thinks will best fulfil the purposes for which the power was granted.[64] This is much more easily apprehended as

[62] The whole ensemble of fiduciary law is only needed where there are discretionary powers (including the giving of advice). If a person is required to do some objectively defined thing, like paying $100 or not causing harm by unreasonably careless action, then we look directly at whether the duty has been fulfilled. We have no concern with the way in which judgment has been exercised. See *Varity Corp v Howe* 516 US 489 (1996) at 504: "the primary function of the fiduciary duty is to constrain the exercise of *discretionary* powers which are controlled by no other specific duty imposed by the trust instrument or the legal regime. If the fiduciary duty applied to nothing more than activities already controlled by other specific legal duties, it would serve no purpose" (emphasis in original).

[63] It is often the case that the objects of the power are the same as the beneficiaries of the trust, in which case the opposition is less clear. Even here, though, their interests as objects of the power are quite distinct from (and opposed to) their interests as trust beneficiaries. For example, the power may allow *all* of the trust property to be given to a single beneficiary, defeating the interests of the others.

[64] *Vatcher v Paull* [1915] AC 372, PC, at 378; *Klug v Klug* [1918] 2 Ch 67, at 71; *McPhail v Doulton* [1971] AC 424, HL, at 449, 457; *Re Hay's Settlement Trusts* [1982] 1 WLR 202, Ch D, at 209; *Turner v Turner* [1984]

a required manner of exercising a power, than as a genuine duty, since it requires the fiduciary to bear in mind an abstract purpose rather than the interests of any person.[65]

Seeing the "duty" of loyalty as a required manner of exercising fiduciary powers also strengthens the relationship with the no-conflict rules. Those rules are not duties in themselves; they partially disqualify fiduciaries from exercising their powers in conflict situations.[66] As we have seen, this is because conflicts are situations where even a good faith fiduciary cannot be certain of complying with the requirement of loyalty. On this view, neither the "duty" of loyalty, nor the no-conflict rules that protect it, are duties in the strict sense. And this is a positive thing, because the cases do not reveal examples of fiduciaries being held liable for loss caused by breaches of either the requirement of loyalty, nor of the no-conflict rule as such. The cases that look *directly* to whether the fiduciary abided by the requirement of loyalty—that is, cases in which there is no invocation of the no-profit or no-conflict rules, nor of the breach of a duty to disclose—are the cases on the review of the exercise of fiduciary powers.[67] When the courts find that the fiduciary has not acted properly, they typically set aside the actions so taken; they do not declare fiduciaries liable to compensate for losses caused, as they presumably would in the context of a genuine duty.[68] Of course, there are cases involving compensation for loss caused by fiduciaries; but these are not based directly on a breach of the requirement of loyalty, nor even on a breach of the no-conflict rule.[69] Some cases may

Ch 100, Ch D, at 109–10; *Re Beatty* [1990] 1 WLR 1503, Ch D, at 1506; *Hayim v Citibank NA* [1987] AC 730, PC, at 746.

[65] Of course rules of standing are still required to decide who can invoke any failure to comply with this requirement, but this has not been overly problematical in trust law; the assumption is generally that trust beneficiaries and objects of dispositive powers have standing.

It should also be noted that this analysis also helps us to understand similar "duties" outside the private law context. For example, a judge in giving judgment is not required to act in the interests of any particular person; rather, in the interests of the administration of justice. Because this is a requirement to exercise judgment in an unselfish way, the law applies similar constraints to those that apply in private law; for example, judges are subject to a version of the no-conflict rule, that can make their judgments voidable (see *Ex Parte Pinochet (No. 2)* [1999] UKHL 1; [2000] 1 AC 119). It is easier to see this set of norms as a required manner of exercising judgment than as a duty in the strict sense; it seems counterintuitive to imagine that judges owe duties (in the strict private law sense) to litigants.

[66] "Partially" because the exercise of powers is voidable, not void. [67] See n 44.

[68] In the case of a fiduciary who holds property accountably, like a trustee, the setting aside of an improper transaction may mean that the transaction is disallowed in the accounting process. In this case the trustee will be obliged to restore the value of any property that was alienated in the disallowed transaction. See for example *Campbell v Hogg* [1930] 3 DLR 673, PC; *Estate of Rothko* 372 NE2d 291 (NY, 1977), discussed in A W Scott, W F Fratcher, and M L Ascher, *Scott and Ascher on Trusts*, vol 4 (2007) § 24.10. This is a very important type of claim, although it is not actually a claim for a loss caused by a breach of duty; the plaintiff's theory is rather the direct enforcement of the original duty, if necessary by the substitution of a money sum. This is why such claims are often called "restitutionary," and why they do not require the plaintiff to show causation or to be concerned with remoteness. The claim is analogous to that of a plaintiff who seeks the monetary value of specific performance of a contract, rather than claiming for the loss caused by the breach (which might be more or less depending on the facts). Both claims enforce the pre-existing obligation, by substitution in money; they are occasioned by a breach, but they are not quantified by the loss shown to be caused by a breach. In the trust context, the beneficiary is enforcing the pre-existing obligation to hold the property in question for the benefit of the beneficiary; once the disposition transaction is disallowed, that pre-existing obligation is restored and can be enforced as a money claim that is not a claim for a loss. But a claim based on that theory is only available against fiduciaries holding property for the benefit of beneficiaries. For a fuller argument, see L Smith, "The Measurement of Compensation Claims against Trustees and Fiduciaries," in E Bant and M Harding (eds), *Exploring Private Law* (2010) 363.

[69] Some authors believe that breach of the no-conflict rule can lead to compensation: see C Mitchell, "Equitable Compensation for Breach of Fiduciary Duty," *CLP* 307 [2013]. But this creates at least two

be based on a breach of the duty of care, skill, and diligence, which is clearly a duty in the strict sense.[70] Other compensation cases arise out of violations of the no-conflict or even the no-profit rules; but when read carefully, they reveal themselves to be about the recovery of losses caused by a *failure to disclose* information that the fiduciary was obliged (in the strict sense of owing a duty) to disclose.[71] Fiduciaries are required to disclose everything about their role, including the presence of any conflict, or of the acquisition of an unauthorized profit.[72] A loss caused by non-disclosure is thus a loss caused by a wrong; by a breach of duty in the strict sense.

The idea that loyalty is not a duty but a required manner of exercising powers helps to explain another feature of fiduciary law. Fiduciaries presumptively owe a duty of care, skill, and diligence; however, this duty can generally be excluded by agreement. Similarly, the no-profit rule and the no-conflict rules can often be excluded in particular cases, or modified prospectively. The "duty" of loyalty, however, cannot be excluded without destroying the fiduciary relationship. A trustee who held property, and the corresponding powers, but who could lawfully use the property for his own benefit, would not be called a fiduciary.[73]

puzzles. First, a person can be in a conflict without even knowing it; if a lawyer has two clients and their interests come into opposition, he is in a conflict situation before he even knows about it. It would be strange to see this as a breach of a duty. We might then ask whether it is only a breach *knowingly* to be in a conflict, although no such distinction is found in the case law. Second, while a claim to avoid a transaction does not need to be framed as based on a breach of any duty, any claim to compensation based on the breach of a duty must establish the breach, the loss, and the causal link between the breach of duty and the loss caused. It is very difficult to see how a beneficiary could show that his loss was caused by the mere *presence* of a conflict, whether or not the fiduciary was aware of it. That would require showing that in the absence of the conflict, the loss would not have been suffered. On the other hand, as the cases in n 71 show, claims to loss can be, and are, framed as having been caused by the breach of a duty to disclose: the beneficiary's claim is that had the fiduciary disclosed the conflict, the loss would not have been suffered because the beneficiary would have behaved differently.

[70] Recent developments in Delaware corporate law have raised the question whether, in that jurisdiction, loyalty extends to a wider range of situations than generally understood. See A Gold, "The New Concept of Loyalty in Corporate Law," 43 *UC Davis L Rev* 457 (2009), especially at 472–83. In my view, however, the kinds of conduct there discussed—for example, deliberate failure to perform one's duties, or dishonesty—clearly involve breaches of other duties: for example, the objective duty of care, skill, and diligence; express or implied terms of a contract of services or employment; or statutory duties. There is some controversy as to whether there is a fiduciary duty of good faith that, being a duty in the strict sense, would stand apart from the requirement of loyalty; if there is, however, it would likely also be breached by such deliberate wrongdoing. To repeat, where the conduct in question is governed by a duty in the strict sense, it is not clear what is gained by another layer of analysis in terms of loyalty; see n 62.

[71] Examples include *Nocton v Lord Ashburton* [1914] AC 932, HL, at 965 ("the duty of making a full and not a misleading disclosure of facts known to him when advising his client"); *London Loan & Savings Co v Brickenden* [1934] 3 DLR 465, PC, at 468 ("the appellant's non-disclosure of these two mortgages was a breach of his duty as solicitor to the Loan Company, particularly in view of his personal interest in them"); *Canson Enterprises Ltd v Boughton & Co* [1991] 3 SCR 534; 85 DLR (4th) 129 (the plaintiff's case, as summarized by both majority and minority, was for compensation for loss caused by non-disclosure of conflict of duty and duty); *Hodgkinson v Simms* [1994] 3 SCR 377; 117 DLR (4th) 161 (the plaintiff's case, as summarized by both majority and dissent, was for compensation for loss caused by non-disclosure of conflict of self-interest and duty); *Item Software (UK) Ltd v Fassihi* [2004] EWCA Civ 1244; [2005] 2 BCLC 91 (liability for loss caused by non-disclosure of breach of the no-profit rule). *Brickenden* is controversial for having applied an irrebuttable presumption of causation; this was not followed in *Swindle v Harrison* [1997] 4 All ER 705, CA, in which causation was not established, but in which the relevant breach was described (at 718) as a breach of a duty of disclosure.

[72] As I have suggested, this is because everything in the sphere of fiduciary management (whether it is rights or information) is attributed to the beneficiary. In the context of information, this attribution creates duties to disclose.

[73] This is exactly why English courts decided, during the nineteenth century, that the relationship between mortgagee and mortgagor is not a trust, even though (in a classic legal mortgage by conveyance)

A person in the position of a corporate director, who held decision-making powers over the corporation, but who could lawfully use those powers to benefit himself, would not be properly called a director. And so on. But why should this be? If one took a contractual view of fiduciary relationships (as I do not), this would be difficult to understand; the incidents of the relationship should be variable according to the wishes of the parties. But even if one does not view all fiduciary relationships as arising by agreement, this is still a puzzle; surely autonomous parties (at least) should be free to vary any legal duty. This feature of fiduciary law actually makes more sense when we see the "duty" of loyalty as a required way of exercising powers; fiduciary relationships are all and only relationships in which powers are held that can only be exercised unassailably if they are exercised in what one perceives to be the interests of another. If the duty of loyalty were really a duty, it would not follow that it must necessarily inhere in all these relationships; but if it is a required way of exercising powers, it follows ineluctably from the nature of the relationship and its defining characteristic. The requirement of loyalty, in other words, is inherent in the powers of fiduciaries.[74]

Does this account move in the direction of the Australian approach, that fiduciary duties are only proscriptive and not prescriptive? Yes and no. Yes, in the sense that it proposes that the core of fiduciary law is the *requirement* of loyalty, which is not a prescriptive duty; but no, in the sense that on my approach, it is not a duty at all; and nor indeed are the no-conflict and no-profit rules. All of them are legal norms which regulate the discretionary powers held by every fiduciary. None of them is properly called a duty, either prescriptive or proscriptive. Moreover, the duties that do fall on fiduciaries as a direct consequence of their fiduciary role—duties to surrender unauthorized profits, and to disclose information—are prescriptive duties.

One potential difficulty with the account I am proposing here relates to advisers. It is clear that some fiduciaries do not have powers, in the strict (Hohfeldian) sense. They only give advice, without making any legal transactions that bind their beneficiaries. Lawyers are often in this category; typically real estate agents are also. Investment advisers, when they are fiduciaries, are usually advisers. In some jurisdictions, physicians are also fiduciaries; they too are advisers, except perhaps in the rare case where their authority goes beyond giving advice and permits the making of treatment decisions on behalf of the patient. Many important decisions on fiduciary obligations concern fiduciaries of this advisory kind.[75]

the mortgagee holds the legal estate while the mortgagor's equity of redemption amounts to the beneficial title: see D W M Waters, *The Constructive Trust* (1964) ch III. Since the mortgagee could act in its own interests, it was not a fiduciary, and the English courts went on to conclude (after much uncertainty) that the relationship was not a trust. I would argue that it is possible for a person to be a trustee without owing fiduciary obligations, as where he has received property that is subject to a constructive trust, but he is not yet aware of the trust or the factors giving rise to it: see L Smith, "Constructive Fiduciaries?," in P Birks (ed), *Privacy and Loyalty* (1997) 249; L Smith, "Legal Epistemology in the Restatement (Third) of Restitution and Unjust Enrichment," 92 *Boston University L Rev* 899, at 907–16 (2012). This turns on how one defines the common law trust, an issue which need not be addressed in the current argument.

[74] J C Shepherd, *The Law of Fiduciaries* (1981) at 48.

[75] *Nocton*, *Brickenden*, and *Canson* (n 71) were all cases involving lawyers, as was *Strother v 3464920 Canada Inc* 2007 SCC 24; 281 DLR (4th) 640; *Hodgkinson* (n 71) involved an investment adviser; *Soulos v Korkontzilas* [1997] 2 SCR 217; 146 DLR (4th) 214 involved a real estate agent.

The idea of loyalty as a requirement for the valid exercise of discretionary (Hohfeldian) powers does not fit so well in the case of these advisers, inasmuch as the giving of advice is only an event, and it cannot be avoided or set aside. But it is still possible to say that there is only one proper way to give advice in these situations, namely in what the adviser believes to be the best interests of the advisee; and this is exactly what the law says. Moreover, since the giving of advice in such a setting is an exercise of other-regarding judgment, the courts have not hesitated to apply the other incidents of fiduciary law, namely the no-conflict rules and the no-profit rule, and the obligations to disclose information, including information about the presence of conflicts. This provides an appropriate juridical structure for the protection of the beneficiary; as in all fiduciary relationships, the law attributes property and opportunities arising from the sphere of fiduciary management to the beneficiary, and it allows the recovery of any loss caused by non-disclosure of the infringement of any fiduciary norm.[76]

Conclusion

Fiduciary relationships are those where one person holds authority to make discretionary decisions that will affect another person's situation and where, on a proper interpretation of the grant of the authority, the authority was granted to permit the grantee to manage the affairs of the other person. In these situations, the law attaches two related sets of norms.

The first set relates to how judgment is exercised. The law imposes a requirement that the fiduciary exercises judgment in what the fiduciary perceives to be the best interests of the beneficiary. This requirement is protected by the no-conflict rules, because even a fiduciary in good faith cannot be certain of excluding improper influences on the exercise of judgment. The rules that forbid delegation (except of ministerial matters, not requiring judgment) are also part of this set of norms. None of the rules in this set are duties or obligations in the strict sense, although infringement of them can create duties under the second set.

The second set of norms relates to the allocation of costs and benefits arising from fiduciary management. Just as its costs must be borne by the beneficiary, so too all the benefits and opportunities accrue to the beneficiary. When the fiduciary acquires rights from fiduciary management, the no-profit rule says that those rights are held for the benefit of the beneficiary. The same principle requires that the fiduciary disclose to the beneficiary all information concerning the sphere of fiduciary management. This creates obligations to provide accounts and information, obligations which are well known in fiduciary law. Less well understood is that it also creates obligations to provide information about infringements of the no-conflict rules or the no-profit rule. These obligations to provide information are obligations in the strict sense, and breach of them will justify an order for compensation of any loss that can be shown to have resulted.

[76] Taking the cases in n 75, *Strother* and *Soulos* involved the allocation of property to the beneficiary via the no-profit rule (although in *Soulos* the opportunity was actually a loss-making one, which shows that the rule is not about profits but about opportunities); *Nocton*, *Brickenden*, and *Hodgkinson* involved the recovery of loss caused by non-disclosure of a conflict. *Canson* actually contemplated both kinds of recovery. The main claim was for loss caused by non-disclosure of a conflict, which would have been available except that the loss was considered too remote as having been caused by third-party negligence. The plaintiff was subsequently able to recover unauthorized profits acquired by the defendants: *Canson Enterprises Ltd v Boughton & Co* (1995) 11 BCLR (3d) 262, CA.

7

Is Loyalty a Virtue, and Even If It Is, Does It Really Help Explain Fiduciary Liability?

*J E Penner**

There is no question that the idea of loyalty has been used to frame the nature of the fiduciary relationship. The following is a typical example:

> A fiduciary is someone who has undertaken to act for or on behalf of another in a particular matter in circumstances which give rise to a relationship of trust and confidence. The distinguishing obligation of a fiduciary is the obligation of loyalty. The principal is entitled to the single-minded loyalty of his fiduciary. This core liability has several facets. A fiduciary must act in good faith; he must not make a profit out of his trust; he must not place himself in a position where his duty and his interest may conflict; he may not act for his own benefit or the benefit of a third person without the informed consent of his principal. This is not intended to be an exhaustive list, but it is sufficient to indicate the nature of fiduciary obligations.[1]

My claim in this chapter is that this characterization of fiduciaries, and what they "owe" their principals, is seriously misguided. The core aspect of fiduciary law, in the view I will espouse, is this: a fiduciary is not, strictly speaking, the bearer of duties qua fiduciary to his principal at all, at least not in the core case of the fiduciary–principal relationship; rather, the fiduciary is subject to a certain kind of liability, to wit, (1) a fiduciary is required to account for any gain he acquires in a situation of conflict of interest (such situations being properly circumscribed by the scope of the relationship), and (2) a fiduciary will be liable to compensate his principal in any case where, owing to the fiduciary relationship, the fiduciary has a duty to disclose an interest in advising his principal, and in failing to do so he causes his principal a loss.[2] In this chapter I will concentrate on the first aspect of

* Many thanks to the participants of the Philosophical Foundations of Fiduciary Law conference held at DePaul University School of Law on 19 and 20 July 2013 and to the participants of the Workshop on Property Law and Theory held at New York University, School of Law, on 23–5 May 2013 for their very useful comments and criticisms. I must also thank Rob Chambers, Hanoch Dagan, Avihay Dorfman, Jamie Edelman, Chris Essert, Josh Getzler, Andrew Gold, Michele Graziadei, Larissa Katz, Dan Kelly, Paul Miller, Irit Samet, Henry Smith, Lionel Smith, Martin Stone, Richard Walker, and Leif Wenar for comments on earlier drafts and for helpful discussion. Any remaining nonsense is my own fault.

[1] *Bristol & West Building Society v Mothew* [1988] Ch 1 at 18 per Millett LJ.

[2] *Nocton v Lord Ashburton* [1914] AC 932 is the classic English case. This is an aspect of fiduciary liability my views on which I have yet to develop in detail, but it has to do with the general idea of a "breach of fiduciary obligation." Loyalty does not only not really capture the normative significance of conflict of interest, but it does not as well make for a plausible *extension* of that normative significance to broaden the concept of fiduciary liability to cases of "breach of fiduciary obligation." There are certain sorts of breach that are called "fiduciary" breaches, for example, the breach of a duty to disclose, which the law lays down as a means of regulating conflicts of interest. The idea here, familiar to company law, is that one way of dealing with conflicts of interest is that where a fiduciary recognizes herself to be in a situation of conflict, disclosure allows the principal either to consent to the fiduciary continuing to act, for example, or brings in train a rule which regulates the conflict, for example a director with a disclosed interest may not be able to vote on a resolution

this liability. On this understanding of fiduciary liability, one of the things Millett LJ (as he then was) says, or at least implies, is false: a fiduciary has no duty not to place himself in a position of conflict of interest—that would be a sensible thing for him to do if he wants to ensure he is not liable to his principal, but that is up to him. This makes perfect sense, for merely being in a position of conflict of interest does not itself amount to a wrong.

I shall proceed as follows: first, I will consider the nature of loyalty, and the sort of value or virtue it amounts to. I shall argue that it is misconceived to think of loyalty as something of value in its own right, and also misconceived to think loyalty, considered as a character trait, to be a virtue. I shall suggest that loyalty is essentially a "negative" value or virtue, ie that loyalty, properly understood, is the absence of a certain kind of disvalue or vice, *disloyalty* or *betrayal*. Moreover I shall suggest that the wrong of disloyalty or betrayal is a wrong of *mens rea*, and to the extent the law should regulate the wrong of disloyalty, it should be restricted to the criminal law—it should have no place in civil law where *mens rea* (as opposed to intentionality) is typically irrelevant. Turning to the law, I shall look at fiduciary liability in the law, focusing in particular on the famous English case of *Boardman v Phipps*.[3] Relying on this case, I hope to demonstrate that attaching a standard of loyalty to fiduciary liability is inapt to explain fiduciary liability. In consequence, the traditional understanding of fiduciary liability framed in terms of discretionary acts undertaken in conflict of interest provides a superior moral understanding of the fiduciary relationship.

I. The Value or Virtue of Loyalty

I want to stick here as much as I can to our commonsense notions of values and virtues. To begin with it seems right to say that values are realized, and virtues are displayed. The value of art, kindness, wit, and so on are realized on those occasions when someone produces a good work of art, when someone is kind, when someone makes us laugh. Virtues, in contrast, tend to be a property or character trait, in the first instance of agents, principally persons, which they display on appropriate occasions. As things that can be realized in the world, courage, kindness, and wit are in this sense values, whereas a person is virtuous when it is part of his character to be prone to act courageously, to be kind, to be witty in conversation. The correlative analysis applies to disvalues and vices, of course. Cowardice, brutality, and dullness are disvalues which are realized when they occur, and a person is 'vicious' to the extent they are prone to act in a cowardly way, are brutal to others, are a tedious bore in conversation.

An institution can be virtuous, in so far as it is shaped in such a way to be prone to realize particular values. A university displays virtue, for example, when it is so organized as to realize the values of freedom of expression, disinterested inquiry, collegiality, and so on.

in which she is interested. Where a fiduciary fails to comply with a duty to disclose, it is fair to say that this is a "breach of a fiduciary obligation," given that the duty was imposed to deal with conflicts of interest. But that does not, I think, detract from the general thrust of this chapter, that fiduciaries are subject to a regime of liability, not a regime of duty, and in particular not a regime reflecting a duty of loyalty.

[3] [1967] 2 AC 46.

The philosophical literature on loyalty is exiguous,[4] and on the sort of duty of loyalty that a fiduciary might owe to his principal, essentially non-existent. Indeed, regarding the latter Fletcher seems to suggest that this sort of loyalty is non-core, or derivative—it essentially requires a professional to act only in the interests of his client.[5] The only sustained examination of the concept of loyalty per se is that by Simon Keller,[6] whose work I shall discuss presently. What passes for discussions of loyalty in the philosophical literature is generally occupied by two issues: (1) whether the partiality that loyalties require, to family, tribe, nation, and so on, is morally defensible given the universalistic aspects of moral reasoning[7]—how could the particularity of attachment to my children, say, count as a reason for preferring their interests to those of other children, or more broadly, any person?—and (2) claims, typically associated with communitarian outlooks, that loyalty is a kind of grounding for morality generally on the view that humans are necessarily social creatures with deep attachments to others.[8] Neither of these issues, important though they may be, have any real bearing on the commonsense idea of loyalty which animates Millett LJ's invocation of the concept.

Simon Keller's analysis of loyalty, on the other hand, is distinctive for illuminating the commonsense concept of loyalty itself. This is his "analysis," so to speak, of the concept:[9]

> Loyalty is the attitude and associated pattern of conduct that is constituted by an *individual's taking something's side*, and doing so with a certain sort of motive: namely, a motive that is partly emotional in nature, involves a response to the thing itself, and makes essential reference to a special relationship that the individual takes to exist between herself and the thing to which she is loyal.

"Taking someone's or something's side" is the essence of the account. Whilst I agree that one may be loyal to entities other than individuals, for example to football teams or charities or nation states, I shall restrict my discussion to individuals, for they, as objects of loyalty, are most relevant to whether or not the concept of loyalty illuminates or obscures fiduciary liability. Keller argues that loyalty may be manifested in different ways, for example by giving another's interests priority relative to others generally in one's deliberations ("deliberative priority"), by defending them in conversation against the adverse views of others, by taking part in rituals honoring the object of loyalty, by identifying with the object of loyalty ("identification"), or by tending to acquire or resist certain beliefs about the object of loyalty (epistemic bias).[10] But what unites these various manifestations of loyalty, not all of which may be present in every instance of

[4] See John Kleinig, "Loyalty," *Stanford Encyclopedia of Philosophy* (2007), <http://plato.standford.edu/entries/loyalty>; Andrew Oldenquist, "Loyalties," 79 *The Journal of Philosophy* 173–93 (1982); John Cottingham, "Favouritism and Morality," 36 *The Philosophical Quarterly* 357–73 (1986); Philip Pettit, "The Paradox of Loyalty," 25 *American Philosophical Quarterly* 163–71 (1988).

[5] George P Fletcher, *Loyalty: An Essay on the Morality of Relationships* (1993) 23.

[6] Simon Keller, *The Limits of Loyalty* (2007).

[7] See, eg, Brian Feltam and John Cottingham (eds), *Partiality and Impartiality: Morality, Special Relationships, and the Wider World* (2010); Simon Keller, *Partiality* (2013); Troy Jollimore, *On Loyalty* (2013); despite its title, this, to my mind, is more of a general work on the partiality question than a work focused on the commonsense concept of loyalty per se.

[8] See, eg, Fletcher (n 5); Keller (n 6), chs 7–10; Jollimore (n 7) ch 4.

[9] Keller (n 6) at 21.

[10] Keller (n 6) at 3–7.

genuine loyalty, is that they all show the loyal person to treat the object of loyalty with an "attitude of positive regard."[11]

The other elements that Keller cites are also essential. Loyalty is a form of emotional commitment. This is shown by the fact that one's emotions are engaged vis-à-vis the individual concerned according to the tenor of the relationship. One feels bound to them, feeling pleasure at their success, and concern when they are in trouble, and so on. This is clearly a necessary, not sufficient condition, as one may be emotionally bound to the fortunes of individuals where one might not manifest any loyalty. I may admire and like Henry Smith, feel pleased when he has an academic success, and disheartened when he publishes nonsense, without my being loyal to him in any sense. Second, it is important that loyalty is directed to an individual qua individual, not someone who fits a generic description. To be loyal to Henry Smith is to be loyal to the person Henry Smith, not to a professor of law at Harvard who works in property, even if only Henry Smith uniquely fills that description.[12] Finally, there must be a special relationship, such as friendship or a family relationship of parent to child (or vice versa), or sister to brother, which forms a sort of substratum of familiar engagement with the object of loyalty. One is not, normally speaking, just a loyal person, but a loyal friend, or a loyal sister.

Is loyalty a value or a virtue? The issues are tricky here, and I can only provide a sketch of the rationale for finding that on balance it is neither.[13] For something to be a value it must have intrinsic, not merely instrumental worth. Friendship itself has intrinsic value, and a life without it would be poorer for that. But should one seek out occasions to manifest loyalty, in the different ways that Keller mentions, for their own sake, that is, to show that one is a loyal person? It is hard to see why. Compare fidelity, in the sense of the value or virtue of keeping one's agreements. It is hard to see why one should seek out agreements, irrespective of the particular value of the end that any particular agreement serves, just for the sake of making and keeping agreements. It is vital to see that having friendships will typically give rise to occasions in which one must, say, defend one's friends against the adverse views of others, or give your friends deliberative priority relative to others. But it would seem odd to think that anything particular of value is manifested on those occasions, except that they may be derivatively required out of respect for the value of friendship itself. One way of thinking about this[14] is to say that one can be perfectly loyal, perfectly manifesting what friendship requires of one in circumstances where one's behavior can be described as loyal, without valuing loyalty itself, without acting "for loyalty's sake." For example, when I am pressed in various ways, the fact that I prioritize seeing my friends over other putative commitments I might undertake can be understood as a reflection of the value I rightly place on my friends' interests and my interest in our friendships. My behavior might be perfectly well characterized as loyal, but I need not (and in my own case, do not) think of my actions *as* loyal, or reflective of any belief I have in the value of loyalty. I act out of the value I find our friendships to have.

[11] Keller (n 6) at 21. [12] Keller (n 6) at 17–18.

[13] I am drawing heavily on Keller (n 6) ch 7, though our accounts differ in important respects.

[14] Emphasized by Keller (n 6) 149–51.

There is another aspect of loyalty which Keller spends a good deal of time upon,[15] which should also weaken any sense we have that loyalty is a value, viz the way in which loyalty tends to lead to certain disvalues. In the case of friendship, the tendency is to an epistemic bias: we are prone to believe the best of our friends, and resist unflattering beliefs about them. Similarly, patriots are prone to hold unjustified beliefs about the special merits of their countries and resist believing unpleasant truths about them, which as Keller emphasizes, typically results in a form of bad faith.

Finally, it seems at least plausible that, where loyalty as an independent value is specifically invoked as a justification for action, this is always mischievous. One does not need to invoke extreme cases like the code of *omertà* to see this. There is no apparent value, when having come to a considered, perhaps arduous, judgment that a friend of mine has behaved discreditably, in my responding positively to my friend's plea that I disregard my own judgment, and believe otherwise, or act as if things were otherwise, on the basis that if I fail to do so I should be disloyal.[16]

Turning to the virtue of loyalty, this would be possessed by someone who values loyalty for its own sake, and would seek out "loyalties," special relationships in which loyalty can be manifested. As the foregoing reasons indicate, there is no such virtue because there is no reason to value loyalty for its own sake, or seek out occasions for its realization. A person who is generically loyalty-minded, displays not a virtue, but a rather minor vice, like indiscriminateness,[17] like someone who makes "friends" too easily.

Unfortunately, in terms of the English language, there is another sense of "loyalty" which I must distinguish from the one I have been concerned to elaborate. "Loyal" can also be a synonym for "committed" or "devoted." A "loyal friend" is one who will, to use the parlance of our times, "be there" for one through thick and thin. But a "loyal" friend in the sense of "devoted" can at the same time not be "loyal" in the sense we have been considering. A devoted friend can betray one, perhaps in a moment of atypical resentment of the friend's success, or more commonly, many devoted friends who are always willing to "be there" can be inveterate gossips who may both breach the obligation of confidence or fail fully to take the friend's side in other ways, such as defending them against adverse comments by others, even if this is mostly with trivial consequences. The two senses of "loyal" are distinct.[18]

II. Loyalty as a Negative Value or Virtue

Where one has a legitimate partiality, say to one's friend, one is in a position where the abuse of that friendship is possible.[19] Take, for example, the typical duty of confidence that arises between friends. I should not discuss intimate aspects of my friendship with you with others. Because of the relation of confidence there is a new wrong

[15] Keller (n 6) chs 2 and 4.

[16] This does not mean, of course, that I cannot act as a true friend in this situation in any number of other ways.

[17] Keller (n 6) 156–8.

[18] Cf Keller (n 6) at 153–5.

[19] Keller's account of disloyalty is at Keller (n 6) ch 10. Our accounts primarily differ in that he regards "disloyalty" as a quite distinct concept from loyalty, whereas I, in the succeeding text, regard loyalty as a negative virtue which more or less directly stands in relation to the disvalue of disloyalty.

I can commit which I could not commit in its absence—if I have no friend I cannot breach any obligations of confidence to which friendships give rise. In short, in the same way that I cannot breach an agreement unless I enter into agreements, or cannot fail in my obligation to hear both sides in a dispute unless I am a judge of that dispute, I cannot wrong a friend unless I have one—these sorts of wrongs are made possible by the agreement, the institution of adjudication, and friendship. They do not exist independently. Because of this, there is a question to be asked about the virtues of fidelity (keeping one's agreements), corrective justice (in adjudication), and loyalty (to one's friends): are these supposed virtues "positive" or "negative"? That is, do they have any sort of positive value which is anything other than the flipside of failing to observe the obligations at stake, so that all the moral content of these virtues really lies in the absence of the vice that represents certain ways of breaching those obligations? If they do not, then they are negative virtues.

The idea of a negative virtue was first most clearly explained (as far as I know) by Joseph Raz in his discussion of the virtue of the rule of law.[20] The basic idea is that there are certain wrongs we can commit only once we have created a legal system, for example the wrong of creating retroactive laws. The basic point of calling the rule of law a negative value or virtue is that, if it, considered as a value, is realized by a legal system or if it, considered as a virtue, is possessed by a legal system, that legal system will, for the most part, avoid committing wrongs which only the law can commit; importantly, however, there is no positive value or virtue which should be associated with the rule of law, such that legal systems are somehow regarded as meritorious per se, ie that governance by law is somehow a value in its own right, irrespective of the problems it solves or gains it achieves. To think otherwise is, in a sense, to fetishize the law. I find this line of thought attractive, though others do not. Jeremy Waldron,[21] for example, believes that regulating our affairs by law, in particular our conflicts through adjudication, is valuable in its own right because of the way it treats the subjects of the law as active centers of intelligence. Whoever is right about this (I will return to the issue in a moment), I take it that the idea of a negative value or virtue is clear enough, so we can proceed.

Consider, for a second example, the so-called value of corrective justice. Waldron's claim about the rule of law as a positive value has some influence on us because we can try to conceive of legal systems as a particularly good way of ordering our affairs in comparison to (at least some of) the alternatives. On the other hand, I think there is reason to be suspicious about saying the same about corrective justice, since, ideally, we should wish that there was no occasion for its instantiation. That is, ideally there would never occur any wrongs which would require adjudicative settlement, and thus, ideally, we would never encounter corrective justice. Another way of putting this is that we would never seek to live in a world that had corrective justice in it, in the same way that we would never seek to live in a world that had wars in it, even just wars, since it would be far better to live in a world without wars at all, irrespective of how just they were. Because, however, there are conflicts that need adjudicative resolution, we therefore need to institute adjudicative bodies to handle them and, as the principles of natural

[20] J Raz, "The Rule of Law and its Virtue," *The Authority of Law* (2nd edn, 2009) 210.

[21] Jeremy Waldron, "The Concept and the Rule of Law," 43 *Georgia L Rev* 1–61 (2008).

justice tell us, there are certain things which an adjudicative body can do which make their decisions unjust. Of course, taking Waldron's line, we could argue that corrective justice is a value because adjudicative resolution speaks to our human nature in a way that makes it a morally superior mode of dispute resolution to (at least some of) the alternatives. But given the growth of ADR and the comparator of civilian trial processes which are very different, I think we are entitled to be at least suspicious of this line of thought. Moreover, it is, I think, very easy to grasp the *wrong* of corrective *in*justice, its vice or disvalue, where, for example, there is a breach of the rules of natural justice, but very difficult to put our finger on what the nature of the "right" or the "good" or the "value" or "virtue" of corrective justice is, other than the absence of corrective injustice. It cannot, to my mind, simply be something like "respect for persons as active centers of intelligence," for that sort of respect should attend all our dealings—that is, after all, just one formulation of the categorical imperative, and that applies all the time in every case to all persons. The fact that good adjudication observes it does not generate a special virtue of adjudication per se.

Carrying on in this vein, I also see no particular content to a virtue like fidelity insofar as keeping one's agreements is supposed to instantiate it. Keeping one's agreements is nothing more than properly discharging the obligations that one has voluntarily undertaken. Attending to one's obligations is a moral duty, but not a separate idea of being under an obligation to attend to an obligation. And I do not see any particular virtue in acting in accordance with one's moral obligations. On the other hand, all sorts of vices can be instantiated in failing to do so: bad faith, dishonesty (eg, undertaking an obligation one has no intention of fulfilling), sloth, greed, and so on. Infidelity is in this sense *interesting*, because it has content. Another illuminating perspective on this is the idea that if fidelity was a genuinely positive virtue, people should try to create those situations in which it can be instantiated. We should enter into agreements for non-instrumental reasons just in order that we could have a chance to be faithful to the obligations they create. I think this is nonsense. Like the law, the value of agreements is purely instrumental. Only an odd sort of fidelity-fetishism would counsel us to enter into agreements just for the sake of being able to be faithful to them. This is not to deny for one moment that the normative power to enter into agreements is a good thing, and indeed, I have elsewhere argued that this power is universal, part of natural law if you will.[22] That being so, however, does not, for the reasons given, generate a particular virtue of keeping one's agreements.

Now back to loyalty and disloyalty. "Betrayal" and "disloyalty" only apply to characterize specific sorts of wrongs to one's friends. Being inattentive to my friend's needs is a failing, but to be so is not disloyal. It may be negligent or slothful of me, but not disloyal. Of course, if I knowingly fail to meet an important obligation of friendship, because I am being greedy and want to put in some extra hours for money, there is a sense in which this is disloyal. But that, I think, tells us that loyalty, and worse, betrayal, are not strict liability offences. They require a *mens rea*. To be clear, one can in a certain sense betray one's friend or be disloyal to him unwittingly, or by mistake. Say I inadvertently

[22] James Penner, "Promises, Agreements, and Contracts," in Gregory Klass, George Letsas, and Prince Saprai (eds), *Philosophical Foundations of Contract Law* (forthcoming, 2014).

forward an email with sensitive information about my friend to a third party who will take advantage of the information. I am certainly going to feel guilty about that, and feel that my act was an act which betrayed the confidence my friend reposed in me. But surely any friend would accept my apology for doing so—this is not an act of betrayal in the full sense, that is, in which I knowingly turned my back on my friend and intentionally divulged the sensitive information. That would be genuine disloyalty, genuine betrayal. And, it seems to me, we think of our friends as loyal just insofar as we think them incapable, or constitutively averse, to betraying us in this sort of way. So on this account it seems right to think that loyalty is a negative value or virtue. Special relationships like friendships, give rise to opportunities for wrongs which wouldn't exist in the absence of those relationships. To commit those wrongs, knowing one is doing so,[23] is to be disloyal.

III. Loyalty as a Source of Duty in Fiduciary Law

In view of the foregoing, it would seem that loyalty, as understood in commonsense terms, is a singularly *inapt* concept to explain fiduciary liability. First of all, consider the manifestations of loyalty that Keller identifies.[24] We can leave to one side ritual manifestations of loyalty and defending one's object of loyalty in conversation, since they clearly have nothing to do with anything a fiduciary undertakes to their principal. Deliberative priority, identification with one's principal, and epistemic bias, however, deserve some attention, though none counts in favor of characterizing the fiduciary–principal relationship as one founded upon loyalty.

At first glance, deliberative priority seems apposite, since is it not the fiduciary's duty to give priority in his deliberations to the interests of his principal (within the scope of his undertaking)? In fact, the answer is no, and this brings out an important disanalogy between the fiduciary's role and that of, say, a loyal friend. Rather than deliberative *priority*, giving prior place to the principal's interests in relation to his own, the fiduciary owes the principal deliberative *exclusivity*. In exercising his discretions, it is only the principal's interests which should be considered. It is not as if the fiduciary can get away with any exercise of his discretion where, whilst considering his own best interests, he can claim the decision is fine because he gave *greater* weight to the interests of his principal (though sometimes reading cases of company directors deciding to forgo an opportunity on behalf of the company, and then going on to take it up themselves, one gets the sense that reasoning of this kind is going on). The clearest case is that of a trustee fiduciary. When exercising, say, the discretion to invest in this or that, the fiduciary's interests are entirely irrelevant, for the very straightforward reason that it is *not his property, but the beneficiary's*.

The case of friends is quite different. In relating to my friends in various ways, it is misconceived to say that I give their interests deliberative priority *over my own*. The deliberative priority in question is one in which I give my friends deliberative priority *over non-friends*. I "take their side" vis-à-vis others that are not friends of mine. In

[23] It is an interesting question whether one can be genuinely disloyal without realizing it, in particular via self-deception or through rationalization. See Keller (n 6) at 204–6.

[24] Text to n 10.

dealing with friends, I do not act "selflessly," discount my own interests, or give deliberative priority either to myself or my friend, considering our own self-interests narrowly conceived.[25] Rather, I act in light of the value my friend has to me, and the value of the friendship, because so to act is to act *in my own best interests*, since both of these values are values to me. Of course, this interest of mine may conflict with other interests I have (including to other friends, friendships), but that is no puzzle. That is just the fact of life that I am unable to fully realize all the values I could to their fullest extent given the limitations of time, effort, and so on. If all this is right then deliberative priority simply fails to capture the attitude fiduciaries should have in relation to their principals; instead they owe their principals deliberative exclusivity in the exercise of their discretions.

Turning to the "identification" display of loyalty, there is a sense, obviously, in which fiduciaries should identify with their principals, generally thinking that their role in serving their principal is worthwhile. This is particularly the case for charity trustees or company directors. This identification is not merely a matter of liking what the charity or company gets up to, but of having a kind of familiarity with its goals and strategy. But discharging the role of charity trustee or company director does not require any sympathy of this kind, in the sense that how the life of the fiduciary will go tracks in any really important way whether the charity or company flourishes. These are jobs, after all. The point can be made more sharply by considering the paradigm fiduciary relationship of that of trustee to beneficiary in the case of the traditional family trust. One of the main tasks of the family trustee-fiduciary is to stand back and take a clear-eyed view of her beneficiaries, untainted by personal "identification," drawing upon personal knowledge of the beneficiaries of course, but not being swayed by likes or dislikes. And beneficiaries, just like some of the rest of the population, can be perfectly dreadful people, with whom it would be personally disastrous to identify. It is not in any way part of the remit of a trustee to think of her identity as bound up with that of her beneficiaries.[26]

Finally, as to epistemic bias. A fiduciary in law undertakes a duty to exercise various powers on behalf of her principal. This duty will not be discharged properly if, in the exercise of those powers, the fiduciary forms false beliefs, however congenial those false beliefs may be to her principal. Indeed, in the case of family trusts, one of the whole purposes of placing powers in the hands of trustees is to provide an antidote to the false beliefs of the beneficiaries regarding how to manage, say, a long-running family business. And consider this: whilst it is not uncommon for one of a number of trustees in a family trust to be one of the family members, and usually a beneficiary, it is overwhelmingly the case that settlors choose trustees for their *impartiality* vis-à-vis the beneficiaries; if loyalty in a fiduciary were genuinely prized, one would see the

[25] I am grateful to Richard Walker for helping me see this point.

[26] I therefore part company with Irit Samet, in this volume, when she argues that a "thick notion" of loyalty involving emotional attachment to one's principal is something to be desired in a fiduciary. It is not a failing for a fiduciary, say a trustee, to be a "cold fish." I also do not think that Kant's idea of "moral strength," a general disposition to comply with the moral law, though it can be cultivated and this cultivation can (must?) involve the emotions, amounts to an endorsement by Kant of any particular virtue such as loyalty, even in the minimal sense of helping one to comply with the moral law.

reverse—settlors would choose close family members to be trustees in family trusts, but this, as I say, is almost never seen.

In summary, to the extent we accept the analysis of the commonsense notion of loyalty elaborated above, it would seem that it is essentially irrelevant, or rather, is positively at odds with, what we legally require of a fiduciary.

IV. Fiduciary Law, the "No-Conflict" Rule, and Disloyalty

The "no conflict" rule is the basic rule governing fiduciaries.[27] A fiduciary who places himself in a position, which is usually to say where he enters a transaction, where his own interests might conflict with those of his principal, is liable to account for any (unauthorized) gain he acquires from such a transaction. The no-conflict rule underlies the more specific rules governing fiduciaries, in particular the 'no unauthorized profit' rule, the self-dealing rule (a transaction in which the fiduciary acts on 'both sides' of a transaction can be set aside as of right, and if not the fiduciary must account for his profit), and the fair-dealing rule (a fiduciary who transacts with his principal must establish that the transaction was fair or it can be set aside, and if not, the fiduciary must account for his profit). Under the no-conflict rule, a fiduciary is liable to account for any profit he obtains in circumstances where his interests *may* conflict with his duty to his principal.

The rule is exceptionally stringent, in that it is framed—"*may* conflict"—in terms of the possibility of conflict, not in terms of there being an actual conflict of interest. Indeed, in some circumstances, one might say that the rule applies even where there is no conflict, because the principal for some reason cannot have an interest in the gain in question. *Keech v Sandford* (1726) is the classic English case. A trustee held a lease for a minor beneficiary, which he sought to renew. The lessor refused to renew the lease in favor of the minor. The trustee took the new lease for his own benefit. King LC required the trustee to hold the lease on trust for the beneficiary, even though his interest when he acquired it could not, strictly speaking, be in conflict with his duty to the beneficiary, since the lessor absolutely refused to renew to a minor. Lord King accepted that the consequence of the rule's application was that:

> . . . the trustee is the only person of all mankind who might not have the lease; but it is very proper that the rule should be strictly pursued, and not in the least relaxed; for it is very obvious what would be the consequences of letting trustees have the lease, on refusal to renew to the cestui que trust.[28]

What the no-conflict rule gets at, it is submitted, is the very well-known idea that a person cannot be a judge in his own cause, and similar ideas about biased reasoning.[29] This has nothing to do with fault or ill will. Take the example[30] of someone who has to

[27] See Matthew Conaglen, *Fiduciary Loyalty: Protecting the Due Performance of Non-Fiduciary Duties* (2010), especially ch 3, for a robust defence of the view that the "no-conflict" rule is the core of the law governing fiduciaries.

[28] *Keech v Sandford*, 2 Equity Cases Abridged 741, 22 ER 629 at 741, 629.

[29] Cf Irit Samet, "Guarding the Fiduciaries' Conscience—A Justification of a Stringent Profit-stripping Rule," 28 *Oxford Journal of Legal Studies* 763 (2008), who justifies the rule somewhat differently as the law's response to the risk of a fiduciary's self-deception.

[30] Which I owe to Lionel Smith.

referee a football match where his own child is on one of the teams. In such a case it is almost impossible to referee fairly—the most honest person is liable to overcompensate and judge his child's team unfairly, just to be sure that he is not taking his child's interests too much into account. A further part of the equation here is the human capacity for rationalization (and this, unlike the predicament of trying to judge fairly when one has an interest, does point to a common human failing). People are liable to rationalize their behavior as acceptable, in particular where it causes "no harm;" the trustee in *Keech* may well have felt that taking the lease could cause no possible harm to the beneficiary. The advantage of explaining the nature of the no-conflict rule in this way is that it frames the rule to match the problem to which fiduciary positions give rise: in cases where people take on the role of fiduciary, that is, take on a role where they must unilaterally direct the legal situation of another by exercising a discretion to do so in one way rather than another,[31] they must act in the interests of their principal. Normally, this is trivially easy. It is no more than complying with one's voluntary undertaking of the discretion under a contract or a trust, and exercising as sound a judgment as one can muster. But where a conflict arises, all of this is undermined given the human inability to overcome bias and the ability to rationalize.

V. *Boardman v Phipps*

Boardman v Phipps has generated a great deal of controversy,[32] but as Michael Bryan points out,[33] except perhaps for Lord Upjohn's view (if it was his view) that the stringency of the "possibly may conflict" aspect of the no-conflict rule should be relaxed, all of the judges both at first instance, in the Court of Appeal, and in the Lords, agreed on the principles of the law; the difficulty at every level was applying the law to the facts. In brief, the facts were these: The defendants were Boardman, a solicitor who had acted for the trustees of the Phipps family trust, and Tom Phipps, son of the settlor and one of the beneficiaries. The other beneficiaries were the settlor's widow (who had died by the time of trial), John Phipps, Tom's brother, their sister and the widow of another brother. The trust held a significant holding in a private company, which was ailing. Boardman and Tom Phipps decided that with new and effective management the company could generate significant profits for the shareholders. With the informed consent of the two active trustees (a third trustee was the settlor's widow, who was suffering from dementia throughout and took no part in or notice of the actions that led to the legal action), Boardman and Tom Phipps, as proxy holders of the trust shares, tried to get Tom elected to the board, and failed. They also failed to negotiate a splitting up of the business between the Phipps holding and the other major bloc of shareholders. The two active trustees made it clear that they would not buy any more shares of the company for the trust. Finally, Boardman and Phipps purchased sufficient shares

[31] On the "discretion theory" of the law governing fiduciaries see also Ernest Weinrib, "The Fiduciary Obligation," 25 *University of Toronto LJ* 1 (1975); Paul Miller, Irit Samet and Lionel Smith in this volume. The classic judicial statement is in *Varity Corp v Howe* (1996) 516 US 489 at 504.

[32] See Michael Bryan, "*Boardman v Phipps*: Doing Equity Inequitably," in Charles Mitchell and Paul Mitchell (eds), *Landmark Cases in Equity* (2012), 581–610.

[33] Bryan (n 32) 585–9.

with their own money to enable them, with the support of the trustees, to take control of the company. As a result, they were able to sell off certain of the company assets, paying out large dividends while at the same time maintaining a high share price. Tom's brother, John Phipps, sued Boardman and Tom Phipps, calling upon them to account for the profits they had earned on the shares they had purchased, as profits acquired for which they were accountable as fiduciaries, because acquired in conflict of interest. The House of Lords, by a 3:2 margin, found Boardman and Phipps liable to account for the profits they earned.

The best explanation for Boardman's and Phipps's liability, as carefully explained by Bryan, is true both to the judgments at all levels taken as a whole, and one which actually establishes their liability on the facts. As found at trial and not overturned, Boardman and Phipps essentially became agents *de son tort*, that is, not properly appointed but de facto agents of those who were interested in the Phipps shareholding in the company, including, of course, John Phipps. Whilst they provided some information to the trustees and John, they did not fully inform them of their activities, but throughout represented to the shareholders of the other holdings that they were acting not only for their own benefit, but on behalf of the Phipps shareholders. They therefore took upon themselves a fiduciary position which made them liable for any gain that they acquired in conflict of interest that was not properly authorized by their principals. Viewed from this perspective, the conflict was clear: by seeking to acquire shares in the company themselves, they were taking advantage of their position as representatives of all of the Phipps beneficiaries to acquire a gain on their own behalf. Unless this taking advantage was authorized by those others interested in the Phipps shareholding, John, their sister, and the widow, they were liable to account for their gains; the Court found that they had not been so authorized, and so they were liable to account. (They were, of course, entitled to deduct the amounts they themselves paid for the shares.)

Viscount Dilhorne's dissent shows that this application of the law to the facts was not necessarily correct, and also explains why readers of the case often have conflicting intuitions about the result. He reasoned that when the trustees firmly insisted they would purchase no further shares, from that time forward Boardman and Phipps and the trustees acted in a sort of joint venture to get the value out of the company; Boardman and Phipps did all the work, and the trustees agreed to vote their shares along with Boardman and Phipps to get control of the company.

In any event, the case stands for an important proposition in the law governing fiduciaries, viz, that acquiring an unauthorized gain in a situation of conflict of interest, for which as a fiduciary one will be liable to account, *does not necessarily disclose any disloyalty whatsoever*. All of the judges in Boardman emphasized that the defendants, in particular Boardman, acted honestly and honourably throughout. Lord Cohen put it this way:

> I desire to repeat that the integrity of the appellants is not in doubt. They acted with complete honesty throughout and the respondent is a fortunate man in that the rigour of equity enables him to participate in the profits which have accrued as the result of the action taken by the appellants in March, 1959, in purchasing the shares at their own risk. As the last paragraph of his judgment clearly shows, the trial judge evidently shared this view. He directed an inquiry as to what sum is proper to be allowed to the

> appellants or either of them in respect of his work and skill in obtaining the said shares and the profits in respect thereof. The trial judge concluded by expressing the opinion that payment should be on a liberal scale. With that observation I respectfully agree.[34]

A second important feature of the judgment is that nowhere does any judge even suggest that Boardman and Phipps had some kind of legal or equitable duty to resolve or remove the conflict of interest—it would be, at the least, morally problematic to say that they had such a duty, as they, in good faith, did not realize they were in one,[35] or they would almost certainly have got a formal consent in writing not only from the trustees but from John Phipps and someone capable of acting on behalf of the settlor's widow. To the extent that a person realizes he is in a conflict of interest, he is wise either to get the consent of his principal to acting despite the conflict, or otherwise resolve it, by resigning or making an application to the court to approve a decision he intends to take. But being in a conflict itself is no wrong; thus there is no duty to escape it. We can emphasize this point with a hypothetical and a fact situation which must frequently occur in practice. Imagine that Boardman, in virtue of a distant relation to one of the non-Phipps shareholders, happened to inherit a block of shares in the company on that distant relation's death. Such an inheritance might have put him in conflict with Tom himself, for he might then have been in a position (let us say) to acquire a majority shareholding on his own account. As a joint venturer with Tom, he would have to disclose his new interest and proceed with Tom as before with Tom's consent, or be liable to account for any further shares he acquired in his own name. But one cannot commit a wrong simply by being in a conflict of interest for, as this example shows, that can occur to one even by operation of law (by application of the rules of succession). That's the hypothetical, so now on to the frequent fact situation. Imagine a trustee that is empowered to purchase shares in the trust of XYZ Co Ltd. As a matter of fact, the trustee himself has shares in the company. So in one sense, the trustee finds himself in conflict of interest because he *could* sell his own shares to the trust. But if the trustee purchases XYZ shares on the open market, his purchase is unimpeachable, because *the very transaction itself* did not reflect that conflict of interest. The liability only arises when a trustee engages in a transaction which itself engages a conflict of interest.

In this respect the law of fiduciary accountability is akin to the law of unjust enrichment. Both are cases of *primary, remedial* duties.[36] No one has a duty not to receive a mistaken payment, but the recipient becomes liable to restore the gain nonetheless, ie to remedy the situation. Similarly, a fiduciary has no duty not to act in conflict of interest, but when they do and acquire a gain thereby, they fall under a duty to account for the gain to their principal.

The idea that one has a legal duty to resolve a conflict of interest does not make sense as a general rule, but it does have a sort of application to a particular case. Boardman and Phipps, though self-appointed agents as the court found, had no obligation to

[34] At 104.

[35] I do not deny that one can be subject to moral norms with which one cannot, as a matter of fact, comply, nor that to be subject to a moral norm requires that one be aware of that moral norm's application to one's situation. My claim here is that this should not be the case with a duty to resolve a conflict of interest.

[36] Stephen A Smith, "Unjust Enrichment: Nearer to Tort than Contract," in Robert Chambers, Charles Mitchell, and James Penner (eds), *Philosophical Foundations of Unjust Enrichment* (2009) 181.

proceed with their share purchase and reorganization of the company. But in certain cases fiduciaries have a duty to act. The best example is the case of a solicitor who undertakes to advise different clients involved at both ends of a transaction where the solicitor knows confidential information from one client that is of material interest to the other vis-à-vis the very transaction about to be undertaken.[37] In such a case a solicitor is in an impossible situation. Either he breaches his duty of confidence to one, or fails in his duty of disclosure to the other. In such a case there is nothing he can do to 'resolve' the conflict—he can only withdraw his services from both clients so as not to act. Any act he takes for either party to the transaction will be a breach of duty to one or the other.

VI. Duties of Loyalty in the Civil and Criminal Law

Besides being regarded as civil actors who owe a duty of loyalty to their principals, some commentators[38] frame the fiduciary relationship as one in which the fiduciary must act "altruistically." I think this is wholly misguided. I can affirm that most professional trust companies do not have any altruism in their veins, or in their outlook; a respect for privacy, confidence, discretion, judgment, managerial competence, yes, but "altruism", no—just look at their charging clauses. The idea that mischievously works here is that certain civil wrongs can be characterized as particularly self-serving, or disloyal. But this has nothing to do with the fiduciary relationship (unless misconceived), or with civil law liability in general, I would submit. As I have already discussed, the fiduciary owes "deliberative exclusivity" to the interests of their principal in exercising their discretions, but this is just a *part of the job*. And doing one's job, fulfilling one's voluntarily undertaken obligations, should never be characterized as an instance of selflessness or altruism, for that would suggest that doing so is somehow exceptional, that in such cases one's own interests are thwarted or neglected for the good of another. This is straightforwardly false, and if it were true no businessperson would undertake the role of fiduciary.

Despite everything I have said so far, it is true that various (to my mind, inappropriate) extensions of fiduciary liability have been made in cases where the person named as a "fiduciary" has committed a legal wrong, a legal wrong that is not "just wrong," but one that can be characterized as an abuse of loyalty. A good example is the decision of the Canadian Supreme Court in *M (K) v M (H)*.[39] In *M (K)*, the plaintiff was sexually abused by her father, the defendant, from the age of 8 until she was 16. She suffered various psychological problems, and it was only following psychological therapy, at the age of 28, that she brought an action against her father for damages for the tort of assault. A jury found for her and awarded $10,000 general damages and $40,000 punitive damages. The trial judge, however, set aside the award and dismissed the action on the basis that the claim was barred by the Ontario Limitations Act. On appeal to the Supreme

[37] For a recent example, see *Hilton v Barker, Booth & Eastwood* [2005] UKHL 8; [2005] 1 WLR 567.
[38] Peter Birks, "The Content of Fiduciary Obligation," 34 *Israel Law Review* 3 (2000). The paper as a whole makes many good points; my objection is only to framing the fiduciary concept in terms of "altruism."
[39] [1992] 3 SCR 6. See also *Norberg v Wynrib* (1992) 92 DLR (4th) 449, Can SC.

Court of Canada, the plaintiff/appellant claimed that for various reasons the Limitation Act should not apply to bar her claim in tort, and her appeal on this ground succeeded. But she also claimed that her father's incestuous assault constituted a breach of fiduciary obligation; in view of the fact that there was no statutory limitation period in respect of breach of a fiduciary obligation, if she succeeded on this ground she would have been in a much better position to avoid any bar based upon the lapse of time between the assaults and her launching her action against her father. The Court accepted her argument that her father had breached a fiduciary obligation in assaulting her.

Child abuse is of course a terrible wrong, and is also a dreadful breach of loyalty and good faith when committed by a parent or guardian, and it seems that the latter consideration is what drove the Court to accept the abuse as a breach of fiduciary obligation.[40] But child abuse is a crime and a civil wrong. No one has a legal power or discretion to commit child abuse, a power or discretion that should be exercised in the best interest of the child or not at all. Fiduciary obligations are intended to ensure that a fiduciary takes decisions *that he is otherwise legally empowered or obliged to undertake in one way or another under his trust or agency or retainer* in a manner that best serves the interests of his principal. In view of a fiduciary's fiduciary obligations, an otherwise *legitimate* use of a *legitimate* power or discretion may be *turned into* a 'wrong', thus rendering the fiduciary liable, because undertaken in conflict of interest. A breach of any old obligation, whether the commission of a tort like assault or child abuse, or a breach of contract, does not become a breach of a fiduciary obligation simply because, besides being wrong in its own right, it *also* reveals self-interest, disloyalty, or bad faith; those acts are not within the range of decisions that make up the extent of the fiduciary's discretion, to which, and only to which, the fiduciary's fiduciary liability applies. As Lord Millett has said in another context:

> Sexually assaulting a boy is not an improper mode of looking after him. It is an independent act in itself, not an improper mode of doing something else.[41]

Thus, just because a wrong manifests, in addition to its wrongness per se, disloyalty, that does not turn it into a "breach of fiduciary obligation." On this view, the parent in *M (K) v M (H)* did not commit such a breach, because the act of sexual assault is straightforwardly a wrong whoever does it. It *aggravates* the wrong that it is committed by a parent, a person one should be able to trust; but that does not turn it into a different sort of wrong, a "breach of fiduciary obligation," because it is not a case of a person using a power or discretion, a power or discretion they have in virtue of their relationship with another which must be exercised in that other's interest, in conflict of interest—no one has the power or discretion to commit a sexual assault against anyone.[42] Indeed, from this point of view, it *belittles* the gravity of the wrong to say that the essence of the wrong is its manifestation of a "conflict of interest"—what's wrong about

[40] R Flannigan, "Fiduciary Regulation of Sexual Exploitation," 79 *Canadian Bar Review* 301 (2000).

[41] *Dubai Aluminium v Salaam* [2002] UKHL 48, para 123; [2003] 2 AC 366, 400. The context was a discussion of strict liability, and Lord Millett was emphasizing that there could be vicarious liability for a wrongful act which could not be conceived of as an improper mode of discharging a duty.

[42] For similar reasoning along these lines, see Lionel Smith, "Deterrence, Prophylaxis and Punishment in Fiduciary Obligations," 7 *Journal of Equity* 87 at 98–100 (2013).

sexual assault is the heinous violation of the victim's bodily integrity, not primarily that it evinced disloyalty, and even less because the perpetrator "favoured his own interests" rather than his victim's. The essence of fiduciary liability is that the fiduciary is the *wrong party* to take part in the transaction, not that the transaction is itself a wrong. A fiduciary is an unsuitable purchaser of his principal's property because in contracting with himself he clearly acts in conflict of interest. But the wrong of sexual assault is not wrong because it was the *wrong person* who carried out the assault. It is a wrong because assault itself is wrong, whoever does it.

I do not deny that when a guardian or parent commits sexual assault, this can be characterized not only as an assault but as breach of loyalty or trust, and that this is rightly an aggravating factor which can properly be taken into account in the criminal law, eg for the purposes of sentencing. The same is true for the case of the security guard who takes a bribe to let the burglars in, or the person who steals from his employer, or an employer who defrauds his employees, eg by systematically under-recording their hours worked. We are angrier with the guard dog than the fox for eating the chickens. But I fail to see how this sort of aggravation is relevant to the civil law, except insofar as the civil law carries out a punitive function, as with exemplary damages.[43]

In *M (K)* McLachlin J said in her concurring opinion:[44]

> I add that were I to enter on the matter of the quantum of damages, I would find myself unable to agree that the measure of damages for battery and assault would necessarily be the same as compensation for breach of fiduciary duty. As I see it, the question is whether the wrong encompassed by the cause of action is the same. The wrong encompassed by the torts of battery and assault may be different from the wrong encompassed by the action for a breach of fiduciary duty. The latter encompasses damage to the trust relationship, for example, which the former does not. The action for breach of fiduciary duty may also be more concerned with imposing a measure which will deter future breaches; as I noted in Canson Enterprises Ltd. v. Boughton & Co., [1991] 3 S.C.R. 534, at pp. 587–88, trustees have always been held to highest account in a manner stricter than that applicable to tortfeasors. In short, while agreeing with my colleague that where the same policy objectives underlie two different causes of action similar measures of compensation may be appropriate (paras. 105–106, supra), I would not conclude that the policy objectives or the wrong involved in breach of fiduciary duty of this nature are necessarily the same as those which underlie the torts of battery and assault.

For the reasons already given, I disagree with almost the entirety of this paragraph. The law of trusts does not compensate for "damage to the trust relationship" in actual trust cases, so why should it here? Given that fiduciary liability can be innocent, why would one want to enhance the award against the defendant? (I take it the clear sense

[43] I am not a purist about the civil law. In certain cases, where circumstances warrant, a civil law court can (and should) take into account the motivation with which wrongs were committed, and fiduciary law is no exception. For an illuminating (and entertaining) example in the realm of director-fiduciaries, see Edward B Rock, "Saints and Sinners: How Does Delaware Corporate Law Work?," 44 *UCLA Law Review* 1009 (1996–7). I am grateful to Andrew Gold for the reference.

[44] At para 118.

from this passage is that "damages for breach of fiduciary duty" would be greater than damages for, or additional to damages for, battery and assault.) It is not the purpose of the civil law to deter, whatever economists may say.[45] That fiduciary liability is strict in the sense that it does not inquire into motive, but only into the circumstances of a gain, ie, was there a conflict of interest, and is therefore sometimes called "prophylactic," does not make it a deterrent. Finally, the idea that "trustees have always been held to highest account in a manner stricter than that applicable to tortfeasors" is hyperbole, if not hogwash. This sentiment is occasionally spouted by judges[46] but has no basis in legal reality. Trustees and fiduciaries, just like other duty-bearers in the law, are required to comply with their duties, no more. They are, because of discretions they hold, liable to have transactions which they have entered into in conflict of interest set aside, and liable to account for gains acquired in transactions entered into in conflict of interest. That is not holding them to a higher standard. It is a perfectly sensible moral response to the way bias and rationalization factor in human decision-making.

[45] See Smith (n 44). Hanoch Dagan advises me to be careful here. The notion of deterrence, he suggests, is a complex one. To the extent that vindicating rights, that is, reinforcing the existence of rights in a community is one of the functions of the civil law, this acts in a way as a *sort* of deterrence, by bringing to attention the structure of our rights and duties. By deterrence here, however, I merely mean the idea of deterrence as a justification for hard treatment, ie that it will act on the consciousness of observers not in an epistemic mode, helping them to realize what rights they and others have, but in a prudential mode, motivating them to avoid certain behaviors because of the (more or less) likely consequences.

[46] The most famous example is *Meinhard v Salmon* (1928) 164 NE 545 at 546 per Cardozo CJ; the pertinent passage is quoted by Michele Graziadei n 2 in this volume.

8

The Loyalties of Fiduciary Law

*Andrew S Gold**

Loyalty matters to the law in a variety of ways—and fiduciary law has no monopoly on the concept. A contractual covenant of good faith and fair dealing is sometimes seen as a type of loyalty in performance.[1] A contract can expressly create a duty of loyalty outside the fiduciary relation. An oath of office might include a pledge of loyalty. And loyalty may be a virtue which legal systems are bound to consider.[2] Yet, while each of these possibilities implicates loyalty, they need not implicate fiduciary law.

On the other hand, fiduciary law is peculiarly concerned with loyalty. While loyalty may show up in diverse settings, it is a hallmark of the fiduciary relationship. Indeed, it is commonly thought that if a purported fiduciary does not owe a duty of loyalty to a beneficiary, then the relationship is not actually a fiduciary relationship. In this sense, duties of loyalty are an essential feature of fiduciary law. I share this view, and will take it as an assumed starting point for the discussion to follow.

A duty of loyalty is not merely necessary to a fiduciary relationship, however. There may well be features of fiduciary law that are trivially true of the field, but loyalty is not one of them. Loyalty duties are a core component of the practice. And this brings us to an interesting puzzle about fiduciary relationships: Although there is broad agreement that the duty of loyalty is a core feature of fiduciary law, theorists produce very different accounts of its content. This chapter will consider whether this essential feature—loyalty—has any essential content. It will conclude that, to a large degree, it does not.

Methodological concerns are an important precursor to this discussion. This chapter will not seek to elucidate the ideal concept of loyalty as it might exist in fiduciary law, nor will it seek to balance the justification for a particular loyalty conception against its fit with precedent. Likewise, this chapter will not offer a normative account of what fiduciary loyalty ought to be if the law were properly reformed. Instead, the aim will be to understand the concepts embedded in our practices of fiduciary law.[3] For these

* I thank Evan Fox-Decent, Scott Hershovitz, Paul Miller, and Deborah Tuerkheimer for helpful suggestions regarding the ideas in this chapter. I am also grateful to participants at the Philosophical Foundations of Fiduciary Law conference held at the DePaul University College of Law, and to participants at the Fiduciary Law Workshop held at the Notre Dame Law School. Lastly, I thank Elise Addis for excellent research assistance. Any errors are my own.

[1] See, eg, D Gordon Smith, "The Critical Resource Theory of Fiduciary Duty," 55 *Vand L Rev* 1399, 1487–8 (2002) ("Fiduciary duty and the duty of good faith are variations on a theme. Both are judicially imposed loyalty obligations designed to attack the potential for opportunism in relationships."). But cf Daniel Markovits in this volume.

[2] See John Gardner, "The Virtue of Justice and the Character of Law," in *Law as a Leap of Faith* (2012) 238, 240 (noting the possibility that a legal system "ought to be honest, loyal, trustworthy, temperate, humane, considerate, charitable, diligent, public-spirited, prudent, and so on").

[3] In this regard, the approach is much influenced by the pragmatic conceptualism adopted by Jules Coleman and Benjamin Zipursky. See Jules Coleman, *The Practice of Principle: In Defense of a Pragmatist*

purposes, the legal point of view will be taken seriously, and the claims courts make when they decide cases will be treated as indicia of which concepts are actually in use.[4]

This is not the only way we might seek to understand fiduciary loyalty, but this approach can be illuminating when we think about fiduciary law, especially given its openness to conceptual changes. Internal accounts of fiduciary law are regularly evolving, both with the arrival of new fiduciary relationships (eg, the Delaware limited liability company), and with the arrival of new doctrines of fiduciary obligation (eg, Delaware's incorporation of fiduciary good faith into loyalty). Fiduciary law also faces regular boundary questions, particularly as fiduciary concepts are extended to public law settings.[5] As scholars develop fiduciary accounts of the state and its administrative apparatus, our ability to revise our fiduciary concepts may become increasingly important for explanatory theories (at least if they are to fit the doctrine announced by courts and legislatures).[6]

This approach may also help us to get past a focus on isolated pockets of law when theorizing about fiduciary loyalty. For example, one theorist has recently attempted a comprehensive theory of fiduciary loyalty—but "as it exists in Anglo-Australian fiduciary doctrine."[7] No doubt we can learn a great deal from such a perspective, but it can also be illuminating to understand fiduciary concepts in all the practices in which they figure, including the law of the United States, Canada, Europe, international law, etc. The same considerations are raised by a parochial focus on particular fiduciary relationships to the exclusion of others. The trust may well be the archetypal fiduciary relationship, but it has long ceased to be the only central case for study.[8] If we insist on limiting our account to English/Australian law or to trust law, we will lose track of the connections that link English/Australian conceptions of loyalty to United States or Canadian conceptions, or the connections that link trust law conceptions of loyalty to corporate law or agency law conceptions.

Finally, despite its focus on legal concepts, this chapter will also take note of extra-legal concepts. Legal understandings of fiduciary loyalty often draw on extra-legal understandings of the nature of loyalty. And, outside the law, the concept of loyalty incorporates a number of distinct conceptions of loyalty. We should be interested in knowing whether fiduciary loyalty is similarly variegated. Loyalty conceptions in the two settings may readily diverge, but it is reasonable to expect that our understanding of the

Approach to Legal Theory (2001); Benjamin C. Zipursky, "Pragmatic Conceptualism," 6 *Legal Theory* 457 (2000). The reader, however, need not adopt the precise interpretive methodology of these authors in order to recognize that the concepts embedded in fiduciary law show the variation described in this chapter.

[4] In other words, this chapter will adopt a transparency criterion. On the importance of adopting a transparency criterion for private law theory, see Stephen A Smith, *Contract Theory* (2004) 24–32.

[5] Recent analyses of fiduciary principles in the public law setting include: Evan Fox-Decent, *Sovereignty's Promise: The State as Fiduciary* (2011); Evan Criddle, "Fiduciary Foundations of Administrative Law," 54 *UCLA L Rev* 117 (2006); Ethan J Leib, David L Ponet, and Michael Serota, "A Fiduciary Theory of Judging," 101 *Cal L Rev* 699 (2013); D Theodore Rave, "Politicians as Fiduciaries," 126 *Harv L Rev* 671 (2013); Andrew S Gold, "Reflections on the State as Fiduciary," 63 *U Toronto LJ* 655 (2013).

[6] This is particularly likely if, as Paul Miller suggests, a public official is a *sui generis* fiduciary. See Paul B Miller in this volume.

[7] See Matthew Conaglen, "The Nature and Function of Fiduciary Loyalty," 121 *LQR* 452, 460 (2005).

[8] Indeed, efforts to apply trust law concepts to non-trust settings may sometimes be problematic. See Edward Rock and Michael Wachter, "Dangerous Liaisons: Corporate Law, Trust Law, and Interdoctrinal Legal Transplants," 96 *Nw U L Rev* 651 (2002).

loyalty duties embedded in fiduciary law can be significantly advanced by our understanding of those loyalty duties prominent outside of the legal sphere.

I. The Multiple Conceptions of Loyalty

As an initial step, I will lay out several leading conceptions of loyalty that are significant to fiduciary law. These are not the only conceptions available in the case law or academic literature. Moreover, some of these conceptions may overlap, or even subsume other conceptions. The conceptions of loyalty under discussion stand out, however, for their salience, or else for their frequent relevance to fiduciary relationships. At this stage, the analysis will be purely taxonomic. Section II of this chapter will assess the possibility that one or more of these conceptions is an essential component of loyalty in fiduciary relationships.

A. Loyalty as the avoidance of fiduciary conflicts

A leading conception of fiduciary loyalty holds that loyalty requires the avoidance of conflicting interests. A broad version of this type of loyalty is set forth in Paul Miller's work. Miller refers to this as a duty of faithfulness. As he describes the duty, it consists of two conflict rules:

> First is the requirement that the fiduciary avoid conflicts between pursuit of his self-interest and fulfillment of his duty to act for the benefit of the beneficiary (the conflict of interest rule). Second is the requirement that the fiduciary avoid conflicts between his duty and the pursuit of others' interests (the conflict of duty rule).[9]

In combination, these anti-conflicts obligations are often considered to be the core loyalty obligation of a fiduciary.

Another version is narrower in scope. Not all would describe the conflict of duty rule as a component of the duty of loyalty. The conflict of interest rule may fully comprise the duty of loyalty on some accounts.[10] This narrower conception of fiduciary loyalty involves an anti-conflicts obligation (a duty to avoid conflicts of interest), but without requiring a single undivided loyalty to one beneficiary. For present purposes, I will group together the different anti-conflicts variations on the duty of loyalty, and simply refer to them as the "anti-conflicts" conception.

Although the anti-conflicts rules may serve the purpose of limiting a fiduciary's self-interested behavior, we should be careful not to confuse an anti-conflicts loyalty obligation with an overarching duty of selflessness. Fiduciaries are generally permitted to engage in self-interested behavior in various aspects of their lives. Rather, the fiduciary "must refrain from self-interested behavior that wrongs the fiduciary."[11] As a result, theorists often distinguish the anti-conflicts obligation from an obligation to engage in other-regarding behavior.

[9] See Paul B Miller, "A Theory of Fiduciary Liability," 6 *McGill LJ* 235, 257 (2011).

[10] See Smith (n 1) at 1410–11 ("[C]ourts typically reserve the label 'loyalty' for self-interested actions. Actions that advantage a third party at the expense of the beneficiary are usually treated as a breach of the duty of care").

[11] See Smith (n 1) at 1410.

Interestingly, the fit between the anti-conflicts conception and existing social norms is doubtful. This common feature of fiduciary loyalty is a questionable match for extra-legal notions of loyalty. For example, it would be unusual to hear Jack describe Jill as a disloyal friend simply because Jill had a conflict of interest when she acted on Jack's behalf. It is quite common, in contrast, to see courts say that a corporate director was disloyal simply because of a conflict of interest while the director engaged in conduct on the shareholders' behalf. This anti-conflicts type of fiduciary loyalty appears to be a peculiarly legal understanding.[12]

Despite this mismatch between legal and non-legal perspectives, anti-conflicts conceptions of loyalty are particularly notable in blackletter legal doctrine, and are one of the more distinctive features of fiduciary law. Anti-conflicts rules are prominent in a broad variety of fiduciary relationships, ranging from the law of trusts, to corporations, to agency. As long as we include legal practices in our analysis, the anti-conflicts rules should provide a leading example of what loyalty requires.

B. Loyalty as affirmative devotion

Another conception of fiduciary loyalty suggests that the fiduciary must act in the best interests of the beneficiary (or more precisely, must intend to act in the best interests of the beneficiary). This conception can readily be linked to the first conception, given the possibility that the rules against conflicting interests are designed to increase the likelihood that a fiduciary will act in the beneficiary's best interests. Nonetheless, the two conceptions are distinct, and they need not overlap.

Lyman Johnson's work offers a good introduction to this conception. Building on George Fletcher's account of loyalty, Johnson has recently suggested that fiduciary loyalty involves two conditions: a "minimum" condition and a "maximum" condition.[13] Under the minimum condition, the fiduciary should not betray the object of his or her loyalty. This means that, for example, corporate fiduciaries should not self-deal or take corporate opportunities for themselves. Under the maximum condition, the fiduciary has affirmative duties of devotion toward the beneficiary. This conception of loyalty requires that the fiduciary should act (or intend to act) in the beneficiary's best interests.

The traditional anti-conflicts rules implicate the minimum condition for loyalty, so defined. Yet a conflicts-based approach to loyalty is not the only approach recognized in fiduciary law. The affirmative devotion requirement is also well established. Delaware,

[12] In noting this distinction, I am in no way calling into question whether these rules are desirable, or whether they qualify as loyalty. Instead, I wish to emphasize that the legal concepts and extra-legal concepts diverge. It is an interesting, but separate, question whether divergence between legal loyalty and extra-legal loyalty is problematic. Arguably, such a divergence could raise accommodationist concerns akin to those potentially raised by a divergence between the norms of contract law and the norms of promissory morality. Cf Seana Valentine Shiffrin, "The Divergence of Contract and Promise," 120 *Harv L Rev* 708 (2007). On the other hand, the requirements of loyalty and the requirements of morality may themselves differ, and the accommodationist concern may thus arise in a different fashion, if at all. I thank Richard Brooks for noting the possibility that fiduciary law may pose accommodationist concerns.

[13] See Lyman Johnson, "After Enron: Remembering Loyalty Discourse in Corporate Law," 28 *Del J Corp L* 27, 37–8 (2003) (citing George P Fletcher, *Loyalty: An Essay on the Morality of Relationships* (1993) 9).

the leading corporate law jurisdiction in the United States, has recently embraced a conception of loyalty that calls for affirmative devotion.[14] The recent Delaware cases on fiduciary good faith—which have now been recast as loyalty cases—provide definitive acceptance of affirmative devotion as a loyalty duty.

In addition, while it may be quite hard in practice to win a case against a director or officer based on a failure to show affirmative devotion, the duty is legally enforceable. Part of a director's fiduciary duty of loyalty in Delaware concerns the aims of the director's conduct. In some cases, this duty has teeth. Liability for corporate waste is an example—but the relevant type of disloyalty can be demonstrated in other ways. A notable instance arises where a fiduciary is held liable for knowingly abdicating his or her responsibilities.[15] Although it is more unusual, a director may also be held liable for intentionally harming his or her corporation. In short, affirmative devotion is an established example of fiduciary loyalty.

C. Loyalty as being true

"Being true" involves a different type of loyalty from the first two types. While somewhat less salient in fiduciary jurisprudence, this aspect of loyalty is notable in extra-legal settings, and has played an increasingly significant role in recent corporate law disputes.

Simon Keller offers an example of this conception:

> There is a sense of "loyal" that is associated with being dependable, or reliable, or dutiful, or true—as in, "straight and true." In telling you that somebody is loyal in this sense, I am telling you that you can trust him; he is not scheming or deceitful or manipulative; he will not sell you out; he takes his promises and commitments seriously; he knows his job and he gets it done.[16]

Joseph Raz's work also offers insights into the idea of being true. In *The Morality of Freedom*, Raz analyzes how some types of conduct and attitudes are incompatible with the existence of certain relationships. As Raz notes, "All social forms involve ways of being true to the project or to the relationship which they define."[17] Raz further argues that it is possible to be false to a pursuit while still having good intentions:

> Indeed people have been known to betray their friends or their employers in the interests of those friends. Many a soap opera has capitalized on the idea of the lover who is disloyal in order to break the relationship because he realizes, correctly, that that is in the best interest of his loved one.[18]

Raz's conclusion is significant: "Such cases may show that being false to one's pursuit or relationship is, sometimes, justified. But even a justified betrayal is a betrayal."[19]

[14] As the court did in *Stone v Ritter* 911 A 2d 362 (Del 2006).

[15] See *In re Walt Disney Co Deriv Litig* 906 A 2d 27, 67 (Del 2006) (indicating that a fiduciary breach can occur "where the fiduciary intentionally fails to act in the face of a known duty to act, demonstrating a conscious disregard for his duties").

[16] See Simon Keller, *The Limits of Loyalty* (2007) 154.

[17] See Joseph Raz, *The Morality of Freedom* (1986) 354.

[18] Raz (n 17) 354.

[19] Raz (n 17) 354.

As these illustrations indicate, being true may have variations. Raz refers to being true with respect to a relationship. Keller's reference to the colloquial sense of "being true" might cover more limited territory—it implicates certain ideas of honesty, reliability, and trustworthiness. For present purposes, both discussions have something important in common. Notice that it is possible to avoid any conflicts of interest or duty, and also to act with affirmative devotion toward another individual, and simultaneously to be disloyal because of a failure to be true. Whether we look to Keller's or Raz's discussions, a type of disloyalty emerges that is neither dependent on breaches of the anti-conflicts rules nor dependent on a lack of affirmative devotion.

A good example is the "white lie." Suppose that Jane is a friend of John's, and she wishes to avoid sharing some information with John that would cause him significant emotional distress. Suppose also that John does not need to know this information for any particular reason. Putting to one side questions concerning the morality of lying, could it be loyal for Jane to tell John a white lie in an effort to prevent him from knowing this upsetting information? It is certainly possible for Jane to conclude that telling a lie in this case will be in John's best interests, and we can posit that Jane has no conflict of interest that would affect her judgment, nor conflicting duties to third parties. If loyalty incorporates a norm of "being true" in Keller's sense, then it would appear disloyal for Jane to lie.[20] If loyalty does not, then Jane's conduct in lying might be a prime example of loyal behavior, at least under some understandings of loyalty. In either case, the question of whether Jane's conduct is loyal will not be reducible to a question of whether she has acted in John's best interests, nor will it be reducible to a question of whether she complied with the anti-conflicts rules.

Courts are now recognizing a conception of fiduciary loyalty that is different from the affirmative devotion and anti-conflicts conceptions.[21] In the recent options-backdating cases, Delaware judges have indicated that a lie to shareholders qualifies as a form of disloyalty.[22] Such lies, however, may occur in cases where there is no conflict of interest, and no failure to act with an affirmative devotion toward shareholder interests.[23] Courts have likewise indicated that breaking agreements with shareholders and engaging in intentional violations of law will qualify as disloyalty.[24] In these cases, a similar pattern emerges. Fiduciaries can be disloyal without conflicts of interest, and while intending to serve the best interests of their beneficiaries. These cases appear to involve loyalty as being true.

[20] Whether or not telling a lie is an example of being true to the terms of the relationship would be a different question. For some relationships, telling a lie would not be true to the terms of the relationship, but it is possible to imagine certain friendships where telling a lie would be precisely what the terms of the relationship call for, or at least permit.

[21] See generally Andrew S Gold, "The New Concept of Loyalty in Corporate Law," 43 *UC Davis L Rev* 457 (2009).

[22] See Gold (n 21) at 477–9 (describing case law). But cf Lionel Smith, "The Motive, Not the Deed," in Joshua Getzler (ed), *Rationalizing Property, Equity, and Trusts: Essays in Honour of Edward Burn* (2003) 53, 81 (suggesting that a white lie can be "an act of loyal deceit").

[23] Nor is it entirely fanciful to imagine that directors might think misleading shareholders would sometimes advance the shareholders' best interests. Cf. *Basic Inc v Levinson* 485 US 224, 234–5 (1988) (discussing the issue of whether corporate officers might advance shareholder interests by keeping information secret from them).

[24] See Gold (n 21) at 479–80 (describing case law).

D. Loyalty as a term in a hypothetical bargain

Another distinctive conception stems from a law and economics analysis of fiduciary law. This perspective sees fiduciary loyalty in terms of a hypothetical bargain. Unlike the affirmative devotion conception or the being true conception, the hypothetical bargain approach has no obvious link to extra-legal conceptions of loyalty. Yet it is one of the leading theories concerning the content of the duty of loyalty.

Judge Frank Easterbrook and Daniel Fischel have offered one of the more influential accounts in this vein. As Easterbrook and Fischel argue:

> What do terms such as "duty of loyalty" mean? Because the process is contractual—because both principal and agent enter this understanding for gain—the details should be those that maximize that gain, which the contracting parties can divide.[25]

Typically, this type of account is understood to be majoritarian: it is thought to reflect the terms that most parties would select under these conditions. The resulting content is protean. In theory, a majoritarian gap-filler could amount to an anti-conflicts rule, or to an affirmative devotion duty, or to some combination of various loyalty conceptions. In the hands of Easterbrook and Fischel, a variety of different permutations on the content of fiduciary duties are all examples of majoritarian outcomes.

Once again, there may be several versions at issue. In another contractarian formulation, courts should adopt the terms that the specific parties to the fiduciary relationship would have chosen.[26] Here, too, we are dealing with a hypothetical bargain, but it is a tailored bargain rather than a majoritarian bargain.[27] Again, this formulation sweeps broadly with respect to content. There is an indefinite number of variations on loyalty that might, in the abstract, count as fiduciary loyalty on a contractarian approach.[28]

E. Loyalty as fairness

Arguably, another conception emerges in those settings where a fiduciary is required to act on behalf of multiple beneficiaries. A good example of this conception is found in Evan Fox-Decent's work. Fox-Decent suggests that state actors may be fiduciaries to the state's citizens.[29] Yet, if the state is viewed as a fiduciary, it is surely not in a position to act in each individual citizen's best interests where doing so would be inconsistent with acting in the

[25] Frank H Easterbrook and Daniel R Fischel, "Contract and Fiduciary Duty," 36 *JL & Econ* 425, 426 (1993). For a recent reassessment, see Robert H Sitkoff, "The Economic Structure of Fiduciary Law," 91 *BU L Rev* 1039 (2011); Robert H Sitkoff in this volume.

[26] For helpful discussion of various permutations on hypothetical bargain methodology, see David Charny, "Hypothetical Bargains: The Normative Structure of Contract Interpretation," 89 *Mich L Rev* 1815, 1821 (1991).

[27] Another possibility is to adopt a bargain-mimicking default. See Omri Ben-Shahar, "A Bargaining Power Theory of Default Rules," 109 *Colum L Rev* 396 (2009). On the relevance of this approach to fiduciary duties, see Andrew S Gold, "Dynamic Fiduciary Duties," 34 *Cardozo L Rev* 491 (2012).

[28] Note that a similar protean quality would seem to follow if we see loyalty as being true to the terms of a relationship. For different social structures, an indefinite number of loyalty variations might qualify as being true to the terms of each resulting relationship.

[29] See Evan Fox-Decent, *Sovereignty's Promise: The State as Fiduciary* (2011).

best interests of the general public.[30] Likewise, the rule against conflicting duties is impossible to meet. The state has obligations to multiple beneficiaries at the same time.

Fox-Decent suggests that, in the private law setting, "the discrete fiduciary duty of loyalty is necessarily transformed into duties of fairness and reasonableness."[31] The basis for this result, he argues, is that the fiduciary principle "can authorize the use of fiduciary power only to the extent that such use respects each person's co-equal status as a beneficiary of the fiduciary principle's authorization of fiduciary power."[32] Public law settings may draw on the same general idea.

Whether or not a duty of fairness and reasonableness is conceptually necessary, it is plausible to think that fiduciary loyalty can have a distinctive content in multiple beneficiary cases. One might contend that this type of loyalty is merely a context-sensitive variation on one or more of the loyalty conceptions described above. This idea may even be implicit in Fox-Decent's reference to the duty of loyalty being "transformed." But even if a loyalty as fairness conception is grounded in another conception of loyalty—such as affirmative devotion—the content of loyalty as fairness represents a distinct content. It may amount to the "next best thing" when compared to other types of loyalty, but acting fairly toward someone is definitely not synonymous with acting in their best interests. Were it otherwise, the state as fiduciary would have an impossible task.

II. The Candidates for a Minimal Core

Of the above conceptions of loyalty, certain candidates stand out as a potential minimum core content to fiduciary loyalty. The anti-conflicts conception and the affirmative devotion conception are both well-known categories, and proponents support each understanding. Other possibilities may exist, however, and are worth consideration. This section will thus assess in general whether there is an essential content to loyalty in fiduciary law.

A. The anti-conflicts view

One leading position is that the bare minimum of fiduciary loyalty is an obligation to avoid conflicts. Consider Paul Miller's work as an example. In an important paper, Miller contends that a fiduciary has no legally enforceable duty to act in the best interests of a beneficiary.[33] In contrast, the duty to avoid conflicts is legally enforceable, and this duty to avoid conflicts can help us understand why disgorgement remedies, among others, are available in cases of fiduciary breach. In fact, Miller doesn't just say that the anti-conflicts rules are central to fiduciary loyalty. He says that avoiding a conflict of interest and duty is what it means to be loyal: "The disloyal fiduciary, in other words, is the conflicted one."[34] Let's begin with this type of claim.

[30] See Fox-Decent (n 29) at 34. The complexities in determining which beneficiaries are the proper objects of fiduciary loyalty for public officers can also be substantial, as demonstrated by Ethan Leib, David Ponet, and Michael Serota in this volume.

[31] See Fox-Decent (n 29) at 34. [32] See Fox-Decent (n 29) at 35.

[33] See Paul B Miller, "Justifying Fiduciary Remedies," 63 *U Toronto LJ* 570, 610 (2013).

[34] See Miller (n 33) at 607.

Initially, we might question whether an anti-conflicts obligation makes sense in the absence of an affirmative devotion account of loyalty. This is what Peter Birks argued. According to Birks: "The obligation of disinterestedness cannot be severed from the obligation to promote and preserve. It does not make sense without that principal obligation."[35] Indeed, Birks goes further—in his view the obligation of disinterestedness becomes "unintelligible."[36]

At the conceptual level, this seems too strong. One could have an obligation to perform a task according to the terms of a contract, for example, and also have an obligation not to perform that task in any way that is self-interested. No affirmative devotion would be required. Fiduciary law might, at least conceivably, have a similar structure. Fiduciaries might be given discretion to act within a range of options and have an obligation not to act self-interestedly with respect to that discretion—without having a simultaneous duty of affirmative devotion.[37] Structural features or reputation costs might protect the beneficiary. It is a separate question whether the law in fact looks that way, but it at least could look that way without being unintelligible.

Yet Birks's argument is not the only challenge. A distinct reason to question the anti-conflicts claim is that, for certain types of fiduciary relationship, it is entirely normal and anticipated that the fiduciary will have conflicts of duty.[38] This is true if the state is a fiduciary, and it is also true under more mundane circumstances. Indenture trustees may have conflicts of duty within the scope of their fiduciary responsibilities. Corporate directors face conflicts of duty all the time. Partners in a general partnership will regularly confront this concern, particularly if there are more than two partners.

In addition, for certain types of fiduciary relationship, the law is designed to permit conflicts of interest, as long as the parties have agreed to this ahead of time. This is evident from the Revised Uniform Partnership Act in the United States, with its provisions for partial waivers of loyalty. It is even more evident in the law of Delaware LLC's, which permits elimination of the anti-conflicts rules altogether. We might say in these LLC cases that the relationships at issue are no longer fiduciary relationships, but without begging the question it is unclear why this must be so. If they are still fiduciary relationships, as many would think based on residual obligations of the LLC managers (which could include a duty of affirmative devotion), then the anti-conflicts rules are not the core minimum content of fiduciary loyalty.

The anti-conflicts rules are sometimes taken to be protective of fiduciary loyalty, rather than an example of fiduciary loyalty itself.[39] If the anti-conflicts rules are merely a prophylactic device to deal with the true loyalty problem—the problem of whether

[35] Peter Birks, "The Content of Fiduciary Obligation," 34 *Israel L Rev* 3, 28 (2000).

[36] See Birks (n 35) ("An independent obligation to abstain from pursuing interests of one's own is unintelligible, certainly unworkable").

[37] Cf Larry Ribstein, "Fencing Fiduciary Duties," 91 *BU L Rev* 899, 909 (2011) ("The fiduciary duty to avoid self-dealing is not defined with reference to the specific parties on whose behalf the fiduciary must act").

[38] For discussion of settings in which this occurs, see Steven L Schwarcz, "Fiduciaries with Conflicting Obligations," 94 *Minn L Rev* 1867 (2010). For a suggestion that corporate directors have some discretion to choose which beneficiaries to favor, see Gold (n 27) at 499–502.

[39] See Smith (n 22) at 56 ("I would say, instead, that [the duty to avoid conflicts] is the most obvious protection of the fiduciary duty, but it is not the fiduciary duty itself").

the fiduciary has shown affirmative devotion—then it seems that there is no necessary conceptual link between fiduciary loyalty and an absence of conflicts. This thesis is consistent with the judicial and legislative willingness, in at least some jurisdictions, to permit the elimination of the anti-conflicts obligation.[40] It is also an entirely mainstream interpretation of loyalty duties.

There are cases, moreover, in which there is no violation of the anti-conflicts rules but there is fiduciary disloyalty. This is especially evident in corporate law, in light of the recent holding in *Stone v Ritter*.[41] By recognizing that fiduciary bad faith can be disloyal, the Delaware courts opened up the possibility of disloyal conduct by unconflicted fiduciaries. Of course, the presence of fiduciary loyalty obligations separate and apart from the anti-conflicts rules does not definitively prove that you can have a fiduciary relationship without those anti-conflicts rules. What these cases do suggest is the plausibility of having a fiduciary relationship with a conception of loyalty other than the anti-conflicts conception.

In short, we can discover cases where a fiduciary is considered loyal despite breaching the anti-conflicts rules, and we can discover cases where a fiduciary is considered disloyal despite *not* breaching the anti-conflicts rules. A conflicted fiduciary is a disloyal fiduciary in many settings, but if we are looking to see whether the anti-conflicts rules are a core minimum, the legal data present an ambiguous picture at best.

B. The affirmative devotion view

Given the possibility that the anti-conflicts rules are designed to prevent a more basic breach of loyalty—ie, a breach of affirmative devotion—it is worth considering whether this is the core conception of loyalty in fiduciary law. This is apparently the position taken by Lionel Smith in his earlier work, where he argues that: "the heart of the fiduciary obligation is the surveillance and justiciability of motive."[42] On this view, the fiduciary "must act (or not act) in what he *perceives to be* the best interests of the beneficiary."[43] Yet this view is also controversial.

One reason to doubt the affirmative devotion view is that, in many settings, a duty of affirmative devotion is not legally enforceable.[44] One could provide a counter-argument to this objection based on practical concerns. After all, the duty of affirmative devotion might rarely be enforceable for epistemic reasons, but it could still exist as a legal duty. Corporate law has long recognized a distinction between fiduciary standards of conduct and standards of review.[45] It is often very hard to know what the fiduciary actually

[40] In some cases, the law is also designed to permit conflicting interest transactions if the parties agree to them *ex post*, or if the transactions are entirely fair. What this signals about the duty of loyalty is open to debate, but these legal practices are also consistent with the view that the anti-conflicts rules serve prophylactic purposes.

[41] 911 A 2d 362 (Del 2006) (concluding that the fiduciary duty of good faith is subsumed within the fiduciary duty of loyalty).

[42] See 911 A 2d 362 (Del 2006) at 67.

[43] See 911 A 2d 362 (Del 2006) at 67.

[44] See Miller (n 33) at 610 (suggesting this type of duty is not legally enforceable and citing a case on parent–child relationships for support). As noted, the duty is legally enforceable in some settings, but it may not be enforceable in all jurisdictions.

[45] See Melvin Aron Eisenberg, "The Divergence of Standards of Conduct and Standards of Review in Corporate Law," 62 *Fordham L Rev* 437 (1993).

intends, and the business judgment rule reflects this fact. Perhaps, even in those settings where the duty is unenforceable, an obligation of affirmative devotion exists as a legal standard of conduct. But the objection might still have some weight to it; for it remains true that courts rarely enforce an affirmative devotion requirement, and in some cases suggest it is unenforceable.

In addition, just as there are cases in which affirmative devotion is enforced absent any conflict concerns, there are also cases in which courts enforce the anti-conflicts rules despite the presence of affirmative devotion. Perhaps there are deterrence reasons for enforcing in these cases (or perhaps courts are worried about a fiduciary's self-deception), but the reality is that, even where we are convinced that the fiduciary intended to benefit the beneficiary, there may still be liability where there was a conflict of interest.[46]

Notice also that, in this setting as well, one could carve away the relevant duty and still have a plausibly fiduciary relationship, indeed a type of loyalty. Suppose in a Delaware LLC that the parties specify that the duty of affirmative devotion is not to be recognized as part of their relationship, and they also specify that the anti-conflicts rules shall apply in full force. Given the established doctrinal status of the anti-conflicts rules as components of the duty of loyalty, it would seem that this LLC would be subject to fiduciary duties of loyalty, despite the absence of the affirmative devotion element. In addition, since the affirmative devotion element is rarely enforced, for practical purposes this LLC would not be much different from many other business organizations.[47]

C. The contractual account

Another candidate for a minimum core of loyalty arises from the contractual account of fiduciary duties. On this view, the content of fiduciary loyalty is the content of a hypothetical bargain in a world of zero transaction costs. With this perspective as a backdrop, we can plausibly see both the affirmative devotion requirement and the anti-conflicts rules as variations on a more fundamental contractual gap-filler. This conception also has the interesting feature that it may provide a bridge between the last two conceptions. While there is much room to debate the content of a majoritarian hypothetical bargain (not to mention a tailored alternative), it is arguable that the contractual approach will provide variable content, but under a fixed test. Under this test, it could be that both the anti-conflicts and the affirmative devotion conceptions of

[46] On the self-deception concern where fiduciaries have conflicts of interest, see Irit Samet, "Guarding the Fiduciary's Conscience—A Justification of a Stringent Profit-stripping Rule," 28 *Oxford J Legal Stud* 763 (2008).

[47] Recently, Stephen Galoob and Ethan Leib have suggested another candidate: the "shaping" account of loyalty. On this view, loyalty necessarily has an intentional dimension, such that accidental compliance is insufficient to satisfy the fiduciary obligation of loyalty. In deliberating on her conduct, they suggest that a loyal fiduciary will attribute non-derivative significance to her beneficiary's interests. See Stephen R Galoob and Ethan J Leib, "Intentions, Compliance, and Fiduciary Obligations" (forthcoming, *Legal Theory*) (draft on file with author). Putting to one side applications in extra-legal settings, the doctrinal features that pose challenges for the affirmative devotion account would pose similar problems for the shaping account as a core minimum for the legal concept of fiduciary loyalty.

loyalty are, in a sense, a core minimum content because both mirror the product of a hypothetical bargain.

A substantial challenge for the contractual account is that it fits so poorly with the internal point of view. There are unquestionably courts that take a hypothetical bargain approach to fiduciary duties—particularly in the business organizations setting.[48] Nevertheless, judicial language and reasoning is frequently inconsistent with the contractual picture, or even with hypothetical bargain reasoning. Whether we take a functional or an interpretive approach to explaining fiduciary law, it is important to understand our concepts from the perspective of legal actors.[49] Yet, in many cases, the contractual account seems inconsistent with this internal point of view.

Assuming these concerns are avoided, there is a more telling weakness. Putting aside the concepts courts reference when they apply fiduciary law, not all fiduciary relationships are plausibly contractual. For example, while not every jurisdiction clearly recognizes parent–child relationships as fiduciary, they are commonly seen in fiduciary terms.[50] The parent–child relationship is not contractual in origin, and the content of the loyalty obligation parents owe their children is not derived from a contract. There is no contractual duty to breach, and, in these cases, a hypothetical bargain is quite alien to legal reasoning.

D. Other possibilities

We might try to adopt some combination of an anti-conflicts obligation and an affirmative devotion requirement.[51] Still, if we have doubts that anti-conflicts obligations or affirmative devotion requirements are essential, then *a fortiori* we will have doubts that the two in combination are essential. Any of the legal settings in which one or the other obligation is absent will also be a setting in which the combined obligation is absent. Of course, we haven't used up all the options yet. There are other conceptions of loyalty available, including the idea of "being true" described above. Being true, however, has only recently become associated with fiduciary loyalty, and it makes for a doubtful core minimum. As we move past the anti-conflicts and affirmative devotion conceptions, the likelihood that we will be able to capture an essential content of fiduciary loyalty recedes into the distance.

The idea that fairness could be the essential content of the duty of loyalty is, if anything, even less likely than the other candidates. Fairness can readily describe conduct that falls short of loyalty, and it can also readily describe conduct that far exceeds the standard requirements of loyalty. In ordinary language use, we do not typically treat

[48] See, eg, *Jordan v Duff & Phelps, Inc* 815 F 2d 429 (7th Cir 1987), cert dismissed, 485 US 901 (1988).

[49] See Andrew S Gold and Henry E Smith, "How Private Law Is Simply Moral" (analyzing areas of convergence between functional and interpretive theories of private law) (manuscript on file with author). For further thoughts on the functional significance of fiduciary judicial language, see Gregory S Alexander, "A Cognitive Theory of Fiduciary Relationships," 85 *Cornell L Rev* 767 (2000).

[50] See Elizabeth S Scott and Robert E Scott, "Parents as Fiduciaries," 81 *Va L Rev* 2401 (1995).

[51] See Birks (n 35) at 28 (describing a conception of fiduciary loyalty under which "[t]he obligation of disinterestedness cannot be severed from the obligation to promote and preserve"); Smith (n 22) at 76 (suggesting that an undertaking to be loyal could issue directly in the fiduciary duty to act in the best interests of the beneficiary, and that it could issue indirectly in prophylactic rules).

fairness and loyalty as synonyms, although sometimes loyalty may call for fairness. And, even if there are settings in which fairness is what loyalty calls for, this is quite different from a demonstration that fairness is always a part of loyalty in fiduciary law.

We might consider another angle on the problem. We might find that fiduciary duties vary in intensity across fiduciary relationships, and conclude that either the anti-conflicts conception or the affirmative devotion conception is simply the more intense form of loyalty. On this approach, the less intense conception of loyalty might count as the core minimum. Lyman Johnson's references to a maximum and a minimum condition of loyalty are suggestive in this regard.

Yet, while it is arguable that fiduciary loyalty varies in intensity, it is not at all clear that an anti-conflicts duty is less intense than an affirmative devotion duty.[52] In some cases, a fiduciary may be liable for disloyal conduct despite an absence of any conflicts of interest (due to a knowing failure to advance the beneficiary's best interests), and in other cases a fiduciary may be liable for disloyal conduct despite showing the most sincere devotion to the beneficiary's best interests (due to conflicts of interest). Depending on the theorist's perspective, either conception of loyalty is a plausible candidate for the more intense category.

A similar point holds for loyalty as being true. We might plausibly think the more intense loyalty duty is one in which the fiduciary must avoid lies to shareholders, intentional violations of the law, or broken commitments to beneficiaries. On the other hand, as Seana Shiffrin has indicated, there is an interesting question whether a fiduciary might have an affirmative duty to breach a contract.[53] Suppose this contract is a contract with shareholders. Imagine a loyalty conception that rejects the requirements of "being true" in Keller's sense, but takes an affirmative devotion requirement very seriously. Under this conception, the fiduciary must break commitments to the beneficiary when it will advance the beneficiary's best interests. A loyalty that gives you a duty to breach or a duty to lie is certainly a powerful form of loyalty. So, too, is a loyalty that prohibits lies. Is there any basis to say that one version of loyalty is more intense than the other? One or the other conception may be more desirable, but that is a separate question.

III. Other Senses of "Core" with Respect to Loyalty

Given the variations among fiduciary relationships, it should not be surprising to discover that theorists disagree on a core minimum content of fiduciary loyalty. Private law theory is rife with divisions concerning the core features of tort law, contract law, unjust enrichment law, and property law, and fiduciary law is not an exception to the rule. There is, perhaps, an unusual level of disagreement about fiduciary loyalty. Theorists disagree not only on the content of fiduciary loyalty, they even disagree on whether fiduciary loyalty is correctly seen as a duty.[54] The existence of disagreements,

[52] It should also be noted that not everyone accepts the idea that fiduciary loyalty varies in intensity across settings. See Smith (n 22) at 77 (dissenting from "the often-expressed view that there are different 'intensities' of fiduciary obligations").

[53] See Shiffrin (n 12) at 729 n 41.

[54] See, eg, James Penner and Lionel Smith in this volume.

however, is not a novel challenge. The question is whether the existing legal doctrine leaves us sufficient room to discern an essential content to fiduciary loyalty.

Part of our problem may be an overly demanding test for what a "core" legal concept is.[55] It is far from clear that the best way to understand the legal concept of fiduciary loyalty is to understand it in terms of its necessary features.[56] In trying to understand the core loyalty duty, it could be counter-productive to seek a content that is essential to all fiduciary relationships. Maybe there is one conception of loyalty that is so predominant or so important that we can usefully work with it to develop our ideas. Or, perhaps there is a type of loyalty that involves the focal meaning of loyalty, where the other conceptions do not. In other words, it may be that our test for "core" content is too demanding, or that it should be adjusted depending on our purposes.

These ideas are promising, but we should not be over-optimistic that they will help us resolve our disagreements, or even that they will lead to one result which is superior to the alternatives. Once we expand our choices in this way, we may end up with multiple candidates for core loyalty duties, each of them plausible, and each of them consistent with leading cases in one or another jurisdiction. This might be a desirable way to theorize fiduciary law, all things considered, yet it probably does not give us the consensus we would hope for.

In any event, if this strategy is to work, we will need to agree on the outlier cases of fiduciary loyalty. (Presumably, these outliers adopt the non-core conceptions of fiduciary loyalty.) This, unfortunately, creates a problem. There is no obvious test for an outlier. And once we allow for exceptional cases when theorizing about fiduciary loyalty, why wouldn't we do the same when assessing fiduciary relationships? Contractarian theorists of fiduciary law will be quick to suggest that the case of parent–child relationships is exceptional. Property-oriented theorists will say that the most important fiduciary cases involve discretion over property, and not those settings where property is hard to identify. A variety of theorists will say that the Delaware LLC is an outlier. Disputed accounts of fiduciary loyalty and relationships are as likely to proliferate as to diminish in number.[57]

These challenges should not deter us from thinking about "core" content in different ways. Disagreements do not mean that a theoretical approach has failed, and there

[55] A roughly analogous concern may arise in the general jurisprudence setting, where some have critiqued efforts to understand the concept of law in terms of its necessary features. See, eg, Frederick Schauer, "Was Austin Right After All? On the Role of Sanctions in a Theory of Law," 23 *Ratio Juris* 1, 11 (2010); Danny Priel, "Jurisprudence and Necessity," 20 *Can JL & Juris* 173, 182 (2007).

[56] We should also be careful not to confuse those features that are necessary in order for fiduciary loyalty to be present with those features of fiduciary law that are legally mandated. This distinction can most easily be recognized by considering the case of a Delaware LLC. In this setting, there simply are no mandatory fiduciary duties. As a matter of law, any fiduciary duties may be eliminated by contract from this type of business organization. That said, it may be the case that, if certain duties were eliminated by contract, their absence would mean that the LLC relationship no longer included a loyalty duty (and, per hypothesis, was no longer a fiduciary relationship). If it turns out that any fiduciary duties have this latter feature, they would be necessary in the sense described in this chapter.

[57] There may also be disagreements concerning the significance of the core to an explanation of fiduciary law. See William Lucy, "Method and Fit: Two Problems for Contemporary Philosophies of Tort Law," 52 *McGill LJ* 605, 623–4 (2007) (questioning a view under which "only those participants whose views of the institution and its constitutive practices capture the core are taken seriously in any theoretical account of the institution").

may well be insights available from efforts to locate those types of loyalty that are most prominent, or functional, or morally legitimate (or otherwise central to our legal practices). On the other hand, the effort to find a core minimum content for fiduciary loyalty may still be worthwhile, assuming it is feasible. Granting that possibility, how are we to do so? Finding an essential content that falls under the leading conceptions of fiduciary loyalty seems unlikely. Seeking the essential content of fiduciary loyalty may instead require a thinner account of the core minimum. The next section will consider this possibility.

IV. The Idea that Loyalty in the Abstract is the Core Obligation

Here is an alternative that allows us to locate an essential content to fiduciary loyalty. Fiduciary relationships require a legal duty of loyalty, full stop. There is no particular conception of what loyalty is that will fit all fiduciary relationships, but all fiduciary relationships must employ some conception of loyalty.[58] This allows for a core minimum—the duty must be a loyalty duty—even if it tells us little about what kind of loyalty is at stake. We can also discern boundaries under this account. For example, the loyalty at issue must be a conception of loyalty that is more expansive than the loyalty (if it is such) that operates in cases of contractual good faith and fair dealing.[59] Yet, while these boundaries between fiduciary loyalty and various other categories of conduct may exist, the core content of fiduciary loyalty itself would remain under-determined.

The above claim may need clarification. The suggestion that the minimum core content of fiduciary loyalty is under-determined is not the same as a suggestion that fiduciary loyalty is an empty vessel. Not every imaginable content will fall within the concept of loyalty—even if a variety of conceptions do. Nor does the above claim commit us to any legal indeterminacy in concrete cases. The core content of fiduciary loyalty may be incredibly vague when we are studying fiduciary law as a whole, but the content of fiduciary loyalty for particular cases, categories of fiduciary relationship, and jurisdictions may be both accessible and well defined.

Note also that the concept of loyalty may still be useful in theorizing about fiduciary relationships, even in the absence of a specific conception. Perhaps there is a family resemblance between the legally adopted conceptions of loyalty. Or, the indeterminacy itself may be informative. Just as we may try to understand fiduciary relationships better based on the view (which I challenge here) that fiduciary relationships involve a specific conception of loyalty, we might also try to understand fiduciary relationships based on the view that loyalty in the law means many things. The reasons fiduciary

[58] By analogy, a basket of fruit must contain examples of fruit in order to qualify as such. It need not hold an apple, or an orange, or a banana. No particular examples of fruit are required, but whichever objects the basket contains must still be fruit. Fiduciary loyalty may work the same way. In order to qualify as such, any one of several types of loyalty may suffice, and there may be no particular type of loyalty that must be present. But there must still be some recognizable conception of loyalty in order for us to find that fiduciary loyalty is present. I thank Robert Sitkoff for this example.

[59] It may also be the case that the content of fiduciary loyalty must always incorporate a particular direction of obligation. That is, the fiduciary must at a minimum owe his or her loyalty to the beneficiary of the relationship. Cf. Markovits in this volume.

relationships come into existence are multiple, and it should not surprise us if the rights and duties that result have different shapes to them.

We should be cautious in considering the implications, however. Adopting the view that fiduciary law incorporates a fiduciary duty of loyalty, but no specific conception of loyalty, may invite several errors. The first error would be to think this is a challenge to loyalty's pride of place in fiduciary law. This need not be true. If there is no specific conception, this does not mean that loyalty is an insignificant component of fiduciary relationships. Games might be a vital component of a particular social relation even if we cannot provide a clear account of the minimum content of a game.[60] By the same token, loyalty may be vital even if it does not have a precise minimum content in fiduciary law.

Moreover, it is still possible for loyalty to have precise requirements at a more abstract level, even if the conceptions of loyalty recognized for particular fiduciary relationships or by particular jurisdictions are not easily assimilated one to another. It might be that loyalty involves particular expressions of an overarching loyalty concept—even if at the ground level these expressions of loyalty may differ in kind, and not just in degree. For example, suppose that loyalty condemns breaches of the trust that is characteristic of the relevant relationship.[61] Different types of relationship may implicate different types of trust, as we see for example when we compare director–shareholder relationships, employer–employee relationships, parent–child relationships, or husband–wife relationships. In turn, different types of conduct may count as a breach of trust in each case. Perhaps some relationships implicate affirmative devotion whether or not there are conflicts of interest, while others prohibit conflicts of interest whether or not there is affirmative devotion. Some relationships allow for white lies (maybe even require them), while others do not. These subcategories of loyalty may not be readily described as variations on the same content, at least not at the ground level, but they may each qualify as examples of what an overarching loyalty concept requires for the particular relationships at issue.

The second error would be to conclude that a comparatively indeterminate concept of loyalty rules out a unifying approach to the explanation of fiduciary law. While that is a possibility, that outcome is hardly entailed by an under-determined concept of loyalty. In the tort setting, for example, civil recourse theorists have offered a powerful wrongs-based account of tort law, yet tort law shows a dramatic variation among different kinds of wrongs. Civil recourse theorists candidly discuss a "Hodgepodge Problem" based on this mix of wrongful conduct, but still offer a unifying account of torts.[62] It is

[60] The classic discussion of games and their characterization is in Ludwig Wittgenstein, *Philosophical Investigations*, trans G E M Anscombe (3rd edn, 1958) §§ 66–71.

[61] I thank Scott Hershovitz for this formulation of a potential overarching concept of loyalty. As I understand this account, it would share some features with the idea of being true to the terms of a relationship, but the trust component may implicate a narrower scope of application. I also thank Paul Miller for emphasizing the idea that what we may be observing are different expressions of a single concept of loyalty. For helpful analysis of how trust plays a role in fiduciary law, see Matthew Harding, "Trust and Fiduciary Law," 33 *Oxford J Legal Stud* 81 (2013); Joshua Getzler, "'As If.' Accountability and Counterfactual Trust," 91 *BU L Rev* 973 (2011).

[62] See John C P Goldberg and Benjamin C Zipursky, "Torts as Wrongs," 88 *Tex L Rev* 917, 941 (2010) ("While admitting the plurality of wrongs and types of wrongs may dash the hopes that some theorists have for a certain kind of essentialist theory of Torts, that is far from making a wrongs-based theory of Torts incoherent").

very possible that particular features of fiduciary law will also involve the application of multiple values and concepts, but that fiduciary law will be amenable to a broadly coherent theoretical structure.

Indeed, it may be that a diversity of loyalty conceptions is itself an indication of something notable in our fiduciary law system. Consider, for example, the arguments for private law pluralism advanced by Hanoch Dagan. As he suggests, private law fields such as property law may incorporate a plurality of values.[63] Particular institutions within those subject areas may then embody specific modes of valuation. On Dagan's account, this structural pluralism is desirable as a mechanism for facilitating autonomy, as it can provide individuals with a range of institutions among which to choose.[64] And, as Dagan and Sharon Hannes argue, fiduciary law may be understood in these terms.[65] An under-determined concept of fiduciary loyalty (writ large) might reflect a structurally pluralist fiduciary law. And, if this hypothesis turns out to be correct, there is even a sense in which it will supply a unifying account. Private law pluralism, on this view, is unified at a more abstract level by a single principle of autonomy.[66]

The third error is related to the first two. It would be a mistake to think we cannot draw conceptual inferences about the nature of fiduciary relationships given the indeterminacy of fiduciary loyalty as such. Admittedly, not everyone thinks we should look to loyalty duties to figure out whether a fiduciary relationship exists. It is a matter of dispute whether it makes more sense to reason from fiduciary relationships to loyalty duties, or to reason from loyalty duties to fiduciary relationships.[67] The arguments in this chapter should not decide this type of question. In either event, fiduciary law may present us with a set of concepts that, roughly speaking, hang together. And, even if some of these concepts do not hang together, there may still be forms of local coherence within the field of fiduciary law.[68]

Particular theories of fiduciary relationships may need reassessment once we reject the idea that fiduciary loyalty necessarily involves a specific conception. For example, if the theorist relies heavily on an anti-conflicts rule in explaining fiduciary relationships, an indeterminate loyalty concept presents a challenge. In contrast, other accounts of fiduciary relationships may be able to build on an indeterminate loyalty concept. For example, Deborah DeMott's suggestion that we can better understand fiduciary relationships based on those circumstances that justify expectations of loyalty may be adaptable to an indeterminate concept of loyalty.[69] Much depends on the chosen

[63] See Hanoch Dagan, "Pluralism and Perfectionism in Private Law," 112 *Colum L Rev* 1409 (2012).

[64] See Dagan (n 63) at 1423–5 (citing Joseph Raz, *The Morality of Freedom* (1986) 372).

[65] See Hanoch Dagan and Sharon Hannes in this volume.

[66] One might also anticipate distinctive loyalty duties under a functional approach like that of Henry Smith, which focuses on the contextual features of equity. See Henry E Smith in this volume (suggesting that "we should only expect a loose tie" between the various fiduciary relationships, in light of variations in anti-opportunism concerns).

[67] Compare James Edelman, "When do Fiduciary Duties Arise?," 126 *LQR* 302, 316 (2010) (describing the view that "the label 'fiduciary' is a conclusion that is reached only once it is determined that particular duties are owed"), with Paul B Miller, "Justifying Fiduciary Duties," 58 *McGill LJ* 969, 978–9 (2013) (suggesting the analytical priority of fiduciary relationship to duty), and Paul B Miller in this volume.

[68] For helpful analysis of local coherence as it relates to legal systems, see Joseph Raz, "The Relevance of Coherence," in *Ethics in the Public Domain* (1994) 277, 314–15 (describing possibilities for local coherence).

[69] See Deborah A DeMott, "Breach of Fiduciary Duty: On Justifiable Expectations of Loyalty and Their Consequences," 48 *Ariz L Rev* 925, 926 (2006) (suggesting that "the law applicable to fiduciary duty can best

theory. While a thick account of the essential features of fiduciary loyalty might be suggestive, a thinner account might offer its own explanatory benefits.

Finally, there is one additional concern worth noting. A theorist might conclude that an under-determined concept of fiduciary loyalty does not provide a sufficiently clear account of loyalty to count as a plausible interpretation. One response would be to assess fiduciary law at a more local level. As noted earlier, legal conceptions of loyalty may be quite precise within specific settings; the proposed indeterminacy arises when we consider fiduciary law as a whole. That said, a potential critic might seek determinacy at the level of fiduciary law as a whole, and not just with respect to individual fiduciary law institutions. This objection is unconvincing. Even if variations in loyalty suggest that fiduciary law as a general subject matter is vague or ambiguous in content, this need not mean that the interpretation under consideration is wrong.[70] For one thing, we may simply have an area of legal doctrine that is less clear than it could be (and assuming that is a weakness, we will accordingly have cause to reform the law). Fit concerns are fundamental for an interpretive account, and it is very hard to locate a thick account of fiduciary loyalty that comes close to fitting all the legal doctrine. Furthermore, an under-determined concept of loyalty need not represent a flaw in the existing conceptual structure of fiduciary law—it may represent a conceptual strength. For example, indeterminate fiduciary duties of loyalty may enable directors to interpret their loyalty obligations in different ways as time passes.[71] This dynamism, in turn, could enable important innovations. And, as Seana Shiffrin has suggested, the vagueness of certain legal concepts may induce moral deliberation among the regulated parties.[72] Loyalty could have similar features.[73] Although these possibilities are contingent, conceptual indeterminacy might sometimes be a desirable feature of fiduciary loyalty, rather than a cause for dismay. This possibility could easily be obscured by an approach to explaining fiduciary law that insists on a more determinate concept of fiduciary loyalty. Indeed, we may overlook some of fiduciary law's most prominent features if we expect loyalty to have a consistent and precise meaning across contexts.

Conclusion

This chapter has sought to discern the minimum content of loyalty in fiduciary law. From a certain perspective, this chapter has come up short. Loyalty duties are an essential feature of fiduciary relationships, but no specific conception of loyalty appears to carry the day. Fiduciaries may have loyalty duties that don't include the anti-conflicts

be understood as responsive to circumstances that justify the expectation that an actor's conduct will be loyal to the interests of another").

[70] But cf Jody S Kraus, "Transparency and Determinacy in Common Law Adjudication: A Philosophical Defense of Explanatory Economic Analysis," 93 *Va L Rev* 287, 302 (2007) (suggesting a determinacy criterion for explanatory theories of private law fields).

[71] See Gold (n 27) at 495.

[72] See Seana Valentine Shiffrin, "Inducing Moral Deliberation: On the Occasional Virtues of Fog," 123 *Harv L Rev* 1214 (2010).

[73] This potential argument implicates the question of how loyalty and morality are linked together. That topic is beyond the scope of this chapter, but it is another question that fiduciary theory might productively pursue. Notably, it is not clear that deliberation over what loyalty requires will involve the same considerations as deliberation over what morality requires.

rules, and fiduciaries may have loyalty duties that don't include a mandate of affirmative devotion. They may certainly have loyalty duties that don't fit the contractual account, and "being true" in Keller's sense is an unlikely choice. It is possible that at least one of these conceptions must be present, but no conception in particular must be.

While we can say that loyalty is essential, most of its common legal features are not. Directedness toward a beneficiary may ordinarily be a minimal requirement, and perhaps loyalty means that a fiduciary must not breach the trust that is characteristic of a particular relationship, but theorists are usually looking for something more. Whether this lack of a specific content that cuts across all relationships and jurisdictions should be considered a problem for fiduciary theory is a separate question. Theories that seek to explain fiduciary law in terms of an essential type of loyalty may need to be reassessed. On the other hand, perhaps part of what is special about fiduciary law is that it requires different kinds of loyalty for different kinds of relationship. Loyalty varies in our social experiences—it also varies in the law.

PART III

ECONOMIC THEORY: CONSTRUCTIVE AND CRITICAL PERSPECTIVES

9

An Economic Theory of Fiduciary Law

*Robert H Sitkoff**

Introduction

Nearly two decades have passed since the publication of the seminal economic analyses of fiduciary law by Cooter and Freedman,[1] and by Easterbrook and Fischel,[2] which together have come to underpin the prevailing economic, contractarian model of fiduciary law.[3] The principal–agent economic theory that motivates those papers has come to permeate the literature on law and legal institutions generally.[4] The law-and-economics movement has matured further, developing new tools and refining its understanding of previously applied concepts. The purpose of this chapter is to restate the economic theory of fiduciary law, providing an updated and improved synthesis.

* This chapter is an expanded revision of Robert H Sitkoff, "The Economic Structure of Fiduciary Law," 91 *BU L Rev* 1039 (2011). In accordance with Harvard Law School's policy on conflicts of interest, the author discloses certain outside activities, one or more of which may relate to the subject matter of this chapter, at <http://www.law.harvard.edu/faculty/COI/2013_Sitkoff_Robert.html>.

[1] Robert Cooter and Bradley J Freedman, "The Fiduciary Relationship: Its Economic Character and Legal Consequences," 66 *NYU L Rev* 1045 (1991).

[2] Frank H Easterbrook and Daniel R Fischel, "Contract and Fiduciary Duty," 36 *JL & Econ* 425 (1993).

[3] In this context, the term contractarian is meant to reference economic contract theory, and the voluntary, agreement-based nature of a fiduciary relationship, not to suggest an identity between fiduciary and contract law.

There is, of course, a thick literature on fiduciary law. See, eg, Matthew Conaglen, *Fiduciary Loyalty: Protecting the Due Performance of Non-Fiduciary Duties* (2010); Tamar Frankel, *Fiduciary Law* (2011); Leonard I Rotman, *Fiduciary Law* (2005); Gregory S Alexander, "A Cognitive Theory of Fiduciary Relationships," 85 *Cornell L Rev* 767 (2000); Rob Atkinson, "Obedience as the Foundation of Fiduciary Duty," 34 *J Corp L* 43 (2008); Henry N Butler and Larry E Ribstein, "Opting out of Fiduciary Duties: A Response to the Anti-Contractarians," 65 *Wash L Rev* 1 (1990); Robert C Clark, "Agency Costs Versus Fiduciary Duties," in John W Pratt and Richard J Zeckhauser (eds), *Principals and Agents: The Structure of Business* (1985) 55; Deborah A DeMott, "Beyond Metaphor: An Analysis of Fiduciary Obligation," *Duke LJ* 879 (1988); Claire Moore Dickerson, "From Behind the Looking Glass: Good Faith, Fiduciary Duty & Permitted Harm," 22 *Fla St U L Rev* 955 (1995); James Edelman, "When Do Fiduciary Duties Arise?," 126 *LQ Rev* 302 (2010); Scott FitzGibbon, "Fiduciary Relationships Are Not Contracts," 82 *Marq L Rev* 303 (1999); Robert Flannigan, "The Economics of Fiduciary Accountability," 32 *Del J Corp L* 393 (2007); Tamar Frankel, "Fiduciary Duties as Default Rules," 74 *Or L Rev* 1209 (1995); Arthur B Laby, "The Fiduciary Obligation as the Adoption of Ends," 56 *Buff L Rev* 99 (2008); Melanie B Leslie, "Trusting Trustees: Fiduciary Duties and the Limits of Default Rules," 94 *Geo LJ* 67 (2005); Paul B Miller, "Justifying Fiduciary Duties," 58 *McGill LJ* 969 (2013); Paul B Miller, "A Theory of Fiduciary Liability," 56 *McGill LJ* 235 (2011); R C Nolan, "Controlling Fiduciary Power," 68 *Cambridge LJ* 293 (2009); L S Sealy, "Fiduciary Relationships," *Cambridge LJ* 69 (1962); J C Shepherd, "Towards a Unified Concept of Fiduciary Relationships," 97 *LQ Rev* 51 (1981); D Gordon Smith, "The Critical Resource Theory of Fiduciary Duty," 55 *Vand L Rev* 1399 (2002); Ernest J Weinrib, "The Fiduciary Obligation," 25 *U Toronto LJ* 1 (1975).

[4] For example, I have elsewhere developed an agency theory of trust law. See Robert H Sitkoff, "An Agency Costs Theory of Trust Law," 89 *Cornell L Rev* 621 (2004); see also Jonathan Klick and Robert H Sitkoff, "Agency Costs, Charitable Trusts, and Corporate Control: Evidence from Hershey's Kiss-Off," 108 *Colum L Rev* 749, 779–83 (2008); Robert H Sitkoff, "Trust Law as Fiduciary Governance Plus Asset Partitioning," in Lionel Smith (ed), *The Worlds of the Trust* (2013) 428.

In restating the economic theory of fiduciary law, this chapter makes three fresh contributions. First, it elaborates on earlier work by clarifying the agency problem that is at the core of all fiduciary relationships. In consequence of this common economic structure, there is a common doctrinal structure that cuts across the application of fiduciary principles in different contexts. However, within this common structure, the particulars of fiduciary obligation vary in accordance with the particulars of the agency problem in the fiduciary relationship at issue. This point explains the purported elusiveness of fiduciary doctrine. It also explains why courts apply fiduciary law both categorically, such as to trustees and (legal) agents, as well as ad hoc, to relationships involving a position of trust and confidence that give rise to an agency problem.

Second, this chapter identifies a functional distinction between primary and subsidiary fiduciary rules. In all fiduciary relationships we find general duties of loyalty and care, typically phrased as standards, which proscribe conflicts of interest and prescribe an objective standard of care. But we also find specific subsidiary fiduciary duties, often phrased as rules, that elaborate on the application of the duties of loyalty and care to commonly recurring circumstances in the particular form of fiduciary relationship. Together, the general primary duties of loyalty and care and the specific subsidiary rules provide for governance by a mix of rules and standards that offers the benefits of both while mitigating their respective weaknesses.

Third, this chapter revisits the puzzle of why fiduciary law includes mandatory rules that cannot be waived in a relationship deemed fiduciary. Committed economic contractarians, such as Easterbrook and Fischel, have had difficulty in explaining why the parties to a fiduciary relationship do not have complete freedom of contract.[5] The answer is that the mandatory core of fiduciary law serves a cautionary and protective function within the fiduciary relationship as well as an external categorization function that clarifies rights for third parties. The existence of a mandatory fiduciary core is thus reconcilable with an economic theory of fiduciary law.

The remainder of this chapter is organized as follows. Section I examines the agency problem that is the common economic structure at the core of fiduciary relationships. Section II examines the fiduciary governance strategy for containing agency costs in such relationships. Section III examines the mandatory core of fiduciary law that has embarrassed prior economic analyses. Section IV examines the remedial structure of fiduciary law, focusing on compensatory and disgorgement remedies. A short conclusion follows.

I. The Agency Problem

The law tends to impose fiduciary obligation in circumstances that present what economists call a *principal–agent* or *agency problem*. An agency problem arises whenever one person, the *principal*, engages another person, the *agent*, to undertake imperfectly observable discretionary actions that affect the welfare of the principal.[6] Agency

[5] See text accompanying n 42.

[6] See Michael C Jensen and William H Meckling, "Theory of the Firm: Managerial Behavior, Agency Costs and Ownership Structure," 3 *J Fin Econ* 305, 308 (1976).

problems therefore arise not only in relationships governed by the common law of agency, but also in trust law, corporate law, and a host of other contexts.

Agency problems are pervasive because no one has the skills necessary to do everything for himself and because every undertaking has an opportunity cost. By delegating a task to an agent, the principal benefits from specialist service and is freed to undertake some other activity. But these benefits come at the cost of being made vulnerable to abuse if the agent is given discretion the exercise of which cannot easily be observed or verified. In such circumstances, the agent may be tempted to favor the agent's interests when they diverge from those of the principal. The losses and other inefficiencies resulting from this misalignment of interests are called *agency costs*.[7]

Removing or limiting the agent's discretion is not a satisfactory answer to an agency problem. Often the principal cannot spell out in advance precisely what the agent should do in all possible future circumstances. This problem of *incomplete contracting* arises from *transaction costs*—the impossibility of anticipating all future contingencies and the infeasibility of reducing to writing instructions for every contingency that can be anticipated. Moreover, in many circumstances the very purpose of retaining an agent with expertise is undermined if the agent is not given room to apply that expertise on behalf of the principal to changing conditions. Disempowering the agent protects the principal from mis- or malfeasance, but it also disables the agent from undertaking acts useful for the principal.

Active monitoring is likewise not a satisfactory answer to an agency problem. Even if the principal has spelled out what the agent should do in a particular contingency, the principal may not be able to monitor the agent's compliance with those instructions. Agents often are retained because the principal lacks the specialized skills necessary to undertake the activity without assistance. In such a case, the skill deficit that prompted the principal to engage the agent renders the principal vulnerable to abuse by limiting the principal's ability to monitor the agent.

To the extent that circumstances outside of the agent's control may affect the outcome, judging the agent on the basis of the agent's results is an imperfect solution to an agency problem. Suppose a real estate agent cannot locate a suitable buyer for a home at a homeowner's desired price. The homeowner can seldom ascertain whether the agent's failure reflects the agent's inadequate effort, the homeowner's overpricing, or a slumping market. The homeowner's inability to assess the cause of the agent's failure is a form of post-contractual information asymmetry known as *hidden action* or *moral hazard*.[8]

Another possibility for ameliorating the agency problem is incentive-based compensation. A real estate agent is typically compensated by a percentage of the sale price to give the agent a financial incentive to maximize that price. But no compensation agreement short of selling the house to the agent will completely remove the possibility of divergence of interest and with it the temptation for the agent to favor the agent's own interests. Consider a real estate agent working on a 5 percent commission. Such an agent will have no incentive to undertake $100 of additional effort to increase the sale

[7] See Jensen and Meckling (n 6) at 308.

[8] See, eg, Jean-Jacques Laffont and David Martimort, *The Theory of Incentives: The Principal-Agent Model* (2002) 3.

price by $1,000, because the payoff to the agent of doing so is only $50 (5 percent of $1,000).[9] By contrast, if the agent owned the home he would undertake the additional $100 in effort for the $1,000 increase in the sale price. But solving the *incentive problem* by selling the house to the agent—in effect, removing the agency—is often impractical. The typical real estate agent could not bear the risk of buying his clients' homes for resale (a *risk-sharing problem*[10]), and his clients would still be dependent on his faithfulness in pricing the home (a *hidden information* or *adverse selection* problem[11]).

In summary, the difficult task for legal institutional design is to "protect[] the principal from the vulnerability that any relationship of agency creates by exposing the principal's property or interests more generally to the risk of self-interested action by the agent."[12] The task, in other words, is to design a body of law applicable to agency relationships that minimizes agency costs while preserving the benefits of agency.

II. The Fiduciary Governance Strategy

A. Categorical and ad hoc deterrence

Agency problems are the defining hallmark of categorical fiduciary relationships, such as those between trustee and beneficiary, guardian and ward, principal and agent (in law), director and corporation, and lawyer and client. If you are a trustee, a guardian, an agent, a director, or a lawyer, you almost certainly have the kind of difficult-to-observe discretionary power affecting the principal's welfare that gives rise to an agency problem. In consequence, as a categorical matter you are a fiduciary, subject to fiduciary duties, and your discretionary powers are held in a fiduciary capacity. The *Restatement (Third) of Trusts* calls this "a basic principle of trust administration," namely, that "a trustee presumptively has comprehensive powers to manage the trust estate and otherwise to carry out the terms and purpose of the trust, but that all powers held in the capacity of trustee must be exercised, or not exercised, in accordance with the trustee's fiduciary obligations."[13]

But the categorical fiduciary relationships do not exhaust the universe of potential agency problems. An agency problem may arise in other relationships, depending on the circumstances. Accordingly, courts impose fiduciary duties ad hoc in relationships of "trust and confidence" that present an agency problem but that are not categorically fiduciary.[14] *Burdett v Miller*,[15] an opinion by Judge Posner, is illustrative. Noting that

[9] This example derives from Frank H Easterbrook and Daniel R Fischel, *The Economic Structure of Corporate Law* (1991) 91.

[10] Agency relationships, in other words, present both incentive and risk-sharing problems. See, eg, Cooter and Freedman (n 1) at 1068; Kathleen M Eisenhardt, "Agency Theory: An Assessment and Review," 14 *Acad Mgmt Rev* 57, 58 (1989).

[11] See, eg, Laffont and Martimort (n 8) at 3.

[12] *Restatement (Third) of Agency* (2006) § 8.01 cmt b. Although the quoted provision refers to common law agency, the point pertains to all agency relationships using that term in an economic rather than legal sense.

[13] *Restatement (Third) of Trusts* (2007) § 70 cmt a.

[14] See, eg, *Wiener v Lazard Freres & Co* 672 NYS2d 8, 14 (App Div 1998) (noting that fiduciary obligation may arise if "a party reposed confidence in another and reasonably relied on the other's superior expertise or knowledge"); *Restatement (Third) of Agency* § 8.01 cmt c (noting imposition of fiduciary obligation "on the basis that one party to the relationship has in fact reposed trust and confidence in the other and has done so consistently with the other's invitation").

[15] 957 F2d 1375 (7th Cir 1992).

"the relation between an investment advisor and the people he advises is not" a per se fiduciary category, the court imposed fiduciary duties on the defendant investment adviser nonetheless.[16] The plaintiff had "reposed trust and confidence" in the defendant, who had held himself out "to be expert as well as trustworthy."[17] The defendant had gained "influence and superiority over" the plaintiff by virtue of his claimed "expert knowledge the deployment of which the [plaintiff could not] monitor."[18]

In both fiduciary applications, categorical and ad hoc, imposition of fiduciary obligation is meant to ameliorate the underlying agency problem. Under the fiduciary governance strategy, an agent who has broad discretionary power may act in the moment, but afterwards the principal is invited to scrutinize whether the agent's action was indeed in the principal's best interests. Stripped of legalistic formalisms and moralizing rhetoric,[19] the functional core of fiduciary obligation is *deterrence*.[20] The agent is induced to act in the best interests of the principal by the threat of after-the-fact liability for failure to have done so. Deterrence in this sense means *ex post* settling up with the principal for any breach of the agent's *ex ante* fiduciary duties.

B. Loyalty and care

The primary fiduciary duties are loyalty and care. The duty of *loyalty* proscribes misappropriation and regulates conflicts of interest by requiring a fiduciary to act in the "best" or even "sole" interests of the principal. The fiduciary may obtain the principal's consent to a conflict, but only in accordance with certain procedural and substantive safeguards, chief among them full and fair disclosure by the fiduciary.[21] The aim is to induce the fiduciary to avoid the conflict or to disclose the material facts of how the conflict might compromise the fiduciary's judgment, thereby enabling the principal to make an informed decision whether to consent to the conflict.[22] In concert with the availability of a disgorgement remedy for breach, the prophylactic ban on self-dealing by a fiduciary thus serves a *disclosure* or *revelatory* purpose.[23]

[16] 957 F2d 1375 (n 15) at 1381. [17] 957 F2d 1375 (n 15) at 1381.

[18] 957 F2d 1375 (n 15) at 1381. See also *Patsos v First Albany Corp* 741 NE2d 841, 849–50 (Mass 2001) (applying fiduciary duties ad hoc to an investment adviser).

[19] The most famous such rhetoric is that of Justice Cardozo in *Meinhard v Salmon*:

> Many forms of conduct permissible in a workaday world for those acting at arm's length, are forbidden to those bound by fiduciary ties. A trustee is held to something stricter than the morals of the market place. Not honesty alone, but the punctilio of an honor the most sensitive, is then the standard of behavior. As to this there has developed a tradition that is unbending and inveterate. Uncompromising rigidity has been the attitude of courts of equity when petitioned to undermine the rule of undivided loyalty by the "disintegrating erosion" of particular exceptions. Only thus has the level of conduct for fiduciaries been kept at a level higher than that trodden by the crowd. It will not consciously be lowered by any judgment of this court.

164 NE 545, 546 (NY 1928) (citation omitted).

[20] See Frank H Easterbook and Daniel R Fischel, "Corporate Control Transactions," 91 *Yale LJ* 698, 702 (1982).

[21] See, eg, *Restatement (Third) of Trusts* § 78 cmts c, d; *Restatement (Third) of Agency* §§ 8.01–8.06; *Principles of Corporate Governance: Analysis and Recommendations* (1994) §§ 5.01–5.02.

[22] See, eg, *Restatement (Third) of Agency* § 8.06 cmt b.

[23] See text accompanying n 55.

The duty of *care* prescribes the fiduciary's standard of care by establishing a "reasonableness" or "prudence" standard that is informed by industry norms and practices. The fiduciary standard of care is objective, measured by reference to a reasonable or prudent person in like circumstances.[24] If a fiduciary has specialized skills relevant to the principal's retention of the fiduciary, then the applicable standard of care is that of a reasonable or prudent person in possession of those skills.[25]

Because agency problems arise from incomplete contracting, the core duties of loyalty and care are phrased in general terms. The duties of loyalty and care are *standards* that allow the court to decide whether, in view of all the circumstances, the fiduciary acted in accord with what the parties would have agreed if they had been able to anticipate those circumstances. In effect, the loyalty and care standards empower the court to complete the parties' contract after the fact. Fiduciary law thus minimizes *transaction costs*. Instead of trying in advance to reduce to writing provisions for every future contingency, the parties need only specify those contingencies that are important and likely enough to warrant the transaction costs of express provision. For all other contingencies, fiduciary obligation fills the gap.

As standards that allow for consideration of all relevant circumstances, the duties of loyalty and care minimize *error costs*. But as is typical of standards (as compared to rules), this reduction in error costs comes at the price of increased *uncertainty* and *decision costs*.[26] The highly contextual nature of a standard makes prediction more difficult and requires a more intensive judicial role.

However, the normal accretive process of common law development has ameliorated this problem by producing a rich body of interpretive authority on fiduciary matters. This mass of authority improves predictability by providing instructive guidance on how the duties of loyalty and care will be applied in various circumstances. It also addresses the extent to which the parties may override fiduciary duties by explicit agreement and the remedies available upon breach of duty.[27]

C. Subsidiary or implementing rules

The uncertainty arising from the nature of the duties of loyalty and care as standards is further mitigated by the development of specific *subsidiary* or *implementing rules* that elaborate on the application of loyalty and care to recurring circumstances. This point is perhaps best explained by way of illustration.

Within trust law, the duty of care (called prudence in trust parlance) is elaborated in application to the investment function by the prudent investor rule.[28] With regard to the custodial and administrative functions, the duties of loyalty and prudence are

[24] See, eg, *Restatement (Third) of Trusts* § 77; *Restatement (Third) of Agency* § 8.08; *Principles of Corporate Governance: Analysis and Recommendations* § 4.01(a).

[25] See, eg, Unif Prudent Investor Act § 2(f) (1994); *Restatement (Third) of Trusts* § 77(3); *Restatement (Third) of Agency* § 8.08.

[26] See, eg, Louis Kaplow, "Rules Versus Standards: An Economic Analysis," 42 *Duke LJ* 557 (1992).

[27] See Sections III–IV.

[28] See, eg, John H Langbein, "The Uniform Prudent Investor Act and the Future of Trust Investing," 81 *Iowa L Rev* 641 (1996); Max M Schanzenbach and Robert H Sitkoff, "Did Reform of Prudent Trust Investment Laws Change Trust Portfolio Allocation?," 50 *JL & Econ* 681 (2007).

elaborated by subsidiary duties to collect, protect, earmark, and not commingle trust property; to keep adequate records of administration; and to bring and defend claims.[29] The duty of impartiality and the principal and income rules elaborate on loyalty and prudence in trusts with multiple beneficiaries with divergent interests.[30] Still another subsidiary rule requires advance disclosure to the beneficiaries of significant developments or non-routine transactions in the administration of the trust.[31]

In agency law, the duty of loyalty is elaborated by more specific duties pertaining to conflicted transactions, competition with the principal, and protection of confidences.[32] In corporate law, the corporate opportunities doctrine elaborates on the application of loyalty to the recurring circumstance of the temptation for a director or officer to usurp a business opportunity that could have been beneficial for the corporation.[33]

The subsidiary rules simplify application of fiduciary obligation to cases that fall within their terms, reducing decision costs.[34] One need not show that the duty of care requires accurate record keeping, for example, if one can invoke a subsidiary rule that imposes such a duty. Moreover, the subsidiary rules offer the typical benefit of simple rules, reduced decision costs, without increasing error costs by providing a roadmap for strategic avoidance behavior. If a fiduciary acts in a manner that is inimical to the principal's interests but that does not fall within one or another subsidiary rule, the principal may invoke the standards of loyalty and care. Operating in tandem, the general primary duties of loyalty and care plus the specific subsidiary rules provide the decision costs advantage of rules and the error costs advantage of standards.[35]

D. Common structure with varied particulars

Because fiduciary law provides for an after-the-fact compliance review of the fiduciary's conduct, and because the nature of the underlying agency problem varies across fiduciary relationships, the precise contours of fiduciary obligation vary across fields. For example, the fiduciary obligation in trust law is generally stricter than in corporate law. But those differences reflect the different contexts. The agency problem in a family trust in which the beneficiaries have no exit option and that is managed by a corporate fiduciary that cannot easily be replaced differs significantly from the agency problem in a publicly traded corporation from which a shareholder can separate easily by selling his shares in a thick securities market.[36]

[29] See Jesse Dukeminier and Robert H Sitkoff, *Wills, Trusts, and Estates* (9th edn, 2013) 646–9.

[30] See Dukeminier and Sitkoff (n 29) at 657–67.

[31] See *Restatement (Third) of Trusts* § 82 cmt d.

[32] See *Restatement (Third) of Agency* §§ 8.01–8.06.

[33] See Stephen M Bainbridge, *Corporate Law* (2nd edn, 2009) § 7.3.

[34] See Sitkoff, "An Agency Costs Theory of Trust Law" (n 4) at 682–3.

[35] I have elsewhere characterized this mode of governance as a "standard tempered by presumptions," in comparison to a "rule tempered by exceptions." Dukeminier and Sitkoff (n 29) at 379–80. The dynamic in fiduciary law thus stands apart from the conventional story in property law. As opportunists find a new trick, the "mud" of loyalty and care becomes a "crystal" of a subsidiary rule addressing that trick. Cf Carol M Rose, "Crystals and Mud in Property Law," 40 *Stan L Rev* 577 (1988).

[36] See Robert H Sitkoff, "Trust Law, Corporate Law, and Capital Market Efficiency," 28 *J Corp Law* 565 (2003); see also Stephen M Bainbridge, "The Case for Limited Shareholder Voting Rights," 53 *UCLA L Rev* 601, 619 (2006).

Likewise, the subsidiary fiduciary rules differ across fiduciary applications in accordance with variations in the underlying agency problems. Because a trust is a fiduciary relationship with respect to property, many trust fiduciary subrules address property management. Because the paradigmatic (legal) agent acts on behalf of the principal in a commercial undertaking, many agency fiduciary subrules concern competition with the principal and protection of confidences.

Accordingly, what has been called the elusiveness of fiduciary law is more properly regarded as context-specific adaptation. The flexibility of fiduciary obligation explains the success of the fiduciary governance strategy. Across the decades, courts and legislatures have adapted the general duties of loyalty and care and have created specific subsidiary duties to fit the particulars of the agency problem at issue.

III. Mandatory and Default Rules

Generally speaking, fiduciary duties yield to a contrary agreement of the parties. This principle follows from the nature of fiduciary governance as a system of deterrence meant to minimize agency costs by allowing the court to complete the parties' contract after the fact. The requirement that a fiduciary act in the principal's best interests, which is informed by what the parties would have agreed if they had considered a given contingency, does not pertain if the parties entered into an express agreement on what the fiduciary should do in the event of a particular contingency. Fiduciary law consists mostly of *default rules* that apply unless the parties have agreed otherwise.

Even the duty of loyalty is subject to modification by agreement of the parties.[37] If the principal gives informed consent to certain self-dealing by the fiduciary, the rationale for the rule against self-dealing falls away. In such circumstances, the fiduciary may engage in the specified self-dealing, provided that the fiduciary acts in good faith and that the transaction is objectively fair and in the best interests of the principal.[38]

As is implied by the good faith, fairness, and best interests qualifiers, there are nonetheless some *mandatory rules* in fiduciary law that cannot be overridden by agreement. It is well settled within trust law, for example, that "no matter how broad the provisions of a trust may be in conferring power to engage in self-dealing or other transactions involving a conflict of fiduciary and personal interests, a trustee violates the duty of loyalty to the beneficiaries by acting in bad faith or unfairly."[39] A trustee may be exonerated, but not "for a breach of trust committed in bad faith or with indifference to the fiduciary duties of the trustee, the terms or purposes of the trust, or the interests of the beneficiaries."[40]

Stated more broadly, if a principal authorizes self-dealing by a fiduciary, fiduciary law imposes substantive and procedural safeguards. The fiduciary must act in good

[37] See, eg, Unif Power of Attorney Act § 114(b) (2006); *Restatement (Third) of Trusts* § 78 cmt c(2); *Restatement (Third) of Agency* § 8.06.

[38] See, eg, *Restatement (Third) of Trusts* § 78 cmts c, d; *Restatement (Third) of Agency* § 8.06; *Principles of Corporate Governance: Analysis and Recommendations* § 5.02.

[39] *Restatement (Third) of Trusts* § 78 cmt c(2); see also Unif Power of Attorney Act § 114(a); Unif Trust Code § 105(b)(2) (amended 2005); *Restatement (Third) of Agency* § 8.06(1)(a), (2)(a).

[40] *Restatement (Third) of Trusts* § 96(1)(a); see also Unif Trust Code § 1008 (2000).

faith and deal fairly with and for the principal, and the fiduciary must apprise the principal of the material facts, the facts that would reasonably affect the principal's judgment, in securing the principal's informed consent.[41]

The existence of a mandatory core of fiduciary law vexed the prior generation of economic analysis. Committed contractarians have had difficulty in explaining why the parties to a fiduciary relationship do not have complete freedom of contract. Easterbrook and Fischel went so far as to assert, erroneously, that in trust law "[a]ll rules are freely variable by contract in advance."[42] The answer is not to deny the existence of mandatory fiduciary rules, but rather to see that they serve an internal protective and cautionary function that protects the principal, and an external categorization function that protects third parties and clarifies the nature of the parties' relationship.

With respect to the internal *protective* and *cautionary function*, the mandatory core insulates fiduciary obligations that the law assumes would not be bargained away by a fully informed, sophisticated principal. True, in an individual case a particular principal might be fully informed and have good reason to want to bargain away something from the mandatory core. But such circumstances are infrequent enough that a prophylactic (if paternalistic) mandatory rule may be justified nonetheless, at least in the traditional fiduciary fields such as trust and agency, in which the principal is commonly not sophisticated and fully informed.

With respect to the external *categorization function*, the mandatory core addresses the need for clean lines of demarcation across types of legal relationships, among other things to minimize third-party information costs.[43] On this view, fiduciary obligation is a necessary constitutive element of certain legal categories, such as trust and agency. Thus, in the Restatement (Third) of Agency, we find the remark that "[a] relationship between two parties in which it is agreed that one party shall have the right to take action that affects the legal relations of the other party without regard for whether the action is for that party's benefit is not a relationship of [legal] agency."[44] Likewise, in the Restatement (Third) of Trusts, we find the statement that "there are limits to the settlor's freedom" to waive fiduciary obligation, "thereby protecting the fundamental fiduciary character of trust relationships recognized by the law."[45]

So the mandatory core of fiduciary law polices the line that differentiates a fiduciary relationship on the one hand from a fee simple or other such arrangement on the other. A person may give property to another person and authorize the other person to act whimsically with respect to the property. But this mode of transfer is an absolute gift, and this mode of holding property is fee simple. Perhaps the leading statement of this

[41] See, eg, Unif Trust Code § 1009 (amended 2001); *Restatement (Third) of Trusts* § 78 cmt c(2); *Restatement (Third) of Agency* § 8.06.

[42] Easterbrook and Fischel (n 2) at 432.

[43] This standardization function has been emphasized in the contemporary learning in property theory. See, eg, Henry Hansmann and Reinier Kraakman, "Property, Contract, and Verification: The *Numerus Clausus* Problem and the Divisibility of Rights," 31 *J Legal Stud* S373 (2002); Thomas W Merrill and Henry E Smith, "The Property/Contract Interface," 101 *Colum L Rev* 773 (2001); Thomas W Merrill and Henry E Smith, "Optimal Standardization in the Law of Property: The *Numerus Clausus* Principle," 110 *Yale LJ* 1 (2000); see also Sitkoff, "An Agency Costs Theory of Trust Law" (n 4) at 643.

[44] *Restatement (Third) of Agency* § 8.06 cmt b.

[45] *Restatement (Third) of Trusts* § 78 cmt c(2).

point in the American cases is by the Supreme Court of Delaware in *McNeil v McNeil*.[46] At issue in that case was a clause in a trust instrument stating that the trustees' decisions were "not subject to review by any court."[47] Observing that courts "flatly refuse to enforce provisions relieving a trustee of all liability," the court reviewed the trustees' action nonetheless.[48] The reason: "A trust in which there is no legally binding obligation on a trustee is a trust in name only and more in the nature of an absolute estate or fee simple grant of property."[49]

The categorization explanation for the mandatory core is strongest as regards fiduciary relationships for which there is no public notice filing, such as agency and common law trusts. The explanation is weaker as regards filing entities, such as corporations and limited liability companies, because the public filing that brings the entity into existence also provides notice of the existence and nature of the entity. For this reason, and because the parties in such contexts are more likely to be fully informed and sophisticated, the mandatory core for filing fiduciary entities is both less robust and more contentious than in agency and trust law.[50] Consistent with this analysis, we find in the recent uniform acts in the fiduciary fields a consolidated scheduling of mandatory rules, but with more flexibility in the filing fiduciary entities than in the non-filing fiduciary relationships.[51]

IV. Compensation and Disgorgement

In the event of a fiduciary's breach of duty, the principal is entitled to an election among remedies that include *compensatory* damages to offset any losses incurred or to make up any gains forgone owing to the fiduciary's breach, or to *disgorgement* by the fiduciary of any profit accruing to the fiduciary by reason of the breach.[52] The former is a standard measure of make-whole compensatory damages. The latter is a restitutionary

[46] *McNeil v McNeil* 798 A2d 503 (Del 2002).

[47] *McNeil v McNeil* (n 46) at 509.

[48] *McNeil v McNeil* (n 46) at 509.

[49] *McNeil v McNeil* (n 46) at 509. A few years earlier, in *Armitage v Nurse*, Lord Justice Millet applied the same principle to an English trust: "[T]here is an irreducible core of obligations owed by the trustees to the beneficiaries and enforceable by them which is fundamental to the concept of a trust. If the beneficiaries have no rights enforceable against the trustees there are no trusts." [1998] Ch 241 at 253 (CA 1997) (Eng).

[50] See, eg, *Gatz Props, LLC v Auriga Capital Corp* 59 A3d 1206, 1218–20 (Del 2012) (remarking that "the issue whether the LLC statute does—or does not—impose default fiduciary duties is one about which reasonable minds could differ"); Larry E Ribstein, *The Rise of the Uncorporation* (2010) 219–22; Andrew S Gold, "On the Elimination of Fiduciary Duties: A Theory of Good Faith for Unincorporated Firms," 41 *Wake Forest L Rev* 123 (2006). Recent legislation in Delaware clarifies that fiduciary law applies to unincorporated entities. Del Code Ann tit 6, § 18-1104 (2013) (Limited Liability Company Act); Del Code Ann tit 6, § 17-1105 (Delaware Revised Uniform Limited Partnership Act).

[51] Compare Unif Statutory Trust Entity Act § 104 (2009), and Revised Unif Limited Liability Company Act § 110 (2006), and Unif Limited Partnership Act § 110 (2001), and Revised Unif Partnership Act § 103 (1997), and Unif Limited Liability Company Act § 103 (1996), and Mark J Loewenstein, "Fiduciary Duties and Unincorporated Business Entities: In Defense of the 'Manifestly Unreasonable' Standard," 41 *Tulsa L Rev* 411 (2006) (discussing mandatory rules in the uniform alternative entity acts), with Unif Power of Attorney Act § 114 (2006), and Unif Trust Code § 105 (amended 2005), and John H Langbein, "Mandatory Rules in the Law of Trusts," 98 *Nw U L Rev* 1105 (2004) (discussing mandatory rules in the Uniform Trust Code).

[52] See, eg, Unif Trust Code § 1002(a) (2000); Austin Wakeman Scott, William Franklin Fratcher, and Mark L Ascher, *Scott and Ascher on Trusts* (4th edn, 2007) § 24.9.

remedy that, within the American tradition, is commonly implemented by way of a constructive trust to prevent unjust enrichment of the breaching fiduciary.[53]

The availability of a compensatory remedy is readily explainable on ordinary contractarian terms. The principal is entitled to the benefit of his bargain, hence to be made whole for his losses incurred or gains forgone owing to the breach. But compensatory damages will deter breach only if the gains from breach to the fiduciary are less than the principal's loss or gains forgone. If only compensatory damages are available, and the gains to the fiduciary from breach exceed the compensatory damages that will be due to the principal, then, for the fiduciary, breach will be efficient.[54] The fiduciary will have no incentive to refrain from breach and return to the principal to negotiate over allocation of the surplus.

The availability of a disgorgement remedy, which allows the principal to take the breaching fiduciary's gain even in excess of making the principal whole, reflects the additional disclosure and deterrence purposes of fiduciary law.[55] Because the fiduciary is not entitled to keep any gains resulting from breach, he is given an incentive to disclose the potential for such gains and to work out with the principal how much of the surplus will go to each party. Put in more formal doctrinal terms, the default rule in fiduciary law is that all gains that arise in connection with a fiduciary relationship belong to the principal unless the parties specifically agree otherwise. This rule, which is contrary to the preferences of the party with superior information, the fiduciary, offers deterrence in the penalty default sense.[56] On this view, the disgorgement remedy is a penalty default rule that induces disclosure.

But what about a cunning fiduciary who reckons that the principal may not be able to discover the fiduciary's secret profits? The recognition in modern law of punitive damages for such egregious fiduciary breaches is a sign of movement toward deterrence of such cases.[57] The *Restatement (Third) of Trusts*, for example, recognizes the need "to deter similar misconduct" as a basis for awarding punitive damages.[58]

Conclusion

In contrast to an arms-length relationship, in which each party is free to be self-serving, in a fiduciary relationship the law requires the fiduciary to be other-regarding because of the potential for abuse inherent to the agency structure of the relationship. What is meant by other-regarding is defined by general primary fiduciary duties of loyalty and care and a host of specific subsidiary fiduciary duties. Fiduciary duties are subject to refinement by agreement of the parties, so long as the fiduciary remains obligated to act

[53] See *Restatement (Third) of Restitution & Unjust Enrichment* (2011) § 55. For criticism of the American tradition, see Lionel Smith, "Legal Epistemology in the *Restatement (Third) of Restitution and Unjust Enrichment*," 92 *BU L Rev* 899, 907–16 (2012).

[54] See, eg, Richard A Posner, *Economic Analysis of Law* (8th edn, 2011) § 4.10.

[55] See nn 21–2 and accompanying text.

[56] See Ian Ayres and Robert Gertner, "Filling Gaps in Incomplete Contracts: An Economic Theory of Default Rules," 99 *Yale LJ* 87 (1989).

[57] See *Restatement (Third) of Trusts* (2012) § 100 cmt d; A Mitchell Polinsky and Steven Shavell, "Punitive Damages: An Economic Analysis," 111 *Harv L Rev* 869 (1998).

[58] *Restatement (Third) of Trusts* § 100 cmt d.

in good faith and in the best interests of the principal. Agency theory, and in particular its emphasis on the problem of opportunism in circumstances of asymmetric information, explains these basic contours of fiduciary doctrine.

In restating the economic theory of fiduciary law, this chapter made three fresh contributions. First, it expanded on earlier work by clarifying the agency problem that is at the core of all fiduciary relationships. The fact of this common economic structure explains the common doctrinal structure that cuts across fiduciary relationships. But the particulars of fiduciary obligation vary across fiduciary relationships in accordance with the particulars of the agency problem at issue. In addition to explaining the purported elusiveness of fiduciary law, this point also explains why courts apply fiduciary law both categorically, such as in trust, agency, and corporate law, as well as ad hoc to relationships involving trust and confidence giving rise to an agency problem.

Second, this chapter identified a functional distinction between primary and subsidiary fiduciary duties. Across fiduciary relationships we find general primary duties of loyalty and care, typically phrased as standards, which proscribe conflicts of interest and prescribe an objective standard of care. We also find specific subsidiary fiduciary rules that elaborate on the application of the duties of loyalty and care to recurring circumstances within the particular type of fiduciary relationship. Together, the general primary duties of loyalty and care and the specific subsidiary rules provide for governance by a mix of rules and standards that offers the benefits of both while mitigating their respective weaknesses.

Third, this chapter revisited the puzzle of why fiduciary law includes a mandatory core that cannot be waived by the parties if they are in a relationship that is deemed to be fiduciary. The answer is that the mandatory core serves a cautionary and protective function within the fiduciary relationship as well as an external categorization function that clarifies rights for third parties and provides clean demarcation across types of relationships.

10

Sharing *Ex Ante* and Sharing *Ex Post*

The Non-Contractual Basis of Fiduciary Relations

*Daniel Markovits**

The *Restatement (Second) of Contracts* observes, among other banalities of contract law, that expectation damages constitute the preferred remedy for breach of contract.[1] As every first year law student learns, this remedy at least permits and perhaps encourages "efficient breach" of contract. By contrast, restitutionary disgorgement of the breacher's gain constitutes a common remedy for the breach of a fiduciary obligation.[2] The law thus rejects a practice of efficient breach of fiduciary duties.[3] Perhaps slightly less familiarly, contract law establishes the mandatory duty of good faith in performance as the

* Thanks to Andrew Gold and Paul Miller for the invitation to join the symposium that has produced this volume and to Erik Stegemiller for outstanding research assistance. Finally, thanks to Andrew Gold, Anthony Kronman, and Alan Schwartz for comments on earlier drafts.

[1] See *Restatement (Second) of Contracts* (1981) § 344. The comments to that section make the preference explicit:

> Ordinarily, when a court concludes that there has been a breach of contract, it enforces the broken promise by protecting the expectation that the injured party had when he made the contract. It does this by attempting to put him in as good a position as he would have been in had the contract been performed, that is, had there been no breach. The interest protected in this way is called the "expectation interest."

Restatement (Second) of Contracts § 344, cmt a.

[2] See, eg, *Restatement (Third) of Trusts* (2012) § 100 ("A trustee who commits a breach of trust is chargeable with (a) the amount required to restore the values of the trust estate and trust distributions to what they would have been if the portion of the trust affected by the breach had been properly administered; or (b) the amount of any benefit to the trustee personally as a result of the breach"); *Restatement (Second) of Trusts* (1959) §§ 205, 206, cmt a ("If the trustee commits a breach of his duty of loyalty he is chargeable with any loss or depreciation in value of the trust property resulting from the breach of duty, or any profit made by him through the breach of duty, or any profit which would have accrued to the trust estate if there had been no breach of duty"); Uniform Trust Code § 1002(a) (2000) 7C ULA 253 (Supp) ("A trustee who commits a breach of trust is liable to the beneficiaries affected for the greater of: (1) the amount required to restore the value of the trust property and trust distributions to what they would have been had the breach not occurred; or (2) the profit the trustee made by reason of the breach"); 29 USC § 1109 ("Any person who is a fiduciary... shall be personally liable... to restore... any profits of such fiduciary which have been made through use of assets of the plan by the fiduciary"). See also Hanoch Dagan, *The Law and Ethics of Restitution* (2004) 237 (treating the disgorgement remedy as characteristic of fiduciary law).

[3] Others have also observed this difference. See, eg, William S Dodge, "The Case for Punitive Damages in Contracts," 48 *Duke LJ* 629, 636 (1999) (noting that contract cases that also involve breaches of fiduciary duty are an exception to the typical bar on punitive damages in contract). The distinction between remedies has introduced tensions at the border of contract and fiduciary law, for example in connection with the "faithless servant" rule. See, eg, Charles A Sullivan, "Mastering the Faithless Servant? Reconciling Employment Law, Contract Law, and Fiduciary Duty," 2011 *Wisc L Rev* 777.

earnest of contract obligation.[4] By contrast, the fiduciary's central duties involve not contractual good faith, but rather loyalty and care.[5]

These two interconnected differences place contract partners and fiduciaries in distinct deliberative postures and constitute contract and fiduciary relations according to distinct models of sharing. Contract partners share *ex ante*; fiduciaries share *ex post*.

These different styles of sharing, in turn, entail that fiduciary relations and the obligations that they involve cannot inhabit a contractual form. The current vogue of approaching fiduciary law on the model of contract may aid efforts to *reform* the substantive rules that govern fiduciary obligations in order to make them better serve the interests of beneficiaries.[6] But the contract model sows only confusion concerning the nature of fiduciary relations and the formal juridical structure of fiduciary law. Contract sharing and fiduciary sharing proceed qualitatively differently; and contract and fiduciary relations display distinct structures. Fiduciary law thus cannot be *understood* on the contractarian model.

Understanding fiduciary law requires a model besides contract. These pages draw a contrast between contract and fiduciary relations and, out of that contrast, introduce a new model of fiduciary law.[7]

[4] See, eg, *Restatement (Second) of Contracts* § 205 cmt a ("Every contract imposes upon each party a duty of good faith and fair dealing in its performance and enforcement"); Uniform Commercial Code §1–304 (2003) [hereinafter UCC] (imposing a mandatory duty of good faith in performance on every contract within the scope of the UCC).

[5] For general observations about fiduciary loyalty, see, eg, Ernest Weinrib, "The Fiduciary Obligation," 25 *U Toronto LJ* 1, 16 (1975) and Hanoch Dagan and Sharon Hannes in this volume ("Like other fiduciaries, these financial fiduciaries are bound by a duty of loyalty, which is oftentimes (justifiably) treated as a (if not the) defining characteristic of fiduciary law overall").

For examples of these duties across a range of fiduciary relations, see, eg, 29 USC § 1104 (pension trustee–beneficiary); 15 USC § 80(b)(6) (investment adviser–client); 29 USC § 501(a) (labor union–employee); Unif Partnership Act § 404(a) (1997) (partner–partner); Indiana Code Ann § 29-3-8-3 (West 2013) (guardian–ward); *Restatement (Third) of Trusts* (2007) §§ 77–78 (trustee–beneficiary); Model Rules of Prof'l Conduct pmbl (2011) (attorney–client); *Perlman v Feldmann* 219 F2d 173 (2d Cir 1955) (majority investor–minority investor); *Osei v Countrywide Home Loans* 692 F Supp 2d 1240, 1249 (ED Cal 2010); *Stone v Ritter* 911 A2d 362 (Del 2006) (corporate manager–investor); *Hoffnagle v McDonald's Corporation* 522 NW 2d 808, 813 (Iowa 1994) (franchisor–franchisee). See also Frank H Easterbrook and Daniel R Fischel, "Contract and Fiduciary Duty," 36 *J L & Econ* 423, 433–4 (1993) (outlining fiduciary duties for the listed relationships).

[6] The contract-model has, for example, sustained a powerful attack on trust law's traditional sole interest rule, which forbids a trustee's contracting with a trust in respect of trust property. The thrust of the critique is that the rule should be abandoned, *tout court*, in favor of a best interest rule. See, eg, John H Langbein, "Questioning the Trust Law Duty of Loyalty: Sole Interest or Best Interest?," 114 *Yale LJ* 929 (2005).

The sole interest rule has long been variously defeasible. For example, the sole interest rule is a default only rule. See *Restatement (Third) of Trusts* (2007) § 78 cmt c(2) ("A trustee may be authorized by the terms of the trust, expressly or by implication, to engage in transactions that would otherwise be prohibited by the rules of undivided loyalty"); *Restatement (Second) of Trusts* (1959) § 170(1) cmt t; Unif Trust Code § 802(b)(1), 7C ULA 229 (Supp). Departures from the sole interest rule may also be permitted where the trustee receives advance approval from a court. See *Restatement (Second) of Trusts* (1959) § 170(1) cmt f ("The trustee can properly purchase trust property for himself with the approval of the court"); Unif Trust Code § 802(b)(2), 7C ULA 229 (Supp). And there exist various categorical exceptions to the rule. See, eg, Langbein, "Questioning the Trust Law Duty of Loyalty," at 968 ff. Finally, nearby fields of fiduciary law permit conflicted persons to act as fiduciaries. See, eg, Langbein, "Questioning the Trust Law Duty of Loyalty," at 942 ff (discussing conflicted fiduciaries permitted by the Uniform Health-Care Decisions Act).

[7] The argument proceeds using ideal types, which fall clearly into either the contractual or the fiduciary camp. This helps to fix ideas and simplify the exposition. At the same time, as Genevieve Helleringer pointed out at the conference devoted to this volume, the life-world produces relationships that invoke both legal categories at once.

I. Contract Sharing *ex ante*

Contract law vindicates promisees' rights through the expectation remedy.[8] This remedy requires breaching promisors to pay their promisees money damages equal to the promisees' value of performance. The expectation remedy thus requires promisors to insure against breach by guaranteeing their promisees' value of performance. This regime aspires to make promisees indifferent, *ex post*, between performance and breach-plus-damages. At the same time, the regime permits promisors to retain for themselves gains associated with efficiencies achieved *ex post*, for example by diverting the promised performance to higher valuing third parties.

Moralists commonly complain that the expectation remedy and the associated practice of "efficient breach" encourage contracting parties to disregard, and indeed to disrespect, their promissory obligations.[9] The complaint rests on a mistake, however. Identifying the mistake opens a window into the structure of contract sharing and the character of the contract relation. The view of contract revealed by the exercise also, by way of establishing a contrast-case, helps to illuminate the character of fiduciary relations.

Parties typically contract because they anticipate that their trades will produce gains. They anticipate, that is, that buyers' values of trade will exceed sellers' costs, so that trade will produce joint surplus.[10] But it is always possible that between the time of contract and the time of trade a buyer's valuation may go down, or a seller's cost may go up. (The seller's cost of course includes her opportunity cost and thus potential gain from dealing with third parties, as in the example above.)

These relationships—which are best thought of as multifarious rather than hybrid—pose complicated moral and legal problems. Contract and fiduciary obligations may reinforce each other or may undermine each other. It may even happen that one form of obligation gives extrinsic, causal support to the other even as it undermines the other's intrinsic structure. An example from personal life illustrates this last possibility: contract-like promises may give causal support to fiduciary-like love relations by protecting vulnerable parties from exploitation and thus encouraging them to remain in the fiduciary relations; but the promises may also, and at the same time, undermine the intrinsic norms of sharing that love properly understood involves. See, eg, Daniel Markovits, "Promise as an Arm's Length Relation," in Hanoch Sheinman (ed), *Promises and Agreements: Philosophical Essays* (2011).

[8] The accounts of the expectation remedy and efficient breach stated here receive more elaborate developments in Daniel Markovits and Alan Schwartz, "The Myth of Efficient Breach: New Defenses of the Expectation Interest," 97 *Virginia Law Review* 1939 (2011) [hereinafter Markovits and Schwartz, "Myth of Efficient Breach"]; Daniel Markovits and Alan Schwartz, "The Expectation Remedy and the Promissory Basis of Contract," 45 *Suffolk Law Review* 799 (2012) (symposium in honor of the 30th anniversary of the publication of Contract as Promise); Daniel Markovits and Alan Schwartz, "The Expectation Remedy Revisited," 98 *Virginia Law Review* 1093 (2012). The account of good faith follows Daniel Markovits, "Good Faith as Contract's Core Value," in Gregory Klass, George Letsas, and Prince Saprai (eds), *The Philosophical Foundations of Contract Law* (forthcoming, 2014) [hereinafter Markovits, "Good Faith"].

[9] See, eg, Seana Shiffrin, "Could Breach of Contract Be Immoral?," 107 *Mich L Rev* 1551 (2009); Seana Valentine Shiffrin, "The Divergence of Contract and Promise," 120 *Harv L Rev* 708 (2007); Richard R W Brooks, "The Efficient Performance Hypothesis," 116 *Yale LJ* 568 (2006); Melvin Eisenberg, "The Disgorgement Interest in Contract Law," 105 *Mich L Rev* 559 (2006); Melvin Eisenberg, "Actual and Virtual Specific Performance, the Theory of Efficient Breach, and the Indifference Principle in Contract Law," 93 *Calif L Rev* 975 (2005); Daniel Friedmann, "The Efficient Breach Fallacy," 18 *J Legal Stud* 1 (1989).

[10] For expositional purposes only, and without loss of generality, I refer to promisors as sellers and promisees as buyers.

Accordingly, even as the parties anticipate gains from trade, it always remains possible that, as events transpire, the parties' joint surplus will be maximized by *not* trading. Typically, although not necessarily in all cases, sellers will be better placed to realize the gains from not trading than buyers—they will be able to identify and pursue these gains at lower transactions costs.[11] For this reason, contracting parties—who seek to maximize the joint surplus available for them to share—will accord sellers the right to capture non-trading gains when they arise. The expectation remedy and the associated practice of "efficient breach" implement this regime.

This logic is of course available to the parties when they fix the terms of their contracts. Accordingly, a seller who retains the right to capture non-trading gains at performance will pay for this right up front, at formation—her payment will be memorialized in a lower price. (The lower price, incidentally, makes the seller's right to "efficient breach" express in the contract, or at least implied in fact rather than in law; and "efficient breaches" are, for this reason, not truly breaches at all, having been contemplated by the parties at formation. Hence the scare quotes.) The lower price, moreover, increases the difference between the buyer's value and the contract price and hence also the buyer's expectation damages in the event of a subsequent breach. Thus, although the expectation remedy appears to allow the seller to capture the entire gains from "efficient breach," this appearance deceives. The price mechanism gives buyers a share of all the gains from contracting, including of the non-trading gains associated with "efficient breach."

Indeed, a buyer who pays the lower price associated with the expectation remedy but subsequently insists on specific performance (or disgorgement of the non-trading gain produced by an "efficient breach") claims a benefit that she has not paid for, and indeed that she forswore in her contract (through its price term). One might even say that such a buyer acts in bad faith.

Explaining this takes some work, because the required explanation engages the structural core of the contract relation. The duty of good faith in performance, which governs all contracts at common law, is notoriously difficult to flesh out. But the best understanding of the duty emphasizes that good faith does not add to the content of contractual obligation but instead expresses an attitude towards contracts whose substantive obligations are fixed on other grounds. As the Uniform Commercial Code emphasizes, the duty of good faith in performance "does not support an independent

[11] Where buyers are better placed to realize non-trading gains, the parties may encourage this by adopting the remedy Richard Brooks has called "efficient performance." See Brooks (n 9). Under this regime, buyers may choose between (1) insisting on trade (as under the traditional specific performance remedy) and (2) *requiring* their sellers to make "efficient breaches" and disgorge the gains therefrom. The efficient performance remedy thus mirrors efficient breach: both remedies cause the party that makes decisions concerning performance to internalize the full costs and benefits of its choices.

Note the degree of buyer control over seller behavior that such an "efficient performance" regime involves: it is tempting to say that a buyer who can command her seller to deal with third parties and disgorge his gains in effect *owns* the seller.

One might even say, borrowing ideas from the Coasean theory of the firm, that the choice between "efficient breach" and "efficient performance" mirrors the choice between coordinating across the firm boundary, by contract, and within the firm boundary, by command and control. This suggests that the expectation remedy and "efficient breach" are almost constitutive of contract. For more on these points, see Markovits and Schwartz, "Myth of Efficient Breach" (n 8) at 1978.

cause of action for failure to perform or enforce in good faith;" rather "failure to perform or enforce, in good faith, a specific duty or obligation under the contract, constitutes a breach of that contract."[12] A prominent opinion thus observes that good faith is "not some newfangled bit of welfare-state paternalism or the sediment of an altruistic strain in contract law."[13] Instead, the duty of good faith merely reflects that, as another court has said, "[i]n every contract there is an implied covenant that neither party shall do anything which will have the effect of destroying or injuring the right of the other party to receive the fruits of the contract." [14] This just *is* the "implied covenant of good faith and fair dealing."[15]

The measure of the duty of good faith in performance is thus the contract itself; and bad faith, in a familiar formulation, "consists of an exercise of discretion in performance to recapture opportunities forgone at formation."[16] "Efficient breach" is consistent with good faith because the breaching seller merely avails herself of a right that she paid to have allocated to her by the contract. And a buyer who insists on specific performance displays bad faith insofar as he seeks, at performance, to recapture a non-trading gain that he forswore at formation and never paid for.

Finally, these nested principles—through which the expectation remedy provides a substantive illustration of the duty of good faith in performance—illuminate the nature of contract sharing and the character of the contract relation. Contract law permits contracting parties to remain as self-interested within the contract relation as they were without it, except that they must limit their pursuit of their private interests according to the terms of their contractual settlement. A promisee may compel his promisor to go the mile that the contract stipulates, but she need not go with him twain, nor indeed one inch further than she agreed to go up front. Contract sharing requires no altruism—no general inclination to promote the interests of one's promisee as they develop nor even any willingness to balance one's promisee's interests impartially against one's own.

Moreover, contract sharing so understood is not simply *less* other-regarding than altruism but rather *differently* other-regarding. The altruist must adjust open-endedly to the interests of the other as circumstances develop *ex post*. But the contractual promisor properly looks not to the changing interests of her promisee *ex post* but rather *to the contract*. Contract sharing is thus sharing *ex ante*. It takes the terms of the contract as its lodestar.

This has profound consequences for the contract relation. Perhaps the deepest concerns the connection between the *ex ante* character of contract sharing and freedom of

[12] UCC § 1-304 cmt 1.

[13] *Mkt St Assocs Ltd P'ship v Frey* 941 F 2d 588, 595 (7th Cir 1991) (Posner J).

[14] *Kirke La Shelle Co v Paul Armstrong Co* 263 NY 79, 87, 188 NE 163, 167 (1933). The case involved a silent-film era agreement to share "motion picture" rights to a play and the question whether rights to make a "talkie" based on the play were within the scope of the agreement. The court held that they were not. It has seemed to many that that this is a mistake on the facts. See *LC Page & Co v Fox Film Corp* 83 F 2d 196, 199 (2d Cir 1936) (words "motion picture" in pre-"talkie" contract held to include "talkies"). See also *Bartsch v Metro-Goldwyn-Mayer, Inc* 391 F 2d 150 (2d Cir), cert denied, 393 US 826 (1968).

[15] *Kirke La Shelle* (n 14) at 167.

[16] Steven J Burton, "Breach of Contract and the Common Law Duty to Perform in Good Faith," 94 *Harv L Rev* 369, 387 (1980).

contract. Because contract sharing is fixed *ex ante*, the parties to contracts engage each other *only* through the medium and on the terms of their contracts. The duty of good faith in performance does, as a court has said, "forbid the kinds of opportunistic behavior" that might undermine the "minimum of cooperativeness in the event unforeseen problems arise" that is required to secure the success of the "cooperative enterprise" that contracts "set in motion."[17] But contractual cooperativeness remains purely a creature of the contract itself and extends only to going the distance, and only along the path, that the contract specifies. A promisor who engages, in good faith, in contract sharing thus takes her promisee's intentions, as expressed in the contract, at face value. She need not, and indeed must not, engage her promisee in any other respect, including altruistically, in respect of her *ex post* beliefs about his interests.

Contract's adoption of good faith in place of altruism is thus connected to contract's anti-paternalism and through this link to freedom of contract. Altruism might always (depending on developments *ex post*) call for paternalistically adding to or even violating an *ex ante* contractual settlement, so that a promisee subjected to his promisor's altruism could not count on contract as a reliable means for pursuing his own purposes. The duty of good faith in performance, including by resisting altruism and ratifying (side-constrained) self-interest within the contract relation, thus promotes freedom of contract by implementing whatever contractual arrangements the parties have made.

Finally, contract partners thereby engage each other abstractly, through their general intentional capacities and for their generic moral personalities—which receive expression in the contract arrangement. Contract partners do not engage each other concretely, through their peculiar interests and for the particular persons that they are or develop into.[18]

II. Fiduciary Sharing *ex post*

The character of contract sharing *ex ante* and the nature of contractual good faith carry considerable interest in their own rights;[19] but the purpose of introducing contract sharing in these pages is to establish a contrast to fiduciary sharing, which proceeds *ex post*. The contrast between sharing *ex ante* and sharing *ex post* illuminates the character of fiduciary sharing.

The label "fiduciary" covers a broad and varied set of relationships. A classic list includes: trustee–beneficiary (in both the pension-context and outside of it); guardian–ward; attorney–client; partner–partner; corporate manager–investor; majority investor–minority investor; investment adviser–client; labor union–employee; lender–borrower; and franchisor–franchisee.[20] Unsurprisingly, the positive law of fiduciary obligation varies substantially across these relations. Possibly the variation is so wide that instances of fiduciary obligation cannot be identified by any set of necessary and sufficient conditions, but rather bear only a family resemblance to one another. Nevertheless, certain prominent markers tend to cast a relationship as fiduciary.

[17] *Mkt St Assocs Ltd P'ship v Frey* 941 F 2d 588, 595 (7th Cir 1991) (Posner J) (internal quotation marks and citation omitted).

[18] I explain this in greater detail elsewhere. See Daniel Markovits, "Contract and Collaboration," 113 *Yale LJ* 1417 (2004); Markovits (n 7).

[19] Here see, eg, Markovits, "Good Faith" (n 8).

[20] See Easterbrook and Fischel (n 5) at 432–4.

Perhaps most important among these is that whereas contract requires good faith, fiduciaries generally must treat their beneficiaries with loyalty and care.[21]

Fiduciary duties of loyalty and care, moreover, reflect a natural response to the structural problems out of which fiduciary relations generally arise. A fiduciary relation becomes appealing partly because a principal requires her agent to act in ways that she cannot substantially specify *ex ante* or cannot directly evaluate *ex post*. In such cases, fiduciary obligation substitutes for the specification of contract duties and the verification of performance. A recent summary statement of the conventional wisdom concerning fiduciary law thus concludes: "In contrast to a normal [read, contractual] relationship, in which each party is free to be self-serving, in a fiduciary relationship the law requires the fiduciary to be other-regarding because of the potential for abuse inherent to the agency structure of the relationship."[22]

The substantive standards imposed by fiduciary loyalty and care vary across areas of fiduciary law, to be sure. Trustees, for example, must by presumption act in the sole interest of their beneficiaries,[23] and "transactions involving trust property entered into by a trustee for the trustee's own personal account [are] voidable without further proof."[24] (Furthermore, where the trust is a pension or welfare plan governed by the Employee Retirement and Income Security Act (ERISA), the sole interest rule is not waivable by contract.[25]) In addition, a trustee's duty of care imposes a standard of high prudence.[26] By contrast, an investment adviser's duty of loyalty to her client requires only that she avoid conflicts of interest. And in this context the fiduciary duty of care imposes only a negligence standard on her.[27] Other circumstances alter fiduciary duties still further. For example, under the Securities Exchange Act of 1934 and the rules promulgated by the Securities and Exchange Commission, a broker or dealer's contract with her customers may even allow her to "trade ahead" of them, buying or selling stock on her own account before filling their orders.[28] And although corporate managers are fiduciaries

[21] For examples of the duties of loyalty and care across a range of fiduciary contexts, see n 5.

[22] Robert H Sitkoff, "The Economic Structure of Fiduciary Law," 91 *BU L Rev* 1039, 1049 (2011) (symposium on Fiduciary Law in the Twenty-First Century).

[23] See, eg, *Restatement (Second) of Trusts* (1959) § 170(1) (the duty of loyalty requires a trustee "to administer the trust solely in the interest of the beneficiary"); Unif Trust Code § 802(a) (2000), 7C ULA 229 (Supp 2004) ("A trustee shall administer the trust solely in the interests of the beneficiaries").

[24] Unif Trust Code § 802 cmt, 7C ULA 230 (Supp).

[25] The general law of trusts permits the sole interest rule to be waived by the terms of a trust. See *Restatement (Second) of Trusts* (1959) § 170(1) cmt t ("By the terms of the trust the trustee may be permitted to sell trust property to himself individually, or as trustee to purchase property from himself individually, or to lend to himself money held by him in trust, or otherwise to deal with the trust property on his own account"). See also *Restatement (Third) of Trusts* (2007) § 78 cmt c(2) (A trustee may be authorized by the terms of the trust, expressly or by implication, to engage in transactions that would otherwise be prohibited by the rules of undivided loyalty"); Unif Trust Code § 802(b)(1) (2000), 7C ULA 229 (Supp 2004) (stating that a transaction is voidable unless "the transaction was authorized by the terms of the trust").

For pension trusts governed by ERISA, the sole-interest rule cannot be waived, even by contract. See 29 USC § 1104(a)(1)(A)(i) which makes the sole-interest rule mandatory and 29 USC § 1103(a), which makes the trust form mandatory.

[26] See *Restatement (Third) of Trusts* § 77 (describing the duty of prudence in trust law).

[27] See 15 USCA § 80(b)(6) (2010) (describing prohibited transactions by investment advisers).

[28] See *EF Hutton & Co*, CCH Fed Sec L Rep para 84,303 (SEC Re No 25887, 6 July 1988) ("It is possible that Hutton could have shown that it was relieved of its agent's duty to refrain from undisclosed self-preferencing conduct. It could have done so either by showing that Manning knew of its practices or by showing that Manning, as a sophisticated investor, must have known of a practice known to all sophisticated investors").

to equity investors, the business judgment rule renders their duty of care effectively less demanding than the negligence standard of general tort law.[29]

In spite of this immense intramural variation, all these versions of fiduciary duty remain qualitatively different from contractual good faith. A contract promisor, recall, must honor her contract but go no further; although the *ex ante* terms of her contract impose a side constraint on her self-interest *ex post*, she may otherwise remain just as single-mindedly self-interested *ex post* as she was *ex ante*. In particular, good faith *never* requires a contract promisor to defer to her promisee in seeking a new opportunity, or even to shoulder a new and unanticipated burden in order to secure the smooth operation of her contract. The common law, it is familiarly observed, has as one of its "hallmark[s] ... that it does not have a doctrine of abuse of rights: if one has a right to do an act then, one can, in general, do it for whatever reason one wishes."[30] This entails that "[e]xcept where the contracting parties are also in a fiduciary relationship, self-interest is permissible, and indeed is the norm in the exercise of contractual rights."[31]

The key to understanding fiduciary sharing is that fiduciary relations do indeed present an exception to the common law's general rule.[32] A fiduciary must take the *initiative* on her beneficiary's behalf. Indeed, the point of the fiduciary relation—written into its generic structure—is for the fiduciary to take the initiative in this way. The beneficiary engages the fiduciary, after all, precisely because she cannot adequately regulate her affairs by contract. One might even say that the beneficiary *buys her fiduciary's initiative*.

This is the sense in which fiduciary relations necessarily involve sharing not *ex ante* but rather *ex post*, as fiduciaries exercise their initiative on their beneficiaries' behalves

[29] See, eg, *Shlensky v Wrigley* 95 Ill App 2d 173, 179 (App Ct 1968) (quoting *Helfman v American Light & Traction Co* 121 NJ Eq 1, 20 (1936) ("In a purely business corporation ... the authority of the directors in the conduct of the business of the corporation must be regarded as absolute when they act within the law and the court is without authority to substitute its judgment for that of the directors")).

[30] Jack Beatson, "Public Law Influences in Contract Law," in Jack Beatson and Daniel Friedmann (eds), *Good Faith and Fault in Contract Law* (1995) 263–88, 266–7.

[31] Beatson (n 30) at 267.

[32] It is commonly thought, for this reason, that fiduciary other-regard exceeds contract other-regard in some general sense, so that fiduciary loyalty and care include all the obligations of contractual good faith and then add some further obligations to them. This thought is mistaken. Fiduciary loyalty and care are not greater than but rather different from contractual good faith, so that neither set of obligations and attitudes includes the other.

That contractual good faith does not subsume loyalty and care is obvious. Any number of cases hold that fiduciary duties of loyalty, in particular, impose duties more demanding than contractual good faith. See, eg, *Stone v Ritter* 911 A2d 362 (Del 2006), *In re Walt Disney Co Deriv Litig* 906 A 2d 27, 66 (Del 2006).

That loyalty and care do not subsume contractual good faith is less so. The structural account of the fiduciary relation in the main text explains why not: very roughly, loyalty and care require paternalism that good faith rejects, so that contractual good faith respects the promisee's freedom in a manner in which fiduciary loyalty and care do not respect the beneficiary's.

Doctrine provides further evidence that loyalty and care are different from rather than simply greater than good faith. For example, there exist cases that hold that statutory remedies for bad faith breach of contract are available only in connection with arm's length contracts and not for breaches of joint venture agreements and associated fiduciary duties. See, eg, *Ray-Tek Services, Inc v Parker* 64 Mass App Ct 165, 831 NE 2d 948, 953 (2005). Joint ventures establish fiduciary rights and duties of their own, of course. But fiduciary relations squeeze out, rather than simply add to, the rights and duties associated with contractual good faith. This is a contested area, however, and not all the cases adopt the approach just set out. See, eg, *Starr v Fordham* 420 Mass 178, 184, 648 NE2d 1261, 1266 (1995) ("Thus, an unfair determination of a partner's respective share of a partnership's earnings is a breach not only of one's fiduciary duty. . . but also of the implied covenant of good faith and fair dealing") (citation omitted).

and, in so doing, balance their and their beneficiaries' interests open-endedly against each other. The various substantive workings-out of fiduciary loyalty and care rehearsed earlier adjust the standards that will govern fiduciary sharing *ex post*. But in spite of their great substantive variety, they all (indeed on their faces) announce abstract standards rather than concrete rules that fix conduct completely in particular cases. These several standards give various shapes to fiduciary other-regard, but none eliminates other regard *tout court* or permits fiduciaries to remain as self-interested within their relations as they were without (subject only to some narrowly rule-like side-constraints). Just what fiduciary initiative consists in may vary with circumstances, but open-ended initiative is always required. And fiduciary sharing may be more or less self-less, but it is always other-regarding, and so it always requires sharing *ex post*.

This entails that while contractual good faith implements freedom of contract, fiduciary loyalty and care build a measure of paternalism into every fiduciary relation. As one prominent court has observed, whereas the contractual duty of good faith "looks to the past" and turns on the parties' intentions at the time of contracting, fiduciary loyalty constitutes a "'free-floating' duty applied at the time of the wrong."[33] A fiduciary must thus engage her independent judgment (concerning her beneficiary's true interests) as she discharges her fiduciary duties. Often fiduciary independence, and the associated paternalism, are written into law: the Model Rules of Professional Conduct, for example, give lawyers ultimate control over the means by which they will pursue the ends that their clients fix;[34] and the rules of medical ethics prevent doctors from employing certain means (for example, unapproved drugs) and adopting certain ends (for example, suicide), notwithstanding that patients choose them.[35] Moreover, even where fiduciary paternalism is not specifically required or permitted by law, it remains woven into the fabric of the fiduciary relation: as observed earlier, the beneficiary has sought precisely the fiduciary's independent and (in commensurate measure) unreviewable judgment and thus also the paternalism that the exercise of this judgment inevitably involves.

This analysis remains accurate, moreover, even where the standards of fiduciary loyalty and care may be altered *ex ante*, by the agreement of the parties. That the parties may choose among standards to govern their fiduciary relation does not entail that the relation is *simply* a creature of their intentions, as on the contract model. Whereas

[33] *Gerber v Enterprise Products Holdings* LLC, 67 A3d 400 (Del 2013), discussing *ASB Allegiance Real Estate Fund v Scion Breckenridge Managing Member* LLC, 50 A3d 434, 440–2 (Del Ch 2012), aff'd in part, rev'd in part on other grounds, 68 A3d 665, 2013 WL 1914714 (Del 2013). Thanks to Andrew Gold for pointing out these cases to me.

[34] See Model Rules of Prof'l Conduct Rule 12(a) (2011) ("[A] lawyer shall abide by a client's decisions concerning the objectives of representation and, as required by Rule 14, shall consult with the client as to the means by which they are to be pursued. A lawyer may take such action on behalf of the client as is impliedly authorized to carry out the representation").

[35] See American Medical Association, *AMA Code of Medical Ethics* (1996), Opinion 8.06 ("Physicians should prescribe drugs, devices, and other treatments based solely upon medical considerations and patient need and reasonable expectations of the effectiveness of the drug, device or other treatment for the particular patient"); Opinion 2.11 ("It is understandable, though tragic, that some patients in extreme duress—such as those suffering from a terminal, painful, debilitating illness—may come to decide that death is preferable to life.... Instead of participating in assisted suicide, physicians must aggressively respond to the needs of patients at the end of life").

contracting parties craft bespoke terms of sharing, and even boilerplate terms derive their meaning from the parties' expectations, the parties to fiduciary relations opt into one or another of a relatively small set of standards provided by background law. Once again, this is an inevitable consequence of the fact that contract sharing is fixed *ex ante*, whereas fiduciary sharing arises *ex post*. The point of the fiduciary relation is that the beneficiary cannot, *ex ante*, fully specify the obligations that he wishes his fiduciary to have. He therefore must opt into a legal regime whose content, *ex post*, is not fully of his own making.

Obligations to share *ex ante* may be specified by the parties and so may, in this sense, be purely chosen—creatures simply of the parties' wills. Even the inevitable incompletenesses in contracts do not change this. Contract partners, aware that their initial agreements will be incomplete, expect to fill in the blanks in their contracts through *renegotiations*, carried out at *arm's length* (on the contractual model), constrained only by the duty of good faith in performance. Fiduciary obligations are very different in this respect. Obligations to share *ex post* cannot be purely party chosen—they are, in substantial measure, creatures of the law. The parties to a fiduciary relation therefore expect the fiduciary *unilaterally* to adjust to new circumstances in an *other-regarding* way, subject to duties of loyalty and care specified by the law and independently and directly enforceable by courts.[36]

Finally, these observations reveal something important about the character of fiduciary engagements. The contrast to contract is again illuminating. The *ex ante* structure of contract sharing, and the associated self-interest and anti-paternalism, reflect that contract partners engage each other abstractly, for their generic personalities—that is, they contract based simply on formal contractual capacity and take each other's stated intentions at face value, never second-guessing each other's substantive purposes. By contrast, the *ex post* structure of fiduciary sharing, and the altruism and paternalism necessarily displayed by fiduciaries who share in this way, reflect that fiduciaries engage their beneficiaries concretely, for the particular persons that they are—a fiduciary, that is, can discharge her duties of loyalty and care only by adjusting her conduct in light of her beneficiary's particular, substantive interests, about which she must form her own opinions. This difference works its way into the administration of the two kinds of relations. A contract promisor need know nothing about her promisee, apart from what is written into the contract, save that he possesses contractual capacity. A fiduciary, by contrast, must pay careful attention to her beneficiary's interests and aims as these develop over the course of the fiduciary engagement. Otherwise, she will not know what to deploy her loyalty and care in favor of.

III. The Fiduciary Relation as a Status

The contractarian model of fiduciary law, which has become the conventional wisdom, emphasizes fiduciary law's continuity with contract law. As Frank Easterbook and Daniel Fischel claimed in a seminal article, "[g]ood faith in contract merges into fiduciary duties, with a blur and not a line."[37] Indeed, Easterbrook and Fischel, pursuing the

[36] This formulation of this important point benefited from an exchange with Alan Schwartz.
[37] Easterbrook and Fischel (n 5) at 438.

contractarian model to its logical conclusion, insisted that fiduciary law does not in fact constitute a unified or distinct doctrinal order: "Searching for the right definition of a fiduciary duty is not a special puzzle. In short, there is no subject here, and efforts to unify it on a ground that presumes its distinctiveness are doomed."[38] Fiduciary law, on this view, is at once too internally various and insufficiently different from its neighbors to constitute a distinctive practice or object of study.

The contractarian approach is not mistaken on its own terms. But its conclusions reflect its presumptions and preoccupations. It thus leaves out important aspects of the truth about fiduciary law.

First, the contractarian approach excessively emphasizes the (correct) observation that the parties may select among substantive specifications of fiduciary loyalty and care and indeed (often) waive certain elements of these duties; and the approach insufficiently acknowledges the ways in which fiduciary sharing *ex post* must be governed not by the parties but by the law. And second, the contractarian approach excessively emphasizes the (again correct) fact that parties employ fiduciary arrangements as instruments to serve antecedently specified ends; and it insufficiently acknowledges that fiduciary relations may possess an intrinsic value for both the legal order and the parties.

In both respects, the contractarian approach to fiduciary law commits not so much error as partial truth. And in both respects, the pattern of what the contractarian approach reveals and what it disguises reflects the strengths and weaknesses of the broader economic approach to law of which it is a special case. In particular, both shortcomings of the contractual account of fiduciary law reflect a preoccupation with the substantive consequences of legal rules for the advance or retreat of pre-legal interests. And both neglect the formal structure of legal relations and the values that inhere, intrinsically, in legal form.

Begin with the first contractarian oversight, concerning the role of choice in fiduciary relations. Parties generally must choose to establish a fiduciary relation and they may indeed often vary the substantive content of fiduciary duties of loyalty and care: an express provision in a trust, to return to an earlier example, may generally modify the sole interest rule and even authorize a trustee to compete with the trust.[39] But the fact

[38] Easterbrook and Fischel (n 5) at 438.

[39] See n 6. But note again that freedom of choice concerning fiduciary duties should not be exaggerated. The sole interest rule, for example, is not waivable in certain substantive areas—including importantly ERISA. See n 25. Nor is this the only example of an unwaivable fiduciary duty. Trust law, for example, makes mandatory the rule that a trust must be for the benefit of the beneficiaries. See *Restatement (Third) of Trusts* (2003) § 27. See also John H Langbein, "Mandatory Rules in the Law of Trusts," 98 *Nw U L Rev* 1105, 1107 ff (2004).

The lawyer–client relation, to pick another example, imposes any number of effectively unwaivable duties on lawyers. A client, for example, cannot consent to her lawyer's representing a party adverse to her in litigation. See Model Rules of Prof'l Conduct R 17(b)(3). And a contract by which a client attempts to transfer the decision whether or not to accept a settlement offer to her lawyer is unenforceable. See, eg, *Jones v Feiger, Collison & Killmer* 903 P 2d 27 (Colo Ct App 1994). More generally, the law absolutely forbids lawyers from turning on their clients and arguing against the clients' cases in court. Where a defense lawyer argues for conviction rather than acquittal, the law considers her assistance constitutionally defective per se, without any further requirement of prejudice to the defense. Indeed, courts regard such conduct as imposing "an actual or constructive denial of assistance of counsel altogether." *United States v Cronic* 466 US 648, 659 (1984). See also *Cuyler v Sullivan* 446 US 335, 359–50 (1980). Needless to say, a client cannot render such conduct acceptable by agreement to vary the lawyer's fiduciary duties.

that parties possess a formal power to abandon or vary certain rules that elaborate a fiduciary's duties of loyalty and care, or even that they may sometimes be free to choose from a menu of alternative constructions of these duties, does not render fiduciary obligation contractual. It is one thing for fiduciary duties to be responsive to the intentions of the parties to a fiduciary engagement and quite another for these duties to arise, as on the contract model, purely as creatures of the intentions of the parties.

The marriage relation vividly illustrates the difference. Although marriage rarely comes up in conventional discussions of fiduciary law, marriage partners do not deal with each other at arm's length but rather subject to the kinds of trust and confidence that generally constitute fiduciary relations.[40] Moreover, although marriage may seem an eccentric rather than a representative fiduciary relation, it is in fact more typical than might at first appear.[41] On the one hand, the feature of marriage that makes it psychologically and morally distinctive—the beneficent motives that marriage partners typically bring to their relation—is legally beside the point. Legal obligations—both contractual and fiduciary—turn on intentions not motives.[42] (The lawyer–client relation, for example, is thus fully fiduciary, and requires lawyers to display client-regarding intentions, notwithstanding the self-interested motives that lawyers bring to their representations.) On the other hand, marriage may well be the fiduciary relation that figures most prominently in lived experience; and scholars are increasingly arguing that impersonal arrangements among sophisticated commercial parties that have traditionally been regulated by fiduciary law should instead be governed simply and openly by contract.[43] Accordingly, although marriage is not much emphasized by conventional discussions, it represents an important example of fiduciary law—perhaps no other case is more important, either practically or theoretically. Marriage thus opens up significant insights into the character of fiduciary relations more generally.

Now, marriage was historically governed by a regime that strictly controlled entry and exit and, through coverture, included mandatory entailments concerning the legal status of married women.[44] Partly for this reason, nineteenth-century lawyers commonly insisted "[t]hat marriage executed is not a contract," including because "the parties cannot mutually dissolve it" and "because its duties are not derived from its terms

[40] See, eg, *In re Marriage of Fossum* 192 Cal App 4th 336, 343 (Cal Ct App 2011) ("[S]pouses occupy a confidential and fiduciary relationship with each other. The nature of this relationship 'imposes a duty of the highest good faith and fair dealing' on each spouse as to any interspousal transaction") (quoting Cal Fam Code § 721(b) (West 2003)) *Dougan v Dougan* 114 Conn App 379, 384 n 6, 970 A 2d 131, 136 (2009); *Billington v Billington* 220 Conn 212 (Conn 1991); *Ramin v Ramin* 281 Conn 324, 349, 915 A2d 790, 805 (2007); *Dunham v Dunham* 204 Conn 303, 322 (1987).

[41] I would like to thank Anthony Kronman for emphasizing the importance of this point.

[42] See, eg, Irit Samet in this volume (quoting Peter Birks's remark that "what the law requires when it requires altruism is at most action in the interest of others, outcomes, not motives." Peter Birks, "The Content of Fiduciary Obligation," 134 *Israel LJ* 3, 17 (2000)). J E Penner makes a related point in his contribution to this volume when he observes, as part of a larger argument best set aside here, that "mens rea (as opposed to intentionality) is typically irrelevant" to civil law. See J E Penner in this volume.

[43] This is the thrust of the approach to the duties of corporate managers taken by Ronald Gilson and Alan Schwartz in Ronald J Gilson and Alan Schwartz, "Contracting about Private Benefits of Control," available at: <http://ssrn.com/abstract=2182781>.

[44] See, eg, Joel Bishop, *Commentaries on the Law of Marriage and Divorce* (6th edn, 1881) 1.

but from the law."[45] (The United States Supreme Court expressly relied on the status character of marriage—"When formed," a marriage is "no more a contract that 'fatherhood' or 'sonship' is a contract"—to explain why legislative divorces did not constitute "Law[s] impairing the Obligation of Contracts" within the meaning of the prohibition of Article I §10 of the United States Constitution.[46]) Today, coverture has been rejected for more than a century (through the Married Women's Property Acts), and the terms of entry and exit have been liberalized (including through the modern law of ante-nuptial agreements and, more recently, through same-sex marriage). But liberalization is not contractualization. And appreciating that the non-contractual character of marriage endures through modern reforms reveals that liberalizing trends in fiduciary law more generally do not render the fiduciary relation contractual.

Even though modern marriage partners may enter and exit the marriage relation increasingly freely, and in increasingly varied combinations, they cannot constitute their marriage relations contractually, simply by their intentions, as merely a creature of their wills. Indeed, the most prominent judicial decision to liberalize marriage by opening up the relation to same-sex partners expressly recognized marriage's separateness from contract:

> In a real sense, there are three partners to every civil marriage: two willing spouses and an approving State. While only the parties can mutually assent to marriage, the terms of the marriage—who may marry and what obligations, benefits, and liabilities attach to civil marriage—are set by the Commonwealth. Conversely, while only the parties can agree to end the marriage the Commonwealth defines the terms of exit.[47]

The tensions between contract sharing *ex ante* and marriage's necessary embrace of fiduciary sharing *ex post* explain why even liberalizers resist the contractualization of marriage. Contract partners engage only each other's abstract, generic intentional capacities (and never their concrete, particular interests and aims), and contract partners remain as self-interested within their contracts as they were without them (and never adopt attitudes of affirmative, altruistic other-regard). By contrast, the traditional wedding vow—"for better or for worse, for richer or for poorer, in sickness and in health"—makes express what every marriage implicitly involves: an emphatic rejection of *ex ante* sharing and its concomitant attitudes. Marriage partners engage each other concretely, as the fully particular persons whom they are and will, over the course of their marriage, become; and they become altruistically committed to support each other's needs and ambitions, as these develop. Marriage partners, being fiduciaries, share

[45] Bishop (n 44) at 1–4. A common habit did call marriage a contract (it was practiced even by Blackstone, who called marriage a "civil contract:" William Blackstone, *Commentaries*, vol 1, *421). Bishop (n 44) rejected this usage in the following terms:

> Plain as [the status view of marriage] is, and incredible as it may seem that any thing contrary to it should be seriously entertained, marriage was generally in our books, prior to the present one, defined as a contract. But this definition, thus broadly stated, was so obviously inaccurate that it was commonly more or less qualified; and, by some, so much was excepted out of it as to leave little or nothing of the original. So that, if marriage was pronounced a contract, it was said also to be more than a contract, and to differ from all other contracts.

[46] *Maynard v Hill* 125 US 190, 212 (1888) (quoting (*Ditson v Ditson* 4 RI 87, 101 (1856)).

[47] *Goodridge v Department of Public Health* 798 NE 2 941, 954 (Mass 2003).

ex post, which is why marriage (like fiduciary relations generally) includes obligations to make new sacrifices in the face of unforeseen developments. Indeed, to grow and to grow together *ex post* (and to endure in the face of unanticipated developments) is the point of the marriage relation. And the mere fact that the parties may vary some terms of their marriages by agreement does not change any of this.

Agreements concerning marriage thus do not—because they could not possibly—constitute the marriage itself, as common lawyers have long understood. In the words of a nineteenth-century treatise:

> This contract of marriage differs from the marriage itself, as the agreement to build a house differs from the completed structure, or as the egg and the incubation differ from the bird produced.... Actual marriage, in any form which makes the parties in law husband and wife, is performance. Nothing short is. At marriage, therefore, the contract ceases.[48]

Nor is marriage alone or indeed unusual among fiduciary relations in these respects. Fiduciary relations—as even the contractarian view acknowledges—arise because the parties cannot achieve their purposes through sharing *ex ante* but only through sharing *ex post*. Lawyer–client, doctor–patient, guardian–ward, and even trustee–beneficiary relations all involve an express juridical recognition that a fiduciary's duties are not cabined by the agreements that establish these relations but may evolve, and become more demanding, as circumstances develop. To pick but one example, a lawyer who receives a better offer from another client or who comes to believe her client's position is harmful overall cannot, simply for these reasons, make an "efficient withdrawal" from a representation.[49] As with marriage, so with fiduciary law more generally, the recognition that parties may vary fiduciary duties by agreement in order better to promote their purposes does not entail any general abandonment of fiduciary sharing *ex post* in favor of contract sharing *ex ante*. The terms of fiduciary sharing may be varied in substance, but not in form. Liberalization, once again, is not contractualization.

A second oversight of the effort to reconstruct fiduciary relations on a contractarian model concerns the contractarian instinct to emphasize the instrumental purposes of fiduciary arrangements and neglect the intrinsic value of the fiduciary form. The contractarian approach is again right insofar as it goes: persons of course do employ

[48] Bishop (n 44) at 1–2.

[49] The Model Rules of Professional Conduct illustrate the point about withdrawal. Even where lawyers may withdraw, they remain under ongoing obligations not to harm their clients' causes, including where harming may be efficient. As the leading treatise on the law governing lawyers observes, "a lawyer may not *sabotage* a client's lawful cause because the lawyer considers the cause repugnant." Hazard and Hodes, *The Law of Lawyering: A Handbook on the Model Rules of Professional Conduct* (2nd edn, Supp 1991) vol 1, § 1.3:101 at 71 (emphasis added). Moreover, the Model Rules require lawyers to comply with their obligations of confidentiality when explaining their withdrawal, Model Rules of Prof'l Conduct R 116 cmt at 2, and insist that even a lawyer who may prejudicially withdraw "shall take steps to the extent reasonably practicable to protect a client's interests," Model Rules of Prof'l Conduct R 116(d) (2003). The *Restatement (Third) of the Law Governing Lawyers* § 33(1) similarly requires a lawyer who withdraws to "take steps to the extent reasonably practicable to protect the client's interests." For all these reasons, withdrawing lawyers must act (even inefficiently) to ensure that substitute counsel is secured in a manner that harms the client's prospects as little as possible. See Hazard and Hodes (2nd edn, Supp 1998) vol 1, § 1.16:303 at 486.

fiduciaries as instruments to serve their antecedent interests; and the liberalization of fiduciary law has importantly improved the law's functioning in this respect. But both the individual parties to fiduciary engagements and the broader legal order also possess interests in fiduciary relations for their own sakes. And such interests cannot be well served by reconstructing fiduciary relations on the model of contract. This is also illustrated by the examples just considered.

Marriage is an obvious case. Partners value a marriage not simply as a means to ends (economic security, generic marital consortium[50]) that they bring to the marriage, but rather as an end in itself. Their marriage becomes—in and for itself—one of the organizing projects of their lives. Indeed, this is among the points of marriage—that it establishes a social and legal support for a form of love whose great value is matched by great difficulty. Guardianship may have a similar intrinsic value. The jointly but asymmetrically pursued project of *Bildung*—of constituting the ward's self-conception and thus his interests—can become one of the great sources of meaning in the lives of both guardian and ward. Nor do fiduciary relations possess intrinsic value in only the personal context. Consider, for example, the lawyer–client relation. Lawyers are essential for both the promulgation of the law and the legitimate resolution of retail disputes, in which generally applicable legal rules cannot be applied to particular, concrete cases in a mechanical or uncontroversial way. Lawyers, one might say, are an essential component of the rule of law. And the law governing lawyers—in particular insofar as it articulates the principle of lawyerly fidelity that organizes lawyers' fiduciary duties to clients—must (and does) depart from general principles of tort and contract in any number of ways in order to establish the rule of law.[51] It would thus be quite incredible to think that the positive law governing lawyers might be adequately explained without any reference to the intrinsic value of the rule of law and as simply a technology for serving lawyers' and clients' prior private interests.

In all these cases, and many others, fiduciary relations constitute meanings and values rather than merely serving as technologies by which antecedent interests may be promoted. But fiduciary relations cannot possess this constitutive character on the contractarian model. Contracts—because of the *ex ante* structure of contract sharing and the purely abstract character of contract recognition—establish only the thinnest form of community among the parties to them. Indeed, that is the point of contract—that the contract relation is available to every person with every other person and requires only the shallowest engagement, based on the narrowest overlap of interest, both absolutely cabined by the contracting parties' intentions *ex ante*. Fiduciary relations, by contrast, bind life-partners into families, educate children into adults, and connect citizens to their states. These activities involve persons deeply and broadly and draw them into fundamentally involuntary commitments. They require sharing *ex post* and cannot be cabined by *ex ante* intentions.

[50] Of course, even though married persons do not value their marriages *solely* as means to these or other ends, they may value them also as means.

[51] See generally Daniel Markovits, "Lawyerly Fidelity," in Sanford Levinson (ed), *NOMOS LIV: Loyalty* (2013) and Daniel Markovits, *A Modern Legal Ethics* (2010).

Conclusion

The contractarian approach that has come to dominate fiduciary law in recent decades made an important contribution to the understanding of fiduciary obligation. Contractarians pointed out that the fiduciary duties of loyalty and care have no fixed or mandatory substantive content; and, along the way, they showed that liberalizing fiduciary law can allow the law better to serve the antecedent interests of the parties to fiduciary relations.

But this worthwhile program of law reform cannot sustain a theoretical account of the nature of fiduciary law or the structure of fiduciary relations. And the contractarians' native instincts to look to contract law as the model for such an account—or, more dramatically still, to insist that there is "no subject" of fiduciary law and that efforts to theorize this body of law are doomed[52]—commit a serious error.

Although the *substantive content* of fiduciary duties varies widely across areas of law, and across cases within an area, the *formal character* of fiduciary duty remains constant across all fiduciary relations. Fiduciaries limit their self-interest according to affirmative duties of other regard and accept the paternalism that these duties necessarily involve; fiduciaries share not *ex ante* but rather *ex post*; fiduciaries engage each other not abstractly, for their universal humanity, but concretely, as the particular persons whom they are and become, as circumstances change; fiduciary relations are not merely creatures of the parties' intentions but instead establish and reflect status-like orders; and, fiduciaries and the broader legal order value fiduciary relations not just as means for serving antecedent ends but also as ends in themselves.

The contractarian approach to fiduciary duty has thus properly liberalized this body of law, but it has not understood it. Liberalization is not contractualization.

[52] Easterbrook and Fischel (n 5) at 438.

11

Knowledge in Fiduciary Relations

*Richard R W Brooks**

One approach to identifying what, if anything, is distinctive about fiduciary law is to begin by asking what is the problem the law seeks to solve. In their provocative article, "Contract and Fiduciary Duty," Frank Easterbrook and Daniel Fischel identify the basic problem as one of contractual incompleteness.[1] In a world of complete contracts, they stress, fiduciary law would not exist. Rational parties would specify the entitlements and duties associated with all possible contingencies and courts would implement a single response, specific performance, whenever asked to intervene by the parties. It is an imagined ideal, of course, this world of completely specified contracts. Real-world contracts are never complete in any proper sense and courts are constantly called upon to use various rules and remedies to address disputes arising from contractual incompleteness. What does this fact tell us about the nature of fiduciary law? Nothing, say Easterbrook and Fischel, "there is no subject here, and efforts to unify it on a ground that presumes its distinctiveness are doomed."[2] The basic problem in their view is contractual and so is the legal response.

Beginning with a premise that fiduciary relations are wholly contractual, it is not at all surprising that Easterbrook and Fischel would conclude that the law guiding those relations is contractual as well.[3] Contract in, contract out. But the initial premise is far from obvious. Though fiduciaries are often created by contract, a contract is not required to form a fiduciary relationship. Nor, according to many scholars, is contract, when present, an essential feature of fiduciary relationships. These scholars search to find the "true" (non-contractual) essence of fiduciary law. They are on a fool's errand, Easterbrook and Fischel scoff; "[t]hey are looking for something special about fiduciary relations. There is nothing special to find. There are only distinctive and independently interesting questions about particular consensual (and thus contractual) relations."[4] Yet this last phrase—"consensual (and thus contractual)"—reveals a critical conflation. Equating consent with contract is an obvious overreach. Consensual sex is not contractual sex, at least not all the time. Nor is a consensual agency, or any number of other fiduciary relationships, of necessity contractual.[5] But again, their seeing consent

* For their thoughtful comments I am grateful to Franklin Ard, Andrew Gold, Sarath Sanga and participants in the 2013 DePaul conference on the philosophical foundations of fiduciary law.

[1] They observe, for example: "We have suggested in earlier writings that the duty of loyalty is a response to the impossibility of writing contracts completely specifying the parties' obligations." Frank H Easterbrook and Daniel R Fischel, "Contract and Fiduciary Duty," 36 *JL & Econ* 425, 426 (1993).

[2] Easterbrook and Fischel (n 1) at 438.

[3] "Because the process is contractual—because both principal and agent enter this understanding for gain—the details should be those that maximize that gain, which the contracting parties can divide." Easterbrook and Fischel (n 1) at 426.

[4] Easterbrook and Fischel (n 1) at 438.

[5] "Agency is the fiduciary relationship that arises when one person (a 'principal') manifests assent to another person (an 'agent') that the agent shall act on the principal's behalf and subject to the principal's

as contract is unsurprising. Departing from an incomplete contracts perspective, there is an overwhelming tendency to view everything that follows as contract.

Complete contracts would eliminate the need for a good deal of existing law (and not only fiduciary law). Even so, that hardly implies that the function of our current law is to replicate what parties would contract for were they able. If tortfeasors and criminals were able to costlessly contract with their victims beforehand, accident and criminal law would occupy greatly reduced roles in our society. Nonetheless, that would scarcely warrant leaping to the conclusion that accident and criminal law exist as a response to the difficulty of contracting. It is perhaps easier to reach this conclusion with regard to fiduciary law—since fiduciary relations are consensual and often commercial—but it is nonetheless a leap to conclude that fiduciary law operates essentially as contract default terms. Had the argument, however, departed from a different premise about the problem that fiduciary law seeks to solve it may have ended up someplace else altogether.

In this chapter I shall take a different problem as a starting point to animate fiduciary law. The problem concerns knowledge and information in the fiduciary context.[6] Attending to this problem is not meant to elide other concerns or to deny the contractual character of fiduciary law. A focus on knowledge and information may complement or even reinforce the "fiduciary as contract" argument. Imperfect and incomplete information are, after all, the central matters underlying contractual incompleteness. Yet by zeroing-in directly on knowledge and information (not mediated by contractual incompleteness) critical, though often obscured, aspects of fiduciary law become prominent. Deborah DeMott's contribution to this volume, concerning instructions in agency relations, provides a good illustration of the kinds of issues that manifest when a fiduciary analysis is specifically oriented around knowledge and information. Such an orientation, moreover, pushes our perspective beyond the overburdened, and often underspecified, duties of loyalty and care. Other vital fiduciary duties—including duties of candor, confidence, and disclosure as well as obligations to be informed, to inquire, and the like—take on greater salience. The payoff of such an expanded perspective is a richer understanding of the distinctive features of fiduciary relationships and the laws that govern them.

In addition to varying the problem of departure, this chapter also varies the unit of analysis. While the "fiduciary as contract" argument takes the rational self-interested individual as the sole unit of analysis, here the fiduciary relationship itself is also taken

control, and the agent manifests assent or otherwise consents so to act." *Restatement (Third) of Agency* (2006) § 1.01.

[6] Knowledge and information are used jointly here, but not interchangeably. One can possess information (written in a sealed envelope, let's say) without being aware of its content. Knowledge requires more. Finer distinctions may be drawn between knowledge and information, but doing so is beyond the scope of this preliminary treatment. The usage "fiduciary context" is meant to represent a setting that goes beyond the strict fiduciary–beneficiary relationship or dyad. It includes all relevant relational pairings in the role-set to which the fiduciary–beneficiary dyad belongs. A role-set is a collection of role-relationships, like that of a medical student, to borrow Merton's example, who occupies the "role of a student *vis-à-vis* his teachers, but also an array of other roles relating him diversely to other students, physicians, nurses, social workers, medical technicians, and the like." Robert K. Merton, 1957, "The Role-Set: Problems in Sociological Theory," 8 *British Journal of Sociology*, 110–20, at110 (1957). Similarly, when considering the occupant of the role we call "fiduciary," we must bear in mind that role with its various pairings to fully appreciate the fiduciary context.

as an undivided whole for legal and economic analytical purposes. The fiduciary relationship is dyadic, not merely bilateral. Law recognizes not only the rational individuals who comprise fiduciary relationships, but also the relational dyads themselves. Recall that some beneficiaries are not rational.[7] Others are not individuals.[8] Yet the fiduciary relationships of which they are a part remain legally cognizable and distinct from both their constitutive fiduciaries and beneficiaries.[9] Hence, while fiduciary relationships often reflect bilateral agreements between rational individuals, those agreements only partially reflect the whole arrangement.[10] More is exposed when third parties are present. Rules regarding the internal order of the relationship may, or may not,[11] be fairly characterized as resulting from bilateral contracting between two rational parties (the internal order appears to be the exclusive domain of the "fiduciary as contract" argument) but when third parties are involved the dyad's separate appearance becomes more visible. Nowhere is this more evident than in matters concerning knowledge and information among the parties.

Legal and economic questions about what anyone knows or can be assumed to know about the knowledge of others must regularly be addressed where fiduciaries are concerned. Duties and presumptions related to knowledge are often established to address challenges arising from tripartite interactions common to the fiduciary context. Moreover, it is not just what is known, in fact or as a matter of law, by or within the fiduciary dyad that is at issue. Information and beliefs shared by fiduciaries and third parties often generate legal authority or power (ie, apparent authority as well as authority by estoppel or other means) leading to liability for even completely uninformed principals and beneficiaries. Fiduciary relations are prone to all sorts of multiparty mischief to which the law must respond. Legal and social structures often arise across role-sets to promote or limit the "observability" of knowledge, in a sense first suggested by Simmel and later developed by Merton, who offers examples of legally protected privileged information and confidential communication. There are a number of other legal rules, as further elaborated in this chapter, through which law manages and structures knowledge and information in the fiduciary context.

But why call these legal rules "fiduciary law," as opposed to bilateral, tripartite, or multilateral contract default rules? One could certainly impose the language and logic

[7] Fiduciaries are often appointed to beneficiaries who lack legal capacity to act on their own behalf. While that need not imply they are irrational (eg, they may be rational minors) in many cases it does.

[8] "A trust can be established for the benefit of a cat or a dog or an unborn child." See Tamar Frankel, this volume (citations omitted).

[9] Just as a partnership (even absent entity status) may attain legal presence distinct from its partners (while not itself a strictly legal unit able to contract, sue, be sued, hold property and such), so too may a fiduciary relationship exhibit a civil trace. See Richard R W Brooks and Timothy W Guinnane, "The Right to Associate and the Rights of Associations: Civil-Society Organizations in Prussia, 1794–1908" (Yale Law School Working Paper).

[10] It is similar in the way two people may come together to form a marriage relationship, after which the marriage itself (separate from the individual spouses) will attain a certain civil and social recognition. See, eg, *The Sociology of Georg Simmel*, trans, ed, and introd Kurt H Wolff (1950) 118–44.

[11] Note that even this internal order needn't be exclusively regulated by the parties' agreement. Not everything that comes about as a consequence of consent or contract is consensual or contractual. Emile Durkheim, *The Division of Labor in Society*, trans Lewis A Coser (1997). In particular, fiduciaries paired with beneficiaries, or with third parties, are subject to social and legal constraints attending the role-set of which they are a part (Merton (n 6)).

of contract on fiduciary dyads and related third parties, although the purpose of doing so is not always entirely obvious. In any event that is not the objective of this chapter. The aim here is to analyze the information structure of fiduciary dealings to gain greater perspective on the function and purpose of the law that regulates them. Labeling the law is a task left for others.

The remainder of this chapter begins with economic considerations. An economic taxonomy of knowledge is presented in Section I. This construction of knowledge is illustrated with the principal–agent model, which is contrasted with the "fiduciary as contract" model. The section concludes with the idea of non-contractibility, revealing a key limitation of the fiduciary contractarian approach and suggesting a broader role for law. Section II presents a legal taxonomy of knowledge with applications to cases and doctrine from agency and other fiduciary relations. This section emphasizes information-related entitlements and duties (eg, confidentiality, candor, disclosure, becoming informed, staying abreast, obligations to inquire and share facts within and outside the fiduciary–beneficiary dyad). Section III provides a brief discussion of the information fiduciary, a somewhat novel application of fiduciary principles to persons possessing information of or about others outside of traditional fiduciary contexts. A short summary concludes the chapter.

I. The Economics of Knowledge

What is the structure of information within the fiduciary context? Economists tend to view the superior knowledge of the fiduciary (ie, the fiduciary's expertise or other insights) as the central challenge with which the parties must contend. That is correct, of course, but it is one thing to generally recognize that a party's expertise or insight motivates the legal and economic arrangement called "fiduciary relationship;"[12] it is another thing entirely to spell it out. Characterizing, from the start, the entitlements and duties associated with this arrangement is an impossible task. Fiduciary law offers a solution. "When one party hires the other's knowledge and expertise, there is not much they can write down," observe Easterbrook and Fischel; thus "[i]nstead of specific undertakings, the agent assumes a duty of loyalty in pursuit of the objective and a duty of care in performance."[13] Though unable to specify *ex ante* what the fiduciary knows and how to apply that knowledge, Easterbrook and Fischel smartly point out that the parties can summon *ex post* the duties of loyalty and care to accomplish the same objective. Their point is undeniable. Fiduciaries are almost always hired for some skill, expertise, or technical knowledge, which is seldom reducible to very specific language in contracts. Duties of loyalty and care in fiduciary law, like good faith performance and enforcement in contract law, provide behavioral guidance when agreements are silent. For proponents of the fiduciary as contract argument, that's all there is to the matter. Fiduciary law is simply a contractual means of dealing with individuals who possess special knowledge and skills that others contract for (incompletely) and monitor (imperfectly). "This is the 'fiduciary' package," as Easterbrook and Fischel sum it up, and "it is still empty."[14]

[12] In many cases the fiduciary is not more informed or knowledgeable than the beneficiary, but simply has more time or attention to spare at some given costs, or can undertake the requisite tasks with less time or concentrated attention than the beneficiary due to advantages of scope, scale, or some other factor.

[13] Easterbrook and Fischel (n 1) at 426.

[14] Easterbrook and Fischel (n 1) at 426.

Fiduciary as contract, like the firm as a nexus of contracts, is not implausible. All forms of economic organization may be imagined as "contract." So what? The value of such reductionist exercises turns on whether they reveal more than they conceal. By this criterion the "fiduciary as contract" abstraction performs ambiguously, but not badly. In some respects, it provides useful organization and clarity to a sprawling and murky area of law. It is difficult, as well as pointless, to deny the many contractual and contract-like features prominent in the fiduciary context. Yet in other respects the contractarian approach cloaks and diverts attention away from salient features of the fiduciary context. For example, the extensive focus on the fiduciary's knowledge and expertise obscures the relational structure of information. Knowledge and expertise possessed by the fiduciary is of course important, but (as Friedrich Hayek warned) it is easy to lose sight of the broader character of information when focusing on the knowledge of any one individual. Hayek emphasized the decentralized nature of knowledge in every economic order—that the requisite knowledge of circumstances "never exists in concentrated or integrated form, but solely as the dispersed bits of incomplete and frequently contradictory knowledge which all the separate individuals possess."[15] Knowledge that is decentralized, but not disconnected, is relational information. The structure of knowledge and information within the fiduciary context is highly relational. Fiduciary law, to a significant extent, supports this structure.

A relational view of knowledge reveals that it is not simply the know-how that the fiduciary brings to the relationship that matters, but also that which is known or acquired in the context of the relationship. Tacit knowledge produced under "local conditions" and in the "special circumstances" of the relationship accrues to "the man on the spot," as Hayek put it. When "the man on the spot" is a fiduciary, the acquired knowledge is subject to heightened duties, including those of care, candor, confidence, and disclosure. This logic is essential for grasping fiduciary law. But even this extension does not go far enough. For it is not merely a question of what facts, *x*, the fiduciary knows; the relational view of knowledge also concerns itself with what others know or can know about what the fiduciary knows and vice versa.

Looking at knowledge in a relational way is familiar to economic contract theorists, who tend to be quite explicit in describing the information structure of their analyses. Four basic modes are typically employed, which are illustrated well with the triad of principal (*P*), agent (*A*), and third party (*T*). First, knowledge of *x* is said to be "common knowledge" among the parties if *P*, *A*, and *T* all know *x*, and each knows that the other two also know *x*, and they all know that they all know that they all know *x*, and so on ad infinitum.[16] Second,

[15] F A Hayek, "The Use of Knowledge in Society," 35 *Am Econ Rev* 519, 519 (1945). Hayek continues:

> The economic problem of society is thus not merely a problem of how to allocate "given" resources—if "given" is taken to mean given to a single mind which deliberately solves the problems set out by these "data." It is rather a problem of how to secure the best use of resources known to any of the members of society, for ends whose relative importance only these individuals know. Or, to put it briefly, it is a problem of the utilization of knowledge not given to anyone in its totality. (519–20)

[16] Common knowledge is an extremely stringent information criterion. Yet, many analyses (and most everyday problems) can be analyzed with constructs that fall strictly short of full-blown common knowledge. Allowing the parties knowledge of what they each know they know to truncate after some finite number of rounds is sufficient for all but the most abstract formulations.

x is "verifiable" if it can be established before some relevant arbiter. Proving x in court is the usual example given to characterize verifiable information, which reveals the contingent nature of this of kind of "knowledge."[17] Third, x is "observable-but-unverifiable" if it is witnessed or known among some parties (for example, if x is common knowledge between P and A) but it cannot be established outside of that association. Fourth, x is "private" information if it is known to either P, A, or T (exclusively) and is neither observable nor verifiable to anyone else. With these four modes of knowledge in mind, now consider the "fiduciary as contract" argument.

Agency, the prototype fiduciary relationship in the contract model, serves well as the exemplary case. To avoid confusion, however, it is important to distinguish what economists call the "principal–agent" model from the "fiduciary as contract" argument. A simple numerical example will do. Imagine an agent who can take only one of two distinct actions. For instance, she can exert high effort or low effort, she may invest aggressively or prudently, she may exercise great care or little care. Let a_H represent high effort and a_L represent low effort. High effort is good, but not always better than low effort. Preferred effort will be determined by the circumstances, the so-called "the state of the world," faced by the parties. For simplicity, let's say there are only two states of the world—prosaically labeled state 1 and state 2, and represented by ω_1 and ω_2, respectively. Assume each state is equally likely to occur. Through some technology, $f(\bullet)$, the combination of chosen action and realized state of the world results in an outcome, x, called the principal's "payoff" or realized value. More x is assumed better than less. The contrived equations below illustrate several possible interaction among these variables.

$$f(a_L, \omega_1) = 10 \tag{1}$$

$$f(a_L, \omega_2) = 50 \tag{2}$$

$$f(a_H, \omega_1) = 0 \tag{3}$$

$$f(a_H, \omega_2) = 100 \tag{4}$$

Equation 1 indicates that when the agent exerts low effort, a_L, and state of the world ω_1 is realized, then the payoff, x, to the principal is 10, whereas high effort, a_H, in state ω_1 generates a payoff of 0 (equation 3).[18] On the other hand, when the state of the world is ω_2, low effort by the agent generates a payoff of 50 (equation 2), while high effort would produce a payoff of 100 (equation 4). These equations are neither interesting nor revealing in and of themselves, but they can help us account for what is known by whom and when.

[17] Verifiable knowledge is neither a dichotomous concept (but typically a question of verifiable at what cost and within what time frame) nor truth-based in a philosophical or scientific sense (but rather what a judge, jury or other arbiter determines).

[18] To make this example simpler, I am treating the payoff to the principal as her net payoff. That is, this is what the principal gets after paying the agent for her effort.

Suppose, for example, that an agent must choose an action before the state is known. Often investments must be sunk before goods are produced, inventory must be purchased before consumer demand is known, demand which may be influenced by such vagaries as the weather. Yet so long as the principal "knows" the technology, $f(\bullet)$, the possible states and their likelihood, and can "verify" the chosen action, then she can specify a contract calling for the agent to take action a_H, which would result in an expected payoff of 50, leaving her with 20 more than expected if action a_L is chosen.[19] The principal can do better still when she knows that the agent knows (or will know) the state of the world before acting. By specifying that the agent should take action a_L if the state of the world is ω_1 and action a_H if the state of the world is ω_2, the principal's expected payoff would increase by 10 percent.[20] Arrangements of this sort, where the agent is given instructions on how to behave in every possible state of the world, are called "fully specified" or "complete state-contingent" contracts.[21]

Variations and generalizations of the simple example above characterize the principal–agent literature in economics.[22] A striking feature of this literature is that nothing resembling "fiduciary law" plays any role in the principal–agent model.[23] When the agent rationally accepts an optimally designed contract offer, it is in her interest to perform as stipulated. Should she fail to do what was specified in the contract the ideal

[19] In stating that the principal "knows" the technology, it is not suggested that the principal has direct access to the technology or expertise herself. She simply knows that actions and states of the world combine through some mechanism to produce outcomes, allowing her to make the calculations to determine what action the agent should take. In reaching this conclusion, note first that whichever action the agent takes, there is a 50 percent chance the state of the world will be bad and a 50 percent chance that it will be good. This means that low effort (a_L) produces a 50 percent chance that the principal will get 10 and a 50 percent chance that she will get 50. Hence, the principal's expected payoff when the agent takes action a_L is 30 (ie, $50\% \cdot 10 + 50\% \cdot 50$). Whereas the principal's expected payoff when the agent takes action a_H is 50 (ie, $50\% \cdot 0 + 50\% \cdot 100$).

[20] Recall that effort level a_H is not the best strategy in every state of the world. Sometimes the principal wants the agent to take effort level a_L. Prudence (ie, a_L) is a better investment strategy in a bear market (i.e ω_1), while an aggressive investment strategy (a_H) is superior in a bull market (ω_2). It may be better for the agent to work for half-days (a_L) when customer demand for the principal's product is weak (ω_1), but show up early and work long hours (a_H) when demand is strong (ω_2). When the contract specifies that the agent should take action a_L if the state of the world is ω_1 and action a_H if the state of the world is ω_2 the principal's expected payoff increases to 55 (ie, $50\% \cdot 10 + 50\% \cdot 100$).

[21] Should the agent not carry out her state-contingent assignment as agreed, then appropriate remedies may also be included in the contract, allowing the court (which must be able to either observe or verify the actions taken and the state of the world realized) to specifically enforce the agreement. In the simple example given in the text, it is enough for the outcome, x, to be verifiable, since there is a unique outcome associated with each action-state combination. Indeed, a unique outcome flowing from any particular action also may be enough for the principal to profitably exploit a "shifting support" to reach a first-best contract.

[22] The literature developed from a basic model seeking to analyze how best to get an agent to pursue a principal's desires or interests when only the agent can fully observe her own actions (a situation known as "moral hazard" or "hidden action") or when only the agent knows some relevant information about the state of the world (often about herself, known as "adverse selection" or "hidden information"). While the underlying assumptions vary from model to model (though many assume that the principal is risk-neutral and the agent is risk-averse; if the agent was risk-neutral a simple solution could involve the principal selling her interest to the agent for its expected value under the optimal action) the objective is always how to align the agent's incentives to match the principal's interest. Incentive alignment is key because all models assume that the agent would pursue on her own interests if not provided with an appropriate menu of sanctions and rewards for her conduct. Law's sole duty rule has no purchase here.

[23] Some law and economics scholars have made noteworthy attempts to infuse fiduciary law into these models. Robert Cooter and Bradley J Freeman, "The Fiduciary Relationship: Its Economic Character

remedy is specific performance, if feasible, or enforcement of a liquidated damage term provided by the parties. Loyalty, care, confidence, disclosure, and other duties common to agents are absent here and are in any case superfluous. The principal–agent model requires a great deal of knowledge among the parties to specify their agreement *ex ante*, but the model places very few demands on law *ex post*.[24]

By contrast the "fiduciary as contract" argument requires much of law *ex post* (although it resists attributing anything special to fiduciary law). The difference in legal orientation taken by these two approaches is largely due to the difference in the problems they seek to solve. The problem addressed by the principal–agent model is incentive misalignment (ie, what to do when the agent's incentives do not naturally align with the principal's interests). Once a contractual solution is devised there is nothing left for law to do, except mechanically enforce the contract terms when asked. As mentioned earlier, the problem to which the "fiduciary as contract" argument addresses itself is contractual incompleteness. It is a problem that calls for a more active court and legal framework.[25]

Contracts involving fiduciaries are especially prone to incompleteness, Easterbrook and Fischel observe: "a 'fiduciary' relation is a contractual one characterized by unusually high costs of specification and monitoring."[26] They present two distinct ways that law responds to contractual incompleteness. First, courts may complete the contract *ex post* by imposing hypothetical bargains.[27] Second, legal rules may encourage the parties to complete the contract themselves at some interim stage.[28] Through these two paths, *ex post* hypothetical bargains or *interim* real bargains, (fiduciary) law significantly solves the problem of incomplete contracts.[29]

and Legal Consequences," 66 *NYU L Rev* 1045 (1991); Eric Talley, "Turning Servile Opportunities to Gold: A Strategic Analysis of the Corporate Opportunities Doctrine," 108 *Yale LJ* 277 (1998) and Robert H Sitkoff, "The Economic Structure of Fiduciary Law," 91 *BU L Rev* 1039 (2011).

[24] The informational demands on the parties are notable. Not only must the contract and the outcomes on which it is based be verifiable (which is all that is required of courts), but the states of the world and some belief regarding their likelihood must be known *ex ante* by the parties, as well as the technology and the agent's utility derived from actions and payments. Assuming so much is no trivial matter.

[25] Contractual incompleteness is not a problem of much consequence in many formal economic models that simply assume it away. "All contingencies (including the process by which the blanks are to be filled in) are covered [by the contract]." Benjamin E Hermalin and Michael L Katz, "Judicial Modification of Contracts between Sophisticated Parties: A More Complete View of Incomplete Contracts and Their Breach," 9 *J Law, Econ & Org* 230, 232 (1993). See also A Konakayama,T Mitsui, and S Watanabe, "Efficient Contracting with Reliance and a Damage Measure," 17 *Rand J Econ* 450 (1986).

[26] Easterbrook and Fischel (n 1) at 427. As Easterbrook and Fischel argue: "*Fiduciary duties are not special duties; they have no moral footing*; they are the same sort of obligations, derived and enforced in the same way, as other contractual undertakings." (Emphasis added.)

[27] For example, they suggest, "[t]he duty of loyalty replaces detailed contractual terms, and courts flesh [it] out... by prescribing the *actions* the parties themselves would have preferred if bargaining were cheap and all promises fully enforced." Easterbrook and Fischel (n 1) at 427 (emphasis added).

[28] "Many legal rules induce people to enter into transactions—not just the stiff penalty for theft, but rules prescribing injunctions or specific performance, rules requiring *disclosure of information*. . ., all of which may send the parties back to the table" to complete the contract. Easterbrook and Fischel (n 1) at 427. See also Ian Ayres and Robert Gertner, "Filling Gaps in Incomplete Contracts: An Economic Theory of Default Rules," 99 *Yale LJ* 87 (1989).

[29] In some cases, Easterbrook and Fischel argue, interim bargains are better than hypothetical ones. "Creating hypothetical contracts is difficult. Judges have less information than the parties.. . . Real transactions, at real prices, are accordingly preferable." In particular, "when it is hard to know the optimal approach,

Importantly, these solutions derive from a particular conception of the contractual problem. In their framework Easterbrook and Fischel stress that contracts are incomplete because transaction costs and, presumably, bounded rationality render fully contingent *ex ante* agreements prohibitive. After contracts are signed, however, parties observe what was difficult or impossible to envision or account for *ex ante*. This allows them to engage in interim bargaining or the court to hypothesize about what the parties would have done had they addressed the relevant contractual gaps *ex ante*. Gaps are filled either by the parties at an interim stage or by the court *ex post*. But this gap-filling activity can only occur if the parties are able to observe the gap and verify their would-be agreements. Often neither is possible, which suggests another source of contractual incompleteness.

Ignorance and uncertainty sometimes do not resolve themselves *ex post*. There are situations where even *ex post* the court is unable to verify the state of things, producing a condition called "non-contractability." Non-contractability leads to a different kind of contractual incompleteness. The parties may know or foresee some important fact that they can write down at trivial expense to make their contract more complete. But why bother writing more terms if the courts cannot verify and enforce them? When contracts are incomplete because of non-contractibility, hypothetical and interim bargains don't help much.

Consider, for example, a principal who gives her agent an asset to manage, initially worth 100 million dollars. Assume the agent may take two different actions, a_L or a_H, the state of the world outside of the agent's control may manifest two conditions, ω_1 or ω_2, and the combinations of actions and manifest conditions will produce one of two possible (outcomes) *ex post* values of the asset, x_A (say, 150 million dollars) or x_B (50 million dollars). All combinations are possible. In this case, the parties could write a fully specified contract, k, with a contingent transfer, s, associated with each combination of (a,ω,x) as shown below.[30]

$$k=\begin{Bmatrix}\{a_L,\omega_1,x_A,s_i\}\\ \{a_H,\omega_1,x_A,s_{ii}\}\\ \{a_L,\omega_2,x_A,s_{iii}\}\\ \{a_H,\omega_2,x_A,s_{iv}\}\\ \{a_L,\omega_1,x_B,s_v\}\\ \{a_H,\omega_1,x_B,s_{vi}\}\\ \{a_L,\omega_2,x_B,s_{vii}\}\\ \{a_H,\omega_2,x_B,s_{viii}\}\end{Bmatrix}$$

when judicial valuation is haphazard, and when transaction costs ex post are small, a contract-forcing remedy is superior." On the other hand, "[r]ules inducing people to bargain are undesirable when bargaining is costly and its outcome is clear. Then courts can save parties the transactions costs by establishing a pre-set rule and leaving those with unusual desires or circumstances to transact for some different approach." Easterbrook and Fischel (n 1) at 445.

[30] The contingent transfer, s, may be thought of as a salary paid to the agent based on her chosen action, the state of the world when her action was taken, and the realized outcome. The transfer may be negative, meaning that the agent pays the principal.

The first term in the contract stipulates that if the agent takes action a_L in the state of the world ω_1 and outcome x_A is realized then she gets a transfer (or salary) s_i. The other terms are similarly read. Suppose that, for whatever reason, the parties did not conceive that high effort, a_H, in the state of the world, ω_1, could possibly lead to a loss of 50 million dollars, leaving a gap in their contract:

$$k = \left\{ \begin{bmatrix} \{a_L, \omega_1, x_A, s_i\} \\ \{a_H, \omega_1, x_A, s_{ii}\} \\ \{a_L, \omega_2, x_A, s_{iii}\} \\ \{a_H, \omega_2, x_A, s_{iv}\} \\ \{a_L, \omega_1, x_B, s_v\} \\ \\ \{a_L, \omega_2, x_B, s_{vii}\} \\ \{a_H, \omega_2, x_B, s_{viii}\} \end{bmatrix} \right\}$$

After such a loss occurs, however, let's say that the parties can verify the actual state of things, $\{a_H, \omega_1, x_B\}$. In this case, as Easterbrook and Fischel suggest, the court may impose the hypothetical bargain that the parties would have struck had they specified a term to deal with this contingency. The perceptive court would identify that the parties would have chosen salary s_{vi} for the agent.[31]

Now moving to a more problematic case, what if the parties failed to anticipate x_B (a 50 million dollar loss!)? Let's say they wrote a contract with just the first 4 terms in k, as below.

$$k = \left\{ \begin{bmatrix} \{a_L, \omega_1, x_A, s_i\} \\ \{a_H, \omega_1, x_A, s_{ii}\} \\ \{a_L, \omega_2, x_A, s_{iii}\} \\ \{a_H, \omega_2, x_A, s_{iv}\} \\ \\ \\ \\ \\ \end{bmatrix} \right\}$$

The gap here is larger than before, but again suppose that it is clear to everyone *ex post* that a 50 million dollar loss has occurred. However, now imagine that the court is unable to verify the action that was taken by the agent. In this case the appropriate salary is either s_v or s_{vi}. What if, moreover, the court is also unable to verify ω? In that case s_{vii}

[31] The salary, which could be positive or negative, is essentially a transfer between the principal and agent. These transfers, when directed through the court, take the nominal form of penalties and rewards for the agent (given her actions and outcomes), but they really are just prices—merely wages chosen from a hypothetical wage schedule.

and s_{viii} must be added to the possible gap-filling salaries. It would not matter if the parties engaged in costless interim bargaining once they realized the state of the world was good or bad for them.[32] The inability of the court to verify whether ω_1 or ω_2 occurred and which action the agent took would make the interim agreement non-enforceable.[33] As this example suggests, contractarian approaches to fiduciary relations are limited by information being verifiable.

II. The Law of Knowledge

A central part of what law does, particularly in the fiduciary context, is to attempt to overcome problems of verifiability through legal rules. Taking this as the problem for fiduciary law to address opens up the scope of contractability, or relational arrangements, that parties may pursue. The structure of information, in law, does a great deal of work to facilitate fiduciary relations and associated transactions. To appreciate this we must look beyond the economics of knowledge and focus on how law construes what parties know.

Law uses four primary constructs to establish knowledge. These constructs overlap and often blend into each other. They are presented here as a heuristics, rather than strict formal categories. First, a party may be shown to have "actual knowledge" of x if she either knows x or knows y and also that y implies x. Actual knowledge is a legal construct, which is typically established directly, such as by an admission, or indirectly, by circumstantial evidence presented before an appropriate arbiter, such as a judge, jury, or arbitrator. Second, a party may be legally charged with knowledge of x if she "should know" x. Knowledge here is imposed by the duty to know x. Third, law will often assume knowledge of x by a party who "should have known" x or who "had reason to know" x. While there may be no prior duty to know x (as with the "should know" standard), knowledge of subsidiary facts and circumstances combined with ordinary intelligence or some level of sophistication or expertise can create legal knowledge of x within a party. Fourth, often a party knows x "by law" through the operation of fictions, presumptions, estoppel, effective notice and other forms of constructive knowledge. These four routes to knowledge in law are all used to support fiduciary relationships. Let's consider them in turn.

Actual knowledge is rather less like the philosopher's "justified true belief" than knowledge that can be verified. In this regard "actual knowledge" in law and "verifiability" in economics are overlapping constructs. It is fair to say that the conventional economic notion of verifiability relies wholly on knowledge that is observable or verifiable to the arbiter. The "fiduciary as contract" argument is grounded in actual knowledge. Judges must be able to observe or verify the realized state of things in order to hypothesize about what the parties would have wanted for themselves. Judges must also be able to observe

[32] Relevant factors that may determine whether the state of the world ought to be characterized as "bad" or "good" (from the perspective of the principal and agent) might include whether lax or stringent regulations are passed, whether there is a bull market or a bear market, strong or weak consumer demand, whether an accident has occurred or not, and so on.

[33] In extreme, though hardly fanciful, cases even the outcome, x, is not verifiable, making gap-filling and interim bargains based on outcomes vacuous.

or verify the terms of interim (actual) bargains if those agreements are to be enforced. Actual knowledge is required for all economic contractarian models because without it, economists will say, a court would not know the terms of the agreements it is asked to enforce.

Knowledge established by legal duties adds something distinctive to the basic contractarian approach. Even if a court is unable to verify the actual knowledge of a party, a legal obligation to know something is enough for the court to treat a party *as if* she knew that thing. Knowledge created by a "duty to know" is common to fiduciaries. Directors have a duty to keep abreast of the business environment of the corporate boards on which they sit. Guardians have a duty to remain informed about the welfare of their wards. Agents are obliged to know certain facts in order to satisfy their duty of care.[34] Agents also have a "duty to inquire" (for example, inquiries directed to subagents are normally required) and they are often treated as knowing that which would have followed from satisfying their inquiry duties. Additional "duties to know" may derive from a fiduciary's expertise and special training, but it seldom ends there. A duty to know may also come out of the particular circumstances faced by fiduciaries and their beneficiaries.

Circumstances also give rise to circumstantial knowledge, which is distinct from knowledge that one "actually possesses" in law or is obliged to have (eg, knowledge based on a strict duty to know or inquire). Persons of ordinary intelligence are held to know that which they "should have known" given the circumstances. As ordinary legal actors fiduciaries are subject to this common standard of knowledge. Moreover, a fiduciary's heightened experience and expertise will often expand the scope of his or her presumed knowledge under the "should have known" standard. Additionally, knowledge based on a fiduciary's skill and experience is usually incorporated in setting the standard for other duties, such as the duties of care and loyalty.[35] A fiduciary will also be held to know that which she "had reason to know" based on what a reasonable person in her situation would have known.[36] As usual, the reasonable person standard may be implemented in a more

[34] Agents also have a duty to share those facts with principals, just as principals have duties to share certain information with agents. "An agent has a duty to use reasonable effort to provide the principal with facts that the agent knows, has reason to know, or should know when. . . the agent knows or has reason to know that the principal would wish to have the facts or the facts are material to the agent's duties to the principal.. . ." *Restatement (Third) of Agency* § 8.11."A principal has a duty to deal with the agent fairly and in good faith, including a duty to provide the agent with information about risks of physical harm or pecuniary loss that the principal knows, has reason to know, or should know are present in the agent's work but unknown to the agent." *Restatement (Third) of Agency* § 8.15.

[35] See, eg, *Restatement (Third) of Agency* § 8.08 ("Special skills or knowledge possessed by an agent are circumstances to be taken into account in determining whether the agent acted with due care and diligence.")

[36] In some cases the "reason to know" and "should have known" standards are conflated and in other cases distinctions are drawn between them. It is better to characterize them differently, though not much is made of that difference here. An example characterizing the "reason to know" standard is found in the US tax code's treatment of prohibited transactions. The Code stipulates that an entity's fiduciary or manager "will be considered to have 'reason to know' if a reasonable person in the entity manager's circumstances would conclude that the transaction was a prohibited tax shelter transaction based on all the facts reasonably available to the manager at the time of approving the entity as (or otherwise causing the entity to be) a party to the transaction." The Code then goes on to describe various factors to consider for determining if a reasonable person in the fiduciary's position would have reason to know a transaction was prohibited, including disclosures received by the fiduciary and "[w]hether the entity manager made appropriate inquiries into the transaction." 26 CFR 53.4965–6(b) (determining whether an entity manager knew or had reason to know).

or less subjective manner by focusing on, or abstracting away from, what similarly situated fiduciaries would be imagined to know given the particular context. As the standard becomes more objective it approaches the fourth means of establishing knowledge in law.

The fourth category, involving fictions, presumptions, estoppel, and so on, is a capacious one with many applications in the law concerning fiduciaries. Legal construction here operates significantly to manage reliance on what the parties to the fiduciary interaction believe about the knowledge of each other. Constructive knowledge in this vein tends to discourage exploitive coalitions and unjust, even if unintended, arbitrage between fiduciaries and beneficiaries that occur at the expense of third parties. For example, the agency law rule presuming that the principal knows what the agent knows—eg, "[n]otice of a fact that an agent knows or has reason to know is imputed to the principal," and "notification given to or by an agent is effective as notice to or by the principal"[37]—protects third parties from negligent or scheming principals. Willful ignorance for unfair advantage is also circumvented by rules calling on agents to disclose relevant facts.[38] Fiduciary law also dissuades exploitive coalitions between agents and third parties by imposing duties of confidence over information concerning principals.[39]

An information focus on fiduciary relations reveals features of legal doctrine that are obscured in the contractarian approach, which relies on verifiable knowledge. Verifiable knowledge as such is just one route to knowledge in law. Law can and often does create the knowledge it needs, particularly in the context of managing fiduciary relations. One could, of course, claim that the legal doctrines used to construct knowledge in the fiduciary context are majoritarian contract default rules—ie, the information-based legal rules described above are simply what most parties would have stipulated had their agreement been more complete. Claims of this sort ring of tautology. Whatever "is," is what the parties would have wanted. Where is the analytical value of a claim with a scope so broad and elastic? In any event, as mentioned previously, the information orientation to fiduciary law is not meant to deny the contractarian model. The objective here is to highlight distinctive features of fiduciary law that seem somewhat lost in conventional approaches.

III. Knowledge and the Information Fiduciary

Fiduciaries tend to acquire special knowledge about their beneficiaries. Oftentimes even more knowledge, in some respects, than beneficiaries possess about themselves. In addition to knowing their beneficiaries' personal and otherwise private information,

[37] *Restatement (Third) of Agency* § 1.04; see also §§ 5.01–5.04.

[38] Although *Restatement (Third) of Agency* § 8.08 speaks of disclosure of those facts "the principal would wish to have," other rules, such as those involving candor, make disclosure less discretionary. Failure to disclose by the agents often offers little protection to principals. For instance, the knowledge or *mens rea* requirement for tortious acts of an agent is transferable in many cases to the principal, as if she had committed the harm herself. "A principal is subject to direct liability to a third party harmed by an agent's conduct when (a) as stated in § 7.04, the agent acts with actual authority or the principal ratifies the agent's conduct and. . . (ii) the agent's conduct, if that of the principal, would subject the principal to tort liability." *Restatement (Third) of Agency* § 7.03 (1)(a)(ii).

[39] *Restatement (Third) of Agency* § 8.05.

fiduciaries normally have or should have superior knowledge concerning the external circumstances to which this knowledge may be put to use in the context of their relationship as well as beyond. As discussed above, there are a number of specific legal rules that promote and regulate the acquisition, possession, sharing, and exploitation of such knowledge within the fiduciary context. But not all parties who possess personal, and otherwise private, information concerning others are fiduciaries. Additionally, someone who is a fiduciary in one context may acquire special knowledge concerning a beneficiary in other contexts, where duties of candor, confidentiality, disclosure, and so on are less well defined or are not currently legally binding. This section briefly considers how the usual rules applicable to fiduciaries might extend to these actors and contexts.[40]

As a point of departure note that there are extant legal rules regulating the possession, sharing, and disclosure of knowledge concerning others in non-fiduciary contexts. Beyond the obvious criminal prohibitions on blackmail and other illegal uses of information, ample bases for regulating the use of knowledge concerning others may be found in ordinary common law doctrine and statutes. For example, a party may have a common law obligation to share information in order to correct a mistaken belief held by a counterparty. Confidence relationships, short of strict fiduciary relations, will also trigger some knowledge-based duties. Securities law and various environmental and consumer statutes also mandate disclosure in certain trading and exchange encounters. These rules show that there is no question of whether law has a role to play managing the dispersed bits of knowledge that parties have concerning others. Of course there is a role for law. The interesting question here is whether the fiduciary approach should be exported or expanded to broader domains, and whether doing so would reveal anything distinctive about fiduciary law—the question that led off this chapter.

Judge Benjamin Cardozo's famous opinion in *Meinhard v Salmon* may be seen as a weigh station along the road to a doctrine of information fiduciaries. The facts of the case are straightforward. Near the end of a joint venture involving a 20-year hotel lease and improvement agreement—where the property and its improvements were largely managed by Salmon, while his off-site joint-venturer, Meinhard, mainly supplied capital in return for roughly half of the profits—the property owner, Gerry, offered Salmon a significant extension and expansion of the lease. Without sharing knowledge of the offer with Meinhard, the on-site Salmon, the man on the spot, pursued the new lease alone. Salmon possessed knowledge of the offer, but it was not his exclusively, argued Cardozo; the information, because of the circumstances through which he came to acquire it, belonged to the joint venture, the dyad, or at least Salmon was obliged to share it with his joint-venturer.[41] Salmon was neither Meinhard's agent nor partner. His fiduciary duty to disclose was derived elsewhere, from his status as co-venturer and his position of unique access to information. Judge Andrews, in his dissenting opinion, argued that the co-venturer's duty of disclosure was not triggered in this case. But

[40] I am grateful to Franklin Ard for his generous and insightful comments in our discussions of information fiduciaries.

[41] Partnership and joint venture opportunity doctrines are clearly relevant here, but I hesitate to conflate ownership of opportunities with access to information. Salmon didn't have to share the opportunity with Meinhard (although Cardozo hints otherwise); rather he had to share the information about the offered opportunity.

looking beyond Salmon's status alone, Cardozo emphasized the context in which the information was acquired. "The very fact that Salmon was in control with exclusive powers of direction," wrote Judge Cardozo, "charged him the more obviously with the duty of disclosure."[42] Whatever his status and obligations to Meinhard in other respects, Salmon's knowledge of the offer made him a fiduciary in one respect: he became an "information fiduciary" by the circumstances through which he was informed.

Salmon and Meinhard were co-venturers. Holding Salmon liable for breach of a duty to disclose followed naturally from his fiduciary obligation as a co-venturer, as Cardozo emphasized with great flair. But could someone without any prior fiduciary obligation become subject to duties of confidence, disclosure, and the like, merely as a consequence of whether and how she comes to possess some knowledge? Yes, of course, is the answer. The US law of insider trading has evolved to recognize an acquisition of duty concerning non-public information. When an "insider" wrongly tips an outsider (or "tippee"), the tippee acquires the insider's fiduciary duty concerning disclosure and trading on that information.[43] In this case there is a prior fiduciary duty resting with the insider. That duty is simply transferred to the tippee when wrongfully informed by the insider. Insider trading analysis has struggled with cases where the outsider was not wrongly tipped, but came upon the non-public information through some other means.[44] To patch this gap, a more general theory of misappropriation has evolved to regulate the exploitation of another's otherwise private information.[45] Beyond securities law, one might imagine a general approach utilizing principles of fiduciary law to regulate actors who come in possession of otherwise private information across various contexts. These actors would be treated as information fiduciaries.

What is an information fiduciary? An early and interesting suggestion was offered by Kenneth Laudon in 1996, when he proposed the establishment of information markets among other market-based mechanisms for managing privacy concerns in the then-upcoming millennium. Laudon argued that "[b]ecause most people would not have the time or interest to participate directly in information markets, a role would emerge for information fiduciaries, or agents acting on their behalf who assume certain legal responsibilities."[46] He envisioned that beneficiaries would hand over their information to agents for management. "Like banks, they [the information fiduciaries] would accept deposits of information from depositors and seek to maximize the return on sales of that information."[47] Laudon's vision presumes a kind of possession or control of information by those who would "deposit" it with their agents, which does not quite capture contemporary privacy concerns involving scores of actors, private and

[42] *Meinhard* 164 NE at 547. Which is not to say that disclosure alone would have satisfied Cardozo: "Joint adventurers, like copartners, owe to one another, while the enterprise continues, the duty of the finest loyalty.... *Not honesty alone*, but the punctilio of an honor the most sensitive, is then the standard of behavior." *Meinhard* at 546 (emphasis added).

[43] *Dirks v SEC* 463 US 646 (1983).

[44] *Chiarella v United States* 445 US 222 (1980).

[45] See eg, *United States v O'Hagan* 521 US 642 (1997). Yet even with the misappropriation doctrine, ambiguous cases remain, such as those involving accidental or innocent acquisition of information. See, eg, *SEC v Switzer* 590 F Supp 756 (1984).

[46] Kenneth C Laudon, "Markets and Privacy," Communication of the ACM, vol 39, no 2, September 1996 (p 101).

[47] Laudon (n 46).

public, managing and manipulating the personal information of others without assuming any obvious legal responsibilities. Hence, rather than looking at the market to bring forth proactive information fiduciaries, Neil Richards has more recently discussed the idea of an information fiduciary in a more defensive stance. "Just as we do not rely merely on market forces and goodwill to mandate confidentiality from our lawyers or librarians, so too should information fiduciaries like search engines and online bookstores be subject to meaningful requirements of confidentiality to safeguard the vitally important interests at stake."[48] Richards would apply the duties of lawyers, librarians, and other traditional agents who handle our personal information to new and novel handlers of such data, like search engines and ISPs.[49]

A fully developed model of the concept of an information fiduciary would incorporate both the affirmative and negative duties suggested by Laudon and Richards. Fiduciaries, as we have seen, have not only duties of confidentiality and disclosure, but also duties to inquire, to inform, to speak with candor and other knowledge-based obligations and presumptions. The entire framework of knowledge in the fiduciary context would potentially apply to the information fiduciary. The difficult task would be to determine what makes one an information fiduciary as opposed to a mere possessor of information in one's own right. Knowing some otherwise private or personal information about another individual could not be sufficient to convert someone into a fiduciary. Only when someone possesses information pertinent to another while in a relation of trust or confidence with that other, could duties with respect to that knowledge arise, causing the information possessor to be treated as a fiduciary. In other words, the information must be connected to a relationship in an appropriate way.

Information is often produced by or in virtue of a relationship. Those so informed may be deemed to hold that information as a fiduciary even absent any contractual duty or other legal relation. Take, for instance, the recent scandal concerning the ubiquitous Bloomberg terminal cluttering desks of financial brokers worldwide. When workers at companies like Goldman Sachs and JP Morgan logged in and out of their terminals *that* information was observed and recorded by Bloomberg LP. Reporters in the news media division of Bloomberg LP then exploited this information to track the comings and goings of financial executives and inform their reporting to the great advantage of the news division.[50] One could argue that the reporters became information fiduciaries when they acquired knowledge about the financial executives on whom they were reporting based on a relationship of trust and confidence that the executives had with Bloomberg LP. The reporters were not fiduciaries to the financial executives per se, they

[48] Neil M Richards, "Intellectual Privacy," 87 *Texas L Rev* 387 at 436 (2008).

[49] "Just as we have recognized in the past that certain professionals were fiduciaries of our information, so too in the Age of Information should we expand our definition to include bookstores, search engines, ISPs and providers of physical and streamed video." Neil M Richards, "The Perils of Social Reading," 101 *Georgetown LJ* 689 at 724 (2013).

[50] It is said that Bloomberg reporters scooped the competition on a number of important stories as a consequence of this advantage. See Tracy Alloway, Andrew Edgecliffe-Johnson, and Robin Harding, "Banks and Regulators Question Access to Bloomberg User Data," *Financial Times*, 12 May 2013; Amy Chozick, "Bloomberg Admits Terminal Snooping," *New York Times*, 13 May 2013.

simply acquired certain duties with respect to the knowledge they gained as a consequence of the relationship between the executives and Bloomberg LP.[51] It is unclear how far this particular approach to information fiduciaries will be taken and further developed. Bloomberg and the financial companies seem to have settled the matter privately. There is, however, little doubt that the application of fiduciary principles to such contexts will continue to grow and acquire salience as commentators and legal officials borrow doctrine from fiduciary law to regulate the possession and sharing of knowledge in our increasingly information-dense world.

Conclusion

All of this is to suggest that not only is a knowledge orientation to fiduciary law important for understanding its doctrines and past practices, but this orientation will be central to understanding the legal management of information going forward. While patents, trademarks, copyrights, and general law of intellectual property can structure the ownership and distribution of patentable objects and the like, the management of relational knowledge (which is expanding faster than patentable objects and the like) will turn to fiduciary law. A legal and economic understanding of knowledge is essential to appreciating fiduciary law and relations. The legal construction of knowledge provides a number of valuable insights into the operation of fiduciary law. The economic approach to knowledge is also revealing in its focus on the nature (not the fiction) of information in relational contexts. While a legal presumption can establish that something is known between a principal and agent, the law saying so does not make it common knowledge or observable between them. Relational knowledge in the fiduciary context is key to the economic logic and the law supporting these relationships.

[51] There is an analogous situation in insider trading, concerning the constructive insider. For example, when a company hires a law firm to represent it, the lawyers at the law firms (even those ones who are not assigned to the matter concerning the hiring company) become constructive insiders of the company and are subject to the same trading rules as the company's fiduciaries. See dicta in *United States v O'Hagan* 521 US 642 (1997).

12

Watering Down Fiduciary Duties

*Tamar Frankel**

Introduction

> Society is a chaotic system. It is interactive and changing. So are the rights we have to and from each other. However, rights and other legal meanings continue to be meaningful because we can continue to recall and reflect on the experience that gave them birth. That is what it means to be human and rational. And that is the way in which law contributes to social structure and institutionalism of social meaning and change.[1]

> The luminaries at the World Economic Forum in Davos have spent a fair amount of their time worrying about restoring trust in business, partly through demonstrating that they are responsible corporate citizens. But it is a curiosity that some of the people in and around business who are most passionate about corporate responsibility also seem to be the most blind to the impediments which can prevent companies doing the "right" things. Some believe implicitly in the "business case" and like to pretend that pursuing responsibility will always pay off financially, even if only in the long term. Others take the moral high ground and suggest that businesses which sign up to the "right" values will become both saintly and rich. Both positions are valid, but only up to a point, as the realities of business life testify.... Many companies can profit by being more responsible. But there are also plenty of occasions when the responsibility and financial equations are not simultaneous.[2]

Legal rights and their meanings are not carved in granite, especially when different parties have different abilities, interests, and goals, striving to reach conflicting legal results. Even the intellectual or personal vision of the ideal society is not shared by all. While few individuals can separate society's needs and desires from their own, some can reverse the emphasis, and envision their own needs and desires as those of the ideal society.

Vagueness may be viewed as the starting point[3] and perhaps as ruling our world. Timing is crucial as well. Adding one grain of sand to another can make a heap, where none existed before. The grain of sand can be used to clarify and reduce confusion and determine where we put the next step to be able to walk.[4] Similarly, "[i]f you

* My thanks to the commentators at the round table discussion at DePaul University College of Law and Andrew Gold and Paul Miller for their suggestions and editing. Many thanks to my colleagues at Boston University Law School, for their comments at the Law School Faculty Workshop presentation, and especially to my colleague Professor David Seipp for his thoughtful and informed suggestions.

[1] Steven L Winter, "Transcendental Nonsense, Metaphoric Reasoning, and the Cognitive Stakes for Law," 137 *U Pa L Rev* 1227 (1989).

[2] Roger Cowe, "When Outrageous Optimism Meets Business Blindness: CSR Visionaries Also Need to Face Reality, says Roger Cowe Especially the Financial Kind," *The Observer*, 2 Feb 2003, Special Supplement, 6 ("What is the moral position, for example, on the highly polluting 4×4s which make huge profits for car makers such as Ford and General Motors while adding to global warming? Or on low-cost, short-haul flights by the likes of EasyJet, which do even more damage to the atmosphere? Or on opening a new superstore which will damage existing small businesses and possibly destroy a town centre?").

[3] Timothy Williamson, *Vagueness* (1996) 249. [4] Williamson (n 3).

keep removing single grains of sand from a heap," then at some point, it no longer remains a heap.[5] It will disappear. More importantly, small changes can be unobserved. Consistently made small changes can become significant yet be unobserved as well. As we get used to them without considering where they are leading to, undoing these large changes will be harder and take longer.

A number of legal arguments can help fiduciaries water down and loosen the strictness of their fiduciary duties, while extending their own benefits from the relationship. These legal arguments help attorneys defend fiduciary clients that have crossed the hard borders of strict fiduciary duties or who seek prior justifications for so doing. A foundational theory, on which arguments for watering down fiduciary duties are based, can be that less law is more profitable for society and beneficial for its members. Expressions can create impressions of trustworthiness, yet lead to reduced legal fiduciary duties and increase fiduciaries' discretion and freedom from duties and liabilities.

Similarly, fiduciaries may expand the variance of their entrusted powers and muddy their precise duties. The purpose of for-profit corporations may be enhanced by broader socially desirable and honorable purposes, be it donations to educational institutions, the purchase of Liberty Bonds in times of a nation's wars, or the use of funds to promote national policies, always for the fiduciaries' benefit. Although the entrustors will have no protection by "voice" they can "exit" by terminating and escape the relationship. This, after all, may be a sufficient protection rather than having small-stake investors dictate their views to the crowd.

This chapter outlines three legal and behavioral approaches and arguments that may reduce the number of fiduciaries under the law, and diffuse the strictness of their duties. It analyzes the sources of these approaches and highlights their justifications and virtues. In each case the discussion evaluates the legitimacy of these interpretations, noting their possible consequences for the parties and for society.

Section I focuses on two legal interpretations or arguments that can reduce the number of fiduciaries and diffuse the strictness of fiduciaries' duties: The first interpretation classifies fiduciary law as a species of contract (coupled with default rules), applying contract concepts, rules, and remedies to fiduciary relationships. That is, even though the balance of power between the two parties is fundamentally different. The second interpretation that would water down fiduciary duties is to concede that fiduciaries are indeed somewhat different from contract parties, but assert that the duties of loyalty, imposed on fiduciaries, require them to act in the "*best* interests" of their beneficiaries rather than in the "*sole* interests" of their beneficiaries. The result of this change is to convert the fiduciaries' duty of loyalty to a duty of care. Yet supporters would claim that trusted persons would not abuse their entrusted power.

Section II considers the watering down of fiduciary duties by reclassifying fiduciaries, within the fiduciary family. For example, this approach moves trustees, and advisers, subject to strict rules, into the category of agents, subject to fewer and lighter rules.

Section III assesses the use of concepts, expressions, and words derived from other disciplines which help "muddy the waters." That is because the focus of other disciplines may be entirely alien to the purpose of the law. A related form of the move to

[5] Williamson (n 3) at first page before the preface.

other disciplines is to "commodify fiduciary services." Viewing fiduciary services as assets presumably helps buyers to evaluate these "assets" more easily, and with such ease of evaluation come reduced fiduciary duties. A "market in fiduciary services" rubs shoulders with a market for shoes and suggests the same or similar treatment for the transactions and their "market environment." Yet, supporters would claim that trusted persons would not abuse their power.

All three approaches reflect attempts at taking smaller or bigger "bites" out of fiduciary law. They do so by reducing the variety of fiduciaries, and their duties, removing or obliterating the more restrictive and burdensome duties and liabilities, and loosening up the rules of fiduciary law. The approaches seem to seek strict clear limits or, alternatively, introduce ambiguities into current rules. The following discussion demonstrates how these approaches are introduced and justified, and where their "softened areas" of fiduciary law are. These methods are not illegal. Violations of the watered down duties may be accompanied by harsher punishments. Whether a balance of watered down duties, even if accompanied by more painful punishments for their breach, is socially desirable and ethically justified, is another matter.

I. Doctrines that Help Water Down Fiduciary Duties

A. Fiduciary relationships are contracts; fiduciary duties are contract duties

To water down fiduciary duties one might argue that, legally, fiduciary relationships are contracts, and that this classification is reasonable. After all, fiduciary relationships require the consent of at least some of the involved parties. The relationship is voluntary. A trustor freely hands over to a trustee property to be managed by the trustee, and the trustee agrees to perform its services in accordance with the trust instrument.[6] The principal and the agent freely agree on their relationship. Is not consent by both parties a contract?

To be sure, the law imposes added rules and duties on fiduciaries. Otherwise, no trustor is likely to offer property to a fiduciary in trust and the principal is not likely to hire an agent whom he cannot fully control. Yet the offer of property by trustor and power to the agent are essential because these fiduciaries cannot perform their services without the transfer of property or power; the trustor and principal cannot control the fiduciaries' use of the property and power without undermining the very utility of the relationship.

But, this situation does not exclude fiduciary relationships from the contract category. There are additional rules, prohibiting fiduciaries from misappropriating power and assets that they hold, but which do not belong to them. However, these additional rules are *default* rules. They are like "form contracts" drawn for efficiency purposes, to reduce the costs of the parties and induce them to interact. Are not such "form

[6] Austin Wakeman Scott et al, *Scott and Ascher on Trusts* (2006–7) vol 1, 175 (trust requires manifestation of intent to create trust); vol 2 at 636 (after valid conveyance of property in trust, trust is created, but "transferee... cannot be compelled to perform unless and until he or she accepts the trust").

contracts," which are impliedly adopted by the parties, contracts? One might further argue that *every interaction among any party with another party constitutes a contract.*

Indeed, one aspect of fiduciary relationships could, but need not, constitute a contract. With few exceptions trustees and other fiduciaries *agree* to serve. In fact, in almost all cases no fiduciary duties can be imposed on anyone without his or her or its consent to serve as fiduciary. In many cases, this consent is demonstrated and recognized by an exchange of the service for payment or another form of consideration. However, this part of the relationship can be, and perhaps should be, severed from the other part of the fiduciary relationship. Yet the focus of fiduciary law is not on the payment but on the fiduciaries' *duties*, and in that terrain the differences between contract and fiduciary relationships are glaring.

The proponents of fiduciary law as contract law do not suggest that fiduciary relationships fall fully into the contract category. They emphasize that contract *law should apply to fiduciary relationships so long as not only the express conditions but also the default rule provisions apply.* These default rules are in fact fiduciary law duties. Yet, the default rules are subject to the parties' contract provisions. They can be erased by the agreement among the contract parties. In fact, it is not unusual for entrustors to waive protective default rules to the utmost limit of contract law. That is even though the default rules impose future duties under circumstances that the parties cannot predict. No wonder that fiduciaries may be willing to "buy" their freedom from unknown duties and liabilities by charging less for their services.

In fact, there are cases in which even at the service contract point, the similarity between fiduciary law and contract law vanishes. First, unlike a contract, a trust relationship may, but need not, involve two parties.[7] A trust can be established for the benefit of a cat or a dog[8] or an unborn child.[9] The rights under the trust belong to the beneficiary; not to the trustor, who handed over the assets and negotiated the trust agreement.[10] It is doubtful whether, after the trust is established, a trustor could agree with the trustee to change the terms of the entrustment.[11] The rights under the trust belong to the beneficiaries, even though they are not parties to the trust document. Further, beneficiaries may not agree to changes in the trust document either. They may agree to waive their rights under the document but not to amend the document. They may agree not to sue the trustee on violation of the document's directives, but not to amend the document.

To be sure, contract law recognizes third-party beneficiaries under a contract.[12] However, the parties to the contract remain the dominant parties. Furthermore,

[7] Scott et al (n 6) vol 1 at 265 (trust does not require notice to beneficiaries nor their acceptance of their beneficial interests).

[8] Scott et al (n 6) vol 2 at 754–5 (trust may be created for specifically identified animals).

[9] Scott et al (n 6) vol 2 at 698 (trust may be created for unborn beneficiaries).

[10] Scott et al (n 6) vol 3 at 808 (beneficiary has property interest in subject matter of trust); Scott et al (n 6) vol 4 at 671 ("Unless the settlor has retained an interest in the trust property, the trustee owes its duties not to the settlor but to the beneficiaries").

[11] Scott et al (n 6) vol 1 at 48 (terms of trust "depend on the manifestation of the settlor's intention at the time of the creation of the trust, not on the settlor's subsequent intentions;" subsequent directions not ordinarily admissible to vary terms unless settlor retained power to modify or revoke trust).

[12] *Restatement (Second) of Contracts* (1981), § 304 (recognizing duty to intended beneficiary).

third-party beneficiaries are vested with very weak rights. And while in a trust relationship each of the parties—the trustee and beneficiaries—may seek judicial release and confirmation of activities, neither the parties to the contract nor the third-party beneficiaries may, or need to, seek the court's counsel, advice, or approval of any changes they make in their relationship. This aspect of contract law constitutes a fundamental contrast to fiduciary trust law.

Second, fiduciary relationships must be accompanied by directives that limit the freedom of the fiduciary to do things with the entrusted assets or power. Suppose the entrustor hands over to the trustee money and says: "Do with this money whatever you think is the right thing." In such an arrangement no fiduciary relationship was created. It seems that a fundamental element of a fiduciary relationship is the imposition on the fiduciary of conditions on how to use the money or power entrusted to him. The absence of these conditions converts a possible fiduciary relationship into a gift. Transfer of power or property without strings attached does not involve fiduciary relationships.

Third, under traditional fiduciary law, fiduciaries, including trustees, are bound by legal fiduciary duties, even though they are neither paid nor receive consideration of any kind. Unlike the requirement of an exchange and consideration in contract law, fiduciary law does not require consideration with respect to entrusted power and property. In fact, fiduciaries are entitled to payment only under a binding contract, or under the provisions of a law.[13] Otherwise, they must carry on their duties unpaid.

Fourth, in contrast to contract law, the remedies against fiduciaries that violated their trust or behaved in contrast to fiduciary duties are not only damages. The remedies signify that entrustment to a fiduciary of power and property does not constitute an exchange. It signifies that the fiduciary does not own the entrusted property or the power, and that the trustee's ownership is to be used solely to perform services for the entrustor. Fiduciary law imposes harsh penalties on fiduciaries that use entrusted assets for their own benefit, or act in conflict of interest (for the benefit of others including themselves).

The penalties imposed on such fiduciaries may include punitive damages,[14] injunction,[15] and specific performance.[16] Some breaches of fiduciary duties, such as misappropriation of entrusted property, may lead to a recognition of a crime—embezzlement.[17] Most of these remedies do not exist under contract law, and others are far less common in contract law.[18] The remedies for breach of fiduciary duties are derived from

[13] Scott et al (n 6) vol 4 at 1589–90 (under traditional rule, trustee not entitled to compensation unless terms of trust so provided). However, most states now have statutes that provide for trustee compensation; in others, courts have held that trustees are entitled to reasonable compensation: Scott et al (n 6) vol 4 at 1590.

[14] Scott et al (n 6) vol 4 at 1694–5 (although "courts have traditionally been hesitant to impose punitive damages," they are now "increasingly willing to do so, at least when the trustee's conduct is especially egregious").

[15] Scott et al (n 6) vol 4 at 1665 (beneficiary may sue for injunction if "reasonable likelihood" of breach of trust, whether or not there is adequate remedy at law).

[16] Scott et al (n 6) vol 4 at 1664–5 (beneficiary may sue for specific performance, even if it has remedy at law).

[17] Wayne R LaFave, *Criminal Law* (5th edn, 2010) § 19.6, 995–1006.

[18] *Restatement (Second) of Contracts* § 359(1) ("Specific performance or an injunction will not be ordered if damages would be adequate to protect the expectation interest of the injured party"); *Restatement (Second) of Contracts* § 355 ("Punitive damages are not recoverable for a breach of contract unless the conduct constituting the breach is also a tort for which punitive damages are recoverable"); *Restatement (Second) of*

the principle that entrusted property and power do not belong to the fiduciary except, and only, for the purpose of performing its services. The property and powers are not intended to belong to the fiduciary, and never did. Thus, the relationship among the parties does not constitute an exchange, which is the basis of contract law. To be sure, the fiduciary receives the legal ownership of entrusted property. But the purpose of that transfer of ownership, as mentioned, is to enable the fiduciary to perform its services; no more and no less.

Fifth, under contract law there is an assumption that each of the parties' interests conflicts with the interests of the other, although their contract benefits both. Much of contract law is based on the premise that each party must be able to protect its interests from the conflicting interests of the other and bargain to enhance its own interests. Therefore, contract remedies involve situations in which one party has made its bargain under the inducement of fraud, or of mistakes that are not easily discoverable, or mistakes affected by truly "black swans"—unanticipated events. Contract law protection is granted to a party that has entered into the relationship under undue influence that renders it incapable of asserting and protecting its interests. Protection is offered to a party that lacked capacity to enter into the relationship in other ways, such as being a minor. Once the parties' ability to advance and protect their interests has not been disproved, it will be assumed and the courts will enforce the substance of the contracts: "the parties made their bed and must sleep in it." Contract law provides remedies for the party that was incapable of advancing and protecting its interests. The remedies are mostly proven damages resulting from a breach of the other party's obligations.

Sixth, characterizing fiduciary relationships as contract renders irrelevant the main focus of fiduciary law: the *relative power relationship among the parties*. Underlying fiduciary law is the assumption that the entrustor cannot protect itself *against the abuse of the entrusted fiduciary's power or property*. This inability to protect one's interests is not necessarily based on the lack of the entrustors' expertise, although in many cases it is. The entrustor's weak position is inherent in the relationship, based on the recognition that supervising the fiduciary would undermine the very usefulness of the relationship. An agent that cannot be supervised must be entrusted and trusted by the principal. A trustee must be trusted by the beneficiaries. And a board of directors as well as partners must be trusted by the investors and the other partners. A requirement that the entrustors police the fiduciaries makes the relationship worthless.

Furthermore, it is recognized that fiduciary relationships strengthen the reliance of society's members on each other. These relationships are crucial to the welfare of the society and its members. In contrast, the view of contracting parties is that each party can and should protect its interests. Society would benefit if they take care of themselves and their own interests. Thus, contract and fiduciary relationships are fundamentally different.

Using the word "contract," entices fiduciaries to view their entrusted power as their own, and their legal ownership as including beneficial ownership. They may feel free to enjoy entrusted power and property, subject to constraints, which the entrustors

Contracts §355, cmt a ("In exceptional instances, departures have been made from this general policy"; states have provided for such damages by statute in some situations).

may agree to waive (sometimes unknowingly by signing on the dotted line). Such breach of trust undermines the social good. With time, the existence of the true owners fades. Fiduciaries may acquire a self-view as owners—a slippery slope to a misguided self-perception. This is the true result of reclassifying fiduciary relationships into contract. The power position, even though a hollow one, is overwhelming. If the fiduciary has not only the power but also the legal ownership and rights with respect to entrusted property (subject to contract terms that can be changed), then why should a fiduciary not use and enjoy it? If the use might be later challenged or even involve damage payments—so be it.

Seventh, the view of fiduciary relationships as contracts bestows on fiduciaries an image of true owners and leaves this same impression on those who deal with them. No one addresses the investors of a corporation for corporate work (except controlling investors). The applicant will seek the Human Relations Department or the corporate CEO. No one would offer investments to the beneficiaries of a trust. An offer of investment would be addressed to the trustee. Thus, by definition a fiduciary is both endowed with and exercises power and is *viewed by outsiders* as the owner. After all, the beneficiaries cannot agree or disagree with the particular transactions. The fiduciary can. Thus, a fiduciary's power is both to deal with others on behalf of the entrustors and to be the principal in representing them to everyone else on their behalf. Anyone who wishes to speak to the owner, whether seeking benefits, offering advice, or proposing a deal, would approach the fiduciary rather than the beneficial owner. It is the fiduciary to whom you go! Therefore, treated like the owner, a fiduciary may acquire the feeling of an *owner*. With this feeling comes the arrogance of power!

The argument that fiduciary relationships are contracts weakens fiduciary duties. The prohibitions limiting fiduciaries' freedom to act are now part of fiduciary law, consisting of actual rules. These prohibitions are likely to be more observed when embodied in *rules of law* than if they were inserted in *contracts* and will be even more watered down when the rules are classified as *default rules which are subject to watering down by the parties' consent*. In his latest book, *Thinking, Fast and Slow*, Daniel Kahneman notes that the operation of associative memory contributes to a general *confirmation bias*. Calling fiduciary relationships contracts affects people's view of fiduciary relationships, rather than the reverse.[19] There are a number of reasons for this conclusion.

The word "contract" is more commonly understood than the name "fiduciary" or even "trustee." *Default rules* are *less deeply impressed* in the actors' minds, especially if the rules are limited by added contract terms. Therefore, to be effective, a rule, without "ifs" and "buts" is needed to prohibit fiduciaries from acting in conflict of interest. In fact, *contract, as the name of the relationship*, colors decisively the entire relationship, including the *default rules* that hover over it.[20]

[19] Daniel Kahneman, *Thinking, Fast and Slow* (2011) ch 7 and especially 81–2 (describing how the confirmatory bias of the system 1 mode of thinking "favors uncritical acceptance of suggestions and exaggeration of the likelihood of extreme and improbable events"). In addition, what is more used and familiar is likely to be more easily accepted.

[20] Cf Kahneman (n 19). As an example of confirmation bias, Kahneman helpfully describes his early experiences grading exams. He found that the grade given to the first question he graded had an influence on an exam's overall grade. Kahneman (n 19) 82–3.

Further, the contract-fiduciary mix confuses the problems that the relationship poses. In a recent case a broker sold obligations to a large bank that he knew were prepared to stack against the buyer. The broker argued that the buyer was sophisticated. Therefore he, the broker, had no duty to offer the buyer information or explanation. Yet, even this type of buyer would have found it difficult to uncover the true facts.[21] The jury rejected the broker's defense and found him liable. Even contract may have a sliver of liability for fraud attached, although some brokers may disagree.

Besides, under certain conditions, even contract law sways towards fiduciary relationships' influence. If inducement to trade is too confusing or misleading, or wrapped in untrue facts, contract law might interfere to protect a buyer. When a bank induced clients to buy a large currency swap, the transaction was classified as a contract. However, when the bank salesman sold the buyer another swap with full knowledge that the buyer of the first swap was definitely going to lose, the parties settled, and the buyer was forgiven most of the amount claimed by the bank under the contract.[22] That is even though the information about the potential loss was available. Thus, there is a point where contract law rubs shoulders with fiduciary law.

Even though the two relationships have consent and agreement in common, the law focuses on the entrustors' need for protection in different ways.[23] I submit that unless there is a modicum of truth and trustworthiness, trading and services that require trust will shrink. In the name of freedom—for fiduciaries and for their trusting (and gullible) entrustors—as well as for the benefits to society, there are arguments for limiting the interference of fiduciary law. The first step is not to eliminate fiduciary law altogether but to exalt contract (and default contract terms). Contract will change the balance of power between entrustors and fiduciaries. It will restrain fiduciary law and its regulators from interfering in the relationship.

B. Change the duty of loyalty from the "sole interest" to the "best interest"

To water down fiduciary duties the suggested argument is as follows: Admit that fiduciaries are indeed governed by fiduciary law. Admit that fiduciaries are subject to the duty of loyalty. However, adopt a proposal to change just *one word* relating to the fiduciaries' main duty of loyalty. A duty of loyalty in its minimal meaning is the duty to use entrusted powers and property that a fiduciary receives for the benefit of the beneficiaries ("entrustor").

[21] Justin Baer, "Tourre Verdict Could Prolong Goldman's Pain," *Wall St J*, 5 August 2013, C1.

[22] Saul Hansell, "Bankers Trust Settles Suit with P & G," *New York Times*, 10 May 1996, D1 (noting that Bankers Trust risked damages if lawsuit had gone to trial).

[23] Cf John H Langbein, "The Contractarian Basis of the Law of Trusts," 105 *Yale LJ* 625 (1995) (attempting to demonstrate the historical sources of fiduciary law as contract; and noting that in the past fiduciary relationships were classified as *status*, and in modern times as contract. Hence, the common law has inherited this history of classifying fiduciary relationships as contractual). This claim is weak. Query whether fiduciary relationships in the past were status relationships or considered contracts. The common law has not recognized the claims of the beneficiary. It was the Chancery Court that offered the beneficiary a helping hand. It was equity and not contract that provided the beneficiary a remedy. Even though we have combined equity and common law together, their history cannot be erased so easily.

The traditional duty of loyalty required that the fiduciaries act in the "sole" interest of the beneficiary. The proposed change suggests that rather than be required to act in the beneficiaries' "sole" interest, fiduciaries will be required to act in the "best" interest of their beneficiaries.[24] What difference can or should *one word* make among friends and trusted people? The answer is: A huge difference.

"Best interest" muddies the waters. It focuses on the action and care rather than on the actor and its loyalty. "Care" denotes the fiduciary's expertise, attention, and avoidance of negligence. "Loyalty" denotes complete and unconditional devotion to other than one-self. Loyalty prohibits the fiduciary from putting itself in a position of conflict with the beneficiary's interests. Instead of "best interest," the duty can also become one of "prudence," "suitability," "diversification," and other words that denote *expertise in investments*.

An expert fiduciary can be disloyal and breach the duty of loyalty. A loyal fiduciary can lack expertise and breach the duty of care. A fiduciary must act with both loyalty and expertise. Meshing the two duties together can effectively confuse and muddy the understanding of these duties. Changing the duties from "sole interest" to "best interest" undermines the very purpose of fiduciary law and clouds its clarity.

In fact, the change from "sole" to "best" converts the duty of loyalty into the duty of care. While the duty of loyalty requires a fiduciary to consider only the interests of the beneficiaries, the duty of care requires the fiduciary to perform services with attention and professional expertise. The word "best" refers to the duty of care. Omitting the word "sole" allows the fiduciary to consider the interests of others, including the fiduciary's interests as well. There is a sufficiently strong temptation, for people who hold other people's money and who have power over other people's assets, to help themselves to some of the entrusted power and money.[25] This, after all, is the temptation that fiduciary law is designed to nip in the bud. The words "best interests" soften the prohibition and open a crack in the door to self-interest.

The word "best" provides a fiduciary with an image of a partnership with the beneficiaries. What is *best* for *you* can be *best* for *me as well*. What is best for *me* can be also best for *you as well*. We are in this together. Thus, in addition to payment for services well rendered, the fiduciary may consider, among the various options given to it under its entrusted power, the option that is good for the fiduciary as well. This is a fine step but a finite step onto the slippery road to misappropriation. The moment the decision-making considers the decision-*maker's interests* the door is opened to consider many other interests as well.

Further, because the beneficiary is not present, nor able to protect its interest, a fiduciary is the only one to determine what is good for both or for the beneficiary and others. This appears in many cases of misappropriation, which started with the "best" intention to act in the "best" interest of the beneficiaries (and the fiduciary as well).[26] The argument of whether a board of directors may consider the public's good in

[24] Scott (n 6) vol 3 at 1078 (trustee must administer trust "solely" in interest of beneficiaries); *Restatement (Third) of Trusts* (2007) § 78(1) (unless otherwise provided by terms of trust, trustee must administer trust "solely" in interest of beneficiaries).

[25] Tamar Frankel, *Trust and Honesty* (2006) 52; also at 90 (noting power of controlling other people's money).

[26] Tamar Frankel, *The Ponzi Scheme Puzzle* (2012) 95.

addition to the investors' interests may lead to the use of corporate funds in the service of many objectives, including political projects that may or may not benefit the enterprise and its investors-owners.

Changing the duties from "sole benefit" to "best interest" undermines the very purpose of fiduciary law and clouds its clarity. Instead of creating a habit of a crystal-clear and rigid distinction between yours and mine it muddies the waters and creates a habit of mixing the fiduciary decision-maker's interests with those of the beneficiary. No habit is more corruptive than the one in which a trusted person bundles others' interests with the beneficiaries' interests.

An example of the problems that arise with the notion of "best" interest is the attempt to identify the interests of corporate management with those of the investors. The idea was that the corporate management should be paid in the corporation's stock, thereby creating an identity of interest between the management and the shareholders. What was not considered is that management has the power while the shareholders do not. What happens when the power can be exercised unequally? The "best interest" offered a slippery slope. Stock options may have driven the management to adopt more risky approaches. But the main test came when the shares fell, and the management, knowing the facts before the stockholders, changed the dates of the exercise of these options.[27] Similarly, it seems that management took advantage of its information regarding corporate events to sell or buy stock at advantageous prices.[28]

Organizations and their management are resisting, and fighting against, any shareholders' influence. The justifications are many: for example, investors are parasites; and that management produces most of their wealth, and is entitled to most of the wealth it creates.[29] The trustees of large trusts may have a similar view of the beneficiaries and a similar attitude. After all, they, the trustees, are the legal owners.

What may start with "best interests" may produce an argument as follows: A trustee plans to act, but is concerned about its liabilities to thousands of investors. It seeks a lawyer's advice to protect itself against liabilities to these investors. The engagement of lawyers serves the investors as well—by making sure that the trustee does not violate its duties to them. There is something perverse in this explanation. It would be different if the trustee sought advice about how best to serve the interests of the investors. But here the advice is in *its* "best" interests and the explanation is that *its* "best" interests would help avoid the actions that might enable the investors to sue it!

Another way to dilute a strict duty of loyalty can be achieved by substituting the duty of loyalty with the duty of care or burying it under the words "prudence," "suitability," "diversification," and other words that denote expertise in investments. The duty of loyalty is then meshed together with the discussion of the duty of care and obtains its color and shallowness. In fact, these two duties are different in a fundamental way. "Care"

[27] Jay M Zitter, "Backdating Stock Options as Breach of Corporate or Fiduciary Duties," *ALR* (6th) 29, 491–506 (2007); *In re Zoran Corp Derivative Litig* 511 F Supp 2d 986, 996–98 (ND Cal 2008).

[28] Donald C Langevoort, "Insider Trading and the Fiduciary Principle: A Post-Chiarella Restatement," *Cal L Rev* 18–24 (Jan 1982); In the Matter of the Purchase and Ret of Ward la France Truck Corp Class A & Class B Stocks, Securities Exchange Act of 1934 Release No 3445, 13 SEC Docket 373 (20 May 1943); *N Trust Co v Essaness Theatres Corp* 348 Ill App 134, 137–9 (1952).

[29] Frankel (n 26) at 94–6.

denotes the fiduciary's expertise, attention, and avoidance of negligence. "Loyalty" denotes complete and unconditional devotion to other than oneself. Loyalty prohibits the fiduciary from putting itself in the position of a conflict with the beneficiary's interests. An expert fiduciary can be disloyal and breach the duty of loyalty. A loyal fiduciary can lack expertise and breach the duty of care. To meet its fiduciary duties a fiduciary must act with both loyalty and expertise. Meshing the two duties together can effectively confuse and muddy the understanding of these duties.

C. Water down the fiduciary duties of advisers imposed on brokers who use "sales talk" as advice to sell securities to retail customers[30]

As advisers, brokers would be subject to the Advisers Act of 1940, which imposes fiduciary duties on advisers.[31] In such a case the brokers' "sales talk" will be considered advice, and brokers will be drawn into the group of professionals, and regulated as fiduciaries-advisers. This category will impose on brokers higher duties and higher punishments upon their violations.[32]

How should brokers contain as much as possible the added burden and disclosure requirements that are likely to reduce returns substantially and impose costs on brokerage services? One approach is similar to the one taken with respect to the "sole interest" to "best interest" change. The argument may be that brokers are already subject to fiduciary duties under the "suitability rule." The approach is to redefine fiduciary duties and render them close to the "suitability rule."[33] In this, like in the "best interest" switch, the result would be to change the duty of loyalty to the duty of care.

Arguably, the social danger that the duty of loyalty is designed to eliminate is that clients would refrain from trusting brokers. If the rule is designed to induce clients to trust the fiduciaries, evidence shows that they do indeed trust their brokers. A duty of loyalty that is almost identical to the duty of care would allow brokers to continue and advise clients while they have conflicting interests without disclosing these interests to clients.

For example, brokers may offer clients shares of mutual funds or similar types of investment management entities. Brokers might offer potential clients "free lunches" and free advice and share a percentage of the management fees with the investment managers of the mutual funds. Regardless of the performance of the assets under management, the fees might grow with the volume of these assets because the management fees are measured as a percentage of the assets (no matter how they grew). This part of the arrangement, however, need not necessarily be disclosed to the clients. It may present conflicting interests, but not necessarily violation of the suitability rule. The suitability rule allows recommendation of a suitable investment even though it might

[30] Dodd-Frank Wall Street Reform and Consumer Protection Act, Pub L No 111–203, § 913, 2010 USCCAN (124 Stat) 1376, 1824–30.

[31] 15 USC §§ 80b-1 to -21 (2006).

[32] See FINRA, Letter of Acceptance, Waiver and Consent No 2008014763601, Re: Merrill Lynch, Pierce, Fenner & Smith Inc (3 June 2013); FINRA, Letter of Acceptance, Waiver and Consent No 2008014350501, *Re: Wells Fargo Advisors* LLC (3 June 2013).

[33] FINRA, Rule 2111, <http://finra.complinet.com/en/display/display_main.html?rbid=2403&element_id=9859> (last visited 27 Aug 2013) (requiring a broker to have a reasonable basis to believe that a security transaction is suitable for the customer).

be more expensive as compared to another similar investment. The same applies to an offer of an investment which is already held by the broker or its employer. The duty of care here embodied the duty of loyalty and is sufficient for investor protection.

A broker's "sales talk" often *sounds like* advice. Indeed, sales talks serve as advice to uninformed buyers. Why should this sales talk be different? More importantly, is the clients' view of sales talk relevant? Don't they know that the broker's objective is to persuade potential clients to trade? So what if clients may not be sophisticated; or if they do not have the mental and temperamental ability to evaluate the sales talk? So do many buyers of other assets. Reliance in and by itself does not create fiduciary relationships if the client is able to protect its interests and make a reasonable decision whether to buy or not. Besides, brokers are regulated with respect to their control of the clients' securities and money. Further, there is a long-standing "shingle theory"—when a broker hangs his shingle he announces to the public that he will treat clients fairly, and there is a rule that requires a broker to offer clients only "suitable" investments. Is not all this law enough?

The arguments on this issue reveal the different tests used for determining whether a service is a fiduciary service. One test may be the actual trust of the service receivers. It seems that investors do trust their brokers. Therefore, the first test is met. A second test may be whether the investors' trust is justified. This measure depends on the subject of the sale. In this case, the securities cannot be easily evaluated by investors at the time of the sale. Securities are promises of future payment. The expertise to evaluate securities involves not only in-depth research but prescience as well. In fact any lawyer or doctor of medicine's advice is similarly advising based on predictions of future results. So what is the difference?

There may be a number of answers. One is: Driven by short term benefits and freedom from responsibility a broker's advice may be harmful to the financial system in the long run, even if it is deemed suitable. Second, suitability does not always factor in costs that may *not* be suitable, especially for long-term investments. If true cost is not clear, the advice may not be entirely truthful. Third, advice to the coming old generation of retirees, if aimed at continuous trading, may be unsuitable, yet limits on trading threatens the lifeline for brokers. Fourth, the threat of withdrawal of brokers' advice may be a blessing. The paucity of independent advice may raise a generation of professional advisers. Their up-front cost may be far lower than the hidden cost that investors may pay brokers. This issue is now on the debating block.

D. Expand fiduciaries' discretion by embodying two purposes, one of which is broader than the other

A recent Delaware law allows the creation of a *for-profit corporation* which provides in its certificate of incorporation *specific public benefits* that the corporation can promote as part of its business.[34] The board of directors of such a corporation must "balance[] the pecuniary interests of the stockholders, the best interests of those materially

[34] Del Code Ann tit 8, §§ 361–8 "'Public benefit' means a positive effect (or reduction of negative effects) on one or more categories of persons, entities, communities or interests..." Del Code Ann tit 8, § 362(b).

affected by the corporation's conduct, and the specific public benefit or public benefits identified in [the corporation's] certificate of incorporation."[35] Shareholders who own 2 percent of the outstanding corporate stock may bring a derivative action asserting that the board is not fulfilling the public benefit mandate.[36] In addition, the legislation blocks some ways in which the corporate objectives may be circumvented.

This legislation represents a thoughtful design to allow and ensure a new mix of business and public interest objectives. First, it reduces the board of directors' discretion to determine the public interest objectives by requiring the objectives to be stated in the certificate of incorporation. Second, it balances corporate management powers with the investors-entrustors' powers to finance and withdraw from financing such corporate objectives which contradict the terms of the entrustment. Third, it enables a significant group of shareholders to seek judicial enforcement of the entrustment directives thus reining in the corporate fiduciaries, if they fail to follow the directions.

Fourth, the legislation narrowed, if not resolved, the arguments about how far corporate fiduciaries may go in using corporate money for political purposes. The legislation expressed recognition of corporate fiduciaries' authority to do so. This expansion may reflect the social move to identify economic power with political power, which is not alien to countries like the United States. In the context of fiduciary duties, however, the legislation broadens corporate fiduciaries' discretion, as it specifies it. As corporations have become depositories of financial power, the legislation presents a balance of power between investors and their managers.

II. Reclassify a Relationship under Fiduciary Law to a Less Regulated Relationship

A. Change the fiduciary's classification, eg, from trust (strictly regulated) to agency (less strictly regulated)

Another method to water down fiduciary duties is as follows: Admit that a particular relationship is indeed a fiduciary one. But change the classification of the relationship to one that is less regulated. Fiduciaries range from those with very little power to those entrusted with enormous power and control over other people's money. "Agents" are defined as fiduciaries that are subject to the control of their principals.[37] Their duties under agency law depend on (1) the degree of entrusted power and property that the fiduciary receives, and on (2) the ability of the clients-beneficiaries-principals to control their agents' activities.[38] When the words "trustee" and "agent" remain fixed or relate to written directives without regard to the degree of their discretion and control, the fixed naming leads to watering down their fiduciary duties.

[35] Del Code Ann tit 8, § 365(a).

[36] Del Code Ann tit 8, § 367. If the corporation is registered at a stock exchange this right is given to shareholders who own at least $2 million in market value.

[37] *Restatement (Third) of Agency* (2006) § 1.01 cmt h (stating that brokers, unlike finders, negotiate on behalf of principal).

[38] Tamar Frankel, "Fiduciary Law," 71 *Cal L Rev* 825–6 (1983).

Agency and trusteeship are very similar except for the ability of the entrustor-principal to control the fiduciary. History offers a number of interesting examples. Three thousand years ago the Code of Hammurabi regulated agency. It provided that an agent, who carried money or goods for trade in Egypt from Mesopotamia (now Iraq), was required to pay *double* the amount with which he was entrusted if he failed to make a higher profit.[39] In addition, under the Laws of Eshnunna, prior to the Code, if goods in possession of a bailee were stolen, he had to show that his own assets were robbed as well.[40] The problem in this case was control; that is what the law addressed. The master could not control the agent in his trading. Traditional Jewish law had a similar provision.[41] To some extent these agents were like trustees, except, perhaps, that their mission was more defined, although some trustees today have a specific mission as well.[42]

Thus, one condition that would change trust into agency is the degree of the entrustor's—principal's—control over the fiduciary in the fiduciary's service. This is a form of reclassification that applies to the same relationship when the circumstances under which the fiduciary serves have changed. For example, even though an indenture trustee is called a trustee, its liabilities before an event of default are very slight. It merely collects payments from the debtor and distributes to the public creditors. When an "event of default" occurs, and the debtor ceases to pay the public creditors, the trustee acquires broader powers and its liability accompanies those powers.[43]

The other transformation of trust into agency is to revise the remedies for violations of the fiduciary's duties or allow for insurance to cover these remedies. Watering down one or both of these two elements would reduce the burden on the fiduciaries and afford them more freedom to deal with entrusted property or exercise broader discretion under a lighter punishment threat. In addition, it is helpful to design a dual fiduciary status during different service periods. In such a case one should start with a lighter fiduciary classification and remedies.

However, allowing a trustee to carry the name of trustee but not the usual liabilities can be confusing to the trustee and the trustors. When a fiduciary is subject to two different regimes, the transition for the fiduciary may be difficult. Each regime has attendant remedies, depending on increased control and power. The fiduciary's habit of dealing under the lighter regime, when the power is slight, may present a barrier to transformation into a more vigilant regime, when the trustee's control expands. A habit in one part of the relationship does not change easily into another habit, especially when the relationship starts with services accompanying lower legal burdens. In sum, changing a fiduciary from one class to another, especially if the latter is stricter than the former, is likely to raise resistance and make difficult the enforcement of the stricter duties.

[39] Russ VerSteeg, "Early Mesopotamian Commercial Law," 30 *U Tol L Rev* 183, 202 (1999); Tamar Frankel, *Fiduciary Law* (2011) 80; Tamar Frankel, *Fiduciary Law* (2008) 7.

[40] VerSteeg (n 40) at 198; Frankel, *Fiduciary Law* (2011) 81; Frankel, *Fiduciary Law* (2008) 9.

[41] Frankel, *Fiduciary Law* (2011) 86–7 (requiring agent for for-profit corporation to maximize principal's profits); Frankel, *Fiduciary Law* (2008) 14 (similar).

[42] Trust Indenture Act of 1939, 15 USC §§ 77aaa-bbbb (2006).

[43] *Ellington Credit Fund, Ltd v Select Portfolio Servicing* 837 F Supp 2d 162, 191–2 (SDNY 2011).

B. Redefine an action that is currently held a wrongful act under fiduciary law

Another approach to watering down fiduciary duties is to start by redefining or eliminating the wrong altogether. Redefinition can begin with denial that an act or a position is wrong. One reason for this posture is that it allows the argument to move to a more neutral ground. One can offer a compromise more easily from a neutral ground. From that claim of absolute innocence, one could start to partially erode the existing definition or position, and bring it to the crossroads. Then it is easier to take the alternative road to freedom from liability. This method draws on the fundamental position that: "everyone is doing it but no one is punished."[44] This argument could render the wrongful act acceptable, even if it is somewhat wrong. The judgment of the society or a group within the society can trump even a strong written prohibition. Besides, if no one else is punished, the unique and signaled punishment becomes unfair and is judged wrong.

In his Article "Defining Deviancy Down" the late Senator Moynihan describes how one can redefine deviancy by "normalizing" situations that the community can no longer afford to recognize as wrongs. This normalization brings the wrong into a no man's land—a neutral place. No longer is the act absolutely bad. When there is no longer a "sense of outrage" "[t]he crime level has been *normalized.*"[45] As he argues:

> [T]he amount of deviant behavior in American society has increased beyond the levels the community can "afford to recognize" and..., accordingly, we have been re-defining deviancy so as to exempt much conduct previously stigmatized, and also quietly raising the "normal" level in categories, where behavior is now abnormal by any earlier standard. This redefining has evoked fierce resistance from defendants of "old" standards, and accounts for much of the present "cultural war" such as proclaimed by many at the 1992 Republican National Convention.[46]

A similar insight is offered by Michael Young: "People with aspirations to power over others are always reinterpreting old customs to their own advantage, trying to shift them so that others will accept their own authority both as a new fact in their society and as properly time-hallowed."[47] While reinterpretation serves to change the status quo, anchoring the change in the more familiar customary behavior makes the change easier to accept. In other words, there comes a point when abuse of trust is widespread, and the situation cannot be tolerated. Society faces a choice of taking strict measures to prevent abuse, or redefining it out of existence and moving towards a different culture. Referring to Senator Moynihan's ideas, Eliot Spitzer, the Attorney General of New York said: "There has been an incremental dissipation of standards over time. We grow more comfortable with improper behavior in steps.... The real issue we're looking at is conflict of interest—how it starts and how it gets institutionalized."[48]

[44] Frankel (n 26) at 31.
[45] Daniel P Moynihan, "Defining Deviancy Down," 62 *American Scholar* 26 (Winter 1993).
[46] Moynihan (n 46) at 19.
[47] Michael Young, *The Metronomic Society: Natural Rhythms and Human Timetables* (1988) 99.
[48] Louise O'Brien, "How to Restore The Fiduciary Relationship: A Conversation with Eliot Spitzer," 82 *Harvard Business Review* 72 (May 2004).

Senator Moynihan listed three categories of redefinition. The last one is normalizing—"the growing acceptance of unprecedented levels of violent crime."[49] In the context of the recent financial scandals the same category appears. We can repeat Senator Moynihan's words but substitute "abuse of trust and deception" for "violent crime." His words would read: Normalizing—"the growing acceptance of unprecedented levels of abuse of trust and deception." Redefining starts with denying that an action is wrong, and attacking the law. It is the law or the prohibition that is wrong.[50]

Redefinition can also be accomplished by exemptions and relaxation of the legal rules. During the 1990s, a number of legal constraints on business were relaxed. For example, Enron Corporation received an exemption from the Investment Company Act of 1940[51] and the Public Utility Holding Company Act of 1935.[52] These exemptions were based on certain assumptions about the business strategy of Enron, as described in the application. Later, Enron changed its basic business strategy, and engaged in abusive prohibited activities. In addition Enron Corporation lobbied successfully for legislation that allowed it to escape other regulation.[53] Redefinition of activities has become permissible. Corruption was more easily achieved.

III. Follow Other Disciplines and "Commodify" Fiduciary Services

A. Use the words and concepts derived from other disciplines to water down fiduciary duties under the law

An additional means to water down fiduciary duties chooses the following method: Introduce terms and concepts derived from other disciplines. Disciplines such as business and economics measure social needs, personal desires, and tempting incentives differently from the measures and principles that guide fiduciary law. The law defines antisocial activities differently and its punishment for such behavior is poles apart from that of business and economics.

So let us draw on economics. First, this use would facilitate confusion. For example, the expression "agency costs" is in fact similar in substance to the expression "conflict of interest." But it involves the word "agency" which has a different meaning in law than in economics. "Agency costs" in economic language involves breach of fiduciary duties by trusted persons. It embraces a broad range of behaviors signifying their joint feature: they are not precisely honest, or they entice dishonesty.

"Agency" in the law is far more specifically defined. As noted, it is a service to a principal and its costs have little to do with violations of fiduciary duties, and more with payment for services. In addition, "cost" is usually unrelated to agency in the legal sense. Law does not measure a violation by its dollars and cents costs. The term "agency

[49] Moynihan (n 46) at 19. [50] Frankel (n 26) at 38.

[51] *In re* Enron Corp, Investment Company Act Rel No 22,515 (14 Feb 1997) (application); *In re* Enron Corp, Investment Company Act Rel No 22,560 (13 Mar 1997) (order granted).

[52] Enron Corp, Public Utility Holding Co Act Rel No 24,428 (23 July 1987) (order granted).

[53] Michael Schroeder and Greg Ip, "Out of Reach: The Enron Debacle Spotlights Huge Void in Financial Regulation," *Wall St J*, 13 Dec 2001.

costs" is not legally precise and may be confusing. It diffuses the image of breach of trust. It equates money with fraud and misappropriation.

In this connection let us remember the introduction: Law reflects our society, which is, as noted, as all societies, a chaotic system. It is interactive and changing. Our "rights" and other legal meanings continue to be meaningful because we can continue to recall the experience that gave birth to these rights. We need fiduciary law to facilitate the reliance of the members of our society on each other. Especially important is reliance on experts in different disciplines and trust in the financial system. However, different disciplines have an environment and guidelines that lead them to different criteria.

No matter what fiduciary law dictates, its rules aim at self-limitation and contained selfishness. Fiduciary rules require full attention to service and commitment to the interests of others. It waters down these values to combine other disciplines with fiduciary duties. Other disciplines can be in service of other aims and interests. Combining law and select other disciplines can justify sacrificing the entrustors' interests under the law for interests which other disciplines serve. Thus, the advice to those who wish to reduce their fiduciary duties is: search for theories that undermine the interests of others—the entrustors—in the service of anyone and anything else, be it the service to society as a whole (instead of service to individuals), service to religion, or the service to the poor and the needy—service to anything and anyone will do *except service to the entrustors*.

There is a very short answer to the search for guidance of other disciplines: Please do all these good things that aim at furtherance of all these marvelous ideas with any source of money except *entrusted* money and *entrusted* power. Please do all these good things with the *money or power of other kindred souls*.

B. Commodify fiduciary services

To reduce fiduciary duties, "commodify" fiduciary services. This approach helps convert *in our minds* services into assets. This form of watering down fiduciary duties is related to a view of the world as a market, and all relationships into business and economic activities. Trustees and other fiduciaries are selling assets; not services. To some extent the view of services as assets for trade comports with the view of the world of capitalism. If *service* becomes the equivalent of *capital*, if we *invest* in *education*, the service providers are capitalists as much as someone who holds dollars. In that situation there is little difference between the service giver and the service receiver, between the trustee and the beneficiary. Besides, an asset is easier to gauge and evaluate than a service, and that image enhances market trading.

In our minds, assets can be viewed, touched, or perhaps smelled and tasted. We have far more ways to evaluate and value assets. Services, on the other hand, can be invisible; the results of financial services in terms of assets are not immediately demonstrated. In fact, it might be years before we convert the results of financial services into real assets. It is difficult to convert the value of a successful operation into an asset. In fiduciary law, the services are performed by managing our assets, or our money, or the body that belongs to us (eg, an operation by a surgeon).

In the financial area, there are instinctive justifications for viewing and converting service givers to property owners. They are, after all, the producers (or losers) of entrusted money. That is accurate especially regarding those who are vested with expansive discretion and carry the burden and the responsibility of decision-making. Why should these persons be deemed servants rather than owners? If not the owners of the money they manage, why not the owners of the services they provide and the profits they produce? That theory is especially enticing when the service givers are in fact and in law the legal owners. And this theory becomes even more attractive when the fiduciaries are the active producers while the capital providers are passive recipients of benefits from the fiduciaries' toils. The owners are the parasites.

There is much to be said about justifying fiduciaries' claims, especially in a society that strives to reach equality and measure it by right deserts. And yet, the commodification of fiduciary services presents a danger to the very foundation of a prosperous society.

In personal relationships or with respect to issues concerning persons directly, the commodification of people has met resistance.[54] But when the issues are more removed from actual persons; for example, when the issues concern personal services in the financial context, the product of the services is identified with the services to become one. The servicers are therefore considered as providing these products.

Yet, the difference between the sale of assets and provision of services for the benefit of others is fundamental. In fact, the difference is similar to some extent to the difference between contracts, which exchange assets for money, and fiduciary relationships, which not only exchange services for money but also entrust assets to the servicer, and these assets do not belong to the fiduciary-servicer. Thus, commodification of fiduciary services is a way to overcome the constraints of fiduciary law. If a fiduciary identifies with the produced tangible asset the distinction of two different items disappears.

As noted, the advocates of fiduciary law as contract argue that fiduciary duties are a contract and the entrusted power or property become the property of the fiduciaries. In this view fiduciaries' services are identified with the entrusted property. They are indeed a mixed asset. But if this view is rejected, and *entrusted assets and power* are not included in the sale of the services, then the services remain just that: services. But the more you describe the service as a commodity and as a sale, the stronger the contractual part becomes and the weaker the entrustment part of the relationship will appear. In fact, the two are then confused and the emphasis moves to their merger. This is a way to water down fiduciary duties.

An example of this development is the commodification of legal advice. When the Supreme Court had encouraged lawyers to compete[55] and when some advertising of legal services was permitted, the idea that legal services will become cheaper was proven false. In fact, the cost of legal services has rocketed for a number of years, until it imploded.[56] From the personal services to the internet legal advice was only a short step.[57] Legal advice is viewed in many instances as a commodity. The result of

[54] Tamar Frankel and Francis H Miller, "The Inapplicability of Market Theory to Adoptions," 67 *BU L Rev* 103 (1987).

[55] *Bates v State Bar of Ariz* 433 US 350 (1977).

[56] Frankel (n 26) at 140.

[57] LawGuru, <http://www.lawguru.com> (last visited 7 June 2013) (website for legal questions and answers over Internet); Avvo, <http://www.avvo.com> (last visited 7 June 2013) (similar).

commodification is to truly commodify human services, including professional services. This trend would reduce fiduciary power and fiduciary duties. That is especially so as long as personal contacts are severed, and the advice becomes entirely impersonal. The rule against conflicts of interest, which is one of the prohibitions that apply to fiduciaries, does not apply to the sender of the advice, and the test is then confined to the written advice.

Conclusion

This chapter outlines various mechanisms that water down fiduciary duties. One may avoid using the terms of fiduciary law, except in those cases when the use of those terms helps reduce the attached duties. Or, one may seek historical incidents, to demonstrate that a reclassification of fiduciary relationships has deep roots in history, with the result of reducing fiduciary duties. For example, it may be argued that fiduciary relationships used to reflect status relationships and were then converted into contract. This approach helps gives the arguments the respectability of age.

There is also the force of a slippery slope. Very little, if anything, is changed in the blink of an eye. If we review the techniques by which fiduciary duties have been reduced or even eliminated, slow small-step movements in that direction are the most effective and long-lasting. The first steps are almost imperceptible. The later steps are more recognizable, but by that later time, the first step has often become accepted and entrenched.

But one should recognize that there is no push in one direction without an opposite push-back. A drive towards reduced fiduciary duties is bound to bring the regulators' drive and an imposition of far harsher punishments than were imposed in the past. As the rules in the book shrink and are diluted, the punishments for violating the remaining rules are bound to "bite" harder. Devious attempts by fiduciaries to avoid responsibilities and raise their benefits may be met not with new rules but with painful punishments for those who are caught. Hopefully, this limitation will lead to fiduciaries' self-limitation, and to a protective culture that encourages justifiable rather than imaginary trust. If fiduciary duties are watered down to reflections without substance, and if fiduciaries' sense of entitlement grows shamelessly, public opinion will likely result in the passage of the appropriate rules, and courts will enforce them.

13

Why Fiduciary Law Is Equitable

*Henry E Smith**

Introduction

The complaints about fiduciary law have a familiar ring. Or a cacophony of rings. Fiduciary law is celebrated as unbound by rules or deplored as unprincipled—and yet is seen as too technical and formal. Fiduciary duties are expressed in moral language of exacting honor, which is treasured by some as the essence of the area and as a flowery show by others. The moralists see in fiduciary law a fixed and mandatory system, even as legal economists and contractarians have cast fiduciary law as the ultimate set of defaults to fill in incomplete contracts. And the confusion over the nature of the fiduciary duty carries over into a vague sense that the remedies for breach of fiduciary duty should be stringent but an inability to say exactly why—is it the vulnerability of the victim, the proprietary status of the interest, or something else? The list could go on, but the fiduciary pudding has too many themes for any one of them to stand out.

This state of affairs is no accident. Fiduciary law is an outgrowth of equity—perhaps the most important and characteristic branch of the tree of equity—and it suffers from the hard times the theory of equity has fallen into, and for the same reasons. Like fiduciary law, equity too is celebrated as unboundedly contextual and abhorred as unprincipled and overexpansive, while at the same time it exhibits pockets of seemingly strange formalism. Equity is sometimes vague and almost always morally inflected, which is alternatively welcomed, deplored, and downplayed. Is equity a direct infusion of morality? If so, is that good? Or is it all epiphenomenal, disguising what is "really" going on? And is there anything special about equitable remedies, or should they—along with fiduciary law and the rest of equity—be treated as standing on their own terms since the fusion of law and equity?

This chapter will argue that a functional theory of equity—of equity as a decision-making mode aimed at countering opportunism—captures the character of fiduciary law. Indeed, fiduciary law is not only a historical outgrowth of equity but is at the functional core of the equitable decision-making mode.

Equity as anti-opportunism explains not only the general tenor, but the overall structure and particular features of fiduciary law. Fiduciary relationships carry more than the usual danger of opportunism. The situation of someone undertaking to act on another's behalf by using discretion carries with it a great potential for opportunism. Engaging in self-dealing and not avoiding conflicts of interest are more or less correlated with

* For helpful comments I would like to thank Andrew Gold, Paul Miller, Peter Turner, and participants at the Conference on the Philosophical Foundations of Fiduciary Law at the DePaul University College of Law and a Faculty Workshop at the University of Virginia School of Law. All errors are mine.

opportunism. In the equitable solutions to opportunism based on proxies and presumptions, fiduciary law gets its main features. Like equity but in a more sweeping way, fiduciary law sets the presumption against the fiduciary when certain proxies are triggered. In the case of fiduciary law, these proxies are very broad and robust. As with the safety valve style proxies and presumptions in equity generally, fiduciary law targets opportunism, and like equity generally it cannot specify explicitly what opportunism is without raising the specter of evasion. What sets fiduciary law apart is its reliance on broad, untailored proxies and presumptions to prevent opportunism. Thus, in situations of undisclosed conflict of interest the presumption of opportunism arises even without regard to the substance of the conflicted deal. For self-dealing likewise the presumption arises in an almost indefeasible way. Like equity generally, fiduciary law features a constrained residuum of open-endedness to deal with new and creative ways of being opportunistic. But as with equity as a safety valve, this open-endedness in fiduciary law is limited. It is *in personam*, here in the sense of only targeting those who have taken on certain duties known to have this quality as well as certain other actors in very special situations, like parents.

This chapter begins in Section I with a sketch of the theory of equity as a decision-making mode targeting opportunists who might abuse the structures of the law. In its origins and functions, fiduciary law is at the core not just of equity jurisdiction. It also presents in especially stark terms the problem of hard-to-monitor and potentially creative misuse of the powers afforded by the law—that is, opportunism. Section II will then show how fiduciary law carries through equity as anti-opportunism with an especially broad and stable set of proxies and presumptions set against potential opportunists. These involve *ex post* standards familiar from equity, coupled with untargeted prophylactic *ex ante* rules to address extreme dangers of opportunism from certain actions by fiduciaries. Section III will show how this theory unifies the best aspects of traditional and modern theories of fiduciary law, and helps explain why fiduciary law has become so disparate and contested after the fusion of law and equity. Cut off from the special rationales of equity, fiduciary law itself threatens to become too expansive or too narrow and hidebound—like equity generally. Finally, the functional theory of equity as anti-opportunism helps explain the similarity of fiduciary law to another much misunderstood area of private law—unjust enrichment—and the relation between the two. Like unjust enrichment, fiduciary law is especially preoccupied with opportunism and so requires a heavier dose of equitable decision-making in the form of more stringent proxies and presumptions. The chapter concludes with some remarks about fiduciary law within the overall architecture of private law.

I. Equity as Anti-opportunism

Fiduciary law, like the rest of equity, tackles a serious problem of potential opportunism. The anti-opportunism theory of equity is a functional one, and this chapter will not claim that equity courts were exclusively concerned with opportunism. Nor were common law courts impervious to the way that their rules and doctrines could be misused. The equitable style of decision-making could be found on both sides of the old law versus equity divide, but, because of its unique role, equity in the Anglo-American tradition did often, and characteristically, reflect the equitable style of decision-making. Nowhere is this more true, both historically and functionally, than in the case of fiduciary law.

A. Origins and function

Although our concern is not mainly historical, the development of equity and the trust help explain their preoccupation with opportunism and their characteristic morally infused *ex post* strategies of countering opportunism.

The equity courts emerged in the fourteenth century out of the dispute resolution activities of the chancellor on the king's behalf. Petitioners would come before the king, and later the chancellor, complaining of oppressive behavior and asking for an order directed at the alleged misdoer to put the matter right. Notions of fiduciary accounting by potential opportunists extend back before chancery,[1] but the tendency for a functionally equitable decision-making mode to be associated with equity courts established itself very early. In particular by the fifteenth century many of the complaints were against "feoffees," persons who held legal title for the benefit of another in a proto-trust (a "use," usually for the purpose of avoiding the tax-like feudal incidents that would be owed the lord on an intergenerational transfer). The arrangement was fraught with danger that the trusted party would take the property for himself—he had legal title after all—and the "faithless feoffee,"[2] was the central character in much of this early litigation. Thus, anti-opportunism was at the center of equity and its most important invention—the trust—from early times. The early chancellors were clergymen, and equity drew heavily on civil and canon law in developing its substance and its procedure. The chancellor was the keeper of the king's conscience and equity courts were known as courts of conscience.[3] Equity bore a close relation to natural law and natural justice, and moral norms infused all of its work.[4]

[1] Joshua Getzler, "'As If:' Accountability and Counterfactual Trust," 91 *BU L Rev* 973, 979–80 (2011).

[2] Austin Wakeman Scott, William Franklin Fratcher, and Mark L Ascher, *Scott and Ascher on Trusts* (5th edn, 2006) vol 1, § 1.5, at 14 ("Petitioners complained frequently to the chancellor. . . about faithless feoffees. Such breaches of faith naturally appealed strongly to the chancellor's sense of justice, and. . . the chancellor began to compel recalcitrant feoffees to do what they had undertaken to do"); John H Langbein, "The Contractarian Basis of the Law of Trusts," 105 *Yale LJ* 615, 634 and n 42 (1995) (citing as an example a petition to the Chancellor from the 1390s, see William P Baildon (ed), *Select Cases in Chancery: 1364–1471*, vol 10 (1896) at 48–9).

[3] See, eg, J H Baker, *An Introduction to English Legal History* (3rd edn, 1990) 112–28; but cf Mike Macnair, "Equity and Conscience," 27 *Oxford J Legal Stud* 659 (2007) (arguing that equity as a court of conscience originally meant that the judge knew and could draw on facts not in evidence). Furthermore, early chancery enforcement of uses drew on earlier notions of accounting by executors in church courts. R H Helmholz, *The Oxford History of the Laws of England: The Canon Law and Ecclesiastical Jurisdiction from 597 to the 1640s* (2004) vol 1, 421–3.

[4] See, eg, Hugo Grotius, *De Jure Belli Ac Pacis Libri Tres* [On the Law of War and Peace: Three Books], trans Francis W Kelsey (1925) vol 2, ii.6, at 193 (1646) ("We must, in fact, consider what the intention was of those who first introduced individual ownership; and we are forced to believe that it was their intention to depart as little as possible from natural equity"); Gulian C Verplanck, *An Essay on the Doctrine of Contracts: Being an Inquiry How Contracts Are Affected in Law and Morals, by Concealment, Error, or Inadequate Price* (1825) 37 ("[Lord Mansfield made] the judgments of the law correspond with the actual practice of intelligent merchants, and with those universal usages, founded partly in convenience, and partly in natural equity, which might be considered as the common commercial and maritime law of the civilized world"); see also *Bright v Boyd* 4 F Cas 127, 133 (CCD Me 1841) (No 1875) (Story, Circuit Justice) ("I have ventured to suggest, that the claim of the *bonâ fide* purchase [in unjust enrichment for improvements made

The equity courts also drew on the tradition of equity stretching back to Aristotle, who defined equity (*epieikeia*) as an invocation of justice where law fails on account of its generality.[5] This tradition came in broader and narrower versions. On the broader one, equity corrects any flaw in the law in the interest of justice; it closes any gaps between the terms of the law and its purpose. I have argued for a narrower version in which one main reason law fails on account of its generality is that law's generality results in exploitable gaps between the law and its purpose. These gaps give an opening to opportunists, which equity seeks to close.[6] Such an interpretation, which I argue for on functional and (tentatively and partially) on historical grounds, is possibly the best interpretation of Aristotle's equity, as Dennis Klimchuk has shown.[7] On this more focused view, equity's domain is not over any and all gaps between the law and its purposes but is especially concerned with gaps and other openings that opportunists intentionally exploit (and even create) in hard-to-foresee ways.

On either the wide or narrow view of equity, not every situation can be anticipated by those framing the law, and so we sometimes need an individualized *ex post* approach. In extreme situations, opportunism can call for broad skepticism toward entire classes of actions or transactions. Either way, opportunism by its nature—a strategic interaction between the opportunist and other actors including courts—cannot be dealt with purely through *ex ante* rules.

This leaves broad, untailored prophylactic presumptions and *ex post* tailored standards as the tools courts can use against opportunism. Whatever the combination of these tools, some *ex post* flexibility is indispensable to equity. In a famous analogy, Aristotle likened equity to the leaden measuring rulers of the builders of the island of Lesbos.[8] Unlike iron rulers, the lead rulers would take the shape of the measured stones, allowing the selection of another neighboring stone that would fit exactly. From the point of view of anti-opportunism, equity cannot be too predictable or else the well-informed opportunists will anticipate it and evade it: *ex post* will collapse into *ex ante*. Further, as we will see it is in the nature of opportunists to be inventive. Equity

to real property] is founded in equity. I think it founded in the highest equity; and in this view of the matter, I am supported by the positive dictates of the Roman law. The passage already cited, shows it to be founded in the clearest natural equity. '*Jure naturae aequum est*.' ['By the law of nature it is equitable.']"); *Moses v Macferlan* [1760] 97 Eng Rep 676, 681 (KB) (Mansfield J) ("In one word, the gist of this kind of action is, that the defendant, upon the circumstances of the case, is obliged by the ties of natural justice and equity to refund the money."). But see Fred F Lawrence, *A Treatise on the Substantive Law of Equity Jurisprudence* (1929) vol 1, § 3 (arguing that it is fallacious to regard equity as based on natural justice).

[5] Aristotle, *The Nicomachean Ethics*, trans David Ross, rev J L Ackrill and J O Urmson (1980) 133; Thomas Aquinas, *Summa Theologica* I-II, q 96, art 6; Christopher St German, *Doctor and Student*, ed T F T Plucknett and J L Barton (1974) 94–107; see also, eg, *Riggs v Palmer* 22 NE 188, 189 (NY 1889) (quoting Aristotle on equity); Eric G Zahnd, "The Application of Universal Laws to Particular Cases: A Defense of Equity in Aristotelianism and Anglo-American Law," 59 *Law & Contemp Probs* 263, 270–5 (Winter 1996) (documenting influence of Aristotelian equity on Anglo-American law); but cf Darien Shanske, "Four Theses: Preliminary to an Appeal to Equity," 57 *Stan L Rev* 2053 (2005) (arguing that Aristotle's equity was not primarily legal).

[6] Henry E Smith, "An Economic Analysis of Law Versus Equity," 22 October 2010 (working paper), available at: <http://www.law.yale.edu/documents/pdf/LEO/HSmith_LawVersusEquity7.pdf>.

[7] Dennis Klimchuk, "Is the Law of Equity Equitable in Aristotle's Sense?," 4 (June 2011) (unpublished manuscript), available at <http://www.law.ucla.edu/workshops-colloquia/Documents/Klimchuk.%20Is%20the%20Law%20of%20Equity%20Equitable%20in%20Aristotles%20Sense.pdf>.

[8] Aristotle (n 5) at 133.

needs to be open-ended and individualized to capture new, hard-to-foresee ways of engaging in opportunism—the problem to which we now turn.

B. The problem of opportunism

In other work I have argued that the theme of equity as a decision-making mode is the fight against opportunism.[9] Historically what has gone under the heading "equity" partakes greatly of this equitable mode. I start with the problem to be solved, but as we will see, in equity the main action occurs in defining the proxies for opportunism and the consequences of the triggering of these proxies and their associated presumptions.

In isolating opportunism a good place to start is the traditional lore of the concerns of equity. A couplet attributed to Thomas More, the first lawyer to serve as chancellor, has it that "Three things are to be helpt in Conscience; Fraud, Accident and things of Confidence."[10] Another version of the equitable domain recites "fraud, accident, and mistake."[11] As we will see, the proxies for triggering the potential for equitable intervention are keyed to fraud, accident, and confidence. Very suggestive is how Justice Joseph Story, who was aware of the importance of equity's role in countering what we could call opportunism,[12] sets out equity jurisdiction by starting with the trust (and confidences), works outward to "mistake, accident, and fraud," and then adds "many cases of penalties and forfeitures; many cases of impending irreparable injuries, or meditated mischiefs; and many cases of oppressive proceedings, undue advantages and impositions, betrayals of confidence, and unconscionable bargains; in all of which Courts of

[9] Smith (n 6).

[10] *Rolle's Abridgement* vol 1, 374; see also *Caco v Clark* [1969] RPC 41 (Ch Div) (Justice Megarry) (quoting More's couplet); Anthony Laussat, Jr, *An Essay on Equity in Pennsylvania* (1826) 67 (stating that "Sir Thomas More used to say that the following doggerel contained all the heads of chancery jurisdiction"). William Blackstone, more a fan of the common law than of equity, gets a little defensive in making the legitimate point that the triggers for equity were not ignored by the common law:

> Again, it hath been said, that *fraud, accident*, and *trust* are the proper and peculiar objects of a court of equity. But every kind of *fraud* is equally cognizable, and equally adverted to, in a court of law: and some frauds are only cognizable there, as fraud in obtaining a devise of lands, which is always sent out of the equity courts to be there determined. Many *accidents* are also supplied in a court of law; as, loss of deeds, mistakes in receipts or accounts, wrong payments, deaths which make it impossible to perform a condition literally, and a multitude of other contingencies: and many cannot be relieved even in a court of equity; as, if by accident a recovery is ill suffered, a devise is ill executed, a contingent remainder destroyed, or a power of leasing omitted in a family settlement. A technical *trust* indeed, created by the limitation of a second use, was forced into a court of equity, in the manner formerly mentioned: and this species of trusts, extended by inference and construction, have ever since remained as a kind of *peculium* in those courts. But there are other trusts, which are cognizable in a court of law: as deposits, and all manner of bailments...

William Blackstone, *Commentaries*, vol 3, *431–2 (footnotes omitted). Interestingly Blackstone cites to 1 Roll Abr 374 despite the slight alteration.

[11] 47 Am Jur 2d Judgments § 718 ("Generally, claimants seeking equitable relief from judgments through independent actions must meet three requirements [, the third of which is that] they must establish a recognized ground, such as fraud, accident, or mistake, for the equitable relief") (footnotes omitted, citing cases); see also William F Walsh, *A Treatise on Mortgages* (1934) 6, 11 (relief from mortgages in equity on grounds of fraud, accident, or mistake); Val D Ricks, "American Mutual Mistake: Half-Civilian Mongrel, Consideration Reincarnate," 58 *La L Rev* 663, 717 and n 277 (1998) (speculating that Chief Justice Allen in *Swift v Hawkins* (1768) 1 Dall 17 (Pa), "considered 'mistake' to be representative of all categories of equity").

[12] See nn 36–7 and accompanying text.

Equity will interfere and grant redress; but which the Common Law takes no notice of, or silently disregards."[13] Again these formulations of the general concerns of equity are susceptible to the broad "fix-it" and narrow anti-opportunism interpretations, and the fix-it approach appears natural if one forgets that formulations like More's couplet delineate a general field of equitable concern, not a rule of its operation. Something like the broad version of equity certainly appealed to the Legal Realists. Thus, Roscoe Pound sounds vaguely proto-Realist when he argues:

> It has been said that the common law will not help a fool. But equity exists to help and protect him. It is because there are fools to be defrauded and imposed upon, and unfortunates to meet with accidents and careless to make mistakes, that we have courts of equity. Surely what equity has done to abridge freedom of contract, legislation may do likewise.[14]

And the Realists and their successors did in effect broaden equitable contextualism, in part to prevent unequal bargains and protect the vulnerable.[15]

But equity, even historical equity, is susceptible to another narrower interpretation—one that does not threaten to swallow all of law. It is true that courts' efforts against forfeitures wind up helping what Carol Rose calls "mopes" and "ninnies,"[16] but as she and other commentators have noticed, courts pay more attention to the sharp practices of the person taking advantage of them than of their vulnerability directly.[17] "Equity abhors a forfeiture," and, as we will see, one of the main and most interesting proxies for opportunism is "disproportionate hardship." Nevertheless the use of the proxy "disproportionate hardship" is in the service of rooting out opportunistic behavior, rather than as an exercise in free-ranging rewriting of rules and contracts in the interest of amorphous and idiosyncratic notions of fairness.

Before turning to the proxies, how should we define opportunism? Nobel laureate Oliver Williamson defines opportunism as "self-interest seeking with guile,"[18] but for our purposes this is too broad and too narrow. Too broad, because Williamson takes

[13] See Joseph Story, *Commentaries on Equity Jurisprudence, as Administered in England and America* (1836) vol 1, § 29, at 28–9.

[14] Roscoe Pound, "Freedom of Contract," 18 *Yale LJ* 454, 483 (1909).

[15] Roscoe Pound, "The End of Law as Developed in Legal Rules and Doctrines," 27 *Harv L Rev* 195, 226 (1913) ("Equity sought to prevent the unconscientious exercise of rights; today we seek to prevent the anti-social exercise of rights"); also at 227 ("Equity imposed moral limitations. The law today is beginning to impose social limitations"). See Owen M Fiss, "The Supreme Court, 1978 Term—Foreword: The Forms of Justice," 93 *Harv L Rev* 1, 2 (1979) ("The structural suit is one in which a judge, confronting a state bureaucracy over values of constitutional dimension, undertakes to restructure the organization to eliminate a threat to those values posed by the present institutional arrangements. The injunction is the means by which these reconstructive directives are transmitted"); but see *Bisciglia v Kenosha* Unif Sch Dist No 1, 45 F 3d 223, 228 (7th Cir 1995) (denying temporary injunction in suit over employment termination and stating: "[T]his court does not possess a roving commission to do good. It must make a decision based upon the record and the law"); Douglas Laycock, "The Triumph of Equity," 56 *L & Contemp Probs* 53 (Summer 1993) (denying "that a court of equity has a roving commission to do good once it identifies a threshold violation of law that justifies its intervention").

[16] Carol M Rose, "Crystals and Mud in Property Law," 40 *Stan L Rev* 577, 587–8, 598–9 (1988).

[17] Rose (n 16); Seana Valentine Shiffrin, "Paternalism, Unconscionability Doctrine, and Accommodation," 29 *Phil & Pub Affairs* 205, 205, 235 (2000). See also Henry E Smith, "Rose's Human Nature of Property," 19 *Wm & Mary Bill Rts J* 1047, 1049–52 (2011).

[18] Oliver E Williamson, *The Economic Institutions of Capitalism: Firms, Markets, Relational Contracting* (1985) 47.

opportunism to include all sorts of rule breaking. But some rule breaking is easily anticipated *ex ante* and detected *ex post*, so there is no reason for equity to be particularly involved. Likewise, other definitions of opportunism based on contravening the spirit of the law or defeating a counterparty's legitimate expectations are helpful, but potentially quite broad,[19] leading to familiar fears of equity's overbreadth, vagueness, and consequent chilling effect (the "Chancellor's Foot"[20]). On the other hand, Williamson's definition is narrow if it is taken to require full-blown deception. Sometimes the opportunist takes advantage of an unexpected opportunity. Conditions change in an unforeseeable way and the opportunist uses the letter of the law or a contract to gain unintended advantage at someone else's expense (More's "accident").[21] Likewise with betraying a confidence: there is some deception in appearing to be trustworthy while not actually being so, but it's a stretch.

Opportunism that is relevant to equity is the kind that is hard to capture explicitly *ex ante*. Elsewhere I have defined opportunism as "behavior that is undesirable but that cannot be cost-effectively captured—defined, detected, and deterred—by explicit ex ante rulemaking.... It often consists of behavior that is technically legal but is done with a view to securing unintended benefits from the system, and these benefits are usually smaller than the costs they impose on others."[22] The intervention of a court based on an equitable proxy can lead non-opportunists to take fewer precautions, thereby improving overall welfare.[23] In contracting, equity can support a "substantial compliance" equilibrium: sellers will substitute into technically noncompliant but less costly and equally high-quality performance (which increases total surplus), but will be discouraged from contracting if they have to pay a cross-subsidy to opportunists who will

[19] See, eg, George M Cohen, "The Negligence-Opportunism Tradeoff in Contract Law," 20 *Hofstra L Rev* 941, 957 (1992) (defining "opportunism" as "any contractual conduct by one party contrary to the other party's reasonable expectations based on the parties' agreement, contractual norms, or conventional morality") (footnote omitted); Timothy Muris, "Opportunistic Behavior and the Law of Contracts," 65 *Minn L Rev* 521 (1981) (opportunism is conduct that is "contrary to the other party's understanding of the contract, but not necessarily contrary to the agreement's terms"); see also, eg, Samuel W Buell, "Good Faith and Law Evasion," 58 *UCLA L Rev* 611, 623 (2011) ("In common parlance, the evasive actor is one whose project is to get around the law. She seeks to avoid sanction while engaging, in substance, in the very sort of behavior that the law means to price or punish"). For a wider definition, see, eg, Richard A Posner, *Economic Analysis of Law* (5th edn, 1998) § 4.1, at 103 (defining "opportunism" in the contracting context as "trying to take advantage of the vulnerabilities created by the sequential character of the contract").

[20] The most famous critique is Selden's humorous one:

> Equity is a Roguish thing: for law we have a measure, know what to trust to; Equity is according to the Conscience of him that is Chancellor, and as that is larger or narrower, so is Equity. 'Tis all one as if they should make the Standard for the measure we call a Foot, a Chancellor's Foot; what an uncertain Measure would be this. One Chancellor has a long Foot, another a short Foot, a Third an indifferent Foot: 'Tis the same thing in the Chancellor's Conscience.

John Selden, "Equity," in *Table-Talk: Being the Discourses of John Selden, Esq.* (2nd edn, 1689) 43, 43–4. See generally J H Baker, *An Introduction to English Legal History* (3rd edn, 1990) 112–33.

[21] There is a tendency to affix the label "fraud" to any nefarious behavior with an element of concealment, which includes breach of trust and underground mining. See *Livingston v Rawyards* (1880) LR 5 App Cas 34, quoted in *Marengo Cave v Ross* 10 NE 2d 917, 923 (Ind 1937).

[22] Smith (n 6) at 10–11.

[23] Kenneth Ayotte, Ezra Friedman, and Henry E Smith, "A Safety Valve Model of Equity as Anti-Opportunism" (Draft, 30 Mar 2013), Northwestern Law & Econ Research Paper No 13-15, available at SSRN: <http://ssrn.com/abstract=2245098>; see also Rose (n 16) at 599.

sue for technical noncompliance.[24] (As where a contractor substitutes a different brand of pipe than the one called for even though it is of equal quality, when the first brand is suddenly much more costly.) The more accurate the proxy for this type of behavior and the more opportunists there are, the more equity is called for.[25]

C. Proxies and presumptions in equity

Equity as anti-opportunism takes a page from history in that it, like the earlier equity courts, focuses on "near fraud" or "quasi-fraud," and, based on certain proxies, shifts the presumption against actors who are both well informed and seek to visit a disproportionate hardship on another. Perhaps the area of equity where this is still half remembered is unconscionability. Modern theories of unconscionability tend to be very broad (expanding historic equity) or narrow (reflecting a formalist backlash), but historical equity employed presumptions keyed to potential opportunism. Two discussions of unconscionability reflect this more historically grounded view, and the theory of equity as anti-opportunism can be regarded as a more general version of them. And this chapter's theory of fiduciary law is a particularly stringent version.

Traditionally, the concern with near-fraud centered on conduct that carried indicia of the danger of fraud without fully demonstrable fraud. This could be either because activity was close to the line of fraud or might well be fraud but cannot be proved as such.[26] Or disproportionate hardship sometimes coupled with a particularly vulnerable party would raise the danger of opportunism so as to set the presumption against the one trying to benefit. As Arthur Leff put it in his famous treatment of unconscionability:

> To summarize, there are two separate social policies which are embodied in the equity unconscionability doctrine. The first is that bargaining naughtiness, once it reaches a certain level, ought to avail the practitioner naught. The second is directed not against bargaining conduct (except insofar as certain results often are strong evidence of certain conduct otherwise unproved) but against results, and embodies the doctrine (also present in *laesio enormis* statutes) that the infliction of serious hardship demands special justification.[27]

Leff notes that equity courts would focus on stock characters like the old, the young, the ignorant, etc, which Jane Mallor summarizes as "particular classes of people who were deemed to be easily duped, such as widows, orphans, farmers, sailors on leave, and the weakminded."[28] Leff calls these classes of persons "presumptive sillies," meaning that the presumption is against enforcing their deals with specific performance.[29] Leff

[24] Ayotte, Friedman, and Smith (n 23). [25] Ayotte, Friedman, and Smith (n 23).

[26] In the nineteenth-century view, "unconscionability" referred to fraud that could not readily be proved, see, eg, *Seymour v Delancey* 3 Cow 445, 521–2, 15 Am Dec 270 (NY Sup 1824) ("Inadequacy of price, unless it amount to conclusive evidence of fraud, is not itself a sufficient ground for refusing a specific performance of an agreement") (citing cases); James Gordley, "Equality in Exchange" 69 *Cal L Rev* 1587, 1639 (1981). See also Richard A Epstein, "Unconscionability: A Critical Reappraisal," 18 *JL & Econ* 293, 293, 293–301 (1975).

[27] Arthur Allen Leff, "Unconscionability and the Code—The Emperor's New Clause," 115 *U Pa L Rev* 485, 539 (1967) (footnote omitted).

[28] Jane P Mallor, "Unconscionability in Contracts between Merchants," 40 *Sw LJ* 1065, 1066 (1986).

[29] Leff (n 27) at 532.

points out that contrary to the assumptions behind the Uniform Commercial Code, most of these traditional equity cases involved land, which is not only often unique but involves one of the parties in a high stakes and once-in-a-lifetime transaction.[30]

In a fashion similar to Leff, Richard Epstein draws out unconscionability's use of presumptions in his theory of procedural unconscionability based on near-fraud.[31] He argues that certain classes of transactions picked out by indicia of near-fraud carry with them such small benefits and such a large danger of fraud (or what we would call opportunism) that they are worth banning at least presumptively. He analogizes unconscionability to the Statute of Frauds, which likewise makes unenforceable a category of transactions, based on a combination of content and the fact of being not in writing.[32] The traditional approach to the defense of incompetence works similarly: contracts with someone underage, insane, or drunk were voidable because of the danger, not the certainty, of fraud, such that not enforcing them minimized decision and error costs (including the costs of not enforcing legitimate deals).[33] Here the fight against opportunism requires a sweeping (perhaps "*ex ante*" but not tailored) presumption against a class of transactions.[34]

Finally, opportunism poses a special problem that requires equity to be at least somewhat open-ended within its domain. Interestingly, Epstein offers as an example of how the doctrine of unconscionability also must be flexible in a case in which the defendants offered unattractive municipal bonds to returning Vietnam veterans, who were vulnerable because of their long captivity and who suddenly came into money in the form of accumulated back-pay.[35] Sharp dealers and unsophisticated purchasers with sudden money fit well into Leff's traditional categories but only loosely. Again it is a combination of a very strange-looking deal and vulnerability that makes the transaction voidable.

Equity would not act if the law was adequate and equitable orders were *in personam*, but the nature of "fraud, accident, and mistake" means that opportunism cannot be explicitly specified *ex ante* in a tailored fashion. This is more than a difficulty in description. It is the strategic interaction between the opportunist and those operating the legal system that precludes a wholly *ex ante* approach. The older courts and commentators on equity too were well aware that equity was aiming at a moving target. As Justice Story put it, "[f]raud is infinite" given the "fertility of man's invention,"[36] and he quoted one explicit judicial pronouncement about the nature of equity:

> Now equity is no part of the law, but a moral virtue, which qualifies, moderates, and reforms the rigour, hardness, and edge of the law, and is an universal truth; it does also

[30] Leff (n 27) at 537. [31] Epstein (n 26).

[32] Epstein (n 26) at 302. [33] Epstein (n 26) at 300–1.

[34] Thus if the rule versus standard distinction is based on timing of decision-making with rules being *ex ante* and standards *ex post*, Louis Kaplow, "Rules versus Standards: An Economic Analysis," 42 *Duke LJ* 557 (1992), then the strategic problem in opportunism tends to call for broad prophylactic rules and more targeted *ex post* standards (if any intervention makes sense rather than tolerating bad behavior).

[35] Epstein (n 26) at 304.

[36] J Story, *Commentaries on Equity Jurisprudence, as Administered in England and America* (9th edn, 1866) vol 1, 184 n 1 (quoting a Letter from Lord Hardwicke to Lord Kames (30 June 1759)). Or, as Chancellor Ellesmere put the point: "The Cause why there is a Chancery is, for that Mens Actions are so divers and infinite, That it is impossible to make any general Law which may aptly meet with every particular Act, and not fail in some Circumstances." *The Earl of Oxford's Case* (1615) 21 Eng Rep 485, 486 (Ch).

> assist the law where it is defective and weak in the constitution (which is the life of the law) and defends the law from crafty evasions, delusions, and new subtilties, invented and contrived to evade and delude the common law, whereby such as have undoubted right are made remediless; and this is the office of equity, to support and protect the common law from shifts and crafty contrivances against the justice of the law. Equity therefore does not destroy the law, nor create it, but assist it.[37]

Further, closing nine loopholes out of ten *ex ante* will do no good if crafty opportunists will all rush through the one remaining open. And, as Williamson pointed out, the more a situation can be characterized by true uncertainty, the more scope there is for opportunism.[38] If risk involves a range of future possibilities that can be captured with a probability distribution, Knightian uncertainty cannot: the probabilities or even the state space is unknown.[39] Uncertainty is important in the theory of the entrepreneur as well, and we can consider the opportunist an entrepreneur in doing bad.[40]

Because of the strategic nature of opportunism, the major features of equity—its use of proxies and presumptions, its lack of tailored *ex ante* rules, its sometime *ex post* operation, its open-endedness at the margin, and its grounding in morality, good faith, and notice—receive a unified explanation. These features of equity run the danger of overexpansion and chilling legitimate behavior, and equity is therefore supposed to intervene only when the law is inadequate and only in a targeted *in personam* fashion.

D. The place of fiduciary law in equity

Consider now how the problem of opportunism in fiduciary law is greater in kind and extent from that addressed by equity more generally. Generically, equity as a decision-making mode manifests itself as an exceptional safety valve. Fiduciary law presents a more systematic problem of potential opportunism that calls for more than a mere safety valve.

Later I will explore the similarities in the contours of general equity and fiduciary law, but it is worth pointing out how fiduciary law lies at the far end of equity in its use of proxies, especially those relating to state of mind. Equity itself responds to the shades of opportunism through its use of intent.[41] Thus, when a clear violation of a boundary—say in a building encroachment—is involved all that is required is knowledge of the boundary in order to be in bad faith. In other instances where the opportunism is not as clear the law uses a combination of a rougher proxy—disproportionate hardship and an intent standard. If someone causes disproportionate hardship, especially of someone very old or young or unsophisticated, the court will look to whether

[37] *Dudley v Dudley* (1705) 24 Eng Rep 118, 119 (Ch) (UK), quoted in Joseph Story, *Commentaries on Equity Jurisprudence* (1836; repr 1972) vol 1, 18–19. Story expresses some qualms about the broad identification of equity with virtue, but endorses this account of equity's function.

[38] Williamson (n 18) at 3–4, 56–9.

[39] Frank H Knight, *Risk, Uncertainty, and Profit* (1921) 19–21, 197–232.

[40] Knight (n 39) at 267–85, 369–73 (developing a theory of entrepreneurship based on an ability to deal with uncertainty).

[41] Smith (n 6).

the advantage taking was intentional and put the burden of justification on the potential opportunist. If potential opportunism is mixed in with activity that is normally unproblematic—say opening a business or erecting a wall—the intent required is pure spite—a desire to inflict harm on another. The stronger the proxy for opportunism (ranging from seemingly incidental harm to disproportionate hardship to violation of a boundary), the weaker can be the state-of-mind-proxy, and vice versa.

Where does this leave fiduciary law? Here the entrusting and vulnerability that give rise to the danger of misbehavior are inherent in the relationship. On the other hand, monitoring the relationship, even with the aid of inquiries into states of mind, is very difficult because the results of and activities involved in opportunism are difficult to measure. Therefore, fiduciary law goes beyond the proxies of general equity: no disproportionate hardship is needed and no intent is required. Self-dealing or conflict lead to liability without any need for a showing of bad faith or fraud; even good faith is no defense.[42] Thus, what is an *ex post* safety valve in equity becomes the general *ex ante* and untailored case in fiduciary law.

Because fiduciary law deals with a broad swath of opportunism it uses a wide range of tools, some more similar to those in general equity and some of a more categorical kind. Some types of fiduciary misbehavior can be foreseen in a general way but not detected *ex post*. Here we might allow limited contracting out of duties. On the present account, contracting out should be the most difficult where someone is quite possibly exploiting the truly unforeseeable and where equity seeks to keep its signals straight. Hence the oft-noted irreducible mandatory and open-ended nature of equity, which are thus two aspects of fiduciary law that we should expect will coincide. Further, if the value of promoting a given type of transaction is not very high but it is extremely hard to differentiate from a class of transactions that involves opportunism, then it makes sense for the former to be swept along in a prophylactic ban, with an apparent lack of concern with mental states.[43] Because fiduciary law needs to be more prophylactic in some situations, presumptions need to be difficult to overcome in those situations.

[42] See, eg, *Regal (Hastings) Ltd v Gulliver* [1942] 1 All ER 378, [1967] 2 AC 134, 144–5 (HL) (appeal taken from Eng) ("The rule of equity which insists on those, who by use of a fiduciary position make a profit, being liable to account for that profit, in no way depends on fraud, or absence of bona fides; or upon such questions or considerations as whether the profit would or should otherwise have gone to the plaintiff, or whether the profiteer was under a duty to obtain the source of the profit for the plaintiff, or whether he took a risk or acted as he did for the benefit of the plaintiff, or whether the plaintiff has in fact been damaged or benefited by his action. The liability arises from the mere fact of a profit having, in the stated circumstances, been made. The profiteer, however honest and well-intentioned, cannot escape the risk of being called upon to account"); *Boardman v Phipps* [1967] 2 AC 46, 104, 105, 112 (HL) (appeal taken from Eng); *Keech v Sandford* [1726] 25 Eng Rep 223, 223–5 (Ch) (UK); but cf *Murad v Al-Saraj* [2005] EWCA (Civ) 959, [85] (Eng); *Warman Int'l Ltd v Dwyer* (1995) 182 CLR 544, 561 (Austl) ("In the case of a business it may well be inappropriate and inequitable to compel the errant fiduciary to account for the whole of the profit of his conduct of the business or his exploitation of the principal's goodwill over an indefinite period of time. In such a case, it may be appropriate to allow the fiduciary a proportion of the profits, depending upon the particular circumstances").

[43] Matthew Conaglen has brought out the prophylactic aspect of fiduciary duty, justifying it on the grounds that it removes temptation from the fiduciary to violate other duties. See Matthew Conaglen, *Fiduciary Loyalty: Protecting the Due Performance of Non-fiduciary Duties* (2010) 59–105.

II. The Structure of Fiduciary Law

As we have seen, fiduciary law was historically at the heart of equity, and historic equity partook to a great extent of the equitable decision-making mode in the service of countering opportunism. In this section, I show that equity as anti-opportunism helps explain and justify fiduciary law. Trusts and trust-like relationships present great dangers of opportunism that call for a broader and more stringent version of equity.

A. The equitable contours of fiduciary law

Consider first the characteristic features of equity. As an outgrowth of equity, it is not surprising that fiduciary law is often untailored and morally inflected. But the connection is more than mere path dependence; it is functional. Because trustees present the greatest dangers of opportunism, they are at the core of equity and the trust is equity at its high-water mark. Deborah DeMott is right that analogies abound in this area,[44] and these analogies are, as Peter Birks argues, based on similarity to the trust and the trustee-beneficiary relationship.[45] Fiduciary relationships are "trust-like" in presenting a similar danger of opportunism and therefore call for untailored—broad *ex ante* or targeted *ex post*—intervention of a morally inflected sort.[46] The safety valve theory of equity leads us to expect that the analogies in fiduciary law will be premised on the theme of threats of opportunism.

The invocation of a high moral standard, associated with Judge Cardozo's ringing endorsement of the highest sense of honor being the standard to which fiduciaries are to be held ("the punctilio of an honor the most sensitive"), is a stronger version of the morals reflected in equity (eg, clean hands, not profiting from one's own wrong). Fiduciary law is like the rest of equity but more so. Indeed, Judge Cardozo explicitly invoked the traditions of the court of equity in his famous pronouncement in *Meinhard v Salmon*.[47] Also, because the ways to be opportunistic as a fiduciary are very hard to foresee in any detail and even difficult to tease apart from general conditions *ex post*,[48]

[44] Deborah A DeMott, "Beyond Metaphor: An Analysis of Fiduciary Obligation," *Duke LJ* 879, 891 (1988).

[45] Peter Birks, "The Content of Fiduciary Obligation," 34 *Isr L Rev* 3, 8 (2000).

[46] Opportunism is one way of specifying what constitutes an "abuse of power." For a theory of fiduciary law built around the notion of abuse of power and the corresponding vulnerability of entrustors, see Tamar Frankel, "Fiduciary Law," 71 *Cal L Rev* 795 (1983); D Gordon Smith and Jordan C Lee, "Discretion," 75 Ohio St LJ __ (2014) (draft, 22 Mar 2013), 12–13, available at SSRN: <http://ssrn.com/abstract=2238287> or <http://dx.doi.org/10.2139/ssrn.2238287>.

[47] *Meinhard v Salmon* 164 NE 545 (NY 1928) (Cardozo J). In holding coadventurers to a fiduciary duty, Judge Cardozo opined (at 546) that:

> Joint adventurers, like copartners, owe to one another, while the enterprise continues, the duty of the finest loyalty. Many forms of conduct permissible in a workaday world for those acting at arm's length, are forbidden to those bound by fiduciary ties. A trustee is held to something stricter than the morals of the market place. Not honesty alone, but the punctilio of an honor the most sensitive, is then the standard of behavior. As to this there has developed a tradition that is unbending and inveterate. Uncompromising rigidity has been the attitude of courts of equity when petitioned to undermine the rule of undivided loyalty by the "disintegrating erosion" of particular exceptions.

[48] Robert Cooter and Bradley J Freedman, "The Fiduciary Relationship: Its Economic Character and Legal Consequences," 66 *NYU L Rev* 1045, 1050, 1057 (1991).

fiduciary law is vague and open-ended around the edges.[49] Like the rest of equity, fiduciary law uses principles like substance-over-form in order to counter opportunism, or in the words of one treatise "[i]n deciding whether a given transaction is tainted with disloyalty the court will look through all the subterfuges and indirections. It will consider the substance and not merely the form."[50] Finally, fiduciary law is *in personam*. The trust is somewhere in between property and contract, but the fiduciary duty is toward the *in personam* end of the scale. Fiduciary duties run in the first instance to beneficiaries. An order to a trustee does not set up a general rule, nor does it bind third parties. Indeed, the duties of third parties to be on the look out for trusts so as not to violate them are as minimal as they can be without calling forth opportunists who would like to pass for good faith purchasers.

Even more striking is the similarity in overall contours of the proxies and presumptions in fiduciary law and those that operate in equity generally, with fiduciary law being a beefed up version of equity. Robert Sitkoff usefully distinguishes "subsidiary rules" or presumptions within the overall fiduciary standard, which as he points out, avoids letting the rules become a "roadmap for strategic avoidance behavior."[51] Similarly, where loophole finding is at its most serious, in tax law, a case can be made for general anti-avoidance standards.[52] Equity is an all-purpose anti-avoidance standard, and fiduciary law not unexpectedly partakes of this approach.

The main difference between fiduciary law and general equity is that the proxies in fiduciary law are even more prophylactic than those in equity generally. One need not show there is an actual injury, and so fiduciary law declares that gains belong to the beneficiary because it was the beneficiary's means that were used.[53] In the core area of trusts, self-dealing or conflict of interest on the part of the fiduciary makes the transaction in question voidable and makes available disgorgement remedies; no showing of fraud or even harm in a narrow sense to the beneficiary is required.[54] If equity seeks to ensure that one not profit from one's own wrong,[55] traditional fiduciary law goes a step further in not allowing one to profit from a situation in which it is hard to tell whether one profited from one's own wrong. Or in the words of one treatise on trusts, "equity deems

[49] See, eg, *Guerin v Canada* [1984] 2 SCR 335, 341, 13 DLR (4th) 321 ("[T]he categories of fiduciary, like those of negligence, should not be considered closed").

[50] Gleason Bogert and George Taylor Bogert, *The Law of Trusts and Trustees* (rev 2nd edn, 1993) § 543(T), at 410. Note that "substance over form" is one of the anti-avoidance doctrines in tax, which aims at the exploitation of loopholes. See Smith (n 6) and the sources cited in n 52 herein.

[51] Robert H Sitkoff, "The Economic Structure of Fiduciary Law," 91 *BU L Rev* 1045 (2011).

[52] See David A Weisbach, "Formalism in the Tax Law," 66 *U Chi L Rev* 860 (1999); see also Sarah B Lawsky, "Probably? Understanding Tax Law's Uncertainty," 157 *U Pa L Rev* 1017, 1032 (2009) (arguing that tax law uses probabilistic doctrines because "the essence of a tax shelter is that it technically complies with the law while nonetheless violating the substance or intent of the law, which is no easy thing to determine"); Stanley S Surrey, "Complexity and the Internal Revenue Code: The Problem of the Management of Tax Detail," 34 *L & Contemp Probs* 673, 707 n 31 (1969).

[53] See Paul B Miller, "Justifying Fiduciary Duties," 58 *McGill LJ* 969, 1019–20 (2013).

[54] See, eg, *Fulton Nat'l Bank v Tate* 363 F 2d 562, 571 (5th Cir 1966) ("[T]he beneficiary need only show that the fiduciary allowed himself to be placed in a position where his personal interest might conflict with the interest of the beneficiary. It is unnecessary to show that the fiduciary succumbed to this temptation, that he acted in bad faith, that he gained an advantage, fair or unfair, that the beneficiary was harmed. Indeed, the law presumes that the fiduciary acted disloyally, and inquiry into such matters is foreclosed."); see generally Austin Wakeman Scott, William Franklin Fratcher, and Mark L Ascher, *Scott and Ascher on Trusts* (5th edn, 2007) vol 3, §17.2, at 1078–80.

[55] See, eg, *Riggs v Palmer* 22 NE 188 (NY 1889).

it better to… strike down all disloyal acts, rather than to attempt to separate the harmless and the harmful by permitting the trustee to justify his representation of two interests."[56]

The duty of loyalty is closely tied to the danger of opportunism, while at the same time sweeping broadly. Under the duty of loyalty, self-dealing leads to per se liability and disgorgement. Conflicts of interest in general lead to a presumption against the fiduciary, and often per se liability. In the corporate context, Delaware law more recently provides that the burden shifts to the fiduciary to prove the entire fairness of the transaction.[57] Consistent with its prophylactic nature and the need to prevent opportunism, fiduciary law may also apply after a fiduciary relationship has ended in order to prevent a fiduciary from evading the requirements of loyalty by terminating the relationship early.[58]

The duty of care works in tandem with the proxies and presumptions that get us into fiduciary law in the first place. Again, where the danger of opportunism is high it makes sense to tailor presumptions to counter the danger. With the duty of care, though, the proxies for opportunism potentially sweep more broadly and more damagingly. Indeed, as in equity generally, the problem is sometimes potential opportunism on both sides. Is the person complaining of a breach just invoking the contract or other law in order to profit from a lawsuit and not out of any true injury?[59] For this reason, the proxies in the area of the duty of care are less sweeping, and in specialized contexts they are reversed, as in the business judgment rule.[60] And, it is worth pointing out that there are even narrower proxies that flip the presumption back into regular fiduciary mode (or prevent the business judgment rule from applying; these include lack of business purpose, conflict of interest, and substantively and procedurally egregiously bad decision-making[61]). Likewise, it is easier to contract out of the fiduciary duty of care than the duty of loyalty—much less the duty of good faith.

[56] Bogert and Bogert (n 50) § 543, at 228.

[57] *Weinberger v OUP, Inc* 457 A 2d 701 (Del 1983); *Sinclair Oil Corp v Levien* 280 A 2d 717 (Del 1971); see also *Nixon v Blackwell* 626 A 2d 1366, 1376 (Del 1993).

[58] Conaglen (n 43) at 188–90.

[59] Ayotte, Friedman, and Smith (n 23).

[60] See *Joy v North* 692 F 2d 880, 885 (2d Cir 1982) (Winter J) ("[T]he fact is that liability is rarely imposed upon corporate directors or officers simply for bad judgment and this reluctance to impose liability for unsuccessful business decisions has been doctrinally labeled the business judgment rule"). Judge Winter goes on to offer several reasons for the business judgment rule, including the implications of portfolio theory:

> [B]ecause potential profit often corresponds to the potential risk, it is very much in the interest of shareholders that the law not create incentives for overly cautious corporate decisions. Some opportunities offer great profits at the risk of very substantial losses, while the alternatives offer less risk of loss but also less potential profit. Shareholders can reduce the volatility of risk by diversifying their holdings. In the case of the diversified shareholder, the seemingly more risky alternatives may well be the best choice since great losses in some stocks will over time be offset by even greater gains in others. Given mutual funds and similar forms of diversified investment, courts need not bend over backwards to give special protection to shareholders who refuse to reduce the volatility of risk by not diversifying. A rule which penalizes the choice of seemingly riskier alternatives thus may not be in the interest of shareholders generally.

Joy v North at 886 (footnotes omitted).

[61] Again, Judge Winter:

> Whatever its merit, however, the business judgment rule extends only as far as the reasons which justify its existence. Thus, it does not apply in cases, e.g., in which the corporate decision lacks a business purpose, is tainted by a conflict of interest, is so egregious as to amount to a no-win

Finally, if good faith is considered a separate fiduciary duty, we should expect it to be similar to but stronger than the general duty of good faith and to involve similar proxies and presumptions. Like the duty of good faith in contract law, the fiduciary duty of good faith cannot be contracted away entirely. I return to this question in Section III.

For situations that go beyond the recurrent hard-to-monitor types of malfeasance, what is important is to find proxies for unforeseeable exploitation of rules. Situations of fraud, accident, and mistake give rise to the problem of near-fraud and exploitation of uncertainty. More particularly, proxies relating to bad faith and disproportionate hardship can be used in a somewhat open-ended fashion to invalidate actions or to throw the burden of justification on a party who wishes to take advantage of them. Fiduciary law is concerned with situations where the discretion of the fiduciary and the vulnerability of the beneficiary call for a gimlet eye on the issue of good faith and disproportionate hardship: any showing that a fiduciary profited from the relationship leads to disgorgement. Fiduciary law combines a stringent version of the open-ended proxies and presumptions of equity with prophylactic *ex ante* rules aimed at dangerous situations of potential conflicts.

B. Equity and reforms

Equity as anti-opportunism suggests caution in loosening traditional stringent rules about fiduciary duties. There has been a tendency to soften some of the per se rules of liability and the strength of some presumptions. Sometimes this is warranted. Thus, in trusts the older prudent investor rule was too cautious in light of modern portfolio theory, and the tendency was for judges to engage in *ex post* hindsight when an *ex ante* standard of appropriate investment of trust assets would allow for higher returns without opening the door to opportunism. The older prudent man rule required that trustees act as "men of prudence, discretion and intelligence, manage their own affairs,"[62] and became encrusted with sub-rules putting entire kinds of investments off limits.[63] The danger in this context is of judicial hindsight bias,[64] not trustee opportunism. Here the *ex post* perspective is simply not needed to combat opportunism, which means that there should be no obstacle to the newer "prudent investor" rule, advocated by scholars like Jeffrey Gordon, John Langbein, and Richard Posner,[65] promoted by law reform

> decision, or results from an obvious and prolonged failure to exercise oversight or supervision. Other examples may occur.

Joy v North (case citations omitted). Interestingly, these categories are versions of the equitable proxies, and are likewise somewhat open-ended. Compare them to disproportionate hardship and forfeiture, which similarly rely on an unexplained extreme imbalance to shift the presumption to one who would benefit from it.

[62] *Harvard College v Amory* 26 Mass 446 (1830).

[63] Max M Schanzenbach and Robert H Sitkoff, "The Prudent Investor Rule and Trust Asset Allocation: An Empirical Analysis," 35 *Am C Tr & Est Couns J* 314, 35–6 (2010).

[64] Daniel B Kelly, "Toward Economic Analysis of the Uniform Probate Code," 45 *U Mich JL Reform* 855, 870 (2012); see also Chris Guthrie, Jeffrey J Rachlinski, and Andrew J Wistrich, "Inside the Judicial Mind," 86 *Cornell L Rev* 777, 804 (2001).

[65] See, eg, Jeffrey N Gordon, "The Puzzling Persistence of the Constrained Prudent Man Rule," 62 *NY U L Rev* 52 (1987); John H Langbein, "The Uniform Prudent Investor Act and the Future of Trust Investing," 81 *Iowa L Rev* 641 (1996); John H Langbein and Richard A Posner, "Market Funds and Trust-Investment Law," 1976 *ABF Res J* 1 (1976).

bodies, and now enacted in all the states.[66] The prudent investor rule sets forth an objective standard for investments appropriate to a trust in light of risk-return trade-offs and the trust portfolio as a whole. The main effect is to increase the proportion of stocks held in trusts,[67] and it is hard to see how this significantly increases the dangers of opportunism.

In contrast, the loosening of the no further inquiry rule in trust law, proposed most prominently by John Langbein, is questionable. In keeping with his contractarian view of the trust, Langbein proposes that fiduciaries who engage in conflicts of interest should be able to prove entire fairness, just as they can in more recent corporate law.[68] The result would be a rule that required trustees to act in the best interests rather than sole interests of the beneficiary. His justifications rely mostly on an improved ability of courts to find facts and on the benefits of conflicted transactions as reflected in statutory exceptions to the no further inquiry rule and in the possibility of getting judicial pre-approval. The exceptions do not, however, prove the rule is unfounded, because they might reflect other policies or are not inconsistent with the no further inquiry rule.[69] To this we can add that the statutory exceptions Langbein points to—allowing trustees to earn commissions and to pool funds for investment purposes—are quite far from the main concerns about opportunism and so dovetail nicely with equitable anti-opportunism. The exceptions do suggest the costs of a sweeping rule—which are true of any prophylactic rule—and, as we have seen, in a system of presumptions there is no reason not to have sub-presumptions that flip the other way. Even though many trustees are financial institutions and many trusts involve financial assets, the no further inquiry rule has a purpose beyond making up for historically bad fact finding procedures. It would be surprising if better civil or even administrative procedures could eliminate the problem of opportunism—they certainly haven't in the area of tax.[70] The worry perhaps should be the opposite: that, as equity judges always feared, the judicial process itself has become a plaything for opportunists.

[66] Uniform Prudent Investor Act (1994); *Restatement (Third) of Trusts* (2007) vol 3, 287–92 (Introductory Note to ch 17).

[67] Max M Schanzenbach and Robert H Sitkoff, "Did Reform of Prudent Trust Investment Laws Change Trust Portfolio Allocation?," 50 *JL & Econ* 681 (2007); Schanzenbach and Sitkoff (n 63) (finding a 3–10 percent increase in trust stock holding at the expense of "safe investments" in the period after the introduction of the prudent investor rule).

[68] John H Langbein, "Questioning the Trust Law Duty of Loyalty: Sole Interest or Best Interest?," 114 *Yale LJ* 929 (2005).

[69] Melanie B Leslie, "In Defense of the No Further Inquiry Rule: A Response to Professor John Langbein," 47 *Wm & Mary L Rev* 541, 567–71 (2005).

[70] Langbein also dismisses equity with some standard references to *Bleak House*. Langbein (n 68) at 945–57. Again, my defense of the equitable element in fiduciary law is not meant to be historic. The problems leading to the breakdown of equity do, as Langbein suggests, flow from the organization of the equity court. In particular, there was only one Chancellor, later joined by one Vice Chancellor. This allowed for more uniformity of judgments, but at the cost of huge delay and expense. I would suggest that the equitable decision-making mode does not require separate courts, and one should concentrate on defining the proxies and presumptions that implement the decision-making mode. Perhaps the lesson to be drawn from Langbein's critique is that we should question whether it is wise to give equitable precedents the same weight in terms of stare decisis, which was also a development of the later equity courts—and which put greater pressure on them to achieve consistency. Perhaps the sorry history of nineteenth-century equity is more a matter of those courts not being equitable enough in the sense of mostly limiting themselves to acting as a safety valve against opportunism.

So the question remains whether it is appropriate for situations called fiduciary, and trusts in particular, to be identified as ones in which the danger of opportunism requires a prophylactic rule. Again, the traditional rule was based, as were other equitable proxies and presumptions, on "near fraud," or the danger of opportunism. In Chancellor Kent's words, the sole interest rule "is founded on the danger of imposition and the presumption of the existence of fraud, inaccessible to the eye of the court."[71] Perhaps there is scope for defining a class of trusts to be similar enough to corporations, and corporate fiduciaries usually do face greater competitive pressures than do trustees.[72] And statutory carve-outs from the equitable prophylactic no further inquiry rule do not conflict with equity as a backstop, either historically or functionally. That reformers like Langbein have—in keeping with the post-fusion loss of awareness of how and why equity does what it does—overlooked the role of opportunism and its special relationship to equity,[73] suggests we should reevaluate such proposals in light of equity as anti-opportunism before taking the plunge. We should not lose sight of the danger of opportunism in the historical core of fiduciary law. At the very least, a residual category of fiduciary liability for the open-ended class of new forms of mischief will be very hard to do without.

C. Fiduciary proxies and presumptions

Let us now consider the proxies. Paul Miller divides previous approaches to fiduciary relationships into status-based and fact-based and argues that neither offers a principled account of fiduciary law.[74] That is true, but on the present account of equity, we should not expect that the status- or fact-based approaches would produce a single principle, let alone a rule. Instead, status and facts reflect different types of proxies for opportunism, with status-based proxies being the more sweeping and stable and fact-based proxies being more targeted and open-ended. What equity needs to avoid is being sweeping and open-ended at the same time. General invocations of loyalty run this danger. James Penner argues for skepticism that loyalty is the content of the duty of fiduciaries.[75] Indeed, if the duty of loyalty is really a shorthand over the system of equitable proxies and presumptions, then we should not expect the "duty" to be infused with content directly. Instead, as he and others have noted, the no-conflict rule is aimed at the human capacity for rationalization.[76]

[71] James Kent, *Commentaries on American Law* vol 4, *438. Langbein finds this and related arguments as reflecting a "logic" that is "dubious." He finds it weird that "because some trustee misbehavior might be successfully concealed, the law should refuse to examine the merits of the trustee's conduct even in a case in which there has not been concealment." Langbein (n 68) at 945. This begs the question. Because we cannot know which case is which we have to make a policy judgment (as in Epstein's theory of procedural unconscionability) whether given the possibility of errors on both sides and their seriousness (in terms of not getting at opportunism, mislabeling, and chilling legitimate behavior), it makes sense to have a prophylactic rule. Langbein's aspersions prove far too much. In any case, as he says, he rests his argument on the changed circumstances, in terms of better courts and more need for conflicted transactions, which I address in the text.

[72] For an argument that corporate law without the Efficient Capital Markets Hypothesis would look like trust law, see Robert H Sitkoff, "Trust Law, Corporate Law, and Capital Market Efficiency," 28 *J Corp L* 565 (2003).

[73] See the discussion in n 71.

[74] Paul B Miller, "A Theory of Fiduciary Liability," 56 *McGill LJ* 235, 241–52 (2011).

[75] J E Penner, "Is Loyalty a Virtue, and Even If It Is, Does It Really Help Explain Fiduciary Liability?", this volume, 169.

[76] Penner (n 75) at 8; Irit Samet, "Guarding the Fiduciary's Conscience—A Justification of a Stringent Profit-stripping Rule," 28 *Oxford J Legal Stud* 763 (2008); see also Andrew S Gold, "The New Concept of

Self-serving rationalization can shade off into evasion,[77] and, as we have seen, fiduciary law needs to be more sweeping than general equity. So the idea that fiduciary duty includes contexts in which self-serving rationalization is the danger, rather than more raw forms of evasion and opportunism, should come as no surprise.

Start with status. Whole categories of relationships have been deemed to be similar enough to the trustee–beneficiary relationship to warrant fiduciary treatment. But analogies imply some basis for considering some similarities more important than others. In the case of fiduciary relationships, the similarities invoked are the same ones that come to the fore when the more open-ended fact-based approach is employed. This is no accident. In equity as anti-opportunism, we can say that sometimes the problem of opportunism as reflected in the most important proxies like disproportionate hardship, hidden action, vulnerability, and the like, point toward a broad shift in the presumption against the one in the informationally advantaged position—the trustee-like actor. Thus, in addition to trustees, fiduciaries include corporate officers and directors, partners, attorneys, and various agents.

Now consider the fact-based fiduciary relationships. The facts in question usually relate to one party's vulnerability and the discretion wielded by the candidate for fiduciary. As with equity, scholars have criticized fiduciary duty for being unpredictable around the edges.[78] And, again as with equity, courts and commentators often state that fiduciary law is not closed, but nervousness about its open-endedness probably explains why courts try to hew to the established categories based on known status relationships.[79] This makes fiduciary law, like equity in general, seem like "a concept in search of a principle."[80]

From the point of view of equity as anti-opportunism, the question is whether the proxies for opportunism and the effect of the presumptions based on them are unpredictable enough to keep the opportunists guessing but without destabilizing the law. Fiduciary law is broader than the general equitable safety valve, as noted earlier, but unlike the rest of the law it has certain special features. First, it is often difficult to become a fiduciary, so the stringent liability of a fiduciary does not affect the mine run of behavior.[81] It is an empirical question whether the proxies implicitly identified by Leff and Epstein are so broad that they chill too much behavior to make the wide prophylactic presumptions worthwhile. Normatively, courts should not forget that fiduciary law has established categories of fiduciary and that the residual open-endedness is simply a protective buffer aimed at opportunism, not a roving commission to rewrite deals in the name of *ex post* fairness. In this sense as in many others, fiduciary law presents in stark form the dilemma facing equity.

Loyalty in Corporate Law" 43 *UC Davis L Rev* 457, 498–9 (2009) (arguing that self-interest may cause director's assessments of the best interests of the beneficiary to be less accurate).

[77] Yuval Feldman and Henry E Smith, "Behavioral Equity," 170 *J Institutional and Theoretical Econ* 137 (2014); see also Louis Kaplow and Steven Shavell, "Moral Rules, Moral Sentiments, and Behavior: Toward a Theory of an Optimal Moral System," 115 *J Pol Econ* 494, 505–6 (2007) (arguing that complex moral rules are susceptible to self-interested rationalizations).

[78] Peter Birks, "Equity in the Modern Law: An Exercise in Taxonomy," 26 *U W Austral L Rev* 1, 17–18 (1996); Miller (n 74) at 249–50; Sarah Worthington, "Fiduciaries: When Is Self-Denial Obligatory?," 58 *Camb LJ* 500, 505 (1999).

[79] Sarah Worthington, *Equity* (2003) 134–5; see also Miller (n 74), at 241.

[80] Worthington (n 79) at 135 (quoting Justice Wilson).

[81] See, eg, Frankel (n 46), at 801.

D. Other equitable features of fiduciary law

As in the case of equity, the fact-based analysis is somewhat constrained by reliance on external standards. Commonsense morality goes some way toward cabining equity, but there has long been skepticism that morality alone would constrain equity judges sufficiently in order to prevent equity from becoming threatening and uncertain.[82] Courts in fiduciary cases look to "community or industry standards."[83] Equity has also long had a role in enforcing community and industry custom.[84]

Moreover, in terms of information costs, there is reason to think that fiduciary law is less threatening to the stability of the rest of private law than is equity in its most general applications. Much of the worry about the role of morality in equity stems from the fear that it will make general declarations, especially in the area of property.[85] These fears are limited in the case of fiduciary law because of the largely *in personam* effect of the fiduciary duties. Impacts on third parties are legally limited to those who knew they were dealing with a trustee qua trustee and those who receive, either gratuitously or with notice, an asset subject to an equitable right transferred in violation of a fiduciary duty. Because the duty to inquire into these matters is minimal, such parties can be expected to avoid involvement in violations of fiduciary duty without great burden substantively or informationally. Returning to the trust itself, the origin of modern fiduciary law, the trust itself is perched between *in rem* and *in personam*, property and contract, and the fiduciary duties relate more to the latter.[86] This is why the contractarian approach to fiduciary law has had the success it enjoys, even though it excessively downplays the residuum of mandatory law that equity as anti-opportunism, by contrast, can handle well.[87]

Notable features of fiduciary law follow from this equitable set of proxies and presumptions. First, the notion that property or a "critical resource" is important receives an explanation.[88] We worry more, as Leff noted, about sharp dealing—opportunism—where the transaction is a large one-off for the (not coincidentally) less informed party. The equitable theory also suggests why fiduciary law is not totally confined to property or critical resources, important though these are. Situations in which the potential for opportunism arise out of an important discretionary agency relationship of great dependence are not limited to ones involving a conventional property interest or other

[82] See n 20 and accompanying text.

[83] *Hodgkinson v Simms* [1994] 3 SCR 377, 411–13, 423–5, 117 DLR (4th) 161; see also Miller (n 74) at 245; Scott FitzGibbon, "Fiduciary Relationships Are Not Contracts," 82 *Marq L Rev* 303, 340 (1999) ("Today as well, many fiduciary relationships are structured outside the positive law: by custom, for example, and by authorities on professional ethics. Social fiduciary relationships are supported by traditional social virtues such as loyalty, civility, self-sacrifice, vocational excellence, and high standards of honesty"); Smith and Lee (n 46).

[84] See Henry E Smith, "Custom in American Property Law: A Vanishing Act," 48 *Tex Int'l LJ* 507 (2013).

[85] See, eg, Charles M Gray, "The Boundaries of the Equitable Function," 20 *Am J Legal Hist* 192, 202–6 (1976).

[86] Ming Wai Lau, "The Nature of the Beneficial Interest: Historical and Economic Perspectives" (MS 2013), available at: <http://www.law.harvard.edu/programs/about/privatelaw/related-content/the_nature_of_the_beneficial_interest-historical_and_economic_perspectives.pdf>.

[87] See nn 96–100 and accompanying text.

[88] D Gordon Smith, "The Critical Resource Theory of Fiduciary Duty," 55 *Vand L Rev* 1399 (2002); see also Daniel Friedmann, "Restitution of Benefits Obtained through the Appropriation of Property or the Commission of a Wrong," 80 *Colum L Rev* 504 (1980).

identifiable resource. Thus, the treatment of physicians as fiduciaries is understandable, and it makes sense to apply quite prophylactic proxies and presumptions against physicians who profit from a physician–patient relationship in any fashion that does not involve informed consent.[89]

Note that because of the nature of the opportunism problem, fiduciary law is "gappy" in the sense that the proxies for opportunism are overinclusive. This leads to the characteristic flavor of fiduciary law as not being based on actual harm. I turn to remedies shortly. It also lends fiduciary law its "exclusive" and perhaps "propertarian" character.[90] In property itself, the exclusion strategies are in many ways overinclusive and prophylactic.[91] Famously the law of trespass does not require a showing of actual harm. In a sense, the problem of someone with access leads to such a large problem of potential opportunism that we flip the presumption against intruders in a very sweeping way in the law of trespass, so that basic entitlements are much lumpier than they would be in a world of much lower transaction costs.[92]

Finally, the equitable theory points to stringent remedies. Violations of fiduciary duties can lead to disgorgement of gains, the imposition of a constructive trust, or the payment of supracompensatory damages. As with the exclusion strategy in property law, a broad proxy calls for remedies with a steep drop-off.[93] Tailoring in the rules should be expected to be paired with tailored remedies, and vice versa. The broad proxies and presumptions not coincidentally sound in morality. Robert Cooter distinguishes between "sanctions," which are payments or even punishments for doing what is not allowed, and "prices," which are payments made to do something permitted.[94] As Cooter shows, the more the law focuses on a defined standard of conduct, rather than aiming at measurable external harm, the law employs sanctions, and the violation of the standard is considered wrong. With sanctions, liability takes a jump at the standard, in contrast to prices, which vary continuously with harm (assuming harm is a continuous variable). When it comes to liability in the presence of potential opportunism, a defined standard coupled with a sanction in Cooter's sense can be more robust in the face of manipulation than a price. Thus, the opportunistic fiduciary is not invited by fiduciary law to consider whether the proxies a court would use for harm might fail to capture the particular kind of opportunism. A blanket approach makes such considerations irrelevant to the fiduciary's thinking.

[89] See, eg, *Moore v Regents of Univ of Calif* 793 P 2d 479 (Cal 1990).

[90] Paul B Miller, "Justifying Fiduciary Remedies," 63 *U Toronto LJ* 570, 602–4 (2013) at 43; Ernest J Weinrib, "The Fiduciary Obligation," 25 *U Toronto LJ* 1, 9–15, 19–21 (1975); see also Gregory S Alexander, "A Cognitive Theory of Fiduciary Relationships," 85 *Cornell L Rev* 767 (2000).

[91] See, eg, Henry E Smith, "Mind the Gap: The Indirect Relation between Ends and Means in American Property Law," 94 *Cornell L Rev* 959 (2009).

[92] See, eg, Robert C Ellickson, "Property in Land," 102 *Yale LJ* 1315, 1327–8 (1993); Lee Anne Fennell, "Lumpy Property," 160 *U Pa L Rev* 1955, 1964 (2012); Carol M Rose, "Rethinking Environmental Controls: Management Strategies for Common Resources," *Duke LJ* 1, 9–36 (1991); Henry E Smith, "Exclusion Versus Governance: Two Strategies for Delineating Property Rights," 31 *J Legal Stud* S453, S467–74 (2002).

[93] Henry E Smith, "Property and Property Rules," 79 *NYU L Rev* 1719, 1748–53 (2004).

[94] Robert Cooter, "Prices and Sanctions," 84 *Colum L Rev* 1523 (1984); see also Guido Calabresi, *The Costs of Accidents: A Legal and Economic Analysis* (1970) 68–9 (outlining scheme of price-like specific deterrence and sanction-like general deterrence).

E. Summary

Overall, then, equity as anti-opportunism combines the best in other accounts. It lies somewhere between the contextualization of factors and policy on the one hand and the more formal principled approach on the other. For functional reasons, fiduciary law is both contextual and principled, but the one or the other element dominates depending on the factors that point to or away from equitable anti-opportunism—the danger of opportunism itself, the availability of cost-effective proxies, and the informational burden on third parties. What most sets fiduciary law apart from equity is a matter of degree: the danger of opportunism is high enough to warrant the addition of broader and more stringent prophylactic proxies and presumptions, and at the same time the informational burden on third parties to the fiduciary relationship is relatively light.

III. The Place of Fiduciary Law in Private Law

Seeing fiduciary law as an extreme example of equity as anti-opportunism allows us to situate fiduciary law within private law. It suggests some new perspectives on the age-old question of how contractarian fiduciary law is (and should be), and it draws out the similarities in fiduciary law to unjust enrichment.

A. Relation to other theories

Overall, seeing fiduciary law as a core of equitable anti-opportunism helps explain how and why fiduciary law is a hybrid of status- and fact-based approaches. Like equity, fiduciary law is moral but not unboundedly so. Like equity, anti-opportunism in fiduciary law lies between open-ended fix-it contextualism and principled formalism, but like equity this relationship has been obscured since the fusion of law and equity.[95]

Strikingly, equity as anti-opportunism can explain why fiduciary law is mostly but not entirely contractarian. Is fiduciary law simply a default contractual term, even in trust law?[96] Or is it mandatory in keeping with its moral flavor?[97] Equity as anti-opportunism suggests that we look for some meta-rule (or meta-standard) for

[95] Sometimes the conflict between expansive and narrow versions of equity results in opinions reflecting one or both extreme points of view rather than an intermediate one based on anti-opportunism that accords better with historical equity. See P G Turner, "Mending Men's Bargains," in "Equity: Mortgage Redemption and Relief Against Forfeiture" (forthcoming, *LQ Rev*, 2014) (analyzing *Cukurova Finance International Ltd v Alfa Telecom Turkey Ltd* [2013] UKPC 20); Smith (n 6) at 51–2 (discussing *Grupo Mexicano de Desarrollo, SA v Alliance Bond Fund, Inc* 527 US 308 (1999)).

[96] See, eg, Frank H Easterbrook and Daniel R Fischel, *The Economic Structure of Corporate Law* (1991) 90–108; Henry N Butler and Larry E Ribstein, "Opting Out of Fiduciary Duties: A Response to the Anti-Contractarians," 65 *Wash UL Rev* 1 (1990); see also Frank H Easterbrook & Daniel R Fischel, Contract and Fiduciary Duty, 36 *JL & Econ* 425, 427 (1991) ("Fiduciary duties are not special duties; they have no moral footing; they are the same sort of obligations, derived and enforced in the same way, as other contractual undertakings"); Langbein (n 2) 657–60; see also Sitkoff (n 51) at 1045–48 (arguing for broadly contractarian approach to fiduciary duty but recognizing need for mandatory standardization of unrecorded interests).

[97] See, eg, DeMott (n 44); FitzGibbon (n 83); see also Robert C Clark, "Agency Costs Versus Fiduciary Duties," in John W Pratt and Richard J Zeckhauser (eds), *Principals and Agents: The Structure of Business* (1985) 55; T P Gallanis, "The Trustee's Duty to Inform," 85 *NC L Rev* 1595 (2007); J C Shepherd, "Toward a Unified Concept of Fiduciary Relationships," 97 *LQ Rev* 51 (1981).

distinguishing situations in which parties have put the problem in question within a domain of contracting (that does not suffer from fraud, unconscionability, and the like), from those in which they have not (potential opportunism). Particularly in the corporate area, we can expect sophisticated parties to be able to deal with opportunism *ex ante*, and Delaware law in particular takes a broad opt-out approach.[98] Nevertheless, even in Delaware one cannot contract out of the duty of good faith altogether, just as in contract law.[99] This mandatory kernel protects the domain of contracting from an unscrupulous party who might do something outside that domain that defeats the contract's purpose. To the extent we can characterize this problem as one of true uncertainty (as opposed to risk), the rationale for some small mandatory core of fiduciary law makes sense.[100]

Equitable theory also helps explain why fiduciary law has been resistant to the type of theorizing that successfully unifies branches of the common law. Thus, many have complained about the unprincipled character of fiduciary law. They seek a principle that will tie the various fiduciary situations or relationships together. But we should only expect a loose tie. These situations are the ones in which, as in unconscionability but more so, the danger of opportunism is great enough compared to the forgone transactional benefits that we are warranted in flipping the presumption against the fiduciary.

One reason for the frustration with fiduciary law is its corresponding open-endedness. Some courts and commentators have asserted that some open-endedness is a necessity in fiduciary law to handle new situations. This is correct but can be overdone. What we need is for fiduciary law, like equity generally, to receive its proper scope based on proxies for opportunism, but the edges of this domain should be somewhat fuzzy and open-ended to respond to the strategic nature of opportunism. The law needs to mirror the open-endedness of opportunism itself. The result looks fuzzy from up close but less so in the larger picture.

Stepping back from this picture, we can see why fiduciary law veers between contextualism and formalism, and commentary is split between contextualizers and contractarians on the one hand and formalists and moralizers on the other. Like equity after the fusion of law and equity, it is hard to justify the mix of formalism and contextualism in a hybrid system if the purpose of the architecture has been obscured.

B. A comparison to unjust enrichment

The equitable approach to fiduciary law also helps explain its similarity and connections with unjust enrichment. This is a plus for the theory, both because there is a

[98] Andrew S Gold, "On the Elimination of Fiduciary Duties: A Theory of Good Faith for Unincorporated Firms," 41 *Wake Forest L Rev* 123 (2006). Coming up with default rules for opting out of or into fiduciary duties is a complex problem in light of how situations vary in terms of opportunism on either or both sides and the incentives to redistribute risk and conceal or reveal information in the process of contracting around defaults. See Jason Scott Johnston, "Opting In and Opting Out: Bargaining for Fiduciary Duties in Cooperative Ventures," 70 *Wash U LQ* 291 (1992). Johnston argues that, among other things, fiduciary duties should be more readily implied when relationship-specific investment is asymmetric (at 298, 318–23).

[99] Johnston (n 98).

[100] Smith (n 6).

general sense that fiduciary law and unjust enrichment share a lot in common and because the theory explains the similarities in detail as reflecting similar justifications.

In private law generally, equity is exceptional. In property, torts, and (especially) contract—in the last of which people can sometimes be expected to contract over possible opportunism—equity is a narrow exception in its role as a safety valve. But there are areas of law in which the problem of opportunism is central. As we have seen, fiduciary law is one such area. Unjust enrichment is another.

This chapter is not the place to offer a theory of unjust enrichment, but I will sketch here how the architecture of unjust enrichment reflects an equitable approach to opportunism. This is true even where aspects of unjust enrichment trace back to the law side of the law versus equity divide.[101] Even areas of the common law like quasi-contract—the main strand along with the constructive trust when they were brought together to form the law of restitution—partook functionally of the equitable decision-making mode.

Unjust enrichment employs broad proxies to set the presumption against the potential opportunist. In unjust enrichment, a major class of these proxies can be cast in terms of a property entitlement. Thus, on Daniel Friedmann's theory of unjust enrichment, most of the law is aimed at vindicating property or quasi-property entitlements, with a residual of cases that he dubs "deterrence."[102] The latter refers to egregious wrongdoing that violates public policy and calls forth a restitutionary remedy. Moreover, unjust enrichment law looks like a collection of disparate situations, such as mistaken payments, with an open-ended fact-based inquiry into bad behavior (wheedling the farm out of the farmer), just as in fiduciary law and the rest of equity. This structure has been celebrated as contextual judicial reasoning or as threatening to the rule of law, just like fiduciary law—and equity.[103] Both unjust enrichment and fiduciary law, like equity, feature a heavy moral flavor and a concern with individualized justice.[104] I suggest that unjust enrichment is a similar hybrid of narrower and broader proxies and presumptions that respond to similar problems of opportunism. The overall architecture of the equitable theory of unjust enrichment is similar to that of fiduciary law but differs in the dividing line between the more per se and rule-of-reason style proxies and in the terms in which they should be couched. Fiduciary law paints with an especially broad brush because the danger of opportunism is at its starkest.

Conclusion

Fiduciary law is and has always been at the heart of equity. The equity courts got their start in dealing with opportunists like faithless proto-trustees. The characteristic approach of proxies and presumptions rather than tailored rules, combined with morally inflected, *ex post* intervention directed in an *in personam* way, is characteristic of

[101] Andrew Kull, "James Barr Ames and the Early Modern History of Unjust Enrichment," 25 *Oxford J Legal Stud* 297, 304 (2005).

[102] Friedmann (n 88).

[103] Compare Hanoch Dagan, *The Law and Ethics of Restitution* (2004) with Emily Sherwin, "Restitution and Equity: An Analysis of the Principle of Unjust Enrichment," 79 *Tex L Rev* 2083, 2083–113 (2001).

[104] See Andrew S Gold and Henry E Smith, "How Private Law Is Simply Moral" (MS 2013), at 41–5.

both fiduciary law and equity generally. Fiduciary law employs especially broad proxies and stiff presumptions because the problem of opportunism is especially acute and some stock situations call for prophylactic *ex ante* rules. Bringing fiduciary law back to its equitable roots promises to allow it to be a hybrid of broader rules and more tailored standards so as to navigate between unconstrained contextualism and rigid formalism. Fiduciary law is central to the role that equity plays in suppressing opportunism.

PART IV

FIDUCIARY PRINCIPLES IN CONTEXT: PRIVATE LAW

14

Virtue and Utility

Fiduciary Law in Civil Law and Common Law Jurisdictions

*Michele Graziadei**

Introduction

Knowledge, in law, is often produced by making explicit what would otherwise remain implicit. An explicit representation of a practice or a norm enables reasoned analysis of it. What once might have gone unrepresented can eventually be labeled, classified, clarified, and reformed, if necessary.

The underlying contours of the law of fiduciaries have been with us for centuries, if not longer. However, the effort to clarify the precise doctrinal contours of the field as well as its core purposes and justification is much more recent. This probably explains difficulties experienced in theorizing fiduciary law and the vitality of academic debates on fiduciary law in common law jurisdictions.[1]

The purpose of this chapter is to explore the intellectual history of fiduciary law from a comparative standpoint, taking English and Italian law as its primary points of reference. It explores why fiduciary law is relatively neglected in countries belonging to the civil law tradition. It also explores the relationship between the civil and common law in the development of fiduciary principles. As will be demonstrated, the jurisprudence in common law countries has a history in which civilian sources played a role. This chapter will also show that there is much more fiduciary law in civilian jurisdictions than most English or American lawyers would think. The belief that fiduciary law is an unimportant minor field in civil law countries is based on false assumptions.

I. More than a Trace of an Old Religion: Fiduciary Law, Interested and Disinterested "Commerce"

We begin with language; the classical language of fiduciary law. By contemporary lights, this language has an unusual moralistic tone, speaking as it does of high duty, of punctilio, of unbending loyalty, of conscience. In Justice Cardozo's famous dictum, this moralistic language is set against that of market transactions, implying that fiduciaries are governed by rules different from those prevailing in the marketplace: "Not honesty alone, but the punctilio of an honor the most sensitive, is then the standard of behavior."[2]

* This publication was partly funded by the University of Torino under the agreement with the Compagnia di San Paolo "Progetti di Ateneo 2011" (Project title: The Making of a New European Legal Culture. Prevalence of a single model, or cross-fertilization of national legal traditions?).

[1] See Paul B Miller, "A Theory of Fiduciary Liability," 56 *McGill LJ* 235 (2011).

[2] *Meinhard v Salmon* 223 AD 663, 229 NYS 345 (App Div 1928).

Justice Cardozo's language recalls a time in which commerce was not yet fully accepted as worthy employment by the higher classes of society, and remunerated work was associated with a lowly social condition.

In that era, trusteeship was presented as a gratuitous, honorary office, to be undertaken for unselfish, rather than for mercenary motives.[3] This reflects the ethos of a world in which markets were not yet universal institutions, and some occupations were considered to be nobler than others. Cases which insist on the gratuitous nature of an undertaking of trusteeship reflect this mindset and this kind of economy. Take, for example, *Foster v William Deacon's Bank*,[4] in which a retiring trustee, being the sole trustee of a family trust created by his deceased father, without power to charge for his service, appointed the defendant bank as trustee to enable it to charge fees under the Public Trustee Act 1906. The court held the appointment of the bank was either invalid, or it was the appointment of an ordinary trustee, not entitled to charge any fee.

Fiduciary obligations spring initially from non-commercial relationships that reflect an economy of honor. This is clearly seen in Roman law sources, which in Europe were handed down over the generations through university teaching. Roman law, which was heavily influential in the formation of the modern law of countries like France, Germany, Italy, and Spain, held certain transactions to be essentially gratuitous, and fundamentally non-commercial in character.

In the Roman law of contracts, mandate was the contractual form corresponding best to this ideal type. Mandate was an honorific contract for services, which was sharply distinguished from contracts like *locatio-conductio*, under which services were to be provided for consideration.[5] Other relationships in Roman law involving one person taking care of another's affairs were also governed by loyalty-based sanctions (*infamia*) affecting the honor of Roman citizens. These included tutorship, deposit, partnership, and *fiducia*. Each of these relationships was informed by the obligation to respect *fides*; all implied a fiduciary dimension, just like *fideicommissa* in the law of succession.[6] Some were properly classified as contractual relationships (mandate, deposit, partnership); others were not so classified (*tutela*, *fiducia*), but all generated a duty to account, which is a distinguishing feature of fiduciary relationships.[7]

[3] *Ayliffe v Murray* (1740) 2 Atk 58, at 60, per Hardwicke LC: "In general this court looks upon trusts as honorary, and a burden upon the honour and conscience of the person intrusted, and not undertaken upon mercenary views; and there is a strong reason too against allowing any thing beyond the terms of the trust, because it gives an undue advantage to a trustee, to distress a cestui que trust, and therefore this court have always held a strict hand upon trustees in this particular." Chantal Stebbings, *The Private Trustee in Victorian England* (2002) 4, 30–1, 41, 194 provides an excellent treatment of this point; for further reflections on this point see: John H Langbein, "Questioning the Trust Law Duty of Loyalty: Sole Interest or Best Interest," 114 *Yale LJ* 929, at 940 (2005).

[4] [1935] 1 Ch 350 (CA).

[5] Alan Watson, "The Evolution of Law: The Roman System of Contracts," 2 *Law and Hist Rev* 1, 12 (1984): "That the contract came into existence at all is a tribute to the great weight that the Romans placed upon friendship—friends were expected to do a great deal for one another. It may seem surprising that such a distinction is made between agreeing to act gratuitously for another and acting for reward, but the Roman attitude that labor degrades sufficiently explains it. This also explains why performance of *artes liberales* could not be the subject of *locatio conductio*." This did not prevent *ex gratia* payments made to the agent, namely an honorarium in return of his services, Reinhard Zimmermann, *The Law of Obligations* (1990) 415 ff.

[6] David Johnston, *The Roman Law of Trusts* (1988).

[7] Joshua Getzler, "'As if:' Accountability and Counterfactual Trust," 91 *Boston Univ L Rev* 973 (2011), rightly notes the duty to account as the key feature of all fiduciary transactions.

Looking at the history of fiduciary relationships from a contemporary perspective one notices a tension between the increasing tendency to view contracts from a market-oriented and utilitarian perspective and the ideals of liberality and honorary service. A good illustration of this tension is found in Hume's treatment of "The Obligation of Promises" in his *Treatise of Human Nature*, first published in 1739.

Hume's *Treatise* took shape in the twilight of the natural law tradition, and his account of promissory obligation opens with a refutation of the Aristotelian view that promise-keeping is mandated by virtue.[8] Aristotle (and the natural law tradition after him) maintained that promise-keeping is mandated by virtues of honesty and justice (as well as liberality in cases of purely gratuitous promises).[9] Hume rejects this approach in favor of one explicitly premised on the pursuit of self-interest,[10] but more nuanced and complicated than that previously advanced by Hobbes.[11]

Hume explains that interested commerce, based on promises, is not the only conceivable form of exchange. He points out that disinterested forms of exchange are often perceived as more gratifying, though they are less secure. In Hume's account, promises have been instituted "to distinguish [those] two different sort[s] of commerce, the interested and the disinterested." Since human generosity is by nature limited and moralists and politicians cannot amend it:

> All they can pretend to, is, to give a new direction to those natural passions, and teach us that we can better satisfy our appetites in an oblique and artificial manner, than by their headlong and impetuous motion. Hence I learn to do a service to another, without bearing him any real kindness; because I foresee, that he will return my service, in expectation of another of the same kind, and in order to maintain the same correspondence of good offices with me or with others.[12]

Selfishness—"the true mother of ingratitude"—undermines older forms of commerce, not explicitly based on pursuit of self-interest, because those forms do not provide enough mutual confidence and security to allow transactions to develop on a large scale:

> Men being naturally selfish, or endowed only with a confined generosity, they are not easily induced to perform any action for the interest of strangers, except with a view to some reciprocal advantage, which they had no hope of obtaining but by such a performance. Now as it frequently happens, that these mutual performances cannot be

[8] David Hume, *A Treatise of Human Nature, Being an Attempt to Introduce the Experimental Method of Reasoning into Moral Subjects* (1739; 2nd edn, 1978) III.II.V, pp 516 ff.

[9] *Nichomachean Ethics*, iv. vii, 1127a–1127b; on this see: James Gordley, *Philosophical Origins of Modern Contract Doctrine* (1991) 10 ff; Martin Hogg, *Promises and Contract Law: Comparative Perspectives* (2011) 69 ff.

[10] In her fine article, Rachel Cohon, "Hume on Promises and the Peculiar Act of the Mind," 44 *J Hist Phil* 25 (2006), notes that Hume's approach does not rely only upon the working on self-interest, but is also premised on the sentiment of morality and duty which assists promise keeping while society develops. I do not deny this, but I agree with Knut Haakonssen, *The Science of a Legislator: The Natural Jurisprudence of David Hume and Adam Smith* (1981) 29 ff: enlightened self-interest, at least in the *Treatise*, is the principal motive of promise keeping according to Hume.

[11] Paul Russel, "Hume's Treatise and Hobbes's the Elements of Law," 46 *J Hist Ideas* 51 (1985), discusses the influence of Hobbes's *Elements of the Law* on Hume's *Treatise*, and why Hume wished to distance his work from that of Hobbes.

[12] Hume (n 8) 521.

finished at the same instant, it is necessary, that one party be contented to remain in uncertainty, and depend upon the gratitude of the other for a return of kindness. But so much corruption is there among men, that, generally speaking, this becomes but a slender security; and as the benefactor is here supposed to bestow his favours with a view to self-interest, this both takes off from the obligation, and sets an example to selfishness, which is the true mother of ingratitude. Were we, therefore, to follow the natural course of our passions and inclinations, we should perform but few actions for the advantage of others, from disinterested views; because we are naturally very limited in our kindness and affection: And we should perform as few of that kind, out of a regard to interest; because we cannot depend upon their gratitude. Here then is the mutual commerce of good offices in a manner lost among mankind, and every one reduced to his own skill and industry for his well-being and subsistence.[13]

The conventional device of promises was therefore introduced to separate interested from disinterested commerce. In the former kind of commerce, "interest is the *first* obligation to the performance of promises."[14] This is signaled by the use of the form of words that "constitutes what we call *a promise*, which is the sanction of the interested commerce of mankind."[15] This innovation shows how selfishness "in an oblique and artificial manner" can ameliorate its otherwise disruptive effects:

> After these signs are instituted, whoever uses them is immediately bound by his interest to execute his engagements, and must never expect to be trusted any more, if he refuse to perform what he promis'd.[16]

Modern commerce, therefore, relies on artificial rules that make the advancement of self-interest a legitimate and avowed goal. According to Hume, the advent of interested commerce did not cause the demise of disinterested commerce. Giving "without any prospect of advantage" can still generate a form of economy that bans explicit calculation from the interaction, grounded as it is on the more generous and noble intercourse of friendship, good offices, and love. According to Hume, this form of economy is based on gratitude and "kindness".

When Hume speaks of kindness he is referring not simply to a character trait but to a mode of action illustrated in Cicero's *De officiis* and Seneca's *De beneficiis*.[17] In law, this mode of action is still referred to as an "act of kindness."[18] This terminology has a rich

[13] Hume (n 8) 519–20. [14] Hume (n 8) 523.

[15] Hume (n 8) 522: "In order, therefore, to distinguish those two different sorts of commerce, the interested and the disinterested, there is a certain form of words invented for the former, by which we bind ourselves to the performance of any action. This form of words constitutes what we call a promise, which is the sanction of the interested commerce of mankind."

[16] Hume (n 8) 522. For a contemporary perspective on utilitarian and moral accounts of promising see Andrew Gold, "Consideration and the Morality of Promising," in Jason W Neyers, Richard Bronaugh, and Stephen G A Pitel (eds), *Exploring Contract Law* (2009) 115–37.

[17] Marion Griffin, "De Beneficiis and Roman Society," 93 *J Roman Studies* 92 (2003), highlights the significance of these works in the Roman context. Edward Andrew, "The Senecan Moment: Patronage and Philosophy in the Eighteenth Century," 65 *J Hist Ideas* 277 (2004), discusses their influence in the age of Hume.

[18] Thus, in *Arnott v Redfern* (1826) 3 Bing 352, 359, Best CJ referred to the general rule that interest was not recoverable neither in debt nor in a claim for money had and received as one which "wisely prevents acts of kindness from being converted into mercenary bargains. . ." (see now *Sempra Metals Ltd (formerly Metallgesellschaft Ltd) v Inland Revenue Commissioners* [2007] UKHL 34).

history.[19] It served as shorthand for a range of cases in which liberality or benevolence was called upon to explain what the parties did, and ultimately linked the world of private law with that of public duty.[20]

This "more generous and noble form of intercourse" has a limited place in modern societies. The ban on the explicit calculation of advantages that is the hallmark of "disinterested commerce" means that this type of exchange is limited to relationships based on love, friendship, and good offices.

Hume would be happy to know that contract law in common law jurisdictions privileges consideration: An exchange is ordinarily a contract only if it involves explicit reciprocation.[21]

English law rejects the notion that trusts are contracts, or that fiduciary obligations are contractual in nature, even when they are undertaken consensually. This is not due to the obvious historical link between trusts, fiduciary obligations, and the equitable jurisdiction of the Court of Chancery, but rather to the fundamental idea that under English law contracts are self-regarding acts in which each party to the transaction must be presumed to be pursuing his or her own interests.

This stance explains why in English law—and here the jurisdictional qualification is salient, from a civilian standpoint—contracts giving rise to fiduciary obligations (eg, agency or partnership contracts) are routinely analyzed in a bifurcated way, by distinguishing claims based on the contract from those based on the fiduciary obligations. Even if these obligations work to the same purpose, they are still considered to be conceptually distinct.[22]

This bifurcated view of contract and fiduciary duty is not universally shared. At least at first sight, the law of contracts of civilian countries leaves little room for it.[23] This is a point of difference that may have practical implications for international litigation as well, raising the question, for example, whether a choice of law clause contained in a contract would be deemed to govern the fiduciary obligations arising under it as well.[24]

[19] Andrew Galloway, "The Making of a Social Ethic in Late-Medieval England: From Gratitudo to "Kyndenesse," 55 *J Hist Ideas* 365 (1994), shows how the word "kindness" originally translated the Latin word *gratitudo*, and notes the rendering of ingratitude with *unkindness*. The concept of "kindness," inherited from the philosophical thought of antiquity, was central to the "gift economy" of the early Middle Ages. Hume's usage of "kindness" is to be understood in the light of that tradition.

[20] On this link: Tamar Frankel, *Fiduciary Law* (2010) 285–87; Getzler (n 7) 931.

[21] The transition to this view of contract was far from smooth, however. Roy Kreitner, *Calculating Promises: The Emergence of the Modern American Contract Doctrine* (2007), brilliantly shows that, although there was an early association between consideration and reciprocity, the development of modern contract theory involved, among other things, cleansing consideration from its non-promissory elements. Contemporary conceptions of contracts thus incorporated the ideal image of the contracting individual, "for whom there is nothing that cannot be calculated in terms of profit and loss" (94).

[22] The present value of this approach is now being carefully considered: *Yam Seng Pte Limited v International Trade Corporation Limited* [2013] EWHC 111 (QB). This is happening because, as Paul D Finn, "Contract and the Fiduciary Principle," 12 *UNSW LJ* 76 (1989), showed, contract law doctrine has now lost the apparent integrity and internal coherence of nineteenth- and early twentieth-century contract doctrine, which exalted individual responsibility and self-reliance, and marginalized other views of contracts.

[23] This point is highlighted in a famous article by John H Langbein, "The Contractarian Basis of the Law of Trusts," 105 *Yale LJ* 625 (1995). Note, however, that gifts and other gratuitous transactions are governed by their own rules in civilian jurisdictions, even though they are classified as contracts: Richard Hyland, *Gifts: A Study in Comparative Law* (2009).

[24] See James Edelman, "Four Fiduciary Puzzles," in Elise Bant and Matthew Harding (eds), *Exploring Private Law* (2010) 298, 309 ff.

Commentators do not always note the collateral effect of having a law of contracts that makes the pursuit of self-interest its cornerstone. This view of contractual exchange invites close scrutiny of gifts and other transactions that "call for an explanation" from a commercial point of view. Strict scrutiny of these transactions is sensible precisely because they are not, on their face, motivated by self-interest. The presumption that parties to a contract will act in mutual self-interest paradoxically serves as a basis to protect parties entering into transactions that cannot be explained in commercial terms.

Consider how the point is made in *Hatch v Hatch*,[25] a case in which Lord Eldon pronounced on the (in)validity of the sale for a nominal consideration of a right to present a candidate to an advowson, which the beneficiary of a trust carried out in favor of the trustee:

> There may not be a more moral act, one, that would do more credit to a young man beginning the world, or afford a better omen for the future, than if, a trustee having done his duty, the *cestuy que trust* taking into his fair, serious, and well-informed consideration were to do an act of bounty like this. But the Court cannot permit it; except quite satisfied, that the act is of that nature, for the reason often given; and recollecting, that in discussing, whether it is an act of rational consideration, an act of pure volition, uninfluenced, that enquiry is so easily baffled in a Court of justice, that instead of the spontaneous act of a friend, uninfluenced, it may be the influence of a mind, misled by undue kindness, or forced by oppression, the difficulty of getting the property out of the hands of the guardian or trustee thus increased; and therefore, if the Court does not watch these transactions with a jealousy almost invincible, in a great majority of cases it will lend to the assistance to fraud; where the connection is not dissolved, the account not settled, every thing remaining pressing upon the mind of the party under the care of the guardian or trustee.[26]

This remarkable passage casts a different light on the egoistic orientation of contract law.

Scholars who study fiduciary law in common law jurisdictions sometimes tend to advance the idea that an obligation to act in some else's interest, with other-regarding motivations, is an unlikely legal duty.[27] The implicit message is that fiduciary law should follow the same path indicated by Lord Atkin for the tort of negligence in *Donoghue v Stevenson*.[28] "The rule that you are to love your neighbour becomes in law, you must not injure your neighbour." If there must be a principle of fiduciary liability, it should

[25] *Hatch* v *Hatch* (1804) 9 Ves 292. The context of the case is set out in Peter Maggs, *Henry's Trials: The Story of Henry John Hatch, First Chaplain of Wandsworth Prison* (2009) 54 ff.

[26] *Hatch v Hatch* (1804) 9 Ves 292, 297.

[27] For a profound discussion of this point: Lionel Smith in this volume. Peter Birks, "The Content of Fiduciary Obligation," 34 *Isr L Rev* 3 (2000), first advanced the idea that fiduciary obligations are premised on altruism in its purest form. But the idea was met with some skepticism: "forced selfless behaviour is hardly altruism" (Anthony J Duggan, "Is Equity Efficient?" *Law Quart Rev* 601, 605 (1997)). An economic analysis of the fiduciary relationship now shows why the law does and should require the fiduciary to be other-regarding by imposing mandatory rules to govern the relationship: Robert H Sitkoff, "The Economic Structure of Fiduciary Law," 91 *BU L Rev* 1039 (2011).

[28] *Donoghue* v *Stevenson* [1932] AC 562, 580.

address the problems raised by instances of disloyalty; an unstructured obligation to be selfless cannot stand. For, as Lord Atkin recognized, the law cannot require you to love your neighbor.[29]

The law of contracts in continental Europe took a different road, including much fiduciary law into its domain, thanks to its flexibility, as will be explained. But first one may query whether the framing of trusts and fiduciary obligations in the language of a non-commercial exchange is completely accurate and satisfactory.

The philosophical attempt to separate commercial and non-commercial transactions fitted into a broader reflection on the evolution of morality in the eighteenth century, a period of dramatic social and intellectual transformations.[30] Nonetheless, recourse to trusts and fiduciary obligations for trading or financial purposes was far from unknown in that epoch. The analysis of contemporary commercial practices shows that the world of fiduciary law did overlap and meet the world of commerce and finance, and that the former supported the development of the latter.[31]

One point is clear: it would be naïve to imagine eighteenth-century England as a place in which trusts and fiduciary obligations were a reservoir of non-commercial values, insulated from contemporary business and financial practices. By the eighteenth century England was a commercial powerhouse, and when Hume published his *Treatise* the South Sea Bubble had just burst.[32] In the aftermath of this crisis, trusts, and fiduciary relationships were regularly called upon to advance commercial purposes and thus to facilitate commercial exchange. Trusts were relied upon as an alternative to incorporation, as a form of organization for business ventures.[33] Agency and partnership law also reflected acceptance of the idea that fiduciary obligations are fully compatible with commercial exchange. Indeed, in many ways the trust law of this period was a precursor of modern companies law,[34] and collective investment vehicles established in the last century or so, such as unit trusts and pension funds, are based upon this historical foundation.

[29] The open structure of much fiduciary law also recalls the open structure of the tort of negligence. See, on this point, Matthew Conaglen, *Fiduciary Loyalty: Protecting the Due Performance of Non-Fiduciary Duties* (2010) 261; Paul Finn, "Fiduciary Law and the Modern Commercial World," in Ewan McKendrick (ed), *Commercial Aspects of Trusts and Fiduciary Obligations* (1992) 9.

[30] They are reflected in the literature of the period: W A Speck, "Eighteenth-Century Attitudes Towards Business," in Arthur Pollard (ed), *The Representation of Business in English Literature* (2000) 9 ff.

[31] For similar observations with respect to France: Amalia D Kessler, *A Revolution in Commerce: The Parisian Merchant Court and the Rise of Commercial Society in Eighteenth-Century France* (2008). She notes how commerce itself in this period developed an ideology embodying virtuous, honorable, and useful qualities which would have been denied by the disdainful, noble-dominated ideologies of earlier times. The same trend prevailed in England.

[32] The influence of this crisis on eighteenth-century intellectual life is investigated in depth by Stuart Banner, *Anglo American Securities Regulation: Cultural and Political Roots, 1690–1860* (1998). He notes that "the market's effect on the nation's social structure remained a subject of interest for the rest of the century" (at 93).

[33] Ron Harris, "The Bubble Act: Its Passage and Its Effects on Business Organization," 54 *J Econ Hist* 610 (1994); Colin Arthur Cooke, *Corporation, Trust and Company: An Essay in Legal History* (1951); Bernard Rudden, *The New River Company: A Legal History* (1985).

[34] Michael Chesterman, "Family Settlements on Trust: Landowners and the Rising Bourgeoisie," in Gerry R Rubin and David Sugarman (eds), *Law, Economy and Society, 1750–1914: Essays in the History of English Law* (1984) 124.

II. The Continental Scene: Fiduciary Obligations in Traditional Civilian Settings

Lawyers trained in common law jurisdictions wishing to learn how fiduciaries are regulated in civilian countries may be tempted to rely on literal translations of local language to make themselves familiar with the relevant law. However, that kind of approach produces a superficial and misleading impression of that law.

The warning concerns in particular the risk of misunderstanding the legal position of intermediaries who take the name of *Treuhander, fiduciaire, fiduciario* in German, French, or Italian, or similar names under the laws of other continental jurisdictions.[35] These intermediaries in many cases serve the function of an agent trustee, or a nominee, holding property for a principal. Their role is ordinarily passive, providing little basis for the development of thick fiduciary obligations which bind most trustees. The diagnosis in this respect remains to a large extent the same even with respect to countries like France that have recently introduced in the civil code rules which should put on a firmer basis the institution in question.[36] The simple fact is that the label "fiduciary relationship" in continental Europe is usually not employed to refer to the same set of facts and problems designated by that expression in common law jurisdictions, except to some extent in company law.[37]

If one can avoid the confusions associated with overly quick translation, one will find that the province of fiduciary law in civilian countries is quite large and rich.[38] It includes the law of guardianship, the law of agency and of contracts for cooperation, of investment management, partnership and corporate law, and so on. Virtually all of the relationships that would be considered fiduciary in common law countries would, in most civilian jurisdictions, be considered to raise issues similar to those known in the common law world. The problem is that the field is highly fragmented, making it difficult to isolate common principles, which constitute a body of fiduciary law. This is the case for several reasons.

The old law of trusts and family settlements, which governed the transmission of wealth across the generations under the ancient regime, was mostly left out of the civil codes enacted in the nineteenth century for political reasons. Therefore contemporary civil law jurisdictions have no key institution of general application like the trust to

[35] For a survey of the relevant law in key European jurisdictions see Alexandra Braun, "Management: Trust, Treuhand and Fiducie," in Sjef van Erp and Bram Akkermans (eds), *Cases, Materials and Text on Property Law* (2012) 553 ff; Esther Arroyo i Amayuelas (ed), *El trust en el derecho civil* (2007); Lionel Smith (ed), *Re-imagining the Trust: Trusts in Civil Law Jurisdictions* (2012); Kenneth Reid, "Conceptualizing the Chinese Trust," in Lei Chen and C H van Rhee (eds), *Towards a Chinese Civil Code* (2012) 209 ff.

[36] See French civil code, arts 2011–30 (on *la fiducie*). Thomas Gallanis, "The Contribution of Fiduciary Law," in Lionel Smith (ed), *The Worlds of the Trust* (2013), notes: "The fiduciary laws governing the French *fiduciaire* lack the breadth and depth of the law governing the Anglo-American trustee." This statement must be qualified, however, to take into account the general law of obligations established by the code, which governs the relationship between the parties.

[37] See Section III.

[38] Cf Rudolf B Schlesinger et al, *Comparative Law: Cases, Texts and Materials* (5th edn, 1988) 783: "It would be a gross mistake to conclude. . . that fiduciary relationships do not exist in civil law countries. The need for such relationships exists in every society which recognises private property and permits a measure of free enterprise."

provide a set of model principles and rules to engender the development of a broad system of fiduciary law. More recent civil codes, such as the Quebec civil code, regulate the institution (arts 1260–98 CCQ) and opt for a systematic approach to fiduciary administration (arts 1299–370 CCQ). This effort shows how fiduciary principles can be given prominence and can be extended to a variety of transactions and relationships. So far this effort is unparalleled in its breadth and ambition, but future developments in this direction in other jurisdictions as well should not be ruled out.[39]

Furthermore, for centuries most countries of continental Europe had separate civil and commercial laws (this is still the situation in France, Germany, and Spain), and in some jurisdictions specialized courts to deal with commercial disputes. This also hindered the development of a common set of fiduciary principles, applicable to both civil and commercial transactions.[40] Under this classificatory plan there was no reason to think that the guardian of a minor in charge of the administration of the minor's property had much in common with the director of a company managing money or other assets.

On the other hand, thanks to its flexibility, in civilian countries the general law of obligations and contracts provides the foundations for certain claims that in common law jurisdictions would be grounded on the application of fiduciary law. For example, an agent's duty to account for profits in civil law countries is typically thought to stem from the contract with his principal, although, interestingly, the duty to disgorge gains from the appropriation of business opportunities extends to gains that are only loosely related to the tasks he was asked to perform under the contract (see eg art 1713 Italian CC; § 667 BGB). Under this regime, there is little incentive to develop fiduciary obligations as distinct from contractual obligations, especially given that the law of obligations as well as contract law incorporates broad notions of fair dealing and good faith, and caters for conflicts of interests.[41]

With this in mind, the most significant area for development of fiduciary principles under the civil codes is provided by cases in which a person is appointed to act as a substitute for another person, either because of incapacity,[42] or because use of an agent is desirable. Broad powers of attorney in civil law jurisdictions perform many functions that in a common law jurisdiction are performed by trusts. The rules on conflicts of interest established with respect to them speak of the fiduciary nature of the task entrusted to the holder of the power of attorney.[43]

The administration of property for incapable persons is subject to court supervision if the administrator is appointed by the court. Quite often, the transactions of this

[39] For the state of play in this field see n 35. The new civil codes of Romania and the Czech Republic have also introduced rules on trusts and fiduciary administration of assets.

[40] For an introduction to the distinction between civil and commercial law in major European jurisdictions see Schlesinger et al (n 38) 590.

[41] For a comparative illustration of the rules on conflicts of interests in key civilian jurisdictions: Association Henri Capitant, *Les Conflits d'intérêts* (2013); Centre Français de Droit Comparé, *Les conflits d'intérêts: fonction et maîtrise* (2013).

[42] For a comparative overview of the civil law in this matter, which is by now dated, but still instructive: S J Stoljar, "Children, Parents and Guardians," in *International Encyclopedia of Comparative Law: Persons and Family* (1982) vol 4, ch 7, 1973; Israel Doron, "Elder Guardianship Kaleidoscope–A Comparative Perspective," 16 *International Journal of Law, Policy and the Family* 368 (2002).

[43] For apt remarks on this point: Schlesinger et al (n 38) 782 ff.

administrator must be approved by the court, if they involve risk of abuse or misappropriation. At least in Italy, the court will approve the transaction if it is necessary or it is for the "evident benefit" (*utilità evidente*) of the person whose property is being managed (art 320 Italian CC). All accounts are also subject to judicial approval (art 386 Italian CC). The rule against self-dealing is strictly applied, and includes the sale of the property at a public auction, as well as dealing in property acquired through a nominee (art 387 Italian CC). Courts cannot authorize these transactions. If administrators must carry out a transaction that may involve a conflict of interest, a special curator will be appointed to protect the interests of the ward (art 320, 321, 360 Italian CC). Administrators must act gratuitously but they may, by judicial decree, obtain an indemnity for services rendered in cases of special difficulty, or for managing considerable wealth, and may employ a remunerated person to be assisted in the discharge of their duties (art 379, 411 Italian CC).

Many of the above-noted rules are of considerable antiquity. The rule against self-dealing is traceable to Roman law of tutorship, for example.[44] Canon and Roman law in the Middle Ages provided regimes which were much more complete and protective of the ward than English feudal law:

> Under Roman law, administration of the child's property was the most important and extensive function of the tutor. He was required to administer the assets for the exclusive benefit of the infant. Unlike the common law of feudal guardianship, Roman law made him a trustee.[45]

Inflexible prophylactic rules striking transactions involving abuses of confidence are also quite venerable and are now in force in civilian jurisdictions, like France. The Napoleonic Code prohibits gifts to doctors and to other people involved in the care of patients in a number of circumstances (art 909 French CC),[46] and this was already the law before the enactment of the Code. Pothier shows that this rule was applied in France during the *ancien régime* to all administrators who could exert undue influence over the persons for which they acted.[47] This point of law proved influential in England. In *Huguenin v Baseley*,[48] a case concerning a donation obtained by a clergyman and his family from a person standing in a relation of confidence towards the female donor, Pothier was relied on by counsel to persuade Lord Eldon to set aside the donation.[49]

[44] Paul. 33 ad edictum, D. 18.1.34.7; C. 4.38.5.

[45] Richard H Helmholz, "The Roman Law of Guardianship in England, 1300–600," 52 *Tul L Rev* 223–57, repr in Helmholz, *Canon Law and the Law of England* (1987) 211, 239 (citation is to the reprint). Helmholz notes in particular that military wardship was a lucrative right, and not a trust for the benefit of the ward.

[46] More recent legislation extends the prohibition to natural persons who own, manage, or work in establishments hosting minors, elderly, disabled, or handicapped people, or to related parties (Code de l'Action Sociale et de la Famille, art L. 331–4).

[47] Pothier, "Traité de donations entre vifs," in *Œuvres Posthumes de M. Pothier*, vol 2 (1778) art 1, § VIII; pp 450 ff.

[48] (1807) 14 Ves 273.

[49] Gerhard Lubbe, "Voidable Contracts," in Reinhard Zimmermann and Daniel P Visser, *Southern Cross: Civil Law and Common law in South Africa* (1996), 296–7, notes that Sir Samuel Romilly's arguments for the donor in this case acquired quasi-judicial authority by being textually adopted in subsequent judgments. On this case and its relationship to civilian sources see Stefan Wagner, "*Huguenin v Baseley* (1807)—Die Bedeutung Pothiers für die Entwicklung von undue influence," in Vanessa Duss, Nikolaus Linder, Katrin Kastl, and Christina Börner (eds), *Rechtstransfer in der Geschichte: Legal Transfer in History* (2006) 354 ff.

French law, according to Pothier, prohibited gifts by a penitent to a confessor, and more generally, all gifts to the religious order to which the confessor belonged, as well as a gift from a patient to a doctor, a surgeon, a pharmacist, or to a nurse. The French code now prohibits gifts to clergymen to the same extent, and under the same conditions, applicable to doctors, surgeons, chemists, who have assisted a patient during an illness of which the patient died (art 909 French CC, although remuneratory gifts are excepted from the rule).[50] Legal systems rooted in French law have in some cases enacted reforms to enable a more flexible approach,[51] but they remain sensitive to the underlying concern over abuse of confidence.[52]

I shall conclude this brief overview of fiduciary principles in civil law by making a few general observations.

First of all, civilian countries now depart from the assumption that to undertake to act in someone else's interest is tantamount to agreeing to act gratuitously. Services which in antiquity were rendered on an honorary basis, involving no remuneration, are now market transactions. Mandate was a gratuitous contract under the Roman law; it is now presumed to be onerous under the Italian civil code (art 1709). Even those civil codes that still pay homage to the old Roman rule, confirming the gratuitous nature of the contract of mandate, like the German civil code (see, eg, BGB § 662), are now to be read in the light of present commercial realities, which feature remunerated agents of various kinds, by agreement of the parties, under the commercial code, or in accordance with company and financial services law.

Second, many fiduciary relationships in civilian countries are framed so to leave title to property subject to fiduciary administration in the name of the beneficiary. Hence, if the property produces profits, those profits automatically belong to the owner. It is unnecessary to distinguish between beneficial and legal owners or otherwise to conceptualize an independent basis of recovery of gains. Problems begin only when the property is sold and the fiduciary invests the profit into property subsequently conveyed to him. The distinction between ownership and obligation may then work to preclude automatic attribution of the property to the beneficiary, although the fiduciary may still be called upon to disgorge profits, by a variety of means.[53]

Third, the administration of justice in civil law and common law countries follows different rules, and the procedural law shapes substantive outcomes. Fiduciary law in continental countries is less robust than it may otherwise be as a result of these differences.[54]

[50] For a comparative discussion see Hyland (n 23) 300 ff (and more generally, on capacity to receive gifts, 296 ff).

[51] Laurie Dearman Clark, "Louisiana's New Law on Capacity to Make and Receive Donations: 'Unduly Influenced' by the Common Law?," 67 *Tul L Rev* 183 (1992–3).

[52] See with respect to wills the penetrating analysis of Ronald J Scalise Jr, "Undue Influence and the Law of Wills: A Comparative Analysis," 19 *Duke J Comp & Internat'l L* 41 (2008).

[53] This is a troublesome and unsettled area of the law, which is developing before our eyes, partly through comparative studies: Mathias Siems, "Disgorgement of Profits for Breach of Contract: A Comparative Analysis," 7 *Edinburgh L Rev* 29 (2003); Michele Graziadei, Ugo Mattei, Lionel Smith (eds), *Commercial Trusts in European Private Law* (2005) 247–405 (cases 3–6); Birke Häcker, *Consequences of Impaired Consent Transfers: A Structural Comparison of English and German Law* (2009) 275 ff.

[54] The point is highlighted by Schlesinger et al (n 38) 783 n 3.

Lastly, a note concerning the nature of the discourse surrounding the application of fiduciary principles and rules. Fiduciary principles and rules in the civil law have been stripped of their original language and cultural frame of reference. Compare the words of Cardozo in *Meinhard v Salmon* with the colorless language of comparable provisions of a code. Much of the meaning, and nuance, of the civic and moral character of the imperative to be loyal is gone![55]

The notion that civilians have neglected fiduciary obligations is belied by the volume of commentary on the relevant articles or paragraphs of the codes and pertinent cases and legislation. But the language of the commentaries reflects that of the sources of law; it does not reflect the psychological and anthropological view of man that inspired the jurisprudence of fiduciary law. The view of man as a moral subject responding to conscience, whose volition is not perfectly free, and whose conduct is driven as much by desire and emotion, as by reason, is not reflected well in the law anymore.[56] The movement towards more neutral language mentioned above is not peculiar to the contemporary evolution of civil law doctrine on fiduciary relationships, however. It is shared by a good number of scholars belonging to the common law world too.[57]

III. Going Uniform—Almost

The law of fiduciaries in Europe today is more uniform than ever, partly as a consequence of the regulatory action of the European Union in the field of company and financial services law, and yet the level of uniformity that has been achieved is still limited, as I will discuss in more detail herein.

The rise of multinationals, the growth of the financial services sector, and the global opening of capital markets has produced increasing pressure for harmonization of company and financial services law throughout Europe. Initiatives to respond to this pressure have transformed the European landscape, and more change is ongoing. The process has given rise to a wave of regulation of conflicts of interests at European and national levels.

With respect to national company law, reforms have focused on enhanced regulation of directors' conflicts of interest, sending an explicit message to international financial markets and investors: fiduciary obligations are far from unknown in civilian jurisdictions.[58] Directors' conflicts of interests have, in most jurisdictions, been regulated for a long time but reforms designed to enhance these rules were inspired by developments

[55] The tendency to do away with this language is also present in common law jurisdictions.

[56] Criminal law, on the other hand, tells a rather different story.

[57] See, eg, Conaglen (n 29) 107–9 (with reference to precedents). Contrast the contribution of Tamar Frankel in this volume. For a far-sighted analysis of why this kind of discourse should be upheld today: James Boyd White, "How Should We Talk about Corporations? The Languages of Economics and of Citizenship," 94 *Yale LJ* 1416 (1985).

[58] For a general view of the subject see: *Study on Directors' Duties and Liability* prepared for the European Commission DG Market by Carsten Gerner-Beuerle, Philipp Paech, Edmund Philipp Schuster (2013) (available online together with the country reports at <http://ec.europa.eu/internal_market/company/board/>), and the contribution of Martin Gelter and Geneviève Helleringer to this volume. Yet, to measure exactly what has been achieved in operative terms is still very difficult: Simeon Djankov, Rafael La Porta, Florencio Lopez-de-Silanes, Andrei Shleifer, "The Law and Economics of Self-Dealing," 88 *Journal of Financial Economics* 430 (2008).

in corporate law in common law jurisdictions, especially the US.[59] In some cases, this has meant departing from mandatory law in favor of default rules, in line with contractarian theories of the firm.[60] It is possible to view these reforms as transplants, although, as is often the case, it is difficult to tell to what extent foreign influences rather than local agency were instrumental in the reform process.[61]

Europe now has a uniform statute on the European company and a proposed statute governing foundations is currently under consideration.[62] The first instrument leaves regulation of conflicts of interest to the jurisdiction in which the company is registered; the latter presently includes embryonic rules on conflicts of interest. Both instruments operate on the assumption that a core of fiduciary obligations ought to be applicable to managers.

The law of financial markets is now almost completely uniform in Europe, at least as far as legislative enactments regarding investment managers are concerned. At the European level, the instrument applicable to unit trusts and investment companies is Directive 2009/65/EC of 13 July 2009 on the coordination of laws, regulations, and administrative provisions relating to undertakings for collective investment in transferable securities (UCITS).[63] Hedge and other alternative funds are regulated by the Alternative Investment Fund Managers Directive 2011/61/EU ("AIFMD") of 22 July 2013. Pension funds are regulated by directive 2003/41/2003 of 3 June 2003. The regulation of financial services is set out in Directive 2004/39/EC on markets in financial services, and by the national implementation of European legislation.

I will not attempt to review this legislation here. It is clear that it marks an important step in the evolution of fiduciary law in Europe, insofar it establishes rules to manage conflicts of interests that are pervasive.[64] Two concerns should be mentioned here. First, under the "single passport" approach, which is fundamental to the market integration policy underlying EU legislation, the above-mentioned European framework by and large pre-empts national regulation.[65] This may be problematic for jurisdictions that have less sophisticated investors, less competitive markets, or less effective regulators.[66] Second, uniform legislation dedicated to companies and investment managers

[59] This is why Klaus J Hopt, "Conflict of Interest, Secrecy and Insider Information of Directors—A Comparative Analysis," *European Company and Financial L Rev* 167 (2013), holds that comparative law itself has been instrumental in preparing or producing legal change.

[60] The point is made for Germany by Hopt (n 59).

[61] See, eg, the nuanced assessment by Hideki Kanda and Curtis J Milhaupt, "Re-Examining Legal Transplants: The Director's Fiduciary Duty in Japanese Corporate Law," 51 *Am J Comp Law* 887 (2003); Holger Fleischer, "Legal Transplants in European Company Law—The Case of Fiduciary Duties," *European Company and Financial L Rev* 378 (2005). In Québec the idea of looking for convergence between civil law and common law in this area meets resistance for the fear of "transplants:" Paul Martel, "Les devoirs de loyauté des administrateurs de sociétés par actions fédérales—impact du Code civil du Québec," 42 *RJT* 149 (2008).

[62] Proposal for a Council Regulation on the Statute for a European Foundation (FE) COM(2012) 35 final.

[63] See arts 12, 13, and 14 of the UCITS Directive cited in the text.

[64] Luc Thévenoz and Rashid Bahar (eds), *Conflicts of Interests: Corporate Governance and Financial Markets* (2007); Anne Peters and Lukas Handschin (eds), *Conflict of Interest in Global, Public and Corporate Governance* (2012).

[65] With respect to the retail sector, this is spelled out in art 4 of the Directive implementing the MIFID directive. National regulation may intervene only in exceptional cases, subject to a proportionality requirement, to target specific risks to investors.

[66] The point is raised by Luca Enriques, "Conflicts of Interest in Investment Services: The Price and Uncertain Impact of MiFID's Regulatory Framework," in Guido Ferrarini and Eddy Wymeersch (eds), *Investor Protection in Europe: Corporate Law Making, The MiFID and Beyond* (2006) 321 ff.

still falls within the general landscape of national law. The question is whether the various remedies available under those laws will actually advance the goal of uniformity.[67] With these observations in mind, one must still ask why regulated actors have so far been accorded so much influence in shaping reform of the policies by which they themselves are regulated.[68]

Concluding Remarks

The modern economy is dominated by intangible wealth. Much has changed in the ways wealth is produced. The economy is increasingly based on services, and those services are remunerated. As Hume noted, there may still be an economy of the gift, but interested, rather than disinterested, commerce has become the rule. Nostalgia may induce us to think that this has left us materially enriched and spiritually impoverished. I am not so sure. In a famous lecture Louis Josserand, a leading French jurist, observed that the decline of gratuitous transactions is a sign of the greater freedom that individuals possess.[69] Charity and generosity, he remarked, reveal deep-seated inequalities. Thus the expansion of commercial exchange may be considered as a progressive rather than a regressive social development.

Given the heightened significance of commercial exchange, it is hardly surprising that fiduciary law has been put under scrutiny in terms of its economic efficiency, or that has been sometimes reformed as a form of contract law especially in the US. This is far from unreasonable. After all, contract law is not monolithic in its constitution and is capable of accommodating a plurality of concerns. When all parties are competent, the main function of the distinction between a contractual and fiduciary relationship lies in signaling the content of the promise or undertaking to be upheld by the law.[70] Comparative lawyers may point out that the law of contracts in civilian jurisdictions is broader and as such better able to accommodate much fiduciary law.[71] This cannot obscure the fact that fiduciary law must still regulate situations for which contract law—even a very broad contract law—was not designed. In particular, fiduciary law regulates the rendering of services where one party is not competent or able to consent. This is a task that goes beyond classical contract law, and that should not be undermined.

From a more general point of view, one may query whether loyalty is really a merchantable good, which can be bought and sold as any other good. The economic theory that emerged after the marginalist revolution tended to answer the question in the

[67] See on this point, Michel Tison, "The Civil Law Effects of MiFID in a Comparative Law Perspective," in Stefan Grundmann et al (ed), *Festschrift für Klaus J. Hopt zum 70. Geburtstag* (2010) 2621 ff, and more generally, Michele Graziadei, Ugo Mattei, and Lionel Smith (eds), *Commercial Trusts in European Private Law* (2009); Marc Kruithof, "A Differentiated Approach to Client Protection: The Example of MiFID," in Stefan Grundmann and Yesim Atamer (eds), *Financial Services, Financial Crisis and General European Contract Law* (2011) 105 ff.

[68] Renate Mayntz (ed), *Crisis and Control: Institutional Change in Financial Market Regulation* (2012).

[69] Louis Josserand, "Le déclin du titre gratuit et sa transformation," in Josserand, *Évolutions et actualités* (1936).

[70] Robert Sitkoff, "The Economic Structure of Fiduciary Law," 91 *BU L Rev* 1039, 1046–7 (2011), speaks of a "categorization function," which mandatory fiduciary law rules perform to minimize third-party information costs about the nature of the relationship involving property entrusted to the fiduciary.

[71] Langbein (n 23).

affirmative. That approach would have surprised the classical economists. They knew that markets have moral effects,[72] and they held that commerce in certain assets shapes the capacities of the human beings involved in it, and thus influences the moral and social environment in which they operate.[73]

We may now see why certain distinctions ought to be maintained. Pricing services and other relationships change their social meaning and may change the nature of the relationships themselves. With respect to information, we distinguish, for example, between journalism, scientific information, and advertising, and we require financial journalists and scientists to disclose material conflicts of interests. Although political and economic theory has made the most of the premise that humans are naturally self-interested we ought to recognize that certain goods—like loyalty—can be enjoyed only if we refrain from appropriating them to our own ends.

[72] Their intuition has been confirmed by empirical evidence: J J Graafland, "Do Markets Crowd out Virtues? An Aristotelian Framework," 91 *Journal of Business Ethics* 1 (2009).

[73] See the profound discussion of this point in Debra Satz, *Why Some Things Should Not Be for Sale: The Moral Limits of Markets* (2010) 44 ff (commenting on Adam Smith's important reflections about the degrading moral consequences of the division of labor and the negative effects it has on the preferences and capabilities of the workforce).

15

Constituency Directors and Corporate Fiduciary Duties

*Martin Gelter and Geneviève Helleringer**

Introduction

Some directors are appointed by individuals or groups who have a specific interest in the manner in which the company operates. Such stakeholders may include shareholders: venture capitalists will often negotiate the right to appoint a director. Yet appointing stakeholders need not be shareholders: lenders and employees may also be represented on the board. Directors appointed to represent the interest of a designated stakeholder are sometimes called "constituency" directors.[1] The law of many jurisdictions requires or facilitates their appointment or election.

Constituency directors may be expected to support their appointer or nominator while they discharge their duties.[2] How would a director representing the interest of employees give primacy to the profit-maximization objective when tackling policy matters? How may a director nominated by a venture capitalist not pay specific attention to the protection of her patron's investment in the company, or not frame issues with the idea that an exit strategy for the venture capitalist needs to remain available? More specifically, an important practical question is how constituency directors deal with their sponsors with respect to confidential information. One of the major issues discussed in the recent US literature is whether directors representing venture capitalists should be permitted to share sensitive information with them.[3]

Nevertheless, despite this source of heterogeneity[4] among beneficiaries, it seems to be a cultural and legal universal for jurisdictions to abstain from formulating any specific duties for individual directors. This uniformity is surprising and needs to be questioned keeping in mind a double commercial reality: appointing stakeholders have different expectations, and directors are appointed on a variety of grounds and their levels and types of expertise are different. May the duties of directors, including constituency directors, nevertheless be thought of as being univocal? Some countries'

* We thank participants at the DePaul Fiduciary Law Conference for helpful comments, particularly Deirdre Ahern and Andrew Gold.

1 Norman Veasey and Christine T. Di Guglielmo, "How Many Masters Can A Director Serve? A Look at the Tensions Facing Constituency Directors," 63 *Bus Law* 761 (2008). In the United Kingdom, the term "nominee" director is more common.

2 We are only looking at directors who are specifically representing stakeholders—and not at independent directors who—by definition—are expected to distance themselves from any particular interest.

3 Section II.B.2.

4 We will subsequently use the terms "homogeneity" and "heterogeneity" when referring to individuals, and "uniformity" and "diversity" when referring to their duties.

corporate laws permit a stipulation in the corporation's charter for the holders of specific registered shares or even other stakeholders (such as employees) of the firm to appoint certain directors. In the absence of a formal arrangement, large shareholders or even creditors often get to nominate a specific director who is then dutifully elected by the controlling coalition of the firm. Such situations create a potential conflict between duties owed to the appointer and duties owed to the company.

In all of these cases, corporate law exhorts directors to pursue the mystifying interest of the corporation instead of pursuing what may appear to an external observer the most obvious course of action, namely to represent their respective constituency. This principle appears from the outset difficult to put into practice. Even if courts affirm that the mere fact that a director has been nominated by certain stakeholders does not impose any duty to benefit such stakeholders, this is an orthodox legal statement that may appear remote from the reality of corporate culture. It appears that the very fact that there is a designated appointer will in general create a specific connection between the constituency director and the appointing constituency, typically reinforced by the latter's power not to reappoint the director: "loyalty inspired by selection, and confirmed by the confidence which the appointers repose in their nominees, is reinforced by the appointer's power of dismissal."[5] In addition, does not the very fact that corporate laws require or enable the appointment of directors by specific constituencies seem to indicate that these directors not only represent these groups or individuals in a symbolic sense, but that they are also intended to be knowledgeable about and sympathetic to their interests?

Looking at heterogeneity on the board is timely and an issue of high practical significance given current developments in corporate case law. On the one hand, the Delaware courts have remained faithful to the traditional approach with respect to directors' decisions: In the 2009 case of *In re Trados Shareholder Litigation*, the Court of Chancery refused to grant the benefits of the business judgment rule to the decisions of directors affiliated to a venture capitalist whose interests were at stake in a decision of the board.[6] On the other hand, in the 2013 case of *Kalisman v Friedman*, Vice Chancellor Travis Laster stated that "[w]hen a director serves as the designee of a stockholder on the board, and when it is understood that the director acts as the stockholder's representative, then the stockholder is generally entitled to the same information as the director."[7] It is not entirely clear whether this statement is consistent with prior case law.[8]

While typically issues such as directors representing venture capitalists and employee representation have been discussed separately, we attempt to address these phenomena jointly.[9] On the basis of what has been explained, the uniformity of directors' duties, which is affirmed across jurisdictions, seems somewhat hypocritical. At a minimum

[5] E W Thomas, "The Role of Nominee Directors and the Liability of Their Appointers," in Ian Ramsay (ed), *Corporate Governance and the Duties of Company Directors* (1997) 148, 150.

[6] *In Re Trados Shareholder Litigiation, Inc.* No Civ A 1512-CC, 2009 WL 2225958 (Del Ch 24 July 2009).

[7] *Kalisman et al v Friedman et al.* 2013 Del Ch LEXIS 100 (17 April 2013).

[8] Contra, eg, *Holdgreiwe v The Nostalgia Network, Inc.* 1993 Del Ch LEXIS 71 (29 April 1993) (suggesting that sharing information with stockholders may violate fiduciary duties).

[9] For a similar synthetic approach, see Deirdre Ahern, "Nominee Directors' Duty to Promote the Success of the Company: Commercial Pragmatism and Legal Orthodoxy," 127 *L Q Rev* 118 (2011).

there is a paradox in providing on the one hand for directors' nomination rules linked to specific constituencies and, on the other hand, for heterogeneity-blind duties. Looking at the law of several key European jurisdictions as well as the US, we suggest that the disjunction between the appointment of directors and fiduciary duties is only sustainable because the purported objective of fiduciary duty—however formulated in theory—is not clearly defined at all. Obscurity conveniently shadows what is an unsettling issue. It is only possible because across jurisdictions the fiduciary duties of directors are delineated primarily negatively; in other words, they almost exclusively say what directors must "not do" and this in quite broad terms.[10]

I. Heterogeneous Directors and Uniform Fiduciary Duties

A. Heterogeneous personal loyalties

In the United States, the courts, in particular those in Delaware, routinely and laconically state that directors are required to act for the benefit of "the corporation;" more often than not "and its shareholders" is appended to the progression of words.[11] Still, the objective corporate directors are expected to pursue is certainly an elusive one. What exactly the "the corporation" and "to work for its benefit" mean are not always clear. Across jurisdictions, the debate oscillates between requiring directors to be loyal "to the corporation and its shareholders" (which provides already for two different beneficiaries), and including the interests of other stakeholders or even the public interest in this overall goal, which creates yet additional classes of beneficiaries.[12]

A more direct way of ensuring that a corporation is likely to consider particular interests is to give them voice on the board. Most jurisdictions start with the basic rule of the board of a public corporation being elected by shareholders. However, shareholders do not all have the same de facto power to elect board members as the corporate charter may provide for a specific repartition of seats. In addition, it is widely acknowledged (and criticized) that the board is often a largely self-perpetuating body whose inside members dominate the selection of their future colleagues and eventual successors. While the classic vision may still accurately describe a certain subset of

[10] See D Gordon Smith, "The Shareholder Primacy Norm," 23 *J Corp L* 277, 284 (1998) ("Some applications of the fiduciary principle in corporate law do not require the identification of any particular corporate constituency as beneficiary, but only that the interests of 'the corporation' in general must be served"); Larry E Ribstein, "Fencing Fiduciary Duties," 91 *BU L Rev* 899, 909 (2011) ("The fiduciary duty to avoid self-dealing is not defined with reference to the specific parties on whose behalf the fiduciary must act").

[11] Veasey and Di Guglielmo (n 1) at 764 n 8; Simone M Sepe, "Intruders in the Boardroom: The Case of Constituency Directors," 91 *Washington University Law Review* 2, 308–78 at 344 n 140 (2013); eg, *Guth v Loft* 5 A2d 503, 509 (Del 1939); *NACEPF v Gheewalla* 930 A 2d 92, 99, 101 (Del 2007). The recent case of *Ebay Domestic Holdings, Inc v Newmark* 16 A 3d 1 (Del Ch 2010) probably contains the clearest verbalization of shareholder primacy in the Delaware courts so far.

[12] See generally Henry Hansmann and Reinier Kraakman, "The End of History for Corporate Law," 89 *Geo LJ* 439 (2001) (arguing that the shareholder model is prevailing). For a discussion of the seminal Berle–Dodd debate in the US, see William W Bratton and Michael L Wachter, "Shareholder Primacy's Corporatist Origins: Adolf Berle and the Modern Corporation," 34 *J Corp L* 99 (2008); for a comparison with the French and German debates, see Martin Gelter, "Taming or Protecting the Modern Corporation? Shareholder-Stakeholder Debates in a Comparative Light," 7 *NYU J L & Bus* 643 (2011); for the UK debate, which culminated in the enactment of a new s 172 in 2006, see Andrew Keay, "Section 172(1) of the Companies Act 2006: An Interpretation and Assessment," 28 *Company Law* 106, 109 (2007).

large, publicly traded corporations even in the US, one strategy of having directors pursue goals beyond (or beside) those of equity investors, however, is to ensure a heterogeneous composition of the board. More so than in the US, in Continental Europe directors are appointed through a more diverse set of processes as a practical matter.

Labor representatives. A number of European countries require employee representation on the supervisory board or board of directors. Comparative corporate law scholars often focus on the German example, in which half of the members of the supervisory board are employee representatives in the largest firms.[13] However, employee representation is common across Central and Northern Europe.[14] In June 2013, even France passed a law that will require employee representatives in very large firms.[15] Where labor representation on the board is not legally mandated, it occasionally happens voluntarily, eg, as a part of a bargain with a union that may trade wage concessions for governance rights in a declining corporation.[16]

Quite obviously, the purpose of putting employee representatives on the board of directors is not merely a symbolic one, but to ensure that employee interests are represented in board deliberation and decision-making. When the UK considered employee representation on boards to be created in the 1970s, it did so under the rubric of "Industrial Democracy,"[17] the implication being that another group affected by the corporation's choices would need to be represented in the decision-making process. One might therefore assume that employee representatives are intended to act as advocates.[18]

Appointed directors. The laws of some jurisdictions permit the corporate charter to stipulate that the holders of specific, registered shares have the right to appoint a certain number of directors.[19] Obviously, this is primarily an instrument for privately held firms, eg to secure the balance of power between founders or their descendants. However, this kind of arrangement also occasionally exists in publicly traded firms. In particular, governments have sometimes used appointment rights to retain a certain degree of control in privatized firms that were in part thought to be of particular national importance, which is illustrated by the "Golden Share" case law of the ECJ on the freedom of movement of capital.[20] While *government representatives* may

[13] Mitbest (Germany) § 1(1).

[14] Countries with such systems include Austria, the Czech Republic, Denmark, Finland, Hungary, Luxembourg, the Netherlands, Norway, Slovakia, Slovenia, and Sweden.

[15] C Com (France) art L225-27-1, introduced by Loi n° 2013-504 du 14 juin 2013 relative à la sécurisation de l'emploi. See S de Vendeuil and O Rault-Dubois, "Représentation des salariés au conseil d'administration ou de surveillance de grandes entreprises," JCP-E 2013, Étude 1379.

[16] Sepe (n 11) at 312 335, 337 (discussing directors nominated by unionized workers).

[17] Lord Bullock, *Report of the Committee of Inquiry on Industrial Democracy* (1977).

[18] Eg, Mathias Habersack, in Wulf Goette and Mathias Habersack (eds), *Münchener Kommentar zum Aktiengesetz* (3rd edn, 2008) vol 2, § 100 para 55 ("codetermination aims at a pluralism of interests, whose basis is not the least in the ability and task of the employee side to contribute employee issues to the deliberations of the board"). See also Klaus J Hopt, "Self-Dealing and use of Corporate Opportunity and Information: Regulating Directors' Conflicts of Interest," in Klaus J Hopt and Gunther Teubner (eds), *Corporate Governance and Directors' Liabilities* (1985) 285, 308 ("it would be naïve to believe that the existing conflicts of interest could be negated this way").

[19] Eg AktG (Germany) § 101(2) (permitting up to a third of board members to be appointed by specific shareholders under the corporate charters). For the UK, see Paul L Davies, *Gower and Davies' Principles of Modern Company Law* (8th edn, 2008) No 14-10.

[20] Since the early 2000s, in the "Golden Share" cases as well as the Volkswagen case, the ECJ has routinely struck down laws and charter provisions that gave special rights to a national government as a shareholder.

constitute a slowly dying species in Europe, state ownership in large firms made a temporary comeback in the US with the Troubled Asset Relief Program (TARP).[21] In some cases, financial institutions that had missed repayment deadlines had to permit the Treasury Department to appoint members to their boards.[22] Government ownership, whether through representatives on the board or not, raises the concern that the board will pursue interests designated as "public."[23] In fact, as government employees, such representatives may be subject to directions given by their superiors, which will likely conflict with their duties under corporate law.[24] While the state will not typically seek to enrich itself, political goals such as full employment may hurt the corporation.

Voluntarily elected representatives of specific shareholders and creditors. Even if there are no specific provisions in the corporate charter, specific shareholders are often informally represented on the (supervisory) board.[25] Publicly traded Continental European companies more often than not have a concentrated ownership structure characterized by the dominance of one controlling or several large strategic shareholders. A wealthy individual with large investments in several companies may not be willing or able to function as a director in all firms, but may deputize a trusted confidant, often a lawyer, to fulfill this function on his behalf.[26] If there are several large shareholders, the dominating groups will typically come to terms with each other and create an arrangement where each of them has some governance role.[27] While an industrial family might send a member,[28] a corporate shareholder will typically nominate an officer or other senior employee.[29] For this

See, eg, Wolf-Georg Ringe, "Company Law and the Free Movement of Capital," 69 *Cambridge LJ* 378 (2010). In some cases, the government had the right to appoint directors. Eg, *Commission v Belgium*, Case C-503/99, 4 June 2002 (only case where the Golden Share passes muster even though government had the right to appoint two directors); *Commission v France*, Case C-483/99, 4 June 2002 (Golden Share allowing the government to appoint two directors struck down by the ECJ); *Commission v Germany*, Case C-112/05, 23 October 2007 (*Volkswagen* case).

[21] Eg, Barbara Black, "The US as 'Reluctant Shareholder': Government, Business and the Law," 5 *Ent Bus LJ* 561, 569–73 (2010) (reviewing bailout legislation).

[22] Sepe (n 11) at 335, 337; William O Fisher, "When the Government Attempts to Change the Board, Investors Should Know," 40 *Pepp L Rev* 533, 536–52 (2013) (describing how the government put directors on the boards of AIG and Bank of America).

[23] See Marcel Kahan and Edward B Rock, "When the Government is the Controlling Shareholder," 89 *Tex L Rev* 1293, 1317–19 (2011) (describing conflicts of interest between the government and other shareholders).

[24] Eg, Bruno Kropff, "Aufsichtsratsmitglied 'im Auftrag'," in Theodor Baums et al (eds), *Festschrift für Ulrich Huber zum 70. Geburtstag* (2006) 841, 849–54 (concluding that instructions contrary to the interest of the corporation are not binding under German law).

[25] Eg, Sujit Sur, Elena Lvina, and Michel Magnan, "Why do Boards Differ? Because Owners Do: Assessing Ownership Impact on Board Composition," 21 *Corp Gov* 373, 376 (2013) (noting the role of Bill Gates as chairman of Microsoft's board.

[26] See, eg, Kropff (n 24) at 842 (example of the former role of the late Leo Kirch in the German Springer media group).

[27] Eg, Kropff (n 24) at 842 (example of different branches of a founding family).

[28] Deborah DeMott, "Guests at the Table? Independent Directors in Family-Influenced Companies," 33 *J Corp L* 819, 823 n 15 (2008) (example of Estée Lauder).

[29] Eg, Roberto Barontini and Lorenzo Caprio, "The Effect of Family Control on Firm Value and Performance: Evidence from Continental Europe," 12 *Eur Fin Mgmt* 689 (2006); Sur et al (n 22) at 376–7 (discussing how corporate owners may use directors to safeguard supply chains or the inflow of resources through affiliated directors).

situation to persist, the various large shareholders will obviously vote for each others' candidates. Sometimes shareholders enter into voting agreements that formalize rights to nominate a specified number of directors for each participant.[30] Nominated directors are also often members of the board in subsidiaries within groups of companies.[31] In the US, the scenario of "constituency directors" representing specific shareholders is becoming more common because of the presence of private equity and venture capitalists.[32]

Important creditors may be part of such a coalition as well, in particular in those cases where the corporation has a close relationship with a specific bank (*Hausbank* in German) that may or may not also be a significant shareholder.[33] While US banks do not play the role in corporate governance that German banks do, the situation may sometimes be not all that different: Studies based on 1992 and 2000 data found that approximately between a quarter and a third of the largest firms had bankers on the board.[34]

Today, the lines between debt and equity are often fluid; whether a venture capitalist takes a debt or equity position is a matter of convenience and the circumstances of the case.[35] Lending contracts sometimes permit creditors to put a director on the debtor's board when it experiences financial distress.[36] In all of these cases, it is obvious that the respective board member was elected to represent the interest of the nominating entity. In fact, directors of this type are often subject to conflicting interests and duties as members of the bodies of different corporations, whose interests may not always be aligned.[37]

Minority representatives: Several jurisdictions have mechanisms that—at least in theory—enable minority shareholders to elect one or more directors to the (supervisory) board against the will of the majority under certain conditions. Examples include (relatively uncommon) cumulative voting in the US,[38] as well as the failed SEC Proxy

[30] See, eg, D Gordon Smith, "Duties of Nominee Directors," in Mathias Siems and David Cabrelli (eds), *Comparative Company Law* 61, 62, 64, 67, 69 (2013) (discussing the US, the UK, France, and Germany); DeMott (n 28) at 823.

[31] Eg, *Kuwait Asia Bank EC v National Mutual Life Nominees Ltd* [1991] 1 AC 187 PC (NZ).

[32] Veasey and Di Guglielmo (n 1) at 763.

[33] See, eg, Hopt (n 18) at 305–6; Gary Gorton and Frank A Schmid, "Universal Banking and the Performance of German Firms," 58 *J Fin Econ* 29, 66 (2000); Andreas Hackethal, Reinhard H Schmidt, and Marcel Tyrell, "Banks and German Corporate Governance: On the Way to a Capital Market-Based System?," 13 *Corp Gov* 397, 398 (2005) (all discussing the role of banks in German corporate governance).

[34] Randall S Kroszner and Philip E Strahan, "Bankers on Boards: Monitoring, Conflicts of Interest, and Lender Liability," 62 *J Fin Econ* 415, 423 (2001); João A C Santos and Adrienne S Rumble, "The American Keiretsu and Universal Banks: Investing, Voting and Sitting on Nonfinancials' Corporate Boards," 80 *J Fin Econ* 419, 437 (2006).

[35] Douglas G Baird and Robert K Rasmussen, "Private Debt and the Missing Lever of Corporate Governance," 154 *U Pa L Rev* 1209, 1217 (2006).

[36] Douglas G Baird and Robert K Rasmussen, "The End of Bankruptcy," 55 *Stan L Rev* 751, 779 (2002).

[37] See, eg, Klaus J Hopt and Markus Roth, in Klaus J Hopt and Herbert Wiedemann (eds), *Grosskommentar Aktiengesetz* (2005) vol 4, § 116 para 174 (recommending that conflicted directors either abstain from voting, recuse themselves, or resign).

[38] Eg Del Gen Corp L §214, 8 Del C § 214.

Access Rule.[39] Italian[40] and Spanish corporate law provide mandatory mechanisms for minority representation.[41] This could raise the question whether the elected minority representative should have a specific duty to look out for the interest of the minority shareholders who elected her, or for minority shareholders in general where their interests are at odds with those of the majority.

B. Uniform fiduciary duties

In spite of the heterogeneity of directors between and within the countries just outlined, all jurisdictions we are aware of developed a strongly uniform duty of loyalty for all directors. In all countries, the historical basis tended to be in the case law as opposed to statutory law. In the United States, the courts have long stated that directors owe an "undivided and unselfish loyalty to the corporation."[42] In the UK, originally the common law formulated that duties of directors were owed to "the company;" the same language has been incorporated into Section 170(1) Companies Act 2006.

In Germany, members of the management board are seen as trustees of other people's assets, from which a fiduciary duty naturally flows,[43] and the same applies to members of the supervisory board by virtue of their membership in a body with monitoring and decision-making functions.[44] In France, scholars and subsequently the courts have—in reference to the requirements present in the common law—begun to use the common law term of fiduciary duties since the mid-1990s.[45] In recent years, French law has progressed from board-level collective duties to individual directors' duties. Traditionally, the board had been considered liable only on a collective basis. However, in March 2010, the Court of Cassation recognized that a director may be held liable on a personal level in the event such director failed to oppose a decision taken in breach of the corporate interest.[46]

All of the corporate objectives mentioned—and all of the jurisdictions discussed—have one thing in common: Courts and legal commentators have consistently stated that directors have uniform duties.[47] In the US, as Sepe puts it, "once a director has been elected to a corporation's board, she owes undivided loyalty to all the shareholders of

[39] The SEC famously introduced Rule 14a-11 in 2010, which would have facilitated the nomination of candidates for directorships by minority shareholders. The rule was subsequently struck down by the Court of Appeals for the District of Columbia. *Business Roundtable v SEC* 647 F 3d 1144 (DC Cir 2011).

[40] Testo unico delle disposizioni in materia di intermediazione finanziaria, art 147-ter (permitting minority shareholders exceeding certain thresholds to present lists for the election of minority candidates to the board of directors). See, eg, Corrado Malberti and Emiliano Sironi, "The Mandatory Representation of Minority Shareholders on the Board of Directors of Italian Listed Corporations: An Empirical Analysis," Bocconi U Leg Stud Res Paper Series No 18 (2007).

[41] Ley dos sociedades anónimas, art 137 (permitting groups of shareholders to designate a proportionate number of directors).

[42] *Guth v Loft* 5 A 2d 503, 510 (Del 1939). See also n 8 and accompanying text.

[43] Gerald Spindler, in Wulf Goette and Mathias Habersack (eds), *Münchener Kommentar zum Aktiengesetz* (3rd edn, 2008) vol 2, § 93 para 92.

[44] Eg, Hopt and Roth (n 37) § 116 para 173.

[45] *Vilgrain*, 94-11.241, Cass Com, 27 Feb 1996 (France); see also *Berley*, 00-15.618, Cass Com, 12 May 2004 (France); *Sté DL Finances*, 10-15.049, Cass Com, 15 Nov 2011 (France).

[46] *Crédit martiniquais* n° 08-17.841, Cass Com, 30 Mar 2010.

[47] For Germany, see Habersack (n 18) § 116 para 11.

that corporation—regardless of how she was nominated or by whom."[48] The Delaware Chancery Court in 1987 explicitly ruled out "a special duty on the part of directors elected by a special class to the class electing them."[49] In the *Trados* case, the court declined to apply the business judgment rule to the decisions of directors affiliated to a venture capitalist. The majority of directors had approved a merger in which their sponsor, by virtue of holding preferred stock, captured all of the residual value of the firm, while nothing remained for common stockholders.[50]

Similarly, the UK Companies Act[51] clearly mentions only the company as the beneficiary of fiduciary duties. There is an expectation that directors will act in a manner that is in accordance with the best interest of the company. The common law has so far rejected the idea that directors might have duties to individual shareholders since this would undermine "the collective nature of the shareholders' association in a company."[52] The courts have recognized that individual directors may owe duties to shareholders on independent grounds, indicating "a special factual relationship between the directors and the shareholders in the particular case" as a result of particular dealings on the individual level,[53] eg, when a shareholder authorizes a director to sell his or her shares on his or her behalf to a potential takeover bidder.[54] However, such duties would not supersede or alter the directors' duties to the corporation; the fact that a director has been appointed by a specific shareholder does not in itself create a duty to this member of the company.[55]

As a consequence, duties based on loyalty owed to the company, ie, the duty to avoid conflicts of interest,[56] the duty to promote the success of the company and the duty to exercise independent judgment, as well as the general duty of loyalty provided for by s 172 (which require directors to keep in mind the success of the company), all described in the Companies Act 2006, are to be discharged in a similar manner by constituency directors and the rest of the board.[57]

It has been argued that because the legislature had not strictly defined the concept of "interest" of the company, there was room for interpretation and taking into consideration the circumstances of a given director's nomination.[58] Yet, s 172 emphasizes the promotion of the interest of the company's members as a whole rather than particular interests.[59] Nevertheless, courts have welcomed a nuanced homogeneity and

[48] Sepe (n 11) at 335–7 (discussing directors nominated by unions).

[49] *Phillips v Instituform of N Am, Inc*, No Civ A 9173, 1987 WL 16285, at 10 (Del Ch 27 Aug 1987).

[50] *In Re Trados Shareholder Litigation, Inc*, No Civ A 1512-CC, 2009 WL 2225958 (Del Ch 24 July 2009). In such a case, the directors and the venture capitalist could still show that the transaction met the "entire fairness" standard, even though the burden of proof may be hard to meet. See Smith (n 30) at 63.

[51] Companies Act, 2006, ss 171–7 (UK).

[52] Davies (n 19) para 16-5.

[53] *Peskin v Anderson* (2001) 2 BCLC 1, aff'd (2001) 1 BCLC 372 confirming *Percival v Wright* (1902) 2 Ch 421.

[54] *Briess v Woolley* (1954) AC 333, HL; *Allen v Hyett* (1914) 30 TLR 444, PC.

[55] *Hawkes v Cuddy* [2009] EWCA Civ 291, LTL 2/4/2009, at 32; see also Ahern (n 9) at 123.

[56] See ss 172 and 175. The rule has been broadly construed and therefore far-reaching, see [1896] AC 44 HL, at 51.

[57] Section 172.

[58] Pearlie Koh, "The Nominee Director's Tangled Lot," *Sing J Legal Stud* 148, 156 (2007).

[59] See Company Law Review Steering Group, *Modern Company Law for a Competitive Economy: The Strategic Framework* (DTI 1999) URN 99/654, para 5; Company Law Review Steering Group, *Modern Company Law for a Competitive Economy: Developing the Framework* (2000); Department of Trade and Industry, URN 00/656, para 2.11; Dan Prentice, "Duties of Directors" in the Companies Act 2006, para 3.21 (2007).

recognized graduated approaches to the duty of constituency directors to act in the best interest of the company.[60]

In Germany, the issue has often been discussed for members of codetermined boards. Employee representatives are supposed to have the same rights and duties irrespective of how they were appointed (although specific duties may arise on an individual level when members are appointed to a committee).[61] The duty of loyalty is said to rule out "one-sided interest group policies of employee representatives."[62] For example, employee representatives have to maintain confidentiality vis-à-vis works councils and unions.[63] The same applies to board members appointed by specific shareholders.[64] The identical treatment of employee representatives has been confirmed in case law of the Federal Court of Justice—at least in dicta—in the context of the duty of confidentiality.[65] The same applies to appointed or nominated representatives of specific shareholders, who, in exercising their function (including voting on the board), must prioritize the interests of the "enterprise" over others.[66] However, it is acknowledged that these interests will typically play a role in defining the "interest of the enterprise."[67] Moreover, sometimes it is suggested that both the interests of shareholders and employees can be taken into account because of their particular bond to the corporation; in the case of employees, this follows from codetermination.[68] The only explicit exception is for board members appointed under special rules by a government entity, who are not required to maintain confidentiality vis-à-vis that particular entity.[69]

In all of these cases, it is generally thought that directors may not be bound (eg, by contract) to follow instructions from their nominator.[70] Some authors argue that instructions are permissible when they are compatible with the interest of the corporation, in which case there would not be a sanction in the form of liability for the decision anyway.[71] According to what is probably the majority view, instructions are not even possible when the corporation is part of a corporate group.[72] Similarly, while the question is disputed, according to the majority view directors appointed by the government are not bound by instructions from the appointing entity.[73]

[60] See Ahern (n 9) at 128.

[61] Habersack (n 18) Vor § 95 para 14.

[62] Hopt and Roth (n 37) §116 paras 176 and 206–11 (discussing whether employee directors may participate in a strike).

[63] Habersack (n 18) § 116 para 12.

[64] Habersack (n 18) §116 para 13.

[65] The court ruled that it cannot be strengthened through a charter provision. Bundesgerichtshof [BGH] [Federal Court of Justice] 5 June 1975, Entscheidungen des Bundesgerichtshofes in Zivilsachen [BGHZ] 64, 325. None of the other reported cases truly concerns directors' duties, but the court simply uses the collegial nature of the collective obligation of all supervisory board members to support another point. Eg, BGH 25.2.1982, BGHZ 83, 106; BGH 15 Nov 1982, BGHZ 83, 293; BGH 28.11.1988, BGHZ 106, 154; see also Bundesverfassungsgericht [BVerfG] [Federal Constitutional Court] 7 Nov 1972, 1973 Neue Juristische Wochenschrift 500 (German constitutional court stating *obiter* that employee representatives are required to consider what the best interest of the enterprise is).

[66] Habersack (n 18) at § 116 para 46. However, such directors can also stand in a legal, often fiduciary relationship to their nominator. Kropff (n 24) at 844–7.

[67] Habersack (n 18) Vor § 95 para 13.

[68] Hopt (n 37) §93 para 115.

[69] Aktiengesetz [AktG] [Stock Corporation Act] §394 (FRG).

[70] Gerald Spindler in Gerald Spindler and Eberhard Stiltz (eds), *Aktiengesetz* (2nd edn, 2010) vol 1, § 111 para 79; Uwe Hüffer, *Aktiengesetz* (10th edn, 2012) § 101 para 10.

[71] Eg, Kropff (n 24) at 848–9; contra Habersack (n 18) at § 101 para 51.

[72] Habersack (n 18) at § 111 para 139; see also Kropff (n 24) at 854–5 (denying a distinction between non-group firms and firms in a de facto group).

[73] Regarding the discussion, see Hüffer (n 70) § 394, paras 28-30.

In France, the issue has apparently not frequently been raised; however, it is thought that worker representatives and representatives of the government as members of the board have the same duties as other directors, given that the law does not stipulate otherwise.[74] In other words, the legislature has not defined the notion of "director" in a prescriptive manner. As a consequence, the "director" legal category may hardly be considered homogeneous, however, for want of legal distinction and subcategories with specific regimes, homogeneous principles apply.

II. Toward Diversity in Directors' Duties?

A. The argument for uniform duties

Private law imposes fiduciary duties in order to remedy the risk of agency costs deriving from representative relationships.[75] Because every board member participates in the collective decision-making process (decisions as to third-party-related transactions being set aside), each is involved in the development of agency cost risks. Moreover, board decisions being collegial, each director enjoys *de jure* the same role and responsibility in the decision. As a consequence, it is therefore also expected that every director will have to abide by the same set of fiduciary duties.[76]

In addition, such a uniform set of fiduciary duties is standardized in its content from the perspective of the board members, because of the needs said set addresses. In any conception of corporations, including models that do not give primacy to shareholders, fiduciary duties are intended to protect shareholders from individuals taking benefits from the corporation to its detriment. Hence, fiduciary duties may be described as a set of rules designed for the benefit of a *class* of corporate actors. They should therefore represent standards uniformly benefiting such a class, and not favoring one shareholder, or category of shareholders, over the others. They are therefore meant to be expressed in an undifferentiated manner from the perspective of the obligated individuals. Not surprisingly, they are often identified as "duties of the board:" They are expected from the collective entity represented by the board, and only by transition, from the directors in their capacity as board members.

It should be emphasized that the uniform and standard nature of fiduciary duties is compatible with the reality of board nomination. Acknowledging the fact that board members are nominated via a process that reflects various constituency interests does not eradicate the grounds for uniformity. The law of agency provides that a representative shall act in the interest of the constituency which authorized him. His or her liability may otherwise be challenged. As Leib, Ponet, and Serota express in reference to the public sphere: a "representative is selected locally and 're-presents' her home district

[74] Anne Chavériat, Alain Couret, and Bruno Zabala, *Sociétés commerciales: Mémento pratique Francis Lefebvre 2010*, ed Francis Lefebvre (41st edn, 2009) paras 7985, 8034.

[75] See John Armour, Henry Hansmann, and Reinier Kraakman, "Agency Problems and Legal Strategies," in Reinier Kraakman et al, *The Anatomy of Corporate Law* (2nd edn, 2009) 39–40, and Luca Enriques, Henry Hansmann, and Reinier Kraakman, "The Basic Governance Structure: The Interests of Shareholders as a Class," in *The Anatomy of Corporate Law* at 55, 79–81.

[76] See Ahern (n 9) at 210 (negatively answering the question whether nominee directors have a distinct legal status among directors under UK law).

in some sense, but she *also* serves the "people" and wields power more broadly."[77] The rationale for this enlarged duty is that others' interests, vulnerable to her legal power over them, may need to be protected in her activities.[78] These authors conclude that "fiduciary duties may apply to a shifting constellation of beneficiaries."[79] They stress that if fiduciary obligation is relational at its core, the contours of the relevant relationship and its configuration can shift during flight.[80] In other words, nomination by a constituency indicates *a moment* in the director's experience but does not participate in drawing the limit of the director's fiduciary duties spectrum.

An argument in favor of more homogeneity within the board has been made and calls for homogeneous duties as well. From an efficiency perspective, a more homogeneous board may be superior since interests of different groups will often conflict.[81] (Such a view may however be questioned in the light of behavioral findings: groups do tend to focus on the portion of knowledge that is already shared rather than engage in more creative thinking.[82] When groups are cohesive, this bias creates a risk of groupthink deriving from a "psychological drive for consensus at any cost that suppresses dissent and appraisal of alternatives in cohesive decision-making groups."[83]) This means that, as to their skills, directors should meet certain shared criteria enabling a more fruitful conversation and decision-making process. Pursuant to this pragmatic logic, there is *conversely* a better case for directors to only owe uniform duties to the shareholders. Any acknowledged diversity in duties is a factor of heterogeneity within the board and may weaken its functioning.

However, in practice, the screening of related party transactions and other questions relating to conflict of interests issues (self-dealing, unfair competition, capture of corporate opportunities) represents an important dimension in the duty of loyalty besides the more traditional information obligations towards the shareholders. Jurisdictions mainly assign responsibility for ensuring compliance with related party transactions law to the disinterested directors only—and it is not the same individuals that are considered disinterested directors for each and every related party transaction. In other words, the uniform standards strategy operates in conjunction with the diverse constituency strategy,[84] the latter providing for duties that are, in essence, diverse and specific to the trust relationship.

B. Non-uniform duties as a solution to incomplete contracts

The question remains whether these arguments justify a uniform duty as mandatory law, as is currently the case (at least in theory) in all of the jurisdictions surveyed here.

[77] See in this volume at 401 (emphasis added).

[78] Leib, Ponet, and Serota at 399–401 (this volume).

[79] Leib, Ponet, and Serota at 401 (this volume).

[80] Leib, Ponet, and Serota at 402 (this volume).

[81] Stephen M Bainbridge, "Much Ado About Little? Directors' Fiduciary Duties in the Vicinity of Insolvency," 1 *J Bus & Tech L* 335 (2007).

[82] Bainbridge (n 81) at 518–19.

[83] Irving L Janis, *Victims of Groupthink: A Psychological Study of Foreign-Policy Decisions and Fiascoes* (1972). A famous example of groupthink is the 1961 invasion of Cuba and the fiasco it amounted to.

[84] See Luca Enriques, Gerard Hertig, and Hideki Kanda, "Related-Party Transactions," in *Anatomy* (n 75) at 153, 174.

The economic theory of contracts, specifically the theory of incomplete contracts, provides a major argument for at least permitting firms to opt out of uniform duties in their charter. Insights from behavioral theory tend to support such a proposal, as it builds upon the likely behavior of directors, instead of ignoring this behavior.

1. *Economic theory*

Traditional Chicago-style economic analysis of corporate law assumes that most groups dealing with the corporation are adequately protected by long-term contracts, thus protecting these from opportunism by shareholders or managers. Only shareholders—as the residual claimants of the corporation—are not, which is why they have residual control rights, including the right to vote for directors.[85] However, economic theory has long recognized that long-term contracts are incomplete in most cases, given that "complete contingent" contracts require determining payoffs for all parties for each possible state of the world,[86] in part because of information asymmetry, opportunism, and bounded rationality.[87] Contracts may therefore not suffice to provide groups entering into a long-term relationship with the corporation with sufficient guarantees to protect their investment.

In the context of US corporate law, Margaret Blair and Lynn Stout have argued that in large, publicly traded corporations in the US the board of directors thus typically takes the role of "mediating hierarch," balancing the interests of various groups and permitting all of them to make specific investment in the corporation.[88] While a "neutral" board may be a solution to this governance problem in a publicly traded corporation with diffuse ownership, this will likely not be the case in a situation where "constituency directors" are voluntarily put on the board. Given the inevitable incompleteness of contracts, a large shareholder such as a venture capitalist, whose investment in the company is specific in the sense that it is difficult for him to withdraw, will seek representation in the process that determines how rents produced by the corporation are distributed *ex post* in situations that were not explicitly stipulated *ex ante*; otherwise, he might not undertake this risk.

Similarly, the economic rationale for employee representation on the board of directors is typically that workers often make firm-specific human capital investments in skills that are difficult to transfer to another job.[89] Employees may be more inclined to

[85] Eg, Frank H Easterbrook and Daniel R Fischel, *The Economic Structure of Corporate Law* (1991) 10–11.

[86] See, eg, Oliver Hart, "An Economist's View of Fiduciary Duty," 43 *U Toronto LJ* 299, 305 (1993) (discussing full protection through complete contracts as an assumption underlying a narrow interpretation of fiduciary duty).

[87] See generally Oliver E Williamson, *The Economic Institutions of Capitalism* (1985) 43–55; Oliver Hart, *Firms, Contracts and Financial Structure* (1995) 23.

[88] Margaret M Blair and Lynn A Stout, "A Team Production Theory of Corporate Law," 85 *Va L Rev* 247, 274 n 57 (1999); see also Hart (n 87) at 306–7 (suggesting that a fiduciary duty that considers stakeholder interests could be used to sustain implicit contracts).

[89] Larry Fauver and Michael E Fuerst, "Does Good Corporate Governance Include Employee Representation? Evidence from German Corporate Boards," 82 *J Fin Econ* 673, 679 (2006). See generally James M Malcolmson, "Individual Employment Contracts," in Orley Aschenfelter and David Card (eds), *Handbook of Labor Economics* (1999) vol 3, 2291, 2311–37 (reviewing the labor economics literature on contractual protection of specific investment); Egon Franck, Stephan Nüesch, and Jan Pieper, "Specific Human Capital as a Source of Superior Team Performance," 63 *Schmalenbach Bus Rev* 376, 377–81 (2011).

invest in specific skills if they are less exposed to threats of opportunistic wage negotiations or termination of pension plans,[90] for which employee directors may provide some assurance.[91]

Discussing "constituency directors" under US corporate law, Simone Sepe argues that boards do not have the discretion to give anything to the "sponsor" of a specific director that has not otherwise been explicitly bargained for.[92] If directors may not represent the interests of their sponsors, but have to strictly pursue the interests of "the corporation" or *all* of its shareholders, and if this duty is strictly enforced, the long-term contracting problem outlined here cannot adequately be addressed with governance rights. A large financial investor who might bargain for a nominee director on the board will have to resort to explicit contractual stipulation of his rights and duties under all foreseeable future situations. The problem should now be immediately apparent: Given that long-term contracts are necessarily incomplete, a potential investor's interest will often not be sufficiently protected. This might discourage investment or require investors to charge a higher risk premium. A similar argument may be made for workers. Workers may be reluctant to invest in firm-specific skills without directors representing them. Contracts, or even strong employment law may not be an adequate substitute given the incomplete contracts problem (which analogously applies to legal rules).

Along the same lines, the commercial reality of the situation shared by nominee directors calls for its legal recognition in the context of contract interpretation. It has been pointed out that, where a company's articles provide for a right of shareholders to nominate a director, they should be read as providing for the following implicit understanding: that it is accepted by the parties that a special responsibility towards a shareholder is in the interests of the company as a whole:[93] If the members of the company provided for these directors to be appointed, than they most likely must have done so to represent their nominators' interests. Thus, it would seem contrary to the intention of the contracting parties to disregard these interests.

2. *Lessons from behavioral theory*

In addition, it is recognized that rationality is only limited: cognitive biases also impact behaviors in practice. Though board members may not deliberately make a decision to take into account their personal loyalty, there are reasons to believe that, in certain circumstances, such loyalty will distort behaviors on the basis of psychological mechanisms. A director willing to discharge his duties according to the principle of "uniform

[90] Eg, Thomas Eger, "Opportunistic Termination of Employment Contracts and Legal Protection against Dismissal in Germany and the USA," 23 *Int'l Rev L & Econ* 381, 384–5 (2004); John C Coffee, Jr, "Shareholders Versus Managers: The Strain in the Corporate Web," 85 *Mich L Rev* 1, 70 n 194 (1986); see also Martin Gelter, "The Pension System and the Rise of Shareholder Primacy," 43 *Seton Hall L Rev* 909, 937–41 (2013).

[91] Eg, John T Addison and Claus Schnabel, "Worker Directors: A German Product that Did Not Export?," 50 *Indus Rel* 354, 358 (2011).

[92] Sepe (n 11) at 342 ff.

[93] See Elizabeth Boros, "The Duties of Nominee and Multiple Directors," 11 *Comp Law* 6 (1989) and 10 *Comp Law* 211; Philip P Crutchfield, "Nominee Directors: The Law and Commercial Reality," 12 *Comp Law* 136 (1991); Pey-Woan Lee, "Serving Two Masters," 2003 *J Bus L* 449.

duties" may find himself in a difficult position due to his own psychological biases that he is often not aware of. It is particularly interesting to observe that such a phenomenon is prone to happen in the context of an incomplete contract situation.

We must first acknowledge that empirical evidence in the context of corporate law and corporate boards is limited and focuses on the independence of directors[94] and not, as we do, on the question whether directors represent a specific constituency outside the corporation. Moreover, for some constituency directors, it is clearly difficult to empirically disentangle the effects of ownership stakes or credit relationships as such on the one hand, and representation on the board on the other.[95]

However, there is some empirical evidence that heterogeneity in the profile of directors sitting at the board has an impact on the corporation. Some experiments suggest that bank representatives have effects on various corporate characteristics such as capital structure.[96] In addition, in the area of employee directors, the literature on German codetermination provides some evidence that suggests that they do.[97] A well-known study by Gary Gorton and Frank Schmid, often cited by critics of the practice, found that firms subject to the strictest regime (where 50 percent of seats are held by employees) traded at a 31 percent discount to firms where employees only held one-third of the seats on the board.[98] A paper by Larry Fauver and Michael Fuerst, however, found a positive effect of the less intrusive regime (one-third of board members), but the results were industry specific.[99] A third study by Felix FitzRoy and Kornelius Kraft found that the introduction of codetermination in 1976 slightly increased productivity.[100] This is clearly not the place to provide an overall evaluation of employee participation systems. In any event, the evidence seems to be clear that employee directors make a difference overall, possibly because of a different distribution between shareholders and employees.

On a more theoretical level, some hypotheses may be grounded in more general behavioral studies. From a legal standpoint, the adequacy of the *decision-making process* tends to receive more emphasis as the review of substantive outcomes decreases in corporate law. This trend is understood as a corollary to (i) the need for flexibility, risk taking, etc, and (ii) the inability of courts to second-guess business decisions. The board is built as a group of individuals. Social psychology insights may help understand the decision process within such groups—and point to potential consequences deriving from the specifically diverse collection of individuals comprising such groups.

[94] See, eg, Sanjai Bhagat and Roberta Romano, "Empirical Studies of Corporate Law," in A Mitchell Polinsky and Steven Shavell (eds), *Handbook of Law and Economics* (2007) vol 2, 945, 992–5.

[95] See Gorton and Schmid (n 33) at 66 (not using bank representation on the board as an explanatory variable because of concerns of endogeneity).

[96] Daniel T Byrd and Mark S Mizruchi, "Bankers on the Board and the Debt Ratio of Firms," 11 *J Corp Fin* 129 (2005).

[97] For a more comprehensive review of the empirical evidence, see Addison and Schnabel (n 91) at 361–9.

[98] Gary Gorton and Frank A Schmid, "Capital, Labor and the Firm: A Study of German Codetermination," 2 *J Eur Econ Ass'n* 863 (2004).

[99] Fauver and Fuerst (n 89) at 679.

[100] Felix FitzRoy and Kornelius Kraft, "Co-determination, Efficiency and Productivity," 43 *Brit J Indus Rel* 233 (2005); see also Thomas Zwick, "Employee Participation and Productivity," 11 *Lab Econ* 715 (2004) (finding an increase in productivity resulting from shop-floor employee participation); but see Olubunmi Faleye, Vikas Mehrotra, and Randall Morck, "When Labor Has a Voice in Corporate Governance," 41 *J Fin & Quant Anal* 489 (2006) (suggesting that employees benefit at the expense of other shareholders when holding considerable stock in US firms).

We may first stress that group decision-making has proven a complicated process. So far, no single model has been established that integrates all of the main factors that have been identified.[101] However, among such factors, the characteristics of the decision (such as its importance or time pressure), the context, and the structure of the group play a recognized role. Psychologists distinguish group decision-making processes in particular along two dimensions, namely the degree of cohesiveness and homogeneity within the group. This characteristic influences the rules according to which decisions are taken. Majority rule is only one option. A weighted linear combination model better explains decision-making processes in those cases that (a) require an active consensus-building and (b) where possible results come along a continuum. In these situations, the opinions of those group members will receive more weight whose position is closer to the group's center.[102] It is thereby implied that group members are influential in direct proportion to how strongly they represent the group. In other words, as a person becomes more cognitively central, the person's influence increases because of the perceived expertise that results from the group agreement.

In relation to our research question this finding tends to indicate that board members with a recognized technical expertise have good chances to be more influential in connection with decisions at the board table relating to their expertise. In this model, the alternative median group decision-making model, the potentially moderating influence of people who disagree is very much diluted.[103] This may in turn indicate that, in cases where there is a dominant group, employee directors and other directors nominated for reasons pertaining to their belonging to a particular group of stakeholders may only have a marginal influence in decision-making.

Group decision-making can polarize individual attitudes as people learn about the attitudes of other members in the group and may tend to conform to the group prototype.[104] As a consequence, decisions taken in a group may be more risky than the original preferences of the individual members in the group.[105] Such findings tend to nuance the effectiveness of subtle networks of powers and counter powers that boards sometimes try to achieve.

In particular, deference bias may induce distorted participation of board members in the collective decision-making process at the board table. In order to enable independence in a board's decision-making, a thorough structural corporate governance design is required. For instance, Randall Morck[106] favors separating the chair and CEO functions in corporate governance. According to his analysis, directors are likely to replicate submission to authority ('obedience' commands) demonstrated in the classic

[101] Ramon J Aldag and Sally R Fuller, *Beyond Fiasco: A Reappraisal of the Groupthink Phenomenon and a New Model of Group Decision Processes* (1993).

[102] J H Davis, P Zarnoth, L Hulbert, W P Chen, C Parks, and K Nam, "The Committee Charge, Framing Interpersonal Agreement, and Consensus of Group Quantitative Judgment," 72 *Org Behav & Hum Dec Proc* 137–57 (1997).

[103] Susan T Fiske, *Social Beings—Core Motives in Social Psychology* (2nd edn, 2004) 520. This is consistent with the findings of group polarization.

[104] Fiske (n 103) at 518.

[105] See the classic experiment, Michael A Wallach, N Kogan, & D J Bem, "Diffusion of Responsibility and Level of Risk Taking in Groups," 68 *J Abnormal & Soc Psych* 263–74 (1964).

[106] Randall Morck, "Behavioral Finance in Corporate Governance: Economics and Ethics of the Devil's Advocate," 12 *J Mgmt & Gov* 179–200 (2008).

social psychology experiments by Milgram.[107] Such excessive deference to a director's influence calls for a counter power that the separation of functions enables. Inferences from psychological findings are however less robust when, as in the Milgram experiment, they are not designed in the corporate context.

Other empirical studies are also of interest in connection with the fact that directors are typically subject to a duty of confidentiality that prohibits them from sharing non-public information from the company with their sponsor.[108] Information-sharing has long been a major issue in the debate about German codetermination. Scholars have often argued that the presence of employee representatives on the supervisory board discourages the company's management, specifically the CEO, from sharing information with the supervisory board.[109] The CEO—together with the chairman of the supervisory board, who frequently plays a prominent role—may decide that certain information (eg, about proposed downsizing) should not be shared with employee representatives because the information will likely leak to the union, politicians, or the business press. It has thus been argued that the absence of a continued flow of information undermines the functioning of the German supervisory board. Others have argued that employee participation may eliminate some information asymmetries between executives and others employees and thus reduce the costs of collective bargaining and the incidence of strikes.[110] Better-informed employees may be less likely to object to necessary restructuring.[111] Moreover, some (highly trained) employees may also constitute a valuable source of information for the board.[112]

Information-sharing between directors and their sponsors is thus a two-edged sword. There are risks, but in some cases companies may benefit because information often flows in two directions.

Two well-known cognitive biases are likely to reinforce behaviors on behalf of directors that relate to constituency-influenced sensitive information sharing. Morck[113] offers some other psychological tendencies that might reinforce the deference to insider authority. In particular, inclination toward *reciprocity* might cause board members to defer—consciously or not—out of gratitude for the invitation to join the board and the perquisites of membership.

In addition, *in-group/out-group biases* might cause board members to reject externally generated threats directed at others on the board "team," especially if the board has developed a fairly close working relationship.

For all these reasons, it is tempting to suggest that a "uniform standards strategy" conforms to a large, publicly traded firm with a dispersed ownership structure and a

[107] Stanley Milgram, *Obedience to Authority: An Experimental View* (1974).

[108] For the US, see Cyril Moscow, "Director Confidentiality," 74 *L & Cont Probs* 197 (2011); Sepe (n 11) at 335; for Germany, see AktG §§ 93(1), 116.

[109] See, eg, FitzRoy and Kraft (n 97) at 236 (citing studies suggesting that information is sometimes deliberately withheld); Mark J Roe, "German Codetermination and German Securities Markets," *Colum Bus L Rev* 171–75 (1998).

[110] Gérard Hertig, "Codetermination as (Partial) Substitute for Mandatory Disclosure," 7 *Eur Bus Org L Rev* 123, 127 (2006).

[111] Hertig (n 110) at 130.

[112] Margit Osterloh and Bruno S Frey, "Shareholders Should Welcome Knowledge Workers as Directors," 10 *J Mgmt & Gov* 325, 330 (2006); Hertig (n 110) at 128.

[113] Morck (n 106).

relatively independent board that is insulated from the pressures of specific interest groups. A "diverse constituency strategy," especially as we look at shareholders, may rather correspond to a corporation with multiple large investors.

Conclusion

From a theoretical standpoint, the prevailing corporate law seems to be in conflict with possibly desirable constituency interest representation on the board. Arguments in favor of non-uniform duties seem more persuasive than those in favor of uniform duties. However, restrictions imposed by positive corporate law may not matter all that much. In other words, fairness may not suffer from the preference given to the uniform duty strategy. Why is that? Beyond the legal logic, what is at stake is the reality of the regulated situation. Corporate law deals with a dual reality: corporate actors are pragmatic and ready to leave a gap in the constraints they undertake to enable the corporation to develop and evolve; and, for the same purpose, they are keen on selecting rules they enforce more diligently than others. The duty of confidentiality, which is relatively strict in the law on the books, is probably the area where the case for turning the currently mandatory directors' duties into default law is the strongest, given that it would facilitate interaction between venture capitalists and firms they invest in.

In addition, there is relatively little enforcement of the corporate purpose directors are expected to pursue, and, therefore, the paradox that this chapter has helped decipher does not matter so much. Most of the conflicts of interest that likely come up between various constituencies represented by different directors are not likely to be reviewed all that intensely by the courts. For example, the shareholder primacy norm in the US is generally not considered to be enforced with any vigor. Robert Clark argues that Henry Ford's mistake in the celebrated case of *Dodge v Ford* was not his decision as such but his purported social motivation.[114] Most decisions that potentially redistribute between shareholders and workers, such as what benefits are offered to employees, whether a plant is to be closed, or how hard to bargain with the union, will typically be protected by the business judgment rule.[115] The same can be said for the main conflict of interest between shareholders and creditors, namely what level of risk is appropriate for the firm (generally, higher risk redistributes from creditors to shareholders). As Douglas Baird and Todd Henderson explain, "the board can even take actions that deliberately benefit creditors at the expense of shareholders, so long as the decision is based in facts, well considered, in good faith, and not conflicted by any personal interests of a majority of directors."[116]

[114] Robert C Clark, *Corporate Law* (1986) 603; see also Jonathan R Macey, "A Close Read of an Excellent Commentary on Dodge v Ford," 3 *Va L & Bus Rev* 177, 182 (2008); Christopher M Bruner, "The Enduring Ambivalence of Corporate Law," 59 *Ala L Rev* 1385, 1419 (2008) (noting that shareholder primacy was only discussed because Ford say that profits for shareholders were only an incidental benefit).

[115] Stephen M Bainbridge, "Director Primacy: The Means and Ends of Corporate Governance," 97 *Nw U L Rev* 547, 582 (2003); see also Einer Elhauge, "Sacrificing Corporate Profits in the Public Interest," 80 *NYU L Rev* 733, 775 (2005) ("So even Dodge, the high-water mark for the supposed duty to profit-maximize, indicates that no such enforceable duty exists"); Macey (n 114) at 181, 190.

[116] Douglas G Baird and M Todd Henderson, "Other People's Money," 60 *Stan L Rev* 1309, 1322 (2008).

The line may be more difficult to draw in cases of conflict of interest between different groups of shareholders. For example, under Delaware law, a director representing a venture capitalist would not be considered disinterested by the courts in a transaction with that shareholder, which is why a decision on a self-dealing transaction in which this director participated would be subject to entire fairness review.[117] Where a transaction would confer an advantage to the sponsoring shareholder, nominee directors are thus not even in the position to promote their sponsors' interests. A corporate objective that requires directors to promote "the interest of the enterprise" or of a broader set of corporate constituencies would make it even more difficult for a court to enforce any specific action.[118]

The lack of enforcement of a strictly binding corporate objective thus leaves considerable decision-making space to be filled by directors. The outcome of board deliberations is obviously determined by how directors are nominated and appointed. Since corporate law does not provide a clear and enforceable objective, one can thus conclude that the "interest of the corporation" is not to be understood substantively, but procedurally. To phrase it differently, the duties imposed on directors emerge largely from corporate objectives which are themselves the product of the process of board deliberation:[119] Directors to a large extent determine via their deliberations the corporate objective—and thus determine the content of the duty of loyalty—themselves.[120]

Inspired by the specific context of German supervisory boards with capital and labor benches,[121] such an understanding of the interest of the corporation fits the broad array of situations of "constituency" or "nominee" directors of all stripes. The interest of the

[117] Veasey and Di Guglielmo (n 1) at 770; Smith (n 30) at 62–3.

[118] See, eg, Mariana Pargendler, "State Ownership and Corporate Governance," 80 *Fordham L Rev* 2917, 2935 (2012) (noting that the broad objective of Brazilian corporate law suited the needs of the government as a controlling shareholder).

[119] See Andrew S Gold, "A Decision Theory Approach to the Business Judgment Rule: Reflections on Disney, Good Faith, and Judicial Uncertainty," 66 *Md L Rev* 398, 436 (2007) ("Thanks in large part to the business judgment rule, directors are free to exercise broad discretion when they interpret what the 'best interests of the corporation' are"); Andrew S Gold, "Dynamic Fiduciary Duties," 34 *Cardozo L Rev* 491, 493–4 (2012) (discussing the indeterminacy of corporate fiduciary duties and suggesting that directors are allowed to select from within a range of corporate beneficiaries); see also Lionel Smith, "The Motive, Not the Deed," in Joshua Getzler (ed), *Rationalizing Property, Equity and Trusts: Essays in Honour of Edward Burn* (2003) 53, 70–1 (noting that both in the US and in Commonwealth jurisdictions, courts require directors to act in what they perceive to be the best interest of the corporation, but do not look at its substance).

[120] Arguably, in recent years the development of the concept of good faith in the Delaware courts may have reduced this discretion by requiring an affirmative devotion to the fiduciary's beneficiaries, thus going beyond the traditional focus of the duty of loyalty on conflicted transactions. Cf. *In re Walt Disney Co Derivative Litigation* 907 A 2d 963, at 755 (Del Ch 2005); *Stone v Ritter* 911 A 2d 362, 370 (Del 2006); see Sean J Griffith, "Good Faith Business Judgment: A Theory of Rhetoric in Corporate Law Jurisprudence," 55 *Duke LJ* 1, 19–21 (2005) (explaining how the duty of good faith, went beyond the duties of loyalty and care in *Disney*); Andrew S Gold, "The New Concept of Loyalty in Corporate Law," 43 *UC Davis L Rev* 457, 461, 468–70 (2009) (explaining how the requirement to act in good faith expands the fiduciary duty of loyalty).

[121] See Habersack (n 18) Vor § 95 para 13 ("[codetermination] primarily aims at employee representatives introducing the concerns of employees into board deliberations, and permitting both the supervisory and management board to open up themselves to these concerns within the boundaries of their entrepreneurial discretion, in other words a *procedural understanding* of the interest of the enterprise" [own translation; original emphasis]); Friedrich Kübler, "Dual Loyalty of Labor Representatives," in *Corporate Governance* (n 18) at 429, 440 ("[the interest of the enterprise] can only require that corporate management adequately respects different needs and interests; it cannot censor or correct the substance of business decisions. . .").

corporation, however defined, is determined primarily by board deliberation; the purpose of permitting a specific type of director on the board is to integrate the interests of his constituency into the determination of corporate policies. In all likelihood, a differently composed board of directors will develop a substantively different "interest of the enterprise" in the individual case depending on what constituencies are represented.

16

The Fiduciary Character of Agency and the Interpretation of Instructions

*Deborah A DeMott**

Introduction

Disputes that turn on the application of agency law often involve situations in which, notwithstanding an agent's foibles, the principal is legally responsible for the agent's actions. Agency doctrine grounds the principal's responsibility in the principal's right or power to control the agent. The principal's fundamental mechanism of control, which may be supplemented by others, is the provision of instructions to the agent, either initially when stating the actions the agent has authority to take on the principal's behalf or thereafter throughout the duration of their relationship.[1] This chapter focuses on how the agent should interpret those instructions. The agent's fiduciary duty to the principal furnishes a benchmark for interpretation and for assessing actions the agent takes in response. The fiduciary benchmark requires the agent to interpret instructions reasonably in light of the principal's wishes as the agent understands them when the agent must decide what action to take, a temporal focus for interpretation that is distinctive to agency relationships. The fiduciary benchmark does not permit the agent to exploit gaps or arguable ambiguities in the principal's instructions to further the agent's self-interest or that of a third party, without the principal's consent. The foundational importance of control in defining agency,[2] and the centrality of instructions to control, make agency distinctive as a common law subject, in particular distinguishing it from other categories (eg, trusts) conventionally treated as fiduciary. Accounts of agency law that ignore or slight the importance of instructions are incomplete because they fail to explain either well-settled doctrine or hard-to-miss facts about how agency relationships function.

Focusing on an agent's interpretation of instructions received from the principal also explains the relative weakness of agency as a mechanism through which a person might bind herself prospectively regardless of future changes in external circumstances or in

* I served as the Reporter for the *Restatement (Third) of Agency*, completed in 2006. Some arguments and examples in this chapter originated in the Restatement project or in my unpublished paper, "Instructions and the Agency Relationship," discussed in Kent Greenawalt, *Legal Interpretation: Perspectives from Other Disciplines and Private Texts* (2010). Thanks to Professor Greenawalt for his reactions.

[1] More formally defined, an instruction specifies "how [an] authorized person is to exercise the power conferred." Scott J Shapiro, *Legality* (2011) 228. Collapsing instructions and initial statements of authority is consistent with common law agency doctrine.

[2] Formally stated, "[a]gency is the fiduciary relationship that arises when one person (the 'principal') manifests consent to another person (the 'agent') that the agent shall act on the principal's behalf and subject to the principal's control." *Restatement (Third) of Agency* (2007) § 1.

the principal's own preferences. A principal's power to terminate an agent's authority or countermand prior instructions stems from the representational character of an agency relationship—remaining a separate person, an agent also functions as an extension of the principal as a legally salient person—as well as from the principal's inability to foresee shifts in the agent's motivations and, more generally, how the agent may act in the future. Although agency doctrine does not treat the principal as personally discontinuous over time, it also does not privilege the principal's prior preferences or intentions over those that the agent reasonably understands the principal presently to have at the time the agent determines how to act. How the agent should understand the principal's instructions is contingent on the circumstances when the agent must determine the action to take and on an honest assessment of what the principal would then wish the agent to do. This assessment has a subjunctive quality—as the principal's representative, the agent should aim to act "as if" the principal personally had taken action and as the principal "would have" acted—which suffices to fulfill the agent's duty although the principal has not, as a matter of historical fact, specifically "consented" to the agent's action. And, acting as the principal's extension, the agent's duty is one of faithful interpretation, aimed at accurate replication of how the principal would have acted at the time the agent determines what to do.[3]

To develop these arguments, the chapter proceeds through a series of examples testing an agent's interpretation of instructions against the fiduciary benchmark: categorically stated instructions that are nonetheless incomplete; instructions that explicitly confer discretion on the agent; instructions conferring authority given after the agent acts; and instructions that countermand prior instructions or withdraw authority altogether. A cumulative discussion of two other accounts of agency doctrine follows, with an assessment of their implications for how agents should interpret instructions.

I. The Categorical but Incomplete Instruction

Most statements of authority and interim instructions are incomplete in one way or another in specifying what the agent should and should not do, distinct from explicit conferrals of discretion on the agent. Although conduct may express meaning without using words, as when a principal points to a painting that the agent should attempt to buy for the principal at an auction, this chapter focuses on verbal expression, which is typical of accounts of legal interpretation. To be sure, not all instructions require interpretation in the sense of raising real doubts what the principal means; the world of agency relationships requires a more workaday understanding of language than one that treats all expressive conduct as requiring interpretation because doubts are always possible.[4]

[3] Agency exemplifies a private law institution that furthers a principal's autonomy. Among its distinguishing characteristics are doctrines enabling a form of self-authorship that is subject to ongoing revision when the principal so wishes. On autonomy-enhancing institutions, see H Dagan and S Hannes in this volume. To be sure, the vocabulary of "extension" and "authority" may usefully be used to analyze fiduciary relationships more generally. See P Miller in this volume. Common law agency, which imposes, directly on the principal, the legal consequences of action taken by the agent, posits an ongoing relationship in which the agent continues subject to the principal's control and thus a distinctive form of "extension."

[4] M Stone, "Theory, Practice, and Ubiquitous Interpretation: The Basics," in Gary A Olson and Lynn Worsham (eds), *Post-Modern Sophistry: Stanley Fish and the Critical Enterprise* (2004) 43, 51, 66.

Nonetheless, although a principal's instruction raises no real doubt as to its meaning as a semantic matter, the agent must always decide what to do in response.[5] The agent's situation, that is, raises questions even when they would not ordinarily be characterized as ones of interpretation.

A. Categorically stated instructions

Consider first an instruction that on its face is categorical. P, who owns a commercial menagerie, employs A as its manager.[6] P says to A, "Buy no more horses." If A thereafter makes a contract in P's name binding P to buy a horse from T, a dealer in horses, has A acted with authority from P?[7] Most likely the answer is no, but explanations are possible for A's purchase despite P's direction to the contrary. First, P's instruction, as understood by A, may not have been as clear as P believed it to be. Lack of clarity takes different forms. Suppose P said, instead and more colloquially, "I'm not into horses anymore." This does not categorically state an instruction to A, and A may understand P to be referring to preferences and choices unrelated to the menagerie business. Separately, P's instruction does not itself define "horse," which might prompt A to wonder whether P should be understood to forbid the purchase of a pony, a zebra, or toy horses for the menagerie's gift shop. Separately, if A has reason to know that P uses the word "horse" idiosyncratically, that understanding of "horse" governs A's authority.[8]

B. Changed circumstances

Second, P's instruction does not state how absolutely or unconditionally A should understand it. It may be necessary for A to decide what to do if circumstances change. Would A contravene P's instruction if A buys another horse when one presently in the menagerie dies? That is, should A understand P's concern to be the menagerie's array of species, or, more literally and narrowly, a prohibition on purchasing horses? A might also wonder whether P's concern is horses as such, or whether monetary issues of relative value are relevant as well. Suppose A has reason to believe that the horse purchased from T is worth more than T's asking price. If A attempts to justify the purchase to P as a bargain, P might respond "That's not the point. Your authority is to buy animals to exhibit, not for investment or trading—what I own is a menagerie, not a mutual fund of animals." Thus, A's understanding of P's overall objectives is key. P may call to mind the speaker in Wittgenstein's well-known example who has said, " 'Shew the children a game,' " to a listener who then teaches the children 'gaming with dice.' "[9] The speaker's

[5] One might characterize this as a form of interpretation nonetheless, see Kent Greenawalt, *Legal Interpretation: Perspectives from Other Disciplines and Private Texts* (2010) 223 and as consistent with Gadamer's claim that applications of legal norms "inevitably involve judgment and create new meaning," (Greenawalt at 161).

[6] "P" and "A" are conventional schematic figures, as is "T" with whom A interacts.

[7] For this basic scenario in somewhat different form see *Restatement (Third) of Agency* § 2.02 cmt g.

[8] *Restatement (Third) of Agency* § 2.02, cmt e.

[9] Ludwig Wittgenstein, *Philosophical Investigations*, trans G E M Anscombe (2nd edn, 1958) 33 n. Wittgenstein continues, "Must the exclusion of the game have come before his mind when he gave me the order?"

rejoinder "'I didn't mean that sort of game'" may imply that the listener misunderstood either the point of the instruction or the speaker's relationship with the children now educated in how to gamble with dice, or that the listener had motives incompatible with the speaker's known objectives.

Agents often resolve such questions by seeking clarification from the principal. Indeed, a prudent third party would often confirm with the principal the nature and extent of an agent's authority. Many older agency cases involving such problems feature agents and principals separated by physical distance and lacking effective means of rapid communication.[10] However, the theoretical ability to seek and achieve clarification that modern technology provides does not mean that such clarification always occurs. Not all agents go about their work armed with cell phones or otherwise engaged in continual exchanges with their principals, and an agent's quest for clarification may, at some point, impede efficient performance of work. Moreover, whatever the mode of contact, the agent may seek clarification but the principal may not respond because the principal is otherwise too busy or wishes the agent to make the decision.[11] A principal may intend to respond but forget to do so; if the principal is an organization, inadvertent slippage from prescribed routines may result in a failure to provide the requested clarification. The principal may attempt to respond but the response goes astray, whether in the mail, amidst or within fax machines, or in cyberspace.

Agency doctrine protects the agent and the third party when the agent's action is reasonable under the circumstances, in light of the principal's present wishes as the agent understands them. This dimension of agency doctrine simplifies matters for the principal by eliminating the need explicitly to update prior instructions in light of changed circumstances.[12] However, circumstances vary, and exigent circumstances may warrant a broader scope for the agent's construction of the principal's instructions. For example, leaving the menagerie for a military illustration, suppose a commanding officer tells his troops to patrol an area but to avoid engagement with enemy troops and to take no prisoners. If the patrol encounters the enemy's general, unguarded, one might initially think that it is reasonable to capture the general, given the overall objectives of armed combat.[13] In some circumstances, that is, an agent may reasonably believe that the need or opportunity to act to accomplish the principal's overriding objective should be understood to expand the agent's authority. This can be a risky choice for the agent

[10] Eg, *Butler v Maples* 76 US 766 (1869). A related consequence of physical distance is the principal's inability promptly to learn that the agent has contravened instructions, as in *Short v Skipwith* 22 F Cas 9, 10 (CD Va 1806) (Marshall CJ). The agent's failure promptly to follow the principal's instructions caused loss to the principal when the market value of the investments specified by the principal rose during the interval of delay. *Short* also articulates the importance of the agent's duty to follow instructions; the agent, a friend of the principal's, was not a professional in investment matters. Observed the court (at 10), "It certainly was not to be expected, that a person under the circumstances of the defendant, could execute the order of the plaintiff with the clarity and adroitness of a professional dealer in certificates; but it was to be expected, that the orders of the plaintiff would not be disobeyed, and his remote situation increased the obligation not altogether to neglect any part of his business." Thanks to Peter Fish for this reference.

[11] Or the principal may acknowledge the inquiry but explicitly refuse to respond. See *Garriock v Walker* 1 Rattie 100 (Sess 1873).

[12] For a related argument supporting a current-preferences default rule for statutory interpretation, see Einer Elhauge, *Statutory Default Rules: How to Interpret Unclear Legislation* (2008) 45.

[13] I owe this example to Mel Eisenberg.

because the principal may disagree after the fact with the agent's assessment of what the principal's overriding objective required, or even what its nature might have been. Moreover, the principal may have information the agent lacks and which the principal has determined to withhold from the agent. In the military illustration, perhaps the commanding officer knew that high-level peace negotiations were underway but did not tell the patrol leader. Capturing the enemy general may destroy the peace negotiations and may also prompt a court-martial, not a medal, for the patrol leader.

C. Departures from instructions

Third, agents at times depart from instructions, well understanding what the principal wished to be done under the immediate circumstances, because the agent believes that the principal's instruction was misguided. Returning to the menagerie example, suppose A contracts to buy the horse from T, fully understanding P's instruction as P meant it, but believing it to be a mistake from the standpoint of the menagerie itself. What appears to be hubris on A's part could have several explanations. A may know from the experience of working for P that P is given to issuing instructions that P later regrets if anyone acts on them. After A ignores P's instructions, P applauds A's good judgment.[14] It may, of course, be difficult and hazardous for A to make an assessment of any particular instruction at the time A acts. A risks ignoring instructions that P intends to be taken seriously, just as the patrol leader in the military illustration risks taking action that is contrary to the organization's objectives as those in control understand them at the time.

Matters are more complicated when the principal is not an individual. Suppose that P is not the owner of the menagerie but instead is the chief executive officer of Zoo, Inc, an incorporated firm. P is A's organizational superior but not A's principal; the common law of agency treats both as co-agents of a common incorporated principal.[15] A may contravene P's instruction because A believes it is an element of P's cash-conservation strategy to enable Zoo, Inc to fund new business ventures believed by A to be unsound. Or P's plan, as understood by A, requires a shift out of horses and into exotic animals to be purchased at inflated prices from P. In either case, by purchasing the horse A has contravened the instruction of A's organizational superior. Does A's duty of loyalty to the interests of Zoo, Inc justify A's actions? If A disagrees only with P's business strategy, although it may be in A's long-term interest in organizational survival to dissent from P's plan, A is not justified in buying the horse. Zoo, Inc's organizational structure allocates authority to make business strategy decisions—some of which likely will turn out to be mistaken—to P, not A. A may resign from Zoo, Inc, or seek reassignment within it, or attempt to persuade P's superiors to override P's prohibition, but if that course fails and A stays in place A should follow the directions of A's immediate superior. Other issues follow when P's instruction is a component of what appears to A to be a plan for self-dealing by P. There may be other avenues within Zoo, Inc that A should

[14] In doctrinal terms, a principal's consistent practice of applauding an agent's departures from instructions may augment the agent's actual authority through implication. *Restatement (Third) of Agency* § 2.02, cmt e.

[15] *Restatement (Third) of Agency* § 1.04(9) & cmt i.

pursue, such as contacting its board of directors, its shareholders, or its general counsel. Additionally, A's justifications for ignoring P's instruction may be more compelling when P has directed A to do something as opposed to prohibiting an action.[16] If A acts affirmatively, as by purchasing exotic animals for Zoo, Inc from P at prices A knows to be inflated, A appears to be aiding and abetting P's breach of fiduciary duty.[17] If A obeys P's instruction to refrain from taking an action, such as buying a horse, A is likely to be less closely and necessarily connected to P's breach of duty.

D. Literal compliance

Before leaving this example of a categorical prohibition, consider whether acting on a literal understanding of the prohibition would necessarily discharge A's duty to P. Suppose that A obeys P and buys no more horses for the menagerie. In A's spare time, A develops a specialized menagerie that displays only horses, having recognized that P's menagerie may no longer appeal to horse fans. Or A tips off P's already-established competitor that P may be abandoning horses. A's literal adherence to P's instruction does not privilege A to do other things inconsistent with P's interests that are related to the scope of A's relationship with P.[18] Additionally, A's duty as an agent requires the disclosure to P of relevant information learned while acting for P.[19] If A learns that P's competitor is developing a horse exhibit, A should tell P. In short, A's literal compliance with P's instruction does not obviate A's fiduciary duties to P.

E. Non-agency relationships

An agent's duties to the principal contrast sharply with those owed by a person whose relationship with the principal consists only of one or more bargained-for exchanges, whether for goods, services, or other things of value. A is in this respect differently situated from T, the third-party dealer in horses encountered earlier. As P's supplier of horses, T's duty to P is to provide the horses P purchases, with qualities as warranted by T. If their supply relationship has had a long history, it may have contributed more to P's success than has A. But T, not having undertaken to act on P's behalf, is free to do what A is not free to do as P's agent. Unless T has explicitly agreed not to do so, T may supply horses to P's competitor and may develop a competing menagerie. T owes no duty to P to reveal relevant information—about P's competitor, for example—unless withholding the information constitutes fraud.[20] Likewise, if T is not a dealer in horses

[16] For starters, an agent is not obliged to follow an instruction to perform an illegal act. See *Restatement (Third) of Agency* § 8.09(2).

[17] Knowingly to assist a fiduciary's breach of the duty of loyalty is a tort. *Restatement (Second) of Torts* (1979) § 874, cmt c and § 876 (b).

[18] *Restatement (Third) of Agency* § 8.04 (agent who competes with principal or assists principal's competitor breaches duty of loyalty).

[19] See, eg, *Evvtex Co v Hartley Cooper Assocs, Inc* 102 F 3d 1327, 1333 n 7 (2d Cir 1996); *Restatement (Third) of Agency* § 8.11.

[20] For example, T must reveal non-obvious defects in the horses offered for sale to P that concern facts basic to the transaction and disclosure is reasonably to be expected in the circumstances. *Restatement (Second) of Torts* (1977) § 551(e).

but a supplier of a service that P uses in the menagerie, such as a veterinarian, T is not P's agent. T's duty is to comply with the relevant standard of care. If P relies on T's advice and trusts T, P may attempt to establish that T should be treated as a fiduciary, for example if P at T's invitation relies on T's professedly expert advice about which animals to buy.[21] Undisclosed self-dealing by T would then become problematic. In contrast, A's fiduciary duties do not turn on whether P is able to establish that P in fact trusted and relied upon A because agency doctrine operates categorically by treating all agents as fiduciaries as to conduct within the scope of the relationship.

II. Instructions That Explicitly Confer Discretion

A. Discretionary authority

An instruction on its face may give an agent discretion to determine what to do. A principal might so structure an initial grant of authority or an interim instruction for many reasons. The principal may believe that the agent's superior training will better situate the agent to decide what to do at the relevant time.[22] Separately, the principal may wish not to hear from the agent again and may wish that the agent not seek clarifications. The principal also may believe that, given the nature of the agent's work, it will be impossible to articulate in advance all contingencies that may occur and how they should be resolved. More concretely, P, the menagerie owner, may tell A, its manager: "We need to enlarge the menagerie. I authorize you to spend up to $100,000 on additional animals, as you see fit." A then purchases an assortment of elephants, giraffes, and cobras. Upon learning what A has done, P reacts negatively. P first says, "But that assortment won't draw crowds, in my judgment." P, however, has expressly allocated discretion to A to use A's judgment, taking the risk that it may not coincide with what P believes, after the fact, that P would have decided to do instead. Alternatively, P reacts, "Cobras! You know I've always refused to exhibit snakes. Too dangerous." Although P's statement on its face imposed only a monetary limit on A, A is not free to disregard what A knows about P's preferences, even if A believes them to be mistaken. But suppose A had no way of knowing about P's aversion to snake exhibits. How widely the menagerie industry shares P's aversion is relevant to whether A acted reasonably. If P's is a general menagerie and only more specialized ones exhibit snakes (especially large and deadly ones), it is not reasonable for A to believe that, without more, P authorized A so radically to shift the nature of P's business.

As discussed more fully in Section IV a principal's initial statement of authority to an agent is subject to later countermand by the principal, as would occur if P, having earlier delegated discretion to A to choose animals to purchase for the menagerie, issues later instructions that limit A's discretion or otherwise alter the circumstances under which A will perform. Suppose that P initially assures A that A will not be required to travel overseas to make the purchases but then later directs A to fly to Ruritania to

[21] On the imposition of duties of loyalty in relationships that are not canonically fiduciary, see D DeMott, "Breach of Fiduciary Duty: On Justifiable Expectations of Loyalty and Their Consequences," 48 *Ariz L Rev* 925 (2006).

[22] K Greenawalt, "From the Bottom Up," 82 *Cornell L Rev* 994, 1020 (1997).

purchase a rare specimen for P's menagerie. Unless P can be persuaded to withdraw the instruction, A has a choice: either comply with the instruction, which may give A a claim against P for the increased cost of A's performance; or resign.[23]

B. Discretion used to self-deal

The fiduciary benchmark disallows (unless the principal consents) interpretations possibly motivated by the temptations of self-dealing. A may use part of the $100,000 to pay for a giraffe, a satisfactory giraffe viewed objectively, but sourced from A's personal collection of exotic animals. Even if giraffes of the type have an ascertainable market price, and A pays no more than that price, A's self-dealing breaches the duty of loyalty that A owes to P unless A discloses the material facts to P and P consents.[24] Free to self-deal without disclosure and the principal's consent, A's judgment as to the assortment of animals to purchase may be biased.[25] Giraffes might then loom larger in the menagerie in more than one sense!

A's breach of the duty of loyalty makes remedies available to P that go beyond compensation for demonstrable loss. Suppose, reversing the example, that P directs A to raise $100,000 by selling animals from the menagerie, and A purchases the giraffe for A's own collection without disclosing this fact to P. Even if A purchases at the then-current market price, P is entitled if P wishes to recover the giraffe itself from A or, if A then resells the giraffe at a higher price to T, to recover A's profit. P may also take the position that A's undisclosed self-dealing forfeits A's right to receive agreed-to compensation for A's services.[26]

In all of these examples, it is beside the point that P's statement did not specifically prohibit A's act. An agent's fiduciary duty furnishes a benchmark for the agent's interpretation of the principal's instructions and for assessing actions the agent takes in response. This benchmark facilitates and simplifies the principal's exercise of control; it means that, to protect the principal's interests, instructions and statements of authority in agency relationships need not resemble trust indentures and other densely drafted commercial instruments. Absent the fiduciary benchmark, the principal would, like a good corporate lawyer drafting a complex loan agreement on behalf of a lender, need to attempt to anticipate contingencies and routes through which the agent might use discretion to the principal's disadvantage. Alternatively, a principal might reduce its use of agents[27] or incur the costs of insuring against agents' decisions skewed by self-interest and other impermissible motivations. Self-protective tactics are not free of transaction and opportunity costs and carry distinct complications and limitations of their own.

[23] *Restatement (Third) of Agency* § 1.01, cmt f(1) & illus 3–4.

[24] *Restatement (Third) of Agency* § 8.03.

[25] Greenawalt (n 5) 220–1 ("Once an agent is encouraged at all to further his own interests or those of worthwhile causes, so long as he does not harm his principal's interests, his judgment about exactly what will satisfy his principal's interests may be skewed. He may convince himself, or hope he can convince others, that her interests did not suffer").

[26] *Cameco Inc v Gedicke* 724 A 2d 783 (NJ 1999). Further on remedies for breach, see D DeMott, "Disloyal Agents," 58 *Ala L Rev* 1047 (2007).

[27] The principal's plan may substitute technology for (human) agents or may reorganize its operation to internalize functions performed by external agents on the theory that employees are easier to monitor or less vulnerable to temptation.

Relatedly, some question why agency is a categorical instance of a fiduciary relationship, even in commercial contexts, and whether or not the principal's instructions explicitly confer discretion on the agent. Linking the principal's right and ability to control the agent to the fiduciary benchmark imposed on the agent's interpretation of statements of authority and of interim instructions, answers the question. In our last example, if A is free to self-deal (by purchasing) without disclosing that fact to P, A may select animals to sell on the basis of A's assessment of their potential for resale at prices higher than the then-current market value. This prospect will affect how A interprets P's instructions. If P tells A, "First sell the animals that aren't drawing the crowds," A may well be tempted to press the definition of "crowd" so as to dispose of the giraffe through self-dealing prior to the horse, if the horse's market value over time is more readily predictable than is that of the giraffe.

To be sure, an agreement between principal and agent may help establish that the parties did not intend a relationship of agency or the scope of any such relationship.[28] However, *ex ante* agreements between principal and agent in which the principal agrees not to hold the agent to any duty of loyalty either are ineffective or create a legal relationship other than agency. Put differently, the definitional components of agency are not default rules. Furthermore, an agent's representational capacity, necessarily tied to the principal's power to control the agent, is also necessarily tied to the interpretive framework through which the agent determines actions to take on the principal's behalf.[29]

C. Well-motivated disregard of principal's preferences

Additionally, an agent's position as the principal's representative calls into question whether the agent may disregard known preferences of the principal when immaterial to the principal's economic interests and when the agent believes that acting on these preferences would be misguided. Returning to the prior example, suppose that A, who cannot immediately consult with P, knows that P has a slight preference that menagerie animals be sold to T, not Z, when both T and Z are willing to pay the same price. P holds this preference for no stated or tangible reason known to A, whether or not economic.[30] A, however, prefers Z and sells to Z, not because A will benefit personally, but because Z generously donates a portion of its profits to the poor.[31] On the one hand, as Kent Greenawalt notes, A has furthered P's objective—reducing the menagerie's cohort of animals—and at no less economic benefit to P.[32] On the other hand, as P's agent, A acted as P's representative, taking action in the world as if P had done so personally, and from all A knows, A has reason to believe that P would have sold to T, not Z. Thus,

[28] *Restatement (Third) of Agency* § 1.02.

[29] For recent recognition of the constitutive nature of an agent's fiduciary duty and the significance of the principal's instructions, see *Hollingsworth v Perry* 133 S Ct 2652, 2666–67 (2013).

[30] Greenawalt (n 5) 228 n 14 ("tangible" interests encompass economic interests as well as preferences known to be based on, for example, sympathy with a particular third party).

[31] Or perhaps A knows that Z minimizes the taxes it pays less aggressively than T.

[32] Greenawalt (n 5) 221 (approving of agent's choice "so long as the peripheral interest is a general good and not the agent's own welfare or particular interests").

even well-motivated departures from P's known preferences are inconsistent with A's position as P's representative.

III. The Tardy Instruction

A. Delayed conferrals of authority

Should it matter what the agent believes the extent of authority to be at the time the agent acts? Suppose P, who owns the copyright interests in books written by her late father, has authorized A, a literary agent, to enter into contracts with publishers for her father's nonfiction works. Later on, P, pleased with the quality of A's work, drafts a letter increasing A's authority to include contracts for her father's novels. P mails the letter to A, but it does not arrive before A executes a contract with T for publication of one of the novels.[33] Is P bound to T? Or is P free to contract with Z, a rival publisher, who offers better terms than T? There are many possible explanations for A's action. A may have failed to focus on or understand the scope of authority granted by P, or A may have known that authority was lacking but hoped that P wouldn't care if A got a good deal with T. Or A may not have wanted to reveal to T that P granted only limited authority to A.

This example illustrates the importance of the prototype or theoretical construct used to define and analyze authority. If authority is defined as a function of the ongoing relationship between an agent and a principal that must reflect the agent's reasonable understanding of the principal's present wishes, an agent may not contravene or exceed instructions even when the agent's action happens to coincide with further instructions that, unbeknownst to the agent, conform the agent's authority to the agent's acts. It is irrelevant to the extent of A's actual authority that P would act grudgingly in objecting to A's action; the letter when it arrived establishes P's willingness to be bound by just such an act by A. In contrast, if conferring authority is like making a gift, it should not matter whether the conferee knows of the conferral. The conferral, if provable, would be analogous to delivery in making a gift, so long as the donor intended to make the gift.[34] Authority would have an autonomous and continuing existence of its own, separate or detached from the relationship between principal and agent. Like a testamentary will, authority would be effective until the principal revoked it but its existence would be detached from the ongoing relationship and communications between the principal and the agent, and perhaps also from the state of facts known to the agent at the time the agent acts.

Although other doctrines—soon to be explored—may bind P (the copyright holder), A lacked actual authority to do so because the basis for actual authority is the agent's reasonable understanding of what the principal wishes the agent to do.[35] The common law does not define authority as a thing that has existence separate from the principal's manifestations to the agent and the agent's reasonable understanding of them. In the

[33] For an illustration in a reported case, see *Ruggles v American Cent Ins Co* 114 NY 415 (1889).

[34] E Allan Farnsworth, *Changing Your Mind: The Law of Regretted Decisions* (1998) 136 (emphasizing importance of donor's intention). To complete the gift, the donee must accept it. *Restatement (Third) of Property: Wills and Other Donative Transfers* § 6.1(b).

[35] *Restatement (Third) of Agency* § 2.01.

example, this understanding is lacking because although P acted to enlarge A's authority, P did so unbeknownst to A.[36] The common law diverges in this respect from civil law systems, which separate questions going to the agent–principal relationship from those concerning the agent's authority to bind the principal in transactions with third parties. For example, under the Louisiana civil code, a principal may confer authority through a unilateral juridical act, addressed to either the agent or the third party.[37] An agent may thus have authority to act without consenting to the conferral itself, which implies that the existence of authority is not dependent on the agent's knowledge of the principal's conferral.

B. Apparent authority

T might nonetheless be able to hold P on the basis that A acted with apparent authority by showing that T reasonably believed A to be authorized, a belief traceable to a manifestation made by P. If T succeeds on this ground, P has a claim against A to recover her loss of the better terms offered by Z because an agent is liable to the principal for losses caused by the agent's failure to act only as directed.[38] Apparent authority is crucial to explaining how the world works, or, more precisely, how agency doctrine accommodates the need for stability in transactions and third-party expectations. As the presence of actual authority depends on events that are often observable only by the agent and the principal, it may be tempting to the principal to deny the existence of actual authority when the principal regrets what the agent has done.[39] Additionally, the principal's explicit imposition of limits on the agent's authority may be accompanied with a nudge and a wink, encouraging the agent to ignore a limit when the agent can conclude a deal that seems advantageous, knowing that the principal has a defense if the deal subsequently proves disadvantageous. That principals only infrequently sue agents—especially employee agents—for overstepping their authority, may suggest that the presence of actual authority often coincides with apparent authority.[40] Apparent authority thus backstops actual authority in circumstances when proving actual authority would likely elude a third party.

Apparent authority resembles shadow boxing because its presence turns on what P has caused T to believe about P's relationship with A. Suppose T first approaches P about her father's novels and P responds, "Talk to A about any of my father's books. I'm too busy to deal with publishers." By deflecting T's inquiry and redirecting T to A, P may lead T reasonably to believe that A's authority encompasses, as P says, "any" of her father's books. Indeed, perhaps, at the time A executes the contract, T knows, but A does not, that P has written and mailed a letter expanding A's authority to encompass what A is about to do. Unless T knows that A executed the contract unaware of the

[36] *Restatement (Third) of Agency* § 3.01, cmt b, illus 1. The same point underlies *Restatement (Second) of Agency* (1958) § 26, illus 1.
[37] La Civ Code art 2987 (defining procuration).
[38] *Restatement (Third) of Agency* § 8.09, cmt b.
[39] For further elaboration, see *Restatement (Third) of Agency* § 2.03, cmt c.
[40] For other possible explanations, see G Schwartz, "The Hidden and Fundamental Issue of Employer Vicarious Liability," 69 *S Cal L Rev* 1739, 1764–767 (1996).

letter, it is reasonable for T to believe that P has authorized A to make the contract for the novel. In contrast, if T knows that A does not know the content of the letter, T has at least reason to suspect that A lacks actual authority. But T may nonetheless reasonably believe that P has also communicated less formally with A. Otherwise, T would not reasonably believe that A has actual authority. Nor would T be reasonable in believing that A acts with actual authority when T has reason to know that A's conduct breaches a fiduciary duty to P, as when T bribes A to induce A to deal with T.[41]

C. Ratification

In contrast, ratification is a consequence of a principal's decision to affirm what the agent has done, after the principal learns the facts.[42] Although ratification has the effect of creating actual authority after the fact,[43] it does not require an instruction from the principal that precedes the agent's action. Accordingly ratification operates differently from actual authority. Suppose P first learns about the contract from T and responds to T, "That's what I've always liked about A—the ability to take the initiative to make a good deal." P is bound because P has affirmed or accepted A's action. That P communicates with T, not A, does not matter because events have moved beyond P's statement of instructions to A.[44] But may P both affirm the contract with T and treat A's unauthorized action as a breach of duty by A? P may wish to affirm the contract to stay on good terms with T,[45] but P may also wish to sue A to recover for her loss of a better deal or to treat A's conduct as a breach that should reduce A's compensation. As to A, P has given no assurances or representations that would estop P from asserting such claims against A. P did nothing to induce A to execute the unauthorized contract binding P to T, nor did their relationship place A in a situation in which executing the contract appeared reasonably necessary to protect P's interests. Nonetheless, P seems to be behaving badly. Given P's manifest willingness to confer fuller authority on A, it is opportunistic for P to assert A's lack of actual authority because P could have gotten a better deal from Z, the rival publisher. Generally, agency doctrine protects an agent against the prospect that a principal may use its unilateral power to ratify as a way of shifting risk on to the agent. Otherwise, a principal might be tempted to ratify an unauthorized transaction, thereby binding the third party, while determining later whether to hold the agent accountable if the transaction with the third party turns out to be one that the principal then regrets.[46] If, however, the agent's unauthorized action places the principal in a predicament requiring that the principal take affirmative steps to avoid loss, those steps do not manifest consent by the principal effective to exonerate the agent.[47]

[41] *Restatement (Third) of Agency* § 2.03, cmt d and § 8.02 (agent has duty not to acquire material benefit from a third party through the agent's use of position).

[42] *Restatement (Third) of Agency* § 4.01. [43] *Restatement (Third) of Agency* § 4.02.

[44] P's attempt to ratify will be ineffective if it is preceded by any manifestation by T of withdrawal, that is, of intention not to be bound by the transaction. *Restatement (Third) of Agency* § 4.05 (1). Once P repudiates A's action, T should not be subject to the risk of P's subsequent ratification. Farnsworth (n 34) 177.

[45] See *Goldstick v ICM Realty* 788 F 2d 456, 460 (7th Cir 1986).

[46] *Restatement (Third) of Agency* § 4.01, cmt b.

[47] *Restatement (Third) of Agency* § 4.02(2)(b) & cmt d.

IV. The Countermanding or Final Instruction

Agency is a fragile legal institution because actual authority terminates whenever the principal or the agent manifests to the other the wish to discontinue.[48] Even when the principal and the agent have agreed that the agent's authority is irrevocable, it is not,[49] subject to two general exceptions. The first reflects a lessening of the theoretical rigors of historical formulations of agency doctrine to further widely acknowledged social needs. Contemporary agency doctrine permits a principal to grant authority irrevocably through a durable power of attorney that becomes irrevocable when the principal loses legal capacity and regardless of that loss.[50] Although a principal who lacks legal capacity may well be unable to provide instructions to the agent that would reflect the principal's wishes, were the principal still legally competent, contemporary agency doctrine respects the principal's designation of a representative made while still competent. The second exception recognizes that the power to affect a person's legal relationships may be granted irrevocably when the grant supports an interest of the agent's that is separate from, or independent of, the agency relationship itself, as illustrated below.

A. Countermanding instructions

These exceptions aside, the relative fragility of authority can seem puzzling because it limits a principal's ability to self-bind against the risk of future changes in the principal's own preferences. Derek Parfit's example, "The Nineteenth Century Russian," is illustrative of instructions that countermand prior instructions: a Russian nobleman, knowing he will inherit large estates in the future, is prompted by his socialist ideals to form the intention "now, to give the land to the peasants."[51] Knowing also

> that in time his ideals may fade... he signs a legal document, which will automatically give away the land, and which can be revoked only with his wife's consent. He then says to his wife, "Promise me that, if I ever change my mind, and ask you to revoke this document, you will not consent."[52]

In the future, Parfit comments, the nobleman's wife "might plausibly regard herself as not released from her commitment," viewing herself as having "obligations to two different people;"[53] she would betray the young man to whom she made the promise to obey the man to whom she was (now) married, the later self of the young man. But, Parfit continues, if in sound mind, "the person to whom we are committed can always release us."[54] Treating the Russian Nobleman's wife as his agent, the fiduciary

48 *Restatement (Third) of Agency* § 3.10.

49 See F Reynolds, "When Is an Agent's Authority Irrevocable," in Ross Cranston (ed), *Making Commercial Law* (1997) 259.

50 *Restatement (Third) of Agency* § 3.08(2).

51 Derek Parfit, *Reasons and Persons* (1984) 327.

52 Parfit (n 51) 327.

53 Parfit (n 51) 327.

54 Parfit (n 51) at 328. Parfit continues, "This is like a similar fact about authority. Suppose that a general tells his troops, 'I order you to attack at dawn, and to disregard any later contrary order.' He later says, 'Disregard my last order and retreat.' Despite the content of the first order, it would be this second order that his troops should obey."

benchmark requires action consistent with her understanding of her principal's present statement of intentions. Although his preferences have changed, the principal's identity has not and his wife is the Russian Nobleman's representative. The Russian Nobleman's situation strikes some commentators as paradoxically self-frustrating.[55] But his situation is troubling only if there's good reason always to prefer one's present projects and wishes over those one may have in the future.[56] Moreover, once he has aged, the Russian Nobleman may understand his youthful fear of middle-aged degeneration to have been only a jejune expression of naiveté.[57] To be sure, his present (middle-aged) perspective may diverge from that of his wife; and the power to revoke that vindicates his autonomy may also be the instrument of her disillusionment with the man to whom she is (now) married.[58]

A principal's power to countermand a prior instruction is not the sole consequence of agency's foregrounding of the principal's present preferences and assessments. Recall that *ex ante* agreements that relieve an agent of fiduciary duties are, in the context of agency relationships, ineffective. However, conduct by an agent that would breach the agent's duty of loyalty does not constitute a breach if the principal consents to it, effective consent requiring a present decision by the principal preceded by disclosure by the agent of material facts relevant to the principal's judgment.[59] That is, whether "consent" is effective turns on the principal's present decision, informed by presently disclosed information, and not the principal's prior assessments.

B. Final instructions

A principal's termination of authority is the principal's final instruction to the agent because it directs that agent cease acting on the principal's behalf. If the agent continues service thereafter, the agent is not entitled to compensation for the post-termination service in most instances. Persisting after the final instruction is not, however, treated as a breach of the agent's duty of loyalty that could forfeit the agent's right to compensation for prior service because the agent has been disobedient, not disloyal.[60] Agency doctrine gives effect to the principal's instruction even when it contravenes an agreement stating that the authority shall be irrevocable, an objective the (young) Russian Nobleman attempted but failed to achieve.

Moreover, a principal has the power to revoke even when exercising the power constitutes a breach of contract. Consider first the distinctive significance of the principal's power to revoke authority, returning to the hypothetical menagerie owner, P. Suppose

[55] Jon Elster, *Ulysses and the Sirens: Studies in Rationality and Irrationality* (1984) 152. As Elster defines paradox, "status X gives you the right to status Z, on the condition that you perform action Y, which automatically disqualifies you from being X." The Russian Nobleman is "setting himself up for a situation in which he cannot make a certain request without ceasing to be himself and thus losing all grounds for being obeyed."

[56] B Williams, "Persons, Character and Morality," A Rorty (ed), *The Identities of Persons* (1976) 197, 206.

[57] Williams (n 56) 206.

[58] Parfit (n 51) 328–9 ("That the young man whom she loved and married has, in a sense, ceased to exist—that her middle-aged and cynical husband is at most the later self of this young man—these claims seem to her to express more of the truth than the simple claim, 'they are the same person'.").

[59] *Restatement (Third) of Agency* § 8.06 (1).

[60] See *Strategis Asset Valuation & Mgmt, Inc v Pacific Mut Life Ins Co* 805 F Supp 1544 (D Colo 1992).

P retains A Corp to manage P's menagerie business. A Corp specializes in managing zoos and amusement parks more generally; properties it manages usually make prominent mention of A Corp's involvement. The management agreement between P and A Corp provides that, in exchange for licensing the use of its name by P's menagerie (which becomes "P's Menagerie. An A Corp Park") and using its specialized management expertise, A Corp will receive a royalty of 3 percent of the menagerie's gross revenues for the first five years, followed by a 5 percent royalty over the next five years. The agreement explicitly provides that P agrees not to terminate prior to the conclusion of ten years, in exchange for A Corp's agreement to accept a lower royalty rate over the first five years.[61] Notwithstanding these terms, if P revokes A Corp's authority at the five-year point, or indeed at any time, A Corp may not remain in control of P's menagerie. If it does not depart voluntarily, A Corp may be judicially ejected. Although A Corp may sue P to recover damages for breach of contract, A Corp will need to prove and quantify its losses.[62] P's power to revoke A Corp's authority is not ousted by A's prior agreement with A Corp, just as the Russian Nobleman's prior instruction to his wife did not cancel his ongoing ability to reconsider in light of his (later) preferences.

In contrast, irrevocability is achievable when authority supports an interest of the agent that is distinct from the agency relationship, which A Corp's interest in recovering the higher royalty rate over the final five years of its management agreement with P would not be. But suppose that P and A Corp agree that A Corp will make substantial physical improvements to the menagerie and will in exchange become a half-owner of the property. A Corp now has an interest separate from its interest in continuing to manage the menagerie, as A Corp would also have if it lends P the money necessary to improve the menagerie, or if it leases the menagerie from P. A Corp's interest as a half-owner, a creditor, or a lessee is distinguishable from its role as an agent.[63] A Corp's distinct interest is enforceable; it also creates a non-agency basis on which to make irrevocable (if the parties' agreement so provides) A Corp's management authority, trumping P's terminal instruction by situating a portion of A Corp's relationship with P beyond the scope of its representation of P.

The principal's ongoing power to give the final instruction to an actor who is simply an agent is an aspect of agency doctrine with wide-reaching consequences. For example, a principal's power to revoke authority helps explain why it is important that a corporation be a legal person distinct from its organizers and its stockholders, although some contemporary theorizing about corporate law appears to assume otherwise.[64] To characterize a corporation as simply a contractually constituted association, in which directors and officers are the shareholders' agents, overlooks the fact that it is often to the advantage of shareholders that directors and officers be able to create contractual commitments with third parties that bind both the corporation and the third party. But

[61] For the specifics, see *Government Guaranty Fund v Hyatt Corp* 95 F 3d 291 (3d Cir 1996). Accord, *Restatement (Third) of Agency* § 3.12, illus 3.

[62] In Maryland, industry-specific exceptions (hotels and retirement communities) oust the application of common law doctrine when an operating agreement does not permit early termination. See Md Com Law Code § 23-104 (2004) & 23-102 (b) (specific performance available as remedy) (2004).

[63] See *Lane Mtge Co v Crenshaw* (1928) 93 Cal App 411, 269 P 672.

[64] See Frank H Easterbrook and Daniel R Fischel, *The Economic Structure of Corporate Law* (1991) 41.

if the shareholders are, individually, the principals, each may revoke authority and do so at any time.[65] This contingency renders unstable the contracting capacity of directors and officers such that, at a minimum, a third party would always want to know, immediately prior to executing a contract, whether all shareholders still assent to their purported representative's authority. The corporate structure overcomes this problem by situating authority between the corporation itself and those who act on its behalf, and not between those agents and the shareholders.[66]

More generally, as a principal's ongoing power to revoke an agent's authority illustrates, agency doctrine consistently privileges the principal's present preferences, which may be expressly stated (as when the principal revokes the agent's authority) or bind the agent when the agent interprets the principal's instructions in light of the principal's present wishes as the agent then reasonably understands them. Viewed instrumentally, this underlying characteristic of agency doctrine reduces the risks inherent in extending one's legal personality by consenting to representation by an agent. Viewed as a consequence of the constitutive elements of an agency relationship, it is consistent with the relational nature of agency itself that agency doctrine mandates loyalty to the principal's present preferences (or persona). A principal's conferral of authority on an agent is unlike making a gift, executing a will, forming a corporation, or authoring a work of literary or artistic art. All of these create a legally salient something that is external to or detached from their creator, whereas an agency relationship remains an extension of the principal throughout its duration.

V. Other Accounts of Agency Doctrine

The central importance of stating and acting upon instructions explains and links elements of common law agency doctrine that otherwise lack a single coherent rationale, in particular the agent's fiduciary duties to the principal and the principal's power to control the agent.[67] Some commentators, most prominently Oliver Wendell Holmes, have doubted whether the common law of agency has any ascertainable intellectual coherence. Justice Holmes asserted that "there is no adequate and complete explanation of the modern law, except by the survival in practice of rules which lost their true meaning," which left, as an unsatisfying residue, only a fictional identification of the agent and the principal, plus common sense.[68] Holmes's pervasive pessimism aside, accounts of agency that slight or ignore the importance of instructions are incomplete. For example, Wesley Hohfeld emphasized an agent's power to create legal liabilities in the principal that are correlatives of the legal power the principal has granted to the agent. The agent's powers, he concluded, are "[e]ssentially similar to... powers of

[65] Each shareholder would be characterized as a co-principal. *Restatement (Third) of Agency* § 3.16, cmt c.

[66] The corporate structure also enables an agent to have an interest in something, the corporation, other than the agency relationship itself. See *Restatement (Third) of Agency* § 3.12(2) (irrevocable proxies granting authority to vote stock).

[67] For a broader theoretical account of fiduciary obligation consistent with this point, see A Laby, "The Fiduciary Obligation as the Adoption of Ends," 56 *Buffalo L Rev* 99, 135 (2008).

[68] O W Holmes, *The Common Law* (1881) 232. For greater optimism about rational or cogent explication, see W Seavey, "The Rationale of Agency," 29 *Yale LJ* 859, 859 (1920) (results reached by courts may be tested, not axiomatically, but "by the use of judicial sense (not common sense) and the needs of commerce").

appointment in relation to property interests," as are a sheriff's power to sell property under a writ of execution and a donor's power to revoke a gift that has been promised but not delivered.[69] Focusing exclusively on an agent's ability to affect the principal's legal interests, Hohfeld's account omits the agent's duties to act loyally on behalf of the principal and as the principal directs and, like civilian treatments of authority, decouples the presence of authority from the agent's duties to the principal. Hohfeld's account also has implications for how an agent should interpret instructions received from the principal. If an agent's authority is comparable to a power of appointment in relation to a property interest, the text in or through which authority is expressed would govern, not the agent's understanding of the principal's wishes at the time the agent takes action. The absence of comparable formal requisites[70] for the creation of agency relationships would be a source of frustration, as would be the absence in many agency relationships of anything comparable to a written power.

Other accounts attempt to capture agency relationships for the turf of bargained-for exchange (in which many agency relationships unquestionably originate) and for the legal domain of contract. James Coleman analyzed agency relationships as the consequence of transactions involving an agent's surrender of the right to control her own actions in exchange for remuneration from a principal who needs the actions of one with the agent's skills or capacities.[71] The principal's dilemma is that "even a directly supervised agent may devote more or less effort toward the outcome desired by the principal."[72] An agent's interests are always disjoint from the principal's, not unified, and an agent always by definition acts differently than would the principal in the agent's place and with the agent's resources. Although Coleman's account explores structures through which an agent may be led to identify with the principal's interests, it does not delve into the nature of direction, supervision, or authority, all highly significant to the functioning of agency relationships. Authority to direct the actions of others is essential to explaining how organized activity occurs because such authority supersedes moment-by-moment negotiation over the terms on which work will be done and by whom.[73] Direction or supervision requires instruction, and by consenting to an agency relationship with a principal, the agent becomes subject to a duty to follow instructions furnished by the principal that are within the broad outer limits imposed by the law. Acting on the basis of those instructions requires interpretation by the agent, a process anchored by the agent's fiduciary duty to the principal, which bridges the agent's interests with those of the principal. But this is not the realm of contractual interpretation, necessarily focused as it is on mutually understood intentions at the time the contract was made and permitting otherwise-legal actions in disregard of the counterparty's interests.[74] Contractual interpretation, as Daniel

[69] W Hohfeld, "Some Fundamental Legal Conceptions as Applied in Judicial Reasoning," 23 *Yale LJ* 16, 46–7 (1913).

[70] See *Restatement (Third) of Property: Wills and Other Donative Transfers* § 18.1 (compliance with formalities requisite to creation of effective power of appointment).

[71] James S Coleman, *Foundations of Social Theory* (1994) 146.

[72] Coleman (n 71) 151.

[73] See R Flannigan, "The Economic Structure of the Firm," 33 *Osgoode Hall LJ* 105, 119 (1995) (observing that employees "do not refuse to take direction. They do what is asked of them, and they do so for very good reasons").

[74] On contractual interpretation, see, eg, Greenawalt (n 5) 255–300; Aharon Barak, *Purposive Interpretation in Law*, trans Sari Bashri (2005) 318–38.

Markovits notes, "takes the terms of the contract as its lodestar," and requires that a promisor look not to the promisee's changing interests but to the contract.[75] Agency doctrine, in contrast, focuses an agent's interpretation on the principal's expressed or cognizable wishes at the time the agent determines how to act.

Conclusion

The fiduciary character of an agent's position explains a principal's exercise of control over the agent through instructions given to the agent, as well as the adaptability of agency relationships across changing circumstances. The fiduciary character of the agent's position stems from an agent's position as a legally salient extension or representative of the principal, as does agency's consistent requirement of loyalty to a principal's present preferences and persona. In striking contrast to other bodies of legal doctrine, agency law is not a basis on which to ground a solution to one's distrust of one's future self, focused as agency necessarily is on assuring a principal's autonomy through time and thus on the principal's present self and preferences.

[75] Daniel Markovits in this volume.

17

On Trust and Transubstantiation

Mitigating the Excesses of Ownership

*Avihay Dorfman**

Introduction

The legal institution of trust gives rise to two basic sets of questions. The first set concerns the respective rights held by the trustee and the beneficiary with respect to the trust property—do these rights feature a structure characteristic of property, contract, or something in between? The second concerns the normative relationship between the trustee and the beneficiary—what explains the existence and content of the obligations owed by the trustee to the beneficiary, especially the fiduciary duty of loyalty? A successful account must be able to address both sets of questions and the nature of the connection between them.

I devote these pages to the second set of questions.[1] Negatively, I seek to show that accounts of the trustee's fiduciary obligations grounded in settlor's intent, the virtue of loyalty, or contract fall short of capturing the idea of the trust. For instance, with respect to the argument from contract, I argue that the trustee/beneficiary relationship features a special notion of beneficiary *passivity* that is deeply incompatible with the formal structure of the kind of contractual relationship said to underlie the trust.

Affirmatively, I argue that the grounds and content of the trustee's fiduciary obligations reflect, at least in part, the special difficulty that the trust institution picks out, namely, the *excesses of ownership*. On this argument, the institution of trust arises in connection with the difficulty of acquiring the standing of ownership. A Trustee makes possible a derivative status of ownership: that which allows *patients* (by choice or by chance) to enjoy access to the institution of ownership but, at the same time, to do without the agential powers characteristic of ownership. The duty of loyalty arises against *this* backdrop, tracking the role of the trustee in possessing, and sometimes even *constituting*, the personhood of the beneficiary and thus acting as his alter ego in relation to the trust property. In this, the duty of loyalty is consequential to the transubstantiation of the trustee into the bearer of the ownership personality of the beneficiary.

I shall use the metaphor of "transubstantiation" to distinguish the proposed account from accounts that cast the relationship in terms of "substitution."[2] The notion of

* This article has benefited from responses received at the Philosophical Foundations of Fiduciary Law Conference at DePaul College of Law. Thanks to Andrew Gold and Paul Miller for the invitation to join the conference. I would also like to thank the participants in this occasion. Finally, thanks to Hanoch Dagan, Joshua Getzler, Michele Graziadei, Ethan Leib, Paul Miller, and Robert Sitkoff, for helpful comments on earlier drafts.

[1] I take up the former question elsewhere. See Avihay Dorfman, "The Letter and the Spirit of Property: The Case of the Trust" (unpublished manuscript).

[2] For a thorough exposition of the substitution-based account of trust and fiduciary law, more generally, see Paul B Miller, "Justifying Fiduciary Remedies," 63 *U Toronto LJ* 570 (2013) (hereinafter: Miller,

substitution implies a transfer of legal capacity or personality from the beneficiary (or settlor) to the trustee so that the latter exercises legal powers that are, in fact, derived from the former. By invoking the metaphor of transubstantiation, by contrast, I seek to emphasize that the trust can, and should, go *beyond* mere substitution. That is, the trust arrangement entails the possibility that the trustee may possess her legal powers *even when* the beneficiary has never held such power to begin with (and even when no settlor is involved in bringing about the trust). It is the creation of the trust that establishes a normative framework within which the trustee can assert the power to author acts and decisions with respect to the trust property in the name of the beneficiary. Such assertion of power need not turn on its being derived (in the right sense) from the beneficiary (or the settlor).

On the account that I shall develop, *the* distinctive feature of the trust form is that of placing a person, the trustee, with the standing to provide ownership, rather than merely management, services to another, the beneficiary, including in cases where the latter does not have the capacity for ownership. This is true both conceptually and normatively. Conceptually, there can be—and, in fact, there are[3]—any number of legal institutions that can solve problems that the trust form addresses, such as the transmission of intergenerational wealth. It is not surprising, therefore, that accounts of the trust form that emphasize management rather than ownership are over-inclusive—much of what they have to say about the trust could equally be said of neighboring legal forms, such as the corporation.[4] What makes the trust form conceptually distinctive is that it enables the trustee to offer *ownership* services, including most importantly to those without the capacity for ownership.[5]

Normatively, the ability of the trust form to mitigate some ineliminable excesses of the institution of private ownership is more significant, morally, than the other problems that this form may help to solve. To see this, consider three alternative societies. In the first society, people who are the immediate bearers of the excesses of private ownership (say, an infant) have absolutely no access to ownership. The second society recognizes a trust institution whose operation is strictly limited to mitigation of such excesses. In the third society, members of the bourgeoisie and other capable adults can invoke the trust form but persons lacking capacity cannot. My claim is that, all else being equal, the private law of the second society is morally superior to that of the other two.[6]

"Remedies"); Paul B Miller, "Justifying Fiduciary Duties," 58 *McGill LJ* 969 (2013) (hereinafter: Miller, "Duties"). See also Paul B Miller in this volume.

[3] See Ron Harris, "The Private Origins of the Private Company: Britain 1862–1907," 33 *Oxford J Legal Stud* 339, 355–63 (2013).

[4] Two familiar accounts that exemplify this suspicion are the economic analysis of trust law, which applies corporate law's agency costs model to trust law, and the autonomy-based account of fiduciary law. See Robert H Sitkoff in this volume and Hanoch Dagan and Sharon Hannes in this volume, respectively.

[5] Civilian arrangements (such as the French *Fiducie*) provide functional equivalents to the trust. However, I suspect that none of them deals with the problem of ownership excesses as comprehensively as the trust form. That is, the trust provides a general, and so systematic, solution to the problem of excesses that I identify in these pages, whereas civilian arrangements provide "local" (ie, context-specific) solutions that may not mirror the trust's comprehensiveness. See, on this point, Michele Graziadei in this volume. Another way to put this point is to say that the trust is juridically, but not functionally, unique. I owe this way of putting the point to Paul Miller.

[6] I further develop this claim in the Conclusion.

I. Setting the Scene: The Methodology of Explaining the Trustee's Duty of Loyalty

I begin with a very brief discussion of the theoretical challenge faced by accounts of the fiduciary duty of loyalty in trust law. The discussion is crucial in order to emphasize the analytical gap between two ways of attending to the interest of the beneficiary. First, that of promoting the beneficiary's *exclusive* interest. And second, that of promoting her *best* (but non-exclusive) interest.[7] An account of the fiduciary's duty of loyalty must explain the law's preference for the exclusive interest rule over the latter formulation.[8] (A structurally similar challenge is familiar from other private law contexts, such as noninterfering trespass to property.[9])

So why is it that acting in the best but not exclusive interest of the beneficiary *must* count as a breach of a duty? A successful answer should begin with two considerations: First, the specific legal *form* against which a particular fiduciary relationship arises—for instance, it may be crucial to focus the inquiry on the fiduciary relation that arises against the backdrop of the trust form as opposed to the complete gamut of fiduciary relations in law; and second, the *point* of this form, trust or otherwise, in particular. To substantiate this claim, I shall critically evaluate two methodological approaches—pluralist and unitarist.

Pluralism. The basic thought that drives the pluralist's analysis is the importance of emphasizing the social and economic context within which a fiduciary acts over and above the formal legal structure of her interaction with the beneficiaries. For instance, consider the contextual divergence of financial markets and the family property relations. On the pluralist view, the appropriate legal treatment of the trust relationship must be influenced at every turn by context. Accordingly, the analysis of the financial and the family trustees will likely set aside similarities in forms of right and duty in relation to the trust property. I maintain that context matters but it *supervenes on* the formal structure of the trust. Moreover, insofar as core legal doctrines, such as the property/contract distinction and the duty of loyalty,[10] apply to the participants in a trust relationship *by virtue of* invoking the trust form, which is to say *across* contexts,[11] it is both necessary and desirable to understand this form before account for context.

Unitarism. Some scholars seek to generate an account of fiduciary obligations by reasoning across different legal forms.[12] Indeed, by moving from the most abstract

[7] John H Langbein, "Questioning the Trust Law Duty of Loyalty: Sole Interest or Best Interest?," 114 *Yale LJ* 929 (2005).

[8] See, eg, *Boardman v Phipps* [1967] 2 AC 46.

[9] See, eg, *Bocardo SA v Star Energy Onshore Ltd and another* [2011] AC 1 at [26] (per Lord Hope) (distinguishing between protecting a person against "interference with the use of the land" and protecting her "ownership").

[10] The property/contract distinction has various important doctrinal implications for the law of trusts. Two such implications are worth noting here: the *numerus clausus* principle (which I discuss in Section III) and the doctrine of pure economic loss. On the latter doctrine, see Avihay Dorfman, "The Society of Property," 62 *U Toronto LJ* 563, 597–9 (2012).

[11] John H Langbein, "The Secret Life of the Trust: The Trust as an Instrument of Commerce," 107 *Yale LJ* 165, 166 (1997) (observing that "The familiar standards of trust fiduciary law protect trust beneficiaries of all sorts, regardless of whether the trust implements a gift or a business deal. . .").

[12] Note that I do not deny the more modest unitarist view, according to which all fiduciary relationships share some basic qualities. The argument in the main text, however, is that such similarities may not render

generalization of the fiduciary relationship *directly* to concrete doctrine (such as the content of the trustee's duty of loyalty), the unitarist approach *necessarily* obscures distinctions that may exist amongst fiduciary relationships that arise in different legal forms. For instance, the formal difference between the trust and the corporation—ie, between ownership and management—vanishes in unitarist accounts of the fiduciary obligation. It is not clear why the content of the fiduciary obligation in these two cases *must* be identical. It may well be that they converge. However, the convergence has nothing directly to do with the formal distinction between trust and corporation and everything with the coincidental overlap of extrinsic considerations. My worry is that the structural characteristics distinctive of the trust relationship (or, for that matter, the corporate form) are no mere empty formalism.

Unitarists may respond by insisting that all fiduciary relationships give rise to one and the same fiduciary duty of loyalty. But this assertion cannot be adequately defended. Consider recent efforts to provide a unitary account of the content of the duty of loyalty.

The non-instrumental strategy. Some non-instrumental unitarist accounts of fiduciary obligations invoke the moral imperative against treating the beneficiary as mere means for the fiduciary's ends.[13] However, this fails to explain the stringent duty to act in the absence of possible conflict of interest. Surely, the Categorical Imperative is consistent with a less stringent obligation.

Another non-instrumental argument resorts to a rather loose analogy to property. The duty of loyalty is a constraint on the fiduciary's power to act in the interest of the beneficiary. The analogy to property implies that the power in question *belongs*, at bottom, to the beneficiary.[14] For this reason, any profit made by the fiduciary qua fiduciary is essentially the beneficiary's. However, the analogy to property is conclusory. To begin with, in many trust cases, the beneficiary has no such power to begin with (as when she is an infant). But even if the idea of a transfer of power is meant only suggestively, there is no relationship of entailment between the power and the content of the duty. All that the property analogy can establish is that fiduciaries cannot disregard the interest of their beneficiaries. At best, the analogy shifts the challenge of divining the precise content of the duty from fiduciary law to property law. At worse, it merely serves as a loose analogy. This is especially the case when the object of the fiduciary relation in question is not property, but rather something else.

The instrumental strategy. The instrumental unitarist account of fiduciary obligations resort to costs–benefit arguments in favor of implementing a clear and simple rule of conduct such as the one associated with the duty to act in the sole interest of

sufficiently precise the connection between the generic duty of loyalty and the content of the particular duty applicable to *trustees*.

[13] Ernest J Weinrib, "The Fiduciary Obligation," 25 *U Toronto LJ* 1, 7 (1975); Ernest J Weinrib, "Restitutionary Damages as Corrective Justice," *1 Theoretical Inq L* 1, 33–4 (2000) (hereinafter: Weinrib, "Restitutionary Damages"); Arthur Ripstein, "Authority and Coercion," 32 *Phil & Pub Aff* 2, 18–19 (2004).

[14] *Boardman v Phipps* [1967] 2 AC 46, 107, 115 (HL); Weinrib, "Restitutionary Damages" (n 13) at 33–4; Ripstein (n 13) at 18–19. On Paul Miller's account, the "fiduciary power [should be] understood as means belonging exclusively to the beneficiary," which is to say it is "one of *her* means." In violating the duty of loyalty, "the fiduciary has treated fiduciary power as a means at his disposal and in doing so has violated the beneficiary's exclusive claim upon the disposition of her means." Miller, "Duties" (n 2) at 1021. In email correspondence, Miller has denied that his account makes any essential reference to property, and explained that the quoted explanation invokes property-like language for the sake of illustration only.

the beneficiary.[15] Certainly, such a rule can bring about desirable economic effects. However, whether these effects warrant the rule is necessarily contingent on the costs of forgoing more accommodating standards, such as the best-interests standard.[16]

Another instrumentalist strategy draws on psychological considerations, according to which fiduciaries are naturally susceptible to biased forms of deliberation when acting in conflict of interest. Conflicted fiduciaries will systematically misjudge relevant reasons when considering how to proceed.[17] Fiduciaries might also engage in insincere forms of deliberation to legitimate impermissible courses of action.[18]

These psychological tendencies, it is argued, provide a straightforward justification of the no-conflict and no-profit rules: A fiduciary must not engage in *deliberation* concerning a particular transaction whenever its pursuit is potentially beneficial to her. A fiduciary who is actuated in part by self-interest might fail to give sufficient deliberative priority to the interest of her beneficiary.

While I see no compelling reason to believe that these tendencies are particularly corrosive of fiduciary relations, I do not deny that they might occasionally be. That being said, it is not clear why they *necessitate* the exclusive interest rule in particular (and its remedial implication, namely, disgorgement). After all, these tendencies and their effects are just as significant in *identifying* possible conflicts.[19] And the same holds with respect to identifying, among different *classes* of action, which is likely to cause bias. The exclusive interest rule does not *eliminate* the difficulties posed by our imperfect nature. Indeed, contra Samet,[20] this rule does not preclude deliberation in the shadow of potentially conflicting interests.

This is not to say that the sole interest rule may not lessen abuse of fiduciary power. Rather, the point is that the psychological justification of the rule does not produce the knock down result claimed for it—namely, the *elimination* of biased deliberation. It is, therefore, an open question whether the benefits of reducing the potential level of bias exceed the costs.

There is a general suspicion aroused by attempts to provide a unitary account of the duty of loyalty. The suspicion is rooted in doubt over the notion that the legal concept of fiduciary is necessary and sufficient to develop a unified account of the duty of loyalty.

To begin with, any theory of the duty of loyalty faces a familiar challenge. Such a duty can figure virtually everywhere in our everyday lives, ranging from some isolated business transactions to the most affective engagements. Moreover, it can arise in connection with any number of legal forms and in diverse contexts. A unitary account is

[15] For an instrumental argument in support of the exclusive interest rule, see Dagan and Hannes in this volume.

[16] Dagan and Hannes (this volume), who seek to defend the exclusive interest rule, are self-consciously aware of the contingency in question.

[17] James E Penner (this volume) discusses the natural tendency to under- and over-compensate.

[18] See Irit Samet, "Guarding the Fiduciary's Conscience—A Justification of a Stringent Profit-stripping Rule," 28 *Oxford J Legal Stud* 763 (2008).

[19] Some anecdotal evidence from the lived experience of trust law is reported in Melanie B Leslie, "Helping Nonprofits Police Themselves: What Trust Law Can Teach Us about Conflicts of Interest," 85 *Chic-Kent L Rev* 551, 551–2 (2010).

[20] See Samet (n 18) at 765 (stressing the importance of "eliminat[ion]" and "prevent[ion]" of fiduciaries' deliberations in the face of potential conflict of interest).

motivated by the correct observation that all fiduciary relationships pick out the challenge of mitigating, or even reconciling, the tension between the demands of right reason, on the one hand, and those associated with our partial commitments. I do *not* argue that the unitarist project is impossible or inconsequential. Rather, the suspicion is that the unitarist approach will likely leave most of the important work, in terms of the existence and content of the fiduciary duty of loyalty, substantially incomplete. In particular, the suspicion is that these aspects of fiduciary doctrine can only be adequately addressed by taking seriously the relevant legal form in which fiduciary duties arise. The argument going forward, therefore, seeks to develop an account of the trust, rather than fiduciary, relationship.

II. The Trust Relationship: Uncovering the Skeletal Framework

A successful theory of fiduciary relationships that arise in connection with trusts must begin with an account of the trust form. And in order to gain precise understanding of the trust form, the preliminary task is to identify a sufficiently thin case of the trust relationship. One familiar attempt to explain the trust relationship proceeds by investigating the difference between the trust and the contract-based alternatives to managing the partitioning of assets.[21] And once the difference has been articulated, the next stage becomes that of comparing between two (or more) proprietary forms of partitioning assets—typically, the trust and the corporation.

But this way of approaching the subject matter is disappointingly inaccurate. To begin with, the contract-trust comparison is over-inclusive, because all that it can establish is that partitioning assets by using *in rem* rights is both qualitatively and quantitatively different from invoking *in personam* rights to achieve a similar effect. The trust form, in other words, is not a unique solution to the disadvantages that are associated with the contract-based scheme of partitioning assets. Other forms of organization equally suggest themselves.[22] At the same time, however, the comparison of the trust and corporation as two *available* forms of asset partitioning that invoke *in rem* rights and duties assumes too much.[23] In particular, it assumes that the trust is just another property form so that, in principle, it is always up to a property owner to decide which property method of asset partitioning would be best for her to invoke.[24] And this assumption, because it simply begins with the *fact* of ownership, misses a key insight concerning

[21] See Henry Hansmann and Ugo Mattei, "The Functions of Trust Law: A Comparative Legal and Economic Analysis," 73 *NYU L Rev* 434, 445–66, 469–72 (1998).

[22] That the trust and corporation are, in some measure, substitutive schemes of asset partitioning goes back to the latter half of the nineteenth century. See Harris (n 3).

[23] I discuss the notion of *availability* in more detail in Section III.A. However, one preliminary observation will be apt. The forms in question are available in the sense that an owner can choose between them according to the appropriate balance of considerations that apply to her case. Thus, "flexibility" is the advantage (or disadvantage) that is most mentioned in connection with the trust as opposed to the corporation. See text accompanying n 46.

[24] This assumption plays an important role in contemporary economic analysis of trust law. It is clearest in recent attempts to apply the agency cost theory to trust law. See Robert H Sitkoff, "An Agency Costs Theory of Trust Law," 89 *Cornell L Rev* 621 (2004); Jesse Dukeminier et al, *Wills, Trusts, and Estates: Teacher's Manual* (8th edn, 2009) § 10-3.

the trust form—as I shall argue presently, unlike the corporation or private ownership itself, trust allows a person who either *cannot* or *would not* exercise ownership rights over a thing to benefit from this thing without being its legal owner. The argument thereby misses the trust's distinctive achievement.[25]

I have two more radical claims about the relationship between trust and contract: that the trust relationship does not turn on contract relations *at all* and that the former is, in some sense, antithetical to the latter. It is not that a trust relationship cannot be created by contract, but rather that a contractual engagement does not and, indeed, should not play an essential role in understanding the structure of this relationship.[26]

Consider the skeletal kind of trust relationship that arises in connection with the control and management of absentees' properties. A notorious case involved Arab-Palestinians who were expelled from their lands and deprived of their goods during the war of 1948 (and, somewhat similarly, during the 1967 war).[27] Most of these owners have not been able to return and reclaim their property. Israel responded by enacting the Absentees' Property Act of 1950 and subsequent legislation. The Act empowers a bureaucrat to act as the absentees' trustee. This apparently bona fide effort has ultimately failed due to several mistakes made by the Israeli government. But this moral failure is beyond the conceptual point I seek to make here. This case provides a helpful analytical lens through which to investigate the formal structure of the trust relationship.

The trust relationship that exists between the trustee and each of the refugees is appropriately thin. It features a trustee vested with legal title over the property in question and, at the same time, subject to an obligation to act in the (sole) interest of the refugee-beneficiary who, in turn, holds a proprietary interest in the trust property. It leaves out several features that are widely associated with the trust relationship that turn out to be inessential. I shall mention the three most important ones: The place of the settlor, the trustee's motivation, and the contractual basis of the trust. I will now take each of these features in turn.

A. Is the trust form reducible to causal questions concerning how it came about?

The usual method of formation of trustee/beneficiary relationships is departed from in the Absentees' Act. Whereas an owner-settlor ordinarily establishes the relationship, here a *non*-owner, the Israeli legislature, initiated the relationship. There are a number

25 To this extent, my critique is entirely different from that developed in Lee-ford Tritt, "The Limitations of an Economic Agency Cost Theory of Trust Law," 32 *Cardozo L Rev* 2579 (2011). Tritt emphasizes the non-economic motivations that typify, on his view, trust law. On my view, his approach also overlooks the distinctive point of the trust.

26 This is not to deny that *historically*, the trust offers advantages that contract may fail to provide. In particular, the doctrines of consideration and (at least in England until the enactment of the Contracts (Rights of Third Parties) Act 1999) privity. Trust can bypass the obstacles posed by these two doctrines, but the key point is that it is conceptually and normatively independent of the idea of contract.

27 I say notorious in recognition of Israel's failure to keep to its official (ie, statutory) commitment to keep the property in question in trust for the absentees. Much of it has been transferred unencumbered to other state agencies. Cf CA 58/54 *Habab v Custodian of Absentee's Property of the State of Israel* PD(10) 912 (1956).

of reasons why this does not undermine my use of the Absentees' case as an example of a trust.[28] But the most important point is that there is no compelling reason to think that formation of trusts is conceptually and normatively inseparable from the normative situation brought about by the trust once formed.[29]

More generally, a trust often arises in ways that do not depend on the active participation of the settlor—consider trusts that arise "by operation of the law." At a more fundamental level, the duty of loyalty takes a relational form. The trustee, after all, owes the duty *to* the beneficiary. Accordingly, the success and failure conditions of acting as a trustee are assessed by reference to how well she attends to the interest of the beneficiary. To be sure, a settlor may influence the manner in which such an assessment is made; for instance, he may determine what counts as serving the interest of the beneficiary and what the interest of the beneficiary requires. However, this does not make him a party to the trust relationship properly conceived.[30] Thus, even though methods of formation play a causal role in trust relationships they form no necessary part in the relationships going forward.[31] This is precisely why through the trust *form* different agents (private individuals, for- and not-for-profit organizations, governments) can achieve any number of different objectives using a *single* formal structure.

B. Need trustees act out of virtue? Need legal trust track or embody the ethics of trust?

The language of trust law is shot through with ethically laden concepts such as trust and loyalty. It thus might seem natural to cast the duty of loyalty in terms of the "duty to act (or not) with the right motive,"[32] in which case loyalty turns on whether the trustee has acquired the appropriate psychological disposition toward the beneficiary.

However, the Absentees' case suggests that there need not be ethically significant meaning imputed to a trustee's undertaking. After all, the trustee here is (just) a bureaucrat whose job is to discharge the state's responsibility to manage the property of an

28 The most straightforward explanation is that the Absentees' Property Act purports to work out a temporary solution to an exceptional situation faced by the State of Israel. Part of the problem is the difficulty, or prohibitive cost, of administering a system of private property rights that allows refugees to act as owners from afar.

29 My account can, therefore, show why theories that reduce the trust to a voluntary undertaking on the part of the trustee fail to account for the trust form, properly conceived. Justice Edelman, for instance, takes this reductionist stance, but does so by explicitly ignoring instances of trust that arise by operation of law (such as by legislative fiat). See James Edelman in this volume. Such a move is artificial, theoretically speaking, because it has no principled justification. Moreover, reducing the trust to a voluntary undertaking may leave nothing theoretically and doctrinally important to say about the trust form. The *law* of trusts, on this view, is merely deciphering the meaning of the undertaking in question. There is nothing interesting to say about the "duty of loyalty" or the "office of trusteeship" to which it gives rise; it all comes down to the actual terms of a particular undertaking.

30 And even then, common law jurisdictions which reject the holding of *Claflin v Claflin* 20 NE 455 (Mass 1889) allow some measure of de facto control of the conduct of the trustee by the beneficiary by exercise of the right to termination of the trust.

31 By analogy, the fiduciary relationship that exists between the US government and its constituents does not include the Founding Fathers even though they exercised overwhelming influence on the terms of the relationship.

32 Lionel Smith, "The Motive, Not the Deed," in Joshua Getzler (ed), *Rationalizing Equity, Property and Trusts* (2003) 53, 65. For a Kantian variation on this theme, see Irit Samet in this volume.

absentee. It is not clear why we should expect such a trustee to act from ethical reasons that apply to virtuous trustees. If anything, a public official is supposed to be motivated by disinterestedness. This means that her commitment to retreat from self-interest is accompanied by a demand, captured by Weberian bureaucratic ethos, to make the public good her regulative ideal.[33]

The Absentees' case also renders vivid a tension inherent in the legal enforcement of virtuous motivation. Insofar as the duty of loyalty makes acting on the right motive *the* defining principle of the fiduciary relation, there is nothing private law can or should do about it. For, just like norms of politeness, legal enforcement of sincere loyalty is contradictory, since compelled loyalty is not loyalty properly so called. Demanding the state bureaucrat to "honestly"[34] display loyalty places the law in the implausible role of fixing the content of the motivation on which the trustee ought to act (or refrain from acting).[35]

C. Is trust a contract?

The third aspect of the trust relationship that the Absentees' case self-consciously sets aside is its allegedly contractual basis. The Absentees' case highlights the independence of the formal structure of the trust from contract. More generally, it is perfectly possible to imagine a society with a private property regime, and so with an institution of trust, but with no legal practice of contract (especially a practice of executory contract).[36]

I shall begin with two familiar versions of the argument that contract underlies the trust relationship. The first has already been mentioned in connection with the formation of trusts. That discussion should be sufficient to set aside this way of explaining the trust relationship by reference to contract: a contract between a settlor and trustee represents a, rather than the, way of forming a trust.

A more plausible version of the argument is that the organizing idea underlying the trustee/beneficiary relation is that of a contract. This argument is best understood as expressing a conceptual claim—that the duty of loyalty is modeled on a contractual engagement. The existence and the content of this duty are explained as reflecting contractual terms that *would* have been agreed upon by the parties to the formation of the trust.

[33] The public official "takes pride in. . . overcoming his own inclinations and opinions, so as to execute in a conscientious and meaningful way what is required of him. . . even—and particularly—when [it does] not coincide with his political views." Max Weber, "Parliament and Government in Germany under a New Political Order," in *Weber: Political Writings*, ed P Lassman and R Speirs (1994) 160.

[34] Paul D Finn, *Fiduciary Obligations* (1977) 15.

[35] Note that in contrast to theorists (such as Penner (n 17) and Dagan and Hannes (this volume)) who criticize the hypermoralization of legal trust, I do not argue that the trust may not accommodate core ethical demands. The fact that the law does not, or should not, compel trustees to act on, rather than in conformity with, ethical considerations of loyalty does not imply that the moral foundations of this body of law cannot be associated with the ethics of loyalty or trust. Such an account may not rest on *motivation*, for there are good reasons why the law does not coercively extract benevolent attitudes or good will. A sound theory of the morality of trust law will take as its main objective the development of reasons that make certain behavior rational and, indeed, morally required.

[36] And at least according to the well-known thesis of Maine, status (to which property belongs) came before contract. Henry Sumner Maine, *Ancient Law* (1861).

The best exposition of this argument comes from economic analyses of fiduciary law.[37] On the economic approach, fiduciary duties are just those duties that economize on the transaction costs involved in fixing the terms of a tailor-made contract and in monitoring compliance with such terms. The thought is that the duty of loyalty obviates the need to specify terms that will govern the conduct of the trustee with respect to the beneficiary's interest in the trust property.

Let me explain why I think this view does not accurately capture the connection between contract and trust. I do not deny that at a high enough level of abstraction—the level at which parties in a Coasean bargaining stand—*all* that efficiency-enhancing private law does comes down to guiding conduct in ways that best approximate the agreements that would be made in a world of zero transaction costs. To this extent, the provocative assertion of Easterbrook and Fischel that "there is nothing special to find"[38] in fiduciary law turns out to be far too modest—they ought to say that there is nothing special in *all* of private law that is not reducible to hypothetical contractual analysis. For instance, the standard economic justification of the standard of reasonable care in negligence law is, in essence, an argument from the (hypothetical) contract that a risk-creator and a risk-taker would make in a world of zero transaction costs.[39]

This expansive view of "contract" is perfectly coherent.[40] More importantly, there may be good reasons to determine the content of the trustee's duty of loyalty at least in part on the basis of the actual or constructive choices of the beneficiary. That said, the emphasis on transaction costs obscures a *distinctive* characteristic of the trust relation. To begin with, the emphasis on transaction costs mischaracterizes the formal structure of the trust relation. The trust does not merely help people specify contract terms and monitor compliance when hiring experts. Rather, it also responds to a different difficulty introduced by beneficiaries who lack *legal personality*. Beneficiaries of trust include members of future generations and infants. And as the Absentee's case also exemplifies, beneficiaries may also be perfectly capable persons who are, nonetheless, legally disbarred from doing business with the citizens and the state where the relevant property is located. The economic approach thus misses a distinctive formal characteristic of the trust—its recognition of a trustee/beneficiary relationship *even when* no such relationship could take a contractual form of interaction.

Furthermore, it is of course true that not all beneficiaries lack the legal capacity to make and carry out contracts. However, even if they have capacity, the contract model overlooks the *passivity* that is built into the position of the beneficiary. Consider a simple case. Suppose that I would love to benefit my father-in-law by giving him my stocks in a promising pharmaceutical company, but I do not trust his judgment in matters of finance. I thus declare myself the trustee of the stocks for his benefit.[41] The beneficiary is in a position of

[37] Frank H Easterbrook and Daniel R Fischel, "Contract and Fiduciary Duty," 36 *JL & Econ* 425 (1993).

[38] Easterbrook and Fischel (n 37) at 438.

[39] The economic interpretation of the duty of care suggests that persons should not engage in acts whose costs exceed their benefits. Thus, the mandatory tort law duty of care *stands in* for the voluntary transaction among participants of the Coasean parable. It induces individuals to fix this tradeoff on their own through incorporating cost-justified precautions into their preferred course of action. William M Landes and Richard A Posner, "The Positive Economic Theory of Tort Law," 15 *Ga L Rev* 851, 854 (1980).

[40] In spite of this, the argument from contract thus understood is extremely simplistic and reductionist.

[41] This is the most prevalent reason to create a trust. *Restatement (Third) of Trusts* (1992) §15 cmt a ("Most trusts are created gratuitously").

passivity that is in tension with contract in two important ways: first, there is no "contract" in this case because I have literally drafted the beneficiary into a legal relationship with me.[42] And second, a unilateral undertaking of a voluntary obligation does not thereby establish a *contractual* relationship, since the beneficiary, whose position is equivalent to that of a "promisee," does not reciprocate and, therefore, is not required to engage the trustee in an active relationship of exchange. Want of engagement, or of consideration if you like, is critical because it can explain why mere voluntary undertaking does not generate a *contractual* obligation owed to, and owned by, the beneficiary.[43] The institution of trust creates the opening for a duty of loyalty to arise *in spite of* these two manifestations of the beneficiary's passivity. Reducing the trust to contract will necessarily lead us to overlook the important ways in which trust does not turn on contract properly conceived.

In this chapter, I have sought to highlight inessential elements of the trust. I will now turn my attention to the essential elements. A first step involves identifying the residuum when the inessential elements are set aside. I shall argue that the trust relationship is formed in and around property and, in particular, private ownership. And it is against the backdrop of the problematics of private ownership that the fiduciary relationship between the trustee and the beneficiary gets its formal shape and (some of its) substance.

III. Trust and the Excesses of Private Ownership: Outline

That the trust form is a creature of property (and ultimately of private ownership) is best understood by reference to the principle of *numerus clausus*.[44] To see the novelty of the trust form, consider the impossibility of establishing a trust by contract alone, as when a property owner seeks the service of an expert in managing her assets. The argument from contract correctly presupposes that, in principle, it is up to the owner and the expert to establish terms of their interaction. However, the trust is no mere contractual engagement—it invokes property rights and obligations that, because of their *in rem* effect, alter the normative situation of third parties.

Accordingly, it is not up to private parties to engage in the private legislation of property *forms* of right and obligation. To this extent, the *numerus clausus* principle imposes, negatively, a restriction on the kinds of normative relations that owners may otherwise establish with non-owners through contract. And affirmatively, the principle publicly recognizes certain other kinds of relation, such as those arising between a lessor and a lessee or in connection with easements.[45] The trust is one of these publicly

[42] Freedom of contract includes the freedom *from* contract so that a person cannot be forced into a contractual engagement.

[43] I do not assume here that contracts must *generally* involve consideration. Most civilian jurisdictions reject the necessity of consideration. Rather, I make a less ambitious assumption: since the kind of contract on which lawyer-economists focus is the one supported by consideration, my counterargument seeks to repudiate the reduction of trust to bargained-for contracts by showing that trust relations can arise even when no bargain is involved. Thus, it is against *this* context that I argue for the incompatibility of the beneficiary's passivity and the economic, contract-based analysis of the trust relation.

[44] See, generally, Thomas W Merrill and Henry E Smith, "Optimal Standardization in the Law of Property: The Numerus Clausus Principle," 110 *Yale LJ* 1 (2000).

[45] I develop the legitimation-based theory of the *numerus clausus* principle in Avihay Dorfman, "Property and Collective Undertaking: The Principle of Numerus Clausus," 61 *U Toronto LJ* 467 (2011).

recognized relations that *operate on* the basic property form, which is to say ownership. Just as the lease form, for example, renders permissible the separation of *in rem* rights and duties associated with the exclusive use of an asset from the right of ownership, so the trust form creates its own distinctive reconfiguration of the ownership form. In particular, it enables the right of ownership to be broken down into two ways of relating to an owned asset—as an agent who authors actions and decisions with respect to the asset and as a patient on whose behalf others act. The duty of loyalty helps to contain the agent/patient separation by announcing that the former speaks and acts directly in the name of the latter.

A. Trust and private ownership

Analogizing the trust with other legal methods of asset partitioning creates the risk of missing its distinctiveness. This also holds true of analogies between the trust and corporation as arrangements for the *management* of other people's assets. It is usually noted that the two arrangements differ in the degree of organizational flexibility that each features and in the efficacy of markets in disciplining fiduciaries.[46] The live question becomes the choice of the fiduciary that would be more suitable to *manage* our assets—the trustee or the corporation's officers and directors.

However, this approach also fails to account for the distinctiveness of the trust. The trust is not merely an alternative mode of managing *privately owned* assets (although it surely is this as well). The trust begins with the premise that the capacity for private ownership itself may be lacking and it provides a *solution* to this difficulty. The trustee provides ownership, rather than merely management, services. This way of casting the distinctiveness of the trust can be extended to other debates as well.[47]

B. The excesses of private ownership and the point of the trust form

Private ownership generates a variety of excesses. These excesses render ownership either categorically unavailable for some or substantially costly to others. The trust form picks out this difficulty, allowing those who could not, or would not, be owners to have access to the ownership institution. It provides access through the familiar division of ownership labor between trustee and beneficiary: The former is vested with title over a particular asset, whereas the latter holds, at the very least, the entitlement to the *ownership of another* over this asset.[48] In other words, the most basic entitlement of the

[46] Concerning flexibility, see F W Maitland, *Equity—A Course of Lectures* (2nd edn, 1936) 23; Tony Honoré, *The South African Law of Trusts* (2nd edn, 1976) 10; Langbein (n 11) at 184; Hansmann and Mattei (n 21) at 472–3; Robert H Sitkoff, "Trust as 'Uncorporation': A Research Agenda," *U Ill L Rev* 31, 44–6 (2005). Concerning market-based disciplining mechanisms, see Robert H Sitkoff, "The Economic Structure of Fiduciary Law," 91 *BU L Rev* 1039, 1045 (2011); Melanie B Leslie, "Trusting Trustees: Fiduciary Duties and the Limits of Default Rules," 94 *Geo LJ* 67, 99–100 (2005).

[47] Precisely how far this argument can go is beyond the scope of this chapter. Suffice it to say that viewing the trustee's position in terms of providing ownership services suggests that the trust form is special relative to familiar cases of fiduciary relations (such as the lawyer/client, public official/constituent, and possibly the parent/child relation). Thus we have another reason to be suspicious of the unitarist's attempt to fix the content of fiduciary law across the different legal forms within which it operates.

[48] Throughout, I shall refrain from deploying the distinction between legal and equitable ownership. I do that to emphasize that my account does not turn on historical idiosyncrasies (such as the then division of jurisdictional labor between common law and equity courts).

trust beneficiary is to have another person in the position of ownership with respect to an asset.

To unpack the argument, I shall commence by sketching the main themes of the idea of private ownership followed by a discussion of the relevant kinds of excesses it generates.[49]

1. *Private ownership as a status authority over (all) others.*[50]

As I have argued elsewhere, the concept of private ownership picks out a kind of a *normative standing*—a power to change the normative situation of others in relation to a particular object. Thus, private owners possess an unusual status, which is to say the standing not just to be in physical or metaphysical control of an object against the backdrop of non-owners' competing claims,[51] but rather to determine what others may or may not be legally entitled to do with this object. This notion of standing in relation to other persons is what unifies the various incidents associated with exclusion and alienation rights often said to be characteristics of ownership[52]—they are incidents *of* the distinctive standing that owners have to address others in a right-conferring and duty-imposing way.

Owners operate as such through a set of complex intentions and attitudes. Consider a simple case. If I own a copy of *Das Kapital* that you would like to briefly consult, I enjoy an unusual standing relative to you. If I restrict your access to the copy of the book, saying "That's mine," what I really am doing is demanding your recognition of my status as *reason-providing* for you. Owners can generate reasons by acting on the special status of private ownership.[53] In particular, by saying "That's mine" under appropriate circumstances, I intend that the reason for your conformity with my judgment concerning the use of the book be that you recognize that it is I, the owner, who judge so, or, in a colloquial sense, say so.

[49] I emphasize *relevant* kinds of excesses in recognition that private ownership may generate more excesses than those discussed presently.

[50] The following two paragraphs draw on Avihay Dorfman, "Private Ownership," 16 *Legal Theory* 1 (2010); Dorfman, "Private Ownership and the Standing to Say So," *U Toronto LJ* (forthcoming, 2014).

[51] The notion that ownership entails a special normative position with respect to the thing, either the position to make an exclusive use or to determine what can be done with the thing, has been emphasized on various occasions. With respect to exclusive use, see J E Penner, *The Idea of Property in Law* (1997) 147 ("normative position vis-à-vis the thing"); Henry E Smith, "Mind the Gap: The Indirect Relations between Means and Ends in American Property Law," 94 *Cornell L Rev* 959 (2009). Concerning the normative power to determine the use to which a thing can be put, see Robert Nozick, *Anarchy, State, and Utopia* (1974) 171 ("The central core of the notion of a property right in X. . . is the right to determine what shall be done with X; the right to choose which of the constrained set of options concerning X shall be realized or attempted"); A Alchian and H Demsetz, "The Property Right Paradigm," 33 *J Econ Hist* 16, 17 (1973) (noting that "[t]he strength with which rights are owned can be defined by the extent to which an owner's decision about how a resource will be used actually determined the use"); Larissa Katz, "Exclusion and Exclusivity in Property Law," 58 *U Toronto LJ* 275, 297 (2008).

[52] See, eg, A M Honoré, "Ownership," in A G Guest (ed), *Oxford Essays in Jurisprudence* (1961) 107; J W Harris, *Property and Justice* (1996) 5, 29, 31, 126, 136; Thomas W Merrill, "The Property Strategy," 160 *U Pa L Rev* 2061, 2068 (2012).

[53] For more philosophical discussion of the distinction between epistemic and practical reasons, see David Owens, "Rationalism about Obligation," 163 *Euro J Phil* 403 (2008); David Enoch, "Giving Practical Reasons," 11 *Philosophers' Imprint* 1 (2011).

The complex set of intentions only grows in complexity and intensity when the interaction between an owner and others involves contractual and other business transactions concerning the asset in question. Furthermore, the stakes are even higher insofar as the background circumstances require the investment of substantial time or special expertise in making decisions with respect to an asset.

2. *The excesses of private ownership: a brief sketch*

Against this backdrop, I shall elaborate on certain kinds of excesses that arise in connection with private ownership. I shall divide them into two kinds—categorical and hypothetical excesses.[54] Whereas some excesses are the necessary outgrowth of private ownership, other cases are merely coextensive with this concept.[55]

Categorical excesses (or the bar of ownership's legal personality). The most obvious class of cases here pertains to persons who fall below the *threshold* of natural competency: infants and mentally disabled adults come to mind. Another class of cases concerns persons who have natural competency but lack legal personality. Some Arab-Palestinians who were forced to leave their homes and land cannot assert their ownership authority and others are effectively excluded from doing so by virtue of state sanctions on those who engage in commercial transactions with residents of enemy states. Furthermore, the so-called Massachusetts business trust was originally developed as a solution to the (then) statutory restriction imposed on corporations against holding ownership rights in land for purposes other than that of carrying on their business.[56] These cases illustrate that sometimes ownership lies beyond the reach for lacking the requisite ownership's legal personality. The trust form creates the legal space within which *patients* (by choice or by chance) could, nonetheless, gain some access to the institution of private ownership.

Hypothetical excesses. Private ownership may generate adverse consequences (in terms, for example, of forgone valuable choices) that far exceed the costs that are *ordinarily* associated with private ownership.[57] Those burdened by the hypothetical excesses of private ownership can in principle gain or maintain ownership status. Nevertheless, the prohibitive cost of ownership motivates recourse to the trust. Cases within this category can be subdivided, for the sake of exposition, into three subcategories: heterodoxy, vocation, and welfare.

[54] I use hypothetical in the Kantian sense of the word to express conditional forms of pursuing ends (eg, you ought to spend some time with a friend if you want to get to know her better).

[55] It is worth pointing out that the excesses I shall discuss focus on the substantial difficulties faced by persons in possessing the standing of ownership. It might be argued that while the trust can mitigate some of these excesses, it also gives rise to others, such as, those associated with the dominance of the settlor's intent. No doubt. The live question is whether these costs exceed the advantage of overcoming the excesses of private ownership. It is not clear (to say the least) that the cases I shall discuss must fall prey to this worry.

[56] Massachusetts, probably due to the traditional anxiety toward mortmain, forbade "organization of cooperations under general laws to deal in real estate" so that "all modern office buildings and hotels had to be financed by voluntary associations. . ." S R Wrightington, "Voluntary Associations in Massachusetts," 21 *Yale LJ* 311, 312 (1911–12).

[57] I say *ordinarily* in recognition of costs that most private owners incur and that circumventing them is clearly illegitimate. Two familiar illustrations are the practice of tax avoidance and bypassing competition law (the root of antitrust law). Both cases involve private owners invoking the trust to avoid costs.

Heterodoxy. Pursuing one's political heterodoxy may sometimes mean ownership deprivation. One familiar historical example occurred during the Wars of the Roses where "[m]en who were interested in politics had been unable to take part in that pastime without the danger of losing all their property" on account of committing treason against the king.[58] These individuals deployed the trust in response to this threat while taking political and military action. More recently, the Zionist movement in Mandate Palestine experienced some private ownership excesses as it went about advancing its goals. The Zionist political program at that time—supporting the settlement of Palestine in preparation for the establishment of a Jewish state—purchased, developed, and then sold land to Jewish immigrants. This required registration of purchased lands; a formal act of asserting private ownership. The assertion of ownership by central Zionist institutions (such as the Jewish National Fund) was bound to be resisted by the Mandate's officials and the local elites.[59] Once again the trust was called upon to address the excesses of private ownership. Indeed, by stepping down as owners and assuming, instead, the passive position characteristic of the beneficiary, Zionist bodies such as the Jewish National Fund made better progress in realizing their political agendas.[60]

Vocation. Now consider the pursuit of a calling in the face of private ownership's excesses to the contrary. Two familiar historical examples are the crusader and the early Franciscan friar whose respective pursuits of religious devotion stood in tension with private ownership. The trust form was enlisted to reduce these tensions. In the absence of the trust (or use), the crusader would have had to choose between going on a crusade and staying at home to keep his property to himself and his family. The friar would have had to face the existential tradeoff between the sanctity of a property-free life and a secured stream of material means of subsistence.

A structurally similar difficulty arises nowadays in the case of high-ranking public officials who cannot hold public office while owning certain commercial enterprises. Lyndon Johnson, for instance, owned a radio and a TV station in Texas when he ascended to the vice presidency of the United States. Johnson created a "blind" trust to ensure his ownership interest did not render ethically impermissible his occupation of public office. Johnson thereby occupied the position of a beneficiary, holding an entitlement to the ownership services of a fully independent trustee.[61]

Welfare (herein of the inconveniences of ownership). The final category of hypothetical excesses of ownership focuses on the welfare of the benefactor, third parties, or society as a whole. The promotion of personal and social welfare is often cited as a central justification of the institution of private ownership.[62] That said, the welfare-enhancing effect of private ownership is not self-generating. It depends, in part, on the conduct of

[58] Austin W Scott, "The Trust as an Instrument of Law Reform," 31 *Yale LJ* 457, 461 (1922).

[59] Adam S Hofri-Winogradow, "Zionist Settlers and the English Private Trust in Mandate Palestine," 30 *L & Hist Rev* 813, 854 (2012).

[60] Hofri-Winogradow (n 59) at 855.

[61] For historical details, see Megan J Ballard, "The Shortsightedness of Blind Trusts," 57 *Kan L Rev* 43, 54–5 (2007).

[62] The *locus classicus* is Harold Demsetz, "Toward a Theory of Property Rights," 57 *Am Econ Rev* 347 (1967).

those who hold ownership rights. Normally, successful performance turns on skill. In many cases, it only takes ordinary skill to make optimal use of an object. But in other cases, special skill is required or is advantageous.

Here, too, examples are revealing. For instance, consider a classic worry among aristocrats—that is, concern over an extremely improvident son or daughter who is destined to be in charge of the family's estate.[63] Or consider a wealthy person who is eager to support excellence in legal theory by granting generous scholarships to a promising junior law faculty. Acting successfully in these circumstances requires expertise that the donor may not possess. *Acting as an owner*—ie, asserting the standing to say so—might be self-defeating. Resort to the trust, and thus the ownership services of another, could make the necessary difference.

The preceding discussion has highlighted a more general theme concerning the point of the trust form, which is that of mitigating certain excesses of private ownership. The trust is not just another form in the menu of property forms from which *private owners* may pick and choose. Instead, it creates the very possibility of access to ownership for those who could not, or otherwise would not, invoke it to pursue their or others' ends. So understood, the trust is a property form that is not reducible to private ownership *simpliciter*. Nor is it reducible to the corporate form; the trustee provides ownership, rather than merely (or even necessarily[64]) management, services.[65]

The trust form is therefore distinctive insofar as it establishes access to private ownership *itself* by way of constituting a legal office—trusteeship—for the provision of ownership services.[66] By virtue of the formation of a trust, a trustee becomes the *author* of the beneficiary's actions and decisions in all matters related to the trust property. Or so I shall argue.

IV. The Trustee's Duty of Loyalty: A Hobbesian Account

Almost all of the familiar approaches to the duty of loyalty are split between two competing accounts. First is the *constraint conception* of the duty, according to which the trustee enjoys the freedom to act as she sees fit subject to the constraint placed on

[63] For a historical discussion of this point, see Ron Harris, *Industrializing English Law: Entrepreneurship and Business Organization, 1720–844* (2000) 149.

[64] See, eg, James Edelman, "Two Fundamental Questions for The Law of Trusts," 129 *LQR* 66, 66 (2013).

[65] The leading discussion of shareholder power is Lucian Arye Bebchuk, "The Case for Increasing Shareholders Power," 188 *Harv L Rev* 833, 837, 843–50 (2005). Note that the argument here is meant to be applicable even in the US context, where shareholders' activism has a very limited scope when compared, say, to England.

[66] For the notion that trusteeship is an office, see, eg, Honoré (n 46) at 4; Bernard Rudden, "Things as Things and Things as Wealth," 14 *Oxford J Legal Stud* 81, 88 (1994); Joshua Getzler, "'As If:' Accountability and Counterfactual Trust," 91 *BU L Rev* 973, 981–2 (2011); Tamar Frankel, *Fiduciary Law* (2011) 279–84. The trustee holds a special office, a legal office rather than mere office, and in particular, an office of ownership. This way of approaching the subject matter of the trust casts doubt on a recent trend to describe private ownership as an office in and of itself. See Christopher Essert, "The Office of Ownership," 63 *U Toronto LJ* 418 (2013); Larissa Katz, "Governing through Owners: How and Why Formal Private Property Rights Enhance State Power," 160 *U Penn L Rev* 2029 (2012). In my view, private ownership has nothing to do, conceptually and normatively speaking, with the idea of an office. See, further, Dorfman, "Ownership and the Standing to Say So" (n 50).

her by the no-conflict rule. The second approach denies that there is such a duty at all. Many such *duty nihilists* are lawyer economists[67] or some reductionist-realists[68] who see (wrongly, in my view) the idea of a legal "duty"—in trust law or otherwise—as something other than a mandatory reason for action. For example, James Penner has recently endorsed the view that fiduciary liability is freestanding in the sense that it does not presuppose a preexisting duty of loyalty, although he provides no support for it.[69]

I shall argue, by contrast, that there is a duty of loyalty. However, I shall also argue that the constraint conception fails to capture its distinctive feature. Unlike the tort duty of care and many other private law duties, the duty of loyalty falls within a *constitution conception* of legal duties. That is, the duty to avoid conflicting interests (and to disgorge profits received through the breach of that duty) is partly *constitutive* of what it is to be a trustee.

A. Setting the stage: trustees and the notion of ownership personality

Recall that our core challenge is that of explaining trust law's preference for an exclusive-interest over best-interest standard of loyalty. The no-conflict and no-profit rules together express this demand.[70] I shall seek to argue that these two rules reflect the formal structure of the trust relationship analyzed above. In particular, I shall argue that, as in Hobbes's argument from political authority, the ownership services provided by the trustee entail *personating* the beneficiary so that the actions and the decisions made by the trustee qua trustee are fundamentally those of the beneficiary.[71] This is precisely what is meant by saying that the beneficiary's basic entitlement is to the ownership of another in respect of the trust property.

[67] See, eg, *Edwards v Honeywell, Inc* 50 F 3d 484, 487 (7th Cir 1995) (Posner CJ) (wondering "[*w*]*hy* duty should be an issue in a negligence case is not altogether clear, however").

[68] See, eg, Percy H Winfield, "Duty in Tortious Negligence," 34 *Colum L Rev* 41, 48–51, 65–6 (1934); W Jonothan Cardi and Michael D Green, "Duty Wars," 81 *S Cal L Rev* 671, 726 (2008).

[69] Penner (n 17). See also Lionel Smith in this volume. It seems to me, however, that Smith does not really deny the existence of a duty. He describes the duty of loyalty (as well as the no-conflict and no-profit rules) as a "*requirement* of loyalty" and as "legal norms" (this volume). I find this description confusing. Semantics aside, talk of "rule," "requirement," and ultimately "norm" implies the existence of reasons for action. And insofar as these reasons are also *mandatory* ones (as Smith probably acknowledges), it is not clear how "duty" can disappear from Smith's account.

[70] There may be room to raise the question whether these rules are intensionally distinct so that each represents a different logic. See, eg, Matthew Conaglen, *Fiduciary Loyalty: Protecting the Due Performance of Non-Fiduciary Duties* (2010) 114–20. It is beyond the scope of the present argument to explain why the two rules are, in fact, intensionally equivalent in the sense that they are *ex ante* and *ex post* manifestations of a single principle of concern and respect for the beneficiary. To provide a rough sense of the basic intuition, a mere profit can hardly justify, morally speaking, a duty of restoration or disgorgement. So there must be something—a prior wrong, namely, a breach of a preexisting duty of some sort—that could turn the *fact* of profiting into a liability-triggering event.

[71] According to Hobbes, the normative power of the sovereign is cast in terms of "the Right of bearing the Person of them all." Thomas Hobbes, *Leviathan*, ed Richard Tuck (1996) 122. In this way, Hobbes believes, every subject coauthors the "Actions[] and Judgments of the Soveraigne Instituted." *Leviathan* at 124. To this extent, the absolutism of the Leviathan lies in its attempt to meet the challenge of governing a polity not so much by adopting the intentions, interests, and preferences of the subjects, but rather by appropriating them entirely. Cf Hanna Fenichel Pitkin, *The Concept of Representation* (1967).

To see this, begin with a property regime featuring only private ownership *simpliciter*. Normally, free and equal individuals negotiate their practical affairs by authoring actions and decisions. The law, and private law in particular, sometimes constitutes and at other times facilitates authorship in this sense.[72] Private ownership enables authorship of actions and decisions in the context of persons' interactions with respect to external objects. It governs one practical arena, albeit quite an important one, among many others.[73]

That said, private ownership, so constituted, excludes persons who cannot or would not assume authority in this sense. The distinctive purpose of the trust is to foster a derivative form of ownership, according to which the law confers upon a beneficiary an entitlement to the very authority, rather than merely to the management, of another in relation to the trust property. To this extent, the trustee becomes the *author* of the beneficiary's actions and decisions in all matters that are related to the trust property.

Note that this argument is *not*, or not necessarily, a causal one; I do not argue for a substitution effect, according to which the beneficiary (or a benefactor) transfers his power to author acts and decisions to the trustee, in which case this power can be said to be derived from the legal personality of the former.[74] As I have observed, the trustee may possess trust powers *even when* the beneficiary has never held such power to begin with.[75] Indeed, it is the trust form that creates a normative framework within which the trustee can assert the power to author acts and decisions with respect to the trust property in the name of the beneficiary.

It might be thought[76] that the law of trusts merely *replicates* domains in which one person, the beneficiary, receives the assistance of another, the fiduciary, in the pursuit of some ends. But this way of characterizing the elation obscures an important distinction between acting *in the name* of the beneficiary and acting *for* him.[77] The trust renders the former possible, but it is not clear that this must hold true of *all* fiduciary relationships; it is not a coincidence, in my view, that leading scholars have emphasized the power of the fiduciary to act *for* another person.[78] Certainly, when I purchase shares in a publicly traded company, I seek to exploit the advantages of this corporation in making business decisions for me; I want it to manage my money. The corporation's decisions, however, are not mine even if they are made for me (ie, in furtherance of my material well-being). By contrast, the trustee does not merely act for the beneficiary or for the beneficiary's interest, but rather "personates" the beneficiary. In particular, the

[72] Of course, the law can and often does place limits on this capacity.

[73] A parallel observation can be made with respect to other, partly overlapping, spheres of interaction such as those pertaining to bodily integrity and to joint ventures (corresponding to the legal practices of tort and contract, respectively).

[74] The causal claim, to which I resist, can be cast in terms of an actual or hypothetical consent on the beneficiary's part to transferring his power to the trustee. The notions of substitution and power being derived from the legal personality of the beneficiary (or settlor) is defended in Miller, "Duties" (n 2); Miller, "Remedies" (n 2).

[75] See the discussion of the categorical excesses of private ownership in text accompanying nn 51–3.

[76] Weinrib, "Restitutionary Damages" (n 13) at 33–4; Ripstein (n 13) at 18–19; Paul B Miller, "A Theory of Fiduciary Liability," 56 *McGill LJ* 235, 262 (2011).

[77] I elaborate on this distinction in Avihay Dorfman and Alon Harel, "The Case against Privatization," 41 *Phil & Pub Aff* 67 (2013).

[78] See Austin W Scott, "The Fiduciary Principle," 37 *Cal L Rev* 539, 540 (1937); Finn (n 34) at 15.

trustee acts from a legal personality—an ownership personality—that the law attributes to the beneficiary *even when*, and indeed sometimes *because*, the beneficiary possesses none.[79]

B. Elaboration: no conflict, no profit, and the role morality of the trustee

It may prove helpful to connect the preceding analysis to the special *role* of the trustee. Arguments from role morality assess the desirable constraints on the conduct of a person by reference to their role.[80] Accounts of the duty of loyalty are typically attentive to the role assumed by the trustee, especially in asset management, with some emphasizing professional responsibility for maximizing the beneficiary's wealth[81] and others the moral commitment to refrain from taking impermissible advantage of the discretionary powers of management.[82] On my proposed account, by contrast, trustees occupy the role of an owner, rather than merely the manager, of the trust property. And in order to assume such a role successfully, the trust form creates a distinct legal personality—*ownership personality*—for the trustee to occupy in authoring acts and decisions with respect to trust property.

Against this backdrop, the no-conflict and no-profit rules can be seen as rules that define the ownership personality built into the position of trusteeship. They reflect a conceptual worry about the trust form and, in particular, the possibility of providing ownership, rather than merely management, services. They effectively demand that the trustee assume the distinctive ownership personality of the beneficiary.

Thus, the rules are not, or not necessarily, about the good or ill manner in which the trustee attends to the task of managing the trust property. On my proposed account, the doctrines that really take up the manner of the trustee's management of the trust property are those pertaining to the administrative *powers* of the trustee.[83] Indeed, a trustee may violate the no-conflict and no-profit rules while acting in the best interests of the

[79] This contrast is not peculiar to the trust/corporation distinction. Consider the case of legislators as public fiduciaries by illustration. In a representative democracy, elected representatives may take their offices only insofar as they are fully prepared to be loyal to the general interest. That said, it is not clear (to say the least) that we should consider their acts of legislation as our own. They speak for us rather than in our names. For a familiar account of democratic representation along these lines, see Bruce A Ackerman, *We The People: Foundations* (1991) vol 1, 181–6. Furthermore, it may also be argued that elected politicians are expected to vote based on their conscience rather than our preferences. See Edmund Burke, "Speech on the Fox's India Bill (Dec. 1, 1783)," in *The Writings and Speeches of Edmund Burke: India: Madras and Bengal, 1774–1785*, ed Paul Langford et al (1981) vol 5, 378. Once again, here is another reason to be suspicious of accounts that seek to provide a unitary account of fiduciary law.

[80] This claim is deeply controversial, to be sure. For instance, one basic question concerns how we ought to proceed with evaluation of the conduct of soldiers. Must they be viewed as *ordinary persons* engaged in certain violent activities or as *soldiers* participating in political acts that take a particularly violent form?

[81] See, eg, Langbein (n 7); Easterbrook and Fischel (n 37); Dagan and Hannes in this volume.

[82] See sources cited in n 13.

[83] As Lionel Smith correctly observes, courts are reluctant to review the wisdom of the trustee's decision to exercise (or refrain from exercising) these powers. See Smith (n 32). That said, there may be good reasons (some of which are familiar from the business judgment rule) for this reluctance that are not inconsistent with the proposition that the object of the trustee's administrative powers is sound management of trust property.

beneficiary.[84] A violation of these rules amounts to a failure on the part of the trustee to respect her capacity to author acts and decisions in the name of another.

On the proposed account, undertaking trusteeship entails holding two *distinct* legal personalities—the one the trustee had all along and the ownership personality held in connection with the assumed office. The no-conflict and no-profit rules provide necessary insulation of ownership personality, keeping it practically separate from the trustee's natural capacity to author acts and decisions. Whereas the no-conflict rule operates in this suggested fashion *ex ante*, the no-profit rule expresses the same purpose from an *ex post* perspective.

Begin with the no-conflict rule. This rule purports to guide the trustee's conduct by demanding that she exclude from consideration her interests as well as those of third parties. It thereby expresses an implication of one person, the trustee, *transubstantiating* himself into the bearer of the ownership personality of another.[85] It does that in the negative sense of specifying what interests should be set aside in the course of authoring acts and decisions in the name of the beneficiary. By implication, the no-conflict rule creates an arena of permissibility within which the interest of the beneficiary remains the sole interest for the trustee to pursue qua trustee.

On this view, the no-conflict rule is no mere side constraint on execution of the office of trusteeship; it is partially *constitutive* of the trustee's claim to hold such an office. The trustee is the bearer of another's ownership personality by virtue of the no-conflict rule; it is the rule that makes her a trustee.[86]

The no-profit rule sets out an *ex post* response to disloyalty; disgorgement of profits.[87] Any successful explanation of this rule must account for three puzzling features. First, the rule reflects a *restorative*, rather than deterrence-based, logic;[88] second, it can take a *proprietary*, rather than personal, form;[89] and third, it triggers a *strict*, rather than fault-based, liability.[90]

On the proposed account, all three features are surface manifestations of a single idea, namely the role of the trustee in constituting the ownership personality of another person.

[84] This is just another way to restate the celebrated argument in Langbein (n 7). As should be clear by now, however, my disagreement with Langbein goes to the essence of the trust.

[85] The metaphor of transubstantiation stands in sharp contrast with other helpful metaphors in the context of fiduciary law. Agency law, as Deborah DeMott has suggested, views the agent as an extension of the principal. Other forms of fiduciary relationships, such as the corporation form, give rise to a substitution effect; that is, the fiduciary assumes powers derived from the beneficiary. The trust is distinctive in that it can *create* a legal power where none existed before.

[86] Of course, the demand to suppress (the trustee's own interest) and defer (to the beneficiary's) need not amount to self-effacing conduct on the part of the trustee.

[87] In fact this conventional way of describing the rule may be somewhat conclusory. See Getzler (n 66) at 978–9. Another way to describe the rule is to say that, unless expressly decided to the contrary, *all* the benefits generated by the trustee in connection with the trust property are the beneficiary's. Thus described, the interesting question becomes that of property (ie, who owns what and why) rather than of fiduciary loyalty. I shall resist this approach, because the real question is not property vs obligation, since even the property question cannot avoid the normative questions that ultimately underlie both.

[88] This is so for two mutually reinforcing reasons. First, a disgorgement remedy cannot deter failed attempts; that is, disloyal behavior that proves unprofitable for the trustee. And second, it cannot provide adequate deterrence insofar as the trustee can often easily hide his gains. This is a structural deficiency, for a disgorgement remedy is *systematically* under-deterring. Any remedy short of punitive damages may fail to produce the appropriate level of deterrence. For general discussion, see Jules L Coleman, *Risks and Wrongs* (1992) 185; A Mitchell Polinsky and Steven Shavell, "Punitive Damages: An Economic Analysis," 111 *Harvard Law Review* 869, 887–97 (1998) (arguing, in the context of tort law, that the chance of escaping liability must be incorporated into the calculus of liability for the harm caused). For more on the restorative, rather than deterrence-based, logic of the duty, see *Restatement (Third) of Trusts* (1992) § 100 cmt d.

[89] See, eg, *AG for Hong Kong v Reid* [1994] 1 AC 324, 336 (PC).

[90] See, eg, *Regal (Hastings) Ltd v Gulliver* [1942] 1 ALL ER 378, 386 (per Lord Russel).

Like its *ex ante* counterpart, the no-profit rule is best understood as an *ex post* expression of what it takes for one person, the trustee, to transubstantiate himself into the bearer of an ownership personality of another. The acts and decisions authored by the trustee (qua trustee) are purported to be the acts and decisions *of* the beneficiary. The profits made by the trustee in breach of her duty of loyalty are, nonetheless, the profits made by a person who purports to act (and, in this case, profit) in the name of the beneficiary, rather than hers. The fact that the trustee has violated her duty of loyalty cannot be invoked as an argument for depriving the beneficiary of his entitlement to the ownership services of the trustee. Indeed, the breach of this duty is a violation of a norm that *defines*, rather than merely constrains, what it means to hold an office of trusteeship.

Conclusion

In these pages, I have developed an account of the trust by reference to the core[91] structural problem out of which it arises—the excesses of private ownership. Against this backdrop, the distinctive point of the trust is to foster a derivative form of ownership, according to which a beneficiary enjoys an entitlement to the very authority of another in relation to the trust property. The trustee is the *author* of the beneficiary's actions and decisions in all matters that are related (in the appropriate sense) to the trust property. More specifically, the trust creates a distinct legal personality—*ownership personality*—occupied by the trustee in authoring acts and decisions with respect to the trust property. The trust *itself* institutes this form of personality and the trustee, by virtue of holding his office, constitutes it. This way of understanding the trust can help explain the duty of loyalty, particularly the no-conflict and the no-profit rules.

Developing an account of the trust in light of the excesses of ownership is important for another reason. The notion that the trust mitigates normatively troubling excesses of ownership can contribute to an underdeveloped subject in property theory—what are the legitimacy constraints on the institution of private ownership?[92] An institution of private ownership cannot count as legitimate where a few own everything and the rest nothing.[93] My emphasis on the excesses of ownership gives rise to a different constraint on the legitimacy of the ownership institution as a whole. An otherwise desirable legal institution may lack legitimacy insofar as it excludes persons, *through no fault or choice of their own*, from the benefits that it confers. Needless to say, these benefits are not picayune. Accordingly, the special normativity of the trust form is intimately related to the legitimacy of the institution of private ownership as a whole—the trust thereby may be understood as a condition of the legitimacy of private ownership.[94]

[91] I explain the two senses in which my use of the notion of "core" is appropriate. See text accompanying nn 2–6.

[92] See, eg, Jeremy Waldron, *The Right to Private Property* (1988) 115–17, 444; Carol M Rose, "Canons of Property Talk, or, Blackstone's Anxiety," 108 *Yale LJ* 601 (1998); Arthur Ripstein, *Force and Freedom* (2009) chs 4 and 9; Ernest J Weinrib, *Corrective Justice* (2012) ch 8.

[93] For a brief discussion of this constraint, see Avihay Dorfman, "The Normativity of the Private Ownership Form," 75 *M L Rev* 981, 1008 (2012).

[94] The proposed argument allows us to see that there is a subtle question of comparative law that lies beneath (or above) the ownership/trust connection. Were traditional civilian jurisdictions to offer absolutely no legal schemes to mitigate the excesses of private ownership, the legitimacy of their private ownership institutions would be wanting. It seems that some civilian jurisdictions provide at least some such institutions, but it is beyond the scope of the present argument to assess whether these are, separately and/or jointly, sufficient to meet the bar of legitimation.

PART V

FIDUCIARY PRINCIPLES IN CONTEXT: PUBLIC LAW

18

Fiduciary Authority and the Service Conception

*Evan Fox-Decent**

Introduction

No contemporary account of practical authority has attracted as much scholarly attention as Joseph Raz's service conception. Raz's account consists in the combination of three theses: the dependence thesis, the pre-emption thesis, and the normal justification thesis. The dependence thesis asserts that authorities should base their directives on first-order or background reasons that apply to their subjects. For example, first-order reasons include the arguments and considerations that two disputants might address to an arbitrator.[1] The pre-emption thesis claims that an authority's directives must be understood to replace and exclude at least some of the first-order reasons a subject might otherwise consider when assessing how to act.[2] Once an arbitrator renders a decision, the "reasons that could have been relied upon to justify action before his decision cannot be relied upon once the decision is given."[3] The centerpiece of the service conception, however, is Raz's normal justification thesis (NJT). This thesis supplies the (main) test for distinguishing legitimate from merely de facto authorities. Whereas de facto authorities, according to Raz, effectively impose their will on others and necessarily *claim* an entitlement to direct them, legitimate authorities *are* entitled to direct others, and those others have a duty to obey.[4]

Under the NJT, Jones is an authority for Smith if Smith's compliance with Jones's directives would help Smith comply better with reasons that apply to her than Smith would if she were to follow her own judgment directly.[5] For instance, when I drive I have prudential and moral reasons to drive safely, and I am more likely to comply better with those reasons if I regard traffic laws as authoritative and obey them than if I decide for myself on every occasion whether to stop at an intersection, drive on a particular side of the street, and so on. The NJT purports to explain the authority of those traffic laws by pointing to how they help me comply better with reasons that apply to

* I thank Michaël Lessard for superb research assistance. For especially helpful comments I thank Evan Criddle, Ian Dahlman, Andrew Gold, Scott Hershovitz, Paul Miller, Stephen A. Smith, the participants of a Legal Theory Workshop held at the University of Toronto, Faculty of Law (17 January 2014), and the participants of a Work-In-Progress workshop organized by the Research Group on Constitutional Studies of McGill University (13 February 2014). Lastly, I thank the Social Science and Humanities Research Council for financial support.

1 Joseph Raz, *The Morality of Freedom* (1986) 41–2.

2 Joseph Raz, *Ethics in the Public Domain: Essays in the Morality of Law and Politics* (rev edn, 1994) 214.

3 Raz (n 1) at 42.

4 Raz (n 2) at 211, 341.

5 For some of Raz's formulations of the NJT over the years, see Joseph Raz, *The Morality of Freedom* (1986) 53; Raz (n 2) at 214; Joseph Raz, The Problem of Authority: Revisiting the Service Conception, 90 Minn L Rev 1003, 1014 (2005). Raz claims that the NJT is subject to an "independence" condition: the directive cannot engage a matter Smith ought to decide for herself; eg, the career she will pursue.

me already (ie, reasons associated with my safety and the public's safety); comply better, that is, than I would were I to follow my own judgment directly.

Various scholars have levelled a particularly devastating critique against the NJT.[6] Roughly, the critique is that even if a purported authority can help its subjects comply better with reason,[7] it does not follow that the alleged authority has standing to rule or its subjects a duty to obey. Raz, the critique goes, confuses counsel with command,[8] and thereby fails to explain the special standing legitimate authorities enjoy when they demand obedience. In Section I I elaborate briefly on this critique, arguing that the problem stems from Raz's construal of authority as a concept that mediates the relation between persons and reasons, whereas authority, properly understood, denotes a particular kind of relation between persons.

In Section II I address a new argument Raz has offered in a draft paper on the right to rule. The argument draws on his interest theory of rights, and while ultimately unconvincing, it brings to the surface two important and related questions. The first is whether the so-called right to rule denotes the state's possession of a claim right or, instead, a moral power. If the state holds a claim right against the subject, then the subject owes a correlative *duty* to the state. If, however, the right to rule is really a moral power, then the subject is under a correlative *liability* to have the state impose duties on her, or change her legal position in other respects. The second question is to whom the duty to obey is owed. If our answer to the first question is that the state holds a claim right, then it follows that the duty is owed to the state. But if, as I will argue, the state's authority consists in a moral power, then it does not follow that the duty is owed to the state. I will argue in Section IV that the duty is in fact owed to others amenable to the state's jurisdiction.

In Section III I suggest that the kind of interpersonal relationship characteristic of authority relations is the fiduciary relationship. The form of this relationship provides the key to understanding the interpersonal normative structure of authority relations. To illustrate, I focus on the parent–child relationship and shipmaster cases of agency of necessity. These relationships supply important pointers to the nature of state authority because both are nonconsensual in nature, and both involve power-holders authorized by law to impose obligations without the duty-bearer's prior consent. Both disclose, in different ways, how a fiduciary theory of authority can explain the standing of legitimate authorities to impose duties on persons who cannot or have not given their consent. In other words, they help us answer what Raz describes as the moral problem of

[6] See eg, Jules L. Coleman, "Beyond Inclusive Legal Positivism," 22 *Ratio Juris* 359–94 (2009); Stephen Darwall, "Authority and Second-Personal Reasons for Acting," in David Sobel and Steven Wall (eds), *Reasons for Action* (2009) 150; Stephen Darwall, "Authority and Reasons: Exclusionary and Second-Personal," 120 *Ethics* 257–78 (2010); Scott Hershovitz, "The Role of Authority," 11 *Philos Impr* 1–19 (2011); Kenneth Einar Himma, "Just 'Cause You're Smarter than Me Doesn't Give You a Right to Tell Me What to Do: Legitimate Authority and the Normal Justification Thesis," 27 *Oxf J Leg Stud* 121–50 (2007); Stephen Perry, "Political Authority and Political Obligation," in Leslie Green and Brian Leiter (eds), *Oxford Studies in Philosophy of Law* (2013) vol 2.

[7] For ease of exposition, I will sometimes use "comply better with reason" to signify "comply better with the moral or prudential reasons that apply independently to the subject."

[8] The command/counsel distinction is from Thomas Hobbes, *Leviathan: with selected variants from the Latin edition of 1668*, ed Edwin Curley (1994) ch xxv, paras 2–3, 165–6. See Darwall (n 6) at 259 (citing Hobbes's distinction).

authority: ie, "how can it ever be that one has a duty to subject one's will and judgment to those of another?"[9]

The answer supplied by the fiduciary model, as elaborated by Evan Criddle and myself in previous writings,[10] is that authority itself is partially constituted by a fiduciary duty to exercise entrusted power in a manner consistent with the Kantian ideal of equal freedom. Here, in the discussion of the parent–child and shipmaster cases, I offer an alternative and Razian account of the fiduciary theory. Under the Razian model, the power-holder's duty takes its inspiration from the NJT: the putative authority is obligated to exercise power in a manner that is likely to help the subject comply better with the reasons that apply to her independently. The idea, in a nutshell, is to resolve the problem of standing that afflicts Raz's theory by embedding its most valuable contribution—the NJT—within a fiduciary framework capable of explaining the authority's standing.

In Section IV I apply the Razian fiduciary model to the question of public authority, by which I mean the authority of a state or state-like body to announce, interpret, administer, and enforce law. In this context, the state's NJT-informed duty is to exercise its law-giving powers in a way that helps its subjects comply better with the reasons that apply to them for having a state at all. Those reasons, I claim, turn on every subject's interest in living within a legal order that provides them security from unilateralism; security, that is, from the dictates of other private parties. This interest is reflected within one of the constitutive properties of the state–subject fiduciary relationship—the juridical incapacity of private parties to exercise public powers—and so it is from within the constitution of this relationship that we draw the argument for the existence and legitimacy of the state. I will conclude with some reflections on how the state's NJT-informed duty can underpin a duty to obey the law that is owed to other subjects rather than the state.

I. The Problem of Standing

Stephen Darwall has recently questioned whether Raz's service conception of authority is in fact a conception of authority at all.[11] Darwall invites us to suppose for the sake of argument that if B would do better in complying with independently existing reasons were B to treat A's directives as pre-emptive reasons, then B has sufficient reason to treat A's directives as pre-emptive, and A's directives actually are pre-emptive reasons for B. In other words, Darwall asks us to suppose that the dependence and pre-emption theses are true (A's directives replace and exclude at least some of the first-order reasons

[9] Raz (n 5) at 1012; but see Perry (n 6) at 38–41 (arguing that Raz's "moral problem" is a mandatory version of what Perry calls the "subjection problem," and that this overlaps with but is not identical to the problem of justifying legitimate authority).

[10] Evan Fox-Decent, *Sovereignty's Promise: The State as Fiduciary* (2011); Evan J Criddle and Evan Fox-Decent, "A Fiduciary Theory of Jus Cogens," 34 *Yale J Intl L* 331 (2009); Evan J Criddle and Evan Fox-Decent, "Human Rights, Emergencies, and the Rule of Law," 34 *Hum Rights Q* 39–87 (2012); Evan Fox-Decent and Evan J Criddle, "The Fiduciary Constitution of Human Rights," 15 *Leg Theory* 301–36 (2009); Evan Fox-Decent and Evan J Criddle, "Interest-Balancing vs Fiduciary Duty: Two Models for National Security Law," 13 *Ger Law J* 542–59 (2012).

[11] Darwall (n 6) at 150.

that previously applied to B), and that the conditions of the NJT are satisfied (B will comply better with reason by treating A's directives as pre-emptive reasons). It still does not follow, Darwall claims, that A has authority with respect to B, in the sense that A has standing to demand B's compliance with A's directives, and B has a duty to obey.

Relying on an example Raz uses in *The Morality of Freedom*, Darwall notes that if all one wished to do was prepare the best possible Chinese meal, and John were an expert on Chinese cooking whose instructions in these circumstances gave one pre-emptive reasons for action, then there is a sense in which one ought to follow John's instructions.[12] Raz himself affirms that with these assumptions in place, "the normal justification thesis establishes the credentials of John" as an authority in his field.[13] Arguably, however, the sense in which one "ought" to follow John's instructions is strictly prudential. As Darwall observes, "one would be foolish not to follow his instructions, but if one didn't it is difficult to see why John would have any standing to complain or otherwise hold one to account."[14] That one is irrational does not, without more, show that one is blameworthy for having breached a duty to obey.

Stephen Perry offers a similar argument, but with an even more generous construal of Raz's premises.[15] Suppose, Perry says, that the issue is how to transport a dangerous substance, and that the relevant background reasons that apply to transporters of the substance are reasons related to the avoidance of creating risks for others, and are therefore moral and categorical (ie, the reasons apply to transporters independently of any desires or goals they happen to have). Suppose as well that a government agency knows much more about the transportation of this substance than I do, and so I will do much better in complying with background reasons of safety if I comply with the agency's directives rather than decide myself how to transport the substance. Assume also that the agency's directives give me pre-emptive reasons for compliance; that is, reasons that preclude me from considering the background reasons directly by replacing those reasons with new ones that are mandatory. Finally, let us suppose that the new reasons, like the background reasons they replace, are categorical. Perry suggests that if the agency's directives give me reasons that are both mandatory and categorical, "that would appear to be sufficient to establish that I have a moral *obligation* to follow the directives."[16] If so, it may appear that the agency has legitimate authority to impose obligations through safety-driven directives.

Perry argues persuasively that even if we follow Raz unflinchingly to the penultimate step in the argument—the generation of a duty to obey—it does not follow that the agency has legitimate authority. Suppose, he says, that everything remains the same except the agency issues optional recommendations rather than directives that are intended to be obligatory. The argument for a moral obligation to obey the agency will still go through, since the background reasons remain categorical, and I will comply better with them if I treat the agency's recommendations as pre-emptive and therefore mandatory. But if this is so, then it is unclear how the final step in the argument, from moral obligation to legitimate authority, can be justified, since the NJT-based argument

[12] Darwall (n 6) at 151 (citing Raz (n 1) at 64). [13] Raz (n 1) at 64.
[14] Darwall (n 6) at 151. [15] Perry (n 6) at 44–8.
[16] Perry (n 6) at 45 (emphasis in original).

generates the moral obligation in the absence of directives that even purport to be authoritative.

More troubling still, the argument for a moral obligation would seem to work even if the relevant recommendations or directives were issued by a friend, or by a black box that may not be under the control of another person. Regardless of the source or standing of the entity issuing the recommendation or directive, if it has the appropriate content such that I will comply better with reason, it appears that under the NJT I am under an obligation to obey. Since it would be absurd to think that my friend or an inscrutable black box possesses legitimate authority to impose duties on me, the fact that I may have a moral obligation under the NJT to do as directed does not show that a putative authority is a legitimate authority. The NJT, Perry concludes, faces a "massive reverse entailment problem:" even if it can produce a moral obligation to comply with a given directive, this obligation in no way entails that the source of the directive is a legitimate authority.[17] Once again, the problem of standing surfaces.

In a draft paper in which Raz replies to Darwall, Raz concedes that, contrary to what he claimed in *The Morality of Freedom* in his discussion of John (the expert in Chinese cooking) and Ruth (an expert on financial investment), "no legitimate authority can be based on superior knowledge alone."[18] In the case of the financial adviser who gives an expert directive to a client, Raz claims that once the adviser tells the client how to invest (and assuming the client has sufficient background reasons to invest), the client will then have the same knowledge as the adviser. Once this happens, Raz says, the client would not comply better with the relevant background reasons by following the adviser's instructions than he would by acting directly on his newfound knowledge; his success at complying with the background reasons would be the same. In other words, once the adviser conveys expert knowledge to a client who has reason to act on it, the adviser "no longer meets the condition of the NJT. [The adviser] does not know what [the client] should do better than he does."[19] As a consequence, under Raz's new construction of the NJT, the adviser is not an authority for her client.

Raz's argument, however, depends on the client taking the adviser's instruction as pre-emptive reasons for action, and under Raz's service conception this presupposes that the adviser is an authority. Were the instruction non-pre-emptive, the client would be entitled, as a matter of practical reason, to rely on his judgment directly when assessing how to act. He would therefore be entitled to add the instruction to a list of background reasons for or against a particular investment. Even if the adviser showed her client that she had taken all such reasons into account, the client would be entitled to reweigh them precisely because the adviser's directive, on our present assumption, is not a pre-emptive reason for action. All the background reasons governing investment remain accessible to the client's unmediated judgment. If so, it is far from clear that the client is likely to comply as well with the relevant background reasons and invest as well

[17] Perry (n 6) at 48.

[18] Joseph Raz, *The Possibility of Partiality* (2008) 21. <http://josephnraz.googlepages.com/ThePossibilityofPartiality-temp.pdf> (last visited 11 Dec 2013). Hershovitz rightly notes that because this is an incomplete draft, it may not reflect Raz's considered views, and so caution is in order in ascribing too firmly to Raz the views he defends in this piece. See Hershovitz (n 6) at 7–11.

[19] Raz (n 1) at 20.

as he would were he to treat the adviser's instruction as authoritative and pre-emptive. It thus appears that the NJT *does* apply to the present case, since the client is likely to comply better with the relevant background reasons by treating the adviser's instruction as authoritative and therefore pre-emptive. It seems that the client, left to his own unmediated judgment, is arbitrarily excluded from the benefit the service conception is specifically designed to provide.

It bears underscoring that if we simply stipulate that the adviser's instruction is a pre-emptive reason for action, as it was taken to be in *The Morality of Freedom*, then the adviser is an authority under the service conception: it is a hallmark of authority under that conception that the directives of authorities alone supply pre-emptive reasons for action.[20] But the whole point of Raz's attempt to divorce expert directives from the NJT is to show that experts are not authorities by dint of their expertise alone. This argument is unpersuasive from the point of view of the service conception, I have argued, because it is plausible only if expert directives are treated as pre-emptive. If they are so treated, then those directives count as exercises of authority under the service conception, and Raz's attempt to remove them from the scope of the NJT is undermined by the presence of the pre-emption thesis within the service conception itself.

There is a further problem with Raz's anti-expertise argument: if it works, it proves too much. On Raz's older interpretation of the NJT, one could readily make sense of a particular species of authority that is frequently invoked as an analogue to state authority; namely, parental authority.[21] To the extent that maturing children capable of understanding and following parental directives are likely to comply better with reason by treating their parents' directives as authoritative, their parents are authorities for them. Why? Because generally, all things being equal, parents know better than their children what is best for them. I will argue that this argument suffers from the aforementioned problem of standing, but at least there is some argument available for parental authority on the older rendering of the service conception. Under Raz's more recent interpretation of the NJT, however, parents arguably have no authority over their children, since once they instruct their children on what is best, the children have the same knowledge as their parents. Like the financial adviser vis-à-vis the instructed client, the parent who has instructed her children, under Raz's newer construal of the NJT, no longer knows better than her children what is best for them to do: they all possess the same knowledge. Thus, it would seem, the parent is not an authority for them, since she "no longer meets the condition of the NJT." To the extent that Raz's newer interpretation of the NJT implies a dismantling of parental authority, we have further reason to doubt it.

Raz now sharply distinguishes claims of authority based on expertise alone from claims based on directives that aim to implement a coordination scheme, such as the scheme implicit in the traffic law example I gave in the introduction: "[w]hen what makes the action best is its role in a co-ordination scheme, and the co-ordination scheme is the one to follow because it is the one the authority instructed people to

[20] It is authority's pre-emptive nature that gives rise to the distinctive "moral problem" of authority; ie, subjecting one's will to another.

[21] See, eg, Himma (n 6) at 137 ("Uncontroversial examples of legitimate coercive authority are very difficult to come by, but parental authority is a familiar example that seems to provide some light on the issue").

follow, knowledge follows instruction, rather than precedes it."[22] What Raz seems to mean is that whereas expert instructions track a fact of the matter that exists independently of anything the expert says or does, the directives that implement a coordination scheme impart knowledge of something there is reason to do that is constituted, in part at least, by the directive itself. Prior to a directive to drive on the right-hand side of the road, and barring any spontaneous coordination, I have no knowledge that driving on the right-hand side is best. But once the directive is given, and assuming general compliance with it, I know now that I have reason to comply with the directive by treating it as authoritative. In this sense, "knowledge follows instruction, rather than precedes it."

This is not to say that expertise plays no role at all in the constitution of authority, but its role, Raz now claims, is always in conjunction with something else: "[m]ost commonly [expert legislative authority] will involve an element of reliance: For example, enabling consumers to rely on products, or on providers of services meeting certain standards, enabling road users, or others who may be affected by the conduct of others, to rely on those others meeting certain standards, and so on."[23] Nonetheless, Perry's "reverse entailment problem" and the problem of standing are still present. It does not follow from the fact (assuming it is a fact) that individuals have a moral obligation to obey directives that establish public standards—whether they are related to product safety, the implementation of a coordination scheme, or anything else—that the putative authority actually possesses authority to set and enforce those standards. The case for the moral obligatoriness of the standards remains the same whether the putative authority proposes them as recommendations rather than directives, and whether the putative authority issuing the directives is my friend or a black box rather than a public agency. To show that an agency issuing directives to set public standards has authority to do so, Raz needs to show that the agency itself enjoys a distinctive entitlement to impose duties on the people subject to it.

II. A Right to Rule?

Raz's draft paper offers an argument intended to address the problem of standing, one based on his interest theory of rights according to which rights protect certain interests. The argument is ultimately unpersuasive, but merits attention for several reasons. First, it brings out a laudable feature of the service conception; ie, that authority is intelligible as such only to the extent it provides a service to its people. Second, in working out the argument's implications, Raz makes the arresting claim that ultimately the duty to obey is not owed to the authority, but rather to oneself. Third, and related, Raz's argument invites inquiry into whether there really is such thing as a right to rule, in the strict Hohfeldian sense of the authority possessing a claim right that is matched by a correlative duty to obey owed to the authority. As should be apparent, Raz's view that the duty to obey is owed to oneself rather than to the authority puts in question his commitment to a right to rule. The better view of authority, I claim, is that authority denotes a Hohfeldian power rather than a right, and that correlative to this power is a liability to have one's normative position changed, most notably through (but not only through)[24] the imposition of duties.

[22] Raz (n 18) at 20. [23] Raz (n 18) at 21.

[24] Law confers powers, immunities, rights, liberties, and privileges as well as imposes duties. But the imposition of duties remains the central case from the standpoint of an inquiry into authority, since the

Drawing on his interest theory, Raz says that authorities are a kind of corporate entity, and corporate entities have rights based on interests "but their interests derive from those of others, normally human, whom—by their constitution—they are meant to serve."[25] Likewise, Raz claims that while "the rights of authorities over their subjects. . . derive from the interests of the authority, which is to be a good authority," the service conception explains authority strictly "by reference to the reasons which apply to the people" under it, and not by reference to the interests of the people who hold authority.[26] Thus, the right of authorities to rule is based on a second-order and derivative interest possessed by the authority, which is the authority's interest in being a good authority inasmuch as it can help its subjects comply better with reason.

The duty to obey is similarly connected to the service conception's underlying rationale for authority: "Duty is owed to the authority in that it arises out of the right of the authority to direct its subjects, which right is itself in the interest of those subjects, each and every one of them. It is in a manner of speaking a duty you owe to yourself, because—according to the service conception—the authority is your servant, and in defying it you fail yourself."[27] Plausibly, the kind of failure Raz has in mind is akin to the failure of an athlete who disobeys a dutiful coach. By disobeying the coach, the athlete fails to comply as well as she could with the relevant background reasons that apply to her (athletic excellence, preparedness for competition, etc), and so, "in a manner of speaking," she fails herself.

It is hard to see how anything Raz says here in relation to an authority's right to rule actually establishes such a right. The most Raz has offered is an account of how a right to rule could conceivably be situated within an interest theory of rights. But he has given no argument to show that an authority's derivative interest in being a good authority is the kind of interest to which a right to rule attaches. Perhaps it is an interest to which only a liberty to advise attaches. And, as Scott Hershovitz observes, Raz's argument appears to be question-begging.[28] The derivative interest that is supposed to ground the right to rule is the interest of an authority to be a good authority, but arguably one can be vested with the relevant interest of an authority only if one already is an authority, which is precisely the question the interest theory of rights is called on to resolve.

In *The Morality of Freedom*, Raz writes that "[authorities] claim [a right to rule]; i.e. they are *de facto* authorities because they claim a right to rule as well as because they succeed in establishing and maintaining their rule. They have legitimate authority only if and to the extent that their claim is justified and they are owed a duty of obedience."[29] Elsewhere he says that "to have authority is to have a right to rule those who are subject to it. And a right to rule entails a duty to obey."[30] Passages such as these suggest that Raz adopts the conventional standpoint that authority involves a claim right on one side and a correlative duty to obey on the other. Yet Raz's more recent statement that the duty to obey is ultimately owed to oneself suggests that Raz views authority not

imposition of duties brings into sharpest relief the moral problem of subjecting one's will to another's. And so I will continue to limit my comments to the justification of a putative authority's entitlement to impose duties.

[25] Raz (n 18) at 17. [26] Raz (n 18) at 18. [27] Raz (n 18) at 18.
[28] Hershovitz (n 6) at 9. [29] Raz (n 1) at 26. [30] Raz (n 3) at 341.

as a claim right, but as a moral power, since were authority a claim right, one would expect that the authority alone would be owed the duty. And indeed, in *The Morality of Freedom* Raz affirms that "[t]he obligation to obey a person which is commonly regarded as entailed by the assertion that he has legitimate authority is nothing but the imputation to him of a *power to bind*."[31]

The immediate implication of viewing authority as a power rather than a claim right is that the duty to obey is not necessarily owed to the authority. Because the correlate of a power is a liability rather than, in the case of a claim right, a duty owed specifically to the right-holder, in principle a liability can be triggered so as to create a duty owed to any number of parties (including, but not necessarily, the authority). Raz's suggestion that a subject ("in a manner of speaking") owes the duty to herself is mercurial, since ordinarily duties are owed to others. But we can amend Raz's claim such that the duty is owed to others subject to the relevant authority's jurisdiction, thus making sense of the other-regarding nature of duties while preserving the valuable idea that authority is the people's servant. I offer an argument for this amended view in Section IV.

First, however, we need to consider whether there is independent reason to view authority as fundamentally a power rather than a claim right. I believe there is, though I will give only a sketch of an argument. The argument assumes that authority is possible. It also assumes that authority must consist in either a power or a right (but not both), so considerations that weigh against one side of this strong disjunction implicitly support interpreting authority as an instance of the other side.

With these assumptions in mind, notice that the idea of a right to rule stands in tension with our usual understanding of rights. In the standard case, rights are self-regarding in the sense that they represent or embody claims that individuals are entitled to make on their own behalves and for their own sakes, with no further justification necessary. On interest theories, rights protect the individual's legally recognized interests. On Kant's theory, a right is a "title to coerce" that protects the individual's equal freedom as she interacts with others.[32] Under both kinds of theory, rights are self-regarding in that their justification traces back to the right-bearing status of the particular agents who possess them. In the case of states or other public entities, no such account is available, since public entities, properly understood, have no self-regarding claims. This is why Raz describes an authority's interest as derivative of its subjects' interest in having a good authority. Authorities have no self-regarding purposes or interests of their own; they are entrusted to pursue public purposes or the public interest only. To the extent that states possess a right to rule, it is arguably a limited and conditional exclusionary right to non-interference in relation to the state's sovereign powers of domestic governance and international representation.[33] The right is limited in the sense that its scope is co-extensive with, and so not greater than, the scope of the state's legitimate authority. The right is conditional in that it can be forfeited (in whole or in part, temporarily or permanently) if the state's agents incorrigibly abuse their position so as to undermine

[31] Raz (n 1) at 24 (emphasis added).

[32] See, eg, Arthur Ripstein, *Force and Freedom: Kant's Legal and Political Philosophy* (2009) 30.

[33] For helpful discussion, see David Copp, "The Idea of a Legitimate State," 28 *Philos Public Aff* 3–45 (1999).

the reasons that warrant their possession of sovereign powers. But the right to rule, as a shorthand description of legitimate authority, is best construed as a moral power to change the normative position of the people subject to it, including through the imposition of duties.[34] Under this construal, legal authorities are public agents empowered to establish legal order through the exercise of moral sovereign powers.

A consequence of viewing authority this way is that the duty to obey may in principle be owed to others subject to the same authority,[35] or possibly to the community as a whole.[36] This consequence may be troubling to some. It may seem offside the conventional view that the duty to obey is necessarily owed *to* the authority. Kenneth Himma, for example, in discussing parental authority, claims that "[w]hat ultimately explains the coercive authority of the parent is that the child owes an obligation to the parent."[37] The moral power view may also seem offside Darwall's second-personal account of morality. According to Darwall, moral claims are intelligible as such only if the claimant is understood to have authority to make valid demands of the addressee, where authority to make demands entails accountability on the part of the addressee *to* the person making the demand.[38] I will argue in Section III that we can distinguish the issue of to whom a subject is accountable from the issue of to whom she owes a duty to obey. The two need not be the same, since one can be accountable to an authority for a duty (including a general duty) owed to someone else. This seems to be what Raz has in mind in his discussion of an authority's derivative right to rule and the duty owed, "in a manner of speaking," to oneself.

Let us collect together the main deficiencies and merits of Raz's service conception. Raz claims that the point of authorities is to "mediate between ultimate reasons and the people to whom they apply."[39] By using the NJT to identify legitimate authority, Raz is able to answer the moral problem of subjection to the will of another because such subjection is justified only if it is likely to help one better comply with reason. As Perry puts it, "Raz fights reason with reason."[40] Moreover, Raz's theory begins with the appealing premise that legitimate authority is necessarily a servant of its people, and that an existence condition of even de facto authorities is that they must claim to be legitimate; that is, they must claim to serve the people under them by purporting to help their people comply better with reason. A power-wielding entity that fails to make such a claim is merely Austin's gunman writ large.

Nonetheless, because the service conception views authority as a relation between persons and reasons, it cannot avoid the problem of standing. It cannot avoid this problem because even if it can be shown that the subject has pre-emptive reasons to follow the putative authority's directives, and even if we assume that these directives impose a moral obligation on the subject, this still does not show that the authority has a right

34 See Perry (n 6) at 24–38 (arguing that authority is a power rather than a claim right, and that understanding it thus places constraints on the shape authority can take); David Enoch, "Authority and Reason-Giving," *Philos Phenomenol Res* 1, 34 (2012) (affirming that authority consists in a Hohfeldian power "to robustly give duties (or duty-like things, quasi-protected reasons)").

35 Enoch (n 33) at 28–33.

36 Stephen Perry, "Law and Obligation," 50 *Am J Juris* 263, 282 n 36 (2005).

37 Himma (n 6) at 137. I will argue momentarily that Himma gets things precisely backwards: what explains parental coercive authority is the parent's obligation to the child.

38 See, eg, Darwall (n 6) at 266.

39 Raz (n 2) at 215.

40 Perry (n 6) at 43.

to demand compliance or complain about disobedience. Perry's "reverse entailment problem" is intractable in the absence of some account of the relationship between the putative authority and the subject that explains the authority's standing to issue binding directives and complain if the subject disobeys. As Coleman says, "[o]ne who has authority stands in a particular relationship, not to reason, but to other persons."[41] In short, what is needed is an interpersonal framework that explains authority as a relation between persons, a framework within which a secondary relation between persons and reasons might eventually be housed. Broadly construed, Raz's idea that authority is an other-regarding service lends itself to the development of just such a framework.

III. Fiduciary Authority

I have argued that a distinctive kind of interpersonal relationship is characteristic of authority relations generally; namely, the fiduciary relationship.[42] Criddle and I have developed a Kantian theory of fiduciary relations that takes as its starting point Kant's discussion of parental duty and authority.[43] The theory draws on Kant's idea of an innate right of humanity (the right to as much freedom as can coexist with the freedom of everyone else) as well as Kant's thought that rights (including the innate right of humanity) embody a moral capacity for putting others under obligation.[44] Kant explains parental obligation as a juridical consequence arising from the child's innate right of humanity and the parents' act of procreation. Procreation particularizes parental duty to the parents on the grounds that they are legally responsible for the child they have created. The child's innate right of humanity explains parental duty as an implication flowing from the child's moral capacity to put her parents under obligation in circumstances in which the child cannot consent to the parent–child relationship. The child's innate right also explains the content of the parents' duty: the parents are under a duty to manage and care for the child solicitously because only thus can parent and child stand in a relation of equal freedom

[41] Coleman (n 6) at 372.

[42] Fox-Decent (n) 10. Scott Hershovitz has suggested to me that the authority of an employer over an employee is hard to reconcile with the fiduciary theory. In the ordinary case, the employee has a duty to obey the employer's instructions, but the employer owes no special or other-regarding duties to the employee beyond payment of her wage. I cannot do justice to this worry here, but it strikes me that the employee's duty is simply contractual. That is, the duty arises at the employment contract's formation, and any instruction that follows formation must be grounded on that duty. Having no power to subject the employee to new duties, the employer does not have authority over the employee, at least not in the relevant sense. Whereas an employer can waive her right to the employee's performance, we do not usually think that authorities can waive their power to subject others to duties. Plausibly, the reason the notion of waiving a power sounds odd is that powers are vested in offices or roles that exist independently of their occupants, and thus for an occupant to disavow a power would be for her to disassemble or abandon her office. I am indebted to Steve Smith for helpful discussion of this point.

[43] Immanuel Kant, *The Metaphysics of Morals*, trans Mary J Gregor (1996) 98–9. See references herein at n 10. In his contribution to this volume, James Penner disputes the idea that parents are fiduciaries of their children. Fiduciary obligations, Penner tells us, "are intended to ensure that a fiduciary takes decisions that he is otherwise legally empowered or obliged to undertake in one way or another. . . in a manner that best serves the interests of his principal". Penner claims that because "no one has the power or discretion to commit a sexual assault against anyone," a parent who sexually abuses a child does not thereby breach a fiduciary duty, since no such duty is owed. But if parents are legally empowered to exercise discretion so as to guide their children's sexual development, as presumably they are, then Penner's argument fails on his own terms, since a parent's sexual assault against her child is a straightforward abuse of this power.

[44] Kant (n 43) 63.

to one another, a relation where neither is subject to the *unilateral* will of the other. The child is subject to the parent's will, but that will is governed by the requirements of the child's innate right of humanity (ie, the requirements of equal freedom), and so the child is subject to a legal regime with substantive moral limits rather than the parent's unilateral will. The parent's authority to direct the child is thus explained as an authority that is both constituted and regulated by the parent's duty to manage and care for the child, a duty Criddle and I characterize as fiduciary in nature.

I continue to find the Kantian theory attractive. But others may doubt the existence, nature, or significance of Kant's innate right of humanity, while others still may doubt that we need to call on it to explain fiduciary relations in terms of the law's internal point of view. In the first part of this section I offer an alternative fiduciary account of parental authority. This alternative account makes no reference to the innate right of humanity, and explains parental authority as a moral power that is constituted and regulated by parental duty. The account is explicitly Razian in that it incorporates the NJT within it. I suggest that the NJT can supply, at a high level of generality, the content of the parent's fiduciary duty to the child, and can thereby serve as a criterion of legitimate parental authority. The account is also Razian in its identification of the child's future self rather than the parent as the person to whom the child's duty to obey is ultimately owed. In the second part of this section I discuss a further kind of fiduciary relationship—agency of necessity—and then conclude the section with a general account of fiduciary relations abstracted from the parent–child and agency-of-necessity cases.

A. Parental authority

As noted earlier, Raz's construal of the NJT in *The Morality of Freedom* supplies a ready-made account of parental authority: a parent whose directives are likely to help her child comply better with reason is a legitimate authority for her child. This account, however, is susceptible to Darwall's and Perry's objections regarding the parent's standing to issue authoritative directives. That a parent's directives give her child pre-emptive reasons does not imply that the parent is an authority for the child, nor that the child has a duty to obey. The following story illustrates the point.

One day, while playing in the park, my daughter and I run into Superdad. He is attentive without being overbearing, authoritative without being authoritarian, generous with praise, gentle with rebukes, and so on. We meet Superdad at a moment when I'm lost in thought pondering the nature of fiduciary relations while listening to music on my MP3 player, with my daughter a few feet behind me drinking water from a not-so-sanitary duck pond. Superdad swoops in and tells her to stop drinking from the pond. I don't hear any of this because I'm distracted, though it is obvious that I'm my daughter's father because we're both wearing the same style of funny hats. My daughter, a surly anarchist, ignores Superdad. He raises his voice and repeats the order to stop drinking. My daughter tells him to go away, using age-inappropriate language (she is, after all, a *surly* anarchist). Superdad now physically pulls my daughter back from the pond, and begins lecturing her on the evils of pond water. My daughter tells him to mind his own business. Superdad lifts her by both arms, places her on a bench, and tells her that she's getting a five-minute "timeout" for bad behavior.

Let us assume my daughter would have complied better with reason had she stopped drinking pond water when Superdad told her to do so. This does not show that Superdad had any authority over her, much less that she had a duty to obey. To the extent (if any) that Superdad had a measure of authority in the early stages of their interaction, it is because he temporarily took on the role of a parent, with its attendant obligations, for the limited purpose of rescue. But after Superdad first told my daughter to stop drinking pond water, he should have advised me, the father, so that I might take action. That is, although by hypothesis my daughter would have complied better with reason by following Superdad's commands, he had no authority to issue and enforce those commands because he had no standing *in loco parentis* with the actual parent (me) standing a few feet away. This explains the impropriety of Superdad's officious lecturing of my daughter, while his manhandling of her constituted battery because he had no authority to touch or punish her, even if his having done so would have led her to comply better with reason.

Himma rightly notes that if "someone else's child steals from me, the child has breached an obligation that is owed *to me*; but it would, in ordinary circumstances, be wrong for *me* unilaterally to punish the child."[45] It is permissible for the child's parents to do so, Himma claims, because "(1). . . the child violated a *content-independent* obligation to do what her parents have told her to do; and (2) . . . this *content-independent* obligation is owed to the parents."[46] Notice first that Himma's argument presupposes that the parents' authority consists in a claim right, whereas I have suggested that authority is better understood as a moral power, which allows for the possibility that the duty is not in fact owed to the parents. Furthermore, even assuming that the child's duty is owed to the parents, it is not clear why they would acquire a right or power to punish from the fact that a duty to do as they say is specifically owed to them. Perhaps all that is acquired is a right or power to reprimand. Himma's argument, then, seems to suffer from the same reverse entailment problem that attends Raz's service conception: a child's duty to her parents, without more, does not entail that they have authority to punish her transgressions. And arguably, the duty-owed-to-the-parents condition is not necessary to the justification of punishment. What is necessary, in addition to the child having breached a relevant duty, is that the child is accountable to her parents and that punishment falls within the scope of parental authority. To whom the duty is owed is irrelevant so long as the parents have authority to punish its breach. Do they?

Under the Razian fiduciary theory contemplated here, parental authority rests in part on the parent's fiduciary duty to issue and enforce directives that are likely to help the child comply better with reason. I owe this duty to my daughter, which helps explain my authority to direct her, whereas Superdad does not. Hershovitz gestures toward this idea when he writes that "it seems unlikely that the story we would tell about parental powers (e.g., to punish or make medical decisions) could be isolated from the story we would tell about parental obligations."[47]

Parental duty arises from the combination of the parent's custody of a legally incapable child and the prohibition on unilateralism, the principle according to which private

[45] Himma (n 6) at 137 (emphasis in original).

[46] Himma (n 6) at 137 (emphasis in original).

[47] Hershovitz (n 6) at 17.

parties are not entitled to dictate terms or enforce justice claims unilaterally against one another.[48] Implicit in the prohibition on unilateralism is the idea that private parties are moral equals, and that equality precludes them from arrogating to themselves unilateral authority.

The custody requirement underpinning parental duty denotes the child's subjection to the parent's de facto control. In this context, where an incapable child is subject to the control of her parent, the prohibition on unilateralism has two major implications. The first is that the law must authorize *someone* to possess parental power over the child and her affairs (neither the parent nor the child nor another private party may do so),[49] since without a guardian there is no one to speak for the child. The child, in effect, would be legally mute, a deprivation of legal personality akin to the deprivation of personality suffered by slaves. In principle, the law could authorize someone other than the biological or adoptive parents to act as guardian, but the most normatively economical way to proceed is for the law to confer guardianship on the parents, since they are already under obligation to the child.

The second implication of the prohibition on unilateralism in this context is that the law's authorization of the parent's guardianship carries with it the requirement that parental powers be exercised in ways that are likely to help the child comply better with reason.[50] Properly elaborated, this requirement warrants that exercises of parental power will be regulated by legal standards that serve the child. So regulated, parent–child relations respect the prohibition on unilateralism because the child's subjection to the parent's will is permissible only to the extent that such subjection conforms to legal standards that serve the child's long-term best interests, interests the child cannot secure for herself. In sum, the parent and child can interact as equals under the law, consistent with the prohibition on unilateralism, precisely because the law sets the terms of their relationship.

Assuming that parent–child relations are fiduciary in nature, we can set out more precisely the law's regulated authorization of parental authority. Parent–child fiduciary relations are structured by a fiduciary principle that authorizes parental power subject to context-sensitive requirements derived from the prohibition on unilateralism. The Razian theory, in other words, puts Kant's innate right of humanity to one side, but adopts one of its entailments—the prohibition on unilateralism—as a context-sensitive juridical principle to which authority relations must conform. In the parent–child context, the prohibition on unilateralism subjects the parent to fiduciary requirements grafted from the NJT, thereby tying conceptually the legitimacy of the parent's authority

[48] For discussion of the centrality of the prohibition on unilateralism in Hobbes's legal theory, see Evan Fox-Decent, "Unseating Unilateralism," in Lisa Austin and Dennis Klimchuk (eds), *Private Law and the Rule of Law* (forthcoming, 2014).

[49] For this reason, Hobbes claims that guardianship is possible in civil society only where a public authority can specify the guardian. Hobbes (n 8) at ch xvi, para 10, 103. The law's authorization of guardianship eliminates the possible problem of children having conflicting duties to other purported fiduciaries (aside from intra-parental conflicts, an issue with which all plausible accounts of parental authority are saddled).

[50] Lionel Smith in this volume suggests that the fiduciary's purported duty is better understood as a "required way of exercising powers," since there is tension between the fiduciary's possession of a discretionary power and a duty to act in a particular way. The theory developed in the text is intended to be consistent with both Smith's view and the conventional view that purported fiduciary duties are actual duties. I make use of both promiscuously.

to the normative requirements that regulate its exercise. As we shall see, fiduciary constraints are a necessary condition of parental authority, while those constraints and the child's incapacity together specify the sufficient conditions which trigger the fiduciary principle's authorization of the parent's legal powers.

Returning to the question of whether punishment is within the scope of parental authority, under the Razian theory it is, but if, and only if, punishment is likely to help the child comply better with reason. The parent's NJT-informed duty to the child supplies content to the normative dimension of the parent's authority, and so the NJT supplies a criterion on which the legitimacy of punishment can be assessed.

The child's duty to obey is implied by the parent's authority, since that authority consists in a moral power to impose duties on the child only to the extent that those duties serve her. The child is accountable to the parent for compliance, but this does not entail that the child owes the parent a duty to obey. I argue now that the child's duty is owed to her future self, and that we can infer this by looking at the content of the parent's duty to the child. Parents of course enjoy wide discretion when it comes to raising their children. But as a first approximation at specifying the content of their general duty to their children, we might say that they ought to take reasonable steps to prepare them to make their own way in the world as competent, decent adults. When parents say "you'll thank me when you're older," they trade on the idea that parenting, in part at least, is about raising a child to become a well-rounded and decent person. To put this into the language of the NJT, the dutiful parent imposes directives on the child that are likely to help her comply better with the reasons she has to become a capable and decent person. If this is right, it is not a stretch to infer that the person to whom the child owes a duty to obey is her future self, the self with an interest in being a capable, well-rounded, and decent person. The parent, in effect, is an agent for the child's present and future selves, and as such she is entitled to impose duties that obligate the present child to do what is best for her future self. The child's duty to obey is a moral duty because the well-being of her future self is a moral concern, and plausibly her future self is a relevantly different person than her present self (one is legally competent, the other is not).

We might yet ask why the parent's subjection to duty gives the parent authority over the child, even if the presence of such a duty lets us distinguish Superdad from me qua my daughter's father. Of course, parental duty alone does not explain parental authority. Parental authority relies as well on the fact that children are incapable or at least immature. In light of this salient feature of childhood, the law, via the fiduciary principle, authorizes parents to direct their children and sometimes act for them. In this context, the parent's subjection to duty explains the scope and content of the parent's authorization. The parent's duty places substantive limits on how the parent may interact with the child, thus delimiting the outer scope of the parent's authority. Furthermore, the substantive content of the parent's authority is explained because it has precisely the same content as the parent's duty—to direct the child so she may better comply with reason.

More significantly still, the parent's subjection to duty offers an explanation of *why* I have authority over my daughter whereas Superdad does not. Because I am legally bound to exercise parental power over my daughter in ways that are consistent with her long-term best interests, my directives are legally guaranteed to be consistent with those interests. While my daughter is accountable to me, I am ultimately accountable to the law. Because Superdad is not accountable to the law for potential abuses of parental power over my daughter, Superdad is not entitled to direct her as a parent might. To put it in a slogan: duty begets authority because duty makes accountability to public standards possible.[51] There is, then, a good sense in which parental authority is a form of public authority: the constitution of parental authority is in part composed of the parent's accountability to legal standards, an accountability that is hard to explain in the absence of parental duty.

I do not wish to overstate the argument. It does not follow deductively that because parents are under a duty to their children and accountable to law that they therefore have authority to direct their children, and their children a duty to obey. The argument, rather, is inductive, and operates on two planes. On the first, it aims to provide a plausible account of parental authority from a Razian and fiduciary point of view under which the legitimacy of parental authority relies on the service it provides to the children subject to it. That is, on the first plane the point is to show that there is a well-justified basis to the conventional view that parents have authority over their children. Parental authority is not a mirage. On the second plane, the argument provisionally takes parental authority for granted, and then proceeds as an inference to the best explanation through an inquiry into the nature of the parent–child relationship from a legal and moral point of view. Himma adopts this same methodology when he concludes that it is the child owing a duty to obey to the parent that explains parental authority, and uses this alleged feature of the parent–child relationship to distinguish actual parents from intermeddling Superdads. I have argued that his argument errantly trades on a claim right to rule, and that the better explanation of the parent's authority is one that looks to the parent's fiduciary duty rather than the child's duty to obey.

Now, the obvious objection to any attempt to transport the fiduciary lessons of parental authority to state authority is that the former relies in part on the child's incapacity, whereas the latter is intended to apply to competent adults. A voluntarist who rests the legitimacy of state authority on consent might accept the fiduciary construal of the parent–child case as a *sui generis* instance of legitimate authority (*sui generis* because children and other incapable persons cannot consent), but resist its extension to legal subjects who are competent to give or withhold their consent. In subsection B I briefly discuss a form of agency—agency of necessity—with a view to loosening the grip of this objection.

B. Agency of necessity

Agency relations are relations in which one party, the agent, has power to change the legal position of another, the principal, vis-à-vis third parties. Typically, an agent can change the principal's legal position by contracting on her behalf or by transferring her property to a third party. The agent must at all times abide by fiduciary constraints by acting in good faith, with reasonable care, and in the exclusive interest of the principal.

[51] For an argument connecting authority to accountability under the rule of law, see Gerald Postema, "Fidelity in Law's Commonwealth," in Austin and Klimchuk (n 48).

Adjusting the NJT to fit this context, we might say that the agent is constrained to exercise her powers in a way that makes sense of the background reasons that apply to the principal and justify, from the principal's point of view, her liability to the agent's power. Of course, many agents, such as brokers and managers, acquire their powers of agency through a contract with the principal. Agency-of-necessity cases are especially interesting in the present context because they arise in the absence of a contract or prior agreement between the agent and the principal.

A common type of such case involves shipmasters who find their ship and cargo in distress, and who contract with third parties on behalf of the cargo's owner so as to sell[52] or safeguard the cargo.[53] In addition to abiding by the aforementioned fiduciary constraints, the shipmaster must make reasonable efforts to communicate with the cargo's owner. If the owner cannot be reached, then the shipmaster is obligated (not just permitted) to act as an agent for the owner and take prudential action so as to save the cargo. The shipmaster's mandate includes contracting with third parties and thereby subjecting the owner to contractual obligations owed to those third parties. In other words, the shipmaster is required and entitled to impose new legal obligations on the cargo owner without her prior consent. How can we explain such an extraordinary power, one that at first blush may seem to fly in the face of the prohibition on unilateralism?

In *Sovereignty's Promise*, I argue that the justification of the law's authorization of the shipmaster's agency flows from the shipmaster's possession of the owner's property—she cannot treat it with indifference—and her fiduciary duty to exercise her power with due regard for the cargo owner's best interests.[54] So constrained, the cargo owner is not subject to the shipmaster's unilateral will, since the shipmaster is required to abide by legal standards in the exercise of her agency. The justification offered takes the relevant law on its own terms while also providing a moral account of the shipmaster's agency. The account is moral because its justification of the shipmaster's agency is tied to her duty of loyalty to the cargo owner. This duty guarantees the parties' moral equality by ensuring that the cargo owner is not subject to the shipmaster's unilateral will, and a concern for equality is a moral concern.

In a penetrating review of my book, Andrew Gold claims that agency-of-necessity cases are plausibly understood through the prism of hypothetical consent, "as the law's best effort to provide what the cargo owner would have agreed to, if a contract had existed."[55] Gold is encouraged by the aspect of the doctrine which stipulates that the shipmaster must make reasonable efforts to obtain instructions from the owner. While recognizing that "the agency of necessity doctrine may arise by operation of law," he nonetheless suggests that "it may be focused on the importance of consent throughout."[56] In these passages, Gold appears to be offering an account of the law's self-understanding with respect to agency of necessity, since he refers to "the *law's* best effort. . ." (emphasis added) and the alleged significance of the communication

[52] *The Gratitudine* (1801) 3 CH Rob 240; *Australasian SN Co v Morse* (1872) LR 4, PC 222.
[53] *China-Pacific SA v Food Corporation of India: The Winston* [1981] 3 All ER 688; 1982 AC 939.
[54] Fox-Decent (n 10) at 134.
[55] Andrew S Gold, "Reflections on the State as Fiduciary," 63 *Univ Tor Law J* 655, 666 (2013).
[56] Gold (n 55) at 667.

requirement within the legal doctrine itself. Yet one will search the cases in vain to find judges asking after what the owner might have wanted were she reached, or whether the shipmaster is under a duty to try to divine the owner's intentions in the absence of communication (she is not). Instead, the cases are about whether the owner could be reached for instructions, and if she could not, whether the shipmaster exercised her agency power in accordance with her fiduciary duty. If she did, the owner is liable to the third party. Indeed, in *Garriock v Walker*[57] a contacted owner declined the shipmaster's request for instructions and advised that the shipmaster would be responsible for any decision he took, but the court nonetheless held that the shipmaster had authority to take action to save the decomposing cargo. The cases reveal that there is no necessary connection between the requirement that the shipmaster attempt to contact the owner and the nature of the agency power that arises in the event of a failure to communicate.

Gold subsequently claims that "the real concern is with locating a moral principle that governs these relationships and not with figuring out the legal understanding."[58] Gold's "real concern," however, presupposes that "the legal understanding" does not contain or point to "a moral principle that governs these relationships." But if, as I have suggested, fiduciary relations can be explained on their own terms by reference to the prohibition on unilateralism and its implicit affirmation of the parties' equality, then we have a moral principle indigenous to law capable of governing these relationships. There is, therefore, no reason to turn to a revisionist account of the doctrine based on an idea—hypothetical consent—that is alien to it.

Gold also points out that the agency-of-necessity cases do not supply a perfect analogue to the state-subject relationship, for if the latter were modelled exactly on the former, we would expect subjects to be entitled to opt out of obeying the state's commands whenever communication with them was possible.[59] But notice that our intuitions on opting-out under agency of necessity may change if multiple cargo owners are involved who have different views on what to do. Suppose the only deal on offer to a beleaguered shipmaster is one that would save all the cargo aboard the ship, and a failure to take this deal means that the entirety of the ship's cargo would be lost. Most of the cargo is owned by companies with whom the shipmaster cannot communicate, while the remainder is owned by a rugged individual who instructs the shipmaster to let his cargo perish. The shipmaster nonetheless makes the deal, and in good faith the salvage company takes the shipmaster's authority as binding and saves the ship's cargo from waste. The rugged individual subsequently refuses to pay the salvage company, and is sued for breach of contract. In these circumstances, a judge must decide either that the recalcitrant owner is allowed a free ride (with the shipmaster possibly liable to indemnify the salvage company), or that the shipmaster had authority to subject our rugged individual to the same contractual obligations as everyone else. The *Garriock* case cited above suggests that a judge would decide in favor of the shipmaster's authority to bind the recalcitrant owner. A finding in favor of the owner would have the prospective effect of giving such owners a veto. I argue that denying or opting out of legitimate public authority is

[57] 1 Rattie 100 (Sess 1873) [*Garriock*].
[58] Gold (n 55) at 667 n 23.
[59] Gold (n 55) at 667.

impermissible because it would grant the anarchist a morally intolerable normative free ride in her relations with others, since the anarchist would be entitled to unilateralism.

Gold is certainly correct, however, to point out that shipmasters cannot subject owners to obligations in anything like the way the state purports to have authority to impose duties on its subjects.[60] This observation may appear to cast doubt on the value of the agency-of-necessity cases to the argument for the fiduciary nature of public authority. But the role of these cases in the overarching argument is quite limited; the cases are simply intended to show that a competent adult can in principle become subject to legal obligations without giving prior consent, and that the best explanation of this form of agency necessarily makes reference to the fiduciary standards that govern the agent. Because it is possible for competent individuals to become subject to new legal obligations without having consented to them, the lessons of the fiduciary theory are not necessarily limited to the parent–child case. While we are still a long way from state authority, this is in part because cases of nonconsensual authority are few and far between. Yet it is suggestive that the parent–child and agency-of-necessity relationships are both fiduciary in nature.

In subsection C, I abstract from these two relationships to set out a sketch of the factual circumstances and normative premises constitutive of fiduciary relations generally. With these general features in place, we can see how the parent–child and agency-of-necessity cases share the same basic fiduciary structure as public authority while not being identical with it. We shall also see that implicit within the fiduciary structure of public authority is an argument for the state.

C. Fiduciary relationships

Parents and agents alike enjoy discretionary powers that have certain common, general elements. Their powers are purposive in that they must be used for certain limited purposes and not others. They are other-regarding in that they must be used for the sake of someone other than the power-holder. And their powers are institutional in the sense that they are necessarily located within a relationship that is structured by a legally permissible institution (eg, a family, but not a kidnapping ring). Their powers are so located because they are authorized by the fiduciary principle with the possibility of persisting stably over time. Criddle and I call this conjunction of purposive, other-regarding, and institutional power *administrative* in nature, since it denotes a kind of power aptly suited to one person's administration of the legal or practical interests of another.[61] It is a constitutive property of fiduciary relations, we argue, that one person, the fiduciary, holds administrative power over another person or their interests.

The second constitutive property looks to the other side of the fiduciary relationship.[62] In the case of cargo owners subject to a shipmaster's agency of necessity, the shipmaster's inability to communicate with the owner discloses that the owner is de facto unable to make her instructions known. The owner, given the special context, is

[60] Gold (n 55) at 668.

[61] See, eg, Fox-Decent (n 10) at 96–101; Criddle and Fox-Decent (n 10); Fox-Decent and Criddle (n 10).

[62] Fox-Decent (n 10) at 101–5.

incapable of guiding or exercising the agent's discretion. To that extent, we might say that the owner is *contextually incapable* of guiding or exercising the agent's discretion. In other circumstances, such as when the shipmaster reaches the owner, the owner is not so incapable, and so the shipmaster does not acquire the discretionary legal power of an agent.

In the parent–child case, however, the beneficiary's incapacity is of a different kind. In this case, the child is *juridically incapable* of exercising parental powers; she is in principle not entitled to exercise those powers, no matter what her factual circumstances happen to be. This is also a different and more comprehensive form of incapacity than the incapacity of the adult beneficiary of a trust who is not legally entitled to exercise the trustee's powers. In this latter case, the beneficiary is *de jure* incapable of exercising the trustee's powers, but the incapacity is *contextual* rather than *juridical* (in the relevant sense) because, in other circumstances, the beneficiary could exercise the powers of a trustee. The second constitutive property of fiduciary relations, then, is that the person subject to a purported fiduciary's power must be incapable of guiding or exercising it on account of her circumstances (contextual incapacity), or on account of the nature of the alleged fiduciary's power (juridical incapacity).

When these two constitutive conditions are met, the fiduciary principle is triggered such that a fiduciary relationship takes hold, and the fiduciary is thereby subject to a duty to exercise her judgment in a certain way vis-à-vis one or more beneficiaries. I have previously claimed that at its most general the duty can be understood as one of "fidelity to the other-regarding purposes for which fiduciary power is held."[63] A Razian way of characterizing this duty is that the fiduciary must make decisions that are faithful to the other-regarding or "service" reasons that warrant the fiduciary's possession of legal power. For instance, when an agent exercises her best judgment impartially when deciding with whom to contract for the good of her principal, she acts with fidelity to the service reasons that justify her power. So understood, the fiduciary theory of authority is also a service conception of authority. The fiduciary's obligation explains her authority to change the legal position of the beneficiary because that obligation binds the fiduciary to exercise her power in a way that reflects the reasons for which she has the relevant legal power in the first place.

IV. Public Authority

On this chapter's construal of fiduciary relations, the state–subject relationship is fiduciary because it meets the two constitutive conditions. The state's legislative, adjudicative, and executive powers are all other-regarding, purposive, and institutional in nature. Just as significantly, private parties are not entitled to exercise the state's public powers; they are juridically incapable of doing so. It follows from the account of

[63] Fox-Decent (n 10) at 37. The duty of loyalty may be the fundamental duty in private law in single-beneficiary cases, but the duty changes in cases with multiple classes of beneficiaries. In these circumstances, the fiduciary must still make decisions without regard for her interest (absent disclosure, in some circumstances), but she must also treat the multiple classes even-handedly and (arguably) reasonably. Self-abnegation cannot explain these latter features of the fiduciary's duty in such contexts, while fidelity to other-regarding purposes can.

fiduciary relationships proposed that the fiduciary principle is triggered such that the state is required to exercise its public powers in certain ways over its subjects and not others. Criddle and I have defended a substantive account of this requirement, arguing that the state must abide by rule-of-law principles elaborated by Fuller and cemented institutionally within common law constitutionalism,[64] and, more substantively still, that the state must guarantee for its subjects a Kantian regime of secure and equal freedom.[65] A state's legitimacy, we claim, rests on the normative necessity of its subjection to this requirement (ie, on the state's normatively intractable subjection to legal standards), and on its compliance with the legal standards constitutive of this requirement. Put slightly differently, the state's overarching fiduciary duty to its people constitutes the normative dimension of the state's authority while regulating the exercise of public powers. The grounds of the state's legitimacy specified by the content of its fiduciary duty are also the public, legal standards to which the state must conform. The constitutive and regulative dimensions of the state's authority are therefore intertwined and inseparable, since the constitutive dimension flows from the same overarching fiduciary duty that governs the regulative dimension.

Understood capaciously, a Razian construal of the general fiduciary duty can accommodate the Fullerian/Kantian interpretation of it. On this NJT-informed construal, the state's general duty is to announce and enforce law in a way that helps its subjects comply better with the reasons that apply to them for having a state at all. The Fullerian/Kantian interpretation is one account of those reasons. But in theory, fair play, voluntarist, natural duty, and other accounts of state legitimacy could operate as the substantive content of the Razian duty, should any of those theories happen to specify the reasons that apply to subjects for having a state. For theorists suspicious of the Fullerian/Kantian account of state legitimacy, or who consider it incomplete, the Razian approach offers a bigger tent within which distinctive or additional grounds of legitimacy may be housed. While I cannot draw out the implications here, there may be a structural parallel between the Razian account and Rawl's understanding of reasonable conceptions of the good: both articulate standards of adequacy whose limits are set by public reasons that must be available to all.

In what remains I reply briefly to two possible objections. The first is that the fiduciary theory, including the Razian construal of it, posits a relationship to which the state and subject are alleged to belong, but does not itself offer an argument for the state. The second objection, closely related to the first, is that the Razian interpretation of the fiduciary theory fares no better than Raz's own service conception at explaining the duty to obey the law, since it does not follow from the state's subjection to a general fiduciary duty (assuming such a duty exists) that the subject has a genuine moral duty to obey the law.

The fiduciary theory's argument for the state begins with one of the two constitutive properties of the state–subject fiduciary relationship—the juridical incapacity of the subject to exercise public powers. This incapacity implies the prohibition on

[64] See, eg, Evan Fox-Decent, "Democratizing Common Law Constitutionalism," 55 *McGill Law J* 511 (2010); Criddle and Fox-Decent (n 10).

[65] See, eg, Criddle and Fox-Decent (n 10); Fox-Decent and Criddle (n 10).

unilateralism, the principle that no private party is entitled to dictate terms to another. While no private party is entitled to unilateralism, every private party has an interest in security against unilateralism, since to be subject to unilateralism is to be dominated, or subject to the arbitrary will of others.[66] In the ordinary case,[67] the fiduciary principle authorizes the state's law-giving branches (the legislature, the judiciary, the executive) to establish legal order in a manner consistent with its overarching fiduciary duty, and on behalf of every subject, since every subject has an interest in security against unilateralism. This authorization thereby secures the state's people from unilateralism and domination.

I have claimed that the Razian construal of the state's fiduciary duty could in theory incorporate various accounts of state legitimacy. Any such account, however, would have to be consistent with the principle of moral equality on which the prohibition on unilateralism rests, since that prohibition is an entailment of a constitutive element of the fiduciary theory (juridical incapacity). Since all plausible theories of state legitimacy assume the moral equality of individuals, this is not an especially high bar. The question for advocates of other theories of legitimacy is whether more is really needed from the point of view of explicating legitimacy, and whether the normative concerns that motivate their views might not be addressed through democratic politics.

It is worth noting as well that the nature of juridical incapacity within the state–subject relationship explains the difference between the state's authority and the much more limited authority of the shipmaster. The shipmaster exercises a limited power in relation to the cargo owner's goods, a power that reflects the owner's contextual incapacity to deal with those goods herself (or through her instructions). Apart from her agency power to obligate the owner to a third party who can save the property from waste, the shipmaster is not entitled to impose duties on the owner, and she is never entitled to simply tell the owner what to do in the way a court might order a remedy. In the shipmaster's case, the prohibition on unilateralism governs her relationship with the owner in two ways. First, it strictly limits the scope of her authority to the imposition of contractual duties necessary to save the owner's goods. Second, the shipmaster's power is conditioned by fiduciary requirements such that its exercise must serve the owner in accordance with legal standards.

In the case of the legal subject, her juridical incapacity to exercise public powers is comprehensive. In the absence of a warrant or license that in effect transforms her into a public actor, the legal subject is wholly incapable of exercising public powers. The comprehensiveness of those public powers in turn determines the comprehensiveness of the subject's juridical incapacity, since the incapacity is defined in relation to those powers. To remedy the problems of unilateralism that would otherwise afflict the

[66] For a crisp Kantian take on various ways the problem of unilateralism can present itself, see Arthur Ripstein (n 32) at 145–76 (discussing problems of unilateral choice, assurance, and indeterminacy as instances of unilateralism).

[67] I cannot address complications that arise from multiple de facto authorities contending for jurisdiction over the same territory any further than to suggest that international law and democratic politics supply the only plausible avenues through which these contests could be settled justly. For the role international law might play, see Patrick Macklem, "What is International Human Rights Law? Three Applications of a Distributive Account," 52 *McGill LJ* 575 (2007).

making, interpretation, administration, and enforcement of law, the fiduciary principle empowers legal institutions to establish legal order. These powers entitle the state to make laws, adjudicate disputes, administer public law regimes, and enforce compliance with public and private law. In short, the subject's juridical incapacity to exercise public powers combines with the threat of unilateralism to supply an argument for the idea of the state, while the fiduciary principle's authorization of state power brings the theoretical idea of the state into actual, practical existence, with actual and practical authority. This brings us to the second objection, the question of the subject's duty to obey.

A skeptic might grant that a state stands in a fiduciary relationship to its people, and grant as well that the state is under a general fiduciary duty to establish legal order consistent with the reasons for having one, but doubt that the subject has a general duty to obey. The skeptic could even grant that the state has authority to impose duties on its subjects coercively, but that subjects have no duty to obey apart from whatever independent moral duties attend their legal duties (eg, there is a duty not to murder but only because murder is an independent moral wrong). On this view, subjects lack a liberty right not to be coerced, but they have no duty to obey arising from the state's authority.

An argument similar in form to the argument for parental authority can be offered here. Suppose there are two states in a world much like ours, Bumbleville and Superstate. Both are liberal democracies committed to multiculturalism. The authorities in Bumbleville are not corrupt, but they are clumsy bumblers. Try as they may, their policies lead to bad roads, poor schools, crumbling infrastructure, substandard health care, and so on. They satisfy their general fiduciary duty to their people, but just barely. In Superstate, on the other hand, the policies are a model of fairness and efficiency. The trains run on time, the parks are clean, and social services are delivered economically and effectively. But Superstate has imperial if well-intentioned ambitions. One day Superstate passes legislation that, if implemented, would greatly improve Bumbleville's roads. All of Bumbleville's citizens would better comply with reasons that apply to them regarding public roads if they and their officials treated Superstate's directive as binding (notwithstanding that they would have to adjust their rule of recognition to do so).

Under the NJT as depicted in *The Morality of Freedom*, it would seem that the people of Bumbleville have reason to treat Superstate's legislation as authoritative. But it is far from clear they have a duty to obey, or that they are accountable to Superstate. One might think that Superstate's legislation is not binding on Bumbleville because it was passed without recourse to Bumbleville's democratic procedures. But that observation only serves to highlight another infirmity of the NJT; without more, it is indifferent to the procedures (democratic or otherwise) through which directives are made.[68] While this procedural objection to the NJT no doubt muddies the analytical waters, it is still plausible to think that Superstate's directive is a nullity vis-à-vis the people of Bumbleville because Superstate does not stand in a fiduciary relation to them. Superstate occupies the position of an officious intermeddler akin to the position occupied by Superdad. Bumbleville's authorities, on the other hand, do stand in a fiduciary

[68] See, eg, Hershovitz (n 6) at 3–6. For discussion of the relationship between a fiduciary theory of administration and democracy, see Evan J Criddle, "Fiduciary Administration: Rethinking Popular Representation in Agency Rulemaking," 88 *Tex Rev* 441 (2010).

relation to their people, they comply (if only barely) with their overarching fiduciary obligation, and so they do have standing to govern their people.

The duty to obey the law follows from the state's legitimate possession and exercise of a moral power to impose duties on its subjects. Like the parent's power, the state's is explained in part by its subjection to fiduciary requirements. The duty to obey which flows from it is a general and moral duty because the justification and nature of the state's power is general and moral; it is the power necessary to secure individuals from unilateralism and domination through the establishment of legal order. However, while subjects are accountable to the state, arguably the duty to obey is not owed to the state. It is owed to every other subject amenable to the state's jurisdiction. The reason the duty has a horizontal rather than a vertical trajectory is that the underlying point of legal duties, on the fiduciary theory, is to allow individuals to interact with one another subject to reciprocal limits that preclude unilateralism. Legal duties, in other words, are part of the institutional answer to the problem of unilateralism. They provide an important means through which the state can satisfy its fiduciary duty because they enable the subject to comply with the reasons for having a state in the first place; they so enable the subject by protecting her (and others) from unilateralism. By respecting a general duty to obey the law that is owed to others, the subject declines to make an exception for herself and implicitly surrenders any claim to unilateralism. Where the state is the "other" with whom the subject interacts and owes a particular legal duty, the general duty to obey is still best understood as a duty owed to all others, since the state is never anything more than a servant and representative of them.

This *may* be a place where the Razian approach to the fiduciary theory comes apart from a Kantian account that hews closely to Kant's views on the matter, depending on how those views are interpreted. Kant characterizes the state's public authority as a matter of "public right,"[69] which could be interpreted to suggest that the state has a claim right and the subject a correlative duty to obey that is owed to the state.[70] For the reasons given earlier and directly above, I think the moral power interpretation of public authority is better, as is the idea that the subject's general duty to obey is owed to other subjects rather than the state (while not denying, of course, that subjects may owe the state various specific legal duties).

Let us turn now to how the state's overarching fiduciary duty contributes to the argument that the subject has a general duty to obey. As in the case of parents, the state's duty places substantive limits on how the state may interact with its subjects, thus determining the scope of the state's authority. In addition, the content of the state's authority is explained because it has the same substantive content as its duty; ie, to announce and enforce law in a manner that helps its subjects comply with the reasons for having a state. Moreover, because the state is required to exercise public power in ways that secure its subjects from unilateralism, state action can be held accountable to legal standards. It is accountable to domestic legal standards and institutions, most notably the judiciary, and ultimately to international legal standards and institutions. But for

[69] Kant (n 43) at 123.

[70] Note, however, that Kant (n 43, at 129) says that the legislative, judicial, and executive branches of the state possess distinctive kinds of *power*.

states to be accountable to law at all, they must be subject to duties or requirements that permit the law to hold them to account. With accountability in place, subjects can properly be held to a moral duty to obey because they have legal assurance that the state is not entitled to subject them to domination. In sum, the state's own subjection to duty makes its power to announce and enforce law normatively effective, since all such exercises of power are legally conditioned so as to serve the subject's interest in security from private and public forms of domination. The subject cannot opt out of the state nor deny her duty to obey the law, since for her to do so would be for her to insist on unilateralism and implicitly deny the moral equality of her fellow subjects.

Conclusion

I have argued that Raz's NJT, as articulated in both *The Morality of Freedom* and his more recent work, is unpersuasive as an account of practical authority because it is invariably subject to the problem of standing. Because Raz views authority as a relation between persons and reason rather than as a relation between persons, he cannot account for the standing authorities enjoy to change the normative position of their subjects.

But I have also argued that there is much of value in Raz's service conception, starting with the basic idea that legitimate authority is necessarily a servant of its people. Of similar merit is the idea underlying the NJT that an authority is legitimate only if its directives help people better comply with reason. Taking these contributions on board, I have elaborated a fiduciary and Razian conception of authority, one that places the NJT front and center by borrowing from it to supply, at an admittedly high level of abstraction, content to the state's fiduciary duty to its people. Properly situated within an interpersonal fiduciary framework, the NJT can fulfil its original mission of providing a means for assessing an authority's legitimacy.

19

Mapping Public Fiduciary Relationships

*Ethan J Leib, David L Ponet, and Michael Serota**

Introduction

"Fiduciary political theory" is an intellectual project that seeks to recover the fiduciary foundations of public authority. It takes seriously the idea that political office is a public trust, which must be administered with sensitivity to the implied fiduciary role officers take on. From Paul Finn's early work,[1] to Evan Criddle's[2] and Evan Fox-Decent's individual[3] and collective work,[4] to some of our own recent scholarship,[5] public law theorists are reintroducing an idea with roots in the writings of Cicero and Locke: that private law fiduciary principles underlie the ethics of public office.

This has been a fertile project for democratic theorists, who now see how the fundamental insight underlying fiduciary law—that the use of discretionary power over the material, practical, and legal interests of others must be constrained by obligations meant to align the interests of agents and principals—can illuminate theories of representation, deliberative democracy, political and administrative power, political consent, and legality. Fiduciary principles once seemed to connect with only environmental and Indian law specialists,[6] where the legal doctrine is most explicitly fiduciary.

* Thanks to Fordham Law School for financial support and to DePaul University College of Law for hosting a symposium for which we prepared this chapter. Martin Gelter provided inspiration and a reality check; Dick Squire and Caroline Gentile provided clarity and expertise; and Andrew Gold and Paul Miller provided challenging written feedback.

[1] See Paul Finn, "Public Trust and Public Accountability," 3 *Griffith L Rev* 224 (1994); Paul Finn, "The Forgotten 'Trust:' The People and the State," in Malcolm Cope (ed), *Equity: Issues and Trends* (1995) 131; Paul Finn, "A Sovereign People, A Public Trust," in Paul Finn (ed), *Essays on Law and Government: Principles and Values* (1995) vol 1.

[2] See Evan J Criddle, "Fiduciary Foundations of Administrative Law," 54 *UCLA L Rev* 117 (2005); Evan J Criddle, "Fiduciary Administration: Rethinking Popular Representation in Agency Rulemaking," 88 *Tex L Rev* 441 (2010).

[3] See Evan Fox-Decent, "The Fiduciary Nature of State Legal Authority," 31 *Queen's LJ* 259 (2005); Evan Fox-Decent, *Sovereignty's Promise: The State as Fiduciary* (2011).

[4] See Evan J Criddle and Evan Fox-Decent, "A Fiduciary Theory of Jus Cogens," 34 *Yale J Int'l L* 331 (2009); Evan Fox-Decent and Evan Criddle, "The Fiduciary Constitution of Human Rights," 15 *Legal Theory* 301 (2009).

[5] See David L Ponet and Ethan J Leib, "Fiduciary Law's Lessons for Deliberative Democracy," 91 *BU L Rev* 1249 (2011); Ethan J Leib and David L Ponet, "Fiduciary Representation and Deliberative Engagement with Children," 20 *J Pol Phil* 178 (2012); Ethan J Leib, David L Ponet, and Michael Serota, "Translating Fiduciary Principles into Public Law," 126 *Harv L Rev F* 91 (2013); Ethan J Leib, David L Ponet, and Michael Serota, "A Fiduciary Theory of Judging," 101 *Calif L Rev* 699 (2013); Ethan J Leib, Michael Serota, and David L Ponet, "Fiduciary Principles and the Jury," 55 *Wm & Mary L Rev* 1105 (2014).

[6] See Joseph L Sax, "The Public Trust Doctrine in Natural Resource Law: Effective Judicial Intervention," 68 *Mich L Rev* 471 (1970); Mary Christina Wood, "Advancing the Sovereign Trust of Government to Safeguard the Environment for Present and Future Generations (Part I): Ecological Realism and the Need for a Paradigm Shift," 39 *Envtl L* 43 (2009); Mary Christina Wood, "Advancing the Sovereign Trust of Government to Safeguard the Environment for Present and Future Generations (Part II): Instilling a

But in recent years the fiduciary rendering of public law has also touched and shaped diverse topics such as constitutional theory,[7] international law,[8] administrative law,[9] and election law.[10] Yet this large and wide-ranging body of sophisticated work seems to be overlooking a fundamental structural complexity within the fiduciary principle.

To wit, fiduciary political theorists have neglected to explore sufficiently the difficulty of mapping fiduciary–beneficiary relationships in the public sphere. This oversight is quite surprising given that the proper mapping of fiduciary–beneficiary relationships lies at the root of one of the most protracted debates in corporate law. After decades of debate over the identity of the beneficiary of corporate fiduciary duties, theorists remain deeply divided. This debate should be of interest to public fiduciary theorists because the cartography of public fiduciary relationships is essential to operationalizing the model. After all, it is only through identifying the relevant fiduciary and beneficiary that one is able to determine the precise contours of the fiduciary framework's ethical architecture. As such, loose mapping of fiduciary–beneficiary relationships in the public sphere precludes a clear understanding of whose interests are pertinent to the public fiduciary's representation, and what the public fiduciary is to do when beneficiaries' interests diverge or collide.

The purpose of this chapter, then, is to explore the debate in corporate law about fiduciary–beneficiary relationships to help translate fiduciary principles into public law configurations. Our effort here is only preliminary: the goal is simply to get clearer on what the options might be, not to choose among them. The hope is that this exercise will be mutually beneficial for private and public law fiduciary theorists.

In the chapter, we first elaborate on mapping efforts in private law (Section I). We thereafter review the limited attention this question has received within fiduciary political theory (Section II). We follow with an exposition of the best way to differentiate the "shareholder primacy" vision from the "stakeholder" view in fiduciary political theory (Section III). By way of conclusion, we suggest that ideas about "Janus-faced" representation in the public political sphere can plausibly shed light on private sphere representation as well.

I. Mapping Private Fiduciary Relationships

It is sometimes easy to specify fiduciaries and their beneficiaries. The agent is a fiduciary for a principal; the attorney is a fiduciary for a specific client; the guardian is a fiduciary for a ward. But intense debate surrounds the mapping of fiduciaries and beneficiaries in the corporate context, where the power relations between corporate

Fiduciary Obligation in Governance," 39 *Envtl L* 91 (2009); Mary Christina Wood, "Indian Land and the Promise of Native Sovereignty: The Trust Doctrine Revisited," 1994 *Utah L Rev* 1471 (1994).

[7] See Robert G Natelson, "The General Welfare Clause and the Public Trust: An Essay in Original Understanding," 52 *U Kan. L Rev* 1 (2003); Robert G Natelson, "The Constitution and the Public Trust," 52 *Buff L Rev* (2004); Robert G Natelson, "Judicial Review of Special Interest Spending: The General Welfare Clause and the Fiduciary Law of the Founders," 11 *Tex Rev L & Pol* 239 (2007).

[8] See Criddle and Fox-Decent (n 4).

[9] See Evan J Criddle, "Fiduciary Administration: Rethinking Popular Representation in Agency Rulemaking," 88 *Tex L Rev* 441 (2010).

[10] See D Theodore Rave, "Politicians as Fiduciaries," 126 *Harv L Rev* 671 (2013).

representatives, those who authorize them, and those affected by their decisions, are significantly more complex. This section explores the core disagreement between proponents of the shareholder view and the stakeholder view. With this background, it will be possible to conduct a corollary inquiry into mapping these relationships in the public sphere.

For decades, theorists of political representation have debated whose interests are to be represented in acts of representation, and what institutional structures are most likely to secure high-quality representation. As to the former, theorists generally agree that any representative must act in the interests of the authorizing constituency, which formally delegates discretionary authority. In many cases of representation, however, this delegation of authority will empower a representative to make decisions that impact the legal and practical interests of additional constituencies that do not take part in direct authorization. Must a representative account for or consider the interests of these additional constituencies in exercising her authority? This is a question over which theorists routinely diverge, and it is not merely one of theoretical interest. The challenge of identifying the appropriate constituency or constituencies to be represented has serious practical ramifications, given that the interests of different groups will often conflict.[11] How to navigate those competing interests—each of which may have a legitimate claim on a representative—is a difficult ethical question for the political representative.

Given how hard it is to monitor representative performance, theories of political representation also struggle with questions of institutional design. Which institutional arrangements best ensure that representatives hew closely to relevant constituencies' interests or welfare? Agency costs lurk in almost all representative relationships, as a representative possesses discretionary authority over vital resources of the represented and tends to have greater expertise and access to information. It is therefore likely that there will exist a significant inequality and asymmetry between the representative and the represented. This imbalance, in turn, renders the represented susceptible to predation and abuse. Accordingly, it is critical to establish some mechanism for aligning representative-represented interests, while also providing representatives with the space to execute their station effectively.

The same lines of inquiry are fundamental to the practice of representation as it arises in the private law, in which corporate entities are governed by diverse representatives whose decisions materially impact a wide range of interests, including those of an authorizing constituency, the corporation's owners, and a variety of other constituencies, such as the corporation's employees, business partners, charity recipients, future shareholders, and the greater community in which the corporation is embedded. In this context, the first issue of representation—the "whose interests?" question—presents itself as the debate about whether corporate decision-making should be based *only* on the interests of the corporation's owners; or, alternatively, whether the board, directors, and officers should consider the interests of all constituencies likely to be affected by their decisions.[12]

[11] See Stephen M Bainbridge, "Much Ado About Little? Directors' Fiduciary Duties in the Vicinity of Insolvency," 1 *J Bus & Tech L* 335 (2007).

[12] This line of inquiry ultimately leads to interesting questions about whether different classes of corporate fiduciaries, such as corporate directors and officers, owe different types of fiduciary duties—or whether

The "whose interests" debate flows neatly into institutional design questions about setting up appropriate governance systems for the corporation that furnish oversight over representatives. The private law copes with the agency costs that inhere in the representative relationships within the corporation by imposing fiduciary obligations over corporate representatives. These duties, most often the fiduciary duties of loyalty and care, can lead to supra-compensatory remedies in order to motivate ethical behavior by corporate fiduciaries toward their beneficiaries. But to whom more precisely do these duties run?

Given the impact of directorial and managerial decision-making, the variety of interests affected, and the frequency with which different constituencies' interests are likely to conflict, much rides on identification of the fiduciary–beneficiary relationship in corporate law. Beginning in the 1930s with the "Berle–Dodd" debate,[13]and carrying through to the present,[14] this has been a subject of intense contestation that continues to divide scholars, courts, and policymakers.

There are basically two approaches to the issue.[15] At one end of the spectrum is the shareholder primacy view. Contractualist in orientation and premised upon the "orthodox assumption [] that corporate law's objective is to develop legal structures that will maximize shareholder wealth,"[16] proponents of the shareholder primacy view contend that the only interests to be represented by a corporation's directors and managers are those of the owners of a corporation. To be sure, denizens of this camp acknowledge that what is in the interests of the shareholders will often be in the interests of other constituencies. Yet to the extent the interests of non-shareholder constituencies would be adversely affected by managerial pursuit of shareholder welfare, the shareholder primacy view dictates that corporate representatives turn a blind eye.

The shareholder primacy view has a singular understanding of the relevant interests to be represented by a corporate representative: a corporation's representatives "owe fiduciary duties to shareholders and to shareholders *alone*."[17] Accordingly, the owners of the corporation—and *only* the owners—have legal standing to enforce obligations in the case of fiduciary default. The board of directors, each individual director, and officers of the corporation are supposed to pursue the best interests of shareholders. True

officers are representatives at all, as they are not subject to shareholder elections. See generally Lyman P Q Johnson and David Millon, "Recalling Why Corporate Officers Are Fiduciaries," 46 *Wm & Mary L Rev* 159 (2005). For our purposes, we work with the traditional assumption that the board, directors, and corporate officers are all similar types of fiduciaries.

[13] See A A Berle, Jr, "Corporate Powers as Powers in Trust," 44 *Harv L Rev* 1049 (1931); A A Berle, Jr, "For Whom Corporate Managers Are Trustees: A Note," 45 *Harv L Rev* 1365 (1932); E Merrick Dodd, Jr, "For Whom are Corporate Managers Trustees?," 45 *Harv L Rev* 1145 (1932); E Merrick Dodd, Jr, "Is Effective Enforcement of the Fiduciary Duties of Corporate Managers Practicable?," 2 *U Chi L Rev* 194 (1935).

[14] See Martin Gelter, "Taming or Protecting the Modern Corporation? Shareholder-Stakeholder Debates in a Comparative Light," 7 *NYU JL & Bus* 641 (2011); Lawrence E Mitchell, "A Theoretical and Practical Framework for Enforcing Corporate Constituency Statutes," 70 *Tex L Rev* 579 (1992); Mark E Van Der Weide, "Against Fiduciary Duties to Corporate Stakeholders," 21 *Del J Corp L* 27 (1996); Jonathan R Macey, "Fiduciary Duties as Residual Claims: Obligations to Nonshareholder Constituencies from a Theory of the Firm Perspective," 84 *Cornell L Rev* 1266 (1999).

[15] See Gelter (n 14).

[16] David Millon, "Communitarians, Contractarians, and the Crisis in Corporate Law," 50 *Wash & Lee L Rev* 1373, 1374 (1993).

[17] Macey (n 14) at 1281.

enough, the action is brought on behalf of the *corporation*—but traditionally, apart from corporate management, only shareholders have standing to sue on behalf of the corporation.

Shareholder primacy theories are not monolithic. However, many of the arguments in support of shareholder primacy are similar in that they revolve around the view that "[a] business corporation is organized and carried on primarily for the profit of the stockholders."[18] On a more conceptual level, a shareholder primacy approach might also be bolstered by a formalistic model of representation: that is, because the corporation's shareholders are the only constituency that authorize directors to serve in a representative capacity, one might think that only their interests are entitled to representation. And from a pragmatist's standpoint, focusing on shareholders' interest avoids complexities associated with fiduciary representation of multiple constituencies. Corporate directors and officers are already challenged by the heterogeneity of shareholders, whose preferences and profit horizons may conflict.[19] Further expanding that relational matrix outwards to include additional classes of beneficiaries might be too much for a governance system to bear. All the same, shareholder primacy proponents assume that other constituencies can protect themselves through contract, such as creditors and (perhaps somewhat less plausibly) employees.

There is much to be said, however, for the alternative stakeholder or "entity" view. Often considered communitarian in orientation and premised upon the view that corporations, as legal entities, owe something to the society and legal system from which they arise,[20] proponents of the stakeholder view contend that corporate representatives must account for the interests of all constituencies whose well-being is tied up with the corporation's future. Constituencies that deserve consideration include a corporation's employees, suppliers, creditors, donees, and surrounding community.[21] On the stakeholder view, the corporation may best be understood as "a bureaucratic hierarchy dominated by professional managers," who are "autonomous actors free to pursue whatever interests they choose (or society directs)."[22] And because the communitarian ethos dictates that many constituencies are given consideration by a corporation's representatives, shareholder interests are to be viewed as "but one variable in an equation with many stakeholder groups' welfare as equivalent variables."[23]

This more expansive approach to interest representation leads to a more complex mapping of fiduciary relationships. Proponents of the stakeholder view tend to see all vulnerable constituencies as beneficiaries in a relational matrix that would "impose a

[18] *Dodge v Ford Motor Co* 204 Mich. 459 (1919).

[19] See Iman Anabtawi, "Some Skepticism about Increasing Shareholder Power," 53 *UCLA L Rev* 561 (2006).

[20] One could also take the view that corporations owe something to the general public interest, whether that orientation benefits shareholders, stakeholders, or is just desirable as a limit to or first principle of fiduciary obligation. See Einer Elhauge, "Sacrificing Corporate Profits in the Public Interest," 80 *NYU L Rev* 733 (2005).

[21] See Margaret M Blair and Lynn Stout, "A Team Production Theory of Corporate Law," 85 *Va L Rev* 247 (1990); Kent Greenfield, "The Impact of 'Going Private' on Corporate Stakeholders," 3 *Brook J Corp & Fin L* 72 (2008).

[22] Stephen M Bainbridge, "The Board of Directors as Nexus of Contracts," 88 *Iowa L Rev* 1, 5 (2002).

[23] Douglas M Branson, "Corporate Governance 'Reform' and the New Corporate Social Responsibility," 62 *U Pitt L Rev* 605, 636 (2001).

fiduciary duty on managers to act in the best interests of all."[24] Still, there is significant variance among scholars as to how this system should operate in practice. Lawrence Mitchell, for example, has argued that managers owe non-shareholder constituencies a more limited duty not to harm, which would "permit[] direct legal action against the board by members of constituent groups... limited by concepts of balance analogous to those developed as pragmatic modifications of close corporation fiduciary duties."[25] Others who subscribe to the stakeholder view argue in favor of creating a more comprehensive set of fiduciary obligations that would apply to particular non-shareholder constituencies, such as a corporation's employees or bondholders.[26] On this model, the fiduciaries are the same—board, individual directors, and officers—but the beneficiaries and their relative priority vary.

Whatever the differences among stakeholder approaches, their arguments tend to be functionalist or moral in nature. Stakeholders—like shareholders—make significant investments of time, money, and/or human capital in a corporation, and are therefore economically or materially dependent on its continued existence.[27] This dependence, in turn, makes stakeholders—like shareholders—highly vulnerable to the manner in which corporate representatives exercise their decision-making authority. And because stakeholders possess little influence over corporate decision-making, stakeholders have no choice but to trust corporate representatives to exercise their authority responsibly (though some of these stakeholders will have contracts that may give them useful rights against the corporation). These functional realities, when viewed in light of the tripartite fiduciary indicia of *discretion, trust*, and *vulnerability*, are understood by stakeholder theorists to provide a sufficient basis for rendering non-shareholder constituencies beneficiaries and making corporate fiduciaries responsible for pursuing their interests.[28]

As the foregoing analysis reveals, there is significant theoretical disagreement and normative complexity frustrating a clean mapping of fiduciary relationships in corporate law. Such disagreement is reflected in positive law, as well. Although the weight of the evidence supports shareholder primacy theorists, proponents of the stakeholder view are also able to marshal significant evidence in support of a multiple beneficiary approach.

The shareholder primacy view is supported by decades of case law. As early as 1891, courts thought of officers and directors as fiduciaries for shareholders: "The officers and directors of a corporation are trustees *of the shareholders*, and in securing to themselves an advantage not common to all the stockholders, they commit a plain breach of duty."[29] Since then, several courts have reaffirmed this proposition, holding that corporate managers do not owe fiduciary duties to non-shareholder constituencies.[30] Probative of the shareholder view's descriptive accuracy may be recent judicial

[24] Van Der Weide (n 14) at 31.
[25] Mitchell (n 14) at 585–6.
[26] See Marleen A O'Connor, "Restructuring the Corporation's Nexus of Contracts: Recognizing a Fiduciary Duty to Protect Displaced Workers," 69 *NC L Rev* 1189 (1991).
[27] See O'Connor (n 26). [28] See Leib, Ponet, and Serota, "A Fiduciary Theory of Judging" (n 5).
[29] *Ark Val Agr Soc'y v Holtz* 45 Kan 164 (1891) (emphasis added).
[30] See *Metro Life Ins Co v RJR Nabisco, Inc* 716 F Supp 1504 (SDNY 1989); *Simon v Cogan* 549 A 2d 300, 303 (Del 1988).

decisions declining to extend beneficiary status to outside constituencies that otherwise seem to be particularly worthy contenders. First, in the context of charitable corporations, for example—organizations which usually exist solely to benefit the public interest—the majority position taken by courts is that stakeholders lack standing to sue for breach of a director's fiduciary duty.[31] Although there is not necessarily a one-to-one correlation between standing to sue and to whom a duty is owed—after all, when shareholders sue, they are often suing *derivatively* on behalf of the corporation—the standing question is some proxy for justiciability of the fiduciary obligation, as shareholder primacy theorists see it. If public interest organizations, where the acceptable profit motive of the organization fades away, cannot be sued by their stakeholders for breach of fiduciary duties, *a fortiori* in for-profit corporate enterprises, only shareholders can have the power to sue for breaches.

Second, although there was ambiguity for some time in Delaware as to the status of the creditors of an insolvent corporation, the issue was recently resolved in favor of the shareholder position, more or less: as the Delaware Supreme Court held, "individual creditors of an insolvent corporation have no right to assert direct claims for breach of fiduciary duty against corporate directors."[32] Admittedly, the creditors of an insolvent corporation may bring a derivative action on behalf of the corporation (as may the shareholders); but creditors do not get direct benefit of fiduciary duties under current Delaware law as beneficiaries themselves. The exception seems to prove the rule that it is the shareholders who must be the primary vindicators of the duties managers owe.

However, as with non-profits, one must be careful in collapsing who has standing to bring a claim on behalf of the corporation—the shareholders usually and the creditors only rarely—and *to whom* the duty is actually owed. Indeed, even shareholder primacy proponents would have to admit that courts focus on director and officer duties to *the corporation*, which could be thought to include a broader set of constituencies of relevance.[33]

For its part, the stakeholder view has a steadily growing chorus of support in legislative bodies, both domestic and abroad, and in the commentary of a diverse group.[34] Stakeholder theorists point out that "[d]espite the traditional view of shareholders as 'owners' of corporations whose interests are superior to all others, no state corporation code in existence specifies that the directors of a corporation owe a fiduciary duty solely to the shareholders."[35] More importantly, state and foreign legislatures currently appear to be heading in a decidedly stakeholder-oriented direction: for example, over 40 US states have recently passed so-called "constituency statutes," which either permit or require corporate representatives to account for interests of outside constituencies such

[31] See Linda Sugin, "Improving Charity Governance with Advance Rulings." Working paper, available at <http://web.law.columbia.edu/sites/default/files/microsites/attorneys-general/Sugin%20draft%20columbia.pdf> (2013); Rob Atkinson, "Unsettled Standing: Who (Else) Should Enforce the Duties of Charitable Fiduciaries?," 23 *Iowa J Corp L* 655 (1998).

[32] *N Am Catholic Educ Programming Found, Inc v Gheewalla* 930 A 2d 92 (Del 2007).

[33] See Adolf A Berle and Gardiner C Means, *The Modern Corporation & Private Property* (1932; 1991) 226.

[34] See Andrew Keay, "Stakeholder Theory in Corporate Law: Has It Got What It Takes?," 9 *Rich J Global L & Bus* 249 (2010).

[35] Edward S Adams and John H Matheson, "A Statutory Model for Corporate Constituency Concerns," 49 *Emory LJ* 1085 (2000).

as employees, suppliers, creditors, and communities, while a similar trend is evident in other Anglo-American countries.[36]

Although the weight of US jurisprudence cuts against the stakeholder position, there is dynamism in fiduciary law, which tolerates multiple beneficiary models in other contexts.[37] This could support a more stakeholder-friendly stance in the future. Consider, for example, that "[c]orporate fiduciary obligations continue to develop, with [American] courts finding that majority stockholders owe fiduciary duties to minority stockholders, and in close corporations, that stockholders owe fiduciary duties to each other."[38] And recent decisions by Anglo-American courts outside the US suggest a growing acceptance of the stakeholder view.[39] Assuming judges could be convinced of the normative desirability of the stakeholder position, they likely already possess the resources to implement it. Courts, for example, apply trust law to enable trustees to represent multiple beneficiaries so long as they treat them fairly and impartially. Courts also apply agency law rules to allow an agent to represent antagonistic interests through disclosure and consent. And courts subject decisions by corporate representatives to an inherent fairness test when those decisions implicate competing interests of majority and minority shareholders.[40] Thus, the potential complexity of administering and enforcing a multiple beneficiary model need not be a stumbling block. But only time will tell if stakeholder proponents can persuade courts to take that step.

These are, in broad strokes, the normative and doctrinal foundations upon which the shareholder and stakeholder positions rest. Strong normative arguments support both singular and multiple beneficiary models, and each camp is able to marshal material evidence supporting its view. Mapping fiduciary relationships in corporate law and elsewhere in private law is a contested, uncertain, and highly complex matter. Still, there is widespread convergence on the identity of the fiduciary: it is the board, the individual directors, and officers of the firm.

II. Fiduciary Political Theory

Despite a long-standing and distinguished tradition of conceiving of political power in fiduciary terms, surprisingly little attention has been paid in recent years—during what might be described as a "fiduciary political theory revival"—to untangling the multiple identities of fiduciaries and beneficiaries in the public context.[41] Otherwise thought-provoking applications of the fiduciary principle to various forms of public office are bereft of explicit engagement with the underlying cartographical questions. But notwithstanding this, all public law applications of the fiduciary principle necessarily implicate some matrix of fiduciary–beneficiary relationships. In this section, we

[36] See Keay (n 34).
[37] Andrew S Gold, "Dynamic Fiduciary Duties," 34 *Cardozo L Rev* 491 (2012).
[38] O'Connor (n 26) at 1248.
[39] See *People's Dep't Stores v Wise* [2004] 3 SCR 461 (Can); *BCA Inc v 1976 Debentureholders* [2008] 3 SCR 560 (Can).
[40] See O'Connor (n 26); Steven L Schwarcz, "Fiduciaries with Conflicting Obligations," 94 *Minn L Rev* 1867 (2010).
[41] See Leib, Ponet, and Serota, "A Fiduciary Theory of Judging" (n 5).

analyze the work of some of the most prominent public fiduciary theorists in the field, with the goal of teasing out the mapping implicit in their models.

Paul Finn in many respects inaugurated the fiduciary political theory revival.[42] Observing that we "cannot ignore the inexorable logic of popular sovereignty," Finn queries: "If the powers of government belong to and are derived from the people, can the donees of those powers under our constitutional arrangements properly be characterized in terms other than that they are the trustees, the fiduciaries, of those powers for the people?" While Finn's application of the fiduciary principle is focused upon the Australian political system, he invokes the American colonists to explain that all institutions of government "exist for the people, to serve the interests of the people and, as such, are accountable to the people."[43]

Most contemporary work in fiduciary political theory identifies all offices of government as fiduciary and posits that "the people" are the corresponding beneficiaries. But this is problematic. Finn's language suggests a unitary referent for all public fiduciary relations—namely, "the people." However, the transition from abstract conceptions of fiduciary relationships in public law to governance of concrete relationships complicates the picture. For example, in a separate essay Finn acknowledges that while in the private domain disclosure to and consent by a beneficiary can immunize a fiduciary from a breach, the corollaries in the public domain are much harder to identify because consent from large collectives is difficult to secure.[44] Finn's public fiduciary model is instructive and is the basis of so much further work in the field, but it falls short of providing precise relational coordinates.

Evan Fox-Decent's groundbreaking work continues the tradition of framing public fiduciary relationships in mostly unitary terms. Fox-Decent acknowledges the "multiple beneficiary contexts typical of public law," but he treats the fiduciary as *the state*, an all-encompassing singular entity.[45] And while implicitly sensitive to the differently situated individuals that reside within a sovereign territory, he refers to these individuals as subjects in generic terms. Thus, Fox-Decent explains that the fiduciary relationship "exists between the state and each person subject to its power and authority. The civil or political status of the person subject to state authority does not matter."[46]

To be sure, Fox-Decent understands that the "state" is divisible. But he does not explain how we are to understand the fiduciary relationships routed through different fonts of sovereignty. Similarly the term "subject" for Fox-Decent takes on a unitary—and very expansive—valence. He concedes that while in the private law the duty of loyalty is generally owed a "discrete beneficiary," public officials "are duty-bound to consider both the interests of the public at large and the interests of individuals directly affected by their determinations."[47] But in his oscillation between the individual, those with affected interests, and "public at large," Fox-Decent goes no further in determining the identity of the beneficiary. This is consistent with his more recent treatment, in which he invokes the fiduciary principle to describe the sovereign–subject relationship,

[42] Finn's papers are cited in n 1. [43] Finn, "A Sovereign People" (n 1) at 14.
[44] Finn, "The Forgotten 'Trust'" (n 1) at 150.
[45] Fox-Decent, "The Fiduciary Nature of State Legal Authority" (n 3) at 256.
[46] Fox-Decent, "The Fiduciary Nature of State Legal Authority" (n 3) at 272.
[47] Fox-Decent, "The Fiduciary Nature of State Legal Authority" (n 3) at 261.

and again posits *the state* as fiduciary.[48] The one-to-one correspondence between public powers and common good makes for an elegant edifice, but it admits too little nuance. Not all subjects, for example, live in the same state or district—and different arms of government may have differing authorizations, obligations, and corresponding principals. These differences have implications in terms of how we construe the public fiduciary obligations that attach to various officeholders.

Evan Criddle deploys the fiduciary principle to resolve the ostensible incompatibility between administrative rule-making and popular sovereignty.[49] In brief, Criddle argues that administrative agencies must exercise their rule-making powers according to principles derived from their status as public fiduciaries.[50] He argues that by mandating a duty to promote "the public welfare," the fiduciary model of administrative law-making reconciles the administrative state with popular representation. To wit, "agency regulators must respect the state's subjects as free and equal autonomous agents, and act to promote the public welfare, not necessarily the public will."[51] Like Fox-Decent, Criddle emphasizes the public fiduciary's obligation to the public welfare, not to the will of the people, which "is usually an abstraction without a reliable referent in the real world."[52] As such, Criddle delinks fiduciary representation from electoral accountability or authorization. The administrative state is thus an "intricate network of nested fiduciary relations."[53] Criddle's conception of public fiduciary office-holding encompasses presidents, legislators, judges, administrators, and all other public officials who act as "fiduciary representatives for their beneficiaries, the people subject to their entrusted administrative powers."[54]

Although all of these theorists recognize the potential for multiple—and sometimes *adverse*—beneficiaries, Criddle, Fox-Decent, and Finn each elide distinctions between individual constituents, "the people," the "public at large," and "public welfare" as the relevant beneficiary. They likewise focus on the state as fiduciary and all of the state's arms as fiduciaries without considering the specific contours of each distinct relationship.

Most recently, Teddy Rave primarily focuses his attention on the individual legislator as fiduciary and her constituents as beneficiaries.[55] He claims that state representatives who draw electoral district lines that may redound to their or their party's benefit are self-dealing and in violation of the duty of loyalty. In choosing the individual state legislator and district as the relevant unit of analysis, Rave concludes that politicians' self-interested line-drawing activity is a taint that should be deemed to invalidate the

[48] See Fox-Decent, *Sovereignty's Promise: The State as Fiduciary* (n 3).

[49] See Criddle, "Fiduciary Foundations of Administrative Law" (n 2); Criddle, "Fiduciary Administration: Rethinking Popular Representation in Agency Rulemaking" (n 2).

[50] See Criddle, "Fiduciary Administration: Rethinking Popular Representation in Agency Rulemaking" (n 2).

[51] Criddle, "Fiduciary Administration: Rethinking Popular Representation in Agency Rulemaking" (n 2) at 466.

[52] Criddle, "Fiduciary Administration: Rethinking Popular Representation in Agency Rulemaking" (n 2) at 473.

[53] Criddle, "Fiduciary Administration: Rethinking Popular Representation in Agency Rulemaking" (n 2) at 491.

[54] Criddle, "Fiduciary Administration: Rethinking Popular Representation in Agency Rulemaking" (n 2) at 491.

[55] See Rave (n 10).

entire redistricting process. Such a conclusion seems plausible; but were Rave to conceive of the *legislature*—as opposed to the legislator—as the fiduciary, he might reach a different conclusion.[56] Consider James Madison's famous argument in favor of representative government in *Federalist* No 10, in which he argues that by admitting numerous private interests and then "filtering" them out through the legislative process, representative bodies can remove the taint of self-interest. This could be viewed in corporate law terms as similar to when a conflicted transaction is disclosed and permitted to stand if a majority of disinterested directors approve it.

In keeping with other work in fiduciary political theory, Rave's application of fiduciary principles to election law pays scant attention to the complexities of fiduciary–beneficiary relationships. In fact, Rave acknowledges that "identifying the relevant group of people to consider as the principal is not straightforward" but thinks such questions "need not detain us long." Rave concludes that "even if opinions differ as to whether representatives should be acting in the public interest or in the interests of their constituents,"[57] they should still not be acting in naked self-interest. Again, this carries intuitive appeal but as the corporate cleansing analogy and the Madisonian filtering idea suggest, the unit of analysis matters in terms of how we calibrate fiduciary duties.

The foregoing discussion highlights how little headway has been made in delineating fiduciary–beneficiary relationships in the public context. Section III brings the private law debate and public law discussion to bear on each other, seeking to provide at least some progress in this mapping enterprise.

III. Mapping Public Fiduciary Relationships

Translating fiduciary principles into public law configurations requires a clear understanding of the relational matrix upon which the translation rests. Just as a determination as *to whom* a corporation's managers serve as a fiduciary is central to the practice of corporate representation, so too is identification of *to whom* a particular public official serves as fiduciary a foundational issue in the practice of democratic representation. In both cases, the cartography determines the fiduciary framework's precise contours. This section thus takes up the cartographical challenge. By juxtaposing the shareholder–stakeholder debate in corporate fiduciary law with previous efforts to translate private fiduciary law into public fiduciary theory, we can expose not only how similarly hard questions in corporate law replicate themselves in public law, but also how such questions can contribute to political theory.

Let us start with a state-level legislator from one of 150 districts represented in a state Assembly, Jane the Rep.[58] For ease and efficiency of exposition, we will mostly focus on state-level elective office; but *mutatis mutandis* the argument could encompass other state and federal officeholders, such as judicial, administrative, and other officers engaged in coercive state action. When Jane is seated, she swears to uphold the

[56] See Leib, Ponet, and Serota, "Translating Fiduciary Principles into Public Law" (n 5).
[57] Rave (n 10) at 719.
[58] Some of this section is drawn from Leib, Ponet, and Serota, "Translating Fiduciary Principles into Public Law" (n 5).

constitution of her state and the constitution of the United States. Here is what Jane's oath would look like in New Jersey, for example:

> I, Jane the Rep, do solemnly swear that I will support the Constitution of the United States and the Constitution of the State of New Jersey, and that I will bear true faith and allegiance to the same and to the Governments established in the United States and in this State, under the authority of the people. So help me God.

Basic fiduciary political theory teaches that Jane is a fiduciary; there is wide convergence on that proposition. But for whom exactly?

Taking the standpoint of the dominant "shareholder primacy" view in corporate law as a point of departure, Jane seems to represent only her authorizing constituency: that is, those individuals authorized by the New Jersey Constitution to select a representative for the particular district Jane represents. Jane thus appears to be a fiduciary for her district's residents—including those who voted for her, those who voted against her, and those who didn't vote at all—as she has been delegated state authority by them and as she holds all of their interests in trust. Traditional fiduciary indicia are present: Jane has *discretionary power* over her district because she controls the legal and practical interests of her constituents. For example, she makes statewide criminal law and passes the statewide budget. Jane must also be *trusted* by her constituents and her constituents are *vulnerable* to possible self-interested exploitation by Jane.

There is more that makes Jane seem like a fiduciary for her constituents, however. To start, the serious expertise gap in the law-making enterprise between representatives and the represented will preclude robust constituent oversight. This means that Jane's constituents will likely have an exceptionally difficult time monitoring her activities. Moreover, it is also likely that Jane's constituents will lack access to meaningful pathways of candidate selection and representative accountability. Elections notwithstanding, the structures of democracy—namely, political party control of access to political office, gerrymandering, and geographical sorting—suggest that the average citizen faces a very narrow set of political choices in state Assembly representation. What's more, Jane may also be term-limited, disabling retrospective accountability. For all of these reasons, *bonding* is essential—and fiduciary constraints capture something true and interesting about the ethics of political representation. Jane is expected to be loyal and careful, attending to her fiduciary duty of loyalty and her fiduciary duty of care.[59]

Yet the shareholder primacy view as extended to the public fiduciary sphere misses another set of potential beneficiaries for Jane: the citizens of the whole state, including those who have no role in Jane's election. This way of thinking about Jane's beneficiaries can be linked to "entity"-based theories of corporate fiduciary duties. Like managers relative to stakeholders, Jane also seems to serve as a fiduciary for the citizens of the state given the state-wide reach of the discretionary policy decisions Jane's office authorizes her to make. Moreover, the citizens of the state may actually be more *vulnerable* than the citizens of the district, who can at least theoretically remove the officer through election. On this analysis, the *discretionary power* and *trust* elements of the fiduciary relational triptych supervene across Jane's relationships (both authorizing

[59] See Ponet and Leib, "Fiduciary Law's Lessons for Deliberative Democracy" (n 5).

district-level constituents and non-authorizing state-level constituents), thereby inviting fiduciary constraint between Jane and the citizens of her state.[60]

This rendering is, however, not without its complexities: namely, the same multi-beneficiary conflicts of interest issues that arise in the private law have corollaries in the public sphere. There is a significant risk that one set of beneficiaries will have interests adverse to those of another. Indeed, in some measure, every instance of pork-barrel politics and every effort to track and capitulate to district preferences in the interest of reelection could be viewed as a derogation of Jane's obligation to pursue a wider public interest. Such conflicts, however, can likely be addressed as they are in private law by providing that Jane's fiduciary obligation is to be "fair-minded" between classes of beneficiaries. Consider Paul Finn on the issue: "It is uncontroversial fiduciary law that where a fiduciary serves classes of beneficiaries possessing different rights . . . the fiduciary is . . . required to act fairly as between different classes of beneficiary in taking decisions which affect the rights and interest of the classes."[61] Or Fox-Decent: "In the multiple beneficiary contexts typical of public law, loyalty manifests itself as fairness and reasonableness."[62]

It is also possible, of course, that neither approach is entirely accurate. For example, conventional political theory—and the oaths taken by political representatives—suggest a different resolution. Although political representation is Janus-faced, at once looking to the "shareholder" in the district and the "stakeholder" outside it, Jane actually swears her ultimate loyalty to the members of the state, not to her constituents.[63] So while we expect her to promote the interests of her constituents in the parliamentary chamber—why else have geographical representation?[64]—most public law theorists recognize the "doctrine of the free mandate."[65] This doctrine requires unmooring representatives from electors or selectors—such that they are not bound by their electors' expressed preferences, "freeing" them to be oriented toward the people more broadly understood. In true conflict between local preferences and the interests of the people of the state at large, then, it is plausible that fiduciary principles require that the state's interests prevail, even if in-district voters alone have the ability to throw Jane out of office. Once this concession is made (and we think it should be made), it starts looking less like the shareholder/constituent is the primary beneficiary; the whole state's people are the primary beneficiary, with the constituents' claims being *derivative*. The constituents are mere limbs of the body politic.

But perhaps we haven't exhausted the potential beneficiaries. Jane may also have at least two other beneficiaries: the nation's citizenry and future generations. After all, both American political thought and contemporary legal theory are "acutely aware that representation of a particular class of individuals at a particular time could include

[60] See Leib, Ponet, and Serota, "A Fiduciary Theory of Judging" (n 5).

[61] Finn, "The Forgotten 'Trust'" (n 1) at 138.

[62] Fox-Decent, "The Fiduciary Nature of State Legal Authority" (n 3) at 265.

[63] See Nadia Urbinati, *Representative Democracy* (2006).

[64] See Andrew Rehfeld, *The Concept of Constituency: Political Representation, Democratic Legitimacy, and Institutional Design* (2005).

[65] See Marc Van Der Hulst, "The Parliamentary Mandate: A Global Comparative Study" (2000), available at <http://www.ipu.org/PDF/publications/mandate_e.pdf>.

responsibility" to both the people of the nation—"who [do] not formally fall within the representative's jurisdiction"—as well as "to [generations] past and future."[66] Accordingly, it may be plausible to think that in those instances in which the entire country is subject to a representative's authority, the representative's oath to the federal constitution requires defending the interests of a different and broader "the people."

For example, imagine that Jane is involved in redistricting in a "swing state"—or voting on a statewide voter ID law that could affect a national presidential race. It seems that her duties may flow outward in light of her work's national repercussions. Similarly, imagine that Jane is governor of her state, responsible for replacing a disabled or deceased member of the federal government from her state.[67] Many states allow state officials to appoint federal officers for a time: must those state officials consider only "the people" of their state—or should they also take account of "the people" represented by the relevant federal body? And what if Jane were to be presented with an expensive appropriations bill that would robustly reinforce the state's social programs, thereby enhancing the welfare of many of her *living* constituents, at the expense of placing great debt upon *future* constituents? To what extent should the impact of the debt levels imposed upon future generations by the bill weigh on her?

These are questions, of course, that lack clear answers, but they also demonstrate the ways in which the Janus-faced nature of representation can confound even the most well-intentioned of representatives. Nevertheless, we think that the shareholder–stakeholder debate in corporate law theory provides a useful frame for productively thinking about this dynamic within political representation. For example, assuming one subscribes to the shareholder primacy view's formalistic understanding of representation, the "people"—of either the nation or the yet-to-be-born—are not entitled to have their interests considered, as the representative stands in as a fiduciary for her authorizing constituency alone. In contrast, the stakeholder view would likely emphasize that although the representative is selected locally and "re-presents" her home district in some senses, she also serves the "people" and wields power more broadly; the interests of others may need to be protected. And when the trifecta of discretionary power, trust, and vulnerability coalesces in an act of political representation, fiduciary duties may apply to a shifting constellation of beneficiaries.

Analogies to corporate fiduciary law not only inform how to think through identification of relevant beneficiaries; they also usefully frame identification of relevant fiduciaries. Thus far, we have assumed Jane the state legislator is a fiduciary. But, as we suggested in Section II in considering Rave's work, it may be that the *legislature* is a fiduciary.[68] After all, in *The Federalist* No 10, James Madison thought that legislative bodies have the unique ability to "pass" private interests "through the medium of a chosen body of citizens;"[69] deliberation and the law-making process are designed to filter

[66] Marci A Hamilton, "Discussion and Decisions: A Proposal to Replace the Myth of Self-Rule with an Attorneyship Model of Representation," 69 *NYU L Rev* 477, 536 (1994).

[67] See Ethan J Leib and David Ponet, "Representation in America: Some Thoughts on Nancy Pelosi, Gavin Newsom, Tim Johnson, and Deliberative Engagement," 16 *Good Soc'y* 1 (2007); Ethan J Leib and Michael Serota, "Christie's Pick: Duty or Politics," *LA Times*, 5 June 2013 at A15.

[68] See Rave (n 10).

[69] *The Federalist* No 10, 78 (James Madison), ed Clinton Rossiter (1961).

and remove the taint of private interests.[70] And, of course, the legislature also satisfies the tripartite fiduciary criteria of discretion, trust, and vulnerability vis-à-vis the citizens it governs. The legislature, accordingly, might also be seen as a political representative of the people, subject to fiduciary constraints.

This does not mean that fiduciary political theorists have it wrong in referring to discrete public offices as public trusts. A board of directors for a corporation is a fiduciary when it acts as a body, but so too are individual board members fiduciaries. Many plaintiff suits for violations of the core fiduciary duty of loyalty focus on the individual directors—and fiduciary obligation flows to each member of the board.[71] Thus, Jane is both a fiduciary and part of a fiduciary institution; both the individual and the institution have relational obligations with their relevant beneficiaries—and the obligations may not be identical.

If this is correct, another question arises: Why stop at the legislature? Why not go bigger? Should we not also call the "political system" or the "legal system" or "the state" a fiduciary?[72] While such an approach is plausible, we would hesitate to adopt it. Our efforts over the years have emphasized the relational dimension of the political fiduciary representative, who has to stand in for different segments of "the people" at different times, subject to different dimensions of fiduciary constraint.[73] However, once one gets abstract about where fiduciary obligation applies, there may be a tendency to think that the "system" owes only wholesale fiduciary obligations to the "people," and that such obligations are fulfilled by fair procedures and diffusing political power among the instrumentalities of the state—judicial review, legislation, executive mercy. Because such a broad rendering comes at the expense of the "retail" fiduciary obligations—running directly from individual public official to individual citizens—that a more individualized framing of fiduciary relations would impose, we find it less persuasive. Ultimately, though, the point here is to open a conversation; our mapping may not be to scale.

Conclusion

This chapter has demonstrated how probing the shifting identities of fiduciary and beneficiary in the private law may help other public law theorists work through some of the most fundamental—and complex—issues in fiduciary political theory. We are optimistic, though, that the cross-fertilization may run both ways: there may also be something that private law theorists can learn from fiduciary political theory in addressing perennial debates in their field.[74]

[70] See Michael Serota and Ethan J Leib, "The Political Morality of Voting in Direct Democracy," 97 *Minn L Rev* 1596 (2013).

[71] See Leib, Serota, and Ponet, "Fiduciary Principles and the Jury" (n 5).

[72] See Fox-Decent, *Sovereignty's Promise: The State as Fiduciary* (n 3).

[73] See Ponet and Leib, "Fiduciary Law's Lessons for Deliberative Democracy" (n 5); Leib and Ponet, "Fiduciary Representation and Deliberative Engagement with Children" (n 5); Leib, Ponet, and Serota, "Translating Fiduciary Principles into Public Law" (n 5); Leib, Ponet, and Serota, "A Fiduciary Theory of Judging" (n 5); Serota and Leib (n 70).

[74] To some extent, Andrew Verstein's recent work may foreshadow a trend along these lines, reviving a line of work inaugurated by Harold Marsh. See Andrew Verstein, "Trustee or Delegate? Understanding Representation to Illuminate Shareholder Governance and Regulatory Change," 9 *Eur Co & Fin L Rev* 74 (2012) (drawing upon the work of Harold Marsh, Jr, "Are Directors Trustees? Conflicts of Interest and Corporate Morality," 22 *Bus Lawyer* 35 (1966)).

For example, from the standpoint of political theory, we have explained the deficits of a version of the "shareholder primacy" view and the virtues of contemplating the "Janus-faced" nature of political representation. We suspect these features of democratic political representation may be instructive for those attempting to figure out just who corporate directors are supposed to be representing in American firms and in firms around the globe. Whether private lawyers are studying the conventional American firm or firms with "constituency directors," a little political theory might help clarify how to think through fiduciary duties to different classes of beneficiaries.[75] Just as further specifications of the public fiduciary obligation of "deliberative engagement" might elucidate useful models for fiduciary best practices on the private law side, further mapping of the fiduciary–beneficiary relationship on the public side could illuminate and reinvigorate the old shareholder–stakeholder debate.[76]

Still, we aren't trying to oversell the private–public symbiosis. Nothing we say here suggests that boundary-crossing work is going to be easy: each context may present *sui generis* problems for institutional design. Although we are optimistic that there is much benefit in getting more public and private law scholars talking to one another about the dynamics of fiduciary representation in their respective domains, we understand that power is exercised in different ways in these different sites, and that people are accordingly vulnerable in different ways. The fiduciary principle is attractive for its ability to scale to context, but we recognize it is not infinitely malleable. Some modesty is essential in this research project going forward.

[75] See E Norman Veasey and Christine T Di Gugliemo, "How Many Masters Can a Director Serve? A Look at the Tensions Facing Constituency Directors," 63 *Bus Lawyer* 1 (2012).

[76] See Leib and Ponet, "Fiduciary Representation and Deliberative Engagement with Children" (n 5).

20

A Sacred Trust of Civilization

Fiduciary Foundations of International Law

Evan J Criddle

Responding to a series of massive human rights abuses during the 1990s, Francis Deng and several co-authors argued in *Sovereignty as Responsibility* that state sovereignty entailed a "responsibility for promoting citizens' welfare and liberty."[1] Of immediate concern to Deng and his colleagues were crises in countries such as Liberia, Rwanda, and Sudan where states had failed "to provide protection and assistance" to groups facing internal armed conflict, genocide, and crimes against humanity.[2] Stressing that all states had a basic responsibility under international law to protect their people from violence, the authors asserted that whenever a state "loses or refuses to use its capacity to provide protection and assistance for its citizens," it must be held accountable to the international community.[3] If a state should prove to be unable or unwilling to guarantee basic security, the international community, acting as "the ultimate guarantor of the universal standards that safeguard the rights of all human beings," must be prepared to shoulder the "responsibility to provide innocent victims of internal conflicts and gross violations of human rights with essential protection and assistance."[4]

Over the next two decades, the idea that state sovereignty entails a "responsibility to protect" would exert a powerful gravitational pull on legal and policy debates at the international level. UN Secretary-General Kofi Annan soon embraced Deng's thesis, arguing that "[s]tate sovereignty, in its most basic sense, is being redefined.... States are now widely understood to be instruments at the service of their people, and not vice versa."[5] In 2001, the International Committee on Intervention and State Sovereignty issued a landmark report in which it endorsed the view that "state authorities are responsible for the functions of protecting the safety and lives of citizens and promotion of their welfare" and bear responsibility "to their citizens internally and to the international community through the UN."[6] Both the UN General Assembly and the UN Security Council would later accept core features of this idea, recognizing that both individual states and the international community as a whole have important roles to play in protecting humanity from genocide, war crimes, and crimes against

[1] Francis M Deng et al, *Sovereignty as Responsibility: Conflict Management in Africa* (1996) xi.

[2] Deng (n 1) xii, xvii, 211. [3] Deng (n 1) xii, xvii. [4] Deng (n 1) xii, xvii.

[5] Kofi Annan, "Two Concepts of Sovereignty," *The Economist*, 18 Sept 1999, available at <http://www.economist.com/node/324795>; UN Secretary-General, "Implementing the Responsibility to Protect," UN Doc A/63/677 (12 Jan 2009).

[6] "The Responsibility to Protect," Report of the International Committee on Intervention and State Sovereignty, 13, para 2.15 (2001).

humanity.[7] Some legal scholars hailed these developments as representing a fundamental shift toward a humanity-centric conception of state sovereignty in which states and the international community would each shoulder burdens for guaranteeing human rights across the globe.[8] Others argued that the international community's responsibility to protect remains primarily a moral or political ideal without a well-established foundation in international law.[9]

In this chapter, I argue that the responsibility to protect under international law is best understood as emanating from the fiduciary character of state sovereignty.[10] The idea that individual states and the broader international community share responsibility for guaranteeing the security and basic rights of human beings can be traced back to international law's colonial-era origins, a time when Western nations rationalized their subjugation of indigenous peoples by casting themselves as benevolent civilizing "guardians" or "trustees" for humanity. Although the historical record suggests that imperial powers abused fiduciary rhetoric as a pretext for subjugating, exploiting, and even destroying indigenous communities, over time the continuing penetration and diffusion of fiduciary concepts has subtly redefined sovereignty itself as a form of legal authority that is entrusted to states for the benefit of humanity. This fiduciary conception of state sovereignty has contributed, in turn, to the progressive development of humanitarian safeguards in many areas of international law, including the law of state recognition, international territorial administration, military occupation, and international human rights.

While states have been entrusted with sovereign authority to serve as the primary guardians for humanity, international law and international institutions are necessary to mediate the fiduciary relationship between states and their people, ensuring that this relationship is not corrupted by domination (ie, vulnerability to arbitrary power) or instrumentalization (ie, the arbitrary exercise of power). The fiduciary character of state sovereignty faces its gravest test, as Deng and his colleagues observed, when states flagrantly neglect their responsibility to protect their people from abuse or affirmatively violate the human rights of their people. In both contexts, international law entrusts the international community as a whole—acting primarily under the UN Security Council's leadership—with a subsidiary responsibility to intercede for the protection of oppressed peoples. Although the international community's responsibility to protect requires further institutional development, it constitutes an essential feature of the fiduciary constitution of international legal order.

[7] 2005 World Summit Outcome, GA Res 60/1, A/RES/60/1, 24 Oct 2005, paras 138–39; SC Res 1970, S/Res/1970, 26 Feb 2011; SC Res 1973, S/Res/1973, 17 Mar 2011.

[8] Ruti Teitel, *Humanity's Law* (2011).

[9] William W Burke-White, "Adoption of the Responsibility To Protect," in Jared Genser and Irwin Cotler (eds), *The Responsibility To Protect* (2012) 17.

[10] The arguments I develop here build on previous collaborations with Professor Evan Fox-Decent: Evan J Criddle and Evan Fox-Decent, "The Fiduciary Constitution of International Law" (manuscript in progress); Evan J Criddle and Evan Fox-Decent, "A Fiduciary Theory of Jus Cogens," 34 *Yale J Int'l L* 331 (2009); Evan Fox-Decent and Evan J Criddle, "The Fiduciary Constitution of Human Rights," 15 *Legal Theory* 301 (2009); Evan J Criddle and Evan Fox-Decent, "Human Rights, Emergencies, and the Rule of Law," 34 *Hum Rts Q* 39 (2012); Evan Fox-Decent and Evan J Criddle, "Interest Balancing vs. Fiduciary Duty: Two Models for National Security Law," 13 *German LJ* 542 (2012).

I. Fiduciary States Abroad

The idea that states serve as fiduciaries under international law can be traced back to the writings of Francisco de Vitoria (1483–1546), a Spanish theologian at the University of Salamanca who is often described as an early "forerunner"[11] or "father"[12] of international law. Although not trained as a lawyer, Vitoria's philosophical reflections on the application of natural law principles to international relations (*jus gentium*) furnished essential building blocks for the subsequent development of international law.

Vitoria lived in the age of Spanish empire, a time when Spain was aggressively expanding its political and military influence, promoting its commercial interests, and spreading Catholicism throughout the New World. The brutality that accompanied Spanish conquest, including the enslavement and forced religious conversion of indigenous peoples, compelled theologians of Vitoria's generation to ask whether Spain's claim to dominion over the Americas could be reconciled with natural law.

The Spanish monarchy initially sought to justify its actions based upon a divine mandate—confirmed by papal bulls investing Ferdinand and Isabella with "full, free and integral power, authority and jurisdiction" over the Americas—to gather all nations under the banner of Catholicism.[13] In exchange for shouldering the spiritual burden of introducing Christianity to "uncivilized" peoples of the New World, Spain received legal title over the Americas and the right to enjoy the spoils of its expanding temporal empire.

Vitoria emphatically rejected this argument. In his seminal 1532 lecture *On the Indians Lately Discovered*,[14] Vitoria argued that indigenous peoples of the Americas, being endowed with reason and moral agency, possessed the same natural rights as Europeans, including the right to hold property. Indigenous peoples therefore "had true dominion in both public and private matters, just like Christians, and... neither their princes nor private persons could be despoiled of their property on the ground of their not being true owners."[15] According to Vitoria, the Pope could not strip Native American political communities of their sovereignty or deny indigenous peoples their natural rights because he lacked temporal authority over unbelievers in the New World.[16] If Spain's assertion of sovereign authority over the Americas could be justified, it would have to rest on some other foundation—one consistent with the innate dignity of indigenous peoples.

According to Vitoria, the best justification for Spanish rule was that foreign intervention was necessary to guarantee respect for natural rights. Vitoria observed that some indigenous communities in the New World had refused to respect the natural rights of

[11] Lassa Oppenheim, *International Law* (2nd edn, 1912) vol 1, 83–4; David Kennedy, "Primitive Legal Scholarship," 27 *Harv Int'l LJ* 1 (1986).

[12] Christopher R Rossi, *Broken Chain of Being: James Brown Scott and the Origins of Modern International Law* (1998) 5.

[13] Robert A Williams, Jr, "The Medieval and Renaissance Origins of the Status of American Indians in Western Legal Thought," 57 *S Cal L Rev* 1, 25–36 (1983).

[14] Francisco de Vitoria, "On the Indians Lately Discovered" (1532), published in Franciscus de Victoria, *De Indis et de Ivre Belli Relectiones* (Classics of International Law edn, 1917) (translation based on Boyer ed 1557, Muñoz ed 1565, and Simon ed 1696) 115.

[15] Vitoria (n 14) 128. [16] Vitoria (n 14) 128.

Spanish citizens "to travel into the lands in question and to sojourn there,"[17] "carry on trade among the native Indians,"[18] "preach the Gospel,"[19] use wild plants and animals for sustenance, extract minerals, and exploit other natural resources.[20] If indigenous peoples violated their duties under the law of nations to respect these natural rights of their Spanish visitors, and if they could not be persuaded to change course through peaceful means, Spain could lawfully go to war, "reducing [indigenous Americans] to subjection," to ensure respect for its own citizens' natural rights.[21] Spanish conquest would also be justified, Vitoria argued, to protect indigenous people from the "tyrannical and oppressive acts" of their own rulers, including human sacrifice and cannibalism.[22] Thus, Spain could establish sovereign authority over the Americas for the benevolent purpose of guaranteeing the natural rights of Spanish citizens, indigenous peoples, and foreign nationals.

In essence, Vitoria's defense of Spanish colonialism cast Western nations in the role of guardians for indigenous peoples. Vitoria noted cautiously that some Spaniards who had spent time in the New World believed Native Americans were "wanting in intelligence" and thus naturally "unfit to found or administer a lawful state up to the standard required by human and civil claims."[23] Vitoria hesitated to rely on these accounts, though he conceded that if they proved accurate, it would lend support for Spain's right under the law of nations to administer the New World as guardian for indigenous peoples, provided that this was carried out "clearly for their benefit."[24] Ultimately, however, Vitoria stressed instead that foreign guardianship could be necessary in some parts of the Americas, as elsewhere in the "uncivilized" world, to guarantee respect for the natural rights of all mankind. On Vitoria's account, the legal basis for this authority was not mere military conquest or papal fiat but the fiduciary character of the relationship thus established. The law of nations entrusted Spain with authority to establish basic security and guarantee fundamental rights in the New World, subject to a fiduciary obligation to use the power thus conferred for the benefit of all people residing within the relevant territory.

This vision of Western colonialism as a legal guardianship would influence international legal theory for centuries. As Robert Williams has observed, Vitoria's account "provided Western legal discourse with its first secularly oriented, systematized elaboration of the superior rights of civilized Europeans to invade and conquer normatively divergent peoples."[25] Within two decades, the Spanish crown formally embraced Vitoria's theory, while largely ignoring its radical implications for the natural rights of indigenous peoples. Whereas Vitoria had emphasized that Spain should seek every opportunity to promote security and individual rights abroad through persuasion rather than the sword, Spanish statesmen pressed Vitoria's guardianship theory into service primarily as a mandate for military conquest and imperialist exploitation.[26]

[17] Vitoria (n 14) 151. [18] Vitoria (n 14) 152. [19] Vitoria (n 14) 157.
[20] Vitoria (n 14) 153. [21] Vitoria (n 14) 155. [22] Vitoria (n 14) 159.
[23] Vitoria (n 14) 161. [24] Vitoria (n 14) 161.
[25] Robert A Williams, Jr, *The American Indian in Western Legal Thought: The Discourses of Conquest* (1990) 106.
[26] Williams (n 13) 93.

Other colonial powers were also drawn to Vitoria's fiduciary theory and invoked it regularly (albeit not uniformly[27]) as justification for their own exercises in empire-building. For example, King James I of England invoked the principle of civilizing guardianship when he authorized the Virginia Company to establish what would become the Jamestown Colony for the purpose of "propagating of Christian religion" and to "bring the Infidels and Savages, living in those Parts, to human Civility, and to a settled and quiet Government."[28] Edmund Burke likewise invoked the fiduciary concept in a 1783 speech before the House of Commons on Fox's India Bill, arguing that "every species of political dominion" is "in the strictest sense a trust" that may "totally cease, when it substantially varies from the purposes for which alone it could have a lawful existence."[29] Such was the power of the fiduciary theory of colonial governance that European nations would continue to characterize Western powers' authority over colonies and protectorates in these terms for over a century, as reflected in the 1884–5 Berlin Africa Conference's affirmation of the "civilized" world's continuing obligation "to watch over the preservation of the native tribes, and to care for the improvement of the condition of their moral and material well-being."[30]

Western nations framed their authority to govern foreign territory in fiduciary terms in the twentieth century, as well, with international institutions assuming a more central role in the entrustment and oversight of territorial governance. For example, in the Covenant of the League of Nations, member states agreed that some "colonies and territories" wrested from the control of Germany and the Ottoman Empire in the Middle East, Africa, and the Pacific during World War I were "inhabited by peoples not yet able to stand by themselves under the strenuous conditions of the modern world."[31] These peoples were thought to require further "tutelage" before they would be prepared to assume the international obligations associated with self-government.[32] The League's solution to the pressure for decolonization was to embrace Vitoria's fiduciary theory with a slight twist; Western powers would continue to govern these territories for the benefit of first nations pursuant to "the principle that the well-being and development of such peoples form a sacred trust of civilization."[33]

The resulting Mandate System of the League of Nations was modeled expressly on private fiduciary law. According to General Smuts of South Africa, who proposed the creation of the Mandate System, the holdings of Germany and the Ottoman Empire after World War I were to be "liquidated," with the League of Nations becoming a trustee or executor for "this great estate."[34] In contexts where newly liberated peoples lacked

[27] *Johnson v McIntosh* (1823) 21 US (8 Wheat) 543.

[28] Williams (n 25) 201 (citing "The First Charter of Virginia," in H S Commager (ed), *Documents of American History* (8th edn, 1968) 8–10). In tension with the fiduciary theory was a competing vision of Native Americans as perpetual enemies (*perpetui inimici*) who could not be induced to civilized governance and must be destroyed. Robert A Williams, Jr, *Savage Anxieties* (2012) 192–6.

[29] Edmund Burke, *Works* (1834) (1 Dec 1783) 276, quoted in George Thullen, *Problems of the Trusteeship System: A Study of Political Behavior in the United Nations* (1964) 11.

[30] General Act of the Berlin Conference, 26 Feb 1885, art VI, 165 Consol TS 485, reprinted in R J Gavin and J A Betley, *The Scramble for Africa: Documents on the Berlin West African Conference and Related Subjects, 1884/1885* (1973) 291; H Duncan Hall, *Mandates, Dependencies and Trusteeship* (1948) 95.

[31] Covenant of the League of Nations, art 22.

[32] Covenant of the League of Nations, art 22.

[33] Covenant of the League of Nations, art 22.

[34] Antony Anghie, *Imperialism, Sovereignty and the Making of International Law* (2004) 119 (quoting J C Smuts, "The League of Nations: A Practical Suggestion" (1928), reprinted in David Hunter Miller, *The*

either the institutional capacity or commitment to establish an independent state, the international community would assume responsibility for the affected peoples through the League. "The best method of giving practical effect to this principle," the Covenant proclaimed, was "that the tutelage of such peoples should be entrusted to advanced nations who, by reason of their resources, their experience, or their geographic position, can best undertake the responsibility and who are willing to accept it, and that this tutelage should be exercised by them as Mandatories on behalf of the League."[35] Individual states would be appointed to administer the "sacred trust" reposed in the international community "in the interests of the indigenous population" by providing interim governance and preparing the former colony or territory to assume the full fiduciary obligations associated with sovereign statehood. Unlike previous iterations of colonial guardianship in which each colonial power was "answerable to his own conscience,"[36] the Covenant itself "embodied" "securities for the performance of this trust" by holding mandatories accountable to a permanent commission, which received annual reports and supervised mandatories' fidelity to their fiduciary obligations.[37]

After World War II, the Mandate System was replaced by a new Trusteeship System supervised by the United Nations.[38] Eleven trusteeships were created from ten former mandates and one territory.[39] UN trusteeships aimed "to promote the political, economic, social, and educational advancement of the inhabitants of the trust territories, and their progressive development towards self-government or independence as may be appropriate to the particular circumstances of each territory and its peoples and the freely expressed wishes of the peoples concerned."[40] Other express purposes of the trusteeship system were "to further international peace and security," "encourage respect for human rights and fundamental freedoms for all," and "ensure equal treatment in social, economic, and commercial matters for all Members of the United Nations and their nationals."[41] The international community sought to ensure that the institutional structures for supervising trusteeships would be "wider and more effective" under the UN Charter than they had been under the Charter of the League of Nations.[42] Like the Mandate System that preceded it, the UN Trusteeship System enlisted Western states as fiduciaries for foreign peoples, with the aim of helping local authorities develop the institutional capacities necessary to guarantee security and basic rights to their people. Responsibility for overseeing the performance of trustee states was divided among the UN Security Council, UN General Assembly, and UN Trusteeship Council.[43]

Drafting of the Covenant vol 2 (1971) 26); and quoting John Fischer Williams, *Some Aspects of the Covenant of the League of Nations* (1934) 205–8 (observing that Article 22 of the League of Nations Covenant established "the Anglo-Saxon conception of the trust… with what may be the beginnings of a system of enforcement" and thereby challenged "the authoritarian doctrine of national sovereignty").

[35] Covenant of the League of Nations, art 22, paras 1–2. [36] Thullen (n 29) 11.

[37] Covenant of the League of Nations, art 22, para 1. [38] UN Charter art 77(1).

[39] Eugene Parker Chase, *The United Nations in Action* (1950) 284–315.

[40] UN Charter art 76(b). [41] UN Charter art 76(a), (c) and (d).

[42] *Legal Consequences for States of the Continued Presence of South Africa in Namibia (South West Africa in Namibia) Notwithstanding Security Council Resolution 276 (1970)*, Advisory Opinion, 1971 ICJ Rep 16 (June 21) 33, para 56.

[43] UN Charter arts 75–91.

The ICJ has affirmed the fiduciary character of the mandate and trusteeship systems on a number of occasions. For example, in a 1950 advisory opinion on the international status of South-West Africa, the ICJ observed that the mandate system "was created, in the interest of the inhabitants of the territory, and of humanity in general, as an international institution with an international object—a sacred trust of civilization."[44] The ICJ emphasized this principle two decades later in another advisory opinion involving South-West Africa. Speaking of the international community's "sacred trust" toward the mandate territories, the court explained:

> It is self-evident that the "trust" had to be exercised for the benefit of the peoples concerned, who were admitted to have interests of their own and to possess a potentiality for independent existence on the attainment of a certain stage of development: the mandates system was designed to provide peoples "not yet" able to manage their own affairs with the help and guidance necessary to enable them to arrive at the stage where they would be "able to stand by themselves."[45]

According to the ICJ, South Africa's fidelity to the other-regarding character of this trust represented an essential requirement for the lawful exercise of entrusted power. "One of the fundamental principles governing the international relationship thus established," the court explained, "is that a party which disowns or does not fulfill its own obligations cannot be recognized as retaining the rights which it claims to derive from the relationship."[46] Thus, the authority of a mandatory or trustee state to administer foreign territory was made contingent upon the administering state using its discretionary powers in a manner that would satisfy fiduciary duties of loyalty and care for the people subject to its powers.

Despite their formal fiduciary structure, both the mandate and trusteeship systems have been justly criticized as devices for perpetuating Western domination. Much as Vitoria's conception of benevolent guardianship paved the way for Western imperialism during preceding centuries, the mandate and trusteeship systems offered legal cover for neo-colonialism in the twentieth century. Antony Anghie, in particular, has argued that "the universalizing mission of international law, by embracing the idea of trusteeship," was able to "continue its task of ensuring that the Western model of law and behavior would be seen as natural, inevitable and inescapable," while entrenching social and economic inequality between established and emerging states.[47] By insisting that the modern nation state was the only acceptable form of governance, colonial powers failed to recognize how tribal systems and other forms of political organization establish legal order within indigenous communities. International oversight of mandates and trusteeships by the League of Nations and the United Nations, respectively, proved to be insufficiently responsive to the legitimate claims of peoples to self-determination.

Undoubtedly, colonial powers' prejudicial attitudes toward indigenous communities also prevented mandates and trusteeships from becoming effective incubators for political self-determination. For example, one widely circulated 1921 tract by a British

[44] *South-West Africa (International Status) Case* 1950 ICJ Rep 128, 132.
[45] *South West Africa in Namibia Case* (n 42) para 46.
[46] *South West Africa in Namibia Case* (n 42) para 96.
[47] Antony Anghie, *Imperialism, Sovereignty and the Making of International Law* (2004) 146.

legal expert on the Mandate for Mesopotamia proclaimed that the Middle East needed the United Kingdom's benevolent trusteeship because "the Arabs" were "wild, turbulent men," who were "not accustomed to self-government."[48] "Full sovereignty will come in due time to the territory," the author suggested, "but only when its people assume the dignity of an independent State."[49] In a similar spirit, General Smuts advocated limiting mandates to Europe and the Middle East because he believed that "German colonies in the Pacific and Africa" were "inhabited by barbarians, who not only cannot govern themselves, but to whom it would be impracticable to apply any ideas of political self-determination in the European sense."[50] Continuing a centuries-old tradition, many Western nations postponed granting political independence to mandates and trusteeships based on professed concerns that the inhabitants had yet to acquire the temperament and develop the institutions necessary to shoulder the full burden of self-government.[51]

Despite these obvious failures, the idea that Western nations were obligated to govern mandates and trusteeships as fiduciaries for indigenous communities arguably did yield some tangible benefits for first nations. For example, Nauru, a Micronesian island and former trust territory under Australia's administration, brought a claim in 1989 against Australia before the ICJ. Nauru claimed that Australia had engaged in self-dealing by managing the island's phosphate deposits for the benefit of Australia rather than Nauru. In addressing Australia's preliminary objections, the ICJ held that Australia was obligated to administer Nauru's resources as a "sacred trust" for the exclusive benefit of the people of Nauru.[52] Australia eventually settled with Nauru, paying an amount that included Nauru's loss caused by Australia's self-dealing.[53]

Alongside the mandate and trusteeship systems, fiduciary principles have informed international law in other areas where states exercise de facto sovereign power abroad. For example, whenever a state establishes military occupation in foreign territory, international law requires that it govern with solicitude for the well-being of foreign peoples, honoring private property rights and refraining from outrages against human dignity.[54] International law does not vest an occupier with sovereignty over a foreign people;[55] rather, the occupier is obligated to stand in as a temporary substitute for the displaced state with "a legal right and duty to enforce public safety, law, and order in accordance with the laws already in force in the territory."[56] As one expert has explained,

[48] Duncan Campbell Lee, *The Mandate for Mesopotamia and the Principle of Trusteeship in English Law* (1921) 22.

[49] Lee (n 48) 19; James Lorimer, *Institutes of the Law of Nations* 1 (1883) 123 (arguing against statehood for peoples governed by "religious creeds whose doctrine renders impossible the presumption of reciprocating will, e.g. the Mohammedan religion").

[50] J C Smuts, *The League of Nations: A Practical Suggestion*, quoted in Hall (n 30) 13.

[51] Williams (n 28) 28.

[52] *Case Concerning Certain Phosphate Lands in Nauru (Nauru v Australia)*, Preliminary Objections, 1992 ICJ Re 240, paras 41–4.

[53] Ramon E Reyes, Jr, "*Nauru v. Australia*: The International Fiduciary Duty and the Settlement of Nauru's Claims for Rehabilitation of Its Phosphate Lands," 16 *NYL Sch J Int'l & Com L* 1 (1996).

[54] Yoram Dinstein, *The International Law of Belligerent Occupation* (2009) 146–209; Hall (n 30) 9.

[55] Martti Koskenniemi, "Occupied Zone—A Zone of Reasonableness," 41 *Isr L Rev* 13, 17–18 (2008) (noting that the Israeli Supreme Court on various occasions has characterized the role of its military in the West Bank and Gaza as a "trustee of the Arab population").

[56] Nils Melzer, *Targeted Killing in International Law* (2008) 154.

the "lodestar guiding the law of belligerent occupation... is the principle that the civilian population of an occupied territory must benefit from maximal safeguards feasible in the circumstances. The protection of the civilian population is the key concern of relevant international legal norms, whether they are engendered by custom or by treaty."[57] In effect, international law entrusts the occupier with guardianship responsibility of establishing basic security and safeguarding human rights for the benefit of those within occupied territory. Thus, principles of trust and fidelity lie at the heart of the international law of occupation—despite the fact that there may be little actual trust, and perhaps even deep-seated enmity, between the occupier and the populace of an occupied territory. As with the mandate and trustee systems, a state that governs territory under belligerent occupation serves as a temporary "guardian" or "trustee" and bears corresponding duties of loyalty and care to the people under occupation.

In sum, Vitoria's vision of powerful states serving as fiduciaries for foreign peoples shaped how international law has regulated colonialism, the neo-colonialist programs of the League of the Nations and the United Nations, and the law of belligerent occupation. Although the fiduciary model has at times invited oppression,[58] this is not its only legacy. It has also provided a conceptual framework that has advanced international law's effort to civilize foreign intervention by prohibiting the barbarous practices that have accompanied intervention throughout history. The fiduciary character of sovereign power in international relations may also have important implications for international law's future progressive development.[59]

II. Fiduciary States at Home

Vitoria introduced the concept of international guardianship as a juridical model for conceptualizing the legal relationship between powerful states and foreign nationals subject to their power. Vitoria recognized, however, that the fiduciary character of public administration was not limited to a state's legal duties to foreign nationals abroad. Embedded in Vitoria's defense of Spanish colonialism was an equally important insight about the fiduciary character of public authority within a state's own borders: not only did the law of nations govern the relationship between Western powers and indigenous communities abroad, but it also regulated the relationship between indigenous communities and their *own* people at home.

Although Vitoria did not expressly characterize the relationship in fiduciary terms, his account of indigenous communities' contingent right to self-government is consistent with a fiduciary conception public authority. Recall that in Vitoria's view the law of nations required indigenous communities to respect the natural rights to travel,

[57] Dinstein (n 54) 286.

[58] As Philip Alston has noted recently, King Leopold of Belgium endorsed a fiduciary conception of colonialist rule at the Berlin Conference, advocating a new European "crusade" to "pierce the darkness which hangs over entire peoples." Philip Alston, "Does the Past Matter? On the Origins of Human Rights," 126 *Harv L Rev* 2043, 2056 (2013) (quoting Adam Hochschild, *King Leopold's Ghost* (1998) 4). History attests that Leopold's ostensibly "civilizing" intervention brought "untold misery to Africa, and caused a population loss of as many as ten million people." Alston, 2056.

[59] Eyal Benvenisti, "Sovereigns as Trustees of Humanity: The Concept and Its Normative Implications," 107 *Am J Int'l L* 295 (2013).

proselytize, hold property, and engage in commerce. Because these freedoms derived from natural law, they could be claimed equally by indigenous people, Spanish traders and missionaries, and anyone else who happened to find themselves in the New World. Natural law also obligated indigenous communities to refrain from "tyrannical and oppressive acts" such as human sacrifice or cannibalism. The violation of these obligations would undermine an indigenous community's right to political independence and could justify foreign conquest. At the core of this account was an implicit theory about the nature of public authority under natural law—namely, that a political community's right to self-government depended upon its commitment to respect and protect individual rights.

The fiduciary conception of state sovereignty also informed the writings of Hugo Grotius, the influential Dutch publicist. As Carsten Stahn has observed, Grotius' conception of the law of nations, like Vitoria's, "was based on the assumption that the rules governing the organization and behavior of states exist ultimately for the benefit of the actual subjects of the rights and duties concerned, individual human beings."[60] One consequence of this conception, Grotius asserted, was that other states could use force to prevent a tyrannical ruler from mistreating his people.[61]

One hundred and fifty years later, Swiss jurist Emerich de Vattel articulated a similar account of state sovereignty. Vattel argued that every monarch

> ought to have his mind impressed with this great truth, that the sovereign power is solely intrusted to him for the safety of the state, and the happiness of the people; that he is not permitted to consider himself as the principal object in the administration of affairs, to seek his own satisfaction, or his private advantage; but that he ought to direct all his views, all his steps, to the greatest advantage of the state and people who have submitted to him.[62]

This duty to consider "the happiness of the people" as the "principal object" of "intrusted" sovereign power was not merely a moral obligation operative on the conscience of the king, Vattel argued; it was, instead, a legal duty upon which the very authority of the crown depended. "When a sovereign does injury to any one" of his subjects, Vattel argued, he "acts without real authority" and, "having lost all the sentiments of a sovereign, ... no longer retains the prerogatives attached to that exalted rank."[63] Thus, a sovereign's "*right* is derived from *duty*"—the legal obligation to exercise public powers to provide basic security and guarantee fundamental rights for their people.[64]

[60] Carsten Stahn, "Responsibility to Protect: Political Rhetoric or Emerging Legal Norm?," 101 *Am J Int'l L* 99, 111 (2007) (citing Hugo Grotius, *De Mare Liberum* (1609), trans Ralph Deman Magoffin (1916) ch V; Hugo Grotius, *De Jure Belli ac Pacis* (1625), trans Francis W Kelsey (1925), bk II, ch 2); Hersch Lauterpacht, "The Grotian Tradition in International Law," *Brit YB Int'l L* 1, 27 (1946) (arguing that for Grotius "[t]he individual is the ultimate unit of all law, international and municipal, in the double sense that the obligations of international law are ultimately addressed to him and that the development, the well-being, and the dignity of the individual human being are a matter of direct concern to international law").

[61] Grotius, *De Jure Belli ac Pacis*, bk II, ch XXV, pt VIII(2).

[62] Emmerich de Vattel, *The Law of Nations: Or Principles of the Law of Nature Applied to the Conduct and Affairs of Nations and Sovereigns* (1758) (trans 1876) 13.

[63] Vattel (n 62) 21–22.

[64] Vattel (n 62) lv.

Vitoria, Grotius, and Vattel were hardly alone, of course, in conceptualizing sovereignty in fiduciary terms. The idea that public institutions and officials serve as fiduciaries for their people can be traced back to the writings of Plato,[65] Aristotle,[66] and Cicero.[67] Puritan revolutionaries in Britain drew upon these ideas to justify constraining the power of the crown. For example, Henry Parker's *Observations* of 1642 rejected royal claims to absolute power by asserting that "all rule is but fiduciarie" and that it would be "unnaturall for any Nation…to subject it selfe to a condition of servilitie."[68] Richard Overton likewise contended that public authority "always is either in the hands of the *Betrusted* or of the *Betrustees*," and that if "the *Betrusted* betray and forfeit their *Trust*,…it returneth from whence it came…: For all iust *humane powers* are but betrusted, confer'd and conveyed by ioynt and common consent" for the protection of the people's "*owne safety and weale*."[69] A generation later, John Locke characterized the "legislative power" as "a fiduciary power to act for certain ends"—with the people retaining "a supreme power to remove or alter the legislative, when they find the legislative act contrary to the trust reposed in them."[70] Across the Atlantic, the authors of the *Federalist Papers* used fiduciary concepts to develop a new theory of popular sovereignty, one premised upon the idea that sovereign powers belonged ultimately to the people, with public institutions and public officials holding those powers in trust to be exercised solely on the people's behalf.[71] Over time, these ideas have influenced political theory and public law throughout the world.[72]

The fiduciary theory of state sovereignty has not gone unchallenged, of course. Over time, many leading publicists of international law have gravitated toward a competing account: Jean Bodin's conception of state sovereignty as a "power absolute and perpetual," "supreme," and "subject to no law."[73] For example, Grotius endorsed aspects of Bodin's definition by characterizing "sovereignty" as power to act without being "subject to the legal control of another."[74] By the end of the nineteenth century, the absolutist account of state sovereignty had become conventional wisdom for a generation of international legal positivists. Rejecting the natural-law underpinnings of Vitoria's fiduciary account of state authority, international lawyers came to accept that sovereign

[65] Plato, *The Republic*, trans H D Lee (1961).

[66] Aristotle, *The Ethics of Aristotle*, trans D Chase (1950); Aristotle, *Politics*, trans H Rackham (1932).

[67] Cicero, "Moral Goodness," in *De Officiis*, trans Walter Miller (1997) I.XXV.85, 87.

[68] Richard Tuck, *Natural Rights Theories: Their Origin and Development* (1979) 146.

[69] Tuck (n 68) 149 (quoting Leveller, *Manifestoes of the Puritan Revolution*, ed D M Wolfe (1944)); John Milton, "The Tenure of Kings and Magistrates," in John Milton, *Areopagitica and Other Political Writings of John Milton* (1999).

[70] John Locke, "An Essay Concerning the True Original, Extent and End of Civil Government" (1690), in *Social Contract: Essays by Locke, Hume and Rousseau*, ed Ernest Barker (1947) 87.

[71] *The Federalist* No 46 (James Madison), ed Clinton Rossiter (1961) 294; *The Federalist* No 65 (Alexander Hamilton) 397.

[72] *Stone v Mississippi* 101 US 814, 820 (1879) ("The power of governing is a trust committed by the people to the government"); *Black River Regulating Dist v Adirondack League Club* 121 NE 2d 428, 433 (NY 1984) (characterizing the legislative power as "akin to that of a public trust to be exercised…for the common good"); Frederick William Maitland, "Trust and Corporation," in *Selected Essays*, ed H D Hazeltine et al (1936) 151, 220 ("[G]overnmental powers should be regarded as being held in trust").

[73] Jean Bodin, *Les Six Livres de la République* (1576) (1986) 179–228, 295–310 (quoted in Paul Gordon Lauren, *The Evolution of International Human Rights: Visions Seen* (1998) 26).

[74] Grotius, *De Jure Belli ac Pacis*, 102.

states possessed "supreme authority," exclusive jurisdiction, and mutual independence in their domestic affairs.[75]

Even during international legal positivism's peak during the late nineteenth and early twentieth centuries, however, the fiduciary conception of sovereignty continued to influence legal theory. For example, international lawyers insisted that aspiring states would have to demonstrate both the practical capacity and the commitment to govern for the benefit of their people before they would receive international recognition. Among other things, this meant that aspiring states would not qualify for independence "until a stable political organization has been created and until the public authorities had become strong enough to assert themselves throughout the territories of the State without the assistance of foreign troops."[76] Respect for the civil and political rights of ethnic and religious minorities also became a firm requirement for formal membership in the society of nations, paralleling respect for minority beneficiaries in private fiduciary law.[77] The failure to satisfy these standards could doom an aspiring state's bid for international recognition, as the apartheid government of Southern Rhodesia learned in 1965.[78] Although the specific conditions that the international community has imposed for state recognition have varied somewhat from one context to the next, the principle that new states must commit to exercise sovereign power in a nondiscriminatory fashion for the benefit of their people remains very much in force.[79]

As the international community linked state recognition to a fiduciary conception of sovereign authority, the fiduciary obligations that existing states owed to their own people came into sharper focus, as well. As applied to states under international law, the fiduciary duty of loyalty dictates that a state must exercise its power impartially for the equal benefit of its people. Expressed in Kantian terms, a state may not treat any of the people subject to its power as mere objects that it may exploit or destroy for its own ends. For Vitoria, a state's fiduciary obligations meant, at a minimum, that the state must refrain from engaging in "tyrannical and oppressive acts."[80] Today, a state's fiduciary duties are best captured by the idea that a state must respect, protect, and fulfill human rights.[81]

By the latter half of the twentieth century, these principles had gained a firm footing in international law. The international community accepted that all states were bound

[75] Oppenheim (n 11) 109, 177–9.

[76] The Aaland Islands Question: Report of the Committee of Jurists, League of Nations *Official Journal*, Special Supp 3 (Oct 1920).

[77] Robert H Sitkoff and Jesse Dukeminier, *Wills, Trusts & Estates* (9th edn, 2013) 657–8 (discussing the duty of impartiality in trust law); Anupam Chander, "Minorities, Shareholder and Otherwise," 113 *Yale LJ* 119 (2003) (observing that corporate directors bear heightened fiduciary duties toward minority shareholders who may be vulnerable to exploitation by controlling shareholders, and drawing lessons for public law).

[78] SC Res 216, S/RES/216, 12 Nov 1965 (calling "upon all States not to recognize [Southern Rhodesia's] illegal racist minority regime"); GA Res 2024 (XX), UN Doc A/2024, 11 Nov 1965 (condemning Southern Rhodesia's unilateral declaration of independence); W Michael Reisman, "Private Armies in a Global War System: Prologue to Decision," 14 *Va J Int'l L* 1, 4 (1973) (asserting that the lesson of Southern Rhodesia's failed bid for independence is that "the prerequisites [for statehood] now include, to some extent, establishing an expectation of present and probable future conformity with minimum standards of human rights").

[79] Paul R Williams and Frencesca Jannotti Pecci, "Earned Sovereignty: Bridging the Gap between Sovereignty and Self-Determination," 40 *Stan J Int'l L* 347, 350 (2004); Michael Scharf, "Earned Sovereignty: Juridical Underpinnings," 31 *Denv J Int'l L & Pol'y* 373 (2003).

[80] Vitoria (n 14) 159.

[81] Fox-Decent and Criddle, "The Fiduciary Constitution of Human Rights" (n 10).

by obligations "to respect and to ensure to all individuals within [their] territory and subject to [their] jurisdiction the" enjoyment of human rights "without distinction of any kind, such as race, colour, sex, language, religion, political or other opinion, national or social origin, property, birth or other status."[82] Some of these human rights constraints (such as the prohibitions against slavery, torture, and apartheid) constituted peremptory norms (*jus cogens*)—prohibitions which states may not transgress under any circumstances.[83] Viewed from a fiduciary-theory perspective, states could not transgress these peremptory norms under any circumstances because a state that did so could not claim to establish legal order for the purpose of guaranteeing rights for each of its people as equal beneficiaries of state sovereignty.[84] Other human rights protections such as freedom of expression and freedom of movement did not qualify as peremptory norms because states could place some reasonable limits on these individual liberties on a nondiscriminatory basis without transgressing their fiduciary obligations. While international human rights law remains a work in progress, the expanding corpus of international human rights represents the international community's best effort to define collectively the legal implications of states' fiduciary obligations toward their people.

The emergence of self-determination as a foundational principle of international legal order also resonates with the fiduciary character of state sovereignty. International law today recognizes the right of all peoples to full political participation and cultural identity within an independent and autonomous state that honors their fundamental rights and freedoms.[85] This "principle of equal rights and self-determination of peoples," as enshrined in the UN Charter,[86] has two dimensions: "external" and "internal."[87] External self-determination entails that national groups are entitled to "freely determine their political status and freely pursue their economic, social and cultural development" without colonial domination.[88] Internal self-determination, on the other hand, entitles subnational groups to full and equal participation in the processes of self-government, affirming that a state's authority to govern depends upon whether it "represents the whole of its population within its territory consistent with principles of equality, nondiscrimination, and self-determination."[89] To satisfy this requirement, states must honor the cultural and linguistic identities of ethnic minorities, provide an opportunity for equal participation in public affairs, devote an "equitable share" of public funds to each group, and create credible institutional mechanisms for vindicating

[82] International Covenant on Civil and Political Rights, art 2.1, 16 Dec 16 1966, 999 UNTS 171.

[83] *Restatement (Third) of Foreign Relations of the United States* (1987) § 702 cmts d–i, § 102 cmt k.

[84] Criddle and Fox-Decent, "Jus Cogens" (n 10) 356.

[85] ICCPR art 1(1); Declaration on Principles of International Law Concerning Friendly Relations and Cooperation Among States in Accordance with the Charter of the United Nations, GA Res 2625, Annex, UN GAOR, 25th Sess, Supp No 28, p 122, UN Doc A/8028 (1970); Convention Concerning Indigenous and Tribal Peoples in Independent Countries, International Labor Organization, Convention No 169, 27 June 1989, ILO Official Bull 59 (1989) (entered into force 5 Sept 1991).

[86] UN Charter art 1, para 2.

[87] Antonio Cassese, *Self-determination of Peoples: A Legal Appraisal* (1995) 67–140.

[88] ICCPR art 1(1).

[89] Patrick Macklem, "What Is International Human Rights Law? Three Applications of a Distributive Account," 52 *McGill LJ* 575, 587–8 (2007).

minority rights.[90] They may also have to consult with indigenous peoples and seek to accommodate their concerns if proposed state action will infringe the rights of indigenous peoples.[91] In some settings, the principle of internal self-determination may even support independent statehood for groups that have suffered systematic oppression at the hands of their state.[92]

What unites these aspects of the principle of self-determination is the idea that all peoples are entitled to representation within a state that treats them as equal beneficiaries of state sovereignty. States exercise sovereign power over legal interests which international law vests exclusively in peoples under the principle of self-determination. Just as a guardian or trustee may exercise discretionary powers on behalf of a beneficiary who possesses the legal right to wield these powers but lacks legal capacity to do so (due to age or other disability), international law permits states to exercise public powers for and on behalf of a people that is unable (both legally and practically) to engage in effective self-governance without institutional representation. And just as a guardian or trustee bears fiduciary duties to respect the beneficial interests of their appointed beneficiaries, international law requires states to use their entrusted discretionary powers for the equal benefit of their people or risk forfeiting sovereign authority through international intervention, partition, federative autonomy for an affected region, or other remedies. Thus, in both the private law and international law contexts, fiduciary principles regulate formally unequal relationships to honor beneficiaries' dignity as autonomous, self-determining agents.

III. The Responsibility to Protect

That sovereign states bear duties under international law to promote human security and safeguard human rights is relatively uncontroversial.[93] Conversely, the idea that the international community also bears an affirmative legal obligation to protect peoples of the world from abuses of state power has been heavily debated. While few international lawyers would dispute today that the UN Charter authorizes the Security Council to prevent massive human rights abuses such as genocide, war crimes, or crimes against humanity, some scholars have resisted the idea that this authority necessarily entails a legal obligation to act, finding a conspicuous lack of support for any such duty in state practice. These scholars caution that the international community's responsibility to protect human rights is best understood as a moral ideal rather than a legally binding obligation.[94]

[90] Brad R Roth, *Governmental Illegitimacy in International Law* (1999) 206–7 (citing the minority treaties of the League of Nations era).

[91] Convention Concerning Indigenous and Tribal Peoples in Independent Countries art 6, 27 June 1989, 28 ILM 1382; Declaration on the Rights of Indigenous Peoples, GA Res 61/295, UN Doc A/RES/61/295 (13 Sept 2007) (supporting self-determination); *Case of the Saramaka People v Suriname*, Judgment, Inter-Am Ct HR, 28 Nov 2007 (Ser C), No 172 (2007); *Seminole Nation v United States* (1942) 316 US 286, 297; *British Columbia v Haida Nation (Minister of Forests)* [2004] 3 SCR 511 (Can); *R v Sparrow* [1990] 1 SCR 1075, 1077 (Can); *New Zealand Maori Council v Attorney-General* [1987] 1 NZLR 641 (HC).

[92] Morton H Halperin and David J Scheffer with Patricia L Small, *Self-determination in the New World Order* (1992) 49–51.

[93] Saira Mohamed, "Taking Stock of the Responsibility to Protect," 48 *Stan J Int'l L* 63, 68 (2012).

[94] William W Burke-White, "Adoption of the Responsibility to Protect," in Jared Genser and Irwin Cotler (eds), *The Responsibility to Protect: The Promise of Stopping Mass Atrocities in Our Times* (2011).

Viewed from the perspective of a fiduciary account of state sovereignty, however, the idea that the international community bears a legal obligation to protect humanity is less easily dismissed. Although states serve as the primary guardians of human rights throughout the world, international institutions are necessary to ensure that the fiduciary character of state sovereignty is respected. The entrustment of sovereign authority to states can be reconciled with international law's foundational commitments to human dignity and self-determination only if institutions are in place at the international level to arbitrate conflicts between a state and its people. Hence, the coherence and credibility of public international law as a normative system depends upon whether the international community, acting through institutions such as the UN Security Council, will honor its responsibility to protect. Indeed, just as private fiduciary law relies upon courts to protect beneficiaries who would otherwise fall prey to self-serving fiduciaries, public international law depends upon the international community's intercession to safeguard humanity from state abuse or neglect.

An important dimension of the international community's protective authority relates to the creation of new states. International legal theory offers two primary explanations for how states qualify for sovereign authority. One theory suggests that international law confers sovereignty on any aspiring state that demonstrates the capacity and commitment to govern within a defined territory and engage in foreign relations abroad on behalf of their people.[95] Under this theory, the international community's formal recognition of new states merely confirms a pre-existing legal status that is based on objective legal criteria (the "declaratory theory"). Another theory posits that formal recognition from the international community is an independent and necessary condition of statehood (the "constitutive theory"). This second approach suggests that the international community must affirmatively entrust authority to aspiring states before aspiring states may claim the right to exercise sovereign powers under international law.[96]

Whether one finds the declaratory or the constitutive theory of state recognition more persuasive,[97] both are compatible with a fiduciary conception of state sovereignty,[98] and both reserve a central role for the international community in protecting humanity. Under the constitutive theory, states and international organizations must use their independent judgment to evaluate whether recognition of a new state will serve the best interests of humanity. The constitutive theory thus places the international community in a protective role analogous to that which courts of equity have

[95] Montevideo Convention on the Rights and Duties of States, 164 LNTS 19, USTS 881 (1934).

[96] Although international law governs the distribution of sovereign authority among states, it also requires states to organize themselves institutionally and exercise their authority in a manner that both enacts and respects the self-determination of their people. State sovereignty under international law may thus be understood to come both "from above" (through international law's distributive function) and "from below" (through the exercise of popular self-determination).

[97] Professor Fox-Decent and I discuss the respective merits of the declaratory and constitutive theories at greater length in "International Law and the Fiduciary Constitution of Sovereignty" (manuscript on file with the authors).

[98] Interestingly, this debate over the international recognition of new states mirrors a similar tension in private law theory over the state's role in either declaring or constituting parent–child relationships. Sarah Abramowicz, "English Child Custody Law, 1660–1839: The Origins of Judicial Intervention in Paternal Custody," 99 *Colum L Rev* 1344 (1999); Jeffrey Blustein, "On the Doctrine of Parens Patriae: Fiduciary Obligations and State Power," 2 *Crim Just Ethics* 39 (1983).

traditionally played in supervising parents and guardians. While perhaps less readily apparent, the declaratory theory also assigns a central role to the international community: when disputes arise regarding whether an aspiring state has satisfied the formal criteria for recognition, the international community as a whole stands in the position of a neutral third-party arbitrator. It safeguards human dignity in such cases by ensuring that new states possess the institutional capacity necessary to meet their fiduciary obligations.

More controversial, but no less important, is the international community's responsibility to ensure that existing states do not subject their people to grave harm through abuse or neglect. This responsibility has several elements. As UN Secretary-General Ban Ki-moon has noted, one crucial part of the international community's protective responsibility is to provide training, resources, and institutional support to empower states to meet their obligations to respect, protect, and fulfill human rights.[99] When states refuse to satisfy their duties of loyalty and care, international tribunals may hold states to account. The international community may use a variety of peaceful coercive measures, including diplomatic pressure and collective economic sanctions, to compel an errant state to meet its humanitarian obligations. International military intervention, in contrast, will be justified only rarely when strictly necessary to protect human beings from grave human rights abuse.[100] Whatever the means employed, the international community must tailor its responsive measures to the exigencies of a particular crisis so as to minimize its intrusion into matters that international law entrusts in the first instance to a state's sovereign discretion.

For better or worse, the international community's responsibility to protect falls principally (if not necessarily exclusively) upon the Security Council. The UN Charter clearly entrusts the Security Council with primary responsibility for determining the international community's collective response to grave human rights abuse. When the Security Council authorizes or requires collective action, the burden of responsibility shifts to UN member states, all of whom "share the responsibility to make [the Security Council] an effective instrument for advancing the principles relating to the responsibility to protect."[101] All member states arguably bear a positive obligation under international law to cooperate with the Security Council to devise effective strategies for protecting humanity from mass atrocities.[102] If the Security Council, its constituent voting members, or other UN member states unreasonably fail to respond to a humanitarian crisis (as was the case, for example, during the Rwandan genocide), the fiduciary character of international legal order suggests that oppressed peoples are entitled to call upon these entities to satisfy their protective obligations in

[99] UN Secretary-General, "Implementing the Responsibility to Protect," UN Doc A/63/677 (12 Jan 2009) 15–22.

[100] UN Secretary-General (n 99) 22, paras 49–50.

[101] UN Secretary-General (n 99) 27, para 61.

[102] Articles on the Responsibility of States for Internationally Wrongful Acts, art 41(1), in Report of the International Law Commission on the Work of Its Fifty-third Session, UN GAOR, 56th Sess, Supp No 10, at 43, UN Doc A/56/10 (2001) (asserting that states have a positive obligation "to cooperate to bring [a serious breach of a peremptory norm of general international law] to an end through lawful means"). But see art 41 commentary, para 3 (observing that this provision "may reflect the progressive development of international law").

order to secure the conditions of "external freedom"—"a world in which everyone's rights are respected."[103]

To be sure, the current institutional mechanisms for enforcing states' fiduciary duties are plainly inadequate to guarantee that states will act in the interests of their people. In a variety of contexts, political gridlock has prevented the Security Council from responding effectively to genocide, war crimes, and crimes against humanity. International human rights courts and commissions cannot always depend upon states to comply with their judgments. Hence, for all of the progress that has been made over the past century in developing international legal standards to formalize states' fiduciary duties, much work remains to be done to develop international institutions that will credibly and consistently enforce these duties. As this work continues, the fiduciary conception of state sovereignty not only illuminates international law's historical development, but also outlines an agenda for the international legal system's progressive development in the twenty-first century.

Conclusion

History suggests that the fiduciary structure of contemporary international law developed through colonial confrontations between imperial powers and first nations. By framing colonial governance as a fiduciary relationship, Vitoria and his followers laid the foundation for an international legal order in which all states would be viewed as fiduciaries charged with a duty to respect, protect, and fulfill human rights for their own nationals and others subject to their care.[104] Whether at home or abroad, a state's responsibility to exercise power for the benefit of humanity has gradually become, in Anne Peters's words, "the α and ω of sovereignty."[105]

In many respects, this emancipatory vision remains a work in progress. As the ICJ stressed in the *South West Africa Case*, the idea that public authority represents a "sacred trust…must be or become something more than a moral or humanitarian ideal. In order to generate legal rights and obligations, it must be given jurisdical [*sic*] expression and be clothed in legal form."[106] In the years that have followed the *South West Africa Case*, the development of international human rights law and other humanitarian safeguards has accelerated the process of translating the international community's moral obligations into positive law. Despite these advances, experience suggests that the legal mechanisms currently available for enforcing states' fiduciary obligations are inadequate to guarantee basic security and freedoms for many peoples around the world. Much work remains to be done, therefore, to clarify the content of states' fiduciary obligations and develop more robust institutions for promoting state compliance. In the interim, states will continue to defend abusive practices based on appeals to sovereignty and self-determination, much as colonial powers exploited first nations under the pretense of benevolent "guardianship."

[103] Christine M Korsgaard, *Creating the Kingdom of Ends* (1996) 21.
[104] Teitel (n 8).
[105] Anne Peters, "Humanity as the A and Ω of Sovereignty," 20 *Eur J Int'l L* 513 (2009).
[106] *South West Africa Cases*, 1966 ICJ Rep 6, 32 para 51 (18 July 1966) (second phase).

Enthusiasm for the fiduciary conception of state sovereignty must be tempered, therefore, by a clear-eyed recognition of the need for states to strengthen their commitment to the fiduciary character of sovereign authority. International law is not unique in this respect, of course. Private law has always relied on fiduciaries' moral commitment to social norms, rather than the threat of legal action alone, to ensure fiduciary diligence and loyalty.[107] Social norms may play an even more important role in public law than private law, because the legal avenues available to redress breaches of the public trust are often relatively ineffective. The challenge of developing an international legal order based on fiduciary obligations may therefore be best understood, as Martti Koskenniemi has observed, not simply as "an architectural project," but as "a programme of moral and political regeneration."[108] Whether this program succeeds or fails will depend upon states' fidelity to the idea that the well-being of their people constitutes a sacred trust of civilization.

[107] Margaret M Blair and Lynn A Stout, "Trust, Trustworthiness, and the Behavioral Foundations of Corporate Law," 149 *U Pa L Rev* 1735, 1794 (2001); Melvin A Eisenberg, "Corporate Law and Social Norms," 99 *Colum L Rev* 1253, 1269–80, 1265 (1999); Edward B Rock, "Saints and Sinners: How Does Delaware Corporate Law Work?," 44 *UCLA L Rev* 1009, 1016 (1997).

[108] Martti Koskenniemi, "Constitutionalism as Mindset: Reflection on Kantian Themes about International Law and Globalization," 8 *Theoretical Inq L* 9, 18 (2007).

Index